Intelligent Tutoring Systems in E-Learning Environments:

Design, Implementation and Evaluation

Slavomir Stankov
University of Split, Croatia

Vlado Glavinić
University of Zagreb, Croatia

Marko Rosić
University of Split, Croatia

Information Science REFERENCE

INFORMATION SCIENCE REFERENCE

Hershey · New York

Director of Editorial Content:	Kristin Klinger
Director of Book Publications:	Julia Mosemann
Acquisitions Editor:	Lindsay Johnston
Development Editor:	Julia Mosemann
Publishing Assistant:	Travis Gundrum
Typesetter:	Deanna Jo Zombro
Production Editor:	Jamie Snavely
Cover Design:	Lisa Tosheff

Published in the United States of America by
Information Science Reference (an imprint of IGI Global)
701 E. Chocolate Avenue
Hershey PA 17033
Tel: 717-533-8845
Fax: 717-533-8661
E-mail: cust@igi-global.com
Web site: http://www.igi-global.com

Library of Congress Cataloging-in-Publication Data

Intelligent tutoring systems in e-learning environments : design, implementation, and evaluation / Slavomir Stankov, Vlado Glavinic and Marko Rosic, editors.
p. cm.
Includes bibliographical references and index.
Summary: "This book addresses intelligent tutoring system (ITS) environments from the standpoint of information and communication technology (ICT) and the recent accomplishments within both the e-learning paradigm and e-learning systems"--Provided by publisher. ISBN 978-1-61692-008-1 (hardcover) -- ISBN 978-1-61692-009-8 (ebook) 1. Intelligent tutoring systems. 2. Web-based instruction--Design. 3. Education--Effect of technological innovations on. I. Stankov, Slavomir, 1947- II. Glavinic, Vlado, 1952- III. Rosic, Marko, 1970- LB1028.73.I65 2010
371.33'44678--dc22
2009052667

British Cataloguing in Publication Data
A Cataloguing in Publication record for this book is available from the British Library.

List of Reviewers

Funda Dag, *University of Kocaeli, Turkey*
Benedict du Boulay, *University of Sussex, UK*
Hersh C. Waxman, *Texas A&M University, and College of Education and Human Development, USA*
Marko Rosić, *University of Split, Croatia*
Sylvain Dehors, *ACACIA team, France*
Dragan Gasevic, *Athabasca University, Canada*
Jeron Geuze, *Radboud University Nijmegen, Netherlands*
David Martens, *Independent Banking Professional Antwerp Area, and Hogeschool Gent, Belgium*
Alke Martens, *University of Rostock, Germany*
Lung-Hsiang Wong, *National Institute of Education, Singapore*
Orazio Miglino, *University of Naples, USA*
Davide Fossati, *University of Illinois at Chicago, USA*
Ig Ibert Bittencourt, *Federal University of Alagoas, and Federal University of Campina Grande, Brazil*
Wei Ding, *University of Massachusetts - Boston, USA*
Larbi Esmahi, *Athabasca University, Canada*
Abdolhossein Sarrafzadeh, *Massey University, New Zealand*
Mingyu Feng, *Worcester Polytechnic Institute, USA*
Xin Bai, *Columbia University, USA*
Rosa Maria Vicari, *Universidade Federal do Rio Grande do Sul – UFRGS, Brasil*
L.M. Brasil, *University of Brasília, Brasil*

Table of Contents

Detailed Table of Contents

In this chapter, Firstly, the appearance of the ITS notion and related literature review will be handled. After then general architecture of Intelligent Tutoring Systems will be presented and information about improvements on ITS will be given up to now. And also best ITS practices will be mentioned, too. In this sense, ZOSMAT - a detailed sample application - will be explained as a demonstration of how an ITS is designed. ZOSMAT can be used for the purpose of either individual learning or real classroom environment with the guidance of a human tutor during a formal education process. This characteristic of ZOSMAT distinguishes itself from other intelligent tutoring systems (Keles et al., 2009). Finally, challenges and problems in the area of ITS and future of ITS will be discussed.

This chapter describes a learning design methodology for creating an intelligent tutoring system (ITS) to support non-violent conflict resolution education in the school environment. The design method is based on a mathematical formalization in which ITS are defined as automata. The aim is to demonstrate that the automata representation facilitates the integration of the domain contents, the pedagogical strategies and the student models in one computational system. The automata structure guides the system design, managing the variables selection of the teaching-learning process. Variables involve the students' characteristics, the interface resources and the pedagogical strategies. Thus the whole teaching-learning process is modeled as an automaton which fits with the ITS structure. The non violent conflict resolution domain was chosen as the case study due to its relevance and its ill structured contents what makes its modeling difficult. The result is a non violent conflict resolution educational process structured as an ITS.

A cognitive framework called REflective Agent Learning environment (REAL) is developed in this study. REAL is a reusable framework that allows researchers to develop a simulation-based learning environment where users can learn through passing their thoughts to some computer-based agents and observe how the agents embodying their knowledge behave as the result of their instruction. Our research benefits from the research in Intelligent Tutoring Systems, game based learning systems, and agent technologies, stressing reflection as part of the thinking processes. It focuses on the design of the framework and the testing of its usability. The external evaluation of specific implementations serves as the guidance for the future design of the REAL applications. We hope, by grounding themselves in the needs of local practice, the REAL applications can give us opportunities to understand how theoretical claims about teaching and learning can be effectively transformed into meaningful learning.

In this chapter, an approach to support the development of ITS based on patterns and pattern catalogues is described. Patterns are means to facilitate inter-project communication. As such, they provide for a clear terminology in an application domain. They support the development process itself by encapsulating information at different levels (e.g. using underlying concepts and tools, adding and integrating new concepts and tools, and fundamentally changing the structure of an existing piece of software). The approach described in this chapter shows two examples of how a catalogue of patterns collected from existing ITS architectures can be used and re-used in different settings. Those settings span the field of plugin frameworks for ITS (i.e. JaBInT), a concrete "proof of concept" ITS (i.e. ChemNom and CoChemEx) using a collaboration script approach.

Section 2
E-Learning Communities Technologies

This chapter describes a mathematical model of virtual learning environment considering both technology and users. Recognized interested users are teachers, parents and students. Interaction between interested parties in elementary and high school education process is presented by using complexity science. The idea is to model and create educational virtual environment that would attract engagement of all parties. Initial engagement would be motivated with the e-grade book. After initial involvement of seeing grades, the users would be motivated for further involvement using forums, blogs, and chats to interact with each other in one place. This would lead to creating groups of students or parents with similar problems and interests. For example, why is mathematics so hard to some students, and for other not? The created virtual environment will enable teachers to additionally inform parents of existing e-learning materials. Virtual environment is modeled as multilevel, multidimensional educational environment, considering communication of all participants, and every aspect of technology that could improve that communication.

Mobile learning, as the "portable and personal" fashion of e-learning, is intended to enhance the efficiency and effectiveness of learning in the context of handheld terminals. Most present-day learning systems run on desktop computers and are not designed for use on mobile devices such as mobile phones, smart phones, Personal Digital Assistants, etc. Mobile learning systems aim to improve the quality of learning by providing mobile learners with an easy, contextualized and ubiquitous access to knowledge. This chapter gives an overview of the current state of knowledge and research in the m-learning domain, describes issues and problems pertinent to mobile learning and offers our approach to solving these problems in the form of a mobile intelligent tutoring model we are currently developing. Given the present absence of relevant literature and referent material we think that this chapter provides developers with some new ideas.

Section 3
Intelligent E-Learning in Different Domains

E-learning has attracted a great deal of interest in educational circles from K-12 to universities. A question that is often rightly asked is how effective current e-learning systems are. It is argued that there is little individualisation of instruction by adapting to the pedagogical needs of each learner in current e-learning systems. Intelligent tutoring systems have tried to fill this gap but even they fail to compete with human one-to-one tutoring. This paper presents Affective Tutoring Systems which are e-learning systems capable of detecting learners' affective state and reacting to it through a life like agent called Eve. This paper presents an Affective Tutoring System in the domain of mathematics and the research that led to its development. It also presents the findings from the study and testing of the system indicating that the animated agent Eve carried a persona effect.

In this chapter, an approach to support the development of ITS based on patterns and pattern catalogues is described. Patterns are means to facilitate inter-project communication. As such, they provide for a clear terminology in an application domain. They support the development process itself by encapsulating information at different levels (e.g. using underlying concepts and tools, adding and integrating new concepts and tools, and fundamentally changing the structure of an existing piece of software). The approach described in this chapter shows two examples of how a catalogue of patterns collected from existing ITS architectures can be used and re-used in different settings. Those settings span the field of plugin frameworks for ITS (i.e. JaBInT), a concrete "proof of concept" ITS (i.e. ChemNom and CoChemEx) using a collaboration script approach.

Tutoring systems for programming help students understand features of target programming languages, and develop their general problem solving skills. Our system guides novices in learning syntax and semantics of programming language, problem decomposition, program design and testing. It is language independent, automatically adjusting course material to the language - subject of learning. Semantic analysis of student's programs is based on comparison of abstract semantics trees of student's and model-program. Model-program is coded by innovative programming language describing goals and variants of possible solutions. The notional machine defined by programming language, its verbal description of instruction actions and visualization of program execution, helps students to understand semantics of teaching language. Advancement through the course material controlled by computer teacher supports connection of new concepts to the present student's knowledge. The system applies distinct teaching strategies to stoppers and movers.

There is great need for collaboration in education and e-learning systems which imply the necessity for group modeling. Since Bloom's experiment, which produced effect size of 2-sigma, there were many attempts to repeat those results with intelligent tutoring systems. Our experiments show effectiveness of xTEx-Sys in measure of effect size. The goal of our research and development is to get as close as possible to effect size of 2-sigma. There is greater need for collaboration in e-learning systems and there are some indications that collaboration could increase effectiveness. Since collaboration is closely coupled with groups, directions for future development and exploration of e-learning systems lay in field of group modeling. Group modeling also implies creation of stereotype models.

In this study, a personalized learning system framework that is KOULearn (Kocaeli University Learning System) has been proposed. It is based on learning object and produces a personalized learning content according to learning style and cognitive knowledge level of an individual. The proposed framework is situated in advanced learning technologies according to educational perspective and is a semantic web application according to development technologies. The proposed framework is aimed to form a personalized learning environment. Three models are included in this system: domain model, user model and adaptation model, respectively. Components of the system have been realized by ontology based knowledge modeling approach. Execution of the personalized learning content structure and learning environment of the system, related to electric education, has been examined by resonance learning module which is constituted considering personalization requirements of the system.

One major direction in research on technology-enabled learning systems revolves round the notion of generating optimal learning pathways. Two examples of the application areas that could be presented as search and optimization problem in the context of Artificial Intelligence are:- (1) Adaptive selection and sequencing of learning objects based on the learning profiles, preferences and abilities of individual learners; (2) Automatic composition of assessment or examination papers based on instructors' specifications. In this chapter, we present a critical discussion of the research which is concerned with the application of the paradigm of "swarm intelligence" in these two areas. The main aim of this survey is to highlight the new trends and key research achievements that have been realised in the last few years. We will also outline a range of relevant research issues and challenges that have been generated by this body of work.

Section 5
E-Learning Systems Effectiveness

This chapter examines part of the broad question: "How compelling is the evidence for the effectiveness of e-Learning in the post-16 sector? It concentrates, largely from a UK perspective, on higher education and on policy issues. In the first section the UK Higher Education Funding Council for England (HEFCE) e-Learning strategy is outlined and previous, partial reviews of e-Learning in higher education are examined. The evidence on the effectiveness of e-Learning in higher education is presented using Kirkpatrick's (1998) levels of evaluation, under the following questions: What are the learners' reactions to e-Learning? What is the student experience of e-Learning? What is the quality of the learning? Does e-Learning in higher education alter the behavior of the learner? What is the impact of e-Learning on the organization. In the final section recommendations for policy and future research.

As the acquisition of knowledge is often an expensive and time-consuming process, it is important to know whether it actually improves the student performance. The e-learning is a revolutionary paradigm that has lately been significantly evolving and it is closely related to the intelligent tutoring systems. Methodology for evaluating the educational influence of learning and teaching process, questions whether and in what amount, students learn effectively. Our contribution to this compulsive field of research is a meta-analysis of a series of experiments based on the same two-group methodology that reveals a more precise effect size of one particular e-learning system - eXtended Tutor-Expert System, a representative of web-based authoring shells for building intelligent tutoring systems.

This study addresses the evaluation of the effectiveness of distance courses and interactive processes in virtual learning environments. It is part of a larger area, which is quality in Distance Education (DE) or evaluation of quality in DE. Our look was theoretically guided by the historical-cultural ap-

Preface

In recent years, information and communication technology (ICT) has become an essential part of educational systems, and more generally, of the learning and teaching process. ICT in this role has served as a support or even as the replacement of human teachers in traditional education. In order to perform such a role, ICT supports both active and interactive learning through combining multimedia with networking and software engineering methods, hence promoting the advanced educational environments. The concept of such environments should be considered in the context of technological diversities used for blended and/or traditional instruction. Blended learning is the combination of traditional face-to-face instruction with the computer-mediated instruction. This new learning paradigm is learner-centered. The learner is positioned in the center of the learning environment with regard to the time, the place and the learning method; consequently, people, knowledge, technology, media, organization and likewise, are all comprised by the concept of learning resources. Nowadays, this learning environment is referred to as the *e-learning paradigm*, or simply *e-learning*, encompassing any learning content or experience affected by electronic technology.

The e-learning represents the meeting point between the world of information and communication technology and the world of education. Its importance is being evident, particularly when used within a well-planned and organized learning environment. Despite all of its advantages, it should be nevertheless noted that the e-learning is not a "magic crystal ball" to replace all of the existing educational methods.

The e-learning is enabled by *e-learning systems* that, according to the way the learning content is delivered, can be subdivided into synchronous and asynchronous e-learning systems. The e-learning systems are further classified according to supporting electronic technologies for learning content delivery into on-site systems (with CDROM and DVD options) and (either LAN or WAN) networked ones. Particular kind of asynchronous e-learning systems are *intelligent tutoring systems* (ITSs), which are a generation of computer systems intended to support and improve the learning and teaching process for certain domain knowledge, respecting the learner's individuality as in traditional "one-to-one" tutoring. The ITSs are knowledge based systems because they possess (i) knowledge about the domain knowledge, (ii) knowledge about the teaching principles and the methods for using them, and (iii) knowledge about methods and techniques for student modeling during the knowledge and skills acquiring process. From the standpoint of pedagogical methodology, the ITSs represent the connection between behavioral approaches as found in traditional systems for computer based instruction on the one hand, and the cognitive paradigm of learning and teaching on the other.

This book observes the intelligent tutoring systems in different research and development environments, as well as approaches of different interest groups to design, implementation and evaluation of abovementioned. It is intended for educators, professionals and researchers working with the intelligent tutoring systems, the e-learning and the e-learning systems. Moreover, the book aims to present the ITSs design, implementation and evaluation methodology trough series of case studies.

The ITSs architectures and technologies are used by various e-learning communities exhibiting differing and special needs with respect to "intelligence". Unfolding domain specific intelligence is a prerequisite for advanced personalization of the respective e-learning environment. The core for personalization is the student, modeled either as an individual or as an aggregate. Following such a personalization, the environment evolves to a personalized advanced e-learning environment. Before "blending" such personalized advanced e-learning environment into educational process, it is very important to evaluate it. In general, an evaluation offers information to make decision about using the product or not. When it comes to e-learning environment evaluation, the most important aspect is effectiveness fortification. Only after evaluation, research in the field of intelligent tutoring systems can take a new direction. This was confirmed by our experience in research and development related to *TEx-Sys* (*T*utor–*Ex*pert *Sys*tem) model that started in 1992 and still lasts, that resulted with the new effectiveness evaluation methodology.

To be more specific, the *TEx-Sys* is a model of an intelligent hypermedial authoring shell for generating ITSs in freely chosen knowledge domains. Authoring shell is based on a number of concepts: the cybernetic model of systems, the paradigm "teaching is control of learning", the teaching principles of the "human" tutor with "one-to-one" tutoring model, and traditional ITSs architecture.

Within this context, it is worth noting that the approach applied in the design of *TEx-Sys* model, brings out some particular features concerning traditional ITSs:

- domain knowledge design is rigorously divided from courseware design; the expert owns the domain area knowledge and skills, providing grounds for teachers to design the courseware;
- authoring shells are considered as systems that have an ontological environment and enable experts to design domain knowledge, teachers to design educational content and students to learn and be tested;
- such an approach to authoring shells makes possible the realization of a number of requirements such as interoperability, reusability, durability and accessibility of knowledge and learning objects which are embedded in the educational content;
- dynamic quizzing enables adaptability by evaluating every step in students testing, where the system generates new questions depending on a student's partial testing results.

The first *TEx-Sys* model implementation was *on-site TEx-Sys*, which supported the learning and teaching process for only two main actors – student and teacher – who were offered the two basic functionalities: (i) the design of learning content for arbitrary domain knowledge, and (ii) learning and teaching, along with knowledge testing. The second implementation phase, known as *Distributed TEx-Sys* (*DTEx-Sys*), was based on dynamic Web documents, and addressed (i) accessibility for as large as possible a number of potential users, and (ii) learning and teaching in arbitrary domains. The *DTEx-Sys,* however, differs from the *on-site TEx-Sys* because it does not have the environment for domain knowledge base design, but uses the ones developed for the *on-site TEx-Sys*. The latest implementation is denoted as *eXtended TEx-Sys* (*xTEx-Sys*) and uses Web services. The *xTEx-Sys* strictly distinguishes the functionalities of experts for domain knowledge design from the ones of teachers for learning content (or courseware) design.

All the three *TEx-Sys* model versions have been, until presently, in effective use as a support for different courses, which also enabled gathering of valuable experimental data. To be more precise, prototype tests with the implemented systems have been carried out with students ranging from primary to academic education, including 7700 knowledge tests that were solved by approximately 2300 students. According to carried out surveys, the implemented systems have satisfied both the required functionalities and the actors' demands. The student's environment has been tested to determine the system's usability and students' achievements in the learning and teaching process at a number of universities, high and primary schools in Croatia, which also resulted in a number of graduate and postgraduate theses.

The *TEx-Sys* model, as framework for research and instructional use, has been extensively studied in a number of research projects funded by the Croatian Ministry of Science, Education and Sport: *Independence of Student Using New Information Technology*, *Computational and didactical aspects of intelligent authoring tools in education*, *Web oriented intelligent authoring shell*, and *Intelligent e-learning systems design and evaluation* as part of the program *Intelligent Support to Omnipresence of e-Learning Systems.* The actual *TEx-Sys* version is publicly accessible and can be found on the following Website: http://proliant.pmfst.hr/xtexsys/

Following all the experience gained in almost twenty years of research and development of intelligent tutoring systems, we have organized the book in 16 chapters divided into six major sections entitled:

- Intelligent Tutoring Systems Architectures (four chapters)
- E-learning Communities Technologies (two chapters)
- Intelligent E-learning in Different Domains (four chapters)
- Personalized Advanced E-Learning Environments (three chapters)
- E-learning Systems Effectiveness (three chapters)
- Intelligent tutoring systems – the future and new directions

The book is meant to unfold a variety of new directions in the fields of mobile computing environments, natural language generation and understanding, applications of natural language processing in testing student's knowledge, computerized tutor for learning and teaching programming, student and group modeling in different kinds of e-learning systems, meta-analyses for determining overall effectiveness of e-learning and e-learning systems.

Both the layout and content of the first five sections substantiate the book title by taking in focus intelligent tutoring systems and their respective environments, from the design, implementation and evaluation point of view, as illustrated by different e-learning technologies. The final, sixth section presents authors views on the future of ITSs and new research directions in the respective field of study.

The first section entitled: *Intelligent tutoring system architecture* consists of four chapters addressing best practice issues in ITS development, intelligent learning environment design methodology, ITS methodology enhancement with the agent paradigm, also providing a concluding overview on the new ITS architecture with pattern approach.

E-learning communities' technology (the second section) describes advanced learning technologies that conform to the virtual and mobile paradigm exploited in ITS environments.

The third section, *Intelligent e-learning in different domains*, describes the positioning of intelligent e-learning system conditions in affective tutoring, learning trough gaming, learning programming and the overlay method in knowledge testing through natural language dialog systems.

Personalized advanced e-learning environment (the forth section) brings into focus the student as the main actor in the process of learning, teaching and testing. Student modeling and cognitive diagnostic assessment are presented as critical issues needed to be addressed for the successful development and application of the ITSs. In modern learning and teaching conditions, it is of great importance to procure collaborative work. Relating to this goal, using effect size for group modeling in e-learning systems provides major contribution in group work evaluation. Semantic Web and adaptive selection and sequencing of learning objects based on learning profiles preferences and abilities of individual learners, along with automatic composition of assessment or examination papers based on instructors' specifications, contribute in the personalization of learning environments.

Effectiveness estimation of e-learning systems along with their respective environments is presented in the fifth section. As first, the factors for determining the overall effectiveness of e-learning systems used in higher education are elaborated. Then, a meta-analytic estimation of a common effect size methodology deriving from a series of experiments at different study levels is used for the evaluation of e-learning system effectiveness. The section concludes with understanding the phenomenon of human learning as an open system establishing relationships with its socio-historical context and the analysis of interactive processes as a path to understanding the quality of distance education.

As already mentioned, we conclude the book by providing a number of views on the future and new directions in the intelligent tutoring systems development. Personal authors' contributions to the discussion on the future of the intelligent tutoring systems are presented. It is considered that this chapter shows different opinions and research directions in the field of the intelligent tutoring systems.

Slavomir Stankov
Vlado Glavinić
Marko Rosić
Editors

Acknowledgment

Following our previous successful collaboration with IGI Global (formerly Idea Press) in contributing a chapter in the edited book *Intelligent Learning Infrastructure for Knowledge Intensive Organizations: A Semantic Web Perspective* (2005), at the end of 2007 we have been offered the possibility to further elaborate the topic of this chapter (titled *Intelligent Tutoring Systems for the New Learning Infrastructure*) in a book to edit. Accepting IGI Global kind invitation, we undertook this project hoping that together with all forthcoming contributors we will provide the reader with the intelligent tutoring systems research, development and implementation results in the teaching and learning process.

During the years 2008 and 2009 we have concluded the organization of the book, having ensured the collaboration of forty two researchers, encompassing both domain experts and teaching practitioners, to contribute with the results of their valuable work. We would like to heartily thank each one of them for their support in this endeavor, and hope that they are satisfied with the resulting book. The interdisciplinary team we succeeded to assemble is formed by experts in their respective fields of research in applying information and communication technology in education, and especially intelligent tutoring systems. Our colleagues thus convened come from the areas of educational technology, cognitive and social psychology, informatics in educations, computer engineering, artificial intelligence, electrical and biomedical engineering, and education. We feel that such as multi and interdisciplinary approach helps to better shed the light on intelligent tutoring systems.

We are most grateful to all reviewers and members of the Editorial Advisory Board, and would especially like to mention the help of Ani Grubišić and Saša Mladenović, without whom this book wouldn't be possible.

We would also like to express our gratitude to IGI Global and especially Julia Mosemann, Director of Book Publications, who has been with us during the preparation of the book, not sparing her effort and time to successfully accomplish the project. It has been truly a pleasure to work with Julia in the production of this book.

March, 2010

Slavomir Stankov
Vlado Glavinić
Marko Rosić
Editors

Section 1
Intelligent Tutoring Systems Architectures

Chapter 1
Intelligent Tutoring Systems: Best Practices

Aytürk Keleş
Atatürk University, Turkey

Ali Keleş
Atatürk University, Turkey

ABSTRACT

Today's education is faced by new challenges and yet new innovations. The key area where innovations are introduced lies on instructional methodology. It becomes necessary for the educators to incorporate new trends and methodologies in instructional methodology. One such aspect that came into existence is intelligent tutorial system. In this chapter, Firstly, the appearance of the ITS notion and related literature review will be handled. After then general architecture of Intelligent Tutoring Systems will be presented and information about improvements on ITS will be given up to now. And also best ITS practices will be mentioned, too. In this sense, ZOSMAT - a detailed sample application - will be explained as a demonstration of how an ITS is designed. ZOSMAT can be used for the purpose of either individual learning or real classroom environment with the guidance of a human tutor during a formal education process. This characteristic of ZOSMAT distinguishes itself from other intelligent tutoring systems (Keles et al., 2009). Finally, challenges and problems in the area of ITS and future of ITS will be discussed.

INTRODUCTION

Instructor-led training (ILT) was the main training method, before computers were widely available. ILT didn't allowed students to get away from the class focus on their studies and to interact with their instructor and classmates. However, in general ILT meant high costs and downtime during office hours, leading training provides to search for better way to train.

Such as windows, Macintosh, CD-ROMs and PowerPoint were the technological advancements of the Multimedia era. Thanks to CD-ROM training more transportable and visually engaging, Computer-Based Training (CBT) courses were delivered. The anytime, anywhere availability of CD-ROMs also provided time and cost savings that instructor-led training (ILT) couldn't, and helped

DOI: 10.4018/978-1-61692-008-1.ch001

reshape training industry. Despite these benefits, CD-ROM courses lacked instructor interaction and dynamic presentations- making the experience slower and less engaging for students.

The rapid growth of the Internet and World Wide Web offers new opportunities and challenges for many areas. One of them is education. Web-based education has numerous advantages such as the convenience of taking a course without leaving the workplace or home and the reduced cost (Berz, Erdelyi & Hoefkens, 1999).

Technological advances – including JAVA/IP network applications, rich streaming media, high-bandwidth access, and advanced web site design – are revolutionizing the training industry. Today, live instructor-led training (ILT) via the web can be combined with real-time mentoring, improved learner services, and up-to-date, engaging, "born on the Web" content to create a highly-effective, multi-dimensional learning environment. These sophisticated training solutions provide even greater cost savings, higher quality learning experiences, and are setting the standard for next wave of e-learning.

E-learning systems have been widely adopted by numerous organizations in recent years. It has also been proved to be effective and efficient to improve learners' knowledge. The most attractive characteristic of e-learning system is that it can provide flexible learning path depending on the learner's skills and learning abilities. Such flexibility can further eliminate some limitations so that learners can decide where and when to learn what materials according to their needs.

Although adopting e-learning systems have been widely accepted by organizations, there still exist some obstacles. For example, e-learning performance is difficult to be evaluated. Meanwhile, learner behavior changes so fast that predefined learning materials cannot catch up the learner's needs. Furthermore, it is also difficult to design an e-learning system that meets all the learner's needs because the computers are not human teachers that can make proper reactions when difficulty occurs. On the other hand, constructing e-learning systems require large amount of time, money, and human resources. Thus, it is required to improve the existed e-learning systems to maximize the learning result while reduces constructing costs as well.

Computational intelligent methodologies used in Intelligent Tutoring System are capable to remove the limitations mentioned above. Intelligent tutoring systems (ITSs) are computer programs that are designed to incorporate techniques from the AI community in order to provide tutors which know what they teach, who they teach and how to teach it.

Firstly, the appearance of the ITS notion and related literature review will be handled in this chapter. After then general architecture of Intelligent Tutoring Systems will be presented and information about improvements on ITS will be given up to now. In progressive parts of this chapter, the integration of ITS with Web oriented technologies will be referred by examples. And also best ITS practices will be mentioned, too. The following questions will be explained: How an ITS is designed, which components are used, how the requirements of a class are responded by a system, etc. Afterwards the problems of ITSs and possible improvements on ITS field will be emphasized.

BACKGROUND

Concept of Intelligent Tutoring System (ITS)

Teachers started using machines to assist in their instructional endeavors before the invention of the computer. After microcomputer systems became more sophisticated, Computer- Assisted Instruction (CAI) allowed for more flexible and comprehensive instruction. Although a student could skim through or skip some of the material using this type of instruction just as one could skip some pages of a book, most CAI programs were not considered intelligent. Intelligent-computer- assisted instruction (ICAI) was introduced by Jaime Carbonell in 1970 when he designed a computer program called SCHOLAR. This program was also considered the first ITS because it separated tutorial capabilities from domain knowledge (Wenger, 1987).

The basic difference in CAI and ICAI or ITS is the knowledge encoded in the program. CAI programs contain only knowledge about the domain while ITS programs contain knowledge about the domain and also knowledge about the student and how to teach that student. The dream of ICAI researchers is to provide each student with a computer-based tutor that has all the qualities of a master teacher. This includes great scope and depth of subject matter expertise, excellent knowledge of teaching techniques, powerful communication skills, and the ability to inspire and motivate students to learn. (Kearsley, 1987).

Much of the research in domain of educational software involving AI has been conducted in the name of "ICAI", an acronym for "Intelligent Computer Aided Instruction". This phase, in turn, evolved out of the name "Computer-Aided Instruction" (CAI) often referring to the use of computers in education. Nevertheless, to all intents and purposes, ITSs and ICAI are synonymous. However, though some researchers still prefer "ICAI" it is now often replaced by the acronym "ITS". The latter, which is also the author's personal preference, is certainly gaining support, as confirmed by the international conference on Intelligent Tutoring Systems held in Montreal, Canada, as recently as June 1988. This preference is motivated by the claim that, in many ways; the significance of the shift in research methodology goes beyond the adding of an "I" to "CAI" (Wenger 1987). However, some researchers are understandably hesitant to use the term "intelligent", instead opting for labels such as "Knowledge-Based Tutoring system" (KBTS) or "Adaptive Tutoring System" (ATS); Wenger (1987) prefers the label Knowledge Communication Systems. Nevertheless, most researchers appear to be reasonably content with the acronym ITS. This fine as long as every one involved with the area understands that the usage of the word "intelligent" is, strictly speaking, a misnomer. This does not appear to be the case, resulting in some very ambitious goals/claims, particularly in the more theoretical parts of the literature: this also appears to be a valid criticism of the entire AI literature. The fact that ITS research spans three disciplines has important implications. It means that three are major differences in research goals, terminology, theoretical frameworks, and emphases amongst ITS researchers (Hyacinth, 1990).

General Architecture of Intelligent Tutoring System (ITS)

Existing ITSs has many variety in architecture. In fact, it is almost a rarity to find two ITSs based on the same architecture. These results from experimental nature of the work in the area: there is yet not clear cut general architecture for such systems (Yazdani, 1986, 1987). Previously, there was considerable consensus in the literature that ITSs consist of at least three basic components (Barr & Feigenbaum, 1982; Bonnet, 1985).

1. The expert knowledge module
2. The student knowledge module
3. The tutoring module

However, more recent research (Wenger, 1987; Burns & Capps, 1988; Mandl & Lesgold, 1988) has identified and added a fourth component to the list.

4. The user interface module

This general form of an ITS architecture can be illustrate such as in Figure 1.

The User Interface module provides to get across with the student in ITS. The expert knowl-

Figure 1. General ITS architecture

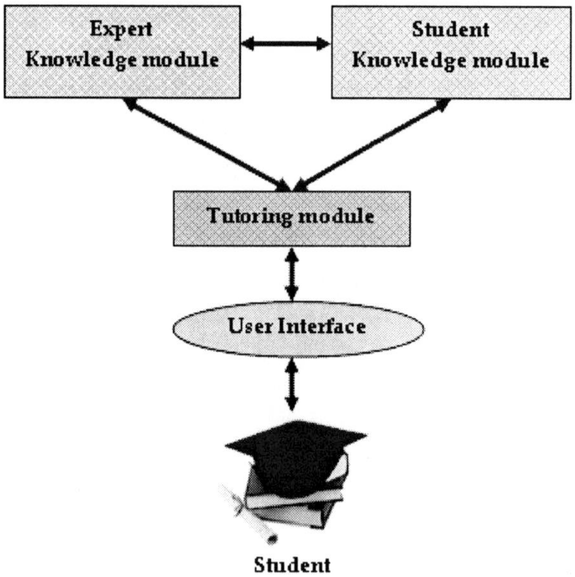

edge module references an expert or domain model containing a description of the knowledge or behaviors that represent expertise in the subject-matter domain the ITS is teaching - often an expert system or cognitive model. The student knowledge module uses a student model containing descriptions of student knowledge or behaviors, including his or her misconceptions and knowledge gaps. An apprentice technician might, for instance, believe a thermostat also signals too high temperatures to a furnace (misconception) or might not know about thermostats that also gauge the outdoor temperature (knowledge gap). A mismatch between a student's behavior or knowledge and the expert's presumed behavior or knowledge is signaled to the tutor module, which subsequently takes corrective action, such as providing feedback or remedial instruction. To be able to do this, it needs information about what a human tutor in such situations would do: the tutoring module.

Intelligent tutoring systems (ITSs) are computer programs that are designed to incorporate techniques from the AI community in order to provide tutors which know what they teach, who they teach and how to teach it. AI attempts to produce in a computer behavior which, if performed by a human, would be described as "intelligent"; ITSs may similarly be thought of as attempts to produce in a computer behavior which, if performed by a human, would be described as "good teaching" (Elsom-Cook, 1987). The design and development of such tutors lie at the intersection of computer since, cognitive psychology and educational research; this intersecting area is normally referred to as cognitive science (see Figure 2).

IMPROVEMENTS ON INTELLIGENT TUTORING SYSTEM (ITS)

Intelligent Tutoring Systems (ITS) are computer programs that use several technological resources to support a teaching–learning process (TLP). Initially based on the programmed instruction paradigm, the evolution of ITS guided them to the Intelligent Learning Environments (ILE) incorporating several pedagogical paradigms. ITS uses techniques of Artificial Intelligence (AI) to represent the three types of knowledge, indispensable to a TLP: knowledge on the domain, on the

Figure 2.

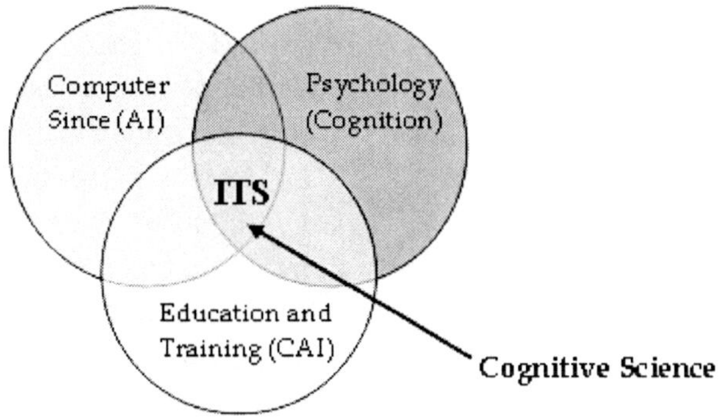

pedagogical strategies and on the apprentice (Dillenbourg & Mendelsohn, 1991). These different kinds of knowledge define the Domain Knowledge Module, the Tutor Module and the Student Module, respectively. The Interface Module allows communication between the apprentice and the system. ITS development shows an evolution in the importance given to each Module. Initially focus was on the Specialist Module, using AI to represent the knowledge on a specific domain (Carbonell, 1970). Next, pedagogical strategies were incorporated into the system, obtaining the Tutor Module (Collins, 1976) and AI was used for the selection of the strategies. Lastly, a Student Model was necessary to make diagnosis for the apprentice (Brown & Burton, 1978; Clancey, 1982), resulting in the Student Module. Recently, the interface has acquired greater importance, enriching interactivity between apprentice and system. Interface became the Learning Environment and its adaptation is fundamental to improve system efficiency (Brusilovsky, 1998).

A key function of any ITS is the ability to adapt, as closely as possible, pedagogical activities to individual student/learner needs. So, ITS try to identify some student's characteristics that allow obtaining criterions to propose activities, as well as to know how to react to some apprentice's actions. Adapting tutoring to individual students significantly increases the speed of learning (Davidovic, Warren, & Trichina, 2003), so adaptability can be observed as a common goal in all the systems developed until today. The new generation of tutoring systems owes its development to the advances of AI and cognitive theories on learning. For example, Atolagbe, Hlupic, and Taylor (2001) discuss the role of pedagogical strategies to facilitate the acquisition of simulation modelling knowledge. The learning environment integrates case-based reasoning with interactive tools to guide tutorial remediation selecting the strategy according to the current problem and student's progress. Davidovic et al. (2003) illustrate and evaluate a generic adaptive tutoring environment, structural example-based adaptive tutoring system (SEAT), using the theory of cognitive knowledge acquisition. Suebnukarn and Haddawy (2004) developed COMET, a collaborative intelligent tutoring system for medical Problem-Based Learning. The system uses Bayesian networks to model individual student knowledge and activity. Kodaganallur, Weitz, and Rosenthal (2004) report the development of a software tool that enables non-software developers to create declaratively intelligent tutors. This intelligent tutor generator creates applications in problem solving contexts, with rich user interaction and theory-based remediation capabilities. As an example of the tendency that incorporates new cognitive theories to model the students, Kelly and Tangney (2004) use Multiple Intelligences and Conati and Maclare (2004) consider student's effective states.

Web-Based Intelligent Tutoring System

An efficient Training System should allow users to take a lesson without time and place constrains. In order to fulfill these requirements, at present days, the best solution has to be naturally Web based. It requires to end-users zero cost installation and provides them the maximum time/place flexibility.

Web-based education has numerous advantages such as the convenience of taking a course without leaving the workplace or home and the reduced cost (Berz, Erdelyi & Hoefkens, 1999). In addition, teachers and educational researchers are encountering both unprecedented opportunities and challenges to adapt networks to their classrooms and research fields (Chou, 1999). However, most of the educational applications that have been delivered through the World Wide Web are just electronic books with very limited interactivity and diagnostic capability. An integration of ITSs and Web-based technologies would be very beneficial for the purposes of education. Indeed, there have been successful attempts to either move existing ITSs to the WWW (e.g. Alpert, Singley, & Fairweather, 1999; Ritter, 1997) or build from scratch Web-based ITSs (e.g. Eliot, Neiman, & Lamar, 1997; Peylo, Thelen, Rollinger, & Gust 2000). However, Web-based ITSs aim at reaching a much more heterogeneous group of learners in settings where no teacher is available to help users during the learning process. In order to match the large diversity of student needs, backgrounds and interests, a careful and extensive knowledge acquisition phase should precede the development of a Web-based ITS. This is even more urging in the case of Web-based ITS authoring tools which are also addressed to a wide range of instructors with varying beliefs, preferences and teaching styles.

Actually, as stated by Hendler and Feigenbaum (2001), the knowledge acquisition bottleneck becomes particularly troubling in the era of the World Wide Web and they continue by saying that the ubiquity of information accessible at the fingertips of millions of users drives a relentless demand for more intelligent computer assistance.

Three kinds of Web-Based Tutoring (WBT) methodologies are available on the scene at this moment (Capuano et al., 2004).

Static WBT: teachers arrange learning material in order to cover one or more topics and convert them in interactive linked HTML pages (or different kinds of Web-deliverable objects). Material is then placed on-line in order to make it visible to everybody. Learners can exploit it only by following the path established by teachers.

Personalized WBT: teachers, using a specific kind of software named Course Management System (i.e. Macromedia Attain) are able to perform manually a set of additional tasks. They can monitor student knowledge by testing them, assign recovery material if necessary, define different paths through learning objects for different kind of learning goals, etc.

Adaptive WBT: includes all features of a Personalized WBT but the teacher is supported/simulated in his activity by using Artificial Intelligence techniques.

When it is mentioned about providing a personalized service in e-learning systems, there are two main research directions: adaptive educational systems and intelligent tutors (agents). Adaptive educational systems adapt the presentation of content and the navigation through these contents to a student's profile. This profile may comprise the student's learning style, knowledge, background, goals, among other features. Different adaptive methods are: adaptive ordering, link hiding, link removal, and adaptive link annotation.

Examples of these systems are: MLTutor (Smith & Blandford, 2003), MAS–PLANG (Peña et al., 2002), KBS-Hyperbook (Henze& Nejdl, 2001) and ELM–ART (Brusilovsky, Schwarz, & Weber, 1996). On the other hand, intelligent tutors recommend educational activities and deliver individual feedback according to the student's profile, which generally includes the student's knowledge or activities within the course he/she is taking. Example of intelligent tutors in different domains are: SQL-Tutor (Mitrovic, 2003); German Tutor (Heift & Nicholson, 2001); ITSPOKE (Forbes-Riley, Litman, & Rotaru, 2008) in the domain of physics problems; CIRCSIM-Tutor (Evens et al., 2001), who helps students solve a class of problems in cardiovascular physiology dealing with the regulation of blood pressure, and KERMIT (Suraweera & Mitrovi, 2002), who teaches conceptual database design using the Entity-Relationship data model. Our agent can be considered as an intelligent tutor, which recommends educational tasks to students depending on their profile. Particularly, it has been used to assists students taking an artificial intelligence course. As regards the problem of student modelling, many works in the two areas discussed above have addressed it (see (Brusilovsky & Peylo, 2003) for a review). These works can be categorized according to different characteristics, such as the content of the student model, the type of student being modelled, how the student model is updated, what the model is used for, among others. Our work can be placed among those modelling psychological features of students, such as ARTHUR (Gilbert & Han, 1999) which considers three learning styles (visual-interactive, reading-listener, textual), CS388 (Carver, Howard, & Lavelle, 1996) and MAS-PLANG (Peña et al., 2002) that use Felder and Silverman styles; and the INSPIRE system (Papanikolaou, Grigoriadou, Knornilakis, & Magoulas, 2003) that uses the styles proposed by Honey and Mumford (Honey & Mumford, 1992).

Consequently, different techniques have been used to represent student models such as rules (Jeremic & Deyedzic, 2004), Bayesian networks, and case-based reasoning (Peña et al., 2002). As regards Bayesian networks, ANDES (Gertner& VanLehn, 2000) and SE-Coach (Conati, Gertner, & VanLehn, 2002) use this technique to model students' knowledge in Physics. IDEAL (Shang, Shi, & Chen, 2001) uses this technique to categorize students into novice, beginner, intermediate, advanced, or expert. In Arroyo and Woolf (2005) the authors build a Bayesian model to detect a student's hidden attitudes, perception towards the e- learning system, and amount learned from observable student behavior recorded in a log file. In Gamboa and Fred (2001) the authors use Bayesian networks to assess students' state of knowledge and learning preferences, in an intelligent tutoring system. In Xenos (2004) BN are used to model the behavior of students in an open and distance education system, aiding student data processing and teachers decision making.

SOME SAMPLES FROM ITS'S BEST PRACTICES

SHERLOCK

Lajoie and Lesgold's (1989) "SHERLOCK" trains Air Force electronic technicians to diagnose problems in a complex device used to service the avionics of F-15 jets. The SHERLOCK computer screen presents a depiction of the device, schematic diagrams of the electrical circuits, and system documentation. The tutor "creates" a fault in one or more of the circuits of the device, and asks the trainee to locate the problem. The trainee selects the circuit diagram he or she thinks should be tested, marks where the probes of the diagnostic equipment are to be placed, "activates" the equipment, and receives simulated readouts. After considering the readouts, the trainee decides whether there is a fault in that tested part of the circuit. The process is usually repeated many times, attaching the probes to various circuits, until the trainee determines the location of the fault. If the trainee is clearly misdirected or proceeding inefficiently, the computer provides feedback and guidance. In addition, whenever the trainee wants help, the computer will provide it. SHERLOCK sequences the various simulated faults in a manner to optimize each trainee's learning.

Cardiac Tutor

The "Cardiac Tutor" of Eliot and Woolf (1994) trains medical personnel in advanced cardiac life support techniques. It consists of a screen-based simulation of the patient's ECG trace, blood gases, and vital signs, and a tutor that provides clues, spoken advice, and feedback. The domain database and the student characteristics database are used to present cardiac problems likely to optimize a given student's learning. The simulated patient presents indications of various cardiac problems, and the student selects various interventions to correct the problem and save the patient's life. At the end of the simulation (the patient either dies or is stabilized), the student can review the entire simulation and his or her responses, receive a critique of the correct and incorrect responses, and request more information about the presented cardiac problems and appropriate interventions.

Mathematics Tutor

The "Mathematics Tutor" of Beal, Beck and Woolf (1998) teaches a student how to solve word problems that make use of fractions, decimals, and percentages. The domain expertise classifies problems by the mathematical operations, by sub skills required to solve them, and by complexity. As the student works problems, the tutor records both success rates for various operations and sub skills and the time needed to solve problems. It selects subsequent problems that are predicted to challenge the student moderately and likely to be answered within a desirable time. The desirable time will be relatively short for students who are not very proficient, lack confidence in their abilities, or give up readily, but will be longer for students with high proficiency and confidence. More than 40 variables are used in selecting the problems, hints, and help provided to an individual student.

AutoTutor

AutoTutor is a computer tutor that simulates the discourse patterns and pedagogical strategies of a typical human tutor. AutoTutor is designed to assist college students in learning the fundamentals of hardware, operating systems, and the Internet in an introductory computer literacy course. AutoTutor presents questions and problems from a curriculum script, attempts to comprehend learner contributions that are entered by keyboard, formulates dialog moves that are sensitive to the learner's contributions (such as short feedback, pumps, prompts, elaborations, corrections, and hints), and delivers the dialog moves with a talking head. AutoTutor has seven modules: a curriculum script, language extraction, speech act classification, latent semantic analysis, topic selection, dialog move generation, and a talking head (Graesser et al. 1999).

ALEKS

ALEKS (Assessment and Learning in Knowledge Spaces) is an example of ITS currently used for the assessment and learning of factual knowledge in arithmetic and algebra. A web-based system, in contrast to compact–disk-based, can easily be used for the monitoring and management of entire courses and even institutions. As an intelligent tutor, this system "teaches" the student, and provides a new and engaging way for students to learn or review the fundamentals of arithmetic and algebra (Canfield, 2001).

CIRCSIM-Tutor

CIRCSIM-Tutor version 2, a dialogue-based intelligent tutoring system (ITS), is nearly five years old. It conducts a conversation with a student to help the student learn to solve a class of problems in cardiovascular physiology dealing with the regulation of blood pressure. It uses natural language for both input and output, and can handle a variety of syntactic constructions and lexical items, including sentence fragments and misspelled words.

Students use CIRCSIM-Tutor to learn to solve problems like those taught in their physiology course. Students are asked to predict the value of the seven parameters at three points in time: the DR or *direct response* stage immediately after the precipitating event, the RR or *reflex response* stage after the nervous system responds, and the SS or new *steady state* stage (Evens et al., 2001).

Why2-Atlas

The Why2-Atlas system teaches qualitative physics by having students write paragraph-long explanations of simple mechanical phenomena. The tutor uses deep syntactic analysis and abductive theorem proving to convert the student's essay to a proof. The proof formalizes not only what was said, but the likely beliefs behind what was said. This allows the tutor to uncover misconceptions as well as to detect missing correct parts of the explanation. If the tutor finds such a flaw in the essay, it conducts a dialogue intended to remedy the missing or misconceived beliefs, then asks the student to correct the essay. It often takes several iterations of essay correction and dialogue to get the student to produce an acceptable explanation (Cerri et al. 2002).

SmartTutor

SmartTutor is an intelligent tutoring system implemented for distance learning in Hong Kong. School of Professional and Continuing Education, The University of Hong Kong (HKU SPACE) has developed SmartTutor to address these two crucial elements: personalization and intelligent tutoring, which are important for life-long/adult education. This project can be treated as a case study of combining Internet technology, education research, and artificial intelligence. The SmartTutor has been integrated into the SPACE Online Universal Learning platform (an online learning platform), which provides support to courses offered by HKU SPACE. The effectiveness of SmartTutor has been evaluated and the results are very positive (Cheung et al., 2003).

Vivids-DIAG and DIAG NLP Systems

Vivids-DIAG, a combination of the Vivids authoring environment (Munro, 1994) and the DIAG framework (Towne 1997a; 1997b), is a tool designed to build Intelligent Tutoring Systems (ITSs). A typical ITS built with Vivids-DIAG provides a student with a visual representation of a relatively complex system. This system is modeled with a set of components called *replaceable units* (RU) and a set of *indicators*. To help the student acquire the skills required to successfully debug the faulty system, DIAG can provide suggestions based on the investigation path of the student, i.e., the parts of the system he/she saw and the indicators he/she read during the current exercise. This advice, given in natural language, answers four types of queries: *Consult RU*, *Consult Indicator*, *Consult Debrief*, and *Show Suspicious RUs*. To answer a *Consult RU* query, DIAG provides an indication of the likelihood that a given RU is the cause of the fault. A *Consult Indicator* query asks for the correlation of a given indicator reading with a set of replaceable units. At the present time, there are four versions of the system: Vivids-DIAG (the original one), DIAG-NLP1, DIAG-NLP2, and DIAG-NLP3 (the NLP-enhanced versions) (Fossati 2003).

ActiveMath

ActiveMath is a web-based, adaptive learning environment for mathematics. These systems strive for improving long-distance learning, for complementing traditional classroom teaching, and for supporting individual and life-long learning. Web-based systems are available on central servers and allow a user to learn in his/her own environment and whenever it is appropriate for her. This system is configurable with pedagogical strategies, content and presentational style sheets as well as with external problem solving systems. It employs a number of AI-techniques to realize adaptive course generation, student modeling, feedback, interactive exercises, and a knowledge representation that is expedient for the semantic Web (Melis E., and Siekmann 2004).

REALP

This system provides reader-specific lexical practice for improved reading comprehension and offers individualized practice to students by presenting authentic and appropriate reading materials. REAP gathers documents from the Web in order to find useful, authentic reading material for these students. The documents are analyzed according to syntactic features, readability, length, and the occurrence of target vocabulary. The tutor uses an extended version of the Lemur Toolkit for Language Modeling and Information Retrieval to annotatethe documents and create an index for language-model based retrieval. When a student uses REAP, the system searches among this set of documents for those that satisfy a number of constraints, including the student's target vocabulary list, document length, his or her user model, and the target reading level for the course, which is sixth to eighth grade. After reading a document, usually from one to two pages in length, the student works through a series of automatically generated exercises based on the target vocabulary found in the reading. The student model is updated after every reading so that the optimal document can be retrieved for the next reading passage (Heilman et al. 2006).

eTeacher

eTeacher is an intelligent agent that provides personalized assistance to e-learning students. It observes a student's behavior while he/she is taking online courses and automatically builds the student's profile. This profile comprises the student's learning style and information about the student's performance, such as exercises done, topics studied exam results. In this approach, a student's learning style is automatically detected from the student's actions in an e-learning system using Bayesian networks. Then, eTeacher uses the information contained in the student profile to proactively assist the student by suggesting him/her personalized courses of action that will help him/her during the learning process (Schiaffino et al., 2008).

HOW AN ITS IS DESIGNED: A DETAILED SAMPLE ZOSMAT

This system was developed to be able to respond almost every needs of a real classroom. ZOSMAT can be used for the purpose of either individual learning or real classroom environment with the guidance of a human tutor during a formal education process. This characteristic of ZOSMAT distinguishes itself from other intelligent tutoring systems. ZOSMAT follows a student in each stage of the learning process and guides him/her about what he/she will need to do. ZOSMAT with a web-based feature presents an equal opportunity of education for both the student in the classroom and the student in the far end of the world. This system is a student-centered one and the progress in student's learning process depends on his/her effort (Keles et al. 2009).

The main architecture of ZOSMAT consists of six components: ZOSMAT manager, question bank, student model, content structure, expert model, and user interface (UI). In summary, the manager coordinates the different ZOSMAT components so they can work together smoothly. Conceptually, the relationship among the six components: ZOSMAT manager, content structure, student model, question bank, expert model and user interface (UI) can be viewed as in Figure 3.

Figure 3. The software architecture of ZOSMAT

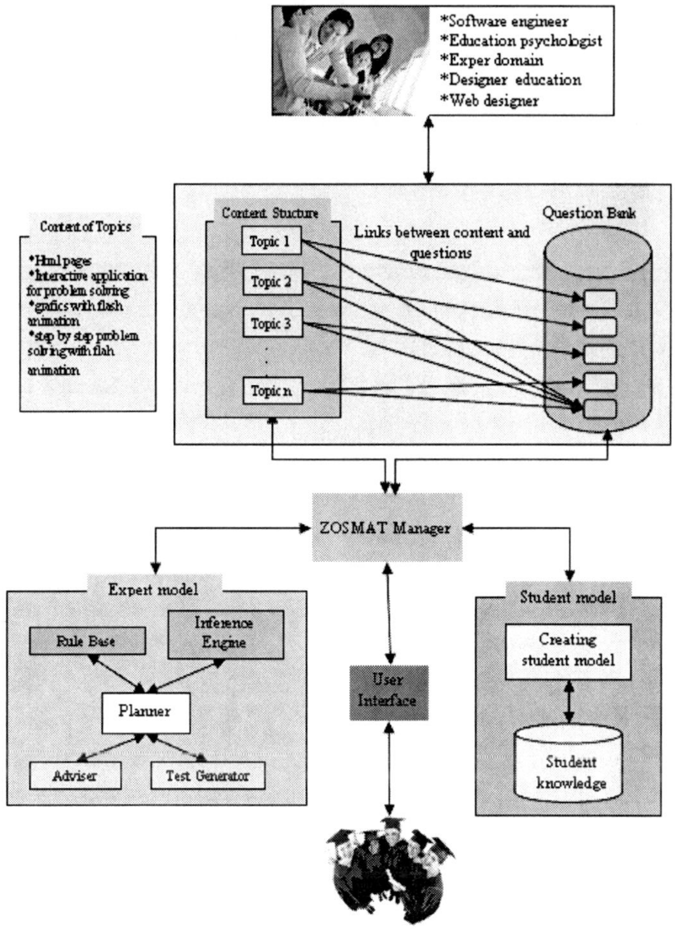

1. ***ZOSMAT manager:*** The ZOSMAT manager is the control center of ZOSMAT. It has the following functions:
   - Analyses the content structure of each courses.
   - Invokes the expert model to create a planned course using the domain knowledge provided by human tutor and developer system, for each student, or to give individualized instructions and suggestions during each student's learning process.
   - Maintains student's personal information, learning status, testing results in the student model.
   - Delivers the course via the UI.
   - Creates adaptive test or examination via the question bank.

In the software design, all data flow and control flow are managed and handled by ZOSMAT manager. Content structure maintains the relationship between course contents so that ZOSMAT Manager can create individual learning maps for students. Question bank stores questions related to topics. There are links between questions and the course contents. Student model maintains student's learning profiles. Especially, it stores the learning performance history of students. Based on this profile, the expert model will analyze and design a plan for the student. From these advices and plans, content structure can create personalized study sequence for students, and planned tests and assessments can be constructed using the questions in question bank to help students. These modules form a feedback loop in every student's study path.

2. ***Content structure and question bank:*** Basically, content structure consists of variety learning materials. These can be any of the following objects: HTML pages, interactive applications, animations, audios, videos, and other files. Question bank is a warehouse of questions that supports the generation of test or examination. It is also an essential part of an online course system. The ZOSMAT controls and evaluates each student's learning process by using the test papers and results, which are the basis of question bank. Only through the tests generated from question bank, ZOSMAT can get learning information of each student and record them in student model. In order to generate one appropriate test easily, question bank must be organized efficiently. Score is the result of marking and is important to system decisions. The score of the test paper is recorded in each student's learning history and can trigger different processes of the system, which makes it possible to achieve various proposed functions of the system. Moreover, if the test paper consists of questions of several topics or concepts, the score of each part will be recorded as the statistic data for future analysis.
3. ***Student model:*** The intelligence of an ITS is largely attributed to its ability to adapt to a specific student during the teaching process. The adaptation involves choosing and presenting each successive teaching activity as a function of the entire scope. The adaptation depends on individual student's knowledge of the subject being taught and other relevant features of the student, thus giving a personalized advice to the student. The knowledge and relevant information about the student are maintained in a student model.Several learning paradigms of education theories were studied (Carbonell, 1970; John, 1988; Johnson, 1986; VanLehn, 1996). To ZOSMAT, each learning paradigm of education theories means a different way to capture information as the student's learning records, and in turn, a different way to build the expert model. For example, in the cognitive approach (Demetriou, 1993; Friedman, 1986), the space of time that a student spends in learning one concept, how many times of repetitions a student has had in a concept, and his/her self-test result about that concept will guide ZOSMAT to advise the student's learning progress. It can also be successfully used in problem-based learning. In the traditional face-to-face education, class is a usual learning group which consists of members who learn the same course or join in the same program. The student's result of each stage of the course is recorded; however, these records are cursory and are not fully utilized to improve student's learning efficiency. Individual learning performance is a serial of testing results attached to each topic. According to the mark distribution through the individual content map, ZOSMAT can give some personalized instructions, corresponding advices, and specific training for everyone during their learning process. Effectively students have their own private Advisor online, so this function of ZOSMAT is called as "Advisor".
4. ***Expert model:*** The expert model is one the core components of ZOSMAT. It is the model that makes the ZOSMAT being "intelligent". It combines the AI technology and domain knowledge provided by the experts in Department of Mathematics Education, Ataturk University. Two-human tutor like-

modules, Advisor and Planner, provide main intelligent functions of ZOSMAT. Advisor focuses on test results and evaluation analysis. Advices are given based on a group of experts in Mathematics Education who design a set of rules using the theory of learning paradigms which best fit Mathematics Education's students in order to achieve the best learning quality. Planner, on the other hand, is like a resource manager and will provide more resource-oriented but personalized planning for the individual students based on the advices from the Advisor. Both the Advisor and Planner need the support from another module, called test generator. All behaviors of ZOSMAT are decided by the rules. The rule-base consists of expert rules that allow the Planner to determine the selection and ordering of materials that should be presented to the student and allow the Planner to determine the selection and ordering of materials that should be presented to the student and allow the Advisor to generate the appropriate instructions and tests that should be presented to the student.

5. ***User interface:*** We aimed to implement the user interface of the ZOSMAT system as user friendly. The program has been implemented in ASP.NET with Visual C# (Microsoft Visual Studio 2005 developer tool) and SQL Server 2005 was used as a database platform. ZOSMAT runs on Windows environment. Finally, a web-based UI is provided for the students. Besides, UI provides displaying results of other ZOSMAT components.

How Does Work and Use ZOSMAT?

Main Screen

This is the main screen of ZOSMAT which appears when the project works. User enters user name and password in this screen (Figure 4). If this user is active in ZOSMAT then it doesn't allow entering and warns to user. Besides, there are visual elements about ZOSMAT system in this screen.

There are four kinds of user in ZOSMAT system.

1. Fully authorized user: This is the most authorized user and can do all of the process

Figure 4. Main screen and selections screen

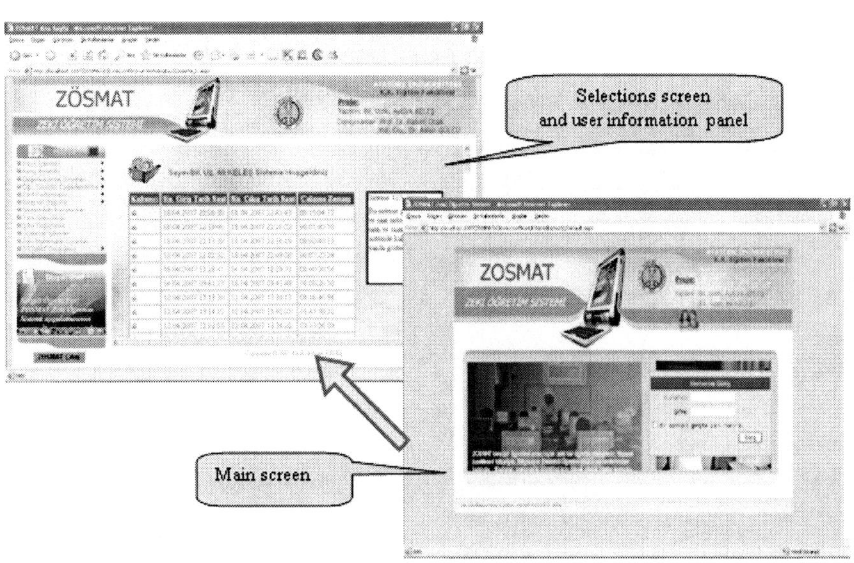

in the system. For example, he can enter all selections and change content of selections and make authorization sharing to users. This kind of user is only defined to system manager and group who developed ZOSMAT.

2. Tutor user: This user can act with authority which fully authorized user defined in ZOSMAT. Mostly, he has got full authority in the educational part of ZOSMAT. He can insert the subjects to be taught in the program and educational visual items and also enter questions to question bank. Besides, He can make all observations deal with student's learning process. Generally, this kind of users consist human tutors.
3. Student user: These are essential users of ZOSMAT which other users type serve. They can select topic that they want to learn and forward direction of suggestion's ZOSMAT in education process. Self performance of student may compare with other student's performance in system. They can extremely benefit from visual education items and interactive applications. In addition, they could examine their own individual learning graphic depending on time. This kind of user authority is given to students.
4. Observer user: this user can see demo of ZOSMAT or part of learning and also follow performances of students in system. They can not make anything without observation in the system. Generally, this kind of users consist experts who is examining system or parents who is following their student's learning situation.

Selections Screen

All of the users of ZOSMAT see this screen (Figure 4). There is a report including information about active users such as when the user entered the system before and how much time student studied and what kinds of things student made in ZOSMAT. Thanks to report, student can inform about (well ground in) his/her individual situation. Menu including selections locates in the left side of this screen. The visual item locates at the bottom of menu which informs to student/students (group or individually) about system or learning program, for example notifications.

Operations of Enrolling

First selection- first screens (enrolling in lesson): This screen is appeared in "inline frame-iframe" (Figure 5). Human tutor enrolls in the student who will take lesson and gives his/her user name and password in this screen. In here, only student user can be defined. First and second type users can use this process.

First selection- second screen (definition of new user): Second, third and fourth type user can be defined in this screen (Figure 5). On accounts of users updating and deleting processes may also be made. This screen is appeared in "inline frame-iframe". Only, first type user has got authority of making operation here. ZOSMAT does not allow other users for this operation.

First selection- third screen (managerial processes): It can be observed which operation has been made by whom. Faulty entries can be deleted or updated in this screen (Figure 5). Besides, different student users' learning performances can be followed. Only first type user can use this screen.

Teaching Topics

The topics which are to be taught in ZOSMAT system locate in these screens (Figure 6). There are a lot of learning materials such as texts, graphics, graphics with flash animation, problem solving with flash animation, interactive applications for more effective learning. All users can use this section. But, authority of adding and subtracting topics and learning materials had given to only first and second type user.

Figure 5. First selection and its sub selections

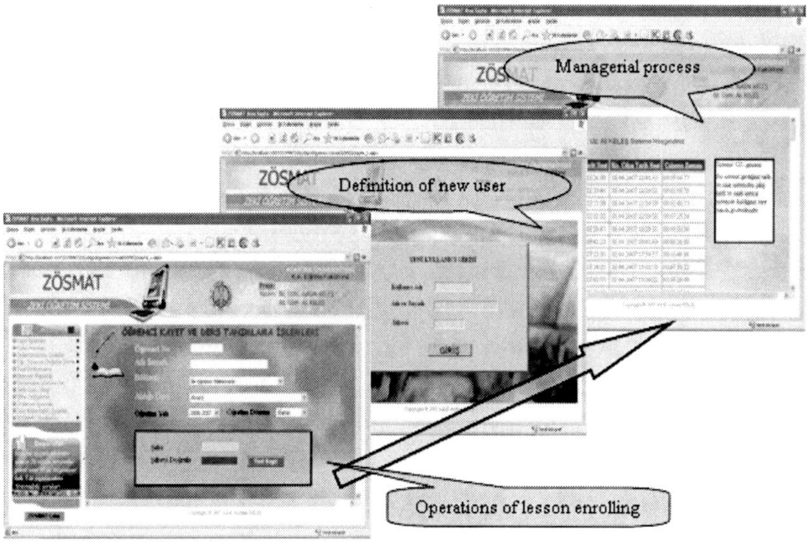

Figure 6. Screens of teaching topics

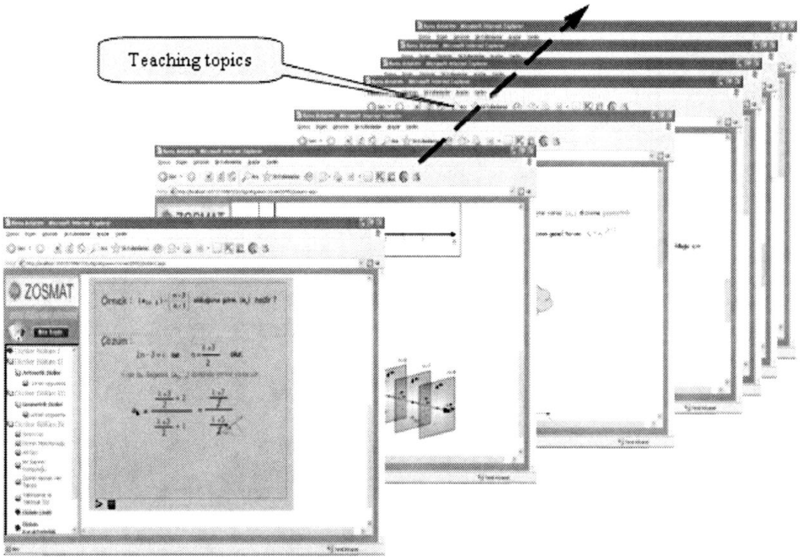

Evaluating Exams

The student is evaluated by means of exams from topic that he/she learned. ZOSMAT ask different questions each student. After the student answers the questions in the exam with limited time ZOSMAT present a report to him/her deal with his/her performance and the student compares his/her own answers and with system's answers. The student is informed with different visual items according to his/her performance by the system. For example, if student is successful then he is applauded otherwise ZOSMAT meets with an unhappy face and says "you must study more and more". Besides, there are a lot of awards such as an intelligence game or entertaining show or a film to encourage the student to solve more exams. These awards have been hided to questions. System warns the student that there is awarded question in his/her test when the student starts. But the student cannot know which question is awarded. ZOSMAT aims to motivate the student by this way. In this section, tests based on one topic or all topics can be applied (Figure 7). All users can enter this section but only first end third type user can make operation.

Performance of Classroom

The student can see self performance in the class' performance and other student's performance according to deal topic. Name of topic locates at the top of the screen and student's name locates at the bottom of it. ZOSMAT show both average of class and student's individual average. In the following list, marks sort descending order according to time. Student's learning performance is expressed with linguistic terms such as "bad" or "good" (Figure 8). Aim of this section is to provide that student can follow both self learning performance and class's performance. This selection includes sub selections as a report for each topic and general situation. All users can see these reports.

Individual Reports

One of the important characteristic of ZOSMAT is that system recognize entering person and direct in system. ZOSMAT gives information only about entering person without any question in this section (Figure 9).

Individual Reports: Screen 1 (report based on topic): Detailed evaluations about topic that the student learned present to him as a table in this screen. In this table, ZOSMAT manager interprets the student's learning situations for each sub topics (concepts) belonging currently topic. Aim of this section is to give the student an opportunity to see his/her lack for currently topic.

Individual Reports: Screen 2 (general report): ZOSMAT manager interprets the student's learning situations for all topics. Aim of this section is to give the student an opportunity to see his/her lack for all topics. General report distinguishes from performance reports with individual evaluation.

Figure 7. Screens of evaluating exams

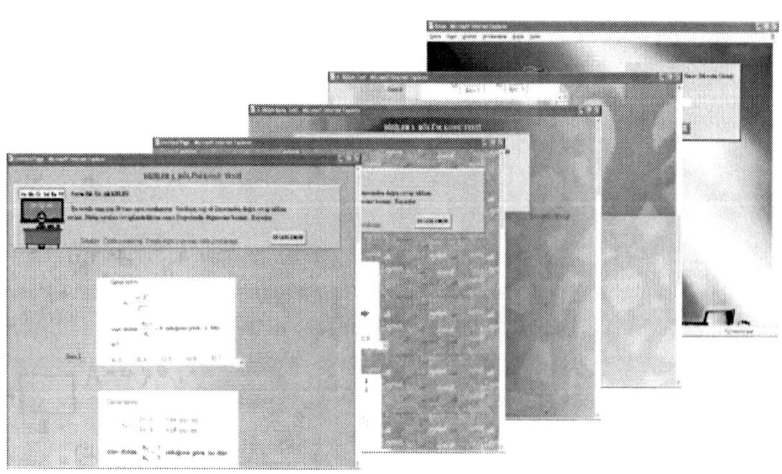

Figure 8. Example screen of performance of classroom

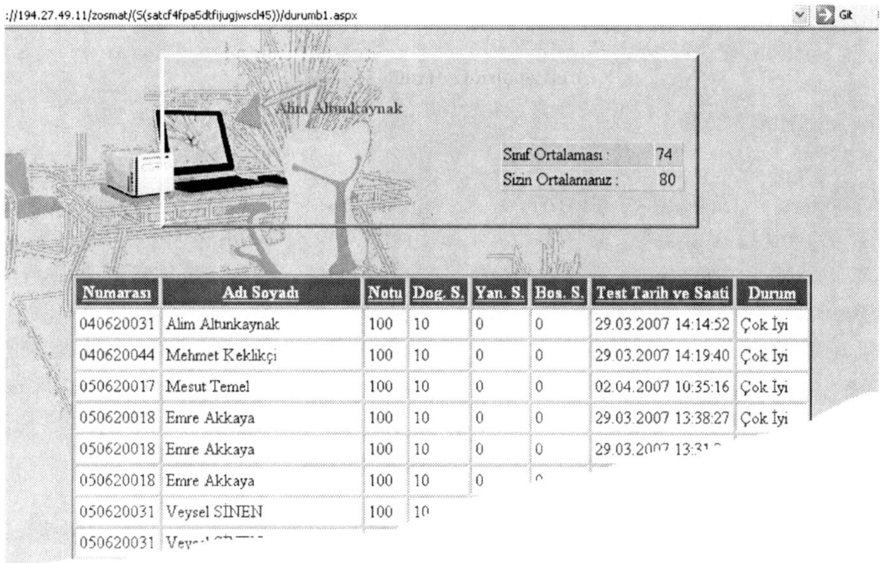

Figure 9. Screens of individual reports

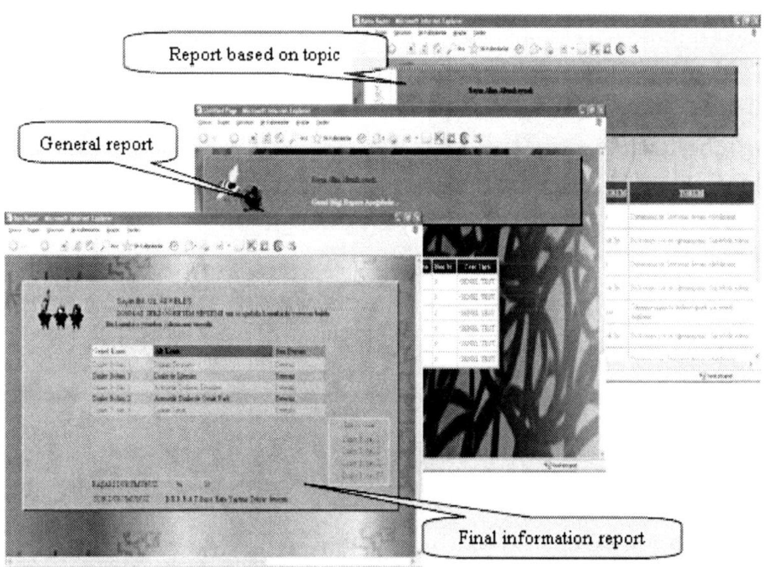

Individual Reports: Screen 3 (final information report): This part of system completely works individually. According to student's final learning situation is made decision what the student must do in learning program and system says linguistically that the student learned which topics and sub topics (concepts). ZOSMAT manager directs student correctly depending on how good he/she is. At top of the screen, there is student's name, under the name there are both general and special advice of ZOSMAT according to topic and sub topic. Successfulness performance expressing as a percent locates at the bottom of the screen. Aim of this section informs individually the student about his lack in topics and concepts. Here, the student is directed with linguistic advices by the system like he is face to face human tutor.

Active Users in ZOSMAT

This screen is appeared in "inline frame-iframe". All users being activated in system are showed and number of activated users via a table. User names, real identity of users, date and time of user entry and what user is doing at the moment in ZOSMAT are given in this table. Thus, human tutor can easily observe all students in the system from his/her armchair. This screen can be used by not only human tutor but also other users.

New Question Entry

There is a question bank in ZOSMAT deal with topics to be taught. In this screen, authority users can add and subtract a question in the bank. At the beginning, authority user can determine question distribution according to topics. ZOSMAT allow only using this screen first and second type user. These operations doing authority users are determined by the system. In this way, the most authority user can find the user doing that operation.

Statistical Operations

ZOSMAT presents statistical information and graphics to authority user deal with the student that he wants to see or to the student deal with his/herself situation (Figure 10). In this way, Human tutor can follow learning performance of his students depend on time. According to situation, Authority users can make necessary changes in ZOSMAT learning process. Besides, Human tutor has got also documentation possibility by saving and printing in format that he wants.

Change Password

All users can change their password at time that they want. During changing operation system defends users by asking their old passwords.

Intelligence Mathematics Games

There are intelligence games, crossword puzzles and flash games etc. deal with mathematics in this section. Aim is to entertain student while he is learning. First and second type user can add these items.

Figure 10. Screen of statistical operations

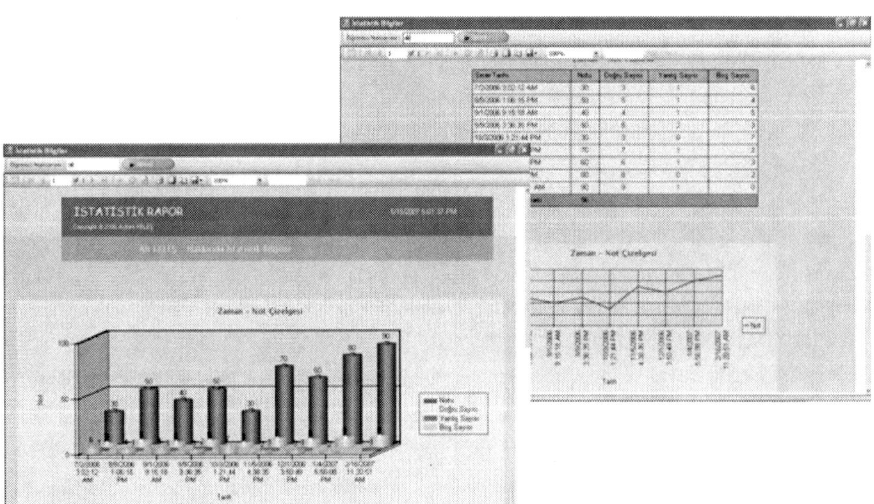

Our ZOSMAT Group

Aim of this section is to create nearness between users of ZOSMAT. Content of this section is filled completely by the users. Idea and feeling about ZOSMAT group or pictures during to lesson, excursions may be located here. Besides, all users can share idea and feeling about ZOSMAT system.

ZOSMAT Application in Real Classroom and its Results

ZOSMAT were applied to the Department of Mathematics Education's students (Faculty of Education, Atatürk University) in 2007 spring semester. On the other hand, in this research, our aim was not to compare ZOSMAT with conventional method of learning. We have only tried to observe the applicability of ZOSMAT and its tutoring performance over a sixteen hour study. Approximately 40 students were taught the topic of sequences as a math subject using ZOSMAT system while the remaining 40 students learned the same topic with the conventional method. In the end of this study, all students took an exam that consists of the same questions from the subject explained above. Moreover, three students from the ZOSMAT group had the same exam by taking advantage of the web-based feature of ZOSMAT and connecting to the system online from their respective hometowns. The average mark of ZOSMAT Group was 90 whereas the other group scored a 66. Supported by the results of this experimental study, we can safely conclude that ZOSMAT is a powerful tool when it comes to improving the learning performance of a student.

CHALLENGES ON ITS AND FUTURE OF ITS

Intelligent Tutoring Systems (ITS) have a multidisciplinary architecture and provide the utility of one-on-one instruction in an automatic way and cost effectively. The challenge remains on transferring to computers the expertise, skills and mode of action of the human tutor, overcoming space, and time, socio-economical and environmental limits. ITS appear as a form of deployment of this issue and have been object of an increasing research.

In order to learn and evaluate in multidisciplinary fields distributed ITS are capable to support on-line tutoring functionalities. ITS must be proficient of accurately diagnose students' knowledge bases, abilities, and styles; diagnose using principles, rather than pre-programmed responses; determine what to do next; adapt instruction accordingly; provide feedback. The improvements of the computer technologies has assisted the use and design of ITS.

"The proliferation of ITS, has spawned many debates about their use and effectiveness: The Degree of Learner Control: How much learner control should be allowed by the systems? Individual vs. Collaborative Learning: Should learners interact with ITS individually or collaboratively? Situated Learning: Is learning situated, unique, and ongoing, or is it more symbolic, following from an information processing model? Virtual Reality and Learning: Does virtual reality uniquely contribute to learning beyond computer aided instruction or multimedia? (Rodrigues et al., 2005 pp. 1)"

According to Kinshuk and Patel (1997), the development of Intelligent Tutoring Systems (ITSs) has suffered since its early days from the fact that the underlying software engineering methodology was not developed specifically for tutoring and did not possess all the desired attributes to facilitate intelligent tutoring. While an ITS inherits powerful functionality at the points of convergence between its objectives and the capabilities of the methodology employed, it also inherits a 'context gap' at the points of divergence between the purpose of the tasks performed within an ITS and the purpose of the methodology. The traditional ITS development was mainly based on the Expert Systems paradigm while the Hypertext paradigm is increasingly becoming popular with the ITS designers. In their pure form, ITS implementations of Expert Systems and Hypertext are respectively 'weak instructionist' and 'weak constructionist' systems, the weakness arising from the 'context gap'. Progress ITS research has been impeded by the lack of modular system architectures, reusable components and sharable knowledge bases. Each new research or development effort typically starts from scratch, without a foundation on which to build.

There are some of the actual limiting problems and future challenges in the ITS area. To eliminate this problems ITS researchers should be concentrated some important principal efforts and characteristics such as Reusable Components, Standardization Efforts, Shared Vocabularies, Ontologies, ITS Shells, Distributed and Agent-Based Architectures, Personalization techniques (web mining), Case based reasoning, Adaptive hypermedia (Rodrigues et al., 2005).

Besides, psychology and education sciences play the crucial role to develop efficient and effective ITS. So psychology and education sciences must be cooperated with computer science to create an effective tutoring strategies in the tutoring module of the ITS. As successful tutoring methods are developed, as along with these methods can be adapted to ITSs, ITSs will be indispensable tools for education and tutoring.

CONCLUSION

Most learners will decide in consideration of prospect of intelligent tutors for the latter. Computer assisted instruction will almost certainly become more "intelligent" in the future. The computing power needed for many applications is already widely available. The biggest obstacle is the difficulty of developing intelligent tutors. There is growing demand for computer and Web mediated learning, and intelligent tutors have great potential for increasing the efficiency and effectiveness of such instruction.

The advances in development of intelligent tutors will exist in the authoring tools that ease the development of intelligent tutors, as there have been advances in all other areas of software. Some computer scientists struggle for simple-minded intelligence that would be easier to develop and perhaps only subordinate to full-fledged intelligent tutors. There are at least two other recent developments that might substantially affect intelligent tutors. Some developers are struggling for tutors that could be easily adapted by teachers, in the hopes that this will make them more attractive to those who control classrooms. Several developers are working on Web-based tutors, and authoring tools to ease the development of such tutors. Further advances in information technologies may open other possibilities (Jackson 2002).

In recent years, the development of intelligent tutoring dialogue systems has become more prevalent, in an attempt to close the performance gap between human and computer tutors. Tutoring applications differ in many ways, however, from the types of applications for which spoken dialogue systems are typically developed. This talk will illustrate some of the opportunities and challenges in this area, focusing on issues such as affective reasoning, discourse and dialogue analysis, and performance evaluation.

REFERENCES

Alpert, S. R., Singley, M. K., & Fairweather, P. G. (1999). Deploying intelligent tutors on the web: an architecture and an example. *International Journal of Artificial Intelligence in Education, 10*(2), 183–197.

Arroyo, I., & Woolf, B. (2005). Inferring learning and attitudes from a Bayesian network of log file data. In *Proceedings of AIED 05, The 12th international conference on artificial intelligence in education.*

Atolagbe, T., Hlupic, V., & Taylor, S. J. E. (2001). GENISA: A Web based interactive learning environment for teaching simulation modelling. In *Proceedings of the 2001 winter simulation conference.*

Barr, A., & Feigenbaum, E. A. (1982). *The Handbook of Artificial Intelligence* (*Vol. 2*). Los Altos, CA: Kaufmann.

Beal, C. R., Beck, J., & Woolf, B. (1998). Impact of intelligent computer instruction on girls' math self concept and beliefs in the value of math. *Paper presented at the annual meeting of the American Educational Research Association.*

Berz, M., Erdelyi, B., & Hoefkens, J. (1999). Experiences with interactive remote graduate instruction in beam physics. *Journal of Interactive Learning Research, 10*(1), 49–58.

Bonnet, A. (1985). *Artificial Intelligence: Promise and Performance*. London: Prentice Hall.

Brown, J. S., & Burton, R. R. (1978). Diagnostic models for procedural bugs in basic mathematical skills. *Cognitive Science, 2*, 155–192. doi:10.1207/s15516709cog0202_4

Brusilovsky, P. (1998). Methods and techniques of adaptive hypermedia. In Brusilovsky, P., Kobsa, A., & Vassileva, J. (Eds.), *Adaptive hypertext and hypermedia* (pp. 1–43). Dordrecht, The Netherlands: Kluwer Academic Publishers.

Brusilovsky, P., & Peylo, C. (2003). Adaptive and intelligent web-based educational systems. *International Journal of Artificial Intelligence in Education, 13*(2–4), 159–172.

Brusilovsky, P., Schwarz, E., & Weber, G. (1996). ELM-ART: An intelligent tutoring system on World Wide Web. *3rd international conference on intelligent tutoring systems ITS 96*, 261–269.

Burns, H. L., & Capps, C. G. (1988). Foundation of intelligent tutoring systems: an introduction. In Polson, M. C., & Richardson, J. J. (Eds.), *In Foundation of Intelligent Tutoring Systems* (pp. 1–19). London: Lawrence Erlbaum.

Canfield, W. (2001, Spring). ALEKS: A Web-based intelligent tutoring system [ProQuest Education Journals.]. *Mathematics and Computer Education, 35*(2), 152.

Capuano, N., Marsella, M., & Salerno, S. (2004). ABITIS. An Agent Based Intelligent Tutoring System for Distance Learning. In *Proceedings of the International Workshop in Adaptive and Intelligent Web-basedEducational Systems.*

Carbonell, J. R. (1970). AI in CAI: An artificial intelligence approach to computer-aided instruction. *IEEE Transactions on Man–Machine System. MMS, 11*(4), 190–202.

Carver, C., Howard, R., & Lavelle, E. (1996). Enhancing student learning by incorporating learning styles into adaptive hypermedia. In *Proceedings 1996 EDMEDIA world conference on educational multimedia and hypermedia* (pp. 118–123). Boston.

Cheung, B., Hui, L., Zhang, J., & Yiu, S. M. (2003). SmartTutor: An intelligent tutoring system in web-based adult education. *Journal of Systems and Software, 68*, 11–25. doi:10.1016/S0164-1212(02)00133-4

Chou, C. (1999). Developing CLUE: a formative evaluation system for computer network learning courseware. *Journal of Interactive Learning Research, 10*(2), 179–193.

Clancey, W. J. (1982). Tutoring rules for guiding a case method dialogue. In D. H. Sleeman et & J. S. Brown (Ed.), *Intelligent tutoring systems* (pp. 201–225). London: Academic Press.

Collins, A. M. (1976). Processing in acquiring knowledge. In Anderson, R. C. (Ed.), *Schooling and the acquisition of knowledge*. Hillsdale, NJ: Lawrence Erlbaum Associates.

Conati, C., Gertner, A., & VanLehn, K. (2002). Using Bayesian networks to manage uncertainty in student modeling. *Journal of User Modeling and User Adapted Interaction*, *12*(4), 371–417. doi:10.1023/A:1021258506583

Conati, C., & Maclare, H. (2004). Evaluating a probabilistic model of student effect. In *Proceedings of the seventh international conference ITS 2004* (pp. 55–66). Maceio, Brazil.

Davidovic, A., Warren, J., & Trichina, E. (2003). Learning benefits of structural example based adaptive tutoring systems. *IEEE Transactions on Education*, *46*(2), 241–251. doi:10.1109/TE.2002.808240

Demetriou, A. (1993). *The architecture and dynamics of developing mind.* Chicago: University of Chicago Press.

Dillenbourg, P., & Mendelsohn, P. (1991). Le Developpement de l'enseignement Intelligemment Assiste par Ordinateur. *Natural and Artificial Intelligence Symposium* (pp. 23–25). Rome.

Eliot, C., Neiman, D., & Lamar, M. (1997). Medtec: a web-based intelligent tutor for basic anatomy. In S. Lobodzinski, & I. Tomek (Ed.), *Proceedings of WebNet '97, World Conference of the WWW, Internet and Intranet* (pp. 161–165). Charlottesville, VA: AACE.

Eliot, C., & Woolf, B. (1994). Reasoning about the user within a simulation-based real-time training system. In *Proceedings of the fourth international conference on user modeling*, 121-126.

Elsom-Cook, M. (1987). *Intelligent computer-aided instruction research at the Open University* (Tech. Rep. No. 63). Computer-Assisted Learning Research Group, The Open University, Milton Keynes.

Evens, M., Brandle, S., Chang, R., Freedman, R., Glass, M., Lee, Y., et al. (2001). CIRCSIM-Tutor: An intelligent tutoring system using natural language dialogue. In *Proceedings of the 12th Midwest AI and cognitive science conference (MAICS 2001)*, pp. 16–23.

Forbes-Riley, K., Litman, D., & Rotaru, M. (2008). *Responding to student uncertainty during computer tutoring: A preliminary evaluation. 9th international conference on intelligent tutoring systems*. Montreal, Canada: ITS.

Fossati, D. (2003). DIAG-NLP: Improving Intelligent Tutoring System with Natural Language Generation Technology. (Master's Thesis), *University of Illinois at Chicago*. (pg. 25).

Friedman, S. L. (1986). *The brain, cognition, and education*. Orlando: Academic Press.

Gamboa, H., & Fred, A. (2001). Designing intelligent tutoring systems: A bayesian approach. In *Proceedings ICEIS 01, 3rd international conference on enterprise information systems.*

Gertner, A., & VanLehn, K. (2000). Andes: A coached problem solving environment for physics. In *Proceedings ITS 2000, intelligent tutoring systems*, (pp. 131–142).

Gilbert, J., & Han, C. (1999). Adapting instruction in search of a significant difference. *Journal of Network and Computer Applications*, 22.

Graesser, A.C., Wiemer-Hastings, K., Wiemer-Hastings, P., & Kreuz, R., & TRG. (1999). AutoTutor: A simulation of a human tutor. *Journal of Cognitive Systems Research*, *1*, 35–51. doi:10.1016/S1389-0417(99)00005-4

Heift, T., & Nicholson, D. (2001). Web delivery of adaptive and interactive language tutoring. *International Journal of Artificial Intelligence in Education*, *12*(4), 310–324.

Heilman, M., Collins-Thompson, K., Callan, J., & Eskenazi, M. (2006). Classroom success of an intelligent tutoring system for lexical practice and reading comprehension. In *Proc. of the Ninth International Conference on Spoken Language Processing.*

Hendler, J., & Feigenbaum, E. A. (2001). Knowledge is power: the semantic web vision. In N. Zhong, Y. Yao, Liu, & S. Ohsuga (Ed.), *Web Intelligence: Research and Development, Proceedings of the First Asia-Pacific Conference, WI 2001*, lecture notes in artificial intelligence, vol. 2198 (pp. 18–29). Springer: Berlin.

Henze, N., & Nejdl, W. (2001). Adaptation in open corpus hypermedia. *International Journal of Artificial Intelligence in Education*, *12*(4), 325–350.

Honey, P., & Mumford, A. (1992). *The manual of learning styles* (3rd Ed.). Maidenhead.

Hyacinth, S. N. (1990). Intelligent Tutoring Systems: an overview. *Artificial Intelligence Review*, *4*, 251–277.

Jackson, G. B. (2002, Janurary-March). Intelligent Tutoring Systems, *Technologies Today, TechKnowLogia*, Knowledge Enterprise, Inc. (pp 73-74).

Jeremic, Z., & Deyedzic, V. (2004). Design patters ITS: Student model implementation. *In IEEE international conference on advanced learning technologies.*

John, K. O. (1988). *Schoolworlds/Microworlds: Computers and the culture of the classroom.* Oxford: Pergamon Press.

Johnson, W. L. (1986). *Intention-based diagnosis of errors in Novice programs*. Los Altos, CA: Morgan Kaufmann Publishers.

Kearsley, G. (1987). *Artificial intelligence and instruction-Applications and methods* (p. 158). Reading, MA: Addison-Wesley Publishing.

Keles, A., Ocak, R., Keles, A., & Gülcü, A. (2009). ZOSMAT: Web-based Intelligent Tutoring System for Teaching-Learning Process. [Elsevier.]. *Expert Systems with Applications*, *36*, 1229–1239. doi:10.1016/j.eswa.2007.11.064

Kelly, D., & Tangney, B. (2004). Predicting learning characteristics in a multiple intelligence based tutoring system. In *Proceedings of the seventh international conference ITS 2004* (pp. 678–688). Maceio, Brasil.

Kinshuk Patel, A. (1997). A Conceptual Framework for Internet Based Intelligent Tutoring Systems. In A. Behrooz (Ed.), *Knowledge Transfer* (pp. 1). London, UK, pp117-124 (ISBN -900427-015-X)

Kodaganallur, V., Weitz, R. R., & Rosenthal, D. (2004). VersaTutor – Architecture for a constraint based intelligent tutor generator. *WWW 2004*. New York.

Lajoie, S. F., & Lesgold, A. (1989). Apprenticeship training in the workplace: Computer-coached practice environment as a new form of apprenticeship. *Machine-Mediated Learning*, *3*, 7–28.

Mandl, H., & Lesgold, A. (Eds.). (1988). *Learning Issues for Intelligent Tutoring Systems*. London: Springer-Verlag.

Melis, E., & Siekmann, J. (2004, June 7-11). ActiveMath: An Intelligent Tutoring System for Mathematics. *Artificial Intelligence and Soft Computing - ICAISC 2004: 7th International Conference*, Zakopane, Poland.

Mitrovic, A. (2003). An intelligent SQL tutor on the web. *International Journal of Artificial Intelligence in Education, 13*(2–4), 171–195.

Munro, A. (1994) Authoring interactive graphical models. In De Jong, T.; Towne, D. M.; and Spada, H., eds., *The Use of Computer Models for Explication, Analysis and Experiential Learning Sciences 5*(1), 49-94.

Papanikolaou, K., Grigoriadou, M., Knornilakis, H., & Magoulas, G. (2003). Personalizing the interaction in a web-based educational hypermedia system: The case of INSPIRE. *User Modeling and User-Adapted Interaction, 13*, 213–267. doi:10.1023/A:1024746731130

Peña, C., Marzo, J., de la Rosa, J., & Fabregat, R. (2002). *Un sistema de tutoría inteligente adaptativo considerando estilos de aprendizaje*. In IE.

Peylo, C., Thelen, T., Rollinger, C., & Gust, H. (2000). A Web-based intelligent educational system for PROLOG. In Peylo, C. (Ed.), *Proceedings of the International Workshop on Adaptive and Intelligent Web-based Educational Systems* (held in Conjunction with ITS 2000), Technical Report of the Institute for Semantic Information Processing, Osnabru¨ ck, (pp. 85–96).

Ritter, S. (1997). PAT Online: A model-tracing tutor on the world-wide web. In P. Brusilovsky, K. Nakabayashi, & S. Ritter (Ed.), *Proceedings of Workshop Intelligent Educational Systems on the World Wide Web at 8th World Conference on Artificial Intelligence in Education* (pp. 11–17). Kobe, Japan: ISIR.

Rodrigues, M., Novais, P., & Santos, M. F. (2005). *Future Challenges in Intelligent Tutoring Systems – A Framework*. Recent Research Developments in Learning Technologies.

Schiaffino, S., Garcia, P., & Amandi, A. (2008). eTeacher: Providing personalized assistance to e-learning students. *Computers & Education, 51*, 1744–1754. doi:10.1016/j.compedu.2008.05.008

Shang, Y., Shi, H., & Chen, S. (2001). An intelligent distributed environment for active learning. In *WWW 01*.

Smith, A. S. G., & Blandford, A. (2003). MLTutor: An application of machine learning algorithms for an adaptive web-based information system. *International Journal of Artificial Intelligence in Education, 13*(2–4), 233–260.

Suebnukarn, S., & Haddawy, P. (2004). A collaborative intelligent tutoring system for medical problem based learning. *In IUI_04*, Madeira, Funchal, Portugal.

Suraweera, P., & Mitrovi, C. A. (2002). A constraint-based tutor for database modeling. In *Proceedings 6th international conference on intelligent tutoring systems ITS*. Kermit.

Towne, D. M. (1997a). Approximate reasoning techniques for intelligent diagnostic instruction. *International Journal of Artificial Intelligence in Education, 8*, 262–283.

Towne, D. M. (1997b). Intelligent diagnostic tutoring using qualitative symptom information. In *AAAI97 Fall Symposium on ITS Authoring Tools*.

Vanlehn, K. (1996). Conceptual and meta-learning during coached problem solving. In *Proceedings of the third international conference on intelligent tutoring systems (ITS96),* (pp. 29–47).

VanLehn, K., Jordan, P. W., Ros'e, C., Bhembe, D., B¨ottner, M., & Gaydos, A. (2002). The architecture of Why2-Atlas: A coach for qualitative physics essay writing. *ITS 2002. LNCS, 2363*, 158–167.

Wenger, E. (1987). *Artificial intelligence and tutoring systems*. Los Altos, CA: Meagan Kaufmann.

Xenos, M. (2004). Prediction and assessment of student behavior in open and distance education in computers using Bayesian networks. *Computers & Education, 43*(4), 345–359.

Yazdani, M. (1986). Intelligent tutoring systems survey. *Artificial Intelligence Review, 1*, 43–52. doi:10.1007/BF01988527

Yazdani, M. (1987). Intelligent tutoring systems: an overview. In Lawler, R., & Yazdani, M. (Eds.), *In Artificial Intelligence and Education* (pp. 182–201). Norwood: Ablex.

ADDITIONAL READING

Abu Naser, S. S. (2001). A comparative study between Animated Intelligent Tutoring Systems "AITS" and Video-based Intelligent Tutoring Systems "VITS", *Al- Aqsa University Journal, 5*(1), 72-96.

Abu Naser, S.S. (2008). Developing Visualization Tool for Teaching AI Searching Algorithms, *Informat techonology Journal, 7*(2), 350-355.

Barry, P., Goettl, H. M., & Halff, C. L. Redfield, Valerie, J. S. (Eds.) (1998). *Intelligent Tutoring Systems.* (Proc. of 4th International Conference on Intelligent Tutoring Systems), Lecture Notes in Computer Science 1452, Berlin Heidelberg: Springer-Verlag, 1998.

Brouwer-Janse, M. D., & Harrington, T. L. (Eds.). (1994). *Human-machine communication for educational systems design*. Springer-Verlag.

Fox, B. A. (1993). *The Human Tutorial Dialogue Project: Issues in the design of instructional systems*. Hillsdale, NJ: Erlbaum.

Glavinic V., Stankov S., Zelic M., Rosic M. (2008). Intelligent Tutoring in the Semantic Web and Web 2.0 Environments. *WSKS*(2), 172-177.

Graesser, A. C., & Person, N. K. (2001). Teaching tactics and dialog in auto tutor. *International Journal of Artificial Intelligence in Education*, (12): 12–23.

Granic, A., Stankov, S., & Nakic, J. (2006). Designing Intelligent Tutors to Adapt Individual Interaction. *Universal Access in Ambient Intelligence Environments*, *2006*, 137–153.

Greer, J. E., & McCalla, G. (1994). *Student modelling: the key to individualized knowledge-based instruction*. North Atlantic Treaty Organization. Scientific Affairs Division.

Jim, E. G., & Gordon, I. M. (Eds.). (1994). *Student modelling: the key to individualized knowledge-based instruction*. Springer-Verlag.

Kenneth, D. F., & Feltovich, P. J. (Eds.). (2001). *Smart Machines in Education*. AAAI Press, 2001.

Looi, C. K., McCalla, G., Bredeweg, B., & Breuker, J. (Eds.). (2005). *Artificial Intelligence in Education: Supporting Learning through Intelligent and Socially Informed Technology* (Proc. AI-ED2005), Amsterdam, The Netherlands: IOS Press.

Murray, T., Blessing, S., & Ainsworth, S. (Eds.). (2003). *Authoring tools for Advanced Technology Learning Environments: Toward cost-effective adaptive, interactive and intelligent educational software. AA Dordrecht*. Netherlands: Kluwer.

Psotka, J., Massey, L. D., & Mutter, S. A. (Eds.). (1988). *Intelligent tutoring systems: lessons learned*. Erlbaum Associates.

Woolf, B. (2008). *Building intelligent interactive tutors*. San Francisco: Morgan Kauffman.

Zhang, Y., & Liu, Z. (2003). A Model of Web Oriented Intelligent Tutoring System for Distance Education. *Fifth International Conference on Computational Intelligence and Multimedia Applications (ICCIMA'03*, 78.

Zhiping, L., Tianwei, X., & Yu, S. (2008). A Web-Based Personalized Intelligent Tutoring System, *2008 International Conference on Computer Science and Software Engineering* CSSE, (5), 446-449.

KEY TERMS AND DEFINITIONS

Computer-Based-Instruction: (1) use of computers in order to provide an interactive educational experience or (2) Use of computer programs controlled by systems of management of education.

Expert Knowledge Module: References an expert or domain model containing a description of the knowledge or behaviors that represent expertise in the subject-matter domain.

Intelligent Tutoring System: A learning technology that dynamically adapts learning content to objectives, needs, and preferences of a learner by making use of his expertise in instructional methods and the subject to be taught.

Student Knowledge Module: A student model containing descriptions of student knowledge or behaviors, including his or her misconceptions and knowledge gaps.

Tutoring Module: Identifies which deficiencies in knowledge to focus on and selects strategies to present that knowledge.

User Interface Module: A module that provides to get across with the student in ITS.

Web-Based Learning: A learning using web-based technologies as a principal means of interaction with learners.

Chapter 2
Design Methodology of an Intelligent Learning Environment Applied to the Non Violent Conflict Resolution Education

G.M. Curilem
Universidad de La Frontera, Chile

B. Vizcarra
Universidad de La Frontera, Chile

A.M. Poo
Universidad de La Frontera, Chile

D. Huenteman
Correo Gorbea, Chile

L.M. Brasil
University of Brasília, Brazil

ABSTRACT

This chapter describes a learning design methodology for creating an intelligent tutoring system (ITS) to support non-violent conflict resolution education in the school environment. The design method is based on a mathematical formalization in which ITS are defined as automata. The aim is to demonstrate that the automata representation facilitates the integration of the domain contents, the pedagogical strategies and the student models in one computational system. The automata structure guides the system design, managing the variables selection of the teaching-learning process. Variables involve the students' characteristics, the interface resources and the pedagogical strategies. Thus the whole teaching-learning process is modeled as an automaton which fits with the ITS structure. The non violent conflict resolution domain was chosen as the case study due to its relevance and its ill structured contents what makes its modeling difficult. The result is a non violent conflict resolution educational process structured as an ITS.

DOI: 10.4018/978-1-61692-008-1.ch002

INTRODUCTION

The introduction of new information and communication technologies into education should support more efficient and customized educational situations, reaching a greater number of people. E-learning allows "any time" and "any where" teaching learning processes to occur. The wide representation facilities provided by the multimedia technology, from text to virtual reality, increase the communication channels with the learners. The possibility to interact with the contents that bring the hypermedia technologies supports more customized learning process, where the speeds, the contents, etc. can be managed by the learner. However, despite the great potential of pedagogical software, their efficiency is still controversial. The limitations, both from the cognitive (it is unknown exactly how learning occurs) and technological (difficulty modeling a learner or the teaching-learning strategies) areas have restricted the impact of these systems and have impelled intense research activity with the aim of determining how technology can increase the efficacy of the educational processes (Alsop & Tompsett, 2007; Albirini, 2007).

One of the most important efforts of this research is to develop adaptive systems. The automatic adaptation of the systems to the students seems crucial to construct pedagogical systems that integrate the potentiality of technology with the requirements of pedagogy. But the integration of technology with pedagogy is not trivial and many works propose design methodologies to support it. With the aim of contributing to new alternatives for learning design, Curilem, Barbosa, & de Azevedo (2007) proposed a methodology to develop an ITS, focused mainly on adapting the learning environment to the learning styles of the learner. In this work, the structure of an ITS was used to develop an Intelligent Learning Environment. The main advantage of the proposed methodology compared to others, is that it enables, through a mathematical formalization based on automata, to integrate all the areas into one computational system. This is done by modeling the teaching-learning process as an automaton. Once all the variables of the pedagogical process are modeled, they are integrated into the ITS in a natural way.

This chapter will show how the teaching-learning process from an extremely ill-structured subject matter such as non-violent conflict resolution, was modeled as an automaton. It will also present how the automaton will allow adapting the contents, the teaching strategies, the forms of representation and the degrees of interactivity to the learner characteristics. As the main result, the chapter presents how all these components are integrated into the ITS structure.

The structure of the chapter is as follows: the next section presents a general background of the work. Then, the methodology to model an ITS and a teaching-learning process as automata (Curilem et al., 2007) is presented. Subsequently, the next section outlines the subject matter of non violent conflict resolution and the premises on which the teaching-learning model are based. The next section presents the results of the modeling processes. Finally, the last section presents a discussion and the main conclusions of this study.

BACKGROUND

The great challenge for educational technology is determining how to give the learner autonomy in his/her learning process while at the same time guiding him/her with assertive interventions when support is required (Rose & Strangman, 2007; Mayer, Johnson, Shaw, & Sandhu, 2006). In light of a pedagogical concept focused on learning, the aim of educational technology is to become a learning moderator. One of the most important results of this endeavor are ITS and their evolution, intelligent learning environments, where the system adapts to the learner, fostering a highly customized and interactive learning environment which integrate more pedagogical paradigms (Stathacopoulou, Magoulas, Grigoriadou & Samarakou, 2005; Curilem, Barbosa, & de Azevedo, 2007).

The learner's adaptation requires the system to be able to identify him/her, taking the characteristics that impact his/her learning into consideration. Advances in cognitive sciences have enabled the discovery of new variables to define cognitive learning states, such as multiple intelligences (Kelly & Tangney, 2004), emotions (Conati & Maclare, 2004; Rodrigues & Carvalho, 2004) and learning styles (Zywno & Stewart, 2005; Yannibelli, Godoy & Amandi, 2006) among others (Rose & Strangman, 2007). These theories make possible the implementation of student models and suggest strategies to design learner-compatible environments.

Different learning strategies suggest how to create more favorable environments for certain types of students. However, both the learner characteristics and more favorable environments depend on the field of study and, despite the advances, one generalized method has not been established that can integrate all these elements into one single system (Rossano, Joy, Roselli, & Sutinen, 2005). Most of the work in the area of educational technology has highlighted specific aspects of the problem, such as student models (Hu & Wu, 2006; Jaques & Vicari, 2007), decision-making mechanisms (Karampiperis & Sampson, 2005; Stathacopoulou, Magoulas, Grigoriadou, & Samarakou, 2005; Mayer, Johnson, Shaw, & Sandhu, 2006) or the implementation of environments (Watson & Hardaker, 2005; Zhu, 2007).

Learning design is the process of modeling a teaching-learning situation. Advances in interface design have enabled varied and flexible environments to be created. One of the most frequently used tools for education interface design are learning objects, used basically in e-learning applications. Learning objects are uniquely identified, modular digital resources that can be combined and that can manage a large amount of hypermedia elements. The sharable content object reference model (SCORM) is used for standardizing the design of learning objects, guaranteeing its reusability, interoperability, accessibility and durability by means of a metadata model (Watson & Hardaker, 2005; Kaczmarek, & Landowska, 2006).

Various languages can be used for learning design purposes and others were created with that aim. For example, OWL (Ontology Web Language), UML (Unified Modeling Language), EML (Educational Modeling Language), IMS (Information Management System), Learning Design (Koper, 2006; Giesbers, Van Bruggen, Hermans, Joosten-Ten Brinke, Burgers, & Koper, 2007) or UDL (Universal Design for Learning) (Rose, & Strangman, 2007). These are appropriate tools to model well known processes using a computational representation. However, teaching-learning process are not well known processes: the great amount of variables involved and their still unknown relevance, makes that their modeling is a difficult task. The need for "guidelines" to know what to model in a teaching-learning process persists, since, despite the languages facility for describing the ontology of the processes, they do not necessarily supply a methodology that aids to select and represent the complex aspects of a real teaching-learning process (Koper, 2006). The absence of such guidelines presents an obstacle to successful modeling because the designer feels lost when facing all the aspects that are present in a teaching-learning process. For example gender is a relevant aspect to be included in the student model of some teaching-learning process but not others. Non verbal communication between a learner and a teacher is difficult to integrate into a computational system. So the problem is which are the variables that most influence a specific teaching learning process and how to integrate them into a pedagogical system? Which aspects of a teaching-learning process should be modeled and which should be discarded? The languages mentioned before do not answer to these questions, thus some modeling strategies have to be proposed.

Mishra & Koehler (2006) proposed a method based on the idea of pedagogical content knowledge. This concept refers to modeling the knowledge of a teacher who interprets the subject matter and finds different ways to represent it and make it accessible to learners. To this concept the authors added the technological knowledge, giving the Technological Pedagogical Content Knowledge (TPCK) which is the intersection of the three areas and enables a procedure for implementing a teaching-learning process model. The interesting thing about this model is that it can identify what is important and what is not in what it calls the use of technologies, which can ease the transition from theory to practice. Wang & Woo (2007) for their part defined the application of information and communication technologies in education as a process that must enable "enhanced student learning", stressing the pedagogical aspects involved in the process. They proposed "a systematic planning model of information and communication technologies integration," based on a logical sequence of steps that must be defined, starting from "problem statements", learning objectives, etc. and finishing with a reflection that resupplies the whole process. These studies demonstrate the difficulty in the modeling process and the diversity of the proposed solutions.

DESIGN METHODOLOGY FOR INTELLIGENT LEARNING ENVIRONMENTS

Intelligent Tutoring Systems

ITS are one of the most important results emerging from current research in the area of educational computer sciences. Using artificial intelligence tools, they try to make interactions between the system and learner flexible, providing customized educational processes. In ITS, the teaching strategies are part of the system's structure. They have four modules that contain the knowledge that the system must have about the field (domain expertise), the learner (student model), the teaching strategies and tactics (pedagogical expertise) and the means of communications (interface) (Carbonell, 1970; Wenger, 1987).

In the 1990s, due to the advance in multi and hypermedia technologies, the interface took on primary importance (Bruillard, 1997). Intelligent learning environments thus emerged and artificial intelligence was used to detect different learner types and make decisions regarding how to offer them an appropriate environment, be it from the point of view of the sequence of activities (Watson & Hardaker, 2005; Stathacopoulou et al., 2005), the type of presentation (Martins & Carvalho 2004) or the system intervention (Suebnukarn & Haddawy, 2006).

One of the most significant issues in the development of ITS is that their design must integrate various areas of knowledge. To facilitate this integration, a mathematical formalization was proposed for these systems. It has been proved (Curilem et al., 2007) that an ITS can be defined by an automata $S = \{ U, Y, X, xo, \lambda, \eta \}$, where:

U: input set formed by all the possible actions of the learner through the interface.
Y: output set formed by the elements that configure the interface (content and form).
X: states set formed by all the different student models considered by the system.
xo: initial state represented by the initial student model, obtained using an initial diagnosis or established by default.
λ: UxX → X: state transition function that updates the actual student model (actual state) depending on the input and the current student model.
η: UxX → Y: output function that updates the interface configuration according to the input and current student model.

Each set is stored in the specific ITS module: the input set is stored in the interface module, the output set in the domain module, the state set in the student module and the η and λ functions in the tutoring module. This last one controls the pedagogical concepts in the system, which is why the η and λ function represent this pedagogical knowledge.

Once the ITS has been formalized as an automata, it is necessary for the teaching-learning process to also be defined as such, giving rise to the concept of "didactic ergonomics".

Teaching Learning Modeling Process

Didactic Ergonomics refers to accommodating pedagogical resources to the cognitive needs of a student to promote learning (Curilem & de Azevedo, 2003). In the present work, it establishes how the learning environment must be configured to facilitate the learning process of a given learner. Didactic ergonomics is then defined by identifying three elements: the learners' types, the environments (contents and means of representation) and the relationship between learners and specific environments. These elements represent the knowledge about the student, the knowledge about the domain and its representation at the interface, and the pedagogical knowledge that relates the cognitive needs of the student with pedagogical resources supplied in the learning environments. This is why the definition of the didactic ergonomics defines the four modules of an ITS and defines the teaching-learning process model.

The teaching-learning modeling process is reduced to identifying the elements of didactic ergonomics. Each teaching-learning process requires a specific analysis to define the three elements of didactic ergonomics: learner characteristics such as gender and age or environments that present problem solving situations and games can be relevant to support one domain and not another. However, the advantage of this modeling method is that any teaching-learning process will be modeled by answering three questions:

1. Which are the students' types relevant for this teaching-learning process?
2. Which contents and technologies will be used to configure the learning environments?
3. How to relate learner's types with specific environments?

Here, the variables that define the learner are called Characteristics, the variables that define the learning environments are called Attributes and the knowledge that associates the Characteristics with the Attributes are called Relationships.

In previous works, we proposed to combine some pedagogical theories to establish the Relationships between the learner styles and the environment definition (Curilem & de Azevedo, 2003). Theories like constructivism (Piaget, 1967) and behaviorism (Gagne, Briggs & Wagner, 1988) were used as pedagogical strategies, that describe the main sequence of activities and contents that should be presented to the student. Theories like Learning Styles (Felder, 1996) and Multiple Intelligences (Gardner, 1993) were used as pedagogical tactics, that define how these contents and activities will be presented at the interface, according to the student styles.

Once the Relationships are defined, the designer that applies the concept of didactic ergonomics to a certain field, has to extract the most pertinent Characteristics and Attributes from this field, based preferably on a team with experience in the specific teaching-learning process, but also on theoretical and empirical antecedents.

The didactic ergonomics can be defined as an automaton where:

U: Input set. Set of Attributes available in the environment that allow the learner to interact with the contents (menus, buttons, edition boxes, etc.).
Y: Output set. Set of Attributes that define the environment (contents and their representation).
X: States. Set of Characteristics that define the learners.

xo: Initial State. Initial Characteristics (obtained from a questionnaire or by default).
λ: Relationships that establishes how changes to the Attributes affect the Characteristics.
η: Relationships that establishes how changes to the Characteristics affect the Attributes.

Once formulated as an automaton, didactic ergonomics can be integrated into an ITS, where each set and function of the former is blended with the latter. It is then necessary to define a tool that enables its computer representation. This is done by means of an Artificial Neural Network.

Computational Representation

An interactive activation and competition (IAC) artificial neural networks was selected to represent the Tutor Module of the system. Several aspects led to the suitability of the IAC networks for the implementation of the adaptive mechanism. The most important is that the variables of the teaching-learning process and their relationships are represented in a very simple way by the structure of this network.

IAC artificial neural networks were proposed by Rumelhart & McClelland (1989) and modified by de Azevedo (1993) in order to solve some original restrictions. In this model, the neurons represent specific concepts and form groups that can be considered categories. Here, they are the variables of the teaching learning process. The knowledge of the artificial neural network is represented by the connections among the neurons, called weights. They represent the relationships between variables. Within the same group, the neurons have inhibitory connections (competition between the learner characteristics and between the interface attributes) but between groups, the neurons can have excitatory connections (active relationship between characteristics and attributes). The detailed explanation of the design of this network is presented in Curilem et al. (2007).

It was demonstrated by de Azevedo (1993) that an IAC network is an automaton. In Hahne & de Azevedo (2007) a learning algorithm was proposed for these networks, facilitating their use. IAC networks also have three properties that make them suitable to model an ITS: parallelism, bidirectionality and treatment of uncertainties. The first guarantees that all the characteristics of the learner are considered simultaneously by the system. Bidirectionality enables the configuration of the interface from the characteristics of the learner (η function) but more than that, the actions of the learner on the interface allow the student model to be updated (function λ). The treatment of uncertainties makes it possible to obtain output, even with incomplete or uncertain data from the input. Finally, their structure based on groups whose concepts or units compete internally and associate externally to other concept categories offers a way to represent the problem very close to reality.

In this study, the Characteristics and Attributes of the problem were represented by the neurons of the IAC network and the Relationships, by the weights. The groups of units were formed by excluding categories of the variables, such as, for example, the learning styles, since there cannot be a learner with all the styles with the same strength. The attributes are similarly grouped.

In summary, for this application, the IAC network can be formulated as follows:

U e Y: input and output sets, formed by the neurons that represent the Attributes.
X e xo: set of states and initial state formed by the neurons that represent the Characteristics.
λ y η: state and output transition functions, given by the value of the weights obtained according to the pedagogical structure that relates Characteristics and Attributes.

Thus, it is demonstrated that using the methodology based on automata, the conceptual model of a teaching-learning process can be represented by a computational model based on an IAC-type artificial neural network (Curilem et al., 2007). This network behaves like a decision mechanism that stores the pedagogical knowledge in its weights.

MODELING THE TEACHING LEARNING PROCESS

Non-Violent Conflict Resolution

Aggressive behavior within the school system has come to be considered from a circumstantial phenomenon to a worrisome question because of its high incidence as well as the alteration that it entails in the school life. Scholastic coexistence and violence are part of the reflection by UNESCO that proposes the concept of a culture for peace as a foundation for sustainable development (UNESCO, 2001). Regulating coexistence is important for maintaining a pleasant learning environment, making it easy to obtain progressive levels of autonomy that permit a constructive social coexistence (Halcartegaray, 1991). However this is a matter that affects the school relationships all over the world, each country may have its own approach to the problem and may define its components in different ways. This is why the implementation of any tool to support the management of violent conflicts must be based on the culture and vision of the region where it will be applied. This is why in this work most references to definitions, concepts and strategies are local, to situate them in the application context.

For the government of Chile, scholastic coexistence constitutes a coherent subject with the idea of an interactive education centered on the student as a subject of his/her own learning (MINEDUC, 2001). School offers a unique opportunity for the primary prevention of violence, since it can reach the at-risk populations at very early ages (Arón, 2000; Leaf & Keys, 2005). The Chilean educational reform proposes transversal objectives that are bound to scholastic coexistence that make reference to the "formation of character in terms of attitudes and fundamental values" (MINEDUC, 1996).

Some authors have established that the violence is part of a pre-existing conflict, which, with no solution, becomes violent (Casamayor, 2000). Thus, they define conflict as a clash of interests or a confrontation caused by a disagreement, which if a solution is achieved, can arrive at mutual enrichment and greater development in scholastic coexistence (Deutsch, 1991; Hocker & Wilmont 1991 as cited in Koch & Girard 1997; Alcalde, Ravenna, & Guala, 1998). Conflict is then considered inherent in the human being, a basic fact of life and a constant opportunity to learn (Darino & Gómez, 2000). Educators are becoming more and more aware of the relevance of the subject, knowing that if the student manages to learn alternate ways to solve problems with others, he/she will possibly not resort to aggression and violence as an expression of his/her dissatisfaction (Antunez, 2000).

Educational institutions are required to have effective programs for solving conflict peacefully. Many school violence interventions are based on the assumption that families, teachers, and schools are not imparting moral values to children, or students lack the basic cognitive skills to handle conflict effectively (Blankeney & Blankeney, 1991; Coie, Underwood, & Lochman, 1991; Guerra, Nucci, & Huesmann, 1994). Programs designed to develop non-violent conflict resolution skills have thus arisen as well as programs to promote changes in policies and procedures to create a more cooperative school environment. These programs require multi-disciplinary teams and a teaching-learning environment that supports the students to experience the different situations that may occur. Nevertheless, as it is frequent in transversal curriculum subjects like this, it is difficult to maintain these proposals over time, because the lack of time and the competences to perform in a sustained way the pedagogical interventions.

Non-violent conflict resolution supposes communication strategies and creative thought to generate acceptable voluntary solutions for those involved in a dispute. These procedures must be studied, observed, acted on and practiced before they can be applied effectively. It is also necessary, to explore the associated values, beliefs and attitudes of the students and consider activities according to their characteristics, creating customized and interactive environments (Deutsch, 1991). Problem-solving methods and the techniques necessary to resolve simple conflicts between pairs constructively (Darino & Gómez, 2000) must be explained to the students. Negotiation, mediation and arbitration (Girard, Rifkin & Townley, 1985) are considered here the most important ones.

Among the wide spectrum of resources required to support an effective educational intervention on non-violent conflict resolution, computers and pedagogical software may support if not all (they never do), at least some important issues of this teaching-learning process (Hobbs & Yan, 2008). Computers may support the students' acquisition of theoretical knowledge on the concepts and definitions of non-violent conflict resolution, like the components of conflicts, their origin, their causes, their consequences, the possible effects on the others, etc. Computers, through the use of multimedia environments, may enrich the representation of real like environments, augmenting different conflict situations, representing the theoretical concepts and allowing the observation of the effects of different resolution strategies. Hypermedia allows interactivity, what gives autonomy to the student and the opportunity to practice the theoretical knowledge, for example by selecting a strategy and evaluating its consequences.

We propose to implement an intelligent learning environment to support teaching-learning processes on non-violent conflict resolution, presenting theoretical and practical aspects of the domain in an adaptive way, according to some student characteristics, that were considered relevant by different educational actors of the region where it is planned to be applied. The learning design for non-violent conflict resolution involves three stages: the definition of teaching strategies and tactics, the definition of student characteristics and the definition of learning environments. The next sections will preset these stages, emphasizing the advantages of the automata representation.

Teaching Strategies and Tactics (λ and η Functions)

Pedagogical strategies and tactics stored in the ITS allows it to decide how to configure the environment, given a student (η function) and how to update the student model according to the actual model and the student's inputs at the interface (λ function).

The pedagogical base of the ITS is extracted from a pedagogical structure where different learning theories are combined to define the learning environments that are better adapted to the student characteristics (Curilem & de Azevedo, 2003). It is emphasized that although all the learning models are valid, their contributions promote their simultaneous use (Savery & Duffy, 1995). The structure is based on pedagogical strategies that define general actions to support learning and pedagogical tactics that define specific actions that should be executed to carry out a pedagogical strategy. The first suggests the kind of activities (tutorial, game, etc.) that will be presented in the environment and their sequence. Pedagogical tactics define the media, interactivity and navigation among the contents. So, if the pedagogical strategy points out that "it is necessary to get the apprentice's attention on the most important matters", the tactics settle down "how to get the attention of each particular apprentice", according to his/her characteristics.

For behaviorist theory, learning means that associations are established between ideas or experiences, known as the stimulus-answer connection. The present study considers that the ITS must support the fulfillment of the phases described by Gagne, Briggs & Wagner (1988) to achieve the desired learning. These phases describe the cognitive stages that must be produced internally in the student during the learning process and establish what elements of the environment can support them. The ITS should provide the student with the necessary external support at each stage.

Conversely, in the constructivist theory, learning implies a modification of the mental structure, reaching a greater level of diversity, complexity and integration. The student becomes an active subject in his/her learning (Denegri, 2004). The ITS in this case must provide an environment of realistic experimentation, where the student can observe the results of his/her actions on the object under study, facilitating the processes of assimilation and accommodation. The system must intervene to cause imbalances and give some brief directions.

Some specific considerations were applied to this proposal, in order to simplify the design of the system. Behaviorist strategies are preferred for students in the first cycle of grade school because they result in more structured environments and guided activities. Constructivist strategies are preferred for students in the second cycle of grade school, because they supply more interactive and free environments.

The teaching tactics are based on learning styles according to the neuro-linguistic programming (NLP) model (Alonso, Gallego & Honey, 1999; Perez, 2001). This model was selected because the measuring instruments used are more pertinent considering the age of the children and because it adapts to the definition of environments since it contains the information input. This model indicates that people differ in the representational system through which they learn (visual, auditory, kinesthetic). The students with a system of visual representation learn better when they read or they see the information; in class they prefer reading over following oral explanations. Auditory students learn better when they receive oral explanations and when they can speak and explain that information to someone else. The auditory system does not enable abstract concepts to be related or elaborated with the same facility as the visual system and it is slower. Kinesthetic students tend to associate information with sensations and body movements and learn better when they have practical experience. The kinesthetic system is slower than the visual and auditory systems; however, it is a deeper kind of learning since what is learned with the muscular memory is very resistant to forgetfulness.

That is why, given the learning style of a student, the ITS should provide a representation based on what the theory suggests. In another hand, when the student interacts with the environment and modifies it, if the changes affect the representation of the contents, the student learning styles have to be updated. So the output and the state transition function involve knowledge on the behaviorist, constructivist and the learning styles theory.

Student Characteristics (Automata States)

The set of characteristics define the states of the automaton. The variables that will define the learner have to be extracted from the analysis of the specific teaching-learning process. To establish the significant characteristics of the non-violent conflict resolution teaching-learning process, a qualitative study was performed, interviewing 18 male and female teachers of basic education from 9 educational establishments in the IXth Region of Chile. The interviews lasted on average one hour and they were done on the basis of a guideline that investigated perception of the level of violence in children, the forms in which it manifests itself and the associated factors.

The teachers all perceived a greater level of violence at the moment and there was a high degree of consensus that the most relevant individual variables related to aggression were age and gender. They said that children from 10 to 12 are more violent in general, although the expression of violence varies according to age. Children between 6 and 7 mainly use direct violence like physical violence, whereas ten-year-olds predominantly use indirect violence, psychological or verbal.

Regarding gender, the teachers recount that boys are more violent than girls in general and the type of aggression is different: girls use more verbal violence or bullying, whereas the boys use more physical violence. They also indicate that the aggressive behavior is expressed predominantly at certain times (entering and leaving school) and in certain places (schoolyard and gymnasium).

From this survey, the basic cycle and the gender were selected as the more relevant, as the other characteristics evaluated, like social and cultural origins, student school performance, among others, were not point out as relevant by the study. In conclusion five characteristics define the states of the automata, that is, basic cycle (related to age), gender, and the learning styles, visual, auditory and kinesthetic.

Environment Attributes (Input and Output Automaton Sets)

Next the attributes that define the environments will be described. Their granularity allows guaranteeing compatibility with the learner characteristics.

1. **Contents:** set of units of information about the field, necessary to achieve the pedagogical objectives.
2. **Activities:** set of specific tasks that are proposed to the learner (game, problem solving, etc.)
3. **Media:** set of forms used to represent the content (images, text, etc.)
4. **Interactivity:** number of hyperlinks offered to the learner. It can only accept "high" an "low" values.
5. **Navigation:** possibility that the learner will have to move around the contents. It can only accept "free" and "predetermined" values.

It can be seen that the first element defines the content of the environment and elements 2 and 3 its form. Both represent system's output. Elements 4 and 5 define the interaction with the learner and represent system's input. These elements will be described in detail in the next section, but their structure is described here.

In this proposal, the learning object concept was used to make the configuration of the attributes viable. In most of the educational applications that use learning objects, the composition of the various objects is given by the strategy defined by a tutor or human designer. However, in this project, an automatic system for configuring these objects is set out.

In the absence of an agreed-upon definition, this study adopted a specific definition of learning object that emphasizes its pedagogical nature: a learning object is designed with an "intention of learning", which is why it considers aspects of form and relation and is not simply a media entity (Flamand & Gervais, 2004). These aspects define the educational sense that the combination of digital resources implies, therefore it is considered that the learning object has pedagogical strategies (relations) and tactics (forms) in its structure (Polsani, 2003).

According to this, the following structure can be defined:

- **Media Objects:** modular digital resources represented by one medium (text, video, link, etc.). In this work, the Media, Interactivity and Navigation attributes are media objects.
- **Activity Objects:** specific activities constructed from the assembly of media objects (tutorial, game, etc.). These do not incorporate teaching strategies, but they can be used to support a stage in the learning process (see Table 2). Here, the Content and Activity attributes are activity objects.
- **Learning Objects:** is the assembly of various activity objects, organized according

to a teaching strategy to respond to a single pedagogical objective. Here a learning object is the entire environment configured by the system, at run time.

The assembly of various media objects and activity objects is performed during the interaction with the learner, so that the learning object is as customized as possible. With this, the design is set out for "Adaptable Learning Objects". Figure 1 shows the resulting structure. The adaptation mechanism based on the IAC network establishes the values of the attributes from the characteristics. This way, it can be seen that the reusability is carried out at the level of media objects and activity objects, but not in the learning object since it is unique for each learner. This way, it can be seen that the reusability is carried out at the level of media objects and activity objects, but not for the learning objects since they are unique for each learner.

RESULT: PROPOSED PROGRAM

Based on the automaton defined in the previous section, this section presents the resulting program implemented to support the teaching-learning process of the non-violent conflict resolution. This program establishes the pedagogical objectives, the contents, the activities and the media, as it is created based on an automaton and its importance lies in its feasibility to be incorporated into an ITS.

The Pedagogical Program on non-violent conflict resolution will be represented in the ITS by the attributes of the interface. To create these Attributes, the content, the activities and the hypermedia have to be defined. So the steps involved in the program design start with the learner characteristics which allow to determine the pedagogical objectives of the ITS. The learning objectives and the learner characteristics allow the identification of the contents that should be incorporated to the system to reach the objectives and the kind of activity and hypermedia that should be present in the environment. The structure is presented in the upper part of Figure 2.

The team with experience in non-violent conflict resolution education decides which objectives, contents and activities should be offered to the learner. The system designer guides the decisions in terms of pointing out the need to consider the learner characteristics, the pedagogical strategies and tactics and the available technology for the interface construction. That is why the program design is oriented, at each step by the automaton previously defined.

Figure 1. Learning object structure based on activity objects and media objects combinations

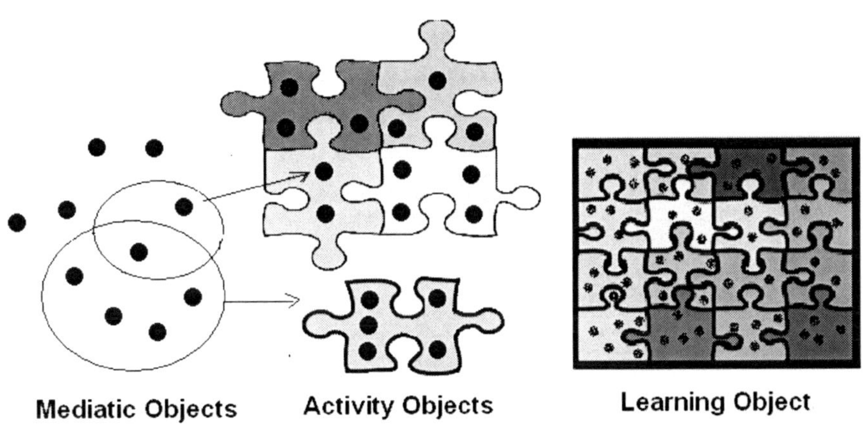

Figure 2. Learner identification and environment configuration flow

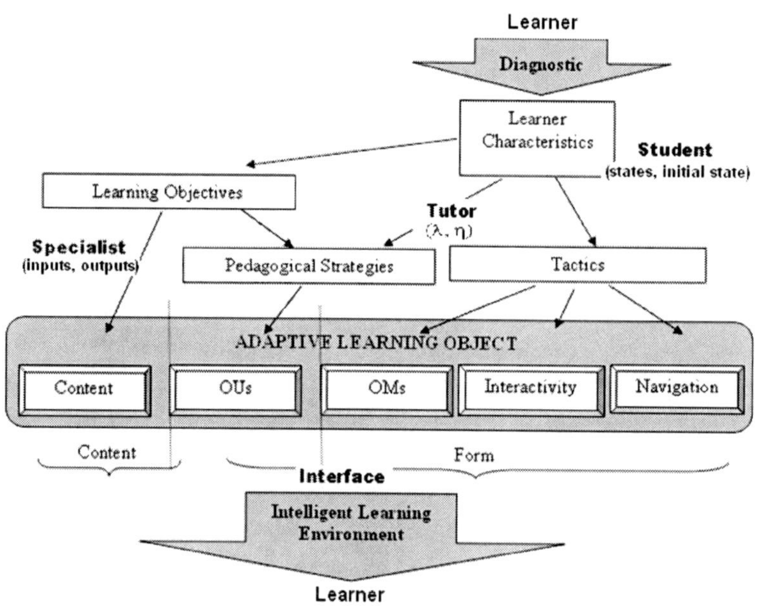

Pedagogical Objectives

The pedagogical objective of this educational process is to know the origins of a conflict and manage collaborative strategies to solve them. However, given the complexity of the subject and the great variety of possible students, these objectives must be divided into objectives of smaller reach, so that the system can combine them based on each situation. Based on the characteristics of the students, cognitive, procedural and attitudinal objectives for the first and second cycle of grade school are proposed. By way of an example, Table 1 presents some of the Pedagogical Objectives suggested for the second cycle.

The Contents

The objectives determine what contents must be incorporated. These are structured to guarantee modularity, so that a student who is already familiar with a subject can interact with another one.

Table 1. Examples of pedagogical objectives in the second cycle

Conceptual Objectives	Define conflict
	Describe a relationship / communication conflict
	Define the elements of a conflict
	Describe the differences between collaborative and NON-collaborative strategies in the approach to conflict
	Recognize the benefits of resolving conflicts collaboratively
	Identify mediation strategies
Procedural Objectives	Develop communication skills that enable conflicts to be prevented
	Develop mediation skills
Attitudinal Objective	Able to describe the advantages and disadvantages of the use of collaborative strategies in conflict resolution

Table 2. Description of activity objects

Activity Objects	Activity
Tutorial	The information is presented in a structured and pre-established manner. The system has control of the interaction.
Interactive Simulation	A hypermedia environment is presented the student has control of the interaction.
Resolution of Problems	Problems are set out that the learner must solve using previous knowledge.
Examples	Resolved problems and situations are set out that enable one to go more deeply into the object under study.
Questions Answers	Questions are put to the learner, who must choose the correct answers.
Game	A challenge and rules to follow are laid out and the learner must achieve the objective using his/her knowledge.
Encyclopedia	An index of subjects appears to the learner where he/she is free to choose the subjects that interest him/her.
Story	An idealized situation is presented, where the learner can project him/herself.

The cycle and gender are the characteristics that define the contents to be presented. The central content structure is detailed as follows:

1. Definition of Conflict
2. Types of Conflict
3. Structure of a Conflict (Person - Process - Problem)
4. Importance of non-violent conflict resolution
5. Non-collaborative Strategies
6. Collaborative Strategies
    a. Negotiation
    b. Arbitration
    c. Mediation

Activity Objects

For this particular Learning Design and based on the criteria of expert judges, the considered activities appear in Table 2.

Teaching Strategies

In order to render the implementation and handling of the system viable, it was decided by the team with experience in non-violent conflict resolution education to grant priority to each strategy using the criteria summarized in Table 3. This table emphasizes more structured environments for younger students and more exploratory environments for older students. Attitudinal objectives should always be evaluated in environments that give more freedom to the student behavior.

Each teaching strategy has an associated set of activity objects that manifests the stages of Gagné in the case of behaviorism or supports the cognitive processes proposed by Piaget (Curilem & de Azevedo, 2003). The corresponding activity objects for each strategy are described in Table 4 and in Table 5, respectively:

Media Objects and Interactivity

Table 6 summarizes the criteria adopted to implement the teaching tactics:

Figure 2 represents the summary of the system output: the learning environment is obtained from the diagnosis of the learner. The underlying structure of ITS is observed in bold and the corresponding automaton components in parenthesis.

Table 3. Relation between cycle, objectives and teaching strategies

Cycle	Pedagogical Objective	Strategy
First Cycle	Cognitive	Behaviorist
	Procedural	Behaviorist
	Attitudinal	Constructivist
Second Cycle	Cognitive	Behaviorist
	Procedural	Constructivist
	Attitudinal	Constructivist

Table 4. Activity objects to support behaviorist strategy

Phase	Process to be supported	Recommended Activity Object
Motivation	Create expectations in the learner by appealing to his/her interest, highlighting subject's importance	Story Example
Apprehension	Direct attention and selective perception towards key points	Tutorial
Acquisition	Facilitate codification, stimulating recall	Examples Resolution of problems
Retention	Support the storage of information, providing reflection.	Questions & Answers Interactive Environments
Recalling	Facilitate recovery of information, providing reminders	Examples Resolution of problems
Generalization	Facilitate generalization applying knowledge in new contexts	Resolution of problems Encyclopedia Examples
Performance	Apply knowledge to real situations.	Games Resolution of problems Questions & Answers
Feedback	Provide reinforcement stimulating the learner when he/she achieves advances in his/her behavior.	Animation

The student characteristics determine the objectives, strategies and tactics, which determine the content and the form of the environment, though the configuration of the Learning Object.

Table 5. Activity objects to support constructivist strategy

Activity	Process to be supported	Recommended Activity Object
Diagnosis	Know the characteristics of the learner, his/her previous knowledge and his/her interests	Questions & Answers
Disequilibrium	Present a new situation that causes a cognitive conflict: the way of thinking does not fit.	Questions & Answers Games Resolution of problems
Assimilation/ Accommodation	Manipulate the learning object in order to modify the way of thinking	Interactive Simulation
Support	Proposals that facilitate the process of accommodation or assimilation	Examples Encyclopedia Tutorial

The use of the IAC network as an adaptation mechanism allows to update the environment according to the student, but also to update the student's characteristics, because this mechanism is bi-directional. In that case, the input process starts off with the learner actions on the interface, which updates its model and generates new outputs.

DISCUSSION

At this stage of the work, the number of characteristics that define the learner is reduced in order to emphasize the teaching-learning process modeling procedure. Nevertheless, the methodology allows the incorporation of new characteristics

Table 6. Relation between characteristic, media objects and interactivity

Characteristic	Media Object	Interactivity	Navigation
Visual Style	Image, Video, Animation	No influence	No influence
Verbal Style	Text, Voice, Sound	No influence	No influence
Kinesthetic Style	Video, Animation	High	Free
1st Cycle	Animation, Voice	Low	Predetermined
2nd Cycle	No influence	High	No influence
Gender	Animated Character (Avatar)	No influence	No influence

(more neurons in the IAC) and new relations with environments (weights of the network).

The basic pedagogical assumption of this work is that when the student learning styles match the tutor teaching styles, the chances of learning increase. This is supported by many theories, like the neuro-linguistic learning styles that was applied here. However, the focus of the paper is not in the learning process but in its representation. The central matter pointed here is how to model an ill-structured domain like non-violent conflict resolution into an ITS. The paper demonstrate that it is possible to model this domain as an automaton, which incorporates all the relevant aspects of the domain, like the educational objectives, the contents, the kind of student, suitable environments, etc. Once the domain is modeled, the ITS is automatically designed.

The main contribution of the proposed methodology is that it allows for a natural integration between what Rossano et al. (2005) defined as "the pragmatic, pedagogical and technological approaches." On the other hand, being based on the definition of Technological Pedagogical Content Knowledge described in Mishra & Koehler (2006), it is possible to say that the formalization facilitates dialogue between the different areas: the concept of the automata is the intersection of all of them. This means that once the teaching-learning process is modeled by means of the definition of its main variables and their relationship, the computational model is simultaneously elaborated.

The main limitation of this work is that it has not been implemented and evaluated in a real context. This is a step that is being worked as it represents a necessary stage to evaluate the ITS and allow refinement of the design methodology. Another limitation is the subjective combination of pedagogical strategies and tactics with the Activity and Media objects. This limitation comes from the lack of consensual knowledge that establishes which elements of the environment support learning. As this is not systematized, the criteria to combine the existing theories is dependant on the educational team, so the elements that are shown in Tables 2 to 6 may be questioned by other teams. This limitation, however, is common to most pedagogical software.

CONCLUSION

The article presented the process for obtaining a pedagogical model of the non-violent conflict resolution education to incorporate it in an Intelligent Tutoring System. The methodology followed was based on the formalization of ITS as automata. It was shown how the concept of didactic ergonomics guided the research of the relevant variables that affect this specific teaching-learning process. These variables were used to define an automaton, defining in a systematic way, the characteristics that identify a student and the attributes of the interface. This systematization guided the design of specific environments to respond to different types of learners, based on teaching strategies and tactics pertinent to the field. A customized interface is thereby generated. In addition, despite having worked with a reduced number of variables, this number can be extended without requiring substantial changes to the original design.

From the point of view of the field, designing an educational software in non-violent conflict resolution is interesting as it can be a contribution to children's coexistence at school. At the moment in Chile, there are few programs for the prevention of violence geared towards students, which are designed to be applied in the classroom by the teacher. Considering the scant availability of teacher time, coverage of these programs is very low. Most educational establishments in the country have the sufficient technological resources to implement the program, so its application should be viable. As the IAC-type network has yielded satisfactory results, the following step is to implement the activities that the pedagogical model suggests and evaluate its performance in real school contexts.

School psychologists and teachers who participated in this work as the educational team had no understanding of automata theory. However, this did not limit the search of the most significant variables for the teaching-learning process. The student characteristics, the strategies, tactics, objectives and contents were given by the educators, but were structured by the designer, using the didactic ergonomy concept to form an automata. So, the method suggests that the person in charge of the learning design must belong to the technological field.

The present proposal offers a customized tool that includes a transversal subject, difficult to handle in the traditional educational curriculum. We believe that this project can work in favor of a shift of paradigm for education, as indicated by Albiniri (2007), as the development of more assertive technologies for learning, mainly in the school environment, can gradually clear the way for the new paradigms that must be adopted in education. If there is no paradigm indicating which technologies support learning and how to put them into practice, perhaps the development of customized educational technologies will aid in the construction of new paradigms.

ACKNOWLEDGMENT

We thank the Research Direction of the La Frontera University for the financial support to the present chapter.

REFERENCES

Albirini, A. (2007). The crisis of educational technology, and the prospect of reinventing education. *Journal of Educational Technology & Society*, *10*(1), 227–236.

Alcalde, S., Ravenna, A., & Guala, M. (1998). *Mediación en la Escuela: Convivir y Aprender*. Argentina: Editorial Homo Sapiens.

Alonso, C., Gallego, D., & Honey, P. (1999). *Los estilos de aprendizaje procedimientos de diagnostico y mejora. España* (Mensajero, B., Ed.).

Alsop, G., & Tompsett, C. (2007). From effect to effectiveness: The missing research questions. *Journal of Educational Technology & Society*, *10*(1), 28–39.

Antunez, S. (2000). *Disciplina y convivencia en la institución escolar*. Barcelona: Editorial Laboratorio Educativo.

Arón, A. M. (2000). Un Programa de Educación para la No-Violencia. *Psykhe Revista de la Escuela de Psicología. Facultad de Ciencias Sociales Pontificia Universidad Católica de Chile*, *9*(2), 25–39.

Blankeney, C. D., & Blankeney, R. A. (1991). Understanding and reforming misbehavior among behaviorally disordered adolescents. *Behavioral Disorders*, *16*(2), 120–126.

Bruillard, E. (1997). *Les Machines a Enseigner*. Paris: Editions Hermes.

Carbonell, J. R. (1970). artificial intelligence in CAI: An artificial intelligence approach to computer-aided instruction. *IEEE Transactions on Man-Machine Systems*, *4*(11), 190–202. doi:10.1109/TMMS.1970.299942

Casamayor, G. (2000). *Disciplina y Convivencia en la Institución Escolar*. Venezuela: Editorial Laboratorio Educativo.

Coie, J. D., Underwood, M., & Lochman, J. E. (1991). Programmatic intervention with aggressive children in the school setting. In Pepler, D. J., & Rubin, K. H. (Eds.), *The development and treatment of childhood aggression* (pp. 389–410). Hillsdale, NJ: Erlbaum.

Conati, C., & Maclare, H. (2004). *Evaluating a Probabilistic Model of Student Affect.* Paper presented at the VII International Conference on Intelligent Tutoring Systems. Lecture Notes in Computer Science. Springer-Verlag Heidelberg, 55-66.

Curilem, G. M. S., & de Azevedo, F. (2003). Didactic Ergonomy for the Interface of Intelligent Tutoring Systems. In Llamas-Nistal, M., Fernandez-Iglesias, M. J., & Anido-Rifon, L. (Eds.), *Computers and Education: Towards a Lifelong Learning Society* (pp. 75–88). The Netherlands: Kluwer Academic Publishers.

Curilem, S. G., Barbosa, A. R., & de Azevedo, F. M. (2007). Intelligent tutoring systems: Formalization as automata and interface design using neural networks. *Computers & Education*, *49*(3), 545–561. doi:10.1016/j.compedu.2005.10.005

Darino, S., & Gómez, M. (2000). *Resolución de Conflictos en las Escuelas. Proyectos y Ejercitación.* Argentina: Editorial Espacio.

de Azevedo, F. M. (1993). *Contribution to the Study of Neural Networks in Dynamical Expert System.* Unpublished Doctoral Dissertation. Facultés Universitaires Notre-Dame de la Paix (FUNDP), Namur, Belgium.

Denegri, M. (2004). *La construcción del conocimiento social en la infancia: reflexiones para la investigación y acción educativa.* Chile: Revista de Estudios y Experiencias en Educación. Universidad de Concepción.

Deutsch, M. (1991). *Koch, S. & Girard, K. (1997). Resolución de Conflictos en las Escuelas*. Argentina: Editorial Granica.

Felder, R. M. (1996). Matters of Styles. [December.]. *ASEE Prism*, *6*(4), 18–23.

Flamand, F., & Gervais, A. (2004). Les objets d'apprentissage: au-delà de la technologie, la pédagogie. *Bulletin Collegial des Technologies de l'Information et des Communications CLIC*, *54*, 1–5.

Gagne, R. M., Briggs, L. J., & Wagner, W. W. (1988). *Principles of instructional design* (3rd ed.). New York: Holt Rinehart and Winston.

Gardner, H. (1993). *Multiple Intelligences: The Theory in Practice.* NY: Basic Books.

Giesbers, B., Van Bruggen, J., Hermans, H., Joosten-Ten Brinke, D., Burgers, J., & Koper, R. (2007). Towards a methodology for educational modelling: A case in educational assessment. *Journal of Educational Technology & Society*, *10*(1), 237–247.

Girard, K., Rifkin, J., & Townley, A. (1985). *Peaceful persuasión: A guide to creating mediation dispute resolution programs on college campuses.* Washington, DC: National Institute for Disputes Resolution.

Guerra, N. G., Nucci, L., & Huesmann, R. L. (1994). Moral cognition and childhood aggression. In Huesmann, L. R. (Ed.), *Aggressive behavior: Current perspectives* (pp. 13–33). New York: Plenum.

Hahne, M. N., & de Azevedo, F. M. (2008). Study on IAC networks models: learning and stability. *Neural Computing & Applications*, *17*(1), 65–74. doi:10.1007/s00521-007-0112-z

Halcartegaray, M. A. (1991). Reflexión en torno a la disciplina y el entorno moral. Corporación de Promoción Universitaria (CPU), 9-19, Santiago. Chile.

Hobbs, L. J., & Yan, Z. (2008). Cracking the walnut: Using a computer game to impact cognition, emotion, and behavior of highly aggressive fifth grade students. *Computers in Human Behavior*, *24*(2), 421–438. doi:10.1016/j.chb.2007.01.031

Hocker, J., & Wilmont, W. (1991). *Koch, S. & Girard, K. (1997). Resolución de Conflictos en la Escuelas*. Argentina: Editorial Granica.

Hu, S., & Wu, Y. (2006). Student diagnosing model based on neuro-fuzzy for web-based educational systems. *Journal of Computer Information Systems*, *2*(1), 377–382.

Jaques, P. A., & Vicari, R. M. (2007). A BDI approach to infer student's emotions in an intelligent learning environment. *Computers & Education*, *49*(2), 360–384. doi:10.1016/j.compedu.2005.09.002

Kaczmarek, J., & Landowska, K. (2006). Model of Distributed Learning Objects Repository for a Heterogenic Internet Environment. *Interactive Learning Environments*, *14*(1), 1–15. doi:10.1080/10494820600566312

Karampiperis, P., & Sampson, D. (2005). Adaptive learning resources sequencing in educational hypermedia systems. *Journal of Educational Technology & Society*, *8*(4), 128–147.

Kelly, D., & Tangney, B. (2004). *Predicting Learning Characteristics in a Multiple Intelligence Beased Tutoring System*. Paper presented at the VII International Conference on Intelligent Tutoring Systems. Lecture Notes in Computer Science. Springer-Verlag Heidelberg. 678 – 688.

Koper, R. (2006). Current research in learning design. *Journal of Educational Technology & Society*, *9*(1), 13–22.

Leaf, P., & Keys, S. (2005). Collaborating for Violence Training Health Professionals. American *Journal of Preventive Medicine 29*(5S2):279–287.

Martins, W., & de Carvalho, S. D. (2004). *An Intelligent Tutoring System Based on Self-Organizing Maps. Design, Implementation and Evaluation.* Paper presented at the VII International Conference on Intelligent Tutoring Systems. Lecture Notes in Computer Science. Springer-Verlag Heidelberg 573-579.

Mayer, R. E., Johnson, W. L., Shaw, E., & Sandhu, S. (2006). Constructing computer-based tutors that are socially sensitive: Politeness in educational software. *International Journal of Human-Computer Studies*, *64*(1), 36–42. doi:10.1016/j.ijhcs.2005.07.001

MINEDUC. (1996). La Reforma en Marcha. Jornada Escolar Completa Diurna para Todos. Santiago de Chile. Retrieved from http://www.mineduc.cl

MINEDUC. (2001). *Convivencia Escolar: Conclusiones de la Comisión sobre Reflexión y Compromiso por el Derecho a la Educación y la Convivencia Escolar*. Retrieved 2001, from http://www.mineduc.cl

Mishra, P., & Koehler, M. J. (2006). Technological pedagogical content knowledge: A framework for teacher knowledge. *Teachers College Record*, *108*(6), 1017–1054. doi:10.1111/j.1467-9620.2006.00684.x

Pérez, J. J. (2001). *Programación Neurolinguística y sus estilos de aprendizaje*. Retrieved October 2006, from http://www.aldeaeducativa.com/aldea/tareas2.asp?which=1683

Piaget, J. (1967). *A psicologia da Inteligência*. Lisboa: Editora Fundo de Cultura S.A.

Polsani, P. R. (2003). Use and Abuse of Reusable Learning Objects. *Journal of Digital Information*, *3*(4), 11–21.

Rodrigues, L. M. L., & Carvalho, M. (2004). *Emotional and motivational ITS architecture*. Paper presented at the IEEE International Conference on Advanced Learning Technologies, ICALT 276-280.

Rose, D. H., & Strangman, N. (2007). Universal design for learning: Meeting the challenge of individual learning differences through a neurocognitive perspective. *Universal Access in the Information Society*, *5*(4), 381-391.

Rossano, V., Joy, M., Roselli, T., & Sutinen, E. (2005). A taxonomy for definitions and applications of learning objects: A meta-analysis of ICALT papers. *Journal of Educational Technology & Society*, *8*(4), 148–160.

Rumelhart, D. E., & McClelland, J. L. (1989). *Explorations in Distributed Processing. A Handbook of Models, Programs and Exercises* (Book, B., Ed.). Massachusetts Institute of Technology.

Savery, J. R., & Duffy, T. M. (1995). Problem Based Learning: An instructivist model and its constructivist framework. *Educational Technology*, *35*(5), 31–38.

Stathacopoulou, R., Magoulas, G. D., Grigoriadou, M., & Samarakou, M. (2005). Neuro-fuzzy knowledge processing in intelligent learning environments for improved student diagnosis. *Information Sciences*, *170*(2-4), 273–307. doi:10.1016/j.ins.2004.02.026

Suebnukarn, S., & Haddawy, P. (2006). Modeling individual and collaborative problem-solving in medical problem-based learning. *User Modeling and User-Adapted Interaction*, *16*(3-4), 211–248. doi:10.1007/s11257-006-9011-8

UNESCO. (2001). *UNESCO y la Cultura para la Paz*. Retrieved in 2001 from http://www.unesco.cl

Wang, Q., & Woo, H. L. (2007). Systematic planning for ICT integration in topic learning. *Journal of Educational Technology & Society*, *10*(1), 148–156.

Watson, J., & Hardaker, G. (2005). Steps towards personalised learner management system (LMS): SCORM implementation. *Campus-Wide Information Systems*, *22*(2), 56–70. doi:10.1108/10650740510587074

Wenger, E. (1987). *Artificial Intelligence and Tutoring Systems*. Los Altos, CA: Morgan Kaufman.

Yannibelli, V., Godoy, D., & Amandi, A. (2006). A Genetic Algorithm Approach to Recognise Students' Learning Styles. *Interactive Learning Environments*, *14*(1), 55–78. doi:10.1080/10494820600733565

Zhu, X. (2007). Extending the SCORM specification for references to the open content object. *Journal of Educational Technology & Society*, *10*(1), 248–264.

Zywno, M. S., & Stewart, M. F. (2005). *Learning styles of engineering students, online learning objects and achievement.* Paper presented at the ASEE Annual Conference and Exposition, Conference Proceedings. (pp. 9615-9623).

Chapter 3
Enhancing Intelligent Tutoring Systems with the Agent Paradigm

Xin Bai
City University of New York, USA

John B. Black
Columbia University, USA

ABSTRACT

A cognitive framework called REflective Agent Learning environment (REAL) is developed in this study. REAL is a reusable framework that allows researchers to develop a simulation-based learning environment where users can learn through passing their thoughts to some computer-based agents and observe how the agents embodying their knowledge behave as the result of their instruction. Our research benefits from the research in Intelligent Tutoring Systems, game based learning systems, and agent technologies, stressing reflection as part of the thinking processes. It focuses on the design of the framework and the testing of its usability. The external evaluation of specific implementations serves as the guidance for the future design of the REAL applications. We hope, by grounding themselves in the needs of local practice, the REAL applications can give us opportunities to understand how theoretical claims about teaching and learning can be effectively transformed into meaningful learning.

INTRODUCTION

Using computers to provide personalized instruction as an alternative to human tutors has drawn the attention of researchers in the fields of education, psychology, computer science, and cognitive science. Thanks to their cooperative efforts, we have Intelligent Tutoring Systems (ITSs), or Intelligent Computer-Assisted Instruction (ICAI), embodying the computer-as-tutor paradigm. In this sense, ITSs/ICAI can be considered as Pedagogical Agents, which have a set of normative teaching goals and plans for achieving these goals (e.g., teaching strategies), and associated resources in the learning environment (Thalmann, 1997). The agent paradigm now allows researchers to collaborate effectively in an effort to develop other efficient user-centered learning environments. Examples include the computer as a collaborator (Blandford, 1994; Dillenbourg & Self, 1992),

DOI: 10.4018/978-1-61692-008-1.ch003

the computer as a learning companion (Chan & Baskin, 1990), and the computer as a teachable agent (Biswas, 2005), to name a few.

However, the design and development of computer-based instruction systems are costly (Murray, 1999; Anderson, 1993). Adaptive and broadly applicable cognitive tools are needed to reduce the development cycle time and the level of the required expertise. This will allow for computer-based intelligent tutoring systems to become affordable learning environments in traditional classroom settings.

The primary goal of this research is to design and prototype an intelligent reflective agent situated in an educational gaming environment based upon a cognitive framework, called REAL (REflective Agent Learning Environment). Attempts were made to encourage reflective thinking through having users explicitly externalize their internal knowledge representations by instructing the agent, which, ideally, generates a sequence of behaviors analogous to those generated by the users' imaginary worlds. It is our hope that when users begin to recognize relationships between their prior knowledge and the newly presented meanings, learning occurs, thus making the new information accessible as part of the learners' active reservoirs of knowledge. The tangible results of this research are some prototypes of the REAL applications.

BACKGROUND

Our research is inspired by our observations of teenagers highly motivated to control the computer-generated characters. It would be ideal if we could create a reusable framework that allows researchers to develop such a motivational computer-based learning environment where users could learn through passing their thoughts to some computer-based agents and observe how the agents embodying their knowledge behave as the result of their instruction. These agents can use the knowledge acquired from the students to achieve intelligent behaviors. For instance, an agent can predict how events will unfold and plan accordingly. When prediction fails or conflicts with reality, students will need to revise the knowledge to help the agent get out of the problematic situation. Learning will occur when they succeed. Some of the procedures they go through will be compiled and available in their long-term memory to aid their understanding. Those steps are missing in traditional learning practices where, most of the time, students are only dealing with the initial problem state and the final outcome state based upon certain solutions. Students do not have opportunities to search through the problem space and apply operators to change the environment and observe the change during which a deeper understanding of "how thing happens" and "why it has happened" is generated. As Black and Bower (1980) stated (pages 247-248),

In a story world, ... the subject can up-date and "see" dynamic changes of characters, objects, and locations in his storyworld: he has available for inspection not only the starting and ending state of a character's motion but also intermediate points along the dynamic path. The reader can "see" that objects afford or suggest certain actions and prevent others. Furthermore, the reader's storyworld model allows him to experiment with hypothetical changes in his imagination. So he can imagine what would have happened had circumstances been different in the storyworld. Thus, readers can answer questions like, "How could this story have been different if Superman had been unable to fly?" or "If St. George hadn't had a lance, how might he have overpowered the dragon? Could he have pacified and domesticated it?"

To have an agent represent knowledge that a user possesses, we need to look at the ways humans and computer-based agents represent knowledge. Next we will give a theoretical literature review that examines the key areas of research that influence the design of the REAL cognitive framework.

Human Knowledge Representation

Acquiring knowledge from users and representing it is crucial in determining what they know before passing it to a computer-based agent. In cognitive science, researchers engage in studying how people obtain, store, and process knowledge. In artificial intelligence, researchers aim to design knowledge bases that programs can process to achieve human-like intelligence. We intend to build a cognitive framework that can benefit from both disciplines.

Several knowledge representation paradigms have been proposed in attempts to understand how people think. Theories like propositional representations (Kintsch, 1988), scripts (Schank & Abelson 1977), and semantic networks (Collins & Loftus, 1975) are examples of using symbols to represent cognitive knowledge in computing systems. They have one feature in common – they all represent declarative facts with a certain (true or false) value. Reasoning is achieved through propositional calculus (Boole, 1854). This enables the computer programs to represent factual objects as well as abstract concepts. The notations by Kintsch (1988) and Anderson (1983) are two of the influential ones used as psychological theories. Anderson's ACT architecture is a well developed propositional network model. In ACT, propositions are represented as entities linked to relations labeled by the roles they play. More recently, the technique of concept mapping was developed by Novak (1998) as a teaching tool for representing the knowledge of students. It has subsequently been used as a visualization tool to increase meaningful learning in the sciences and other subjects. However, reasoning with uncertain facts is not possible using these networks. Bayesian networks (Pearl, 1988) have been designed in computer programs that serve as a natural mirror of these kinds of knowledge structures in the human mind. They have formal probabilistic forms that can model human reasoning and optimal decision-making based upon probabilistic facts or uncertain knowledge.

As semantic networks, propositional networks, concept maps, and Bayesian networks can all be represented as networks with nodes chained together through propositional, functional/causal, and system relations, we have decided to categorize them as network diagrams in our efforts to adopt a broadly applicable knowledge format in the REAL framework.

Network diagrams, such as semantic networks, propositional networks, and concept maps, are good at representing declarative knowledge. Newell and Simon (1972) suggested that human problem solving behavior could be viewed in terms of goals, plans, and other complex mental structures as well. This knowledge of knowing how to achieve goals is procedural in nature. To accomplish a goal, certain operations need to be carried out based upon certain conditions. A goal is achieved through using if-then rules called production systems. A complex goal can be broken down into several smaller pieces of sub-goals. The SOAR architecture (Newell, 1990, 1972; Laird, Newell, & Rosenbloom, 1987) is one of the production systems using a goal-orientated approach. Anderson (1983) states that there is evidence to suggest that knowledge is also stored in the brain in the form of if-then production rules that act on declarative propositions. Therefore, the REAL framework needs to allow for the construction of production rules as another type of knowledge representation.

But thinking is more than the manipulation of symbols by rules. Black (1992, 2007) states that mental images are a type of knowledge that exists in human cognition. In his SaW cognitive model, he proposed "knowledge can be represented in symbolic level and deeper abstract level; imaginary world, in abstract level, makes it complete for representing human cognition, together with propositional networks, production systems and mental images." This model becomes the basis for the knowledge representations in the REAL cognitive framework.

Agent Knowledge Representation in Games

In video games like Sims (http://thesims.ea.com), Second Life (http://secondlife.com), or World of Warcraft (www.worldofwarcraft.com), the characters are controlled by the users who can dress them, feed them, rest them, entertain them, clean them, and engage them in social activities. For instance, in Warcraft, people control a character avatar to explore the landscape, fight enemies, and interact with other players, all achieved through users' immediate commands using either the classic "point and click" control or the analog stick. Those characters themselves do not have the abilities or knowledge to plan or solve problems. In other words, they are more like passive puppets waiting for users to tell them what they need to do next. Thus, users are not able to plan ahead strategies that a character can use for dealing with specific situations or solving problems. For instance, a Sim, a computer-generated character in the Sims video game, may not have such knowledge as a tiger is a kind of carnivore or energy flows from a producer to an herbivore. Therefore, it is not able to make decisions such as assigning enough plants to a planet to maintain a balanced energy flow. Or, to operate a machine, a Sim may need to know a rule like this: if a machine malfunctions and the light turns red, turn off the power immediately; otherwise, turn on the fan to cool it down. It is not easy to develop an interface that allows a Sim to understand and use such rules.

Also, in Sims, the emphasis is more on relations between some Sims and other Sims or the Sims and their environment. The knowledge about how the systems work is not exposed for users to reflect upon. This is because, like any other games, once all the tricks are exposed, the Sims game will lose its motivational factor. Users will soon get bored in a transparent environment where there is nothing mysterious to explore. In other words, the mechanism of how a system works is purposely hidden from the user to sustain their engagement.

We would like our learning environment to be transparent as well as motivational. To make it transparent, we need to develop tools for users to construct knowledge to be passed to the agents. We also need to have tools to represent knowledge of how a system works. We believe users will benefit from the opportunities to observe the consequences of an agent's behaviors in a simulation and reflect upon the knowledge represented that drives the events.

There are other attributes of agents that implement concepts that apply more to humans: for example, notions like knowledge, belief, desire, motivation, emotion, intentions, and obligation. In REAL, the reflective agent is designed to have the potential of reflecting users' mental models and personalities, exposing their knowledge and reasoning processes, and displaying their emotions.

Game-Based Learning Systems

Simulation game based learning systems are the exact learning environments we are looking for to expose mental models learners need to (re) construct to "change their perception and interpretation patterns of reality (Kriz, Puschert, Karl, & Dufter-Weis, 2004)".

Game-based learning systems are eLearning systems that use "a computer games-based approach to deliver, support, and enhance teaching, learning, assessment, and evaluation (Kriz, et al., 2004)". They claims game-based learning systems, the latest generation of eLearning, are more collaborative learning environments based much more on the constructivist epistemology, promoting reflective practice through tools like ePortfolios, blogs, wikis, online communities, and using interactive technologies such as online visualizations, games, and simulations (Kriz, et al., 2004). Gee (2003) states that games are "not only pushing the creative boundaries of interactive digital media but also suggesting powerful models of next-generation interactive learning environments."

Of all the games available, simulation games stand out for their enormous educational potential. According to Hmelo-Silver (2004), making sense of complex systems requires that a person construct a network of concepts and principles about some domain that represents key phenomena and the interrelationships among different levels of the system, whether it is macro to micro or structure to function. Thus, computer-based science simulation games offer the potential to improve students' understanding of scientific concepts (Jacobson & Kozma, 2000). Video games have also been adopted as simulated learning environments. They present players with simulated worlds: worlds which, if well constructed, are not just about facts or isolated skills, but embody particular social practices (Shaffer, Squire, Halverson, & Gee, 2005).

Computer games have highly desirable qualities and build on theories such as motivation, constructivism, situated learning and problem-based learning (Connolly & Stansfield, 2007). However, empirical studies have also shown that, although educational games are usually highly engaging, they often do not trigger the constructive reasoning necessary for learning (Conati & Zhao, 2004; Klawe, 1998). It is often possible to learn how to play a game effectively without necessarily reasoning about the underlying domain knowledge. Most educational games to date have been produced in the absence of any coherent theory of learning or underlying body of research (Shaffer, et al., 2005).

Integrating ITSs with Game-Based Learning Systems

In this study, the potential of educational games will be further explored by integrating ITSs with simulation games, thus helping students learn effectively with the help of the intelligent tutors while maintaining a high level of engagement and motivation.

With the rapid progress of computer technology, researchers have attempted to adopt artificial intelligence (AI) to develop computer-aided instruction systems (CAI). There is a strong argument in AI in education which advocates that computer-based learning systems need to adapt to the needs of learners if they are to provide for effective personalized instruction (Self, 1999). For a computer-based system to provide such an adaptive instruction, it needs to reason about the subject domain and the learner. This leads to the development of ITSs, which are characterized by the philosophy of high tutor control – the system plays the active role of domain expert, controlling the selection of task for problems, while the students are supposed to solve the problem. The knowledge base is organized in such a way that it is not only composed of the traditional components in such a format as practice-and-drill, but also contains a student model that depicts the students' cognitive capacities, which is a crucial issue in building adaptive systems. Furthermore, it has defined goals for learning, which may be the mastery of factual knowledge and procedural skills. Such a system achieves its intelligence through its ability to make pedagogical decisions about how and when to provide pedagogical assistance based on individual students needs and learning objectives. ITSs have been proved to be highly effective at improving students' performances and increasing motivation (Anderson, Boyle, Corbett, & Lewis, 1990; Koedinger, Anderson, Hadley, & Mark, 1997; Mark & Greer, 1991; Lajoie & Lesgold, 1989; Shute, Glaser, & Raghaven, 1989).

Learning contents are important components in learning management systems (LMSs). SCORM (shareable content object reference model) has been a widely adopted eLearning standard for defining, packaging, and managing learning objects. In December 2004, the US Department of Defense mandated that all its e-learning purchases must comply with SCORM standards. The goal is to enable interoperability, accessibility and reusability of eLearning content for industry, government, and academia. Today, most major LMSs and educational software vendors comply with this standard for creating and deploying eLearning. SCORM-compliant game-based learning systems therefore have great potential to be readily plugged in to any existing LMS. Once built, these self-contained learning modules can be easily maintained and re-purposed, thus cutting costs in the long run. With this vision in mind, we would like to design a generic framework that supports sustainable knowledge base that can grow over time and supports multi-disciplinary collaboration.

We hope, with the goal of winning a game, students will actively review instructional material, revise game rules and appreciate just-in-time feedback, in the process of which they master the target cognitive skills. Next, we will discuss other approaches applied in REAL in an effort to facilitate learning.

Betty's Brain (Biswas, Schwartz, Bransford, & The Teachable Agents Group at Vanderbilt, 2001) is one of the relatively recent approaches to designing computer-based learning environments that place learners in the role of teachers. It is about teaching an agent, Betty, so that it can answer questions based upon what is taught. Betty is a generic agent that is domain-independent. The benefit of this is that it can be applied to any knowledge domain without the cost of re-inventing the wheel. Such an approach emphasizes the learner's beliefs about the domain, but lacks the correct world view embodied in the traditional expert model of an ITS. Therefore, the system can not reason beyond the students' teaching scope. Hence students lose the opportunity of getting the "deeper" feedback that domain experts can provide. It would be helpful if we could add a correct mental model, i.e., an expert model, which could provide insightful domain-specific guidance that is beyond students' current understanding capacities.

A domain expert may not necessarily be a good teacher, who can provide "intellectual scaffolding" to help students learn and progress through the different stages of knowledge development. We need to have a pedagogical model that contains teaching strategies and essential instructions. These strategies should be tailored to students' needs. Hence, based on students' performances, instructional feedback can be given to students in different ways including immediate, delayed, informative, motivational, positive, or negative. The main purpose of this model is to reduce the differences between the expert and the novice to a minimum or none using adaptive instructional strategies.

THE REAL COGNITIVE FRAMEWORK AND ITS APPLICATIONS

We designed the REAL cognitive framework in Figure 1, which contains the components for constructing intelligent agents in the REAL learning environment. As in a traditional ITS, the REAL framework consists of expert knowledge, instructional strategies, the student model, and human-computer interaction components. These components are modularized and represented by such agents as the reflective agent (i.e., student model), the expert agent (i.e., expert model), the pedagogical agent (i.e., pedagogical model), and the communication agent (i.e., communication model) in REAL. They are the electronic human alternatives of the student, the domain expert, the teacher, and the collaborator.

The knowledge bases of these agents are acquired differently. Users pass their thoughts about how a system works to the reflective agent in the form of network diagrams, production systems, and images in Design Mode. These symbolic knowledge representations become the knowledge base of the reflective agent in the simulation, which is another form of users' knowledge representation, their imaginary world. Together, they give the reflective agent the ability to reason and make decisions. The use of the term reflective gives the agent two layers of meaning: it reflects the users' domain knowledge back to them (similar to looking into a glass box and seeing their own

Figure 1. The REAL system architecture

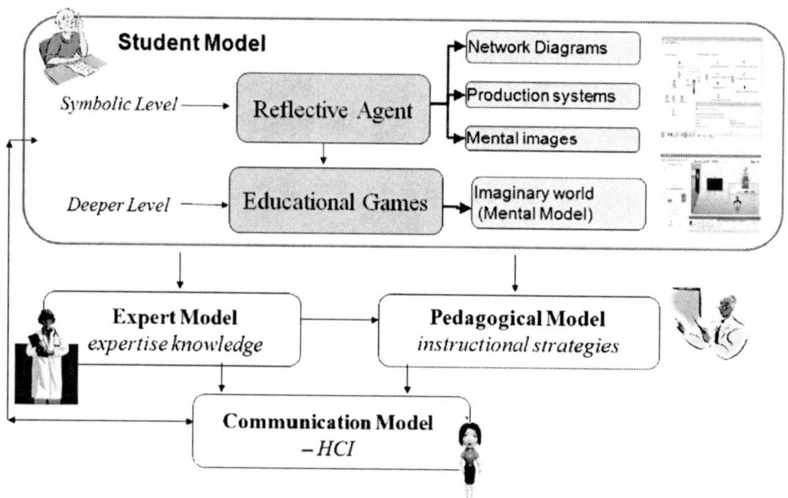

reasoning); the users reflect on that knowledge (similar to looking at a mirror, criticizing their own thinking processes).

The expert agent's knowledge base is predefined and domain-specific. It contains what a user should know ideally. The pedagogical agent relies upon the teaching strategies designed by the researchers to figure out when to give feedback, critique, instruction, or more learning materials. The communication agent acts as a collaborator for facilitating human-computer interactions. It is an animated character that communicates with the user via synthesized speech, facial expressions, and simple hand gestures.

This kind of complex system can be best built with people from different areas involved. There have been about a dozen doctoral students involved in the design of the system in its different phases. They have been trying to improve REAL from different perspectives. Figure 2 is a use case diagram illustrating how users, instructional designers, and domain experts (represented as stick figures in the diagram) collaborate in the REAL environment.

For instance, in REAL Business, a researcher, who had taught math in high school, worked as a domain expert. He collected the learning material and learning objectives on probability (Figure 2). The instructional designers analyzed the cognitive tasks, designed the knowledge contents and structure, and put them to a local context in simulation – running an ice cream store using the knowledge on probability. Together with the expert, they identified the typical misconceptions a user might have and designed how to diagnose and correct them. These strategies were stored in the pedagogical module. The instructional designers design the story scripts, the simulation layout, and other game features, such as game scores and levels. The information is stored in the game module, which the game coordinate agent can get access to for generating simulation games. After the REAL application is developed and deployed, users start the program in Design Mode. They pass their thoughts to the reflective agent in the form of network diagrams, production systems, and visual representation using images. These knowledge representations are then stored in the student module saved in a user's local computer. This module is used by other agents in the REAL system to generate Reflection Mode in real-time and the dynamic simulated world.

The result of the compiling of these knowledge representations is the unfolding of a simulation where the reflective agent makes decisions based

Figure 2. Use case diagram of the REAL application

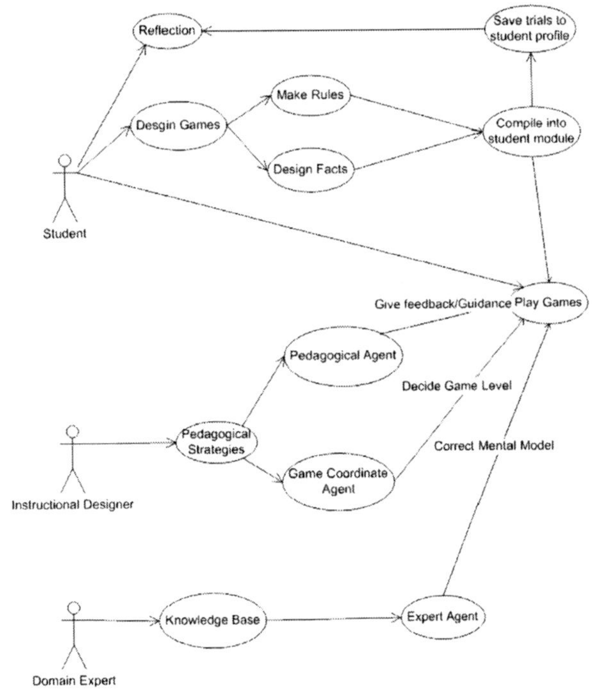

upon what is taught. The pedagogical agents provide just-in-time feedback which is generated through comparing the knowledge processed by the expert agent and the reflective agent. The communication agent guides students throughout the running of the REAL application to ensure they know how to use different sets of tools.

REAL Planet as a Proof of Concept

The first REAL application, REAL Planet, was developed in the domain of ecology. We chose ecosystems as our initial prototype because they are complex emergent systems. Emergent phenomena result from the local interactions among many individual entities with different characteristics. The interactions result in unanticipated patterns that emerge in a macro level. Therefore, designing such dynamic emergent systems involves consideration of individual agent behaviors as well as system functions. Simulation is a powerful tool for illustrating the dynamics of such complex systems. In agent-based simulations, where each entity is modeled as an autonomous agent following its own goals, the interaction among the agents produces the emergent phenomena. As Holland (1998) stated, one of the characteristics of emergence is it occurs in systems composed of small components that obey simple laws. It helps students gain insights into situations where simple local rules can lead to emergent macro-level structures. For instance, in an ecosystem simulation, each animal's goal can be as simple as hunting for food in order to survive. Observing that the tigers do not have enough food in a simulation, students may add more rabbits to feed the tigers. The tigers will eat the rabbits following the simple a predator goes after a prey law. But more rabbits demand more grass as food. This may result in less grass available, thus fewer rabbits left due to the lack of food. In the end, the tigers still do not have enough food. Hence, adding more rabbits to a system where tigers are starving has not solved the problem. The emergent phenomenon generated in this process can be a teaching moment that gives students opportunities to understand how the food-chain system works in the macro-level, thus determining how problems can be better solved through changing the law (e.g. maintaining a certain amount of bio-energy in each category in the food chain) in the micro-level.

In REAL Planet, students are supposed to embody knowledge about how to design an ecological system on an alien planet, which has environmental conditions similar to that of the Earth. To do so, users pass their thoughts to the reflective agent (the alien) through building propositional networks in Design Mode. The nodes in the propositional networks represent entities in the physical world such as tigers, fungi, and grass. These entities have virtual representations as images at the bottom of the screen (Figure 3). Users construct a network through dragging these images to the main screen and connecting them with relations through arrows. Users can click on an entity to modify its properties (e.g., age, size, energy level, food preferences) or click on a relation (e.g., energy flow) to update it. When the teaching is done, users can click on Game Mode (Figure 4) at the top of the screen and launch the simulation game, where the quality of their teachings will be evaluated. The simulation is controlled by the rules of Mother Nature embedded in the expert agent. The pedagogical agent decides which event to trigger, with the goal of exposing users' missed concepts and misconceptions. For instance, students can observe how many organisms are created at the beginning of the game. As time progresses, some organisms may be consumed by others based upon the energy-flow relations defined by students. If there is a conflict between the expert agent and the reflective agent, say, on whether tigers should eat grass, the pedagogical agent may intervene, illustrating tigers have no desire to eat grass or they find it yucky. Later, users or teachers can save their propositional network in Design Mode and load them again when they would like to improve or make changes. Anytime users switch from Game to Design Mode, their propositional networks are saved as XML files to the local computer. This allows them to roll back to an earlier session through loading in that file in Design Mode and continue from there.

Figure 3. REAL Planet in design mode (This is REAL Planet in Design Mode. Each entity is represented as an image icon and a title. Users can drag and drop entities to the canvas and choose relations from a drop-down list to connect two nodes. This screen shot displays an example network a student designed illustrating how energy flows in the food chain.)

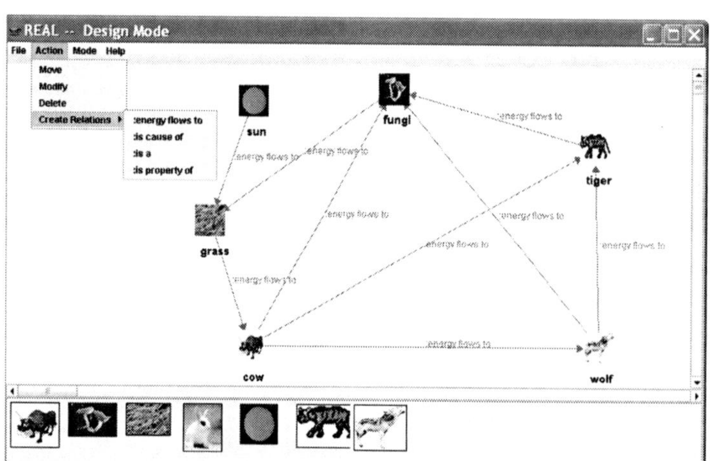

Figure 4. REAL planet: Game mode (In this version of REAL Planet, each animal agent has a "biological clock" that starts to tick once the agent is born. The result of the time decay is the decreasing of energy, the increasing of age and size. The property status in each agent affects the agent's cognitive states. For instance, energy below threshold may cause an agent to pursue a goal of hunting for food. But if the health level is also extremely low, the agent might decide not to take risks to get the food that is difficult to obtain. "Yummy" appears in a wolf's thought bubble (in the white oval) when that wolf eats a cow. The reflective agent (in the white square) can walk around observing what is happening in the imagery world.)

We benefited from creating this prototype when applying REAL to other domains like probability. The design of an agent with complex characteristics makes it possible to represent an agent in almost any possible domain.

REAL Business

The time and efforts on the design of REAL Planet paid off when we started to design the second REAL variant, REAL Business, in the domain of probability. It took two weeks to program the application. The design team spent the rest of the semester putting together instructional strategies that are mostly relevant in this specific domain (Bai, Black, Vikaros, Vitale, Li, Xia, Kim, & Kang, 2007; Bai, Black, & Vitale, 2007).

REAL Business simulates the running of an ice-cream store in order to present the probability concepts and problem solving skills in an authentic context. It can be used to facilitate the development of probabilistic reasoning in middle school students, who will have opportunities to predict the chance of an event happening, observe the data generated in the process, identify the patterns that emerge, compare the results with those they predicted, and draw conclusions. Simulation is a good tool for emerging students in this kind of learning environment.

Unlike the knowledge representation in REAL Planet, REAL Business requires users to apply production rules in the macro-level or abstract level. It asks users to observe interactions between elements of the system in the micro-level over time, derive patterns, and provide production rules that can be used in the macro-level based upon those patterns. For example, in REAL Business, users are asked to help the reflective agent (i.e. an ice-cream store owner) figure out the proper amount of ice cream to purchase for each day. Then they are challenged further – the same rules they provide should also work for running ice cream stores in other communities with a totally different set of probabilistic data. Thus, they need to learn to go beyond the basic rules governing a local context in the micro-level and think about business strategies in the macro-level.

In REAL Business, when the program starts, a communication agent jumps to the center of the screen (Figure 5) and tells users what they are supposed to do to win a game. She explains what problem is to be solved and what users can do to solve it. When she starts to introduce Design Mode, the researchers open Design Mode. The communication agent points to the left side of the screen in Design Mode and asks users to observe some statistical data in a tree diagram. Then she flies to the right side of the screen and tells users that they need to design mathematical formulas that the store owner can use to decide how many servings to buy each day. After users provide formulas, the communication agent tells users to click on Game Mode and observe how the business goes in the simulation. When Game Mode (Figure 6) starts, users will see customers walking in the store and the storeowner selling ice creams behind the counter. As customers have different flavor preferences, they may be happy or sad depending on whether they can get the flavor they want. The store owner and customers have thought bubbles illustrating what they are thinking. Users can switch back to Design Mode in the middle of the game to improve the business formulas. Data is collected, reorganized, and displayed in such formats as bar charts, line charts, or dynamic tree diagrams in Reflection Mode (Figure 6) so that users can justify and evaluate their strategies.

Agent Design

The agent technologies allow us to embody objects with Belief-Desire-Intention (BDI) (Bratman, 1999), hence giving those otherwise abstract symbolic objects human or animal-like decision-making abilities. The intelligent agents in REAL are entities empowered with their own thread of control. They are able to initiate actions in order to achieve goals, thus being able to behave autonomously in an environment.

Figure 5. Design mode in REAL business

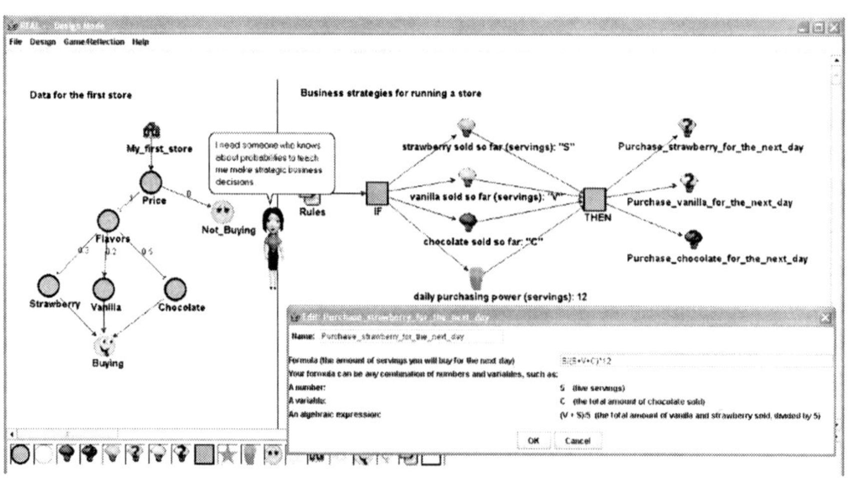

Figure 6. Game mode (right) and reflection mode (left) in REAL business

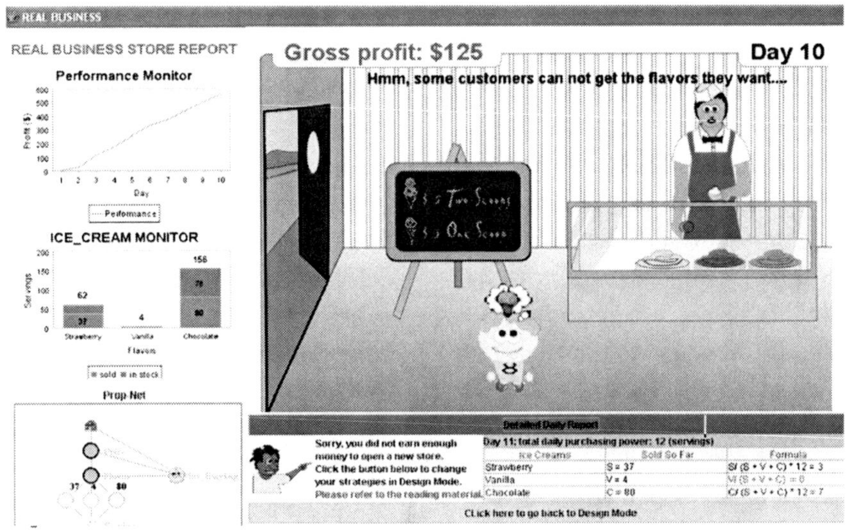

Some of these agents are embodied with visual representations. They can interact with the simulation environment with a body that is represented graphically. For instance, organisms, such as animals, are displayed as cartoon-like characters wandering around hunting for food in REAL Planet. Customers and store owners are represented as animated characters that can walk and have facial expressions in REAL Business.

There are two types of agents in REAL: (1) entity agents in simulation in a subject domain, whose beliefs, goals, and intentions users must incorporate into their knowledge representations within Design Mode. Most of these agents are embodied agent; (2) cognitive agents, which represent human alternatives in a classroom. They include a reflective agent (modeling learners), expert agent, pedagogical agent and communication agent. Only some of these agents have graphical embodiment. For instance, a reflective agent (e.g., the store owner in REAL Business) can be seen serving customers in an ice cream store in REAL Business. Most of the current cognitive agents function as invisible automated agents that manage the learning processes and control the simulation games.

Agents as Transparent Entities in Design Mode

Upon launching a REAL application, users are presented with an overall goal, such as creating a zoo in REAL Planet or developing a successful ice cream shop in REAL Business. These goals require the user to correctly predict or direct entity behaviors in the simulated world and provide effective instruction to their reflective agents. Constructing effective knowledge representations of entity behaviors, relations, and properties in Design Mode allows the reflective agent to deal with the emergent events successfully within the game world.

The basic knowledge units in Design Mode are nodes and relations. Nodes may represent either a single biological agent or a specific state of an agent. In the case of REAL Planet, each node is a separate organism, such as fungus, grass, and tiger, which resides in the simulated world. In REAL Business, nodes represent the possible actions that the customer agent may take within the simulation.

The interaction between these various entities or states is guided by relations. In Design Mode, a relation connects two entities. Each relation is associated with some relational property, such as "is a," "energy flows to," or "35% (chance of causing)." In REAL Planet, the reflective agent needs to design the energy flow to maintain energy balance, e.g., each agent should have enough food to survive although they may be food of other agents. The energy flows from the agent as food to the agent as the food hunter. In REAL Business, the relations establish the set of behaviors that a customer will engage in while shopping. Thus a behavior can only lead to a finite set of other behaviors and is determined probabilistically.

Furthermore, each entity may maintain properties which represent either static characteristics of the entity or possible temporary states. For instance, an entity "tiger" may have such properties as "birth rate," "category," or "hunting for food." An entity "customer" may have properties like "price preference" or "flavor preference." The user typically decides how the characteristics of the entity should affect its actions. For example, a user may decide that a customer will decide to buy ice cream if his or her preferred flavor is in stock. Thus, in Design Mode the user is able to create production rules to adjust daily purchase amount in order to make each customer agent achieve their goal of getting the ice cream.

Autonomous Agents in Game Mode

When Game Mode is launched, the rule engine grabs the entities and their associated properties and relations from the XML file, converts them to shadow facts and loads them to the REAL system in the form of Java Beans. The thread in each Java Bean will immediately start a heart beat – an agent is born at this point.

The user-constructed information is stored in Java Beans. The Genuts (http://www.genuts.com) game engine picks up these Java Beans and provides them with visual representations in the form of Sprite objects. A sprite in Genuts is an animation of pictures in one image. Its goal is to provide an object with animated picture along the time with a sequence of pictures. These sprites are contained in a playfield with a collision manger handling the collision detection. The agents represented visually by these sprites have different kinds of mobility. Some agents, particularly those representing humans or other animals, are active. They move around in the simulation, while other entities, such as grass or a cashier, remain in a relatively fixed location. Sprites can be static images or animations (with a sequence of images that loop over). They can be wrapped with other sprites (which layer to unwrap depends on which behavior to display in the real time). For instance, a "customer" sprite" can be wrapped with a sprite representing a thought bubble.

Agents' Reasoning Abilities

Such agents embedded in a rule-based system reason through pattern matching. A rule-based system consists of facts, rules, and a reasoning engine that acts on them. Facts represent an agent's goals, beliefs, desires, and physical conditions. Rules represent procedural knowledge, instructing how an agent should act at certain conditions (patterns).

These shadow facts are represented by observable java objects in the REAL game (Figure 7). The change of the status of these java objects triggers a notification that is sent to the rule engine. The rule engine checks on the working memory and decides which patterns are matched, thus triggering the corresponding rules.

The Jess reasoning engine monitors agents' statuses as declarative facts in a virtually parallel fashion. It will trigger events whenever it finds pattern matches in the pre-defined rules residing in the expert module or the student module, thus allowing an agent to sense, reason and act. These agents can decide whether or not to perform an action in a conflict situation according to their goals and beliefs. They are also capable of flexible (reactive, pro-active, social) behaviors (Wooldridge,

Figure 7. REAL agent architecture

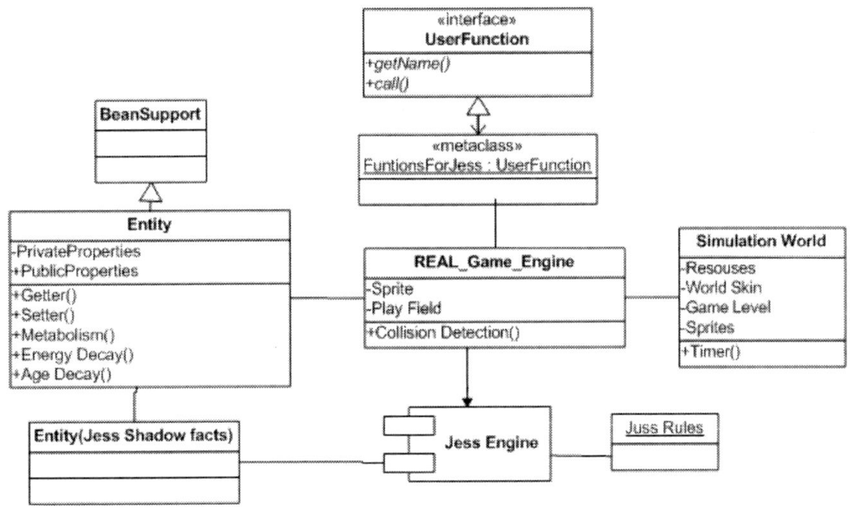

1995). For instance, if a customer has the desire to buy ice cream of a chocolate flavor, but that flavor is out of stock, this customer leaves the store without achieving his or her goal. The store owner identifies this situation and decides to order more ice cream of this flavor for the next day.

Cognitive Agents

Cognitive agents in REAL are software entities that carry out some set of operations on behalf of a user in a learning environment with some degree of autonomy, and in so doing, employ some knowledge or representation of the users it represents. In REAL, cognitive agents are employed to represent the goals or desires of the user, an expert, and a teacher. Not all the cognitive agents are necessarily embodied as visual characters in a specific simulation environment. Rather, some may be designed as software agents that serve as a paradigm for developers to engage in intelligent agent design and for researchers to explore ways of using computers to embed teaching strategies, model learners, or design knowledge base in a subject domain.

Reflective Agent

This agent represents the mental states of users. Built in Design Mode by the user, this agent combines the knowledge representations for the entity agents with specific rules to guide its actions. Like the entity agents, reflective agent behaviors are constructed in the form of propositional networks, production rules and mental images. In the case of REAL Business, the reflective agent is a store owner who is given the task of establishing an effective business. This requires the reflective agent to not only understand the behavior of his customers, but to act appropriately in response to these behaviors. The user is given the task of constructing production rules for the reflective agent that prompts it to buy more ice cream. To engage in this task effectively the user must incorporate information from the entity (i.e. customer) agent's knowledge representation, including such concepts as sample size, decision trees, and probability formulas.

In Game Mode the reflective agent, along with the entity agents, will act according to the knowledge representations given by the user. Furthermore, the Game Mode itself should simulate the user's mental model for the specific scenario.

Thus, the reflective agent can be viewed as the user's own embodiment within the simulation.

Pedagogical Agent

The strategies in pedagogical agent are designed by instructional designers. They may learn appropriate pedagogical practices for REAL applications in the design team as well as through pilot studies with some students. The procedure of developing pedagogical strategies requires designers to generalize common misconceptions students make and record human teacher interventions that get students back on track. These misconception patterns and the corresponding pedagogical strategies are implemented in the pedagogical module in the rule-based system that allows the pedagogical agent to decide what misconceptions to look for, what feedback to give and when. Although the developers are required to create rules for capturing common misconceptions, the process has been designed in such a way that it allows non-technical researchers to modify the feedback texts and the timing of certain feedback in a notepad with no recompilation needed. Thus the researchers can change the wording and adjust the feedback to fit his or her own style (Table 1). The feedback is sent to the user in the form of thought bubbles next to the storeowner.

Table 1. Message feedback in the pedagogical agent module

Misconceptions in Student Model and the corresponding pedagogical intervention	**Description**
(defrule game2Diagose ?et <- (ActiveEntity (type "messenger")) (test (= ?*gameLevel* **2**)) ?c <- (changeDay ?day&**2**) ?gc <- (game2SVC ?d) => (printout t "game2Diagose" crlf) (assert (addnew ***"Should I use S, V, C to represent sales?"*** 3)) (retract ?c) (retract ?gc))	*Misconception 1:* Constant numbers, instead of variables, are used. This will result in a poor business performance in Game Level II. *To customize, change:* Game level: # in green When: Day # in red Message: Wording in blue
(defrule diagnose_g1 (or (S ?s&~3&~4) (V ?v&~2&~3) (C ?c&~6)) (test (= ?*gameLevel* **1**)) ?c <-(changeDay ?day&**2**) => (printout t "diagnose_g1" ?*score_walkout* crlf) (assert (addnew **"Hmm, some customers can not get the flavors they want."** 3)) (retract ?c))	*Misconception 2:* The formula does not fit in the data model for Game I. *To customize, change:* Game level: # in green When: Day # in red Message: Wording in blue
(defrule diagnose_g2 (or (S ?s&~1) (V ?v&~1) (C ?c&~9)) (test (= ?*gameLevel* **2**)) ?c <-(changeDay ?day&**2**) => (printout t "diagnose_g2" crlf) (assert (addnew **"Hmm, some customers can not get the flavors they want."** 3)) (retract ?c))	*Misconception 3:* The formula does not fit in the data model for Game II. *To customize, change:* Game level: # in green When: Day # in red Message: Wording in blue

This serves as a template for non-programmers to design pedagogical strategies based upon the pattern explained in the "Description" column

Expert Agent

An expert agent exhibits mastery of knowledge in a domain and can perform a task in an optimized way. Discrepancies between the behaviors of the reflective and expert agents can be seen as missed concepts or misconceptions in student understanding and may lead to interventions within the game to help the user overcome his or her conceptual difficulties.

In the case of REAL Planet, the expert agent incorporates the rules by which animals behave. If a user creates a behavior which does not match the expert's (e.g. a buffalo taking energy from a lion), the user will receive feedback from the pedagogical and communication agent.

In REAL Business, an expert agent possesses strategies that allow one to run a business successfully. For instance, it tends to ignore sales data on specific days, instead paying more attention to accumulated data in a longer ranger of time. The skill involved is the understanding of the concept of "sample size." If the reflective agent's profits are significantly lower than the expert agent then the user may be prompted to redesign his or her agent. The expert agent is also capable of providing assistance through statistical charts to facilitate the discovery of meaningful patterns in data.

Communication Agent

A communication agent acts as a collaborator that facilitates user-computer interaction. It is designed using Microsoft Agent, utilizing configurable features such as speech, tonality, gesture, facial expression, gender, and screen navigation that can be combined together to emulate a human face-to-face communication act. It can also stay on top of different REAL modes and is disposable upon a user's request. For instance, in REAL Business, the communication agent introduces the REAL tools and game rules with a female voice. It asks for help from the users to design business strategies for the store owners. It can navigate to different locations in the screen and make gestures. Text in thought bubbles and a machine-generated voice are both available to users.

EVALUATION

We evaluated REAL Planet using the internal evaluation method and evaluated REAL Business with both the internal and external evaluation methods. We focused on system design for REAL Planet. The time and efforts on its design paid off when we started to design REAL Business, which took two weeks of programming by one developer to build. The external evaluation of REAL aims at testing the usefulness of the REAL system for the user, such as its ability to foster learning, motivate learners, and encourage scientific exploration. The evaluation of the learning outcome is not a focus in this study. Lessons derived from the process are intended to be used for the design of specific REAL applications and studies in the future. The result will influence the direction for the future research and development.

Our main focus is on the internal evaluation of system performance, addressing the question: "what is the relationship between the REAL cognitive framework and the performance of the REAL application?" More specifically, internal evaluation answers the following questions: "What agents do we need? What do these agents need to know? How do these agents do what they do based upon what they know?" This is an iterative design process. We evaluated the advantages and disadvantages of using different sets of technologies. We also tested out a few reasoning engines and game engines in our platform. We then looked at ways to standardize our design so that this framework can be developed and deployed to other local contexts easily.

Internal Evaluation

Originally, we had planned to set up REAL in a 3D virtual reality environment where users could interact with the computer-generated images, observe the happening of events in a 3D environment, and get the look and feel of the simulation in a realistic way as much as possible. At the same time, we had intended to have these entities in the simulation to be controlled by a rule-based engine in the back-end, which could make critical real-time decisions regarding the control of the entities. Since the sequences of the events as well as the interactions among entities are not and should not be pre-defined, we needed to find an efficient solution that allowed the graphical game modules and the reasoning modules to collaborate seamlessly.

When we started to develop REAL Planet, we chose Virtual Reality Modeling Language (VRML) as the 3D virtual reality scripting language. VRML is a standard file format for representing 3D interactive vector graphics that can be viewed through an Internet browser. In the back-end, we used a traditional artificial intelligence programming language, called LISP, to handle rule-based reasoning. But we found this architecture could not meet one of our development goals - efficient real-time control of the virtual agents. The rendering of a complex simulation like this involved tedious coding in VRML, and the resulting VRML file was big in size. This made it difficult to control a 3D environment through sending dynamic data from the rule-based system. This lack of efficient direct communication kept us from getting full control of the virtual agents. Also, because of the lack of support of LISP from other industrial vendors, we might have had to think about the compatibility issues for every component we would have needed to add to REAL in the future stages. Most of the time, no application programming interface (API) is available to LISP. In the long run, this might have posed serious risks to REAL as it might have ended up as an obsolete application quickly due to its lack of scalability.

We decided to look for other technologies that would allow us to have efficient control of the simulation. JESS is similar to LISP. Both have rule-based engines with similar syntaxes. JESS, written in Java, has the ability to interface with other components through a Java-based adapter. This gives JESS an edge over other rule-based shells, because Java-based systems are platform independent – this allows for a program to be compiled once and run on any other platform. Later, we found that we had greatly benefited from this design, which makes REAL extensible and scalable.

Flash was adopted as the GUI developmental environment. It has built-in support for socket connection with the XML Socket object. This object allowed us to establish a communication channel with a socket server application. It used XML as the format for data transfer between the client and the server. For instance, when a tiger encountered a rabbit, a collision was detected. The event was sent to other interested parties through a dedicated socket channel. The corresponding feedback from those parties was also sent back to Flash through the same channel. Thus, our concern about the real-time two-way communication was solved.

We developed a game engine written in Action-Script in Flash and used a socket server to push the collision detected in the simulation back to JESS in XML. However, we had a bottleneck later when the number of entities increased beyond a threshold – a single thread looping through entities was not able to manage all the changes and the corresponding updates. The computational demand for processing these entities increased in exponential order. As a result, it slowed down the simulation. This contradicted our original goal – designing a system that is scalable. Later, we tried Director, which has a built-in 3D Havok physics engine. We found that although Flash and Director can provide fancier and more user-friendly interfaces and can communicate with other components, they are not able to handle a complex situation where each component in the virtual environment demands constant attention. Also, in our case, we wanted the data to be processed through a rule-based engine based upon users' knowledge construction. Therefore, a front-end component like a tiger only needed to be a passive receiver of instructions for what to do next from a rule-based engine.

Finally, we decided to choose a game developmental environment that came with a built-in game engine – Genuts. Another advantage of adopting a java-based game engine is that a Java-based object (e.g., a Sprite in Genuts), once attached to a Java Bean, can be directly manipulated as a native shadow fact in the JESS rule engine. This greatly simplifies the development process. For instance, no XML files are needed for data exchange between the client and the server. Also, once entities are defined in Design Mode, they are automatically converted to Sprites for visual representation in Game Mode and to shadow facts for knowledge representation in JESS. This approach helps streamline the development process and makes REAL a generic platform where knowledge construction, representation, and manipulation can be achieved with less programming effort.

External Evaluation of REAL Business

The external evaluation of REAL Business examined the usability of the REAL application through surveys, interviews, a pre-test, and a post-test. As the participants have had background knowledge on the basics of probability, pre-test and post-test were not used for evaluating learning outcomes. Rather, they were designed and improved by the research team to gain a better understanding of the design of the tests in terms of content and structure.

Participants

Twenty-seven students participated in the study. They were all graduate students from Teachers College, Columbia University. Twenty students finished the evaluation, while seven spent too much time playing with the REAL application to finish the evaluation.

Procedures

The study was conducted by eight researchers working on the REAL project. At the beginning, the participants were told that they would teach a virtual storeowner to run a virtual ice cream store in REAL Business. They were instructed to review reading material for 5 minutes on how to run a successful business. The goal was to provide participants with some basic knowledge of the concepts of probability including sample size, probability tree diagrams, and probability formulas. Then, participants received pre-test handouts that evaluated the level of their understanding. The pre-test consisted of multiple-choice and short-answer questions. The multiple-choice questions checked for the understanding of the concepts and formulas; the short-answer questions evaluated whether a learning transfer occurs. Next, a computer-based communication agent informed the students of the goal of the game and some basic rules of the game. This agent navigated to different parts of the screens, pointing out what the game challenge was and what the participants could do to solve the problem. Audio and thought bubbles displaying the audio scripts were both available (Figure 5). Audio, with a female voice, was generated by a text-to-speak engine. This agent had the ability to take in simple oral or mouse-click commands. For instance, users can issue commands verbally through a microphone. The computer agent has the ability to capture those commands that have been pre-defined, find the corresponding answers, and read it aloud with texts displayed in thought bubbles over its head.

Next, our researchers gave a brief orientation on REAL, showing participants the application tools they could use and giving them some examples illustrating how to run the game. The text version of the orientation was handed out to each student at the same time.

Finally, students started to design and run the REAL simulation. Each time a user switched from Design Mode to Game Mode, a copy of the knowledge representation in Design Mode was saved to the users' local computer in the data format of XML. Users could (re)load in any of these saved sessions in Design Mode and continue their design work. This allowed users to roll back to a previous version of their design and investigate why it worked well or not satisfactorily.

Last, students worked on post-test, which is the same as pre-test. They filled out a survey evaluating the usability of the REAL application. Some students voluntarily participated in a brief interview afterwards.

Results

The survey results in Table 2 display the evaluation the usability of REAL on the scale of 1 – 5. A scale with "Yes/No" was used in the first study session. It was converted to "4.5/1.5" and compiled into the rest of the evaluation result. Some students were not able to finish the survey due to the lack of time.

Discussions

To efficiently simulate a learning environment, we found it essential to design an eLearning framework that not only allows users to get just-in-time help from different resources (e.g., teachers, experts, or coordinators), but also provides designers and programmers opportunities to engage in efficient collaboration using a metaphor that is meaningful and intuitive to both parties. We found the agent paradigm allows programmers to use agent-based technologies to communicate effectively with non-programmers, such as researchers or educators. These intelligent agents should work together to understand what the learners know and how to help improve their learning skills.

Although the sample participants showed a high degree of prior knowledge, many expressed that the REAL environment could have a positive impact on their learning (Table 2) and they would be interested in learning more about this subject in the future.

Here is an example illustrating how REAL has been designed to encourage reflective thinking through giving users various cognitive tools to explore a problematic situation. One participant told us that he had experience running a real ice-cream store a few years ago. Therefore, he approached the REAL task with a great deal of confidence, believing that he could find an effective solution without running the simulation. Instead of launching the REAL Game Mode, he attempted to simulate its workings in his own

Table 2. The survey result on REAL business

Question	Mean	Scale	Size
Does playing REAL increase your interest in probability?	4.0	1 = strongly disagree 2 = disagree 3 = neutral 4 = agree 5 = strongly agree 4.5 = Yes* 1.5 = No*	20
Does REAL give you greater confidence that you can understand and use probabilities?	3.7		
Do you want to learn more about probability?	3.9		

The scale of "Yes/No" was used in the first session; it was converted to "4.5/1.5" in the other sessions imaginary world using pencil and paper. In the study, based upon the provided reference material and the specific data about the community's flavor preferences, he progressed through the calculation of each day of simulation. He plugged in constant numbers starting from Day One according to the flavor preference probabilities provided in the tree diagram in Design Mode. Based upon the results (the leftovers and the possible demand), he decided the supply purchases for the next day. Soon he got lost in the calculation and numbers, and decided to start all over again. After regaining some momentum, he got stuck at around Day Four. At this point, the researcher intervened and suggested that he run the simulation game, thus gaining a concrete idea of how such a system worked. During the running of the game, he began to pay more attention to the data in Reflection Mode, in addition to the activities in Game Mode. Immersion in the simulation facilitated a more global perspective of the situation. He realized that he had paid too much attention on the day-to-day values, which limited his ability to generate effective business strategies that could be applied to a global business environment. He told us that it was a "leap' for him to look at the system mechanism from this perspective, and it was not easy for him to mentally simulate this kind of situation on his own, either. We asked how he had made decisions about ice cream purchases when he ran the real ice cream store years ago. He told us he did it through observing/feeling the demand first and deciding the supply accordingly. That was exactly what he was doing in his pencil and paper simulation.

Clearly, the prior knowledge, combined with the reading material, was not sufficient for solving the problem presented in REAL. This case demonstrates the difficulty many students have when transferring their concrete real-world knowledge to the abstract problems encountered in educational environments. Although the provided text did contain the necessary information for solving the problem, we suspect that it did not systematically integrate with his pre-existing mental model for running an ice cream store. Thus, his design decisions were constrained by the limitations of his model. However, by interacting with and reflecting upon the environment within REAL, this participant was able to represent knowledge about the complexities of a dynamic system abstractly. Therefore, a constructive environment, such as REAL provides, encourages reflection through facilitating users' ability to extend and elaborate upon pre-existing mental models.

Although the pedagogical, reflective, and expert agents are not new, our integration of all three agents within an educational simulation game based upon a generic framework is unique. Certainly, the non-digital analog of these agents (i.e. teacher, student, and expert) is a common feature of many educational designs. However, it is not currently within our expectations that we could accurately model the knowledge of a student, teacher, or expert. Rather, our attempt is to provide just enough information as to allow the user to successfully accomplish goals and construct appropriate mental models. A few questions we constantly asked among ourselves were, in such a straightforward domain as REAL Business, whether agents can accurately diagnose students' misconceptions the same way as a human tutor does. If the answer is no, we would like to know how we can design cognitive agents that can better understand learners. If the answer is yes, we want to explore whether agents embedded in such systems can efficiently and effectively replace the human alternatives. As we continue to improve REAL and develop other REAL implementations, we expect to further our own understanding of the role of each agent in a user's learning processes (Bai et al., 2007).

FUTURE RESEARCH DIRECTIONS

With our approach of designing ITS with agents embedded in simulations, it is natural to think about extending REAL to multiple-user and mobile-learning versions. The modularized design of the reflective agent over a common interface makes it possible for a user to develop his/her own agents in Design Mode and share it with other users in Game Mode over the internet, where each reflective agent can carry out actions representing its creator. This will allow users to observe the consequences of their actions interacting with other reflective agents in simulations. The current java-based reasoning engine and game engine allow the applications to be developed once and deployed to different platforms, including mobile platforms. The advantage of developing the REAL applications over mobile devices is that such portable devices can encourage learners to observe the emergent phenomena and collaborate with peers anywhere anytime. For instance, certain situations may trigger a communication request from a reflective agent to another reflective agent. Users can thus talk over the phone and work together to solve a problem. Or a pedagogical agent may capture a moment when it needs to inform a reflective agent what goes wrong and what needs to be done to correct it. This can be achieved by having the pedagogical agent send text messages to a user's mobile phone with detailed pedagogical feedback. The multi-level communication among the reflective agents and the users will make REAL a rich motivational learning environment where users are willing to collaborate to solve problems with active reflection of their internal thinking processes.

CONCLUSION

From the design and study on the REAL applications, we found the following value for REAL as a cognitive framework. (1) The learning environment is motivational. Through survey and interviews, participants in our studies showed great interest in our application. Most of them indicated that the game was very fun and playing with REAL increased their interest in the target domain. (2) The REAL framework is reusable and extensible. We had a quick turn-around time in terms of application development, for instance, in the second implementation – REAL Business. The intelligent agents, embedded in a rule–based system hooked up to a game engine, can be easily extended for representing humans or organisms. The modules were well defined, thus the developers were able to easily jump in and work on specific areas. (3) The REAL platform encourages collaboration among researchers with interest in such areas as artificial intelligence, intelligent computer-aided instruction, human computer interaction, human cognition, and educational games, to name a few. It can serve as a generic platform for those researchers to embed their ideas and test out their hypotheses.

This study builds a cognitive framework for developing intelligent agents in simulation games to encourage reflective thinking and engaged learning. We believe that our cognitive framework could contribute to the much-needed ongoing effort to develop intelligent agents for simulation in a constructive eLearning environment.

REFERENCES

Aguilera, M., & M'endiz, A. (2003). Video games in education. *Computers in Entertainment*, *1*(1), 1–14.

Anderson, J. R. (1983). *The architecture of cognition*. Cambridge, MA: Harvard University Press.

Anderson, J. R. (1993). *Rules of the Mind*. Mahwah, NJ: Lawrence Erlbaum.

Anderson, J. R., Boyle, C. F., Corbett, A., & Lewis, M. (1990). Cognitive modeling and intelligent tutoring. *Artificial Intelligence*, *42*, 7–49. doi:10.1016/0004-3702(90)90093-F

Bai, X., Black, J. B., Vikaros, L., Vitale, J., Li, D., & Xia, Q. (2007). *Learning in One's Own Imaginary World.* Chicago: American Educational Research Association.

Bai, X., Black, J. B., & Vitale, J. (2007). REAL: Learn with the Assistance of a Reflective Agent. *Agent-Based Systems for Human Learning Conference*, Hawaii.

Biswas, G., Schwartz, D. L., & Bransford, J. D. The Teachable Agents Group at Vanderbilt. (2001). *Technology support for complex problem solving: From SAD Environments to AI.* Menlo Park, CA: AAAI/MIT Press.

Biswas, G., Schwartz, D. L., Leelawong, K., & Vye, N., & TAG-V. (2005). Learning by teaching: A new agent paradigm for educational software. *Applied Artificial Intelligence*, *19*, 363–392. doi:10.1080/08839510590910200

Black, J. B. (1992). *Types of Knowledge Representation CCT Report.* New York: Teachers College, Columbia University.

Black, J. B. (2007). Imaginary Worlds. In Gluck, M. A., Anderson, J. R., & Kosslyn, S. M. (Eds.), *Memory and Mind: A Festschrift for Gordon H. Bower.* Mahwah, NJ: Lawrence Erlbaum Associates.

Black, J. B., & Bower, G. H. (1980). Story understanding as problem-solving. *Poetics*, *9*, 223–250. doi:10.1016/0304-422X(80)90021-2

Blandford, A. E. (1994). Teaching through collaborative problem solving. *Journal of Artificial Intelligence in Education*, *5*(1), 51–84.

Bloom, B. S. (1984). The 2 sigma problem: The search for methods of group instruction as effective as one-to-one tutoring. *Educational Researcher*, *13*, 4–16.

Boole, G. (1854). *An investigation of the laws of thought on which are founded the mathematical theories of logic and probabilities, Macmillan, 1854/1958.* New York, NY: Dover Publications.

Bratman, M. E. (1999). *Intention, Plans, and Practical Reason.* CSLI Publications.

Chan, T. W., & Baskin, A. B. (Eds.). (1990). *Learning companion systems. Intelligent Tutoring Systems: at the Crossroads of Artificial Intelligence and Education.* Norwood, NJ: Ablex.

Collins, A. M., & Loftus, E. F. (1975). A spreading-activation theory of semantic processing. *Psychological Review*, *82*, 407–428. doi:10.1037/0033-295X.82.6.407

Conati, C., & Zhao, X. (2004). Building and evaluating an intelligent pedagogical agent to improve the effectiveness of an educational game. In *Proceedings of IUI '04, International Conference on Intelligent User Interfaces*, Island of Madeira, Portugal (pp. 6-13).

Connolly, T.M. and Stansfield, M.H. (2007) From eLearning to Games-based eLearning, International *Journal of Information Technology and Management, 26*(2/3/4), 188-208.

Dillenbourg, P., & Self, J. A. (1992). A computational approach to socially distributed cognition. *European Journal of Psychology of Education*, *3*(4), 353–372. doi:10.1007/BF03172899

Friedman-Hill, E. (2003). *Jess in Action: Rule-Based Systems in Java.* Greenwich, CT: Manning Publications.

Gee, J. P. (2003). *What video games have to teach us about learning.* New York: Pal grave.

Hmelo-Silver, Merav, G. (2004). Comparing expert and novice understanding of a compex system from the perspective of structures, behaviors and functions. *Cognitive Science*, *28*, 127–138. doi:10.1207/s15516709cog2801_7

Holland, J. (1998). *Emergence: from chaos to order*. Reading, MA: Addison-Wesley.

Jacobson, M. J., & Kozma, R. B. (2000). *Innovations in science and mathematics education: Advanced designs for technologies of learning*. Mahwah, NJ: Erlbaum.

Kintsch, W. (1988). The role of knowledge in discourse comprehension: A construction–integration model. *Psychological Review*, *95*, 163–182. doi:10.1037/0033-295X.95.2.163

Klawe, M. (1998). *NCTM Standards 2000 Technology Conference*. Arlington, VA: When Does the Use of Computer Games and Other Interactive Multimedia Software Help Students Learn Mathematics.

Koedinger, K. R., Anderson, J. R., Hadley, W. H., & Mark, M. (1997). Intelligent tutoring goes to school in the big city. *International Journal of Artificial Intelligence in Education*, *8*, 30–43.

Kriz, W. C., Pushert, M., Karl, J., & Dufter-Weis, A. (2004). Effective *Learning through Gaming Simulation Design*. In: R. Shiratory, K. Arai & F. Kato & (Eds.), Simulation & Gaming (pp. 217-227)

Laird, J., Newell, Allen and Rosenbloom, Paul. (1987). SOAR: An architecture for general intelligence. *Artificial Intelligence*, *33*, 1–64. doi:10.1016/0004-3702(87)90050-6

Lajoie, S. P., & Lesgold, A. (1989). Apprenticeship training in the workplace: Computer coached practice environment as a new form of apprenticeship. *Machine-Mediated Learning*, *3*, 7–28.

Mark, M. A., & Greer, J. E. (1991). The VCR tutor: Evaluating instructional effectiveness. InHammond, K.J. and Gentner, D.Q. (Eds.): Proceedings of *13thAnnual Conference of the Cognitive Science Society*, Hillsdale, NJ: Lawrence Erlbaum Associates.

Murray, T. (1999). Authoring intelligent tutoring systems: An analysis of the state of the art. *International Journal of Artificial Intelligence in Education*, *10*, 98–129.

Newell, A. (1990). *Unified theories of cognition*. Cambridge, MA: Harvard University Press.

Newell, A., & Simon, H. (1972). *Human Problem Solving*. Englewood Cliffs, NJ: Prentice-Hall.

Novak, J. D. (1998). *Learning, creating, and using knowledge: Concept maps as facilitative tools in schools and corporations*. Mahwah, NJ: Lawrence Erlbaum Associates.

Pearl, J. (1988). *Probabilistic Reasoning in Intelligent Systems: Networks of Plausible Inference*. San Francisco: Morgan Kaufmann.

Schank, R. C., & Abelson, R. P. (1977). *Scripts, plans, goals, and understanding: An inquiry into human knowledge structures*. Hillsdale, NJ: Erlbaum.

Self, J. (1999). The defining characteristics of intelligent tutoring systems research: ITSs care, precisely. *International Journal of Artificial Intelligence in Education*, (10): 350–364.

Shaffer, D. W., Squire, K. D., Halverson, R., & Gee, J. P. (2005). Video Games and the Future of Learning. *Phi Delta Kappan*, *87*(2), 104–111.

Thalmann, D., Noser, H., & Huang, Z. (1997). Autonomous virtual actors based on virtual sensors, in: Creating Personalities (Ed. R.Trappl, P. Petta), *Lecture Notes in Computer Science*, Springer Verlag, (pp. 25-42).

Wooldridge, M. J., N. (1995). Intelligent Agents: Theory and Practice. *The Knowledge Engineering Review*, *10*(2), 115–152. doi:10.1017/S0269888900008122

KEY TERMS AND DEFINITIONS

Imaginary World: It's a subject's story world, where he can update and "see" dynamic changes of characters, objects, and locations in his imaginary world. That is, he has available for inspection not only the starting and ending state of a character's motion but also intermediate points along the dynamic path.

Pedagogical Agent: A pedagogical agent has a set of normative teaching goals and plans for achieving these goals (e.g., teaching strategies), and associated resources in the learning environment (Thalmann, 1997).

Reflective Agent: It's an autonomous intelligent agent based upon a generic cognitive framework called REAL (Reflective Agent Learning environment). REAL allows researchers to develop a simulation-based learning environment where users can learn through passing their thoughts to some computer-based agents and observe how the agents embodying their knowledge behave as the result of their instruction.

Chapter 4
Intelligent Tutoring System Architecture Rebuilt:
A Pattern Approach

Alke Martens
University of Rostock, Germany

Andreas Harrer
Catholic University of Eichstätt-Ingolstadt, Germany

ABSTRACT

In this chapter, an approach to support the development of ITS based on patterns and pattern catalogues is described. Patterns are means to facilitate inter-project communication. As such, they provide for a clear terminology in an application domain. They support the development process itself by encapsulating information at different levels (e.g. using underlying concepts and tools, adding and integrating new concepts and tools, and fundamentally changing the structure of an existing piece of software). The approach described in this chapter shows two examples of how a catalogue of patterns collected from existing ITS architectures can be used and re-used in different settings. Those settings span the field of plugin frameworks for ITS (i.e. JaBInT), a concrete "proof of concept" ITS (i.e. ChemNom and CoChemEx) using a collaboration script approach.

INTRODUCTION

Projects which aim at the development of Intelligent Tutoring Systems (ITSs) are usually interdisciplinary projects. Some ITSs are developed based on psychological theories (e.g. (Anderson et.al., 1990), (Künzel & Hämmer, 2006)), some are tailored for specific application domains (Bergin & Fors, 2003), some are developed as "playground" for ideas of computer scientists (Martens & Himmelspach, 2005). Often, these fields overlap in one and the same project (Illmann et.al., 2000).

However, ITSs projects are cost intensive when it comes to development time and man power (Murray, 1999). Thus, approaches to allow re-usage of ideas or even of components, system parts, databases, training content, and the like are highly desirable. Other research fields under the e-Learning umbrella have identified re-usability, especially of content, as one major contribution a computer system can have in educational settings (e.g. (Forte et. al., 1999)).

DOI: 10.4018/978-1-61692-008-1.ch004

This article is based on research described in (Harrer & Martens, 2006), where a generic pattern catalogue for ITSs has been introduced. We want to clarify some fundamental concepts and terms, we will show how patterns can be used by different ITSs developers (given their different research background), and we will show examples, how we have used the pattern language in the last two years.

AN ARCHITECTURE AND THE PROBLEM OF INTERDISCIPLINARITY

Having its roots in the Greek term "arkitekton" (αρχιτεκτων), an architect is etymologically spoken the "leader" or "chief" of the "builders". The architecture, being related to the Latin term "architectura", denotes something which is man-made. Traditionally, it is related with built environment, which means man-made surroundings, buildings, and the like. Nowadays, the term's meaning has been extended and is used in additional areas, e.g. mathematics, computer science, but also biology (e.g. architecture of cells). The core of today's usage of the term is that an architecture is a structure plan of something, which is either man-made or found in nature.

In the context of computer science, the notion of architecture is often related to the abstract structural description of the underlying software system. The architecture describes the fundamental structural organization of the system. An architecture pattern thus sketches established solutions regarding the development of software. Moreover, the architecture pattern usually provides structure but no details (Buschmann et. al., 1996). The notion of design patterns and architecture patterns has been proposed for the field of ITS early (e.g. Devedžić; 1999). Surprisingly, patterns still have not been taken up as a major method for systematic ITS development.

One possible reason for this is that, when it comes to concepts and terms in an interdisciplinary field like teaching and training systems, the computer science perspective is only one among several other perspectives. The history of ITS development is an interdisciplinary history: ITS have been developed by psychologists (e.g. (Anderson et.al., 1990)), by application domain experts, and by computer scientists (e.g. (Illmann et.al., 2000)). They sometimes work hand in hand with experts from pedagogy and design. Each of these groups of people developed their system with a different scientific background, and, moreover, based on different ideas about the finally resulting system (see Figure1). For example, a psychologist might want to investigate hypotheses or teach a theory (Künzel & Hämmer, 2006) - however, usually his main interest will not lie in the design of the underlying software system. The computer scientist might be interested in the re-usability of components or in formal system descriptions (e.g. (Harrer, 2003)), but in most cases his knowledge about the learning theory which shall be realized with the system, or his knowledge about the training content might be comparably low. The same situation arises when it comes to content development. Usually, the developer of teaching and training content has not much knowledge about software engineering processes - and vice versa, the computer scientist does not need to have knowledge of the teaching and training domain. All these different needs and interests have to be merged and integrated productively to create mature and maintainable ITS, otherwise only specific aspects of the field can be explored with little perspective to use the synergy of the knowledge of the different stakeholders in the ITS area.

Summarizing, in ITSs development, psychologists, computer scientists, training domain experts, and designers have to communicate about the intended resulting system - which naturally has "an architecture", in the sense that it has a fundamental structural organization. To find this underlying

Figure 1. Interdisciplinary perspectives on ITS

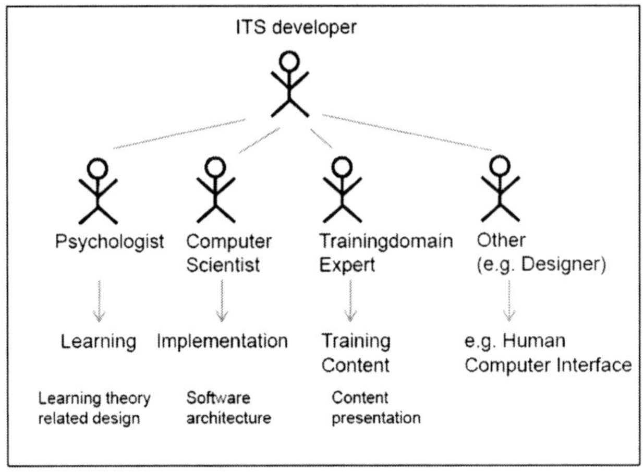

fundamental structure, an investigation of architecture descriptions in teaching and training system development has been performed (e.g. (Martens, 2004), (Oertel, 2007)). Not only the constituents of the architecture have been located – moreover, there exist a plethora of heterogeneous names and interpretations of functionality, which potentially have occurred due to the inherent interdisciplinary concepts. The aim of the approach described in this chapter has been to find re-occurring patterns, and to organize these patterns in an ITS architecture.

THE CLASSICAL ITS ARCHITECTURE

In the context of Intelligent Tutoring System development, the state of the art still is a system architecture which has been described by Clancey in the 1980s (Clancey, 1984). In his article, Clancey distinguishes between four system constituents, which are

1. The expert knowledge base,
2. The learner model,
3. A user interface,
4. The pedagogical knowledge model.

Historically seen, the pedagogical knowledge model is the "youngest" component. It joined the circus of components based on the insight of Woolf and McDonald, and of Clancey. Woolf and McDonald claimed that the learner's task is best supported not only with expert knowledge but also with cognitive knowledge (Woolf & McDonald, 1984). Clancey later describes an extension of the expert knowledge with pedagogical knowledge (Clancey, 1987).

The investigation of existing ITS systems revealed that these parts of the ITS architecture are still in use - even if naming of the components varies. A small excerpt of the results is shown in the following Figure 2.

However, one problem, which hinders re-use of parts of the architecture, is that the interpretation of role and functionality of each of those parts varies. For example, sometimes the expert knowledge base is realized as a complete subsystem – with data and execution, sometimes it is only realized as a comparably simple database. Even the variation itself is not the problem - the problem is that the functionality of each part is not explicated when it comes to system architecture descriptions. One reason for this can be seen in the fact that the ITS architecture has not been designed or engineered (in the sense of software design as described for

Figure 2. Table of naming of parts of ITSs

Reference	Expert Knowledge	Pedagogical Knowledge	Learner Model	User Interface
(Corbett & Koedinger & Anderson, 1997)	Domain Knowledge	Pedagogical Module	Student Module	Problem Solving Environment
(Lelouche, 1999)	Domain Expert Module	Tutorial Module (Pedagogy Expert)	User Model	User Interface
(Alpert & Singley & Fairweather, 1999)	Expert Solver	Tutorial Module	Student Module	User Interface
(Melis & Siekmann, 2004)	MBase (Course Generator)	Pedagogical Rules (Course Generator)	Student Model	Presentation Engine

example in (Ghezzi, Jazayeri, & Mandrioli, 2003)) but has evolved over the years.

ITS ARCHITECTURE AND PATTERNS

Patterns can be used to facilitate communication in interdisciplinary team (e.g. Martens & Hambach & Lucke, 2009)). The notion of pattern in design processes can be traced back to the much cited architect Christopher Alexander (e.g. in (Alexander & Ishikawa & Silverstein 1977).). Also in computer science, patterns have been adopted and used for quite some time now. Patterns exist on multiple levels, e.g. software engineering patterns, which focus directly on the development of software (Gamma & Helm & Johnson & Vlissides, 1995), and special purpose patterns for design of special software, as for example Patterns for computer mediated interaction as described in (Schümmer & Lukosch, 2007). An architecture description which provides a template for a specific system type, like an ITS, might be written up as an architectural pattern, a collection of patterns in form of a generic pattern catalogue, and as an entry pattern of a pattern language (see e.g. (Harrer, 2003), for the notion of pattern language see (Noble, 1998), and (Cap & Martens, 2009)).

A step from this initial pattern toward a pattern language for ITSs has been described in (Harrer & Martens, 2006). The result is shown in Figure 3. The intention is to use the pattern language for system design from early stages of project development as a means for communication in interdisciplinary teams. Potentially, if new developments take place, the pattern language can be extended by introducing new patterns and their relations to the existing ones (such as "pattern is alternative to", "pattern supports another pattern", "pattern conflicts with another pattern" etc.). Such a pattern language is most likely never complete, especially in complex domains, as ITS are: for example relevant aspects, such as logging of actions for later evaluation or data mining purposes is currently not included, but can be integrated if patterns on this issues have been written up.

Such a pattern language can be used as a tool when designing and implementing intelligent tutoring systems (as sketched for general pattern languages in Buschmann et al. 1996): starting from the "entry pattern" ITS with its decomposition in the typical 4 components, the different components can be instantiated in different variants based on the requirements and needs (also called "forces" in the terminology of patterns) of the system to be developed. For example, overlay models are well suited for expert modules in well-defined and stable domains, while for ill-defined and dynamic expansion they are less well suited; as another example, if flexibility in the process regulation is desired, the separation of the process steering-module into a stable process-steering component and exchangeable process description is the preferable solution, because no code changes are necessary when changing the process description that is just taken up as an interpretable model for the process steering component. The refinement of each of these components using suitable "continuation patterns" can inform and guide the design process of the ITS to be developed.

REALIZATIONS

Based on the ideas sketched in the section above and on the work described in (Harrer & Martens, 2006) two projects have been started in the last two years. In both cases, the pattern language described in (Harrer & Martens, 2006) (shown in Figure2) has been used to help system

Figure 3. Approach toward pattern language, (Harrer & Martens, 2006)

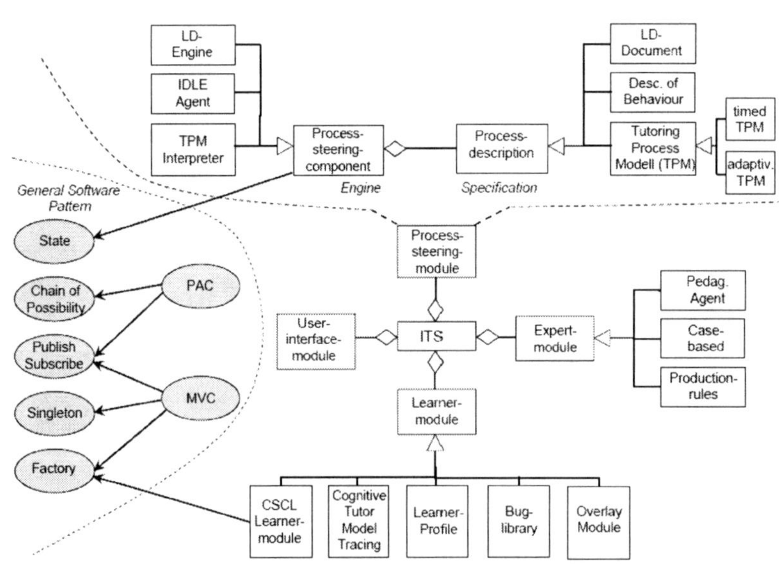

development regarding systematic design and construction of the systems. In the first phases of project development, the main architecture pattern has been used as basis for communication and clarification of roles and competencies in the system development. At a later stage of project development, the computer scientists used the pattern language for development of the system by applying single patterns and connecting them, as described by the relations given in the pattern language. The work described in the first subsection resulted in a framework for ITS and training simulation development. The work described in the second subsection is located in the field of CSCL (Computer Supported Collaborative Learning): a collaborative inquiry scenario that is scripted / regulated by a formal description of the pedagogical model has been realized here. For the development of the system several pre-existing components have been integrated into a complex CSCL system by means of a pattern and framework approach.

THE PLUG-IN BASED APPROACH

Computer science concepts, which can support the work in interdisciplinary teams, are patterns, architectures, and frameworks. Given the framework definitions described by (Hansen, 1997), a computer science framework can be summarized as a collection of something (e.g. classes, components, objects) which together define a pattern, template, or design of a system. It takes into account special domain requirements. Usually, frameworks have an architecture. Madsen (Madsen, 2003) summarizes that a framework provides a template, which can be reused to build many related applications. The re-usable structures of a framework are realized as concrete and abstract classes, which contain the core functionalities of the system. Parts of the abstract classes are concrete and abstract operations, which define interfaces. The interfaces provide for the basic structure of the application. This basic structure can be used by developers for extending the framework and realizing the resulting system, e.g. the concrete teaching and training system.

Frameworks can be used at different user levels. A similar distinction as shown in Figure 1 has been described by (Hansen, 1997) in the context of framework development. Hansen distinguishes between three levels of user

1. Users at level one are application builders - they don't need to know details of implementation, but just use the framework "out of the box". In our case this would for example be experts from the teaching and training domain.
2. Users at level two are advanced users - they can modify the framework. These might be for example psychologists or computer scientists with focus on system realization and not on system design.
3. Users at level three are system developers, which need to understand the framework design itself. In most cases, in our application domain this would be computer scientists or other researchers with deep system engineering understanding.

Our main idea was to take the architecture sketched in the previous section and the pattern language and develop a framework for teaching and training systems. The resulting system (Oertel & Martens & Himmelspach, 2008) realizes a plug-in approach. The idea of providing a core system which is then extended by plug-ins has been adopted from the Plugin pattern, which allows adding new functionality to an existing system without re-designing or re-implementing the system itself. The approach has been for example used in the Eclipse framework (see www.eclipse.org). The "Plug-n-train" concept, which has been realized in JaBInT (Java Base Intelligent Tutoring), shall support teaching and training system developers at the three levels described above.

Level one developers can re-use a predefined framework "out of the box" and add teaching and training content. Level two developers can re-use existing components, plug them together in the predefined framework, try new compositions of components, and potentially develop new components. Level three developers might wish to extend the framework itself.

The framework JaBInT is based on the research sketched in the previous section - it is based on the analysis if existing ITS and theoretical ITS descriptions, and it has been realized based on the pattern language described in (Harrer & Martens, 2006) and (Harrer & Martens, 2007). The framework development started with the basic pattern, which has been used as starting point in the generic pattern description (ibid.), as can be seen on the left side in Figure 4. The core elements are four components, i.e. expert component, pedagogical component, learner component, and user interface component. Each component has at least two interfaces, i.e.:

- Expert component:
- getData: Extraction of knowledge data
- setData: Adding of knowledge data
- Pedagogical component:
- evaluate: Evaluation of data
- prepareData: Pedagogical preparation of data
- Learner component:
- getData: Extraction of learner data
- setData: Adding of learner data
- User interface component:
- show: Prepare and display data
- getInput: Transfer data about learner interaction and activity

Currently, only three characteristics of these components have been distinguished. Components can be realized as databases, as processes, or as simulations.

As can be seen in Figure 4, the teaching and training system core is a composition of components. Each component, as can be seen on the right side of the figure, is realized as a kind of frame which contains several (at least one) modules. Each module has in- and output ports. These modules provide for the functionality of the component in the ITS - they characterize the component, e.g. as expert component. In the expert component, there might for example be a module for evaluation of user input. As the modules are completely independent, they can be easily ex-

Figure 4. Architecture of JaBInT framework. Sketched exchange of components (left). Component with exchange of modules (right) (Oertel & Martens & Himmelspach, 2008)

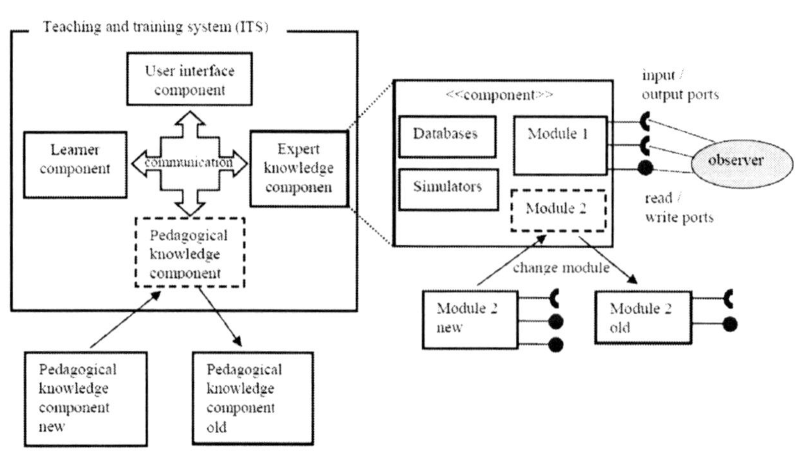

changed and replaced. As can be seen in Figure 4 on the left side, also complete components can be exchanged. Here, the only restriction is that a component must be replaced by a component of the same type (e.g. learner components can only replace learner components).

The JaBInT framework has been realized based on several different patterns, e.g. the training system itself is based on the MVC (model view controller) pattern. Intra-module communication is realized by observers, which are based on the observer pattern. Observers are responsible for data transfer between output port of one module to the input port of another module. Modules are based on the plugin pattern, and components have been developed according to the singleton pattern.

The applicability of the framework for ITS development has been tested. Based on JaBInT, the ITS ChemNom has been realized as a proof of concept (Oertel, 2007) ChemNom has been developed for 2nd semester Pharmacy students and allows training of the chemical nomenclature, i.e. the systematic naming of organic compounds (see Figure 5). The user interfaces provides a toolbox, which allows to graphically combining atoms and chemical bonds (single, double, and triple bonds) to a chemical structure. This structural formula is then evaluated by the system's pedagogical component. This component also generates new tasks for the learner. For this purpose, it uses the underlying expert knowledge, provided by an expert knowledge component. The user component stores the user related information, as usual.

On the system level, the ITS consists of an expert component (implemented by module named Knowledgedata, and a database, where the module can access the data), the pedagogical component (realized as the module Preparation, which is responsible for selection of tasks for the learner, correction of mistakes and offering of solution steps based on an overlay model), the learner component (which is the UserData module with the database containing the user profiles), and the user interface component (realized as the UserInterface module, which contains the design of the user interface, and the EventTimer module, which e.g. generates interactive help after a certain amount of time). The modules communicate via ports. Which ports exist in an application is stored as XML information. For example, ChemNom provides 28 unidirectional port connections (more detailed information can be found for example in (Oertel, 2007)).

Figure 5. ChemNom: Training of chemical nomenclature with ITS

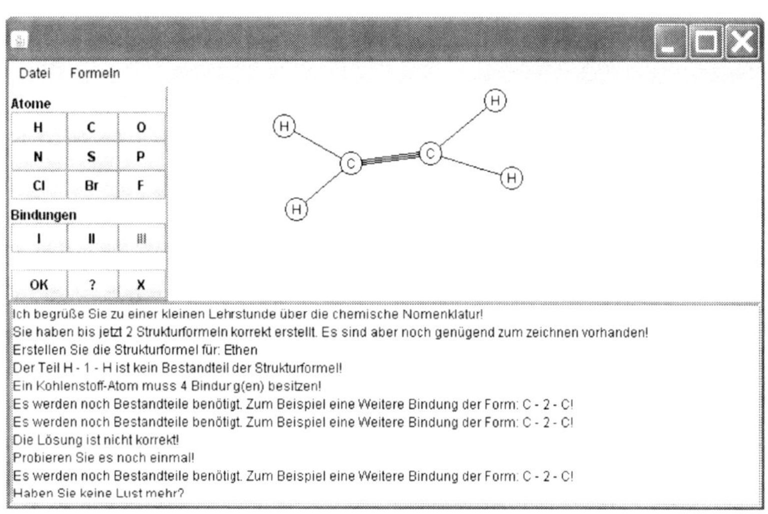

After successfully realizing the ChemNom system, this approach has been used as a basis in a second project for game-based learning. Here, our goal was to show that the pattern based plug'in approach also lends itself for the development of different instructional settings and system types, and that communication and data exchange with other dataformats, e.g. Macromedia Flash, can be realized. From ChemNom, we took the expert knowledge component, the pedagogical component, and the learner component. We exchanged the complete user interface component, but we had to keep the ports to stay compatible with the rest of the components. The user interface component of ChemisTris (shown in Figure 6) is realized based on Flash, the communication with Java is realized by XML via socket server communication. The approach was very successful, as we needed a very short time to develop ChemisTris based on ChemNom.

The game idea behind ChemisTris is to show the chemical molecules in the lower part of the window, and to let game bricks, which are labelled with molecule names, drop from the window's top in a Tetris-like manner. The learner has to navigate the bricks to the fitting chemical molecule representation. After a set of correct answers, the chemical molecules are exchanged. Over time, the bricks become faster, thus the learner's decision has to be quicker.

Figure 6. ChemisTris: Game-based ITS for training of chemical nomenclature as extension to ChemNom

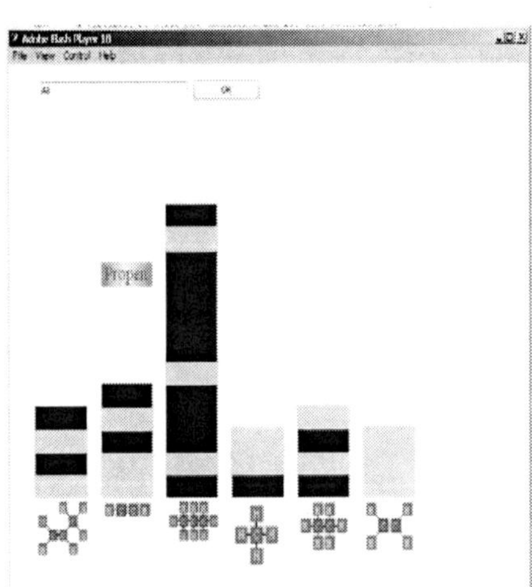

Our main idea, to provide for a set of implemented modules with interfaces, which are more or less domain independent, and thus to facilitate re-use and in general the development of diverse types of eLearning systems, is very successful. Ongoing work is to extend the collection of modules, e.g. to develop a multi-purpose evaluation component for the framework, which shall be re-usable in different teaching and training systems. Moreover, as the framework is able to work with the simulation system JAMES II (Java based Agent Modeling Environment for Simulation II a JAva based Mulitpurpose Environment for Simulation) (Himmelspach & Uhrmacher, 2007), the TutMoSi system (Tutoring of Modeling and Simulation) will be re-factored based on the framework.

Summarizing, the resulting framework should provide independence of the teaching and training domain, the components should be independent of a certain programming language, the framework should allow for integration of different plug-ins, and interfaces for databases and simulation systems should be provided.

SCRIPTED CSCL APPROACH

The principles of re-use of design and components in the spirit of our pattern language proposal have been recently applied in the development of a learning support environment for a study on collaborative learning in the context of the Pittsburgh Science of Learning Center (PSLC). The subject of the CoChemEx (Collaborative Chemistry Experimentation) study was conceptual understanding of chemistry, that should be trained by using a virtual laboratory for chemical experimentation, the Vlab system (Yaron et. al., 2005). To support the students in their scientific inquiry process (De Jong & van Joolingen, 1998) the system was required to provide scaffolds, such as specific tools for the different phases of problem solving. The original chemistry lab is a powerful experimentation tool to be used for a multitude of purposes and was designed as a single-user system. Because of the specific requirements of the scenario - collaboration and specific support of the given task - additional features had to be provided in the final system: On the one hand it had to allow for collaboration in small synchronous groups (in the actual experiment 2 student experimenters and 1 human tutor to guide their collaboration) and on the other hand it had to scaffold the process of problem solving by providing appropriate tools in specific phases of the scientific inquiry process, i.e. a collaboration script had to be integrated into this scenario.

Interestingly, this scenario required all the different perspectives involved in ITS development in the introduction and in Figure 1: Psychology was needed to define a sound script that supports the inquiry process, while computer science was needed to formally represent it and interpret it with our scripting component, a coarse-grained type of tutoring module. For the development of the system based on pre-existing components, re-usability and integration of the components was a major issue for the computer science perspective. The definition of the problem to be solved on the content level was the concern of the educational perspective and addressed aspects related to the domain of expertise. And finally, the HCI perspective was also of importance to allow the human tutor to regulate and intervene into the collaboration, if needed.

The practical implementation of the system relied heavily on the re-use of design ideas and existing components that could be put to use in an integrated system. Our pattern language was used as a development aid as presented earlier in this article and because of the multiple perspectives involved in the development of the scenario, different types of patterns have been used to address the required forces imposed by the requirements:

- The script for inquiry and collaboration was designed by our psychological project partners in accordance with the literature in science inquiry (De Jong & van Joolingen, 1998), adapted to the specific aspects of the chemistry experimentation, and the type of communication between the students we wanted to research; to support the structured elaboration of the pre- and post-experimentation phases we used graphical discussion maps, while the interactive character of collaborative experimentation afforded a chat as a more immediate type of coordination. The resulting script (more details about this can be found in Tsovaltzi et el., 2008) can be seen as a blueprint for other science inquiry scenarios and was in this study also adapted for a modified task using the same basic script with slightly different setup. In pattern terms, the science inquiry cycle could be considered a high-level pedagogical process pattern, while the chemistry script is a more specific pedagogical pattern for collaborative experimentation.
- To prepare the script to be re-usable with other learning support environments in the future, we followed our design pattern engine + specification' (Harrer & Martens, 2006, in Figure 3 labelled as process-steering component / process description) that separates the description of a pedagogical model from the execution. This was deliberately in contrast to most current scripted CSCL environments, where the script is usually tied closely to the code, or is even hard-wired into the user-interface: The separation allows adaptation and exchange of the script conveniently without having to re-compile any code, and thus enables the script designer to make adaptations on short notice without deep technical proficiency. This claim is supported by the fact, that during the experimentation

with the full system, the researcher (a psychologist) was able to change the instructions of the script on her own, with only little support from the technical partners for larger changes in the script structure. As for the technical solution of the design pattern we took up our earlier implementation "remote control approach" (Harrer & Malzahn & Roth, 2006) that uses the third-party CopperCore engine which is able to interpret educational models compliant to the IMS/LD format, the de facto e-learning standard for educational models. Details about this work, that uses a loose-coupling between the LD engine and the learning environment the user interacts with, can be found in (Harrer & Malzahn & Roth, 2006).

- Since the scenario uses a computer-mediated collaboration, i.e. each participant works on an own computer in a potentially remote setting, the virtual chemistry lab Vlab was extended into a collaborative lab. Technically, it was embedded into an existing distributed synchronization framework called MatchMaker (Jansen, 2003). The Vlab itself, which formerly has been a Java applet, was wrapped into a component that is compliant with the plug-in mechanism of the collaborative modeling application FreeStyler that uses MatchMaker. The general design pattern Adapter (Gamma, 1995) was chosen for that end to keep the original code of the Vlab untouched, yet providing the plug-in interface to use the Vlab as a learning tool in FreeStyler just as the other tools used in the script, e.g. the graphical discussion language, the chat, a glossary with explanation texts on chemistry concepts, and the student's notepad to document their notes/comments.
- As mentioned above, the adaptation required for the Vlab did not have to be implemented from scratch, but used the MatchMaker synchronization middleware, that coordinates/synchronizes the work context for every participant of a collaboration session with each other. Actions conducted by one of the student are sent via the MatchMaker synchronization server to the other student machines and the result of the action is then re-created for the student, so that they have the same task context in a relaxed WYSIWIS (What you see is what I see) HCI paradigm style, i.e. the pages show the same content, but individual scrolling and resizing of the window and browsing through pages is possible without changes at the partners' side. The propagation of the actions is performed via the Publisher-Subscriber design pattern or change-propagation mechanism that notifies all participants in a collaboration session that previously have registered at the MatchMaker server. From the pattern perspective the middleware uses a combination of two architectural CSCL patterns, synchronization server' and replicated model' (to allow continuation of work in case of a server crash and re-configuration of the session content after re-launch of the server), that is realized in the MatchMaker/FreeStyler combination. As a subordinate pattern the general Publisher-Subscriber' (Buschmann et. al., 1996) aka. Observer' (Gamma, 1995) is used.
- The third human participant of the experimental setup, the so called Wizard (This term was chosen to reflect that a longterm goal of the research on scripted collaboration is to create an intelligent artificial tutor handling this task; thus, this first experiment can be considered a Wizard-of-Oz design, with a human tutor acting according to a pre-defined) behaviour that is similar to the one of the imagined artificial tutor), is a human tutor that supervises the experimentation and collaboration of the dyad

and gives feedback and hints according to instructions provided by our psychological partners. On the one hand this required to take into account HCI principles for the design of the feedback transmission and the layout of the instructions, on the other hand a technical implementation was required. The graphical interface (see Figure 7) for the Wizard showed a decision tree that was traced through decision steps toward a feedback message by unfolding/folding the currently active tree elements. By choosing a feedback message in the tree, the message was automatically sent to an editable text section, where the Wizard can modify the text and finally send it to one or both of the students. On the students' side the message is displayed as a pop-up window with the text and graphical avatar of the Wizard's choice. Besides these carefully designed HCI aspects, the propagation of the Wizard message to the FreeStyler has been implemented in a similar event propagation design pattern for distributed communication as above, this time using the JSDT middleware. A substantial part of the intervention mechanism and interface was already developed in a similar project, which made it possible to re-use this code and reduce the implementation work to the programming of the decision tree.

The implementation of the system supporting the whole scenario would have been an enormous effort if the solution was to be developed from scratch (our estimates are 2-3 person years). Yet, the re-use of design ideas, that was guided by our pattern language for ITS and CSCL systems, and the re-use of existing components along the pattern ideas made it possible to finish the overall system with substantially less effort: including the technical preparation of scripts and instruction, and the deployment of the system in a network setting, this feat was achieved in approximately 3 months of part time student programmers coordinated by the project's investigators. All the

Figure 7. Screenshot of the wizard interface (on the right with dynamic decision tree and message window) and the resulting feedback in the FreeStyler environment (on the left with popup at the bottom))

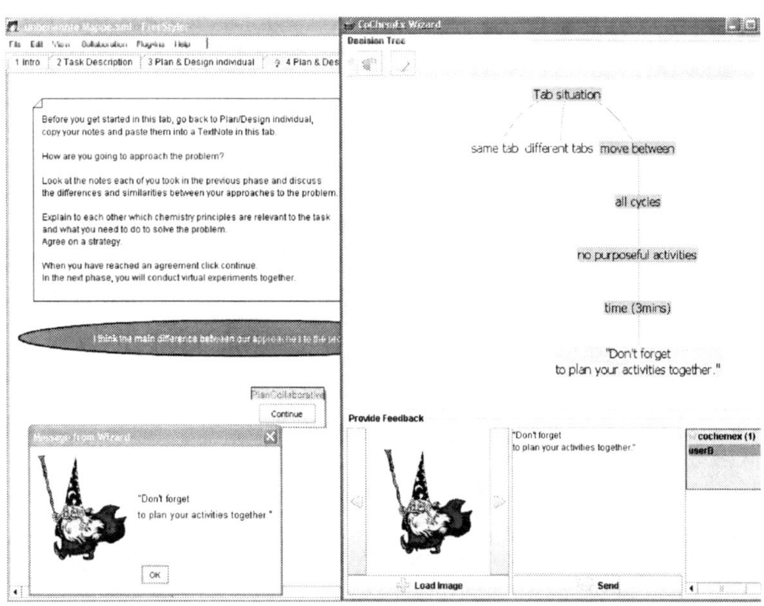

components used have been developed in the Java programming language, which allowed us to transfer the whole system from our testing environment to the experimental environment on a different operating system without any problems of platform-dependency. The results of the first studies with the system have been published in (Tsovaltzi et al., 2008).

CONCLUSION

The chapter describes a pattern based approach for the Intelligent Tutoring System architecture and shows exemplary developments. It continues the research introduced in (Harrer & Martens, 2006), where a pattern language for ITS has been proposed. The presentation of (Harrer & Martens, 2006) has lead to further intensive discussions. One of these discussions was centred on the question, how research groups from different scientific fields (e.g. computer science, psychology, and training application fields like law or medicine) communicate the underlying system architecture during system development. In this discussion, one position has been that the ITS architecture is existing in more or less well known shape, which mainly arose from Clancey's description (Clancey, 1984). So our question was why this architecture seemingly does not help to support re-use and re-engineering of existing systems or at least part of systems. From our perspective, the major flaw was (however not surprising) the different usage of the same terms. Thus, this chapter starts with an analysis of the related concepts. Subsequently, an exemplary design process based on the patterns described in (Harrer & Martens, 2006), is sketched, to show, which developer group can have which gain when using our approach. Two examples how the pattern approach has been used in different projects in the last two years demonstrate the viability of the approach.

REFERENCES

Alexander, C., Ishikawa, S., & Silverstein, M. (1977). *A Pattern Language – Towns Buildings Construction*, Vol. 2 of Center for Environmental Structure Series. New York: Oxford University Press.

Alpert, S. R., Singley, M. K., & Fairweather, P. G. (1999). Deploying Intelligent Tutors on the Web: An Architecture and an Example. *International Journal of Artificial Intelligence*, *10*(2), 183–197.

Anderson, J. R., Boyle, C. F., Corbett, A. T., & Lewis, M. W. (1990). Cognitive Modeling and Intelligent Tutoring. *Artificial Intelligence*, *42*, 17–49. doi:10.1016/0004-3702(90)90093-F

Bergin, R. A., & Fors, U. G. H. (2003). Interactive Simulated Patient - An Advanced Tool for Student-activated Learning in Medicine and Healthcare. *Computers & Education*, *40*(4), 361–376. doi:10.1016/S0360-1315(02)00167-7

Buschmann, F., Meunier, R., Rohnert, H., Sommerlad, P., & Stal, M. A. (1996). *System of Patterns*. Chichester, UK: John Wiley & Sons.

Cap, C., & Martens, A. (2009). Patterns for eLearning Systems. In Hambach, S., Martens, A., Urban, B. (eds.) *Proc. of the eLBa 2009 e-Learning Baltics International Scientific Conference* (pp. 115-124) Stuttgart, Germany: Fraunhofer IRB Verlag.

Clancey, W. J. (1984). Methodology for Building an Intelligent Tutoring System. In Kintsch, W., Miller, J. R., & Polson, P. G. (Eds.), *Methods and Tactics in Cognitive Sciences* (pp. 51–84). Hillsdale, NJ: Lawrence Erlbaum Associates.

Clancey, W. J. (1987). Methodology for Building an Intelligent Tutoring System. In: Kearsley (ed.): *Artificial Intelligence and Instruction*. Reading, MA: Addison Wesley.

Corbett, A. T., Koedinger, K. R., & Anderson, J. R. (1997). Intelligent Tutoring Systems. In M. Helander, T. K. & Landauer, P., & Prabuh (Eds.), *Handbook of Human-Computer Interaction*. Elsevier Science B.V., 2nd completely revised edition (pp. 849-874).

de Jong, T., & van Joolingen, W. (1998). Discovery learning with computer simulations of conceptual domains. *Review of Educational Research, 68*, 179–201.

Devedžić, V. (1999). Using design patterns in ITS development. In: S.P. Lajoie, & M. Vivet, (Eds.) Artificial IntelligeNce in Education (pp. 657-659). Amsterdam: IOS Press / Tokyo: OHM Ohmsha.

Forte, E., Haenni, F., Warkentyne, K., Duval, E., Cardinaels, K., & Vervaet, E. (1999). Semantic and Pedagogic Interoperability Mechanisms in the ARIADNE Educational Repository. [SIGMOD]. *SIGMOD Record, 28*(1), 20–25. doi:10.1145/309844.309870

Gamma, E., Helm, R., Johnson, R., & Vlissides, J. (1995). *Design Patterns: Elements of Reusable Object-Oriented Software*. Reading, MA: Addison-Wesley.

Ghezzi, C., Jazayeri, M., & Mandrioli, D. (2003). *Fundamentals of Software Engineering* (2nd ed.). Prentice Hall, Pearson Education.

Hansen, T. (1997). Development of Successful Object-Oriented Frameworks. in Proc. of the OOPSLA 97, Addendum to the 1997 ACM SIGPLAN conference on Object-Oriented Programming Systems, Languages, and Applications. New York: ACM Press, 115-119.

Harrer, A. (2003). Software Engineering Methods for re-use of Components and Design in Educational Systems. *International Journal of Computers & Applications, Special Issue on Intelligence and Technology in Educational Applications, Anaheim, CA, 25*, 1.

Harrer, A., Malzahn, N., & Roth, B. (2006). The remote control approach - how to apply scaffolds to existing collaborative learning environments. In Dimitriadis, Y., Zigurs, I., & Gomez-Sanchez, E. (Eds.), *Groupware: design, implementation, and use; proc. of CRIWG, Vol. LNCS 4154* (pp. 118–131). Berlin: Springer. doi:10.1007/11853862_10

Harrer, A., & Martens, A. (2006). Towards a Pattern Language for Intelligent Teaching and Training Systems. In T.-W. Chan & M. Ikeda & K. D. Ashley (Eds.): Proc. of the 8th International Conference on Intelligent Tutoring Systems. Lecture Notes in Computer Science LNCS 4053, Springer. 298-307.

Harrer, A., & Martens, A. (2007). An Integrated Approach for Teaching/Tutoring Process Models using Meta-Models. In Proceedings of the International Conference CELDA.

Himmelspach, J., & Uhrmacher, A. M. (2007). Plug'n simulate. In *Proceedings of the 40th Annual Simulation Symposium*. IEEE Computer Society. (pp. 137-143).

Illmann, T., Weber, M., Martens, A., & Seitz, A. (2000). A Pattern-Oriented Design of a Web-Based and Case-Oriented Multimedia Training System in Medicine. 4th World Conference on Integrated Design and Process Technology, Dallas, US.

Jansen, M. (2003). Matchmaker - a Framework to Support Collaborative Java Applications. In U. Hoppe, F. Verdejo & J. Kay (Eds.), Proc. of the 11th Int. Conf. on Artificial Intelligence in Education AIED. Amsterdam: IOS Press. 529-530.

Künzel, J. & Hämmer, V. (2003). Simulation in University Education: The Artificial Agent PSI as a Teaching Tool. *Simulation - Special Issue on Modeling and Simulation in Teaching and Training, 82, 11*. 761–767.

Lelouche, R. (1999). Intelligent Tutoring Systems from Birth to Now. In: KI-*Künstliche Intelligenz, 4,* 5-11.

Madsen, K. (2003). Five Years of Framework Building - Lessons Learned. In *Proc. of the OOPSLA Conference*, Anaheim, CA: ACM Press. (pp. 345-352).

Martens, A. (2004). *Ein Tutoring Prozess Modell für fallbasierte Intelligente Tutoring Systeme.* AKA Verlag infix.

Martens, A., Hambach, S., & Lucke, U. (2009). Multi-perspective Cooperation based on Boundary Objects. In: In *Proc. of the ICALT 2009, pp. 476-488, The 9th IEEE International Conference on Advanced Learning Technologies.*

Martens, A., & Himmelspach, J. (2005). Combining Intelligent Tutoring and Simulation Systems. In *Proc. of the Internat. Conference on Simulation in Human Computer Interfaces, SIMCHI, Part of the Western Multi Conference WMC '05.* New Orleans, LA. (pp. 65-70).

Mayo, M., Mitrovic, A., & McKenzie, J. (2000). An Intelligent Tutoring System for Capitalization and Punctuation. In *Proc. of the Int. Workshop for Advanced Learning Technologies IWALT* (pp. 151–157). CAPIT.

Melis, E., & Siekmann, J. (2004). Activemath: An Intelligent Tutoring System for Mathematics. In R. Tadeusiewicz, L.A. Zadeh, L. Rutkowski, J. Siekmann, (Eds.), *7th International Conference 'Artificial Intelligence and Soft Computing' (ICAISC) Lecture Notes in AI LNAI 3070.* Springer-Verlag 91-101.

Murray, T. (1999). Authoring intelligent tutoring systems. *International Journal of Artificial Intelligence in Education, 10*(3/4), 98–129.

Noble, J. (1998) Towards a pattern language for object oriented design. In Proceedings of Technology of Object-Oriented Languages. *TOOLS 28*, 2-13.

Oertel, M. (2007). *Entwicklung eines Frameworks für intelligente Lehr-/Lernsysteme. (Masterthesis).* Germany: University of Rostock.

Oertel, M., Martens, A., & Himmelspach, J. (2008). Teaching and Training System Plus Modeling and Simulation - A Component Based Approach. to appear in: Proc. of the EUROSIM.

Schümmer, T., & Lukosch, S. (2007). *Patterns for Computer-Mediated Interaction, Wiley Software Patterns.* New York: Wiley & Sons.

Szyperski, C. (2002). *Component Software. Addison Wesley, Component Software Series.* New York: ACM Press.

Tsovaltzi, D., Rummel, N., Pinkwart, N., Harrer, A., Scheuer, O., Braun, I., & McLaren, B. M. (2008). Cochemex: Supporting conceptual chemistry learning via computer-mediated collaboration scripts. In *Proceedings of the European Conference on Technology Enhanced Learning.*

Woolf, B. P., & McDonald, D. D. (1984). *Building a Computer Tutor: Design Issues* (pp. 61–73). IEEE Computer.

Yaron, D., Cuadros, J., Leinhardt, G., Evans, K. L., & Karabinos, M. (2005). Virtual Laboratories and Scenes to Support Chemistry Instruction, in About Invention and Impact: Building Excellence in Undergraduate STEM (Science, Technology, Engineering, and Mathematics) Education. In *Proceedings from National Science Foundation Course, Curriculum, and Laboratory Improvement (NSF-CCLI) program conference.* Arlington, VA, 2004, edited and prepared by NSF.

ADDITIONAL READING

Aleven, V., McLaren, B. M., Sewall, J., & Koedinger, K. R. (2006). The Cognitive Tutor Authoring Tools (CTAT): Preliminary evaluation of efficiency gains. In M. Ikeda, K.D. Ashley, & T-W. Chan (Eds.), *Proceedings of the 8th International Conference on Intelligent Tutoring Systems* (ITS-2006), Lecture Notes in Computer Science, 4053 (pp. 61-70). Berlin: Springer.

Aleven, V., McLaren, B. M., Sewall, J., & Koedinger, K. R. (in press). A New Paradigm for Intelligent Tutoring Systems: Example-Tracing Tutors. *International Journal of Artificial Intelligence in Education (IJAIED)*, Special Issue on ". *Authoring Systems for Intelligent Tutoring Systems.*

Hambach, S., & Martens, A. (2008) Systems Engineering for Technology Enhanced Learning In *Proc. of the ECTEL European Conference on Technology Enhanced Learning*, vol. LNCS 5192, Springer. LNCS.

Harrer, A., & Martens, A. (2008). Software Engineering in e-Learning Systems. In Tomei, L. (Ed.), *Encyclopedia of Information Technology Curriculum Integration*. Hershey, PA: IGI Global.

Maciuszek, D., & Martens, A. (2009to appear). *Patterns for the Design of Educational Games. Educational Games: Design, Learning, and Applications*. New York: Nova.

Martens, A., Diener, H., & Malo, S. (2008). Game-based Learning with Computers -- Learning, Simulations, and Games. *Transactions on Edutainment*, *5080*, 172–190. doi:10.1007/978-3-540-69744-2_15

Martens, A., Hambach, S., & Müsebeck, P. (2009). ROME - a Generic Process Modell for Interdisciplinary E-Learning Systems Design and Development In: Proceedings of the ED-MEDIA 2009-World Conference on Educational Multimedia, Hypermedia & Telecommunications, pp. 1372-1377, Chesapeake, VA, AACE.

Martens, A., Himmelspach, J., & Ewald, R. (2008). Modeling, Simulation and Games. In: *Workshop Proceedings der Tagungen Mensch und Computer 2008, Delfi 2008 und Cognitive Design 2008*, ed. by U. Lucke, M.C. Kindsmüller, S. Fischer, M. Herczeg, S. Seehusen, pp. 349-354, GI, Berlin, logos Verlag.

Mitrovic, A., Martin, B., & Suraweera, P. (2007). Intelligent Tutors for All: The Constraint-Based Approach. *IEEE Intelligent Systems*, *22*(4), 38–45. doi:10.1109/MIS.2007.74

KEY TERMS AND DEFINITIONS

Architecture: In software engineering the term is related to the abstract structural description of a software system.

Game-Based Learning: An approach to combine classical learning with insights from game related learning research. Game-based learning systems aim towards keeping the learner's motivation at a high level.

Intelligent Tutoring Systems: Intelligent Tutoring Systems (ITS) are computer-based systems for teaching and training, which are based on expert knowledge of the application domain, some sort of pedagogical knowledge model, a model of the learner and a user interface. In contrast to other computer-based teaching and training systems, ITSs are flexible and adaptable.

Pattern: A pattern is an abstract description of something, which is re-occurring. Patterns can be described by pattern languages, and they can be organized in form of pattern catalogs.

Section 2
E-Learning Communities Technologies

Chapter 5
Virtual Learning Environment

Saša Mladenović
University of Split, Croatia

Haidi Kuvač
University of Split, Croatia

Maja Štula
University of Split, Croatia

ABSTRACT

This paper describes a mathematical model of virtual learning environment considering both technology and users. Recognized interested users are teachers, parents and students. Interaction between interested parties in elementary and high school education process is presented by using complexity science. The idea is to model and create educational virtual environment that would attract engagement of all parties. Initial engagement would be motivated with the e-grade book. After initial involvement of seeing grades, the users would be motivated for further involvement using forums, blogs, and chats to interact with each other in one place. This would lead to creating groups of students or parents with similar problems and interests. For example, why is mathematics so hard to some students, and for other not? The created virtual environment will enable teachers to additionally inform parents of existing e-learning materials. Virtual environment is modelled as multilevel, multidimensional educational environment, considering communication of all participants, and every aspect of technology that could improve that communication.

VIRTUAL LEARNING ENVIRONMENT AND WEB 2.0

Before beginning to talk about virtual learning environment it is necessary to define meaning of terms that are used in everyday communication. We hear on a daily bases the term Web 2.0, but the question is: What is Web 2.0? At its simplest, the term 'Web 2.0' denotes a transition from a classic content delivery system to a collaborative system. Sometimes it is referred to as the 'participatory web', which is perhaps a more appropriate term to use.

The term 'Web 2.0' first appearance came in 1999.(DiNucci, 1999) The term originally coined by Darcy DiNucci relates mainly to Web design.

DOI: 10.4018/978-1-61692-008-1.ch005

She argues that the Web is 'fragmenting' due to widespread use of portable Web-ready devices.

The Web we know now, which loads into a browser window in essentially static screenfuls, is only an embryo of the Web to come. The first glimmerings of Web 2.0 are beginning to appear, and we are just starting to see how that embryo might develop The Web will be understood not as screenfuls of text and graphics but as a transport mechanism, the ether through which interactivity happens. Darcy DiNucci, 1999

The article is written for designers, emphasising the need to code for an ever-increasing number of Web-ready devices. Although her use of the term announced, it did not directly relate to the current use of the term.

'Web 2.0' term as we use it today is closely associated with Tim O'Reilly because of the Web 2.0 conference organised by O'Reilly Media in 2004. At the time it was supposed to mean using 'the web as a platform'. The term suggested a new version of the World Wide Web, but did not refer to any update to any technical specification. It addressed cumulative changes in the ways end users and programmers used the Web.(Oreilly, 2007)

Like many important concepts, Web 2.0 doesn't have a hard boundary, but rather, a gravitational core. You can visualize Web 2.0 as a set of principles and practices that tie together a veritable solar system of sites that demonstrate some or all of those principles, at a varying distance from that core. Tim O'Reilly

World Wide Web inventor, Tim Berners-Lee challenged the term by calling it a 'piece of jargon'.(Laningham, 2006) After a lot of criticism O'Reilly offered new, compact definition of Web 2.0(O'Reilly, 2006)

Web 2.0 is the business revolution in the computer industry caused by the move to the internet as platform, and an attempt to understand the rules for success on that new platform. Chief among those rules is this: Build applications that harness network effects to get better the more people use them. (This is what I've elsewhere called "harnessing collective intelligence.") Tim O'Reilly

To summarise we can say that the Web 2.0 is a term to describe a variety of developments on the web and a shift in the way the Web is used. This is often characterised as the evolution of web use from passive consumption of content to more active participation, creation and sharing – to what is sometimes called the 'read/write' web.

From the students perspective Web 2.0 is seen as set of internet activities and tools that are encouraging communication and participation among internet users. Web 2.0 covers a range of technologies, services and trends underpinned by the growth of a critical mass of internet users. Technologies used by the students are helping change some characteristics of actual and future students.

The current situation has to also consider and the other populations that are directly connected to changing population. Before all we are talking about teachers and parents populations taking an active role in virtual environments, and the most important one is the environment containing elements of virtual learning environment. Changes in student population trigger changes in teaching and learning methods. Students participating in learning process are part of digital natives, so called digital generation that have grown up with digital technology. They are native to deal with multiple tasks simultaneously and quickly. Digital environment to which population members have been exposed during the development had an impact on reasoning development. Although those students are less patient and less thoughtful regarding the subject under consideration they posses better visual knowledge and skills and are able to follow multiple media simultaneously. In teaching and learning process the learning group is composed of students with different cognitive competences if compared with previous students groups.(Prensky, 2001) Students have computer literacy, they are very accustomed to internet technologies, network connected, expecting immediate answers to questions posed, prefer learn by experience, have highly expressed social component so therefore are willing to accept into group anyone who is friend of their friend, prefer working in group, look for interactivity within rich interface environment.

Beside the common student population, the importance of part time student population is growing. Part time student population is composed of individuals belonging to different age groups but exhibiting the same behaviour as the digital generation members. The behaviour can be explained by extensive use of technology with the intention to reach the goal in minimum time interval. To answer the question whether is necessary to change learning methods considering the students population change, it is necessary to analyse interaction between all participants involved in the virtual learning environment. Migrations of VLE towards social networks like Facebook have to be taken into account because students engagement in such kind of activities. Many students are emphasising issue of learning environments invading their private virtual space, so it is necessary to examine students' response to the approach mentioned.(Hewitt & Forte, 2006)

Although previously mentioned indicates the conclusion that the technology and its choice is relevant factor in teaching efficacy, research denies that. From that reason it is important to evaluate influence of technology like VLE on teaching for which it is appropriate using automatic evaluation methods.(Grubišić, Stankov, & Žitko, 2007) Students aren't burdened with teaching techniques as long as the teaching process is well founded.

Virtual learning environments are designed as collaboration tools. Collaboration between students is efficient as already shown by many studies, but some conditions for either failure or success are still unknown.(Dillenbourg & Schneider, 1995) Virtual learning environment integrates a set of tools supporting functions like: information, communication, collaboration, learning and management.(Peraya, Piguet, & Joye, 1999)

Virtual learning environment usage is not restricted to well-structured information space but content management becomes main issue for all participants in virtual learning environments. Better understanding of the functional relationship between information structure and representation has to be developed to be able to use it in learning. The representation of the virtual learning environments can range from text-based to the most complex 3D interface. Representation can be important but it is not the key issue. What is important is what participants actually do with the representation. Set of activities in which participants construct and share objects makes the virtual learning environment specific. Most of shared objects are web pages (study reports, news, useful links...) and participants are both information consumers and producers.

Usually study group is composed of two well known participants, student and teacher. Neglected participant of the educational environment system is a parent. Parent plays active role in educational process both by acting as positive or negative motivator to student, and mediator in student teacher communication. Parental influence is more important in elementary and high school than in later education where parental role is taken over by mentors. In classic educational environment system parents are involved trough grade book and regular teacher-parent meetings. The main disadvantage of the classic approach mentioned is lack of information fidelity provided by student or teacher. The learning success has been identified as a common interest of all parties involved in the educational process. In most educational environments grade is defined as measure of success, and grade book is basically grade repository. The e-grade book is important element of the

CMS educational environment system motivating involvement of all parties (Figures 1 and 2).

There is uncertainty does the on-line grades put extra pressure on the student population. That pressure could endanger overall education process improvement. The main goal of the educational environment proposed is to ease and improve information exchange process for all participants. There are numerous commercial and open source solutions that can be used to build educational multilevel, multidimensional educational environment. The intention is to show that a general Content Management System with implementation of a simple e-grade book extension component represents multilevel, multidimensional educational environment. In this way, emphasis is switched back from the technology to the functionality.

Numerous studies show that student's perception of studying using internet technologies is positive. However, students are not ready to embrace e-learning as an exclusive way of learning,

Figure 1. The main diary grade view for particular pupil

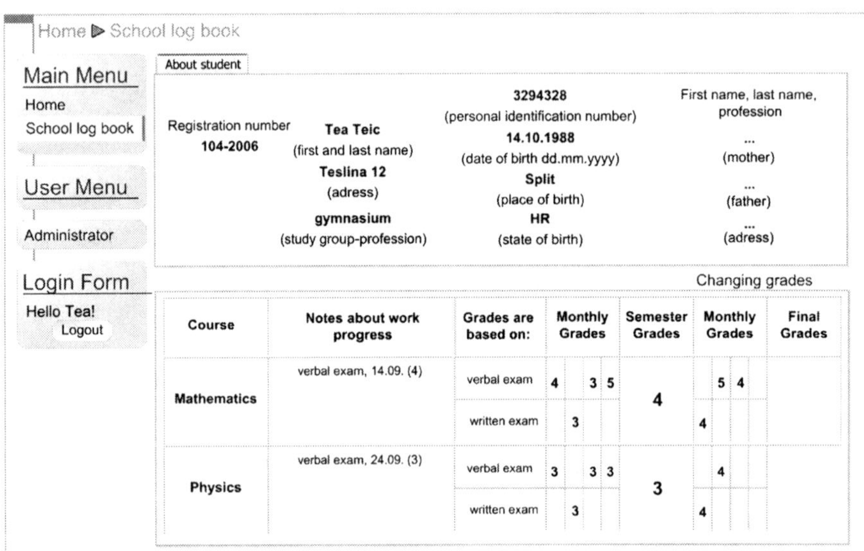

Figure 2. The main diary behaviour view for particular pupil

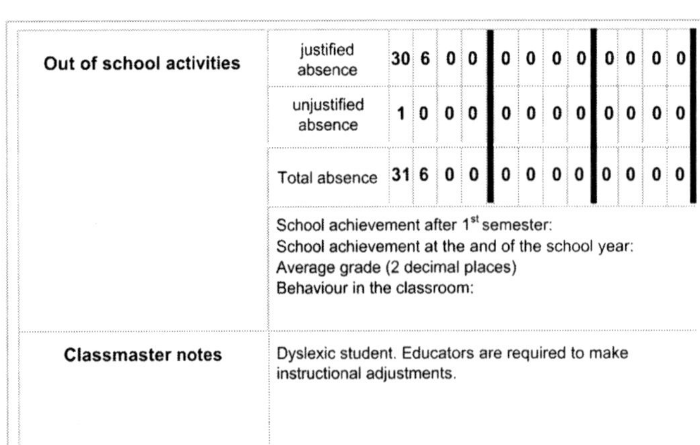

but are requiring some kind of blended system. (Burger, 2003)

Before internet era students had to initiate in-person communication if they wanted to improve social inter-connectivity. One additional e-learning system element recognised is social network enabler. Today, all that students have to do is to use CMS social elements.

Social networks, detected by the system, should be used as guidance to choose appropriate approach in learning process, with the goal to maximise knowledge transfer for the recognised social group. Dynamics of the educational group emerge from interactions between group participants.

Any existing or future technology can be understood as complex collaborative educational system with premise that additional components could provide functionality required by educational environment. It is recommended to use technology like CMS as a starting point to encourage creation of educational social networks, expected to emerge from the proposed educational environment.

VIRTUAL LEARNING ENVIRONMENT COMPLEXITY

Virtual learning environment is complex environment, if it is looked from the participants' perspective, both technologies and humans. Multiple programs and applications used are making the VLE difficult to model with the purpose to understand interactions found in the system. Taking into account all the above mentioned facts, complexity science is a good candidate to be used to create the VLE mathematical model. Such a model will enable researchers to analyse interdependencies in the VLE. Modelling method involves ways of building "grounded" multidimensional constructs bottom-up from a "soup" of lower level constructs, in the context of resolving systems into lower level multidimensional constructs top-down.

Complexity Definition

There are many definitions of complex system, therefore in this paper it will be mentioned only few of them. One of complexity definitions says that a complex system can be seen as a system that consists of many parts that interact in a non simple way. In such systems the whole is more than the sum of its party, not in an ultimate, metaphysical sense but in the important pragmatic sense that, given the properties of the parts and the laws of their interaction, it is not a trivial matter to infer the properties of the whole. (Simon, 1996) Also there is suggestion for a division between and "old science" of simple systems, and "new science" of complex system.(Ashby, 1956) One characteristic of the old science is linearity: analyse the parts and add them together, with the whole being the sum of its parts. Most complex systems exhibit both linearity and non-linearity in their subsystems. Concluding from a variety of complexity definitions, we can say that a necessary condition for complexity is that there are interactions between parts of the system, with system properties emerging.(Johnson, 2006)

The idea of a measure for complexity is some procedure that maps any system to a number, where systems with the highest complexity have the highest (or lowest) numbers. Emergence is one of the central ideas in the science of complex systems. The meaning of the emergence can be explained by saying that constitutive characteristics of the complex is some like new and emergent against those many parts put together. (Bertalanffy, 1968) The behaviour of the system can be derived from behaviour of the parts that constitute system and relations between them. Complex systems are characterized by interactions between their parts. Discrete systems have (usually finite) sets of elements and (usually finite) sets of relationships between them. Relationships can be represented by networks in which the elements are represented by vertices and the relationships are represented by directed links.

A set can be any collection of objects, called objects' elements. Elements can be abstract or concrete. In this paper attention is restricted to finite sets, i.e. those sets whose elements can be counted from 1 to N, for some finite number N. A set X is well-defined if there is an operational procedure, P_x, for recognizing its elements. The notation $P_x=True$ means that x passes the operational procedure P_x, in which case we say that x belongs to X. This is written: x belongs to the set X if x passes the operational procedure P_x $X=\{x|P_x(x)=TRUE\}$.

Learning systems have many heterogeneous sets and many heterogeneous relations between them. There are sets of educational participants and learning technologies. There are many relationships between the sets elements, like relations between participants themselves or, relations between them with some technologies.

The starting point is finding all recognized elements at intermediate levels between "the system" at the highest level and the all the minutiae of the lowest level. This is the process of set definition, which requires operational procedures for recognizing members of well-defined sets and recognizing patterns of relational structure that make elements at one level well-defined in terms of structured sets of elements at lower levels. Network theory has been very successful in analyzing binary relations and related dynamics and flows. Learning systems also characterized by higher level relations between many elements, can lead to a multidimensional generalization of network theory. Many dynamic system properties are dependent on the underlying multidimensional connectivity.

Relational Structure

It is known that networks represent a powerful method for presenting relationships, but also that they are only a special case of a more general structure, called the simplicial complex or hypernetworks. Hypernetworks are a self extension of networks with two-vertex edges, and every edge in hypernetworks can have many vertices. Hyper-edge can also be called simplex. In general, hypernetworks are related to hypergraphs, and represent more powerful representation and reconstruction of the dynamics of complex multilevel systems then networks.

The first step is representing relationships between n things so that a mathematical theory of multilevel systems with its own theory of discrete multidimensional time and multilevel multidimensional dynamics as system activity flows through the polyhedra within and between levels could be built.

Let V be a set of objects called vertices, and E a set of objects called edges. Each edge e_i is associated with a pair of vertices (a,b). We write $\rho:e_i \rightarrow (a,b)$. The pair (V,E) is called a graph. We allow $\rho(e_i)=\rho(e_j)=\rho(e_j)=(a,b)$ for $i \neq j$, with more than one edge between pairs of vertices.

Generally dynamics emerge from interactions between parts of systems, sometimes with associated flows. The abstraction of edges (a,b), is ideally suited for representing interactions and flows between a and b. A general network is a graph in which the edges are oriented so that $(a,b) \neq (b,a)$. Usually a network has mappings from its vertices and edges to many sets that represent flows and associated entities. Therefore, network topological connectivity constraints above mentioned. Although graphs and networks have powerful analytic power, there is some essential disadvantage that is they can represent only binary relations between pairs of things.

For example, consider three recognized parties in learning environment, teacher, student and parent, having meeting or some conversation in the school. This is not the same as they having meeting or conversation as three pairs at three different times. Thus, the combination (a,b,c) is not the same as (a,b) with (a,c) with (b,c), which can be written as $(a,b,c) \neq (a,b)+(a,c)+(b,c)$.

Figure 3. $(a,b,c) \neq (a,b)+ (a,c)+ (b,c)$

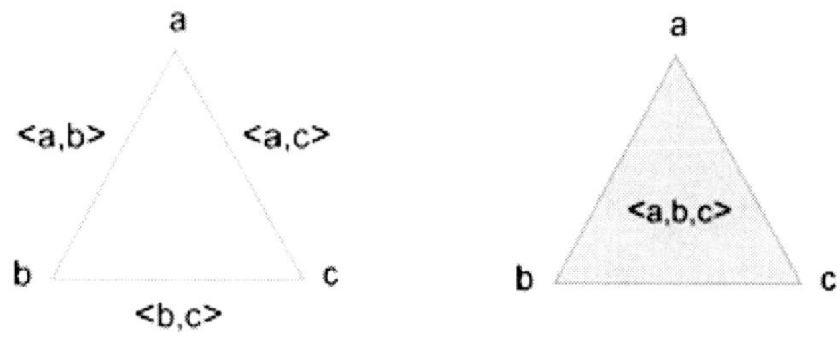

Since (a,b) is represented by a line the natural generalization is to represent (a,b,c) as a triangle, as illustrated in Figure 3. The relationship of three people having meeting together is a 3-ary relation, and this cannot be expressed in terms of 2-ary relation (binary relations). Although each person is inherently individual, making a group of them, defines something that we can perceive as a whole. Such n-ary relations are primary in complex systems, respectively relations assemble elements into structures that exist at a higher level to the elements.

Hypergraphs

We define hypergraph on the finite set $X=\{x_1, x_2,\cdots,x_n\}$ to be a family of subsets of X, $H=(E_1, E_2,\cdots,E_m)$ such that (1) $E_i \neq \emptyset$ for all $i=1,2,\cdots,m$ and (2) $X=\cup_i E_i$ for $i=1,2,\cdots,m$.(Berge, 1976) A *simple* hypergraph has the property that no hyper-edge is a proper subset of another. The sets, E_j are called hypergraph edges or simply edges. Later on it will be allowed that empty set belongs to hypergraphs. Thus, any finite class of finite sets $\{E_1, E_2,\cdots,E_m\}$, will be called a finite hypergraph with vertex set $X=\cup iE_i$, for $i=1,2,\cdots,m$. There is a binary relation, R, between the vertices and edges of a hypergraph with E_iRx_j if and only x_i belongs to E_j. This can be represented in the usual way by an incidence matrix, M, where $m_{ij}=1$ if x_iRE_j and $m_{ij}=0$ otherwise.

Figure 4 presents relational structure of the proposed virtual learning environment. There are three main educational participants (student, teacher and parent) that communicate with virtual learning environment which can be seen as the fourth educational participant because of its educational communication properties.

According to definitions about hypergraph domain, we can now define appropriate definitions for virtual learning environment (further VLE).

We define hypergraph (Figure 5) on finite set $X = \{x_1, x_2, x_3, x_4, x_5, x_6, x_7\}$, where follows: x_1 = {student}, x_2 = {teacher}, x_3 = {parent}, x_4 = {student, teacher}, x_5 = {student, parent}, x_6 = {teacher, parent}, x_7 = {VLE}, and $H = (E_1, E_2, E_3, E_4)$; E_1 = student, E_2 = teacher, E_3 = parent, E_4 = VLE. For hypergraph $H_E(X,R)$ is defined incidence matrix shown in Table 1.

Figure 4. The graph of a relation from a set to itself

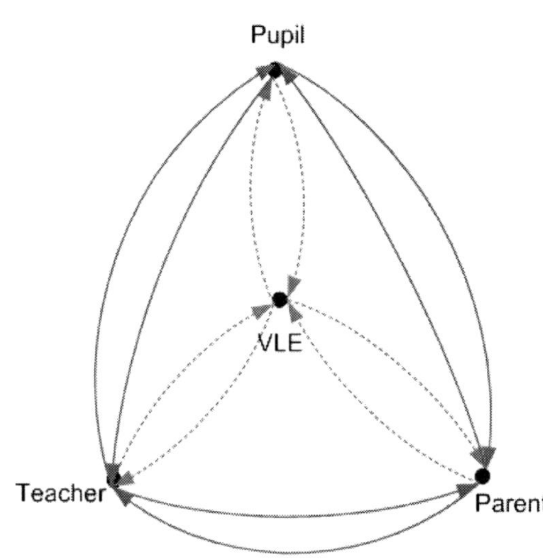

Figure 5. The hypergraph $H_E(X,R)$ and the conjugate hypergraph $H_X(E,R)$

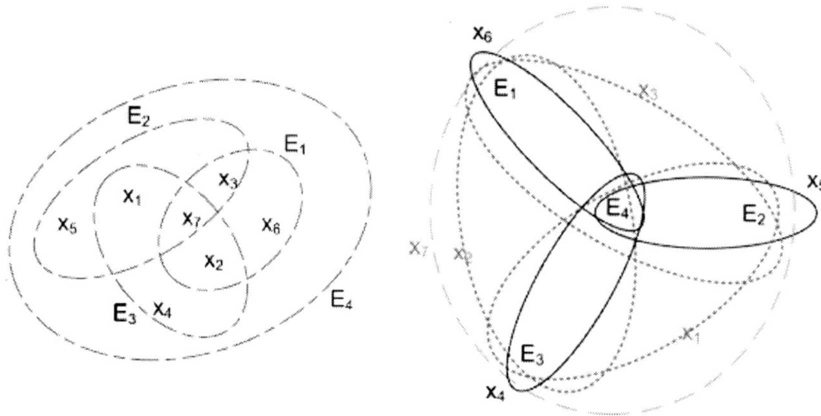

So, hypergraph $H_E(X,R)$ is defined by the elements of E being related to subsets of X. The conjugate hypergraph, $H_X(E,R)$ is defined by the elements of X being related to subsets of E (Figure 5).

Therefore, a class of subsets of X for hypergraph $H_E(X,R)$ is given by,

$$\{E_1\rightarrow\{x_2,x_3,x_6,x_7\}, E_2\rightarrow\{x_1,x_3,x_5,x_7\}, E_3\rightarrow\{x_1,x_2,x_4,x_7\}, E_4\rightarrow\{x_1,x_2,x_3,x_4,x_5,x_6,x_7\}\}$$

and class of subsets of B for hypergraph $H_X(E,R)$ is given by

$$\{x_1\rightarrow\{E_2,E_3,E_4\}, x_2\rightarrow\{E_1,E_3,E_4\}, x_3\rightarrow\{E_1,E_2,E_4\}, x_4\rightarrow\{E_3,E_4\}, x_5\rightarrow\{E_2,E_4\}, x_6\rightarrow\{E_1,E_4\}, x_7\rightarrow\{E_1, E_2\, E_3,E_4\}\}$$

Table 1. The incidence matrix of $H_E(X,R)$

	X_1	X_2	X_3	X_4	X_5	X_6	X_7
E_1	0	1	1	0	0	1	1
E_2	1	0	1	0	1	0	1
E_3	1	1	0	1	0	0	1
E_4	1	1	1	1	1	1	1

Hypergraph Connectivity and the Galois Lattice

Two hypergraph edges are k-near if they share k vertices.(Wasserman & Faust, 1994) This is an immediate generalization of two network edges being connected by a single vertex. The edges E_i and E_j are k-connected if there is a chain of edges $E_{(1)}, E_{(2)},\cdots, E_{(n)}$, with $E_i = E_{(1)}$, $E_j= E_{(n)}$, and $E_{(h)}$ κ-near $E_{(h+1)}$, $\kappa \geq k$, for $h = 1,\cdots,n\text{-}1$. This is analogous to the existence of a path in a network, and generalizes the notion of connectivity. Intuitively, two edges are "more highly connected" for larger values of k. There is also some other connectivity that is "stronger" than k-connectivity, called star-hub structure. Figure 6 illustrates how the class

Figure 6. Star-hub configuration

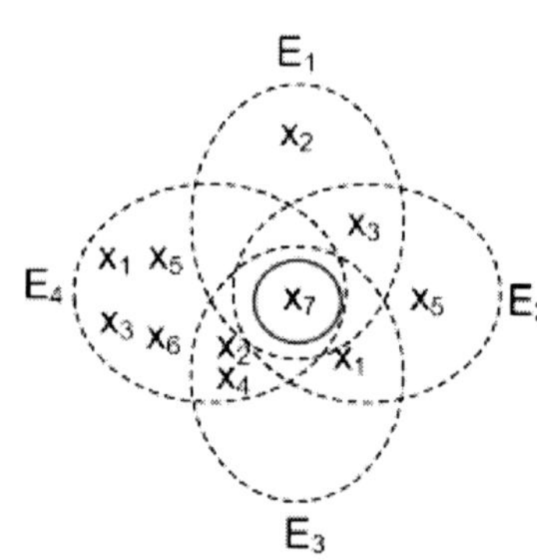

$\{E_1, E_2, E_3, E_4\}$ form a star-like configuration, with the set $E_5=\{x_1\}$ as its hub.

Hypergraphs $H_E(X,R)$ and $H_X(E,R)$ have a close interrelationship. Every hyper-edge of $H_E(X,R)$ is associated with a hyper-edge in $H_X(E,R)$, with all associated elements. For example, $\{E_1, E_2\}$ is associated with $\{x_3,x_7\}$, with both of E_1 and E_2 related to both of x_3 and x_7. These pairs of sets can be arranged in Galois lattice (Figure 7). In the lattice Ø means empty set, and the expressions $(\{E_1, E_2, E_3, E_4\},\emptyset)$ means that no member of X is related to every member of X, while $(\emptyset,\{x_1,x_2,x_3\})$ means that no member of X is related to every member of X.

A lattice is partially ordered set in which every two elements have a supremum and an infimum. We say that $(x,y) < (x',y')$ if $x \subset x'$ and $y \subset y'$. For any (x,y) and (x',y'), $(x \cup x', y \cap y')$ exists by construction. It is the supremum of (x,y) and (x',y'), since $(x,y) < (x \cup x', y \cap y')$ and $(x',y') < (x \cup x', y \cap y')$. Similarly $(x \cap x', y \cup y')$ belongs to the system, and is the infimum of (x,y) and (x',y'), since $(x \cap x', y \cup y') < (x,y)$ and $(x \cap x', y \cup y') < (x',y')$. In Figure 7 a line is drawn between each pair of sets and their supremum and infimum, to produce the lattice.

Multilevel Structure in Virtual Learning Environment

Multilevel mathematical theory lays the basis on very common and elemental idea that wholes are assembled from parts.(Klir, 1991) Let P be the set of parts of an object W, then these parts have to be assembled into W under a relation R. *We* write $R{:}P \rightarrow W$. If P has n elements, then R is an n-ary relation.

Multidimensional polyhedra can be used as a mathematical representation of emergence (that is related with idea of multilevel systems), and therefore enable the definition of multilevel structure. If vertices exists at one level then structures assembled from vertices, exist at a higher level. Thus the mapping from the set to the simplex moves up the hierarchy of representation, from *Level N* to *Level N+1*.

Figure 8 presents fundamental diagram of multilevel systems, in which hierarchical cones present the assembly of vertices into a polyhedron. Euler circle (ellipse) as the base of the cone represents the set, and apex represents vertex and all together at a higher hierarchical level represent simplex. Assembly relation maps base set to a structure at a higher level in the representation.

Figure 7. The Galois lattice of the relation R between X and E

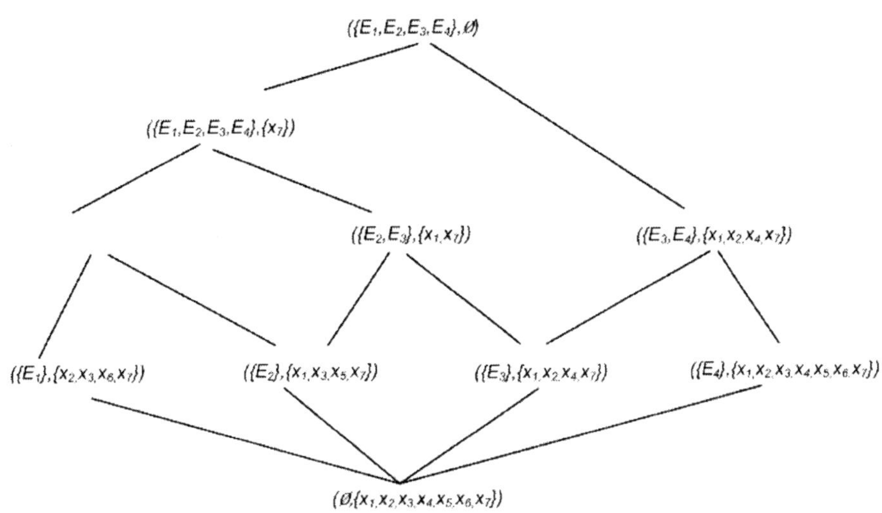

Figure 8. The fundamental diagram of multilevel systems

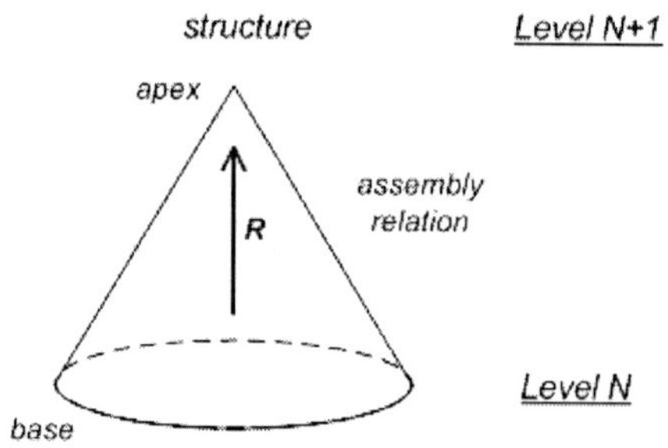

Since the same set can be assembled in many different ways, the cone construction illustrates a many important options. Simplex is represented with set of vertices and relation that assembles vertices into structure. It's related notation is $\langle v_0,v_1,\cdots v_n; R\rangle$.

Figure 9 illustrates multilevel structure of virtual learning environment with its all participants, student, teacher, parent and environment itself, because of its mutual interaction with all other participants. In the *Level N*, on the left side there are group of, each independently, students, teachers and parents, assembling them on *Level N+1*, by relations R_1, R_2 and R_3.

On the right side of the Figure 9, there is virtual learning environment decomposition by its main functionalities (based on Figure 3). They are Community (forums, blogs, wikis, chat), Social network (friendly list, activity streams, contacts) and Participation (open add-ons, content contribution). They are assembled on the *Level N+1*, under the relations R_4, R_5 and R_6. In the *Level N+2*, under the relations R_7 and R_8, educational participant and VLE are incorporated into VLE as its communication participants. Under the relation R_9, elements from *Level N+2* are assembled into multilevel multidimensional virtual learning environment on the *Level N+3*

Figure 9. Hierarchical aggregation in multilevel virtual learning environment

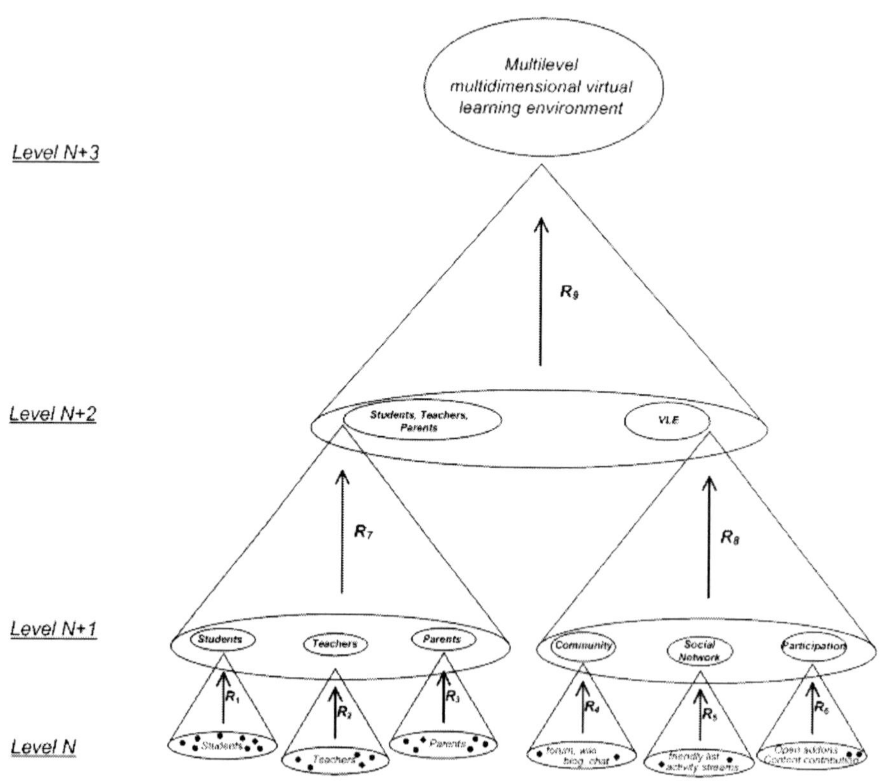

Multidimensional Structure, Q-Analysis and Connectivity

Although Galois lattice construction and hypergraphs can show some major characteristic like showing relations based on sets, or showing the sets of components in multilevel systems, they cannot also represent the structured sets of components.(Kemp & Lee, 2000) Therefore, it is necessary to make assembly relations explicit and develop algebraic properties of the relations as a natural multidimensional generalization of network theory.

N-ary relations are a natural generalization of binary relations that can be represented by a natural generalization of the vertices and directed edges of network. For example, a 3-ary relation can be represented by a triangle, a 4-ary relation can be represented by a tetrahedron, and in general an *n*-ary relation can be represented by an *n*-hedron. Polyhedra can be seen as a multidimensional generalization of vertices and edges in a network: vertices have dimension zero, lines have dimension one, triangles have dimension two, tetrahedral have dimension three, and in general *(p+1)*-hedra have dimension *p*. An abstract *p*-dimensional simplex, or *p*-simplex, σ_p, is defined by an ordered set of vertices, $\sigma_p=\langle v_0,v_1,v_2,\cdots v_p\rangle$. Although polyhedra graphical presentation of simplices can carry the intuition of relation structure, their algebraic formulation provides the basis for rigorous theory.

Since multidimensional polyhedra (simplices) with all their faces can be used for representing *n*-ary relationships, it can also form multidimensional networks called simplicial complexes.

Hypernetwork is a set of simplices that contains just the shared faces. Simplices within hypernetworks have a connectivity structure analogous to connectivity in networks. However, this connectivity exists at different dimensional levels.

Two simplices are said to be *q*-near if they share a *q*-dimensional face. Thus the simplices are 0-near if there is a single vertex in common and has dimension zero; 1-near if there are two vertices that make a one-dimensional line, and 2-near if there are three vertices that make a two-dimensional triangle, and so on.

Two simplices are *q*-connected if there is a chain of pairwise *q*-near simplices between them. A listing of *q*-connected components is called a *Q*-analysis. *Q*-analysis is based on the connectivity of pairs of simplices.

In the next section we will define algebraic formulation for proposed virtual learning environment.

Let $\langle v_0,v_1,\cdots,v_p\rangle$ be a simplex σ_p. Then $\{v_0,v_1,\cdots,v_p\}$ is defined to be its vertex set. The simplex $\sigma_G=\langle v'_0, v'_1,\cdots,v'_G\rangle$ is a face of $\sigma_p=\langle v_0,v_1,\cdots,v_p\rangle$, written $\sigma_G \lesssim \sigma_p$, if $\{v'_0,v'_1,\cdots,v'_G\}\cdots\subseteq v_0,v_1,\cdots,v_p\}$.

Virtual learning environment system is composed of four simplices σ_p: σ_1 representing virtual learning environment (VLE), σ_2 representing students group, σ_3 representing teachers group and σ_4 representing parents group.

A simplicial complex, or a set of simplices with all its faces for virtual learning environment, is presented in Figure 10, and it was structured following these assumptions.

Virtual learning environment (VLE) has the largest access rights and it is connected to all possible educational participants, therefore it is represented by 6-hedron. Since virtual learning environment is the centre of educational communication in this system, all other participants

Figure 10. The simplicial complex

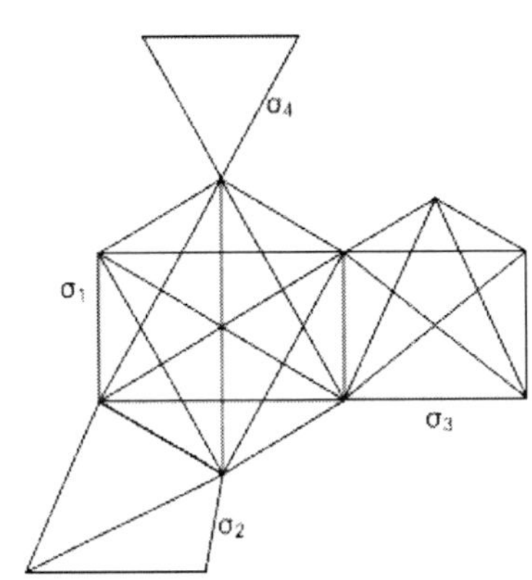

(students, teachers and parents) have access to it following different types of access rights. Since parents have the smallest access rights, it has only one shared vertex toward VLE. Teachers and students have the same number of shared vertex, two, because even they don't have the same enabled possibilities managing the virtual learning environment, they still have the same scale of it (students have their portfolios, wikis, etc. while teachers have management through students learning progress). But when we are talking about polyhedra that are going to represent group of teachers and students, there is some difference in hierarchy. Although students have many kinds of activities on virtual learning environment, still teachers have some higher authority managing major part of it. Therefore, teachers are represented by 5-hedron and students by 4-hedron. Parents with the smallest range of activities over VLE are represented by 3-hedron.

The q-connected components in simplicial complexes are the sets of mutually q-connected simplices. For example, Figure 11 presents components connected by lines or components through one-dimensional face, of simplicial complex in Figure 10.

Table 2 presents the shared vertex matrix, which shows the number of shared vertices between the

Figure 11. Components connected by lines

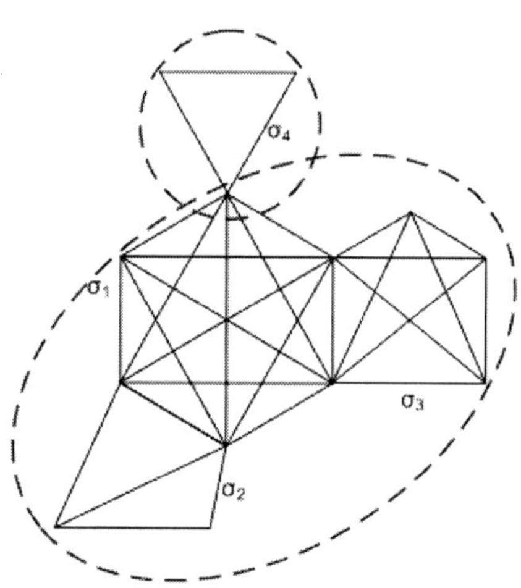

Table 2. Shared vertex matrix

	σ_1	σ_2	σ_3	σ_4
σ_1	6	2	2	1
σ_2	2	4	0	0
σ_3	2	0	5	0
σ_4	1	0	0	3

Table 3. Q-analysis for Figure 10

q=5	$\{\sigma_1\}$
q=4	$\{\sigma_1\},\{\sigma_3\}$
q=3	$\{\sigma_1\},\{\sigma_2\},\{\sigma_3\}$
q=2	$\{\sigma_1\},\{\sigma_2\},\{\sigma_3\},\{\sigma_4\}$
q=1	$\{\sigma_1,\sigma_2,\sigma_3\},\{\sigma_4\}$
q=0	$\{\sigma_1,\sigma_2,\sigma_3,\sigma_4\}$

simplices in Figure 10. From this we can make a listing of q-connected components, or make Q-analysis shown in Table 2.

For example, there are two distinct components at $q=1$, which become connected as a single component at $q=0$ (Figure 11).

Figures 12 through 14 shows the relationship between a group of students, teachers and parents independently, in other words it shows how information can pass through social structure determined by relations. For example, among students there can be several different groups in which information can flow in different ways, depending on priority of that information in that group and how is that group connected. In general the more highly connected the structure, the more rapidly information is transmitted.

Dynamics of Multidimensional Multilevel Virtual Learning Environment

Many complex systems have multidimensional and multilevel structure, and all possible changes can be represented with numerical functions or with relational structure.(Foote, 2007)

Figure 12. The transmission of information on educational participant structure (students)

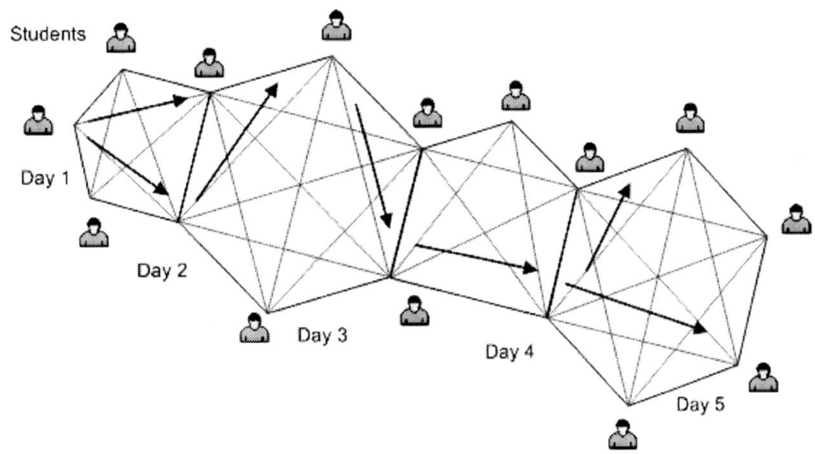

Figure 13. The transmission of information on educational participant structure (teachers)

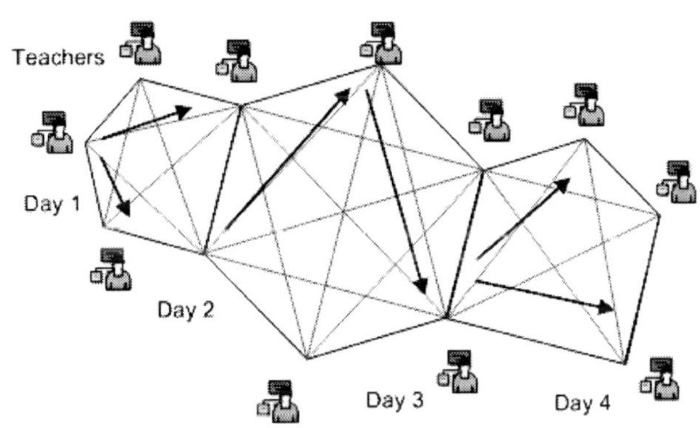

Figure 14. The transmission of information on educational participant structure (parents)

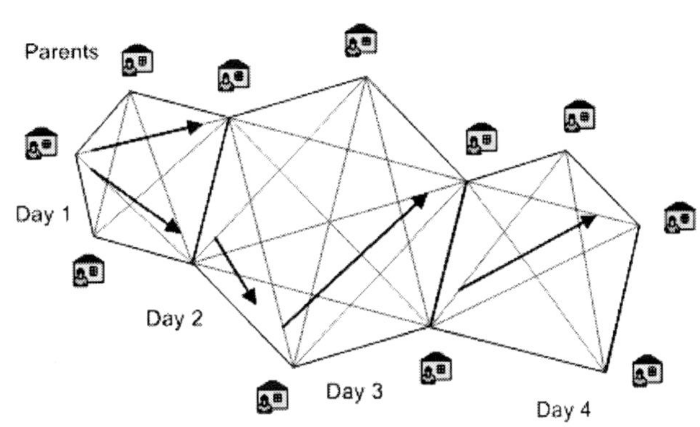

The formation of a relational polyhedron can be considered to be an event in a system. The event gives a way of marking system time. For example, before and after polyhedron existed.

The event of a clock can be used to measure time in physical systems, but for example, in socio-technical systems, time can be measured with some structural events. Moreover, system events measure time in systems in a natural way, for example, the event of getting some information will determine when some kind of action can be done according to obtained information and not a schedule in clock time.

Figure 15 illustrates the example of gathering all educational participants through social elements of virtual learning environment, and therefore getting information about all kind of activities in educational process. That kind of system is presented with simplex at *Level N+2*. Before all needed events, all elements that make the mentioned simplex were just a set of vertices. So, the situation before and after can be discriminated, and we say that the formation of the simplex is a polyhedral event. Polyhedral events mark the passage of system time, and since the events occur at different levels on multilevel systems, they have to be coordinated.

Forming above mentioned system involves a few levels to go through. *Level N-1* to *Level N* represents gathering all educational participants (students, teachers, parents and virtual learning environment), and on the other side represents impact of Web 2.0 on e-learning systems. *Level N* to *Level N+1* on the one side represents including all participants of e-learning into system, and on the other side represents requests for different kind of educational activities. *Level N+1* to *Level N+2* represents the main event of involving all educational participants into all educational activities. Each of these events creates higher level structure in the hierarchy.

Figure 15. The formation of multilevel multidimensional events

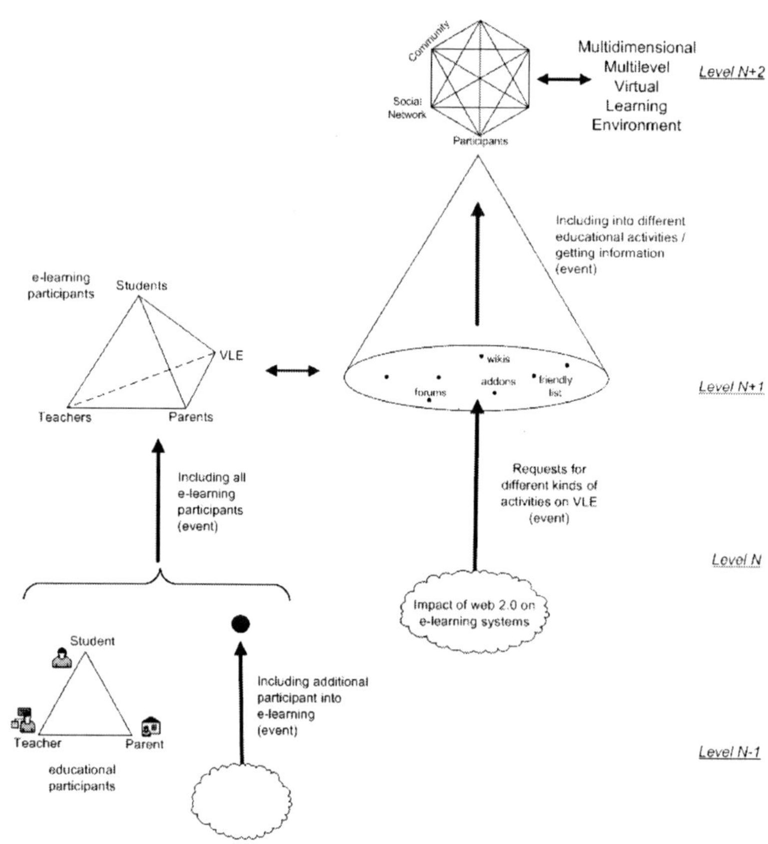

CONCLUSION

Virtual learning environment can be seen as complex system considering both technology and users.

Namely, there is an issue about modelling VLE system, its efficacy and productivity evaluation, which usually presents evaluation of only one or few aspects of VLE system.

The main issue is how to model VLE system that would be able to show overall system efficacy and productivity, and not only part of it as we can find in most of nowadays systems' evaluations.

Nowadays communication encompasses not only communication of new users' generation (called also digital population), but also communication with software modules, that can stand for technology part of any VLE system. Therefore, every communication participant should be involved in VLE according to users' structure representation. Speaking about technology complexity, there are many technologies that could be implemented, but the main point is how to use any kind of it to build some educational environment that could ease the process of learning and exchanging information among all system users.

Complexity science is one of mathematical methods that can help in system modelling process. It allows representing VLE as multilevel, multidimensional educational environment, considering communication of all participants, and every aspect of technology that could improve that communication.

Although complexity science is not yet mature, and there are still many questions to be answered, still complexity science enables us to understand better why some system are complex, offers new methods for modelling complex systems as VLE.

REFERENCES

Ashby, W. R. (1956). *An introduction to cybernetics*. London: Chapman & Hall.

Berge, C. (1976). *Graphs and hypergraphs*. Amsterdam: North-Holland Pub. Co.

Bertalanffy, L. (1968). *General System Theory: Foundations. Development, Applications*. New York: George Braziller.

Burger, T. (2003). Percepcija i stavovi studenata prema" u enju putem Interneta. *EDUpoint časopis o informacijskim tehologijama u obrazovanju, III*(16). Retrieved from http://edupoint.carnet.hr/casopis/broj-16/clanak-01/sazetak.html

Dillenbourg, P., & Schneider, D. (1995). *ICCAI 95 article*. Retrieved October 27, 2009, from http://tecfa.unige.ch/tecfa/research/CMC/colla/iccai95_1.html

DiNucci, D. (1999). Design & New Media: Fragmented Future-Web development faces a process of mitosis, mutation, and natural selection. *PRINT-NEW YORK*, *53*, 32–35.

Foote, R. (2007). Mathematics and Complex Systems. *Science*, *318*(5849), 410–412. doi:10.1126/science.1141754

Grubišić, A., Stankov, S., & Žitko, B. (2007). EVEDIN: A System for Automatic Evaluation of Educational Influence. *International Journal WSEAS Transactions on Computers*, *6*(1), 1109–2750.

Hewitt, A., & Forte, A. (2006). Crossing boundaries: Identity management and student/faculty relationships on the Facebook. *Poster presented at CSCW, Banff, Alberta*.

Johnson, J. (2006). Can Complexity Help Us Better Understand Risk? *RISK MANAGEMENT-LEICESTER*, *8*(4), 227. doi:10.1057/palgrave.rm.8250023

Kemp, Z., & Lee, H. (2000). A Multidimensional Model for Exploratory Spatiotemporal Analysis. In *Proceedings of the 5th International Conference on GeoComputation*.

Klir, G. J. (1991). *Facets of systems science*. Springer.

Laningham, S. (2006, August 22). *Developerworks Interviews: Tim Berners-Lee*, CT316. Retrieved September 16, 2009, from http://www.ibm.com/developerworks/podcast/dwi/cm-int082206txt.html

O'Reilly, T. (2006, October 12). Web 2.0 compact definition: Trying again. *O'Reilly radar*. Retrieved September 15, 2009, from http://radar.oreilly.com/2006/12/web-20-compact-definition-tryi.html

Oreilly, T. (2007). What Is Web 2.0: Design Patterns and Business Models for the Next Generation of Software. *SSRN eLibrary*, Communications & Strategies, (65), 17-37.

Peraya, D., Piguet, A., & Joye, F. (1999). *Rapport d'information sur les mondes virtuels. Rapport rédigé pour l» office fédéral de la formation professionnelle et le la technique*. Suisse: Berne.

Prensky, M. (2001). Digital natives, digital immigrants. *Horizon*, *9*(5), 1–6. doi:10.1108/10748120110424816

Simon, H. A. (1996). *The sciences of the artificial*. Cambridge, MA: The MIT Press.

Wasserman, S., & Faust, K. (1994). *Social network analysis: Methods and applications*. Cambridge, UK: Cambridge Univ Pr.

Chapter 6
Mobile Learning

Marija Zelić
University of Split, Croatia

ABSTRACT

Mobile learning, as the "portable and personal" fashion of e-learning, is intended to enhance the efficiency and effectiveness of learning in the context of handheld terminals. Most present-day learning systems run on desktop computers and are not designed for use on mobile devices such as mobile phones, smart phones, Personal Digital Assistants, etc. Mobile learning systems aim to improve the quality of learning by providing mobile learners with an easy, contextualized and ubiquitous access to knowledge. This chapter gives an overview of the current state of knowledge and research in the m-learning domain, describes issues and problems pertinent to mobile learning and offers our approach to solving these problems in the form of a mobile intelligent tutoring model we are currently developing. Given the present absence of relevant literature and referent material we think that this chapter provides developers with some new ideas.

INTRODUCTION

The use of information and communication technology (ICT) in education is becoming more and more common as the price of technology drops and its general availability is increased. Along with recent information and communication technology developments, learning and teaching has moved towards new paradigms, one of which is certainly e-learning. In fact, e-learning systems base their operation on information access, electronic transition and communication services, which are all to be provided by artifacts of the information infrastructure (Rosić, Glavinić & Stankov, 2001).

Furthermore, developments in the wireless infrastructure have paved the way to a new e-learning paradigm named mobile learning. Mobile learning (m-learning) is nowadays attracting a lot of attention as the next kind of computer supported learning, the respective implementation issues

DOI: 10.4018/978-1-61692-008-1.ch006

however still being the object of more detailed further elaboration (Glavinić, Rosić & Zelić, 2007). Most present-day learning systems run on desktop computers and are not designed for use on mobile devices such as mobile phones, smart phones, Personal Digital Assistants (PDAs), etc. We have to consider the fact that we live in an information age and expect to have fast and reliable ways of accessing any kind of information, anytime and anywhere, by using whatever technology we have at hand. In fact, we are now at the break of a new world of ubiquitous computing that will bridge the gap between our largely sedentary lives and new forms of nomadic life (Glavinić, Rosić & Zelić, 2007). Education is not an exception. Mobile learning systems aim to improve the quality of learning by providing mobile learners with an easy, contextualized and ubiquitous access to knowledge. Latest achievements in the mobile technology compel us to expand the world of e-learning to this new environment and explore the potential benefits. The systems are intended to blend into a mobile learner's daily routine, by being at the reach of a hand, hence enabling the learner to brush up on her/his knowledge, review some referent material, take a short quiz and the like; all this while waiting for a friend at an airport, waiting in a queue at a bank, traveling by train, etc. The global intention is to make learning "a way of being".

The chapter is organized as follows. Section 2 gives an overview of the m-learning domain in terms of different perspectives and definitions, literature review and discussion on the most interesting projects in the field. Section 3 describes issues and problems pertinent to mobile learning and offers our approach to solving these problems in the form of a mobile intelligent tutoring model we are currently developing. Section 4 gives an overall discussion and some conclusion remarks as well as guidelines for future work.

OVERVIEW OF THE M-LEARNING DOMAIN

This section gives an overview of the current state of knowledge and research in the m-learning domain including various definitions, motivation for employing mobile technologies in the learning and teaching process, technical and pedagogical considerations, relation towards e-learning as well as a description of the most commonly referenced m-learning projects. The objective is to explore global trends and investigate an emerging field of great interest to the international education and training communities. The new learning environment incorporates the physical and the digital, the sedentary and the nomadic, and the online, the offline, and the wireless. The section focuses on presenting a set of visions for application and development of the m-learning paradigm and provides the best practice framework to guide the design of high-quality learning experiences.

M-Learning Definitions

M-learning is a term coined to represent the convergence of new mobile technologies, wireless infrastructure and the e-learning domain. M-learning has been variously described and there are many attempts to give a complete definition encompassing pervasive philosophies and practices of education, interpersonal communication, technological implementations as well as the concept of mobility. There are a few interesting definitions containing terms inherent to the m-learning domain.

Quinn (2000) defines m-learning as the intersection of mobile computing and e-learning: accessible resources wherever you are, strong search capabilities, rich interaction, powerful support for effective learning, and performance-based assessment; e-learning independent of location, time and space. Mobilearn (2003) project explores the new m-learning architecture that would support creation, brokerage, delivery and tracking of learning and information contents, using ambient intelligence, location-dependence, personalization, multimedia, instant messaging (text, video) and distributed databases. Vavoula and Sharples (2002) suggest three ways in which mobility may be conceived: in terms of space, in relation to different pursuits in life, and with respect to time. Wagner (2005) asserts that effective mobile learning programs require new digital communication skills, new pedagogies, and new practices. These statements represent visions rather than definitions and it is important to identify the respective assumptions and implications about the m-learning field (McLean, 2003):

- The crucial common element is the intersection between the use of mobile devices and wireless access. As Singh (2003) says: "Mobile computing relates to the ability to interact with the device from anywhere, whereas wireless access defines the communication between computers and devices" (p. 2).
- The concept of delivery and access anywhere, any time is central to the vision.
- The distinction between e-learning and m-learning becomes blurred in much of the analysis.
- Most of the key proponents highlight the promise of rich interactivity, total connectivity and powerful processing.
- Transformation of learning is the ultimate assumption behind the m-learning paradigm.
- The capacity for customization, personalization and flexible adaptation are constant themes in the current discourse.
- The lifelong learning vision underpins much of the m-learning debate.
- Pedagogical debate has gained momentum- as it has in the e-learning space, but remains problematic.
- Ubiquitous access through the use of mobile devices is perhaps the most persistent driver in the m-learning paradigm.
- The potential return on investment is often cited, although unproved in current practice.
- There is very often confusion between the issues involved in providing mobile device/wireless access in fixed locations such as the classroom and the challenge of providing distributed asynchronous access within dispersed learning communities.
- There is a tendency to reinvent the wheel in terms of many of the issues already addressed in e-learning communities.
- The difficulties of preparing and delivering and evaluating relevant learning content in the form of learning objects are invariably underestimated.
- The need to link m-learning technologies to institutional infrastructure is recognized but, as yet, little explored.
- Convergence of technologies, standards and services is very often assumed but the understanding of how, and when, such convergence will happen remains elusive.
- There is a considerable amount of semantic confusion in the attempts to conceptualize the m-learning paradigm.

Obviously there is a lot of potential as well as open questions when it comes to m-learning. Rapid development of new technologies makes it difficult for e-learning communities to apply the technological infrastructure in a systematic way. E-learning (and consequently m-learning) needs to be considered in a much wider context taking into account the pedagogical, cultural, ethical and many other issues, something that is often underestimated and neglected. Additionally, m-learning should also account for a learner moving freely in her/his physical and virtual environment. Laouris and Eteokleous (2005) discuss mobile learning as a function of the available and dynamically changing technology. A socially and educationally responsible definition should also consider time-varying levels of attention, interest, preferences and motivation of the learner. Therefore it is important to evaluate the state-of-play in current m-learning initiatives and provide a conceptual framework to support the design of mobile learning.

M-Learning Objectives

Motivations for employing mobile technologies in the learning and teaching process have been summarized by Kukulska-Hulme and Traxler (2005) in their book "Mobile Learning: A Handbook for Educators and Trainers". The main objectives involve improving access, exploring changes in the learning and teaching process, and alignment with institutional or business aims:

Access:

- Improving access to assessment, learning materials and learning resources;
- Increasing flexibility of learning for students;
- Compliance with special educational needs and disability legislation.

Changes in teaching and learning:

- Exploring the potential for collaborative learning, for increasing students' appreciation of their own learning process, and for consolidation of learning;
- Guiding students to see a subject differently than they would have done without the use of mobile devices;
- Identifying students' needs for just-in-time knowledge;
- Exploring whether the time and task management facilities of mobile devices can help students to manage their studies;
- Reducing cultural and communication barriers between staff and students by using channels that students like;
- Wanting to know how wireless/mobile technology alters attitudes, patterns of study, and communication activity among students.

Alignment with institutional or business aims:

- Making wireless, mobile, interactive learning available to all students without incurring the expense of costly hardware;
- Delivering communications, information and training to large numbers of people regardless of their location;
- Blending mobile technologies into e-learning infrastructures to improve interactivity and connectivity for the student;
- Harnessing the existing proliferation of mobile phone services and their many users.

Mobile learning, as the "portable and personal" fashion of e-learning, is intended to enhance the efficiency and effectiveness of learning in the context of handheld terminals. Wagner (2005) identifies three main reasons for the global uptake of mobile learning: a) there are more wireless networks, services, and devices than ever before, b) consumers are demanding better mobile experiences than ever before, and c) people want "anytime, anywhere" connections more than ever before. The value of deploying mobile technologies in the service of learning and teaching seems to be both self-evident and unavoidable.

Technical Considerations

Mobile computing environment possibly introduces some complex implementation issues. Namely, the wireless environment (GSM, UMTS, WLAN) is much different from the standard "wireline" one: bandwidth, delay, error rate, interference and the like, may change dramatically as the learner changes her/his location. Another thing to consider is the characteristics of different mobile devices used for accessing the m-learning systems, spanning from low-performance mobile phones to high-performance laptops. Features like processing power, amount of memory and display qualities have to be taken into account. There is however a relatively common agreement that handheld devices will outsell PCs and laptops in the very near future; tablet PCs are becoming more and more powerful with strong potential for m-learning. Nevertheless, it is important to make some assessment of the current state of mobile technologies, connectivity and applications. McLean (2003) lists some of the obstacles in terms of implementing any significant m-learning application: a) limited memory and storage are major inhibitors, b) screens are generally too small for the use of any sophisticated application, c) intermittent connectivity is a potential barrier, d) links to learning management systems or enterprise systems are in an embryonic stage of development, e) the industry is plagued by proprietary solutions, f) existing applications are not easily integrated to the mobile technology environment, g) start-up costs are invariably high, h) tracking outcomes is difficult, i) security is a major issue, j) continuous technology development militates against stability and sustainability in terms of mounting viable m-learning applications. There are initial reports on using various mobile devices for some kind of m-learning: tablet PCs, iPods, palmtop computers, PDAs, mobile phones and so on. Widespread availability of the technology is fundamental but by itself insufficient for effective learning environments.

The common mobile system components as well as technical characteristics that should be taken into account are summarized by Singh (2003) as follows:

- Authoring tools for content capture and conversion for mobile delivery;
- Mobile games and simulation templates;
- Mobile learning content management systems (mLCMSs) that download and manage a repository of mobile content;
- Mobile learning management systems (mLMSs) to track mobile learning use;
- Enterprise application integration tools such as Customer Relationship Management (CRM) and Human Resources Information System (HRIS).

Pedagogical Considerations

Mobile learners usually work alone and have little time on hand for educational activities. With this in mind the m-learning systems should be able to "play the role of a human expert" and provide the learners with intelligent help and support. This requires personalization i.e. adaptation of the systems to the learners, their individual characteristics, abilities, learning backgrounds, preferences and so on. Obviously we are talking about intelligent tutoring systems extended to the mobile computing environment. Many pedagogical issues are inherited from the e-learning domain. Even though e-learning has been rapidly developing over the last few years, there is not a lot of research on pedagogical effectiveness of learning through technology enhancements. Lately there are signs of growing interest in this direction. The m-learning community faces even more difficult challenges due to limitations of the mobile computing environment. Interestingly enough terms like adaptability, personalization, ambient intelligence and context awareness appear on regular basis in the m-learning literature; there is yet little evidence however that present-day m-learning systems actually provide these capabilities. It is important to emphasize that the pedagogical issues need to be constantly reevaluated due to evolving learner behaviors, technology advances as well as changes in organizational and institutional needs.

Cobcroft, Towers, Smith and Bruns (2006) in their "Literature review into mobile learning in the university context" identify a new breed of students evolved from a constant exposure to digital technologies, gadgets, games, and mobile devices: 'the natives': those learners who think and process information fundamentally differently from their predecessors, 'the immigrants', whose interaction with these tools is not innate. Generational differences are measured by the ease by which they adopt and adapt to new technologies. Oblinger (2004) describes the 'millennial student' as being digitally literate, 'always on', mobile, experimental, community oriented, focused on 'connectedness' and social interaction, and as having preference for group-based activities in study and social occasions. The millennial generation, being in possession of an information technology mindset and a highly developed skill in multitasking, stays in contact through SMS, mobile phones, chat rooms, and email, while simultaneously playing computer games, listening to music, and watching television (Frand, 2000; Oblinger, 2003). Today's learners have desire to be creative, to collaborate and gain celebrity, which brings focus to the do-it-yourself (DIY) user-led creation of content. Thomas (2005) describes the potential for institutions as 'pervasive learning', where a learner "authors himself, in a location that the learner finds meaningful and relevant" (p. 1). Development of such pervasive learning models cannot be the end in itself, but is a response to learners' new ways of being. In addition to this new kind of learners, mobile learning encompasses a range of learners varying from mature-aged, gifted, international and remote learners, as well as those with cognitive, behavioral or social problems, or with physical or mental difficulties. Attewell (2005) enumerates some benefits of learning by using mobile devices:

- Improving literacy and numeric skills;
- Encouraging independent and collaborative learning experiences;
- Identifying areas where learners need assistance and support;
- Mitigating resistance by using ICT;
- Engaging reluctant learners;
- Enabling learners to remain more focused for longer periods and promote self-esteem and self-confidence.

By offering flexibility, ubiquity of access to information, and motivating increased engagement, mobile technologies and infrastructure facilitate the revolution of "always-on learning, accessible to the masses, but tailored to the individual" (Thomas, 2005, p. 5). Many authors emphasize the possibilities of coordination, communication, organization, negotiation, interactivity and mobility, within the learning and teaching process taking place outside the classroom.

Organizational and institutional aims, described in the section "M-learning objectives", are the result of external factors (market trends, competition, government policy) as well as internal (student preferences, pedagogical approaches). Technology advances inevitably affect the learning and teaching process, and it is imperative that institutions adjust their methods to the new learning paradigms. Terms like blended learning, intelligent tutoring and user-centered approach are now in the focus of attention. There are some issues however that need to be addressed: a) selecting the appropriate technology infrastructure (based on device cost, quality, compatibility, reliability, ease of use, suitability, security, privacy, ethical concerns, pedagogical approach, etc.), b) learning management, c) gaining institutional support for m-learning, d) deciding which curriculum is best suited for the m-learning environment, e) lack of teacher confidence and training, f) technical difficulties with devices, g) evaluation and quality assurance, and so on. Obviously there is a need for the conceptual framework that would guide the design of user-centered learning environment based on the mobile technology. Despite the issues, mobile learning offers great possibilities and novelty approaches to the learning and teaching process. Cobcroft, Towers, Smith and Bruns (2006, p. 30) made a very interesting observation about a 'tipping point' where the uptake of mobile and wireless technologies gains a critical mass thus compelling institutions to adopt effective and efficient mobile learning plans. It is beyond this tipping point that the potential for pervasive and seamless m-learning pedagogical approaches will be realized for learners, teachers, and institutions.

Relation towards E-Learning

Information and communication technology (ICT) has become an integral part of the educational system for either assisting a teacher in realizing a traditional lecture or in completely substituting the teacher. E-learning implies using various aspects of ICT in education, and most commonly refers to teaching contents on the Web, multimedia discs, Web sites, forums, blogs, animations, simulations, games, and so on. The American Society for Training and Development (ASTD) defines e-learning as "instructional content or learning experience delivered or enabled by electronic technology" (ASTD, 2001). Due to developments in the wireless infrastructure the e-learning paradigm was inevitably expanded to mobile devices. The mobile learning systems are viewed as an extension of the existing e-learning systems and certainly not as their replacement. The m-learning systems are intended for support and improvement of the learning and teaching process by providing learners with "anytime, anywhere and any device" access to knowledge. The global intention is to support the new philosophy of ubiquitous and pervasive computing. Therefore e-learning and m-learning can be viewed as a continuum based on deployment of more sophisticated technologies. Distinction between e-learning and m-learning is often ambiguous and most of the advantages as well as limitations of e-learning are inherited in the m-learning paradigm. Wagner (2005, p. 47) states that "the employment of mobile devices will be far from a panacea for the problems currently faced in education unless implementations of m-learning take heed of lessons 'e-learned'. Sharma and Kitchens (2004) summarize the transition from e-learning to m-learning in the following table.

The emphasis is on rich communication, collaboration and student creativity, as well as flexible timing. Development of both e-learning and m-learning programs should be iterative and based on feedback from students, teachers and administrators. McGovern and Gray (2005) conducted a qualitative survey on e- learning at five universities in the Australian Technology Network. The organizational and management questions can also be applied to m-learning and used for evaluation and quality assurance of the programs: a) from the student perspective, what are useful online learning resources and activities, b) what can a wide range of staff do that provides useful online learning support for their students, c) what functionality must the technology support, d) what is online learning doing for the University as a whole. These questions provide a normative framework for implementation of successful evaluation structures.

M-Learning Projects

In order to appreciate the impact of mobile learning both as an everyday practice of learners as well as a technology-based educational phenomenon, it is important to give an overview of the m-learning projects being carried out in this domain. The most commonly referenced projects are described in the following.

The MOBIlearn project, coordinated by GIUNTI Ricerca and co-funded by the European Commission (IST Programme) exhibits its latest achievements in the research of next-generation paradigms and interfaces for technology supported

Table 1. Various changes for the m-learning environment (Adapted from (Sharma & Kitchens, 2004))

Pedagogical Changes	
Current e-Learning Methods	*M-Learning (Wireless)*
More Text-based and Graphics-based instructions	More Voice, Graphics and Animation-based instructions
Lecture in classroom or in internet labs	Learning occurring in the field or while mobile
Instructor to Student Communication	
Current e-Learning Methods	*M-Learning (Wireless)*
Time-delayed e-mail (students need to check e-mails or web sites for communication)	Instant announcement of e-mail delivery (as soon as e-mail or communication arrives, students are informed through instant messaging)
Passive communication	Instant communication
Asynchronous	Interactive
	Spontaneous
Student to Student Communication	
Current e-Learning Methods	*M-Learning (Wireless)*
Face-to-Face	Flexible
Audio-teleconference is quite common	Audio-teleconference and Video-teleconference both possible
e-mail-to-e-mail	24/7 instantaneous
Private location	No geographic boundaries
Travel time to reach the internet site	No travel time since wireless internet connectivity
Dedicated time for any group meeting	Flexible timings on 24/7 basis
Poor communication due to group consciousness	Rich communication, due to one-to-one communication, reduced inhibitions

learning in a mobile environment. The project involves 24 partners from the European Community, Israel, Switzerland, USA and Australia. This project explores new ways to use mobile environments to meet the needs of learners, working by themselves and with others. A new m-learning architecture will support creation, brokerage, delivery and tracking of learning and information contents, using ambient intelligence, location-dependence, personalization, multimedia, instant messaging (text, video) and distributed databases. Field trials cover "blended learning" (as part of formal courses); "adventitious, location-dependent learning" (during visits to museums); and "learning to interpret information sources and advice" (acquiring medical information for everyday needs). The high connectivity and functionality may lead to new group behaviors, akin to the SMS phenomenon. The economic benefits of this project will be substantial at European level. The key actors include public bodies, mobile operators, software and learning technologies production companies, mobile devices manufacturers, publishers and content providers, and participants in standards initiatives. The total cost of the project is €7.505.312 of which the European Commission's contribution is €3.505.385. http://www.mobilearn.org/

One of the biggest initiatives in the m-learning domain is **the HandLeR project** at the Educational Technology Research Group, University of Birmingham. The HandLeR (Handheld Learning Resource) project aims to develop personal mobile technologies for learning, based on a deep understanding of how people learn in multiple contexts over their lifetimes. The project brings together researchers with expertise in educational technology, human-centered systems design, education, psychology, communications and digital systems. The main investigated concepts are concept mapping and knowledge sharing, lifelong learning, wearable learning technologies and conversation between mobile learners. http://www.eee.bham.ac.uk/handler/

M-Learning (2001-2004) is a €4.5m 3 year pan-European research and development program supported by the European Commission's IST Programme within the 5th framework. The program is coordinated by Learning and Skills Development Agency (LSDA) and participant organizations include universities and commercial companies from Britain, Italy and Sweden. The m-learning project addresses social and educational problems related to many young adults in the EU: a) poor literacy/numeric skills, b) non participation in conventional education/training, c) lack of access creating ICT "haves"/ "have nots" resulting in inequality of opportunity. The aim is to develop prototype products and services which will deliver information and learning experiences via technologies that are inexpensive, portable and accessible to the majority of EU citizens. The products and services are designed to capture the interest of young adults (16 to 24) who are not currently taking part in education or training. The learning themes focus on subjects of interest to young adults, e.g. football and music, and the modules include activities designed to develop aspects of literacy and numeric skills. M-learning's target audience includes young adults who are unemployed, under-employed or homeless. http://www.ultralab.ac.uk/projects/m-learning/

LearnTone was a Canadian Learning Management System (LMS) called Isopia before Sun Microsystems acquired it in 2001. Sun LearnTone LMS is the only e-learning infrastructure in the marketplace that offers both e-learning and m-learning capabilities delivered entirely using Java. With power and functionality of Sun LearnTone LMS extended to mobile devices, Sun enables enterprises to offer a seamless, blended learning experience extending from classrooms and desktops to PDAs, two-way pagers, mobile phones and hybrid devices. The following scenario is presented. You are checking in at the airport. The line is long - so how do you fill your time? In the line-up, you pull out your PDA and decide to brush up your knowledge on the course you downloaded. At the end of this course you take a short quiz to test your knowledge. When you arrive at the destination, you set up your laptop and the PDA, linking up to your learning portal. You connect- "hot-synch"-directly with your company's LMS which will read the results of your completed courses and automatically update your learner profile. You then decide to download a number of materials and courses for study on the road and at home. Sun's m-learning benefits include convenience, portability, accessibility, flexible learning options, quick access to information and much more. http://www.isopia.com/ILMS/ILMS.html

In 2001 Global Learning Systems announced their system **Learning to Go**, an interactive training solution for wireless mobile users. Learning to Go is ideal for departments intent on providing their mobile workforce with a convenient alternative to a desktop learning environment. You can now extend the learning sessions from the confines of the desktop to true anywhere, anytime convenience. The PDA gives learners the ability to learn wherever they are. Learning to Go provides an organization with an enterprise-wide, scaleable, re-usable learning tool. With GLS's PDA delivered solution, you can: a) review up-to-the-minute product information, b) access key reference materials, c) interact with instructional guides, d) evaluate behaviors and skills, e) upload test results/Q&A, f) download courseware, g) manage the learning process. The entire system is integrated with a central database, allowing end users to learn either at their desktop PC or on the road via their PDA. http://www.globallearningsystems.com/collateral/LearningToGo.pdf

The MIT Teacher Education Program, in conjunction with The Education Arcade, has been working on creating Augmented Reality simulations to engage people in simulation games that combine real world experiences with additional information supplied to them by handheld computers. The first of these games, **Environmental Detectives** (2003), is an outdoor game. Students play the role of environmental engineers who are presented with a scenario at the beginning of the simulation. The spread of toxin is simulated on a location-aware Pocket PC, which functions as a tool which students can use to investigate the toxic spill. Each Pocket PC is equipped with a GPS device, which allows players to sample chemical concentrations in the groundwater depending on their location. This game has been run at three sites, including MIT, a nearby nature center, and a local high school. Early research has shown that this mode of learning is successful in engaging university and secondary school students in large scale environmental engineering studies, and providing an authentic mode of scientific investigation. http://www.educationarcade.org/

The Electronic Guidebook is an Exploratorium research project investigating the use of handheld computing devices and wireless networks to support a richer learning experience for science museum visitors. In collaboration with HP Labs and the Concord Consortium, and with funding from the National Science Foundation, the Exploratorium is testing a network of mobile devices, wireless systems, and Web-based content that supplement the Museum's interactive science exhibits. The goal of the project is to investigate how such a network will allow individuals and groups to engage in a continuum of activities before, during, and after a museum visit to support a deeper engagement with the exhibits and the ideas they can communicate. http://www.exploratorium.org/guidebook/

TenseITS is a mobile intelligent tutoring system for the use of tense in English, designed primarily for Chinese learners of English. The learning environment adapts interaction to the individual learner's needs as well as to contextual features of the learner's location that may affect their ability to study – the likelihood that they will be interrupted by others, their general ability to concentrate at that location, and the amount of time they have available for study. Comparing time, concentration, likelihood of interruption to the learner model attributes (knowledge, difficulties, misconceptions), the system offers an interaction appropriate for that location, time and current learning needs – e.g. in a situation where the learner is likely to be frequently interrupted, the interaction will not require continued focus. Depending on the learner's needs, this may be revision of a previous topic or questions on a current topic. If the learner can concentrate and is unlikely to be interrupted, they may get new material. If the learner has enough time, a combination of activities may be offered (e.g. a tutorial followed by questions, feedback). http://www.eee.bham.ac.uk/bull/papers-pdf/system-05.pdf

mGBL (mobile Game-Based Learning) is a joint venture of ten partner organizations from Great Britain, Italy, Croatia, Austria and Slovenia to work on the development of a platform for the presentation of educational content in a playful and emotional way on mobile devices. The largest challenge within this project is the idea of communicating content from the fields of career guidance, e-Health and e-commerce in an involving and emotional way to different target audiences. Based on innovative methods from the fields of m-learning and the latest research results from the field of didactics, new forms of game-based learning on mobile phones will be developed. The results of this project will enable new forms of learning as well as offering support for traditional learning processes and will offer the opportunity to involve the mobile channel for presentation and training of learning content. The project is being supported by funding from the European Union within the 6th framework Programme amounting to €2.4 m. http://www.mg-bl.com/

MULTI-AGENT SYSTEMS FOR M-LEARNING

The projects described in section 2 have very little regard for social processes and emergent behavior of learning communities. Concepts like adaptation, student management and activity management, adequate m-learning content as well as context awareness do not receive enough attention. The idea of intelligent tutoring as such remains a considerable challenge. Our approach puts emphasis on the intelligent tutoring theory and discusses in detail an agent-based architecture for m-learning that would solve the above mentioned problems. The section gives a theoretical background of the intelligent tutoring theory as well as the agent paradigm, and describes our approach to development of the m-learning systems within the TEx-Sys model, an evolving series of intelligent tutoring systems we have been developing for the last fifteen years. Given the present absence of relevant literature and referent material we think that this section provides developers with some new ideas.

Intelligent Tutoring Systems

Intelligent tutoring systems (ITSs) are the generation of systems intended for support and improvement of the learning and teaching process. Their work is based on simulation of a human teacher in the learning and teaching process. The teaching paradigm of intelligent tutoring systems is based on the following features of a human teacher (Patel, 2001; Stankov, 1997): a) possession of domain knowledge, b) possession of knowledge on teaching methods, c) capability of diagnosing student's knowledge, d) capability of comparing the level of student's knowledge with the domain knowledge, i.e. determining the level of student's domain knowledge acquisition and e) capability of adjusting the teaching methods to students. According to Major (1995) the intelligent tutoring systems are adjusting themselves to individual student's needs in the following ways: a) by varying the difficulty level of teaching contents presented to a student, b) by adjusting the presentation manner, c) by providing help to a student depending on her/his behavior during the system use and d) by adjusting the processing order of individual teaching units. ITSs base their work on an iterative comparison of student's knowledge with a referent model and act after getting information on differences, if there are any.

The Agent Paradigm

In order to discuss a potential multi-agent architecture of the m-learning systems it is necessary to give some basic definitions and explanations. Intelligent agents represent a relatively new software paradigm that brings concepts from the theories of artificial intelligence into the mainstream realm of distributed systems. Agent-Oriented Programming (AOP) models a system as a collection of autonomous interactive agents who share the same goal (e.g. ant colony) or follow their own (e.g. free market economy). The term agent is very broad and it can have different meanings depending on the context. Even though there is no standard definition of an agent, the Wooldridge definition is most commonly used. This definition provides the weak and the strong notion of agency. The weak notion of agency implies the minimum set of properties that most researchers agree on, while the stronger notion is more controversial and a subject of active research (Wooldridge & Jennings, 1995). The weak notion of agency encompasses agents with the following properties:

- Autonomy implies performing complex and often long-term tasks without direct user intervention and complete control over actions and internal state;
- Social ability implies communication with other agents or entities in order to accomplish the given tasks;

- Reactivity refers to monitoring the environment and reacting quickly and efficiently to changes in that environment;
- Proactiveness additionally involves exhibiting goal-directed behavior by taking the initiative.

The strong notion of agency is extending the weak notion with additional human characteristics such as desire, belief, intention, and so on. Furthermore, an agent can be mobile i.e. it can migrate from one computer to the other, it can be benevolent always trying to accomplish the given task, rational by acting in accordance with the goal and not contrary to it, it can have learning possibilities and adjust itself to the environment and user needs, and so on. The architectural model of an agent-oriented system is p2p (peer to peer), as any agent is able to initiate communication with any other agent or be the subject of an incoming communication at any time. There are several development environments for developing multi-agent systems (JADE, ZEUS, RETSINA, IMPACT, etc.), each one with its own characteristics regarding low-level and high-level services, agent architecture, interoperability and so on (Bellifemine, Poggi & Rimassa, 2001; Nwana, Ndumu, Lee & Collis, 1999; Rogers, Ross & Subrahmanian, 2000; Sycara, Giampapa, Langley & Paolucci, 2003).

Agent technology has been the subject of intensive research within the scientific community for several years, but it has only recently been somewhat used for commercial purposes. Multi-agent systems are being used in a variety of applications, ranging from relatively small systems for personal use to complex industrial systems. Examples of industrial domains where multi-agent systems have been deployed include process control, system diagnostics, manufacturing, transportation logistics and network management. Intelligent agents are considered to be a promising approach to developing complex and high-quality systems due to the fact that the agent paradigm enables modeling of the systems in an intuitive and natural way, resembling to human perception of the problem domain. There are a few issues however holding back the agent technology from a global breakthrough. Developing the agent systems requires skills in many different fields such as distributed systems engineering, communication infrastructure, etc. More significantly there is no general consensus on the methodology for analysis and design of such systems: even though a lot of methodologies have been developed (such as Gaia, ROADMAP, SODA, etc.), none of them have reached a high level of maturity (Juan, Pierce & Sterling, 2002; Omicini, 2001; Wooldridge, Jennings & Kinny, 2000). There are also no adequate templates or guidelines for porting existing applications (as well as developing new ones) to the world of agents. Further development of methodologies as well as templates and scenarios for planning multi-agent systems is required (Luck, Ashri & d'Inverno, 2004).

An Agent-Based Architecture for M-Learning

Our analysis of a potential multi-agent architecture for mobile learning is the basis for extending our intelligent tutoring system TEx-Sys to mobile devices. The intention is to enrich the system with delivery of personalized educational contents to mobile devices. This of course would only be the main function of the system; others would include short quizzes, course notifications, adequate chat applications, and so on. The key ideas of the presented analysis can certainly be applied to any similar system. It is important to note that identifying the agents and their responsibilities, modeling of agent acquaintances, agent refinement as well as deployment is system dependent and should be discussed in detail as the specific system requires (Glavinić, Rosić & Zelić, 2008).

Overview of the TEx-Sys System

In order to gain some insight into both functionality and architecture of the system, in the following we give a short overview of TEx-Sys (Tutor-Expert System). By outlining some basic ideas of the system, we can further discuss porting (a part of its) functionality to mobile devices and contemplate on the agents enabling such a migration. The detailed description of the system, its history, pedagogical framework, specifications and methodologies, evaluation, comparison to other similar systems and the like, can be found in (Stankov, Rosić, Žitko & Grubišić, 2007).

The formalism for knowledge representation in the TEx-Sys system is based on semantic networks with frames. Knowledge is represented by concepts (i.e. domain knowledge objects) and semantic relations between them. The concepts can have structural attributes such as textual descriptions, pictures, presentations, documents, sound and animation, URL addresses and the like. Figure 1 shows an illustration of the concept "Heat" in the course "Physics 1". The left side of Figure 1 shows a hierarchical structure of the courseware. A course can be decomposed into the following elements: units which generally include one or more lessons, lessons which include one or more topics, and finally topics which include one or more instructional items. An instructional item is a collection of related concepts from various knowledge bases, but it can also take the form of a dynamic quiz. The system exhibits intelligent behavior by proper sequencing of course elements, adjusting the difficulty level of teaching contents to the student and providing interactive problem solving support.

The TEx-Sys system has its shortcomings, primarily concerning the limited expressiveness of the knowledge representation formalism as well as insufficient adaptation of the system to the student. The future version will include natural language processing (NLP) techniques to provide students with more fluent and intelligible reading materials.

The Analysis

The system analysis should clarify the problem in detail. The resulting tables and diagrams form the basis of the system design which should provide enough technical detail to enable a relatively straightforward implementation of the system. The design phase targets a specific agent platform and it is outside the scope of this section. Following the guidelines provided in the Methodology for the analysis and design of multi-agent systems using JADE (Nikraz, Caire & Bahri, 2006), the

Figure 1. Presentation of a concept in TEx-Sys

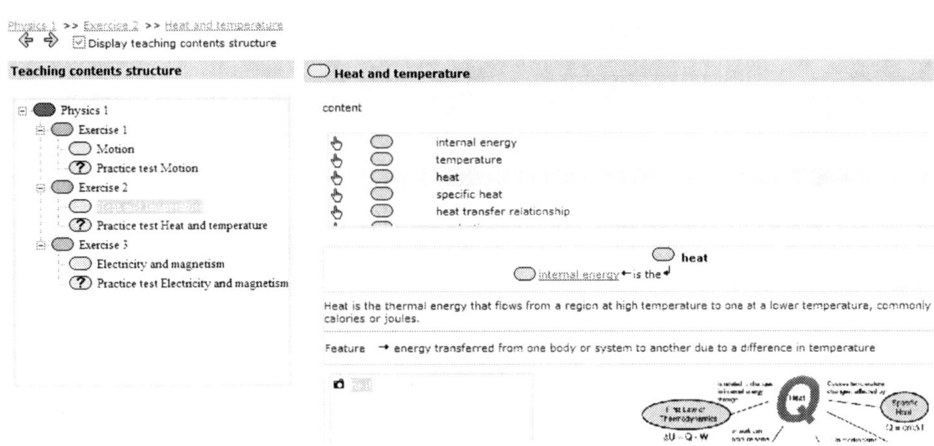

analysis is carried out through a number of steps described in the following sections.

Functional Specification

The first step of the analysis is writing a preliminary list of the system's functions, based on the required functionality and different user requirements. Users of the m-learning system are students, teachers, experts and administrators. Our focus however is transferring the student's environment for learning and testing to the mobile computing environment. Initially the students are prompted to register or login to the system, but they can also view information on the system's services and eventually decide whether or not they are willing to participate. After authentication the students are presented with the main menu comprising the following items:

a) **Profile:** The profile module enables editing of personal information as well as learning preferences. Personal information includes data like name, address, email, username, password and the like. Learning preferences define favorable display properties (e.g. fonts, colors, text size) and learning styles (e.g. visual/auditory, working individually or in a group, different study habits). This information is stored in the student's personal profile.
b) **Scheduler:** The scheduler displays a customizable calendar of the student's activities, plans and tasks. The student can schedule appointments, meetings, events, seminars, exams, subscribe to course notifications, etc.
c) **Learning and Testing:** The learning and testing module is the heart of the system enabling students to learn from adequate teaching materials, test their knowledge and view their efficiency score. A student can select a course, view teaching units' contents, browse related material, take a short quiz or examine her/his previous test results.
d) **Collaboration:** The collaboration module enables various forms of communication among students. This primarily includes the chat functionality for exchanging messages with other students or groups, creating or joining different chat rooms, transferring files, etc. The second functionality is the message board for discussion and comments on distinct topics. A useful feature of this module would be forming of different interest groups based on the students' personal profiles.

Agent Types

After writing the functional specification of the system, the next step involves identifying agent types that would perform the defined functions. These agent types form the backbone of the system. There are two simple and intuitive rules to be followed: a) one agent type should be added per user/device, and b) one agent type should be added per resource. Contemplating the agent types results in an agent diagram as shown in Figure 2 (at this point only the elements in bold are present). The agent diagram is constantly refined with each step of the analysis. The following four element types are present: a) agent types, represented by circles, b) humans, represented by Unified Modeling Language (UML) actor symbols, c) resources, represented by rectangles, and d) acquaintances, represented by arrows (at this point only the agent-human and agent-resource acquaintances are present in the diagram, agent-agent acquaintances are added later). The agent diagram is based on the following agent types, which are discussed in more detail in the following sections:

a) The personal agent assists the student while she/he is using the system;
b) The pedagogical agent guides the learning and teaching process;
c) The device agent enables adaptation of content to mobile devices;

Figure 2. Agent diagram

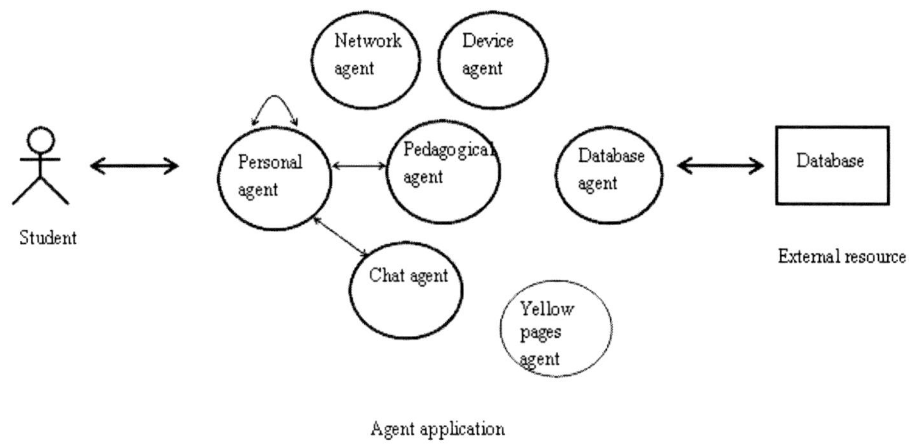

d) The network agent enables adaptation of the system to different networks;
e) The database agent communicates with the system's database, and
f) The chat agent enables communication among students.

a) **Personal Agent:** The first agent newly included in the system is certainly the personal agent. The personal agent resides on a student's mobile device, interacting with her/him usually via a graphical user interface. This agent is responsible for assisting the student while she/he is using the system, providing intelligent help and support, updating her/his personal profile, reacting to the system's notifications, etc. It basically behaves like a secretary, accomplishing routine support tasks thus allowing the student to concentrate on her/his real job. The above specified functionality implies a complex internal architecture of this agent. First of all, the personal agent should contain the student's profile with her/his personal information as well as preferences (e.g. beneficial display properties: fonts, colors, text size; different study habits and learning styles). The way the personal agent builds a student's profile is an area of vast and extensive research (Kuflik & Shoval, 2000). The personal agent containing the student's profile can provide her/him with a more friendly and enjoyable learning environment. Secondly, the personal agent should manage the student's calendar containing her/his appointments, meetings, events, seminars, exams, etc. The above described functions imply that the personal agent maintains its internal knowledge in some form of semantic markup. The agent should be able to manage the knowledge accumulated from different sources and draw inferences from it. Therefore it should be equipped with a reasoning engine. The TEx-Sys mobile version (although at a very early stage) is being developed within the JADE agent platform (Bellifemine, Poggi & Rimassa, 2001). The agents' mental attitudes are modeled by the Jadex BDI reasoning engine (Braubach, Lamersdorf & Pokahr, 2003). Information is structured using the OWL language (OWL, 2004). There are of course different agent platforms, reasoning engines and semantic markup languages, and developers should make their own choice depending on application requirements, personal preferences and the like. Applying some of the above mentioned features to TEx-Sys includes for example: coloring different elements of the course tree (e.g. elements the student has already reviewed), applying preferred themes and styles, alerting the student when a course notification arrives, etc. The agent should be able to communicate with other students' personal agents, collect information, recommendations and so on. Privacy and other security issues should be taken into account.

b) **Pedagogical Agent**: Closely tied to the personal agent is the pedagogical agent responsible for guiding the learning and teaching process. The pedagogical agent represents the heart of the system enabling students to learn from personalized teaching material. The agent is equipped with the student's profile containing information on her/his learning background, previous test results, learning goals, etc. Depending on this information the agent can suggest to the student a revision of previous lessons or some additional material, an exercise, a related test and so on. The educational contents should be customized based on the student's profile, for example a lesson might include more or less explanations, examples and such. The agent should also provide help to the student either explicitly (e.g. a "help" button) or implicitly (monitoring the student's performance and appearing when needed). There already exists a lot of research in this area, especially dealing with animated agents, peer agents, etc (Sklar & Richards, 2006). Our focus however is on the mobile computing environment. This automatically assumes some "downsizing" of the pedagogical agent. Viewing the TEx-Sys mobile version as an extension of the system enabling "study on-the-go", it is clear that the student will not be engaged in an exhaustive learning process but rather in a quick review of learning matter, a short quiz, a simple educational game and the like. With this in mind, the agent should be able to parse educational contents and show the student only the relevant parts. For example, the TEx-Sys student can initially be presented with a course tree as shown in Figure 1. After selecting a course element the associated lesson's summary might be presented along with a link to a short exercise. Content adaptation should be done in close cooperation with the device agent that is described in the following section. It is important to understand that there is no clear boundary between these agents; they have to engage in constant communication, negotiation and information sharing in order to accomplish their tasks. For instance, the pedagogical agent might request data from the database agent, tailor the collected data to fit the student, pass it along to the device and network agents for further content adaptation, and eventually engage the personal agent to apply the appropriate display styles.

c) **Device Agent**: Mobile devices are quite restrictive in terms of screen size, memory and processing power. They typically display less than 20 lines of text, run on different operating systems of restricted functionality, support different markup languages, etc. When displayed directly on mobile devices the content designed for desktop computers is usually aesthetically unappealing and difficult to navigate. So far the content adaptation implied creating different versions of the same content for different target devices. Obviously this approach is device dependent and inflexible. The device agent should be used for dynamic content adaptation which includes layout changes, reconfigurations of content format and so on. This should be coupled with client-side navigation techniques enabled by the personal agent. Additionally the device profile containing physical characteristics of the device (color depth, screen size, memory) can be used, e.g. the CC/PP profile (CC/PP, 2007). There are some simple ways of adapting content to mobile devices based on device profile and student preferences (Zhang, 2007):

- The "fit to screen" approach produces a scaled-down version of the content by removing or shrinking images, using smaller fonts and casting out irrelevant parts;
- The "hierarchical display" of the content is suitable for navigating a large document, providing the student with a global view of the document and enabling selection of a particular section;
- Different visualization techniques for maximizing the display space (e.g. the fisheye view, the circular interface, etc.);
- Methods for multimedia content adaptation (e.g. layered encoding, rate shaping, etc.).

The device agent of the TEx-Sys mobile version can use a combination of the above mentioned techniques for content adaptation. The agent can, for example, remove the header and footer of a page, replace images of different course elements in a course tree with smaller ones, use the fisheye view to display focal content of a course tree in a larger font size and peripheral content in a smaller font size, etc. The applied techniques are obviously application dependent.

d) **Network Agent:** The device agent works in close cooperation with the network agent. The network agent provides information on the Quality-of-Service (QoS) values of the wireless network currently in use. WLAN, UMTS, GSM and other networks have different characteristics regarding bandwidth, bit rate, delay, roundtrip time, and so on. Other agents in the system can request these values from the network agent or subscribe to notifications about changes in the values. Adaptation of the system to changes in the mobile environment is obviously an important issue. The deployed agents should be able to make necessary corrections in a transparent fashion. For instance, if the connection is slow, the personal agent might fetch only email headers to the mobile device and not entire emails, the device agent might use different compression methods on a document, etc. The network agent should also have knowledge about advanced error recovery methods, techniques for handling disconnected learning and so on. In addition to the main agents there are a few other supporting agents that are discussed in the following section.

e) **Database Agent:** The database agent is responsible for communication with the system's database. Interaction with an external resource such as a database, file or legacy software requires some careful consideration since resources might change their status independently of the agent (Nikraz, Caire & Bahri, 2006). The TEx-Sys system uses Web services as a database front end, therefore the Web services agent is deployed instead of the database agent.

f) **Chat Agent:** The chat agent enables communication among students, registering different personal agents as clients. Students can engage in conversation with other students, create or join different chat rooms, form buddy lists, transfer files and the like. A useful feature of the chat agent would be forming of different interest groups based on the students' personal profiles. Figure 3 shows a simple chat module of our TEx-Sys mobile version.

Figure 3. Simple chat module of the TEx-Sys mobile version

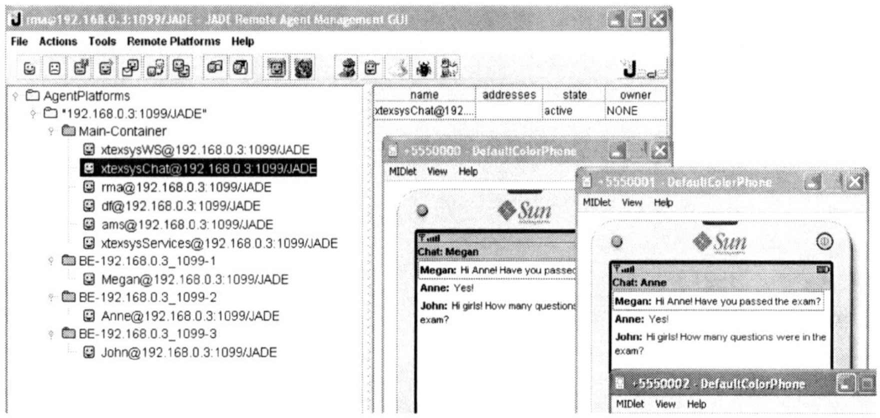

Agent Responsibilities

An initial list of responsibilities is defined for each identified agent type in an informal and intuitive way. There are a few rules to be followed: a) responsibilities should be inferred from the functional specification, b) responsibilities of the agent types with clearer functionality should be defined first, while those for the others should be postponed for a later moment. This results in responsibility tables such as Table 2.

Agent Acquaintances

At this point the agent-agent acquaintances are identified and added to the agent diagram (see Figure 2). The main acquaintances in the system are those between the personal agent and the pedagogical agent, as well as the personal agent and the chat agent. Some important acquaintances are not shown in the diagram for clarity reasons; they are mostly relations between the agents and the database agent responsible for retrieving data from the system's database, as well as relations between the agents and the network/device agent used for adaptation of the system to the mobile environment. Acquaintances are also added between different personal agents that may communicate directly without the chat agent as the mediator. Updating the agent diagram immediately implies updating the responsibility tables, e.g. some new responsibilities added to the personal agent are:

- Retrieve teaching materials from the pedagogical agent;
- Ask the pedagogical agent to generate a quiz;
- Request the chat agent to create a chat room.

Table 2. Responsibility table for the personal agent

Agent type Personal agent
Responsibilities Enable the student to set her/his learning preferences. Alert the student about scheduled activities and tasks. Determine possible conflicts in the student's schedule. Respond to course notifications. Present adequate teaching materials. Provide intelligent help to the student. Enable collaboration with other students/groups.

Agent Refinement

The set of identified agent types is now refined with additional agents related to support, discovery, management and monitoring. These issues are discussed in more detail in the following:

a) **Support:** Support implies supplementary information the agents need in order to accomplish their tasks. This information is highly dependent on the domain. Following the scenario the additional agents that can be added to the system are, for example, the XTalks agent that recommends talk announcements to registered users, the Mapquest agent that provides information on distance, driving time and driving directions between two addresses, and so on (Cost, Finin, Joshi, Peng, Nicholas, Chen, Kagal, Perich, Zou, Tolia & Soboroff, 2002; Kagal, Perich, Chen, Tolia, Zou, Finin, Joshi, Peng, Cost & Nicholas, 2003; Kumar, Kunjithapatham, Sheshagiri, Finin, Joshi, Peng & Cost, 2002). Adding new agent types automatically involves updating the agent diagram as well as the responsibility tables.

b) **Discovery:** Discovery assumes discovery of the service providing agents. The agents in the system should be able to discover stationary agents that provide specific services, such as the chat agent, the database agent as well as the network/device agent. This can be solved by introducing the yellow pages mechanism that enables discovery of agents based on the services they provide. The agents wishing to advertise their services register with the Yellow pages agent. This agent is added to the agent diagram and the responsibility tables are updated. Agent platforms in conformance with the FIPA standards implement their own version of the yellow pages mechanism (FIPA, 2004).

c) **Management and Monitoring:** Additional agent types should be added for dealing with issues such as monitoring of agents, dynamic creation of agents, killing agents, and so on. However these issues are usually addressed in the agent platform itself.

After the agent refinement, the previous steps of the analysis are iterated until sufficiently detailed information on the agent types, their responsibilities and acquaintances are acquired.

Agent Deployment

Finally the agent deployment diagram provides basic information on deploying the agents to physical devices (see Figure 4). This diagram only shows the essential deployment information required in the design phase for possible agent splitting/merging or considering communication efficiency.

The System Interoperability

A very important issue when developing the m-learning systems is undoubtedly the system interoperability and reusability. Development of (mobile) intelligent tutoring systems is a multidisciplinary process which requires engagement

Figure 4. Agent deployment diagram

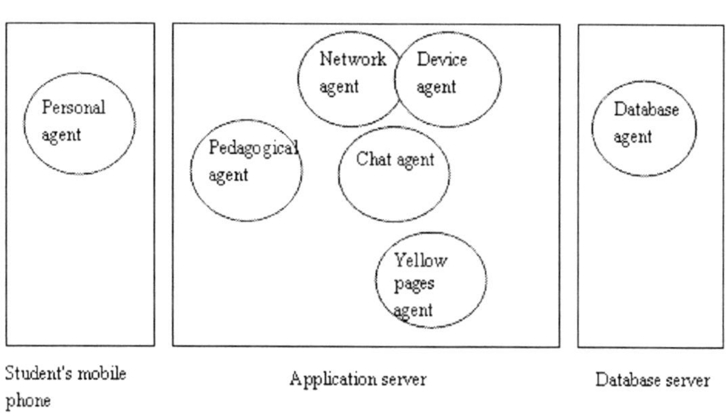

of experts in computer science, education, domain knowledge, cognitive psychology, philosophy, artificial intelligence, linguistics and related fields. This is obviously a difficult and expensive process. The respective costs however can be minimized by ensuring the system interoperability and sharing of knowledge. The TEx-Sys mobile version is therefore devised as a multi-agent system functioning over the common information space.

Reusability and interoperability of intelligent tutoring systems are considered to be the most important elements in reducing the respective development costs: the amount of time and money invested into development is increased exponentially due to multidisciplinary nature of the systems. Researchers design their own system architecture, develop knowledge representation strategies and reasoning mechanisms, acquire the relevant domain and instructional knowledge, etc. Present software design methodologies emphasize the importance of system modularity and interoperability, yet little has been done in this context when it comes to intelligent tutoring systems.

Our model proposes the basic approach to ensuring the system interoperability in form of sharing different types of knowledge in the common information space and deploying a distributed agent-based application over the information space (Figure 5). This architecture addresses issues like modularity and reusability; standardization efforts however should be made to make it applicable in the real world.

First of all, let us note that sharing knowledge in the common information space may be complicated due to the fact that different systems differently display and store knowledge. Furthermore, different systems use: a) different terminology for the same domain knowledge elements, b) the same terminology for different elements, c) different ways of connecting these elements as well as d) different inference rules on the elements. The common solution to this problem is the use of ontologies, which define domain concepts and their attributes, relationships between the concepts as well as inference rules within the domain (Poli, 1996).

The common information space should include different types of ontologies, which are to enable publishing along with sharing of domain knowledge, knowledge on teaching methods, students, the environment as well as social, economical and other aspects of tutoring. These ontologies should obviously be attached to their instances, i.e. knowledge bases containing the knowledge described by using the ontologies. Agents in the multi-agent application access these ontologies and their respective instances by using adequate Web services. This is yet another aspect of ensuring the system interoperability.

Figure 5. The common information space

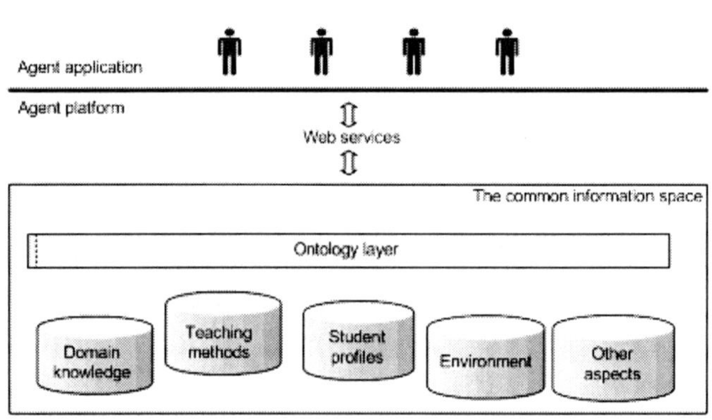

Therefore the TEx-Sys ontological environment, which presently includes specifications for both domain knowledge and courseware design, should be extended with additional ontologies and knowledge related to students, different teaching techniques, pedagogical issues and so on. The agent-based architecture of the TEx-Sys mobile version functioning over the common information space brings the intelligent tutoring theory to its full potential.

CONCLUSION AND FUTURE WORK

This chapter gives an overview of the new learning paradigm intended to enhance the efficiency and effectiveness of learning in the context of handheld terminals. The m-learning systems support the new philosophy of ubiquitous and pervasive computing by providing learners with "anytime, anywhere and any device" access to knowledge. The global intention is to integrate learning into our everyday lives in a simple, pleasant and interesting manner. Naismith, Lonsdale, Vavoula and Sharples (2004) made a very interesting remark about the success of mobile learning: "In the future, the success of learning and teaching with mobile technologies will be measured by how seamlessly it weaves itself into our daily lives, with the greatest success paradoxically occurring at the point where we don't recognize it as learning at all" (p. 36). The chapter describes different perspectives and definitions, various interesting projects as well as issues and problems pertinent to mobile learning. Our approach to solving these problems is presented in the form of an agent-based architecture for m-learning. The basic examples are related to the TEx-Sys mobile version but the discussion itself is quite general and grants its application to a broader range of related systems. The main research challenge is modeling of the agents, their functionality, internal structures and mechanisms. Future work foresees writing a thorough specification of the system based on the presented analysis in order to obtain sufficient insight which would enable a relatively straightforward implementation of the system. This specification should include items like agent interaction tables, message templates, service registrations, agent behaviors, ontologies, content languages and the like. Additional issues to be addressed comprehend security, persistency, performance and scalability of the system.

On a more global scale, potential areas of future research and development have been outlined in the Manolo project (Wentzel, van Lammeren, Molendijk, de Bruin & Wagtendonk, 2005):

- The technology infrastructure is not yet ready for truly mobile learning. Stability, device availability, and course support problems remain unresolved.
- Personalization is crucial but is not yet sufficiently implemented - not because personalization tools don't exist, but because many courses' monolithic nature makes tailoring educational material to personal preferences difficult.
- Mobile learning works only when its practical use during the course is unmistakable and logical.
- The impact on educators is large, but little guidance exists on how to achieve the best results for mobile learning.
- Clear relationships seem to exist between what constitutes good and bad use of mobile learning. These relationships are not fully spelled out in educational terms.
- Wireless and mobile learning impact logistics, resources, and costs. These impacts must be identified and modeled to provide guidance for future implementations.
- Communication - both teacher-student and student-student - seems to find new channels and opportunities within mobile learning. This positively affects community building but must be streamlined from both the ICT and educational sides.

- The course Web site should be accessible by mobile devices.
- Batteries pose serious limitations to PDAs' usefulness in fieldwork. An average usability of four hours is too short for a normal fieldwork workday.
- PDAs will do an excellent job as "fieldwork computers" in most cases, since in fieldwork weight and size are defining factors. (p. 17)

REFERENCES

Agent Management Specification, F. I. P. A. (2004). *FIPA Standard SC00023K*. Reterieved from http://www.fipa.org/specs/fipa00023/index.html

American Society for Training and Development. (2001). *A Vision of E-Learning for America's Workforce*. Report of the Commission on Technology and Adult Learning.

Attewell, J. (2005). From Research and Development to Mobile Learning: Tools for Education and Training Providers and their Learners. In *Proceedings of mLearn 2005*. Retrieved December 20, 2005, from http://www.mlearn.org.za/papersfull.html

Bellifemine, F., Poggi, A., & Rimassa, G. (2001). JADE: a FIPA2000 compliant agent development environment. In *Proceedings of the 5th International Conference on Autonomous Agents (Agents 2001)* (pp. 216-217). Montreal, Canada.

Braubach, L., Lamersdorf, W., & Pokahr, A. (2003). Jadex: Implementing a BDI-Infrastructure for JADE Agents. *EXP - in search of innovation, 3*, 76-85.

CC/PP. (2007). *Composite Capabilities/Preferences Profile Home Page*. Retrieved from http://www.w3.org/Mobile/CCPP

Cobcroft, R., Towers, S., Smith, J., & Bruns, A. (2006). *Literature review into mobile learning in the university context*. Brisbane, Australia: Queensland University of Technology, Creative Industries faculty.

Cobcroft, R., Towers, S., Smith, J., & Bruns, A. (2006). Mobile learning in review: Opportunities and challenges for learners, teachers, and institutions. In *Proceedings of the Online Learning and Teaching Conference 2006 (OLT'06)* (pp. 21-30). Brisbane, Australia.

Cost, R. S., Finin, T., Joshi, A., Peng, Y., Nicholas, C., Chen, H., et al. (2001). Ittalks: A case study in the semantic web and daml. In *Proceedings of the 1st International Semantic Web Working Symposium (SWWS'01)* (pp. 477-494). Stanford, CA.

Frand, J. (2000). The information age mindset: Changes in students and implications for higher education. *EDUCAUSE Review, 35*(5), 15–24.

Glavinić, V., Rosić, M., & Zelić, M. (2007). Agents in m-Learning Systems Based on Intelligent Tutoring. In C. Stephanidis (Ed.), *Universal Access in Human-Computer Interaction. Applications and Services: Vol. 4556. Programming and Software Engineering* (pp. 578-587). Berlin: Springer.

Glavinić, V., Rosić, M., & Zelić, M. (2008). Analysis of an Agent-based m-Learning System. In *Proceedings of the 14th IEEE Mediterranean Electrotechnical Conference (MELECON'08)* (CD-ROM Proceedings pp. 1-6). Ajaccio, France.

Juan, T., Pierce, A., & Sterling, L. (2002). Roadmap: Extending the Gaia methodology for complex open systems. In *Proceedings of the 1st ACM Joint Conference on Autonomous Agents and Multi-Agent Systems (AAMAS 2002)* (pp. 3-10). Bologna, Italy.

Kagal, L., Perich, F., Chen, H., Tolia, S., Zou, Y., Finin, T., et al. (2002). Agents making sense of the Semantic Web. In *Proceedings of the Innovative Concepts for Agent-Based Systems: 1st International Workshop on Radical Agent Concepts (WRAC 2002)* (pp. 417-433). McLean, VA.

Kuflik, T., & Shoval, P. (2000). User profile generation for intelligent information agents. In *Proceedings of the 2nd International Workshop on Agent-Oriented Information Systems (AOIS 2000)* (pp. 63-72). Stockholm, Sweden.

Kukulska-Hulme, A., & Traxler, J. (Eds.). (2005). *Mobile Learning: A Handbook for Educators and Trainers*. London: Routledge.

Kumar, S., Kunjithapatham, A., Sheshagiri, M., Finin, T., Joshi, A., Peng, Y., & Cost, R. S. (2002). A personal agent application for the semantic web. In *Proceedings of the 2002 AAAI Fall Symposia on Personalized Agents*. North Falmouth, MA.

Laouris, Y., & Eteokleous, N. (2005). We need an educationally relevant definition of mobile learning. In *Proceedings of mLearn 2005*. Retrieved December 20, 2005, from http://www.mlearn.org.za/papers-full.html

Luck, M., Ashri, R., & d'Inverno, M. (2004). *Agent-Based Software Development*. Norwood, MA: Artech House Publishers.

Major, N. (1995). How Generic can Authoring Shells Become? In *Proceedings of the Workshop on Authoring Shells for Intelligent Tutoring Systems (AI-ED-95)* (pp. 75-82). Washington, DC.

McGovern, J., & Gray, K. (2005). Directions for organisation and management of university learning: Implications from a qualitative survey of student e-learning. In *Proceedings of ASCILITE 2005*. Retrieved January 12, 2006, from http://www.ascilite.org.au/conferences/brisbane05/proceedings.shtml

McLean, N. (2003). *The M-Learning Paradigm: an Overview* (A Report for the Royal Academy of Engineering and the Vodafone Group Foundation). Sydney, Australia: Macquarie University, IMS Australia.

Mobilearn (2003). *The Mobilearn Project Vision*. Available at http://www.mobilearn.org/vision/visiton.htm

Naismith, L., Lonsdale, P., Vavoula, G., & Sharples, M. (2004). *NESTA Futurelab Report 11: Literature Review in Mobile Technologies and Learning*. Bristol, UK: NESTA Futurelab. Retrieved December 27, 2005, from http://www.nestafuturelab.org/research/reviews/reviews_11_and12/11_01.htm

Nikraz, M., Caire, G., & Bahri, P. A. (2006). A methodology for the analysis and design of multi-agent systems using JADE. *International Journal of Computer Systems Science and Engineering*, *21*, 99–116.

Nwana, H., Ndumu, D., Lee, L., & Collis, J. (1999). ZEUS: A Tool-Kit for Building Distributed Multi-Agent Systems. *Applied Artificial Intelligence Journal*, *13*, 129–186. doi:10.1080/088395199117513

Oblinger, D. G. (2003). *Boomers & gen-Xers, millennials: Understanding the "new students"*. EDUCAUSE Review.

Oblinger, D. G. (2004). The Next Generation of Educational Engagement. *Journal of Interactive Media in Education*, 2004(8). Retrieved January 16, 2006, from http://www-jime.open.ac.uk/2004/8/oblinger-2004-8-disc-paper.html

Omicini, A. (2001). SODA: Societies and infrastructures in the analysis and design of agent-based systems. In *Proceedings of the 1st International Workshop on Agent-Oriented Software Engineering (AOSE '01)* (pp. 185-193). Montreal, Canada.

OWL. (2007). *Web Ontology Language OWL*. Retrieved from http://www.w3.org/2004/OWL

Patel, A. Kinshuk, Russell, D., & Oppermann, R. (2001). Intelligent Tutoring Systems: Confluence of Information Science and Cognitive Science. In *Proceedings of the 2001 Informing Science Conference* (pp. 392-397). Krakow, Poland.

Poli, R. (1996). Ontology for Knowledge Organization. In Green, R. (Ed.), *Knowledge organization and change* (pp. 313–319). Frankfurt: Indeks.

Quinn, C. (2000). M-Learning. Mobile, Wireless, In-Your-Pocket Learning. *Linezine, Fall 2000*. Available at http://www.linezine.com/2.1/features/cqmmwiyp.htm

Rogers, T. J., Ross, R., & Subrahmanian, V. S. (2000). IMPACT: A system for building agent applications. *Journal of Intelligent Information Systems, 14*, 95–113. doi:10.1023/A:1008727601100

Rosić, M., Glavinić, V., & Stankov, S. (2001). DTEx-Sys – A Web Oriented Intelligent Tutoring System. In *Proceedings of the International Conference on Trends in Communications (EUROCON'01)* (pp. 255-258). Bratislava, Slovakia.

Sharma, S. K., & Kitchens, F. L. (2004). Web Services Architecture for M-Learning. *Electronic Journal on e-Learning, 2*(1), 203-216.

Singh, H. (2003). Leveraging Mobile and Wireless Internet. *Learning Circuits, September 2003*. Available at http://www.learningcircuits.com/2003/sep2003/singh.htm

Sklar, E., & Richards, D. (2006). The Use of Agents in Human Learning Systems. In *Proceedings of the 5th International Joint Conference on Autonomous Agents and Multiagent Systems (AAMAS 2006)* (pp. 767-774). Hakodate, Japan.

Stankov, S. (1997). *Isomorphic Model of the System as the Basis of Teaching Control Principles in the Intelligent Tutoring System*. (Unpublished doctoral dissertation), University of Split, Split.

Stankov, S., Rosić, M., Žitko, B., & Grubišić, A. (2008). TEx-Sys model for building intelligent tutoring systems. *Computers & Education, 51*, 1017–1036. doi:10.1016/j.compedu.2007.10.002

Sycara, K., Giampapa, J. A., Langley, B. K., & Paolucci, M. (2003). The RETSINA MAS, a Case Study. In Garcia, A. (Ed.), *Software Engineering for Large-Scale Multi-Agent Systems: Research Issues and Practical Applications* (*Vol. 2603*, pp. 232–250). Berlin: Springer. doi:10.1007/3-540-35828-5_15

Thomas, S. (2005). Pervasive, persuasive eLearning: modeling the pervasive learning space. In *Proceedings of the 3rd International Conference on Pervasive Computing and Communications Workshops (PERCOMW'05)* (pp. 332-336). Kauai Island, Hawai'i: IEEE Computer Society.

Vavoula, G. N., & Sharples, M. (2002). KLeOS: a personal, mobile, knowledge and learning organisation system. In *Proceedings of the IEEE International Workshop on Wireless and Mobile Technologies in Education (WMTE'02)* (pp. 152-156). Vaxjo, Sweden: IEEE Computer Society.

Wagner, E. D. (2005). Enabling Mobile Learning. *EDUCAUSE Review, 40*(3), 40–53.

Wentzel, P., van Lammeren, R., Molendrijk, M., de Bruin, S., & Wagtendonk, A. (2005). *Using Mobile Technology to Enhance Students' Educational Experiences*. Boulder, CA: EDUCAUSE Center for Applied Research.

Wooldridge, M., Jennings, N. R., & Kinny, D. (2000). The Gaia methodology for agent-oriented analysis and design. *Journal of Autonomous Agents and Multi-Agent Systems, 3*, 285–312. doi:10.1023/A:1010071910869

Wooldridge, M. J., & Jennings, N. R. (1995). Intelligent Agents: Theory and Practice. *The Knowledge Engineering Review, 10*(2), 115–152. doi:10.1017/S0269888900008122

Zhang, D. (2007). Web Content Adaptation for Mobile Handheld Devices. *Communications of the ACM, 50*, 75–79. doi:10.1145/1216016.1216024

KEY TERMS AND DEFINITIONS

E-Learning (Electronic Learning): Instructional content or learning experiences delivered or enabled by electronic technology. E-learning can include a wide variety of learning strategies and technologies, from CD ROMs and computer-based instruction to videoconferencing, satellite-delivered learning and virtual educational networks.

Intelligent Agent: An autonomous software component that observes and acts upon its environment, directing its activity towards achieving goals.

Intelligent Tutoring Systems: A generation of e-learning systems intended for support and improvement of the learning and teaching process. The systems are based on simulation of a human teacher.

M-Learning (Mobile Learning): A subclass of e-learning enabled by mobile technologies; "anywhere, anytime and any device" portable and personalized learning.

Mobile Intelligent Tutoring Systems: Intelligent tutoring systems designed for the mobile computing environment, with regard to different mobile devices and wireless networks.

Multi-Agent Systems: A collection of interactive intelligent agents having common or conflicting goals. The agents may interact with each other both indirectly (by acting on the environment) or directly (via communication and negotiation). The agents may decide to cooperate for mutual benefit or may compete to serve their own interests.

Ubiquitous Computing: Model of human-computer interaction in which information processing has been fully integrated into everyday objects and activities. This model is usually considered an advancement from the desktop paradigm.

Section 3
Intelligent E-Learning in Different Domains

Chapter 7
E-Learning with Affective Tutoring Systems

Abdolhossein Sarrafzadeh
Unitec, New Zealand

Jamshid Shanbehzadeh
Tarbiat Moalem University, Iran

Scott Overmyer
Baker College, USA

ABSTRACT

E-learning has attracted a great deal of interest in educational circles from K-12 to universities. A question that is often rightly asked is how effective current e-learning systems are. It is argued that there is little individualization of instruction by adapting to the pedagogical needs of each learner in current e-learning systems. Intelligent tutoring systems have tried to fill this gap but even they fail to compete with human one-to-one tutoring. This paper presents Affective Tutoring Systems which are e-learning systems capable of detecting learners' affective state and reacting to it through a life like agent called Eve. This paper presents an Affective Tutoring System in the domain of mathematics and the research that led to its development. It also presents the findings from the study and testing of the system indicating that the animated agent Eve carried a persona effect.

INTRODUCTION

Using computers in education is a topic of great interest in today's schools and universities as well as the e-learning market. The global e-learning market is projected to exceed $52.6 billion by 2010 (Kopf, 2007). Due to the paucity of recently published literature containing empirical data on the effectiveness of e-learning, many are (rightly) asking: "Are computers being used as effectively as they could be for education?"

In fact, e-learning has been a significant issue since before desktop computers were invented, with the work of the American psychologist B.F. Skinner, who used "teaching machines" to present and assess basic flashcard exercises (Hill 1997). As technology improved, computers replaced the teaching machines, and Computer Assisted Instruction (CAI) came into being (Hayes 2001).

DOI: 10.4018/978-1-61692-008-1.ch007

What CAI systems lacked, however, was a means of individualizing instruction by adapting to the pedagogical needs of each learner (Urban-Lurain 2003). This meant that all students were instructed in exactly the same way, and the strengths, weaknesses, and learning styles of individual students were rarely considered.

The successor to CAI was the Intelligent Tutoring System (ITS), which came into existence during the early 1970s and is still in vogue today. ITSs are characterized by the 'intelligent' ability to adapt their teaching strategies to the knowledge and abilities of individual learners. This is so that the instruction is as effective and efficient as possible (Urban-Lurain 2003). ITSs represent a significant improvement over CAI systems. They have proven to be effective, resulting in increased learning (Aleven et al. 1999; Aleven & Koedinger 2001; Anderson et al. 1995; Conati & VanLehn 2001; Mitrovic et al. 2002; Whitehurst et al. 1998). Studies have shown that ITSs even outperform traditional classroom instruction: they are always available, non-judgmental and provide tailored feedback (Anderson et al. 1995; Holt et al. 1994; Johnson et al. 2003; Self 1990). Even so, we assert that one-to-one human tutoring remains the most effective means of instruction, and would, were enough tutors found to teach and enough money found to pay them, quite certainly provide the best solution. There are, however, some characteristics of human tutors that are not optimal. First, human tutors are typically not available at the convenience of the student. Rarely does one find a human tutor who is available 24/7 and ready to go at a moment's notice. Secondly, human tutors become tired and fatigued. Most human tutors are good for 1-2 hours at best, and after that are not at their best from either personality or performance perspectives. Finally, unless providing services *pro bono*, human tutors are beyond the reach of many students of limited means. So, the ultimate aim of an ITS – to create a tutor as effective and efficient as a human, but without the human cognitive and emotional weaknesses or often, great expense.

If human tutors are the "ideal" solution from a learning perspective, however, what are the capabilities of humans that machines lack? For example, human tutors can perceive the cognitive and emotional state of the human learner in real time, and adjust their pedagogical approach according to this perception. Is it reasonable to suggest that we could embed these naturally occurring perceptual characteristics of human tutors into an ITS? We believe that the answer is "yes", and have evidence to support our assertion (Sarrafzadeh et al., 2008). We outline our rationale and approach in the following sections. This paper, presented in five sections, covers various aspects of affective tutoring systems (Alexander, Sarrafzadeh, Hill, 2008) and how they can improve e-learning.

THE SIGNIFICANCE OF AFFECT IN E-LEARNING

Why is it that computer based tutoring systems are generally less effective than one-to-one human tutoring? Overmyer (Overmyer 1999) asserts that today's ITSs lack the 'personality' of human tutors, which greatly reduces their ability to adapt to the precise needs of each individual learner. In fact, studies show that 35% of comments by human tutors have affective content (Self 1990), and estimate that a staggering 93% of affective communication takes place either non-verbally or paralinguistically (Mehrabian, 1971), through facial expressions, gestures, or vocal inflections (Picard 1998). Yet, nearly all existing ITSs adapt their teaching strategies based only on a model of the cognitive state of the learner (i.e., the state of learner knowledge). Naturally, human tutors do this too, but good human tutors also regulate their teaching strategies based upon the non-verbal (including affective) feedback given by the learner, which tells the tutor whether the learner is happy, confused, frustrated, surprised, bored, or content with the material that the tutor is presenting. For example, a human tutor who can see that a learner is visibly confused will naturally try to simplify the material being presented, present the material in an alternative manner, or perhaps revisit prerequisite material. This immediately meets the learner's need, and leads to greatly increased learning. As ITSs lack this ability to sense, interpret, and respond to non-verbal, affective communication, we assert that their ability to reliably select the most appropriate teaching strategies in real time is greatly reduced.

In our opinion, the evidence is clear that affective state is a factor in learning. The selection of teaching strategies by a tutoring system would be significantly enhanced were its model of the learner extended to incorporate the affective, as well cognitive state of the learner.

DETECTING A LEARNER'S AFFECTIVE STATE

If we assume that tutoring systems would benefit from extending the learner model to include affective state, how can we use a computer to detect affective feedback?

Given that human tutors do not have access to biometric affective cues, we regard these kinds of cues as auxiliary confirmation for research purposes, but not particularly interesting for real-time intelligent tutoring. Human tutors DO have access, however, to facial expressions and occasional posture and gesture cues, and this paper focuses on these kinds of cues, primarily facial expressions, as the most important and immediate medium of non-verbal, affective communication. That spontaneous (or unconscious) facial expressions are indicative of underlying affective state is supported by several studies that found a high correlation between facial expressions and self-reported emotions (Ruch 1995; Rosenberg & Ekman 1994). Physiological activity has been found to accompany various spontaneous facial expressions (Ekman & Davidson 1993), which also bears witness to a link between emotions and facial expressions. We can conclude that both spontaneous facial expressions and their accompanying physiological activity illustrate an underlying affective state.

Computers can interpret facial expressions of emotion with reasonable accuracy thanks to the recent development in automated facial expression analysis. Automated facial expression analysis systems identify the motion and position of muscles in the face by comparing several images of a given subject, or by using neural networks to learn the appearance of particular muscular contractions (Fasel & Luettin 2003). This builds on the classic work of Ekman and Friesen, who developed the Facial Action Coding System for describing the movement of muscles in the face (Ekman & Friesen 1978). Affective state can then be inferred from analysing the facial actions that are detected (Pantic & Rothkrantz 1999). Detection and estimation of learner affect will be discussed in the following paragraphs.

We have developed a facial expression analysis software for incorporation into e-learning systems. Figure 1 shows the overall architecture of this system. The facial expression analysis system recognises learners who have used the system before and estimates their affective state by analysing face images captured using a webcam mounted on the top of the learner's monitor.

From a functional point of view, as discussed above, there are three main components in this system, face detection, facial feature extraction, and facial expression analysis.

Face Detection

The first stage is face detection. Real time face detection requires rapid identification of the face in the image captured from the camera. Researchers have had success designing algorithms suitable for detection of various objects (e.g., Xu and Aliaga, 2007), but detecting faces is particularly difficult as the face is a special kind of object that does not have a well-defined shape and strictly uniform set of features.

Figure 1. Overall structure of the real-time facial expression analysis system

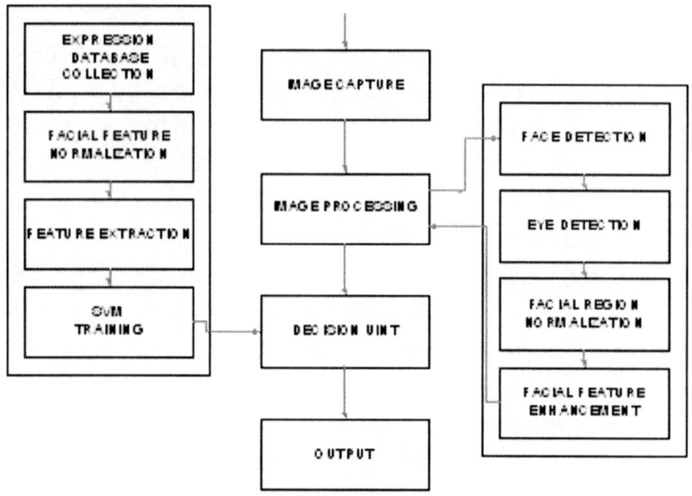

In general, face detection occurs using the following process. Firstly, an image is captured by a digital camera. These images are then sent to the face detection system, which determines whether the image contains a face. The face detection system in this research uses two different filters to determine whether an image contains a face. First a fast template matching algorithm makes the initial decision about whether a face is present. Images which are considered to contain a face are then sent to the second, more accurate filter which consists of a trained support vector machine (the training is conducted offline). A support vector machine (SVM) is a relative of the neural network used primarily for pattern recognition. The SVM performs classification that separates the data into two categories, by constructing an N-dimensional hyperplane. Support vector machines are used because they are accurate at detecting faces as they have a strong learning ability and converge easily (Michel and El Kaliouby, 2003; Sahbi and Geman, 2006). While the support vector machines are accurate to a certain degree, they are not yet very good at detecting faces which are even slightly rotated – beyond approximately 10 degrees in either direction. In order to solve this problem, which would clearly have an adverse affect on any face detection system designed to operate in a real world environment, we have developed a real time face detection algorithm that is able to detect a face with a wide variety of angle rotations. This will be described in more detail in the following section. This technique can be applied to any type of object, and ability to detect fully rotated objects has a variety of useful applications.

Following the face detection, the next step is to normalize the face region. The size of the face image is not always the same, so it is necessary to modify it to the same size before continuing with further processing. In order to do this correctly without deforming or degrading the image, the eyes must be detected using an eye classifier. In previous systems (e.g., Wang and Yang, 2006), eyes were detected by using a known parameter that the eye region is a darker region within the face. Using this knowledge, a histogram equalization algorithm can be applied and the approximate position of the eyes can be found by assuming that they are the darkest region within the face. Obviously this can lead to inaccurate results as sometimes other parts of the face can be the darkest region in the image. However, this problem has been resolved as our research has introduced a novel iris detection algorithm which detects and locates the actual eye, rather than just the approximate region of the eye.

Facial Feature Extraction

The second stage is facial feature extraction. Human face images are inherently different due to variations of age, sex, skin color, and external factors such as lighting conditions. In order to have an accurate facial expression recognition system, it is important that these features are normalized as much as possible.

After conducting testing of a variety of different methods, a number of techniques have been combined to achieve this normalization. These include effective lighting correction, sigma filter and contrast-limited adaptive histogram equalization, and edge preventing smoothing algorithms. When these techniques are organized and implemented in a coherent, effective way, the system is able to enhance and extract facial features from a wide variety of human faces and still achieve the goal of real time operation.

To remove the effects of skin color and variations in lighting conditions, the facial region of the image is converted to gray scale and the lighting is corrected using a linear lighting correction algorithm. This algorithm averages lighting in all directions, which nullifies the effect of differences in lighting and skin color. Image noise can also affect feature extraction quality, and there are many existing algorithms which eliminate noise from images. Lee's (1983) sigma filter was chosen as the face region noise removal algorithm because the sigma filter does not destroy edge information which is important for the recognition of facial features. An edge smoothing algorithm is applied to make the facial features more consistent. The facial features are then further enhanced by contrast-limited adaptive histogram equalization (CLAHE).

Facial Expression Analysis

The last stage is the detection, analysis and recognition of the facial expressions themselves. In this part of the system, a trained support vector machine is used to classify different facial expressions. The SVM is trained offline using a database containing a variety of facial expressions. To produce a large facial expression database for better training results, the faces in the facial expression database for training were collected from many different sources, and FaceGen software (Singular Inversions, 2009) was used to generate additional facial expressions. This means that the training database was a combination real and generated facial expression. The facial expression database also includes faces of individuals of different age, sex, and race. Furthermore, to achieve the best performance for the classifier, an exhaustive parameter searching algorithm is applied.

Accurate representation of facial features and reducing feature dimensions is also important in improving the machine learning ability. The novel algorithm developed in this research, which reduces features dimensions by radon transformation and discrete cosine transformation, made this possible. Figure 2 shows a screen shot of the facial expression recognition system.

ANIMATED PEDAGOGICAL AGENTS

Although existing ITSs cannot recognise emotions, many ITSs have been developed that can show emotions through an animated pedagogical agent (Johnson, Rickel and Lester, 2000; Prendinger and Ishizuka, 2004). Animated pedagogical agents are "lifelike autonomous characters that cohabit learning environments with students to create rich, face-to-face learning interactions" (Johnson, Rickel and Lester, 2000). Animated agents carry a persona effect, which is that the presence of a lifelike character can strongly influence students to perceive their learning experiences positively (van

Figure 2. A screen shot taken from the facial expression analysis software

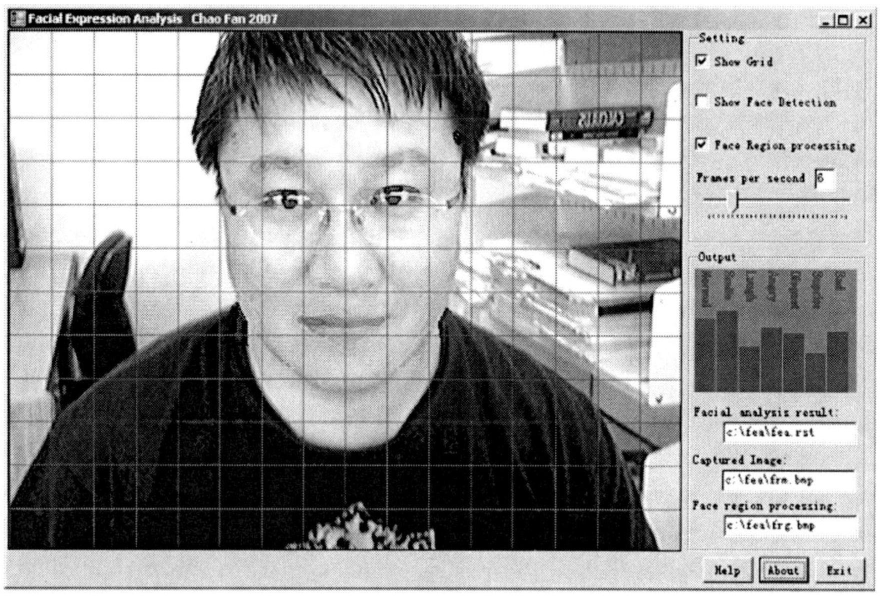

Mulken, André and Muller, 1998). The persona effect has been shown to increase learner motivation, especially in technical domains, although its overall benefits remain unclear (van Mulken, André and Muller, 1998).

Burleson (2006) at has developed an *Affective Learning Companion* that is able to mirror several student non-verbal behaviors believed to influence persuasion and liking. The Affective Learning Companion is also able to detect frustration/help seeking behavior from students using input from the nonverbal sensors with an accuracy of 79%, but that result is based on offline computation. Future work will be needed to refine the system to accurately sense these frustration/help seeking behaviors in real time, so that the agent can be continuously aware of the student's affective state. According to Burleson, exactly how and when the agent will choose to intervene (or not) will be based upon the real time information from the sensors as well as the personality type of the student.

We used an animated pedagogical agent called "Eve" which is capable of using the detected facial expressions of the learner. Eve then displays emotions and gestures based on the perceived affective state of the learner. Eve's decisions are driven by a case-based reasoning program that was constructed based on the cases extracted from a study of human tutoring. For this purpose, 62 students were tutored by three experienced human tutors. Each tutoring session was 20 minutes which was videoed. These video recordings were then analysed using a coding scheme developed for this purpose to extract the knowledge required for the case base. Figure 3 shows a snapshot of Eve in action.

The study of human tutors revealed many interesting results including the fact that students most frequently show a neutral emotion. The frequencies of student and tutor facial expressions are shown in Figure 4. For both students and tutors, neutral expressions were by far the most common: this was especially the case for tutors, for whom 86% of all expressions were neutral.

This might be because of the nature of the topic tutored (i.e., mathematics). The second and third most commonly appearing expressions were also the same for both students and tutors: Low and High intensities of smiling. However, smiles

Figure 3. Pedagogical agent Eve is capable of displaying emotions and gestures

were much more common for students than tutors: students smiled for a total of 29% of student turns, whereas tutors smiled for only 12% of tutor turns. Students also appeared apprehensive for 4% of turns and confused for 3% of turns, but the combined occurrences of all other student expressions totaled only 2% of student turns.

Similarly for tutors, the combined occurrences of all expressions other than neutral and smiling (including confusion and apprehension) totaled only 2% of tutors' turns. Expressions of frustration, disappointment, boredom, surprise and disgust were almost entirely absent for both students and tutors.

There are a number of reasons why this might be the case, and we need to investigate ways in which students may be encouraged to be more emotionally and socially engaged with an affective tutoring system. On the face of it, if adult tutors have low intensity or flat affect, one would expect students to display similar affect. We suggest that it is likely that students would display affect in response to a display of affect on the part of one in which students are more socially engaged. To this end, affective tutors, such as Eve, should actively engage student socially, if they expect to elicit social and affective responses.

One manner in which ATS agents can engage students is via the use of both parallel and reactive empathy. Empathy has been demonstrated to be important in everyday human discourse

Figure 4. Frequencies of tutor expressions following student expressions

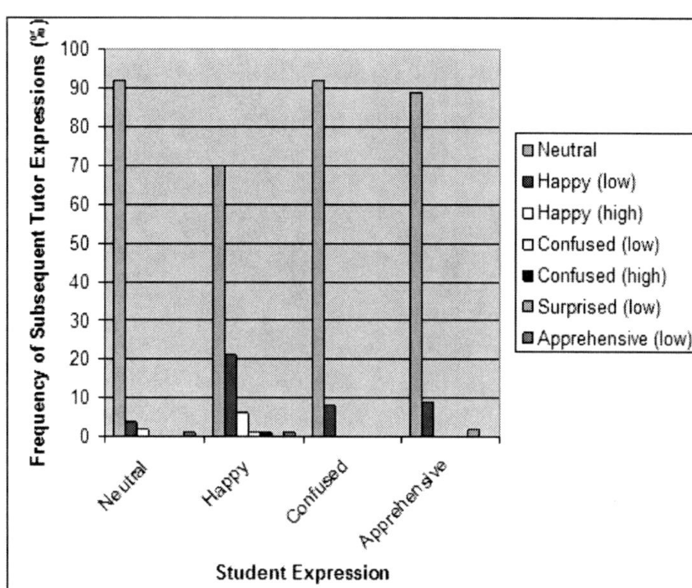

and motivating to students (Bickmore, 2003). McQuiggan et al (2008) have presented an inductive framework for modeling parallel and reactive empathy, and shown how a combination of parallel and reactive empathy can be modeled for use in an ATS. While we did not utilize this model in our ATS, future work will likely employ this model as a component of the system to further engage students with the ATS tutor and encourage more outward expression of emotional state. It is through this kind of stimulus that we anticipate student affective responses will become more apparent, and in turn, be more useful in adaptive pedagogical strategy.

AFFECTIVE TUTORING SYSTEMS AND E-LEARNING

An affective tutoring system is an intelligent tutoring system that takes into accounts not only the knowledge state but also affective state of the learner to individualize learning. The student model of an affective tutoring system is therefore different than an intelligent tutoring system. An affective tutoring system also has components for detection and expression of emotion. An overview of the architecture of affective tutoring systems is presented in Figure 5.

As Figure 5 shows, the overall architecture of an affective tutoring system is made up of four main components: a facial expression analysis module; a student model, which is made up of both a set of proficiency scores for several mathematics concepts and a coded representation of the interaction history; a tutoring strategies module; and a set of tutoring actions in the form of agent animations and tens frame and counter animations. As Figure 5 shows, both the actions and the emotions of the student are taken into account by the tutoring system.

AN AFFECTIVE TUTORING SYSTEM FOR MATHEMATICS

A functioning Affective Tutoring System (ATS) for mathematics has been implemented at Massey University, and is the first ever of its type. Emotion detection is carried out using facial expression analysis, and the system adapts to the student via an emotionally expressive animated lifelike agent, Eve. Tutoring actions are guided by a case-based method for adapting to student states that

Figure 5. Architecture of an Affective Tutoring System

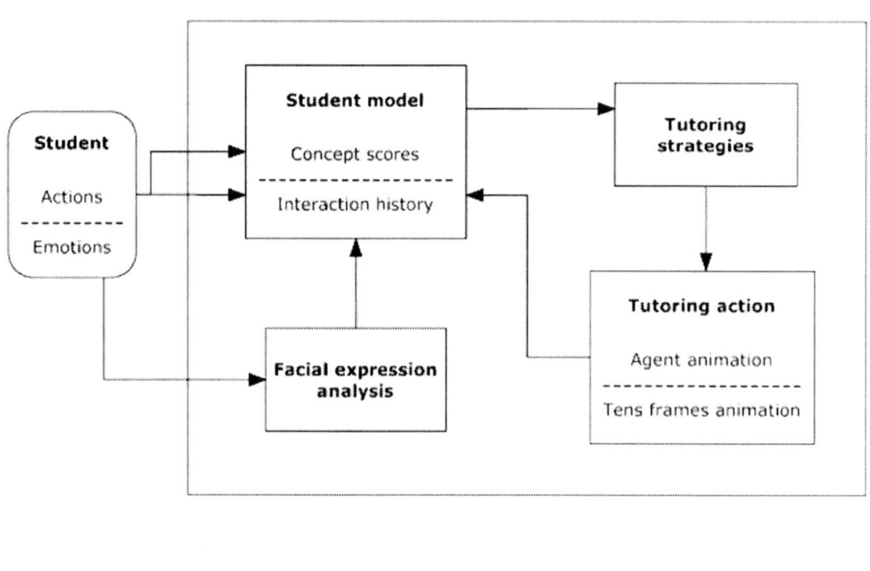

recommends a weighted set of tutor actions and expressions. The data that this case-based program uses was generated by an observational study of human tutors. Figure 6 shows a snapshot of one of the screens of the affective tutoring system.

The implications of this system are potentially very significant: it represents another step towards tutoring systems that are fully aware of the cognitive and affective states of the student, and are fully capable of adapting to these states wisely. Future work will build on the current ATS, and work towards making Eve increasingly lifelike in her interactions with students.

FUTURE RESEARCH DIRECTIONS

The work presented in this paper has scope for future research to work towards improving affective tutoring systems in electronic learning environments. Some of these are:

- To extend the study of human tutors to include other subject areas as well as a larger number of students and tutors as well as different ages and genders
- The appearance of the lifelike agent could be improved by animating her in real time, but without sacrificing the quality of the current animations. A larger range of possible gestures and facial expressions, would allow the agent to adapt to students in a more immediate manner; this would help to amplify how believable she appears to students.
- The accuracy and range of facial expressions could also be improved
- Other channels for emotion detection such as physiological measures and voice can be investigated.
- Finally, although the system was tested in two schools in New Zealand, a more extended study of the effectiveness of the system needs to be carried out.

In addition to our current research direction, we would like to extend this work to the realm of 3D virtual worlds and "affective" pedagogical agents. Baylor (2001) suggests a number of possible roles for pedagogical agents, including assistants, mentors, and/or learning companions for students. We would like to explore some of

Figure 6. A screen shot of the Affective Tutoring system

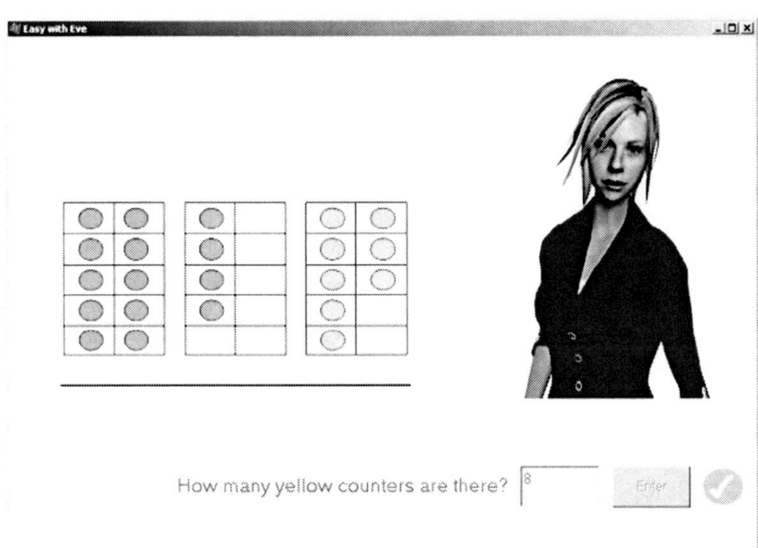

these possibilities using "affective avatars" in Second Life, ActiveWorlds, and other virtual environments.

She reaches additional conclusions regarding the nature of the learner-agent relationship, and suggests that the learner must have confidence in the agent for the agent to be effective. In order to gain the learner's confidence, she concludes that: "... the agent must be believable, motivational, competent, and trustworthy, all of which require the agent to assert control in the learning process" (Baylor, 2001; p. 413). It is unlikely that, in the absence of an affective component, that these goals can be realized. We plan to further develop agent models that employ affective computing in these more "naturalistic" settings, in which affective state is utilized to not only modify pedagogical strategy, but create human-like relationships with agents making the system even more compelling for students.

As suggested in this section, there is ample scope for this work to be extended and further explored. May the days of frustrating, confusing interactions with artificial tutors be coming to an end.

CONCLUSION

This paper has briefly presented work on the development of an affect-sensitive animated tutoring character named Eve, as well as a new ATS that helps students with a counting and addition exercise. The research leading to the development of this ATS has shown that:

- It is possible to develop an emotion-sensitive tutoring system.
- It is possible to model the interaction with the student based on the interactions of human tutors with students using a case based approach.
- The findings from the study and testing of the system indicate that the animated agent Eve carried a slight persona effect. Thus it could be said that an ATS may increase student motivation and perception of learning gains. However, this conclusion would need to be verified further by future studies.

REFERENCES

Aleven, V., & Koedinger, K. R. (2000). Limitations of student control: Do students know when they need help? In *Proceedings of ITS'2000*.

Aleven, V., Koedinger, K. R., et al. (1999). Tutoring Answer Explanation Fosters Learning with Understanding. In *Proceedings of AIED'99*.

Alexander, S., Sarrafzadeh, A., & Hill, S. (2008). Foundation of an Affective Tutoring System: Learning How Human Tutors Adapt to Student Emotion. *International Journal of Intelligent Systems Technologies and Applications*, *4*(4). doi:10.1504/IJISTA.2008.017278

Anderson, J. R., & Corbett, A. T. (1995). Cognitive Tutors: Lessons Learned. *Journal of the Learning Sciences*, *4*(2), 167–207. doi:10.1207/s15327809jls0402_2

Baylor, A. L. (2001). Permutations of control: Cognitive considerations for agent-based learning environments. *Journal of Interactive Learning Research*, *12*(4), 403–425.

Bickmore, T. (2003). *Relational Agents: Effecting Change through Human-Computer Relationships*. (Ph.D. Thesis). Cambridge, MA: Massachusetts Institute of Technology.

Burleson, W. *(2006, September)* Affective Learning Companions: Strategies for Empathetic Agents with Real-Time Multimodal Affective Sensing to Foster Meta-Cognitive and Meta-Affective Approaches to Learning, Motivation, and Perseverance, *MIT PhD Thesis*.

Conati, C., & VanLehn, K. (2001). *Providing adaptive support to the understanding of instructional material*. Santa Fe, New Mexico: Proceedings Intelligent User Interfaces.

Ekman, P., & Davidson, R. J. (1993). Voluntary smiling changes regional brain activity. *Psychological Science* 4: 342-345. Ekman, P. and W. V. Friesen (1978). *Facial Action Coding System*. Consulting Psychologists Press.

Fasel, B., & Luettin, J. (2003). Automatic Facial Expression Analysis: A Survey. *Pattern Recognition, 36*(1), 259–275. doi:10.1016/S0031-3203(02)00052-3

Hayes, B. G. (2001). Where's the data: Is Multimedia Instruction Effective in Training Counselors? *Journal of Technology in Counseling, 1*(1).

Hill, W. E. (1997). *Learning: A Survey of Psychological Interpretations*. Reading, MA: Addison-Wesley Educational Publishers Inc.

Holt, P., & Dubs, S. (1994). Student Modeling: The Key to Individualized Knowledge-based Instruction. In Greer, J. E., & McCalla, G. I. (Eds.), *The State of Student Modeling*. Berlin, Germany: Springer-Verlag.

Johnson, W. L., Rickel, J. W., & Lester, J. C. (2000). Animated pedagogical agents: Face-to-face interaction in interactive learning environments. *International Journal of Artificial Intelligence in Education, 11*, 47–78.

Johnson, W. L., Shaw, E., et al. (2003). Evolution of user interaction: the case of Agent Adele. In *Proceedings Intelligent User Interfaces*.

Kopf, D. (2007*). E-Learning Market to hit $52.6B by 2010*. Retrieved June 27, 2008, from http://www.thejournal.com/articles/21046

Lee, J. S. (1983). Digital image smoothing and the sigma filter. *Computer Vision Graphics and Image Processing, 24*, 255–269. doi:10.1016/0734-189X(83)90047-6

(2004). Life-Like Characters, Tools, Affective Functions, and Applications. InPrendinger, H., & Ishizuka, M. (Eds.), *Cognitive Technologies Series*. Berlin Heidelberg, Germany: Springer.

McQuiggan, S. W., Robison, J. L., Phillips, R., & Lester, J. C. (2008) Modelling parallel and reactive empathy in virtual agents: an inductive approach. In *Proceedings of the 7th international Joint Conference on Autonomous Agents and Multiagent Systems - Volume 1*. International Conference on Autonomous Agents. International Foundation for Autonomous Agents and Multiagent Systems, (pp. 167-174).

Mehrabian, A. (1971). *Silent messages*. Belmont, CA: Wadsworth.

Michel, P., & El Kaliouby, R. (2003). Real time facial expression recognition in video using support vector machines. In *Proceedings of the 5th international Conference on Multimodal interfaces* (ICMI '03), (pp. 258-264). New York: ACM.

Mitrovic, A., & Martin, B. (2002). Using evaluation to shape ITS design: results and experiences with sql-tutor. *International Journal of User Modeling and User-Adapted Interaction, 12*(2-3), 243–379. doi:10.1023/A:1015022619307

Overmyer, S. P. (1999). If only my intelligent pedagogical agent could! *Journal of Educational Technology & Society, 2*(1).

Pantic, M., & Rothkrantz, L. J. M. (1999). An Expert System for Multiple Emotional Classification of Facial Expressions. *IEEE International Conference on Tools with Artificial Intelligence*, Chicago.

Picard, R. W. (1998). Towards Agents that Recognize Emotion. In *Proceedings of IMAGINA*, Monaco.

Rosenberg, E. L., & Ekman, P. (1994). Coherence between expressive and experiential systems in emotion. *Cognition and Emotion, 8*, 201–229. doi:10.1080/02699939408408938

Ruch, W. (1995). Will the real relationship between facial expression and affective experience please stand up: the case of exhilaration. *Cognition and Emotion*, *9*, 33–58. doi:10.1080/02699939508408964

Sahbi, H., & Geman, D. (2006). A Hierarchy of Support Vector Machines for Pattern Detection. *Journal of Machine Learning Research*, *7*, 2087–2123.

Sarrafzadeh, A., Alexander, S., Dadgostar, F., Fan, C., & Bigdeli, A. (2008). How do you know that I don't understand? A look at the future of intelligent tutoring systems. *Elsevier Journal-. Computers in Human Behavior*, *24*(4), 1342–1363. doi:10.1016/j.chb.2007.07.008

Self, J. A. (1990). Theoretical foundations for intelligent tutoring systems. *International Journal of Artificial Intelligence in Education*, *1*(4), 3–14.

Singular Inversions, Inc. (2009). *The FaceGen Modeler User Manual*. Retrieved January 8, 2009 from http://www.facegen.com/modeller_help.htm

Urban-Lurain, M. (2003). An Historic Review in the Context of the Development of Artificial Intelligence and Educational Psychology. Retrieved October 24, 2009, from http://www.cse.msu.edu /rgroups/cse101/ITS/its.htm

van Mulken, S., André, E., & Muller, J. (1998). The persona effect: How substantial is it? In *Proceedings of Human Computer Interaction*. Berlin.

Wang, Q., & Yang, J. (2006). Eye Detection in Facial Images with Unconstrained Background. *Journal of Pattern Recognition Research*, *1*, 55–62.

Whitehurst, R. A., Powell, C. L., et al. (1998). Utilizing the student model in distance learning. In *Proceedings of ITiCSE'98*. Dublin, Ireland.

Xu, Y., & Aliaga, D. G. (2007). Efficient multiviewpoint acquisition of 3D objects undergoing repetitive motions. In *Proceedings of the 2007 Symposium on interactive 3D Graphics and Games, I3D '07*. (pp. 113-120). New York: ACM.

Chapter 8
E-Learning through Gaming: Unfolding Children's Negotiation Skills

Jeroen Geuze
Donders Instiute for Brain Cognition and Behaviour, The Netherlands

Egon L. van den Broek
Human-Centered Computing Consultancy, The Netherlands

ABSTRACT

A generic theoretical framework on teaching children to negotiate is presented, founded on Piaget's child development and Thompson and Hastie's negotiation theories and validated through an experiment. The framework was implemented as CLIPS knowledge base, the back-end of an Intelligent Tutoring Agent (ITA). Negotiation skills were assessed through an online JAVA implementation of the board game Settlers of Catan (SoC). The CLIPS knowledge base was connected by JCLIPS to SoC. The ITA was thoroughly tested and found to be robust, with an excellent multithread handling. After installing a client, SoC can be played over Internet against other artificial or/and human players. The integrated ITA helps children to improve their negotiation skills and helps science to improve the theoretical framework, which makes it unique in its kind.

Tell me and I forget. Show me and I remember. Involve me and I understand. -- Old Chinese Proverb

INTRODUCTION

Almost half a century ago, Roberts & Sutton-Smith (1962) started their influential paper "Child Training and Game Involvement" with: "Games are systemic culture patterns which are distinctive, ancient, and widespread..." (Roberts & Sutton-Smith, 1962). In their paper, they explain that games are of all times and places. Moreover, they illustrate the importance of games for our development both as individuals and as society. The statements of Roberts & Sutton-Smith can be considered as a specific instantiation of the old Chinese proverb shown above.

With the rise of the computer, a new type of games was given birth. With the increasing availability and speed of Internet, gaming over Internet evolved rapidly. Similar to traditional (e.g., board)

DOI: 10.4018/978-1-61692-008-1.ch008

games, these "digital games" can help its players develop themselves (e.g., on mental or motor skills), provide distraction, or both. In this paper, an intelligent tutoring system (ITS) is introduced that facilitates e-learning through gaming. Such a system should be able to provide individualized instruction, while dynamically adapting to level of knowledge, intelligence, and needs of individual students. Compared to traditional teaching scenarios, an ITS has various advantages; e.g., it is always available, is non-judgmental, and provides tailored feedback (Sarrafzadeh, Alexander, Dadgostar, Fan, & Bigdeli, 2008).

ITSs are developed for a range of purposes; e.g., military (Doesburg, Heuvelink, & van den Broek, 2005). This research deviates from most other research on two aspects: 1) it focuses on a rather fixed age span and 2) its topic: learning negotiation skills. Where other researchers have also focused on specific target groups, in most cases the students were adult or adolescent, we focus on children with the age of 8–12. Negotiation processes are of interest to a range of settings and, consequently, have been studied from a range of perspectives. However, the combination of these two aspects has not been made so far. This, while also children negotiate with both other children and with their parents.

With the aim to train children in negotiating using an e-learning environment, a game was sought that could be utilized for this purpose. The popular board game Settlers of Catan (SoC) was chosen; Table 1 provides a brief description of the game. The use of SoC has another advantage: an open source JAVA implementation of the game was available. Consequently, not the complete game including all its rules had to be implemented.

This chapter introduces an Intelligent Tutoring Agent (ITA) that helps children understand the negotiation processes through playing SoC. It is connected to the open source implementation of SoC. After providing some background information on Games in Education and ITSs, the paper describes the complete process of development of the ITA. It starts with a new theoretical framework on negotiation processes with children, which is founded on 1) Piaget's theory of child development and 2) adult negotiation strategies, as will be described in the section 'Theoretical framework'. Next, the validation of this theoretical framework is described. The development of the ITA itself is described in the section 'Design and implementation'. Next, the testing of the ITA is described in the section 'The ITA in practice'. The paper ends with a Discussion in which we reflect upon the work presented.

Table 1. Short description of the Settlers of Catan board game, taken from the Mayfair website: http://www.mayfairgames.com/

Players are recent immigrants to the newly populated island of Catan. Expand your colony through the building of settlements, roads, and villages by harvesting commodities from the land around you. Trade sheep, lumber, bricks and grain for a settlement, bricks and wood for a road, or try to complete other combinations for more advanced buildings, services and specials. Trade with other players, or at local seaports to get resources you might lack. The first player to achieve 10 points from a combination of roads, settlements, and special cards wins.

GAMES IN EDUCATION

In order to explain the usefulness of games for education, let us start with a definition of a game. Salen and Zimmerman (2004) define a game as: 'A game is a system in which players engage in an artificial conflict, defined by rules, that results in a quantifiable outcome.' (p. 80). This definition contains a number of important elements that need further clarification. We explain these elements in line with the work of Salen and Zimmerman (2004). A system is a set of parts that interrelate to form a complex whole. All systems have four common elements: objects, attributes, internal relationships and an environment. Systems can manifest itself in different ways; e.g., a mathematical system, a social system. A game has to be played by one or more players; they interact with the system to experience the play of the game. Games are artificial; they are separate from the real world. They occur in the real world, but they themselves are not real, artificiality is one of the defining features of a game. A game always contains an element of conflict or contest. This can manifest itself in different ways, there can be cooperation between players, or there can be competition between them, there can be conflict between players or conflict between a player and the system, but there is always an element of conflict. A crucial part of a game is made up by its rules. They provide the structure of the game, by (de)limiting the possibilities within the game. At the end of the game, a player has won or lost, or a numerical score can be given: its quantifiable outcome, which distinguishes games from more informal forms of play.

The sheer amount of different kind of games shows the importance of games in society. There are for instance games that are played outside with friends (e.g., hide and seek, hopscotch, marbles), official team games / sports (e.g., soccer, baseball, basketball), puzzles and riddles, digital games, etc. In the last decades, the interest in computer games has increased dramatically, and its potential for educational purposes has been duly noted. As indicated by Salen and Zimmerman (2004), there are four special traits that distinguish computer games from regular games. First, computer games have immediate but narrow interactivity. One of the most compelling qualities about digital games is that they provide immediate feedback, offering the player real-time game play. Though most people think that the interactivity of digital games is very broad, it is in fact, very limited. The user has only a (small) set of options from which to choose. Second, digital games manipulate information, as becomes apparent when studying them from an information system perspective. Everything in the game, audio, graphics, and even the program code itself, is information and can be manipulated. Third, a digital game can be seen as an automated complex system. Hence, things that are impossible in "regular" games, because they are too complex, become possible. Fourth and last, digital games are able to utilize networked communication and consequently can facilitate communication between distant players; e.g., players of the game World of Warcraft1 can play the game together, even when on different sides of the continent.

Games may be important to society and are often associated with children and childhood, but are children able to understand games? In particular, games as they are defined by Salen and Zimmerman (2004)? According to Gobet, Voogt, and Retschitzki (2004): "children understand the concept of rules [...] at about 6 years of age, even if they sometimes forget specific rules or change them during play. They also understand the concepts of winning and losing. But they only apply rules consistently [...] at 11 or 12 years of age." (p.139). They also state that there exists "an association between level of games played by children and their presumed level of cognitive development based on their age." (p. 140). Hence, games can be used in education from the age of 6 but their difficulty has to be tailored to the mental development of the children (from ages 6 to 15). Coleman (1967) poses that children do not learn by being taught, but by experiencing the consequences of their actions, as is facilitated through using games in education. Games have i) an attention-focusing quality, which enriches the depth of involvement and ii) students experience the consequences of their actions in games with no teacher to blame in the case of failure, as their role is diminished to that of judge and jury.

For educational purposes, games are also interesting because they are challenging, which is defined as that: "an activity should have a goal, whose outcome is uncertain." (Malone, 1983) (p. 241). This is confirmed by Salen and Zimmerman (2004): "Uncertainty is a key component of every game. If a game is completely predetermined, the players actions will not have an impact on the outcome of the game and meaningful play will be impossible." (p. 189). This all makes games very useful for educational purposes.

Despite all their advantages, computer games on their own can hardly be used for educational purposes, since didactic functionality is missing (Leutner, 1993). There is a trade-off between learning to play the game and acquiring the intended skills or domain knowledge. Students that play games without instructional support learn to play the game, but acquire only limited domain-specific concepts, facts, rules, and principles, where students that play games with instructional support learn to play the game only to a limited degree, but do acquire a high degree of domain knowledge (Conati & Zhao, 2004; Leutner, 1993). This holds for different age groups and educational standards (Leutner, 1993).

To improve the efficiency and effectiveness of instruction using games, instructional support should be embedded. The latter can be achieved through, i) provide essentially unlimited examples and problems, ii) facilitate visualization and manipulation; link visualization with symbolic representations, iii) provide adaptive sequencing and feedback, and iv) provide sustained contextualization in a meaningful and engaging application (Klawe, 1998). When adding this functionality to games, a game is transformed into a, so called, ITS, as will be described in the next section.

INTELLIGENT TUTORING SYSTEMS (ITS)

"An Intelligent Tutoring System allows for errors to occur and provides the student with feedback and associated remedial action" (Siemer & Angelides, 1995, p. 1377). An ITS can deliver personal (tailored) instruction to a student, taking his or her progress into account (Beck & Woolf, 2000).

An ITS should be able to give personal instruction in an automatic and cost effective manner, mostly within a highly interactive learning environment. An ITS assesses the actions of the learner and develops a model of the learners knowledge, skills, and expertise. Based on this model, it can offer explanations, hints, examples, and demonstrations (Craighead, 2008; Gulz & Haake, 2006; McQuiggan, Mott, & Lester, 2008; Romero & Ventura, 2007; van Rosmalen, et al., 2008; Wang, Johnson, Mayer, Rizzo, Shaw, & Collins, 2008; Keleş, Ocak, & Gülcü, 2009).

An ITS consists of four knowledge modules: the domain knowledge module, the user or student model, the pedagogical module, and the communication module (Sarrafzadeh, Alexander, Dadgostar, Fan, & Bigdeli, 2008).

The domain knowledge module includes an explicit representation of domain-specific knowledge. It contains a computer representation of the knowledge that has been elicited from domain experts by knowledge engineers. The knowledge in this model is compared to the student's actions to determine what the student's state of knowledge is.

The student model contains information on student. It includes a model of the current knowledge of the student; i.e., which concepts does he understand, which can be understood with a minimum of guidance, and which are out of reach (for the moment). To model the student either single or hybrid formalisms can be used. Single formalisms are based on one theory; e.g., symbolic rules (as used in this project), case-based reasoning, neural networks. Hybrid formalisms combine multiple formalisms.

The pedagogical module contains teaching expertise; i.e., how to present the information in such a way that it aids the student in learning.

The communication module is responsible for all communication with the learner.

Generally, there are three types of users of an ITS: domain experts, who provide knowledge concerning the domain of the ITS, knowledge engineers, who manage the development of the ITS, and learners, who are the end-users of the ITS. Each of these users pose their own requirements on the system. For a more detailed description of these requirements, see the article by Hatzilygeroudis & Prentzas (2004). In this research, the domain expert and knowledge engineer are embodied by the researcher and the learners or end-users are children, who will be guided while playing the game.

THEORETICAL FRAMEWORK

The amount of research done on either children and board games or children and negotiation is very limited (Gobet, Voogt, & Retschitzki, 2004). Therefore, we choose to develop a new theoretical framework founded on two theories: 1) the child development theory of Piaget (Lourenço & Machado, 1996) and 2) Thompson & Hastie's (1990) theory on negotiation between adults. The combination of the latter theories enabled us to determine the initial level of understanding of the negotiation process in children. We will now first briefly introduce both theories and derive some general cognitive notions. Subsequently, the general cognitive notions are related to the stages Piaget distinguishes. Knowledge gathered through the latter three steps is merged to a new theoretical framework.

Piaget's Stage Theory

Although various theories on child development have challenged Piaget's stage theory, his work is still and by far the most influential. Moreover, much of the criticism on Piaget's work is founded on misconceptions and misinterpretations of his work, as is shown by Lourenço and Machado (1996). They defent Piaget's work through rejecting 10 common criticims on it. This article also provides an excellent overview of both Piaget's most important works and those of others who either agree or disagree with Piaget. More than anything else, this shows that although Piaget's theory is well known its interpretation is a source for discussion and child development is general is a challenging topic.

Piaget defined four stages, which make up his Stage Theory; e.g., see Lourenço and Machado (1996) for an overview. These four stages are also called periods and are provided with an indication of the period in life they apply to.

In the sensorimotor period (birth to 2 years), children look at the world around them in terms of physical, overt actions on that world. They move from simple reflexes to organized behavior in six sub stages: modification of reflexes, primary circular reactions, secondary circular reactions, coordination of secondary schemes, tertiary circular reactions, and invention of new means through mental combinations.

The preoperational period (2-7 years) is mainly defined by: Egocentrism: children a) do not have a complete differentiation between themselves and the world and b) have the tendency to look at the world in terms of the self. This makes it difficult to take another person's view; Rigidity of thought: a) centration, the tendency to focus on one salient feature of an object or event and ignore the other features and b) the tendency to focus on states rather than on transformations linking the states emerges; and Semi logical reasoning: thought is often linked together in a loose way instead of in a logical relationship. Limited social cognition entail that social development undergoes a similar process as cognitive development.

In the concrete operational period (7-11 years), the regulations, functions, and identities turn into operations as they become more complete, differentiated, quantitative, and stable. With the ability to use operations, the child's representations are no longer isolated, rigid, or simply juxtaposed. In the formal operational period (11-15 years), adolescents carry the concrete operations one step further: they generate hypotheses that follow the results of concrete operations. With that, thought has become truly logical, abstract, and hypothetical, which is often called the scientific method. Children generate hypotheses and test them against reality. Consequently, they can reflect on their own and others, thinking and can act through a tightly organized system of thought – a unified whole.

Six Judgments with Negotiation

An excellent up-to-date book on negotiating is that of Saner (2008). This book has both a scientific merit and is of high value in practice. Moreover, it explores the process of negotiating from a generic perspective, which is illustrated by a range of cases. Although the book has an extensive bibliography, it is far from exhaustive. More than anything else, this illustrates the vast amount of research that has been done in the field of negotiating.

An exhaustive overview of theories on negotiation is beyond the scope of this chapter. For the interested reader, we refer to Saner (2008) and Thompson and Hastie (1990), which are complementary and as such make a good pair for an overview on the topic.

We have chosen for the theory of Thompson and Hastie (1990) on negotiating. This choice if founded on two reasons: 1) it is explicit, which enables its use for a rule based system, such as ours and 2) It maps reasonably well on Piaget's stage theory (Lourenço & Machado, 1996).

According to Thompson and Hastie (1990), six judgments are of importance when negotiating: 1) Judgments of the Other Party; e.g., the other party's strength or firmness, competitiveness, and fairness; 2) Judgments of the Self: the negotiator's own tastes, values, and preferences; 3) Interpersonal Judgments of Utilities: the negotiator's perception of his own utilities and those utilities of the other party and the amount of resources that will be negotiated about; 4) Judgments of Offers and Counter-offers: predictions about future moves; e.g., if one sees that the other really wants a resource, one might expect the next offer to be higher; 5) Judgments of Outcomes: the final outcome of the negotiation, the worth of the solution to the negotiator and the other party as well as the joint payoff for both. This determines the satisfaction of both parties and can influence future negotiations; 6) Judgments of Negotiation Process: the fairness and satisfaction of the whole negotiation process, including the rules, fair play, norms, etc. As is specified through the six judgments, the negotiator makes judgments about the other party, the self, the interpersonal utilities, offers and counter-offers, outcomes and the negotiation process itself.

The six judgments imply the utilization of various cognitive resources throughout the process of negotiating (Thompson & Hastie, 1990). To be able to make judgments about the other party, the negotiator has to be able to imagine what the other party wants and values. For self-reflection, a clear self-image and goal are needed (Saner, 2008). With judging offers and counteroffers, the negotiator requires an image of both himself and the other party and has to be able to hypothesize about the future. Judgments about the outcomes of the negotiation can only be made when the negotiator has a feeling for the utility (value) for himself, but also for the other party. In order to make judgments about the negotiation process itself, the negotiator has to know about the rules, about fairness, and about norms surrounding the negotiation (Saner, 2008). Though this last part is more of a goal in this research. Another important ability needed when negotiating it to keep one's goal in mind, and not get sidetracked by less important dimensions of the negotiation. The judgments give rise to the following cognitive aspects needed for negotiation: Feeling for numbers, fairness, utility for self, and utility of other party as well as the ability to keep one's goal(s) in mind and to predict/hypothesize.

A Theory on Negotiation Processes with Children

The general cognitive aspects were determined taking in consideration they should be: 1) based on the judgments put forward by Thompson and

Table 2. Overview of the Cognitive aspects and the judgments on negotiation (Thompson & Hastie, 1990) they are based upon

Cognitive Aspect	Judgment(s)
Feeling for numbers	4
Feeling for fairness	4
Feeling for utility to self	2, 3, 4, 5
Feeling for utility to other party	1, 3, 4, 5
Ability to keep one's goal in mind	
Ability to hypothesize	4, 5

Hastie (1990), 2) applicable on the domain of Settlers of Catan and be generalizable to a broader domain, and 3) able to match with the stage theory of child development to tailor these aspects to children. The general cognitive aspects and the judgments they are based upon are summarized in Table 2.

The fourth and last step in setting up the theoretical framework was to denote for each stage defined by Piaget (Lourenço & Machado, 1996), whether or not each of the general cognitive aspects is already present in children in that stage of development. Let us illustrate the latter by sketching the decision process for the Feeling for utility to other party aspect. In the pre-operational stage, this aspect is not yet developed since children have a limited social cognition and are egocentric. Children in this stage have problems taking another's' viewpoint; e.g., when a child is looking at a picture in a book and draws his mother's attention to this picture, it does not realize that the mother is not able to see the picture when she is sitting opposite the child. From this, one can deduce that they will not be able to determine the utility of a negotiation to another party. In the concrete operational stage, the egocentrism fades away and children's limited social cognition is improved, enabling them to make judgments about utility to another by the end of the concrete operational stage. Once a certain level of development has been reached there will be no regression; therefore, once a cognitive aspect has been developed, it will not be lost. This explains why the Feeling for utility to other is also developed in the formal operational stage.

Table 3 summarizes the results of mapping the cognitive aspects to Piaget's stage theory. This table denotes that in the concrete operational stage, most of the cognitive aspects are developed. From these results, the target group age could be determined. According to Piaget (Lourenço & Machado, 1996), the developments are only complete at the end of each stage. He also showed, using the containment experiment (Lourenço & Machado, 1996), that children are not able to learn a certain task when they have not yet reached the required level of development. Keeping this in mind, the target group age was determined to be around 10 years of age. The mapping of the aspects to Piaget's theory was confirmed by a semi-experiment, in which three 10-year-old children played a game of Settlers of

Table 3. Overview of the combination of the Piaget's Stage Theory (Lourenço & Machado, 1996) and the cognitive aspects derived from the judgments on negotiation (Thompson & Hastie, 1990)

Aspect / Stage	Pre-operational	Concrete operational	Formal operational
Feeling for numbers	No	Yes	Yes
Feeling for fairness	No	Yes	Yes
Feeling for utility to self	Yes	Yes	Yes
Feeling for utility to other party	No	Yes	Yes
Ability to keep one's goal in mind	Yes	Yes	Yes
Ability to hypothesize	Yes	No	Yes

Catan. This is also the lower age limit set by the makers of Settlers of Catan.

The findings presented in Table 3 are also confirmed by Gobet, Voogt, & Retschitzki (2004) who states: "Parker argues that children understand the concept of rules... at about 6 years of age, even if they sometimes forget specific rules or change them during play. They also understand the concepts of winning and losing. But they only apply rules consistently... at 11 or 12 years of age." (p.139) and "Sutton-Smith... reports an association between level of games played by children and their presumed level of cognitive development based on their age." (p. 140).

VALIDATION OF THE THEORETICAL FRAMEWORK

The theoretical framework, described in the previous section, is based on two theories. The next step is to validate this framework in practice, as is done by a validation experiment. The experiment utilized a Likert scale questionnaire (Likert, 1932). In the first subsection, the pilot study that was executed to determine the size of the intervals for the Likert scale is described. The actual validation experiment is described in second (and last) subsection.

Pilot

A questionnaire was developed to be able to determine whether or not a certain cognitive aspect has evolved. For each cognitive aspect, a number of questions were posed that would determine whether or not the aspect has been developed. These questions were specific to the context of Settlers of Catan.

An overview of all questions in the questionnaire is provided in Table 4. The answers could be provided through a Likert scale that denoted three intervals. The size of these intervals was determined in this pilot study.

Table 4. Questionnaire used in the validation of the theoretical framework. For each of the cognitive aspects, there are a number of questions that can be asked to poll their development. The questions in italics where answered by the experimenter in the pilot study and the other questions were answered by the subjects.

General considerations:
How many times does he stray from the rules?
In the beginning (First 20 minutes)?
Middle (middle 30 minutes)?
At the end (Last 20 minutes)?
Which rules, simple or complex ones?
How many times does he have to ask for certain rules?
In the beginning (First 20 minutes)?
Middle (middle 30 minutes)?
At the end (Last 20 minutes)?
Which rules, simple or complex ones?
Feeling for numbers:
How often does the subject offer a ratio to a player that he can also trade with a bank or port?
Does the subject understand probabilities? Does he choose places with high probability (5, 6, 8, and 9)?
Feeling for fairness:
How often does the subject try to close an unfair (asking more than giving) deal?
How often does the subject accept an unfair deal?
Feeling for utility to self:
How often does the subject trade resources that he needs himself?
Feeling for utility to other:
How often does the subject offer to someone who is about to win?
How often does the subject accept offer from someone who is about to win?
Ability to hypothesize:
Does he pick strategic starting places?
Does the subject form an consequent strategy (city building, longest road, monopoly, etc.)?

Method

Three university students (one male, two females) participated in the pilot experiment on voluntarily basis. They were between 21 and 25 years old. The experiment was performed in a natural setting; i.e., at on of the student's homes. The questionnaire as depicted in Table 4, was divided into two parts. One part that was answered by the experimenter (marked with italics). The other part was answered by the subjects. With that, the factor of awareness was taken into account. For some questions, the action would not occur if the subject is aware of it; e.g., trade with player instead of bank. These questions were allotted to the experimenter. Other questions are difficult for the experimenter to determine; e.g., conscious strategy changes. These questions were allotted to the subject.

Summarizing, the subjects were asked to keep track on how often they performed certain key actions; e.g., changed their overall strategy or negotiate with an almost winning player. In parallel, the experimenter kept track on how often players did violate the rules, how often they traded for resources with players instead of with the bank or port, etc.

Results

The results of the pilot experiment are given in Table 5 and Table 6. The experimenter observed that all students abode the rules: they did not trade for a resource with a player while they could also trade with the bank. In addition, each player chose strategic starting places and no unfair deals were made.

Summarizing, the questionnaires the subjects filled in indicated the following:

- The number of questions concerning the rules dropped while playing the game;
- Multiple strategy changes were made, some as a reaction to actions of opponents;
- Trades were more for required resources;
- No (conscious) decisions were made not to trade;
- No trades with winning players were initiated;
- Offers of winning players were accepted.

Discussion

The questionnaire was updated with the three item Likert scales for a number of questions. It was assumed that the score of the students would be the ideal case; i.e., when all cognitive aspects are fully developed. These scores determined the range of the Likert scales. An example of this can be seen in Table 7.

Table 5. Results of the pilot study, questions answered by the experimenter

Question	Subject 1	Subject 2	Subject 3
Stray from rules beginning/middle/end	0/0/0	0/0/0	0/0/0
Trade with player instead of bank	0	0	0
Choose strategic starting places	Yes	Yes	Yes
Number of unfair offers	0	0	0
Number of unfair accepts	0	0	0

Table 6. Results of the pilot study, questions answered by the subjects

Question	Subject 1	Subject 2	Subject 3
Ask for rules beginning/middle/end	8/5/1	4/0/0	1/0/2
Change overall strategy	6	2	1
How often determined by opponent	3	1	1
Trade for resources needed now	12	1	1
Not decide to trade	0	0	0
Initiate trade with winning player	˙0	0	1
Respond to offer from winning player	2	1	0

Table 7. Example of a question used in the experiment. Here, the Likert scales have been added. The expected interval when the cognitive aspects if fully developed it marked with an asterisk.

• How often does the subject offer a ratio to a player that he can also trade with a bank or port? ○ 0 - 5 * ○ 5 - 10 ○ 10 • Does the subject understand probabilities? Does he choose places with high probability (5, 6, 8, and 9)? (YES)

Please note that subject one, who won the game, has higher values for all questions than the other subjects. The answers she gave on the questions possibly indicate the use of more fruitful strategies compared to the other two players. However, the higher values could also be attributed to her paying more attention to the questionnaire, due to her mathematical background. Moreover, it could be that the other players performed the key events as much as subject one, but in the heat of the game forgot to write it down.

Validation Experiment

The aim of the experiment was to validate the newly developed theoretical framework. The experiment should determine whether children (10-13 years) have effectively developed the cognitive abilities, as described in the framework. To test this, the questionnaire shown in Table 4 was used.

Method

In the experiment, the board game Settlers of Catan was played with three 10-year-old boys, who already knew each other. Two of the boys were in group six, and one in group seven of the Dutch education system. The research was explained to the boys and they were asked whether or not they were willing to participate. In parallel, their parents were given an informed consent, which they signed.

The game was played in a natural setting; i.e., at one of the children's homes. This eliminated the period where the children have to acquaint themselves. The game was recorded on video of which a transcription was made afterward. Based on the transcription, the actions of the children were identified. A frame of the video is shown in Figure 1 to give an idea of the experimental situation. The questionnaire was used in the analysis of the game, where the experimenter tallied the occurrences of the events of interest.

Figure 1. Frame taken from the video recorded during the validation experiment

Results

The complete results of the validation experiment are given in Table 8. This table shows all the questions in the questionnaire and the score of each of the subjects. For the questions with a Likert scale, the intervals are indicated with "Low", "Middle", and "High". Whether or not a cognitive ability was developed by a player was determined by checking whether the answer found in the experiment is the same answer that would be expected if the aspect has been developed (indicated in the "Desired" column). The results of this analysis are summarized in Table 9. As can be seen, all players have developed all cognitive aspects except for the ability to hypothesize, which has only been developed by one subject. One of the children made the following remark to a fellow player: "I will give you a tip, put it at what you want, that one will probably have it.", where 'it' denotes the robber, the piece that allows a player to steal from another (see Table 1) and 'what' refers to a resource tile, showing an understanding of probabilities. Another observation was that one of the players showed an obvious strategy (largest army), by buying a large number of development cards in a row.

Table 8. Complete results of the validation experiment, sorted by cognitive aspect, where 'L', 'M', 'H', denote the Low, Middle, High Likert intervals

Question	Desired	S1	S2	S3
General Aspects				
Stray from rules beginning/middle/end	L/L/L	L/L/L	L/M/L	L/M/L
Which rules	Complex	Simple	Both	Both
Ask for rules beginning/middle/end	L/L/L	M/L/L	M/M/M	L/L/L
Which rules	Complex	Complex	Complex	Simple
Feeling for numbers				
Trade with player not bank	Low	Low	Low	Low
Understand probability	Yes	Yes	Yes	Yes
Feeling for fairness				
Offer unfair deal	Low	Low	Low	Low
Accept unfair deal	Low	Low	Low	Low
Feeling for utility to self				
Trade for resources needed	Yes	Yes	Yes	Yes
Deny trade when resources needed	Yes	Yes	Yes	Yes
Feeling for utility to other				
Offer to winning player	Low	Low	Low	Low
Accept from winning player	Low	Low	Low	Low
Ability to hypothesize				
Pick strategic starting places	Yes	Yes	Yes	Yes
Form strategy	Yes	No	Yes	No

Table 9. Overview of the developed cognitive aspects for each of the three subjects in the validation experiment

Aspects / Player	Subject 1	Subject 2	Subject 3
Feeling for numbers	Yes	Yes	Yes
Feeling for fairness	Yes	Yes	Yes
Feeling for utility to self	Yes	Yes	Yes
Feeling for utility to other	Yes	Yes	Yes
Ability to keep goal in mind	Yes	Yes	Yes
Ability to hypothesize	No	Yes	No

Discussion

The children in the experiment show the same cognitive aspects that could be expected from children at the end of the concrete operational period; thus, sustaining the theoretical framework. An advantage of the experiment is that it was done in a natural setting and that the children were familiar with each other, making it easier for the children to forget they are participating in an experiment, which facilitates the natural behavior of the children. Three improvements could be made to enhance the results of the experiment: (i) The game could be played multiple times to determine if the results hold over multiple games. (ii) It could be played with only girls, and a mixture of boys and girls to determine if there is difference between genders. (iii) The age could be more varied over the interval of 10-13 years old. The experiment could also be performed with children under 10 years of age, to determine whether or not the theoretical framework holds for children that are not at the end of the concrete operational period; e.g., with children between 5 and 7 or children between 7 and 10 years of age.

DESIGN AND IMPLEMENTATION

This section describes the development of the Intelligent Tutoring Agent itself. First, a short introduction to JSettlers to which the ITA was added. Next, the design of the agent is discussed and some of the design decisions are highlighted. Last, the actual implementation is documented.

JSettlers

JSettlers has been developed by Robert S. Thomas at Northwestern University2. It has been designed and implemented using a client/server architecture, this has been done to be able to collect data about games being played at a central location. The JSettlers server can host a number of games and manages all the game state information for each of the games initiated on the server. One or more clients are connected to each game. If there are not enough real players the remaining number of players can be filled by robot clients. The client/server architecture could also facilitate the addition of the ITA to be developed. There are not many operational versions of Settlers of Catan. Another operational version called Pioneers3 has been found. This program was developed under Linux, and using the C programming language. It is not portable to any other operating system. This was the main reason for choosing JSettlers, which is developed under JAVA and is, therefore, platform independent.

Design of the Intelligent Tutoring Agent (ITA)

The ITA was designed as an integrated part of the original JSettlers client. This way, the agent is able to retrieve information about the game through the client. Alternatively, the agent could have been implemented as a stand-alone application; however, then all game information had to be retrieved and interpreted from the JSettlers Server manually.

In the section Intelligent Tutoring Systems, an architecture for ITSs was presented. There are four important components in an ITS: a Domain Knowledge Base, a Student Model, a Pedagogical Module, and a Communication Module. The design of the ITA was based on these four components, as can be seen in the conceptual architecture in Figure 2. The player interacts with JSettlers, the game upon which the ITA is built. JSettlers has a link with the Agent user interface (UI), through which the interface is presented to the user and the actions of the player are communicated to the agent. These actions are passed on to the Strategy DB and the Offer Judge components. The Strategy database (DB) component contains domain information about the possible strategies within Settlers of Catan. The Offer Judge contains domain information about negotiations; e.g., how to recognize an unfair offer or an offer for a trade that could also have been made with the bank. The Strategy DB, communicates its findings to the Strategy Monitor, which maintains information about which strategy the player is or is not employing. The Strategy Monitor relays this information to the Generate Hypotheses component. The Offer Judge relays information about the negotiations to the Generate Hypotheses component. This component then generates hypotheses about the development of the cognitive aspects in the monitored player. These hypotheses are tested in the Test Hypotheses component. When a hypothesis has been judged true, an advice is generated in the Generate Advice component. This advice is relayed through the Agent UI and JSettlers to the player. The Check Effect component keeps account of the number of times an aspect has been disproved. This influences the advice generated through the generate and test hypotheses cycle. Each of these components (see also Figure 2 is explained in more detail below.

Agent UI provides the UI of the agent. It is also the direct link between the ITA and JSettlers and, thus, the only link between the agent and the player. All actions of the player and information

Figure 2. Schematic overview of the design of the ITA. The circles denote the different modules traditionally found in ITS: Communication Module, responsible for all the communication with the user, the Pedagogical Module, responsible for tailoring the information provided to the learner, the Domain Knowledge Module, which contains the information about the domain: Settlers of Catan, Student Model, which contains information about the learner. In boxes the specific sections of the ITA and how they interact with each other.

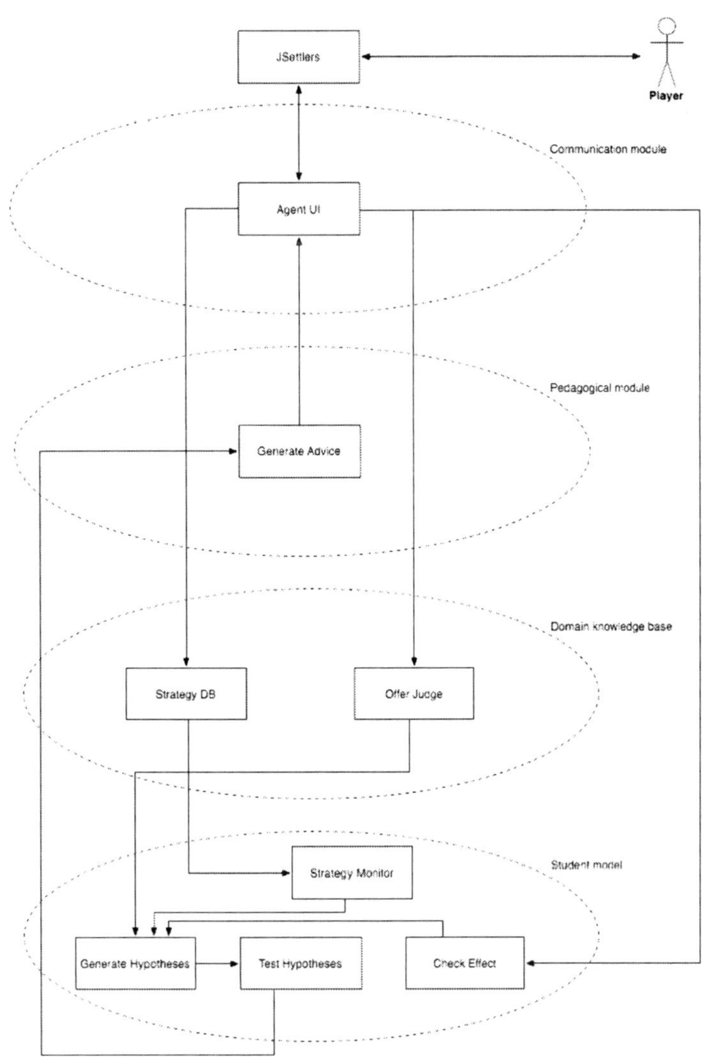

on the state of the game arrive at the Agent UI, which relays some of this information to the other modules for further processing.

Strategy DB receives game information from the Agent UI concerning the placement of game pieces and a buy history. It contains domain information about the possible strategies in Settlers of Catan. For each of these strategies, it also contains information on how it can be determined whether or not a player is employing this strategy. By combining the game information and the knowledge about strategies, it is able to determine which strategy or strategies are employed by the player. In determining these strategies from the game information, it also takes the number of parallel strategies into account; other conditions apply when multiple strategies are employed than when a single strategy is used.

Offer Judge receives information about negotiations in the game from the Agent UI. It is able to keep track of all offers that have been made and is able to judge these offers. A judgment could for instance indicate whether a certain offer is fair or not.

Strategy Monitor receives information on the strategies detected by the Strategy DB module and compares these to the strategies the player indicated in the interface. The information whether any strategy is being used and whether the indicated strategies match with the detected strategies is passed on to the Generate Hypotheses module.

Generate Hypotheses This component receives information from different components about the game and the player, and generates hypotheses about the cognitive aspects of the player. When there is an indication that a certain cognitive aspect may not be fully developed, it generates a hypothesis that states this.

Test Hypotheses receives the hypotheses that have been generated by the Generate Hypotheses component and tries to confirm them. This is done by checking whether all conditions to falsify a certain cognitive aspect have been met. If this is the case, the confirmation of this hypothesis is relayed to the Generate Advice module. If not all conditions have been met, nothing happens and the module waits for more game information to become available.

Generate Advice This component generates the advice that is presented to the player when the system has detected that one of the cognitive aspects has not been fully developed. This advice is specific to the aspect and depends on how often advice on the same cognitive aspect has been given before. The advice starts out generally and becomes more explicit.

Check Effect keeps track of how often a cognitive aspect has been disproved. If an aspect is not falsified again after advice has been given to the player then it can be concluded that the advice had an effect.

The last four modules: Generate Hypotheses, Test Hypotheses, Generate Advice, and Check Effect, together form an expert system architecture for a diagnosis expert system. When choosing an expert system architecture, there are many different model templates that can be used as a basis, or architecture. These model templates vary with the task that needs to be performed; the continuous detection of errors and the reason for them. Schreiber et al. (2000), suggest three models that can be of use in this case: the assessment, diagnosis, and monitoring templates. Of these three models, assessment only takes one point in time into account and monitoring only registers a discrepancy and does not look at the cause of it. Diagnosis does incorporate both these characteristics and is, therefore, applied. See also the Student model in Figure 2.

The rules in the diagnosis modules were designed from global to specific, with the cognitive aspects as starting point. The agent assumes that all the cognitive aspects have been developed and tries to disprove them: First, the system determines whether or not a cognitive aspect needs to be elicited. Next, the system checks whether or not that aspect has been developed by asking a set of questions.

Determining the Symbolic Rules

For each of the six cognitive aspects, questions were defined and, subsequently, converted into symbolic rules. As an example we take the *Ability to hypothesize* aspect. The first step consists of determining how this aspect manifests itself in the game. For the ability to hypothesize, in other words to think ahead, two actions in the game are of importance. The selection of strategic starting places when setting up the board and the employment of a general game strategy. These were turned into two questions that could be tested when playing, for our example, the questions are given in Table 10. These questions are then transformed into symbolic rules that could disprove the cognitive aspect in question. For our example the resulting symbolic rules are given in Table 11. For each of the conditions in the general rules, more specific, or auxiliary, rules were constructed to determine when these generic conditions were met. An example for the Not using strategy condition is given in Table 12, including rules for two of the six strategies.

Table 13 through Table 15 provide some another example for the *Feeling for numbers* aspect Hence, Figures Table 11 trough Table 15 illustrate the three phases in which the cognitive aspects

Table 10. Example questions used for the cognitive aspect: Ability to hypothesize

• Does he or she pick strategic starting places? (YES/NO) • Does the subject form a consequent strategy (city building, longest road, monopoly, etc.)?

Table 12. Example of auxiliary rules used to determine one of the conditions of the generic rules shown in Table 11

IF ANY Strategy THEN NOT Not using strategy IF More than 2 same resource incomes AND Port of that resource THEN Strategy Monopoly IF Built more than 3 roads in short interval AND Longest road is less than 2 roads away THEN Strategy Road building

Table 14. Example of how the system determines a specific fact, in this case Offer to player instead of bank, which is used in the rule depicted in Table 15

Given Negotiation(fromPlayer, toPlayer, giveSet, getSet), IF fromPlayer == monitoredPlayer AND resourceAmount(resources, giveSet) == 4 AND size(getSet) == 1 THEN Offer to player instead of bank

Table 11. Example of how the questions in Table 10 are transformed into symbolic rules used in the edxpert system

IF No strategic starting place OR Not using strategy THEN Hypothesis(NOT ability to hypothesize) IF Hypothesis(NOT ability to hypothesize) AND No strategic starting place AND Not using strategy THEN NOT Ability to hypothesize

Table 13. Example questions used to test for the cognitive aspect: Feeling for numbers. This table is identical to Table 7 and is replicated for convenience

• How often does the subject offer a ratio to a player that he can also trade with a bank or port? ○ 0 - 5 * ○ 5 - 10 ○ 10 • Does the subject understand probabilities? Does he choose places with high probability (5, 6, 8, and 9)? (YES)

Table 15. Example of how the questions in Table 13 are transformed into symbolic rules used in the expert system

IF Offer to player instead of bank OR No strategic starting place THEN Hypothesis(NOT feeling for numbers) IF Hypothesis(NOT feeling for numbers) AND Offer to player instead of bank AND No strategic starting place THEN NOT Feeling for numbers

from the theoretical framework are implemented into the Student model.

Implementation

The ITA has been divided into two packages. One package, developed in JAVA, handles the interaction with the game, the interpretation of game information, and the extraction of user actions from this game information. The other part, representing information about the player has been captured in symbolic rules. These symbolic rules have been implemented in CLIPS (Riley), a symbolic rule language developed by NASA. The JAVA components make up one package (the JAVA Agent package) and the CLIPS components make up the other package (the CLIPS package). A package diagram of the implementation of the system can be found in Figure 3 where the JAVA package can be seen in the middle of the figure. At the top of the figure, the link to the slightly adapted JSettlers client; at the bottom, a more elaborate representation of the Student model is presented, as it is implemented in CLIPS. The KBCommunicator component in the ITA is the only component communicating with the CLIPS package. This communication goes through JCLIPS (Menken). JCLIPS is able to assert and retract facts in the fact base that is shared by all components in the Student model. JCLIPS is also able to start the inference engine of CLIPS that evaluates all the rules in each of the Student model's components. These rules can assert and retract facts in the fact base, that is observed through JCLIPS by the KBCommunicator, which relays this information back to the relevant JAVA component. Each of the classes in the package diagram are explained in more detail below.

- **JAVA client:** This package contains the original JSettlers interface with some minor changes that attach the ITA to this package. The adaptations were necessary for the agent to be able to receive important game information. The JAVA client package uses a number of events that indicate actions by players or important game states. Some of these events are now forwarded to the ITA. This package is represented by the box with JSettlers in Figure 3.
- **SOCAgent:** This class is an implementation of the Agent UI from Figure 3. It contains the interface of the agent and communicates with the user through a connection with the SOCPlayerClient, which is the standard client that is included in JSettlers. The SOCAgent class uses the SOCStrategyMonitor, SOCOfferJudge, and KBCommunicator classes to handle specific tasks.
- **SOCStrategyMonitor:** This class is responsible for handling information about the strategies the user is employing. It is able to determine whether a certain strategy is being used or not and compare this with the strategies that are manually selected by the player from the interface. In order to do this, it utilizes the Strategy Module in the CLIPS package, by communicating with the KBCommunicator. If there is a discrepancy between the deducted strategies and the indicated strategies, the SOCAgent is alerted and a message can be sent to the user. The SOCStrategyMonitor is an implementation of the Strategy DB in Figure 3.
- **SOCOfferJudge:** The SOCOfferJudge is an implementation of the Offer Judge from Figure 3, and is responsible for monitoring all the negotiations that the player is engaged in.
- **KBCommunicator:** The KBCommunicator is responsible for all the communication between the JAVA agent package and the CLIPS package. This class contains methods that are specific for the communication between the classes in the two packages. This class was added to keep application specific functions separate from JCLIPS.

Figure 3. Class diagram of the implementation of the ITA. It is subdivided into three packages: JAVA Client, JAVA agent, CLIPS. Each of these packages contains a number of communicating classes. The lines indicate with which other classes a class communicates. Links between packages are indicated with dashed lines.

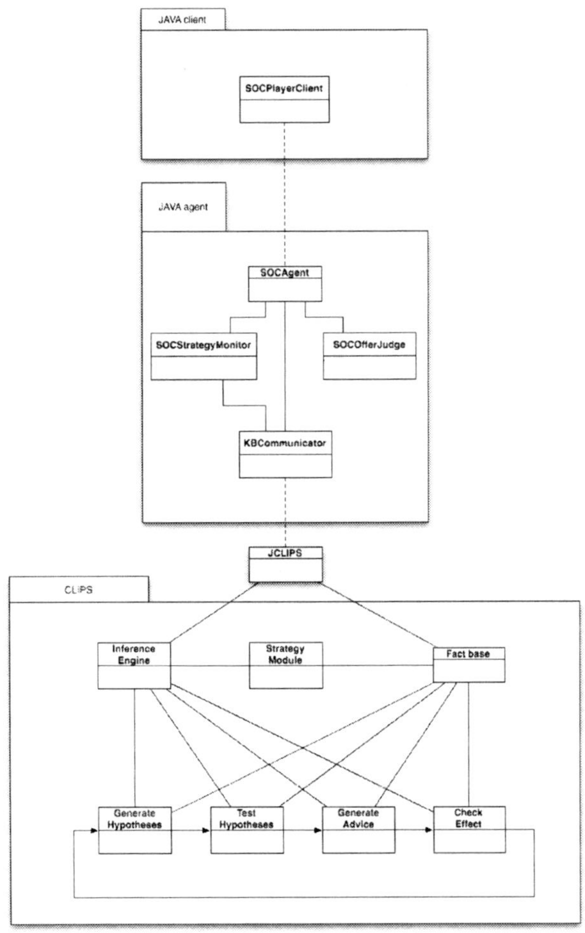

- **JCLIPS:** functions as a bridge (Gamma, Helm, Johnson, & Vlissides, 1995) between JAVA and CLIPS. It is able to manipulate the CLIPS fact base and control the inference engine. JCLIPS is written in JAVA with native methods written in C that control CLIPS.
- **Inference Engine:** This class corresponds to the inference engine in CLIPS. This inference engine interprets the symbolic rules in each of the components in combination with the facts in the fact base. The inference engine is incorporated in a CLIPS distribution.
- **Fact Base:** This class represents the fact base that is incorporated in CLIPS. This fact base contains all the facts that are used by the symbolic rules in the different components.
- **Strategy Module:** This class contains the symbolic rules that pertain to the monitoring of the strategies employed by a player.

It corresponds to the Strategy Monitor in Figure 3.

- **Generate Hypotheses:** This class holds the symbolic rules that generate the hypotheses concerning the development of the cognitive aspects.
- **Test Hypotheses:** The symbolic rules that test the hypotheses from the last component are stored in the Test Hypotheses class.
- **Generate Advice:** This class generates the advice that is presented to the player. This is also done with symbolic rules. Because of this, the generate advice class is contained within the CLIPS package and not in the JAVA agent package where it would be expected when looking at the conceptual architecture.
- **Check Effect:** This class contains the symbolic rules that determine whether a certain

Figure 4. The different UI screens of the ITA: On the left hand, the main interface. The green colored screen at the bottom is the status screen of the ITA. It is used to communicate which strategies are being followed and to give tips to the user based on this information. On the right: Top: Offer statistics, indicates how many offers have made and how many accepted and rejected. Middle: Cognitive Aspects, shows which of the cognitive aspects are developed according to the ITA. Bottom: Message pop up, shows a text message to the user containing guidance.

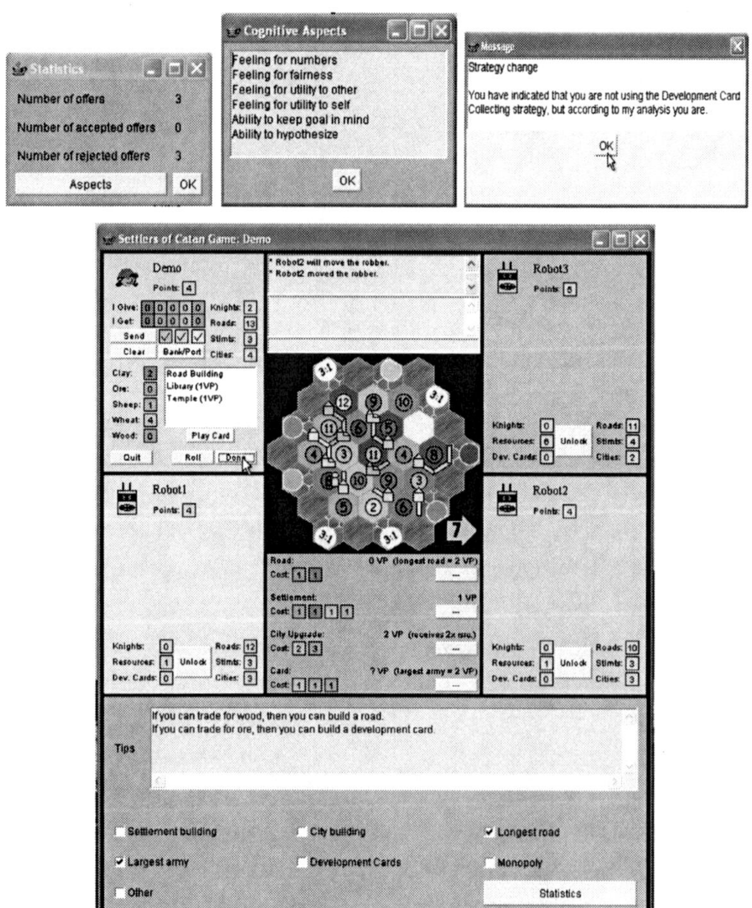

cognitive aspect has been disproved more than once, i.e., whether or not the generated advice had a effect on the player.

In order to generate transparent programming code, the domain knowledge base was implemented in JAVA.

The interface is an added panel to the JSettlers interface, which is shown in Figure 4. This panel contains an area where the user can communicate the strategies he is using to the agent. It contains a button that opens a new window that contains statistical information on the negotiation history. It also contains an area where tips to the user can be displayed. Tips are only displayed inside the panel itself. Changes in the cognitive aspects detected by the agent, and the corresponding text messages, are provided to the user inside a dialog window. These windows pop-up at the end of a turn. The agent collects messages until the user ends his turn and they are displayed then.

THE ITA IN PRACTICE

Throughout its developed, the ITA has been iteratively tested. Each of the symbolic rules used in the CLIPS package were first tested by manually asserting the required facts in the fact base and running the inference engine. In such way we were able to determine whether or not the required behavior emerged. When this was the case, the CLIPS package was connected to the JAVA agent. Next, JSettlers was played in such a way what the circumstances for each symbolic rule were satisfied. Debugging continued until all symbolic rules functioned correctly under the required game circumstances. Through this iterative testing procedure, the following implementation issues were solved:

The first version of the Test Hypotheses and Generate Hypotheses modules were initially only able to disprove an aspect once. This would not enable the Generate Advice module to offer different messages each time a mistake was made again. To enable this feature, an aspect has be able to be disproved more than once. In the first version, an aspect was a condition for a rule that disproved it, but this means that if it is disproved, the rule will not be activated again. To be able to disprove the aspect more than once, the aspect was removed from the condition list. Consequently, it was needed to keep track of the occurrences of each action and to remember the occurrence of the action when the facts are retracted and only regenerate when the occurrence changes. For example, when the Feeling for fairness was disproved the first time, the occurrence of Offer unfair deal was 2 and the occurrence of Accept unfair deal was 1. When both occurrences have changed, only then may be concluded that the mistake has been made again (Offer unfair deal > 2 AND accept unfair deal > 1).

When the user selects a strategy in the user interface, the facts that are the basis of this strategy are asserted into the knowledge base. The Strategy Monitor looks at the buy history of the player and concludes which strategies the player has employed. The problem here is that when the user selected the strategy in the interface, the Strategy Monitor looked at the buy history and concluded that the selected strategy was not used and it was immediately disabled again. The cause of this, was that the Strategy Monitor did not give the user any time to demonstrate that he was going to employ the selected strategy. The solution to this problem was to have the Strategy Monitor check whether the strategy has been selected when updating the facts. When the strategy has not been selected (the Monitor is trying to prove that the strategy is being used), the monitor will look back in time to see whether or not the strategy has been employed. When the strategy has been selected (the Monitor is trying to prove that the strategy is not being used), the Monitor will withhold judgment until the interval, associated with the selected strategies, has passed since the strategy was selected and then determine if it was used or not.

At the start of the game, no strategy has been selected yet (neither manually or deducted from the buy history). The agent immediately concludes that the player is not using strategies at all and asserts the hypothesis that the player is not able to hypothesize. This was not desirable, the player should have a certain interval to be able to select or start employing strategies. To be able to support this, the turn numbers that were already being monitored by the agent, were also asserted into the knowledge base and incorporated into the rules. The no-strategy rule was adapted to take the turn numbers into account.

When the knowledge bases had been largely implemented and the link to the JAVA agent had to be made an exception occurred. It was determined that the exception occurred because JCLIPS was not thread-safe while the JSettlers Client was using threads. The JCLIPS code was rewritten to make it thread-safe, which solved the problem.

To conclude, all major problems have been solved and the ITA is operational. On our website (http://eidetic.ai.ru.nl/e-learning), a number of videos of the use of the agent are available. Moreover, the software packages can be downloaded.

DISCUSSION

After the introduction of the project, the concept "Games in Education", a rapidly evolving field of science is presented; e.g., Doesburg, Heuvelink, and van den Broek (2005), Kelly (2005), and Squire and Jenkins (2003). In the section on *Intelligent Tutoring Systems*, a brief explanation of these systems is given. Next, the domain of application is introduced: negotiation processes with children. Subsequently, Piaget's stage theory (Lourenço & Machado, 1996), Thompson & Hastie's (1990), and the combination of both are discussed. The latter resulted in a new theoretical framework, which is validated through an experiment. After the theoretical framework was found to be valid, it was used as foundation for the development of the ITA. The usage as well as the pros and cons of the ITA in practice are presented in *The ITA in practice*.

As was already denoted in 1962 (Roberts & Sutton-Smith, 1962), without any doubt games are among the most powerful means to enhance education (Squire & Jenkins, 2003). With the acceleration of processing power of PCs and the advances in computer graphics, the involvement (or presence) of users of games brought to high levels, as is ultimately done through Virtual Reality techniques (Doesburg, Heuvelink, & van den Broek, 2005; Murray, Fox, & Pettifer, 2007; Takatalo, Nymana, & Laaksonen, 2008). However, also 'classic' 2D screen games can be very appealing as is illustrated by a new type of addiction that evolved this century: game addiction. In addition, various other risks are denoted; e.g., see "Harnessing the power of games in education" of Squire & Jenkins (2003) for an overview. Despite the drawbacks, it is (still) envisioned that games will become more important for educational purposes (Doesburg, Heuvelink, & van den Broek, 2005; Kelly, 2005).

The theoretical framework that is developed within this project has a solid foundation and is validated. Nevertheless, one can debate its foundation with respect to both its origins. Within the field of education, various theories on the development of human beings exist. Happily, these theories have their foundation in the same field of research. In contrast, the topic negotiation is assessed from various fields of science (e.g., psychology (Bazerman, Curhan, Moore, & Valley, 2000), management (Nadler, Thompson, & Boven, 2003; Wolfe & Murthy, 2006), and artificial intelligence (AI) (Jonker, Robu, & Treur, 2007)). We will now briefly denote both theories and explain our choice for Piaget's theory (Lourenço & Machado, 1996) and Thompson and Hastie's judgments (Thompson & Hastie, 1990).

Piaget's theory has been a topic of heavy debate (Lourenço & Machado, 1996; Palmer, 2001) and still there are groups either strongly in favor or against Piaget's work. Lourenço and Machado (1996) provide a concise overview of ten common criticisms and counter them. However, despite the excellent defense of Lourenço and Machado (1996), one can argue to replace Piaget's stage theory by another theory; see Palmer (2001) for a recent overview of the most important alternative theories.

As a consequence for the broad interest in negotiation processes (Bazerman, Curhan, Moore, & Valley, 2000; Boven & Thompson, 2003; Jonker, Robu, & Treur, 2007; Nadler, Thompson, & Boven, 2003; Wolfe & Murthy, 2006), an enormous variety of theories, perspectives, and methods exist with respect to negotiation research. This makes it very hard to provide an overview of the field. There has also been research conducted specifically on training or teaching negotiation skills; e.g., Druckman, Harris, and Ramberg (2002), Gillespie, Thompson, Loewenstein, and Gentner (1999), and Shell (1995). In addition, since roughly a decade, in parallel with theoretical models often founded on qualitative data, computer applications were developed that either analyzed negotiation processes, modeled them (Jonker, Robu, & Treur, 2007), or supported them (Wolfe & Murthy, 2006). Within this broad palette of research, the work of Thompson and Hastie (1990) is prominent and has been quoted frequently; e.g., Bazerman, Curhan, Moore, and Valley (2000), Boven and Thompson(2003), Nadler, Thompson, and Boven(2003), and Wolfe and Murthy(2006). Therefore, we also adopted the theory of Thompson and Hastie on negotiation processes.

For both Piaget's (Lourenço & Machado, 1996) and Thompson and Hastie's (1990) theory, multiple alternatives are available. However, the theories adopted are (at least among) the most generally excepted. Moreover, in particular criticism on Piaget's theory is often founded on misconceptions and misinterpretations of his work (Lourenço & Machado, 1996). Therefore, these two theories were chosen to develop the new theoretical framework on negotiation processes with children.

The development of robust rule-based systems requires a tremendous effort. Moreover, rule-based systems often lack the ability to be generically applicable, again this is true for our system. However, in the development of the system, future adaptations were taken into account. Its modular setup, as depicted in Figure 3, allows smooth adaptations of the system. Although the ITS as implemented works according to plan, some issues can be addressed that would probably enhance the ITS and improve children's learning. The ITS consists of four modules: the domain, student, tutoring, and communication module; we will denote three of such possible improvements on these modules:

1. In the current study, the communication module is simply the interface between the ITS and the child. However, since communication is of the utmost importance in the communication between a child and his teacher, we expect that the implementation of a good communication would support the effect of the ITA substantially (Vugt, Konijn, Hoorn, Keur, & Eliëns, 2007). For example, a Virtual Reality environment could enhance the communication substantially (Doesburg, Heuvelink, & van den Broek, 2005; Murray, Fox, & Pettifer, 2007; Takatalo, Nymana, & Laaksonen, 2008) and even probe their experience (Westerink, Ouwerkerk, overbeek, Pasveer, & Ruyter, 2008).
2. The pedagogical model generates the advice that is given to the child through the communication module. Advice can be given trough various strategies, depending on domain and student's features. Hence, it would be of interest to extend this model with various strategies on generating advice.
3. Sarrafzadeh, Alexander, Dadgostar, Fan, and Bigdeli (2008) present a paper on "a look at

the future of intelligent tutoring systems", which addresses the exploitation of emotion in ITS. They baptize this next generation ITS as: Affective Tutoring Systems. Without any doubt, empathic ITS would substantially advance the communication process and with that the learning of the student. The ITS should be able to sense the student's emotional state and act appropriately to it. This sensing should be done unobtrusively; for example, through speech signal processing (Sarrafzadeh, Alexander, Dadgostar, Fan, & Bigdeli, 2008; van den Broek, 2004) or psycho physiological measurements (e.g., galvanic skin response and facial electromyography) (Westerink, Ouwerkerk, overbeek, Pasveer, & Ruyter, 2008).

Where the first two improvements only require adaptations to one of the systems modules or models, bringing empathy into the ITS requires substantially more effort (Sarrafzadeh, Alexander, Dadgostar, Fan, & Bigdeli, 2008; van den Broek, 2004; Westerink, Ouwerkerk, overbeek, Pasveer, & Ruyter, 2008). The incorporation of the signal processing techniques and their interpretation has to be embedded in the pedagogical model, the communication model, and the student model. Consequently, the complete architecture would have to be adapted.

Throughout the research presented in this chapter, the complexity of the project's aims became evident. Subtle shifts in strategy of explaining by human tutors that fit the student's understanding remain striking (Person & Graesser, 2003). Despite the progress in behavioral research and the technological advances, true advances in the evolution of agent technology, expert systems, ITS, and AI in general still have to come (Shoham, Powers, & Grenager, 2007; Spector, 2006). However, various forms of AI exist that have proved their use (Doesburg, Heuvelink, & van den Broek, 2005; Jonker, Robu, & Treur, 2007; Sarrafzadeh, Alexander, Dadgostar, Fan, & Bigdeli, 2008). In this line, the project has delivered a unique ITS founded on a newly developed and validated theoretical framework on negotiation processes with children. It has proved to be stable and shown its value in learning children to negotiate. Moreover, it can be used to further specify the theoretical framework. Hence, the value of the online ITS system introduced in this paper is bi-directional: it helps science to understand children's negotiation processes and helps the children to improve their negotiation skills through gaming by use of an artificial tutor.

REFERENCES

Bazerman, M. H., Curhan, J. R., Moore, D. A., & Valley, K. L. (2000). Negotiation. *Annual Review of Psychology*, *51*, 279–314. doi:10.1146/annurev.psych.51.1.279

Beck, J., & Woolf, B. P. (2000). High-Level Student Modeling with Machine Learning. In *Intelligent Tutoring Systems* (pp. 584-593).

Boven, L. V., & Thompson, L. (2003). A Look into the Mind of the Negotiator: Mental Models in Negotiation. *Group Processes & Intergroup Relations*, *6*, 387–404. doi:10.1177/13684302030064005

Coleman, J. (1967). Learning Through Games. *Play, its Role in Development and Evolution*, 460-463.

Conati, C., & Zhao, X. (2004). Building and Evaluating an Intelligent Pedagogical Agent to Improve the Effectiveness of an Educational Game. In *Proceedings of IUI '04, International Conference on Intelligent User Interfaces*, (pp. 6-13). Island of Madeira, Portugal.

Craighead, J. (2008). Distributed, game-based, intelligent tutoring systems — The next step in computer based training? *Collaborative Technologies and Systems, 2008. CTS 2008. International Symposium on*, (pp. 247-256). Irvine, CA.

Doesburg, W. A., Heuvelink, A., & van den Broek, E. L. (2005). TACOP: A Cognitive Agent for a Naval Training Simulation Environment. In M. Pechoucek, D. Steiner, & S. ThompsonM. Pechoucek, D. Steiner, S. Thompson (Eds.), *Proceedings of the Industry Track of the Fourth International Joint Conference on Autonomous Agents and Multi-Agent Systems* (pp. 34-41). ACM.

Druckman, D., Harris, R., & Ramberg, B. (2002). Computer-Assisted International Negotiation: A Tool for Research and Practice. *Group Decision and Negotiation*, *11*, 231–256. doi:10.1023/A:1015281906202

Gamma, E., Helm, R., Johnson, R., & Vlissides, J. (1995). *Design Patterns. Elements of Reusable Object-Oriented Software*. Reading, MA: Addison Wesley.

Gillespie, J. J., Thompson, L. L., Loewenstein, J., & Gentner, D. (1999). Lessons from Analogical Reasoning in the Teaching of Negotiation. *Negotiation Journal*, *15*, 363–371. doi:10.1111/j.1571-9979.1999.tb00734.x

Gobet, F., Voogt, A., & Retschitzki, J. (2004). *Moves in mind: The psychology of board games*. New York: Psychology Press.

Gulz, A., & Haake, M. (2006). Design of animated pedagogical agents-A look at their look. *International Journal of Human-Computer Studies*, *64*, 322–339. doi:10.1016/j.ijhcs.2005.08.006

Hatzilygeroudis, I., & Prentzas, J. (2004). Knowledge Representation Requirements for Intelligent Tutoring Systems. *7th International Conference on Intelligent Tutoring Systems,* (pp. 87-97.). Maceio, Alagoas, Brazil: Springer.

Jonker, C. M., Robu, V., & Treur, J. (2007). An agent architecture for multi-attribute negotiation using incomplete preference information. *Autonomous Agents and Multi-Agent Systems*, *15*, 221–252. doi:10.1007/s10458-006-9009-y

Keleş, A., Ocak, R., & Gülcü, A. (2009). ZOSMAT: Web-based intelligent tutoring system for teaching-learning process. *Expert Systems with Applications*, *36*, 1229–1239. doi:10.1016/j.eswa.2007.11.064

Kelly, H. (2005). Games, Cookies, and the Future of Education. *Issues in Science and Technology*, *21*, 33–40.

Klawe, M. (1998). When Does The Use Of Computer Games And Other Interactive Multimedia Software Help Students Learn Mathematics? *NCTM Standards 2000 Technology Conference*.

Leutner, D. (1993). Guided Discovery Learning with Computer-based Simulation Games: Effects of Adaptive and Non-adaptive Instructional Support. *Learning and Instruction*, *3*, 113–132. doi:10.1016/0959-4752(93)90011-N

Likert, R. (1932). A Technique for the Measurement of Attitudes. *Archives de Psychologie*, *140*, 5–53.

Lourenço, O., & Machado, A. (1996). In Defense of Piaget's Theory: A reply to ten common criticisms. *Psychological Review*, *103*, 143–164. doi:10.1037/0033-295X.103.1.143

Malone, T. (1983). Guidelines for Designing Educational Computer Programs. *Childhood Education*, *59*, 241–247.

McQuiggan, S. W., Mott, B. W., & Lester, J. C. (2008). Modeling self-efficacy in intelligent tutoring systems: An inductive approach. *User Modeling and User-Adapted Interaction*, *18*, 81–123. doi:10.1007/s11257-007-9040-y

Menken, M. (n.d.). *JCLIPS - CLIPS for Java*. Retrieved on July 28, 2010, from http://sourceforge.net/projects/jclips/

Murray, C. D., Fox, J., & Pettifer, S. (2007). Absorption, dissociation, locus of control and presence in virtual reality. *Computers in Human Behavior*, *23*, 1347–1354. doi:10.1016/j.chb.2004.12.010

Nadler, J., Thompson, L., & Boven, L. (2003). Learning Negotiation Skills: Four Models of Knowledge Creation and Transfer. *Management Science*, *49*, 529–540. doi:10.1287/mnsc.49.4.529.14431

Palmer, J. A. (2001). *Fifty Modern Thinkers on Education: From Piaget to the Present Day* (1 ed.). London, UK: Routledge.

Person, N. K., & Graesser, A. C. (2003). Fourteen Facts About Human Tutoring: Food for Thought for ITS Developers. In C. P. Rosé, & V. Aleven, (Ed.), *Supplementary Proceedings of the 11th International Conference on Artificial Intelligence in Education (AIED2003), VI: Workshop on Tutorial Dialogue Systems: with a view on the classroom*, (pp. 335-344).

Riley, G. (n.d.). *CLIPS: A Tool for Building Expert Systems*. Retrieved July 28, 2010, from http://clipsrules.sourceforge.net/

Roberts, J. M., & Sutton-Smith, B. (1962). Child Training and Game Involvement. *Ethnology*, *1*, 166–185. doi:10.2307/3772873

Romero, C., & Ventura, S. (2007). Educational data mining: A survey from 1995 to 2005. *Expert Systems with Applications*, *33*, 135–146. doi:10.1016/j.eswa.2006.04.005

Salen, K., & Zimmerman, E. (2004). *Rules of Play*. Cambridge, MA: MIT Press.

Saner, R. (2008). *The expert negotiator: Strategy, tactics, motivation, behaviour, leadership* (3rd ed.). Leiden, The Netherlands: Koninklijke Brill NV.

Sarrafzadeh, A., Alexander, S., Dadgostar, F., Fan, C., & Bigdeli, A. (2008). How do you know that I don't understand? A look at the future of intelligent tutoring systems. *Computers in Human Behavior*, *24*, 1342–1363. doi:10.1016/j.chb.2007.07.008

Schreiber, G., Akkermans, H., Anjewierden, A., Hoog, R., Shadbolt, N., & Velde, W. (2000). *Knowledge Engineering and Management, The CommonKADS Methodology*. Cambridge, MA: MIT Press.

Shell, G. R. (1995). Computer-Assisted Negotiation and Mediation: Where We Are and Where We Are Going. *Negotiation Journal*, *11*, 117–121. doi:10.1111/j.1571-9979.1995.tb00052.x

Shoham, Y., Powers, R., & Grenager, T. (2007). If multi-agent learning is the answer, what is the question? *Artificial Intelligence*, *171*, 365–377. doi:10.1016/j.artint.2006.02.006

Siemer, J., & Angelides, M. (1995). Evaluating intelligent tutoring with gaming-simulations. In *WSC '95: Proceedings of the 27th conference on Winter simulation* (pp. 1376-1383). Arlington, VA: ACM Press.

Spector, L. (2006). Evolution of artificial intelligence. *Artificial Intelligence*, *170*, 1251–1253. doi:10.1016/j.artint.2006.10.009

Squire, K., & Jenkins, H. (2003). Harnessing the power of games in education. *Insight (American Society of Ophthalmic Registered Nurses)*, *3*, 5–33.

Takatalo, J., Nymana, G., & Laaksonen, L. (2008). Components of human experience in virtual environments. *Computers in Human Behavior*, *24*, 1–15. doi:10.1016/j.chb.2006.11.003

Thompson, L., & Hastie, R. (1990). Judgement tasks and biases in negotiation. *Research on Negotiation in Organizations*, *2*, 31–54.

van den Broek, E. (2004). Emotional Prosody Measurement (EPM): A voice-based evaluation method for psychological therapy effectiveness. [Medical and Care Compunetics]. *Studies in Health Technology and Informatics*, *103*, 118–125.

van Rosmalen, P., Sloep, P., Kester, L., Brouns, F., de Croock, M., & Pannekeet, K. (2008). A learner support model based on peer tutor selection. *Journal of Computer Assisted Learning*, *24*, 74–86. doi:10.1111/j.1365-2729.2007.00245.x

Vugt, H. C., Konijn, E. A., Hoorn, J. F., Keur, I., & Eliëns, A. (2007). Realism is not all! User engagement with task-related interface characters. *Interacting with Computers*, *19*, 267–280. doi:10.1016/j.intcom.2006.08.005

Wang, N., Johnson, W. L., Mayer, R. E., Rizzo, P., Shaw, E., & Collins, H. (2008). The politeness effect: Pedagogical agents and learning outcomes. *International Journal of Human-Computer Studies*, *66*, 98–112. doi:10.1016/j.ijhcs.2007.09.003

Westerink, J. M., & Ouwerkerk, M. overbeek, T., Pasveer, W. F., & Ruyter, B. (2008). *Probing Experiences: From Academic Research to Commercial Propositions*. Dordrecht, The Netherlands: Springer.

Wolfe, C. J., & Murthy, U. S. (2006). Negotiation Support Systems in Budget Negotiations: An Experimental Analysis. *Journal of Management Information Systems*, *22*, 351–381. doi:10.2753/MIS0742-1222220312

ENDNOTES

1. World of Warcraft is a Massive Multiplayer Online Role Playing Game (MMORPG), where thousands of people can play with and against each other in a fictive virtual world. http://www.worldofwarcraft.com/
2. For details about JSettlers, see http://jsettlers.sourceforge.net/
3. For details about Pioneers, see http://pio.sourceforge.net/

Chapter 9
Intelligent Tutoring System for Learning Programming

Tonći Dadić
University of Split, Croatia

ABSTRACT

Tutoring systems for programming help students understand features of target programming languages, and develop their general problem solving skills. Our system guides novices in learning syntax and semantics of programming language, problem decomposition, program design and testing. It is language independent, automatically adjusting course material to the language - subject of learning. Semantic analysis of student's programs is based on comparison of abstract semantics trees of student's and model-program. Model-program is coded by innovative programming language describing goals and variants of possible solutions. The notional machine defined by programming language, its verbal description of instruction actions and visualization of program execution, helps students to understand semantics of teaching language. Advancement through the course material controlled by computer teacher supports connection of new concepts to the present student's knowledge. The system applies distinct teaching strategies to stoppers and movers.

INTRODUCTION

Intelligent tutoring systems for programming are an interesting area of artificial intelligence application. Since early seventies, tens of systems have been designed and hundreds of papers published, related to procedural (Adam 1980, Barr 1976, Johnson 1984, Ueno 1994), functional (Anderson 1985), logical and object languages (Butz 2006, Chee 1993), including problem analysis, program specification, planning (Eisenberg 2003) and coding. In addition, researchers focused to adaptive navigation (Brusilovsky 1992), visualization of program execution and intelligent debugging (Eisenberg 2003).

Regardless significant research effort in field, there are very few intelligent tutoring systems or integrated learning environments used regularly

DOI: 10.4018/978-1-61692-008-1.ch009

for teaching programming in a real classroom, and most of them can not be used outside the university where they were created (Brusilovsky 1995). Author explains such situation by complexity of intelligent systems, where research and development of each component requires a couple of man-years. Design of an environment supporting efficient teaching of programming is a challenging domain with many open issues to explore (Guzdial 2004).

In this chapter we present our system for teaching to program by procedural languages. We based design of our system to fundamentals referred in section Learning programming and tutoring systems. Many attributes of our system are typical, while we believe that some characteristics make it unique in the field. Section History of intelligent tutoring systems for programming depicts history of the field through characteristic of some specific systems, leaving reader to compare our work. We explain our system in necessary details. In The system evaluation section we present findings of our students in using the system in real classroom.

BACKGROUND

We believe that students have to acquire computer programming knowledge, skills and capabilities already in primary education. Educational contents that would enable this process, starts with problem solving formalism (in individual and group work), and proceed with programming paradigm using some appropriate programming languages as LOGO, Basic or Pascal. Our consideration is directed toward goals presented in Croatian Educational National Standard (CENS) for elementary school computer science. This standard was carried out in Republic of Croatia during 2004-2005. (Budin et al. 2006). Our long experience of working with students enrolled in basic computer programming courses (Introduction to computing and Programming 1), undoubtedly imply many difficulties that have occurred due to late beginning of learning computer programming. Sometimes teachers wonder about programming language to use as a starting point. Our opinion is that choice of programming language is not the most important point, but more relevant is an early start of computer programming during elementary education.

We believe that programming course may be introduced to primary education if an efficient framework supporting students in learning programming is available. Motivated by this problem, we have started developing of prototype model of computerized tutor for learning and teaching programming. In this chapter we introduce our system that helps student to acquire basic programming knowledge. We believe that application of this system in real classroom may greatly improve process of learning and teaching of computer programming. It should realize assumptions for students and teachers to solve mentioned problems in an individualized computer-based approach combined with traditional education. Development of the computerized tutor for learning and teaching of programming is based on age-long research and development of the Tutor–Expert System, a hypermedia authoring shell model for building intelligent tutoring systems (Stankov 1997).

LEARNING PROGRAMMING AND TUTORING SYSTEMS

Researchers and experts of the field agree that learning and teaching programming is a complex activity for students and teachers. Understanding and visualization of abstract processes make problem to students when they learn programming as well as other fields with similar characteristics.

Programming Knowledge to Acquire

Linn and Dalbey (1989) have identified the ideal chain of cognitive achievement by learning to program. They propose their model as a standard in comparison of different teaching methods. The three main links of the chain are features of programming language, design skills and general problem solving skills.

Features represent syntax and semantics as well as significance of programming language. Knowledge at this stage helps students read program examples, code their own solutions of tasks, and it is the necessary assumption of advancement through the next links of the chain. The assessment of student's achievement at this stage can be provided by tasks of program reformulation and tracing. We find from our experience, that mental simulation of program execution is a very powerful method helping to understand programming language. Lister et al. (2004) elaborate that program tracing skills are prerequisite for program designing.

Design skills are the group of techniques that combine language features into program that solves given programming task. It is necessary that students acquire knowledge of specific algorithms that solve common programming problems, like sorting, array and tree traversal etc. Experienced programmers decompose the programming task into sub-problems, solve each of them and compose partial solutions back into the program as a whole. Finally, programmers validate solution and localize bugs by program testing.

General problem solving skills play important role in learning new programming languages. It is found that various languages share many common attributes. Once when students are familiar with common algorithms and design methods, they are able to transfer knowledge to the new languages they start to learn. This stage is identified as the goal of learning programming.

What Makes Problem to Novices?

Lemut et al. (1993) explain difficulties in learning to program by many complex activities that novices have to perform at once. For example, in order to localize and prune out bugs, program has to be run supplied by specific inputs. Selection of such inputs requires knowledge of instruction semantics. Since novices are learning instructions, it isn't very likely that they can find such inputs on their own.

DuBoulay et al. (1989) identifies possible sources of difficulties in:

1. Orientation – general meaning of program and programming
2. Notional machine – virtual machine defined by programming language
3. Structures – knowledge of programming constructs that solve specific requirements
4. Pragmatics – skills needed to design correct programs, including planning, problem decomposition, coding and testing.

Traditional Course of Programming

In traditional course of programming, teacher explains language features introducing programming examples. Students try to understand instructions deeply, designing programs that solve given tasks. The students' group of single course is very often heterogeneous, regarding motivation, previous knowledge students bring to the course, learning styles and abilities. Commonly, students are very creative in inventing unpredictable programming errors. It is challenging for the single teacher to localize and explain errors to each individual. Learning and teaching process may be significantly enhanced, extending traditional course by an intelligent tutoring system capable to understand and explain individual errors.

Evaluation of LISP Tutor (Anderson 1985) proved that students acquired the same level of knowledge learning 11.4 hours with human tutor, 15 hours with help of computerized tutor or 45 hours in traditional course.

Cognitive Psychology of Learning Programming

Cognitive psychology finds an important role of meaningful learning in new information acquisition. The activation of present knowledge from learner's long term memory helps assimilation of new knowledge. Mayer (1989) elaborates how concrete models, familiar to novices improve understanding of new technical information. He argues that verbal description of statements execution helps novices to understand programming language features.

Generally, teaching approaches are distinguished by kind of feedback (Lane 2004).

Preliminary teaching tutor explains upfront how to solve a category of problems. Tutor doesn't watch student's actions in problem solving and can not provide help if she or he is faced with trouble.

Interactive tutor watches student's activity solving given task, character by character it is typed in source code editor. Whenever students are not able to find step towards correct solution, tutor interrupts their work offering help. There is strong evidence that interactive tutoring method with immediate help is appropriate for many students.

Reflexive tutoring is scenario where students approach to the final solution on their own, without tutor's help. Later tutor evaluates solution and informs student about errors. Feedback of this kind may be too late, allowing accumulation of many errors, where one error implies others. Some students are confused with many errors and just tend to disengage from the task.

LISP Tutor diagnoses students' knowledge providing interactive tutoring, keeping novices on the path of correct solution. Applying reflexive tutoring, PROUST (Johnson 1984) performs late semantic analysis of programs compiled by standard Pascal compiler.

Question arises if there is a single tutoring method preferable for all students regardless of their knowledge, learning styles and abilities? We find that program testing and bug localization is an important skill. Very often industrial programmers are faced with bugs in deployed programs. Fast bug localization and fixing is a mandatory attribute of professional programmers. It argues that novices have to practice debugging technique at early stage of learning. Systems that apply interactive tutoring with immediate feedback avoid opportunity to practice testing and debugging, since it doesn't allow propagation of bugs to testing stage. The approach is appropriate for students with difficulties in correct program construction, while students performing well can't improve their testing skills.

Our system distinguishes students performing well and those with difficulties. Students are allowed to experiment with program without system intervention, and to localize bugs by testing when found ready to advance to this stage of course.

History of Intelligent Tutoring Systems for Programming

Research and development of intelligent tutoring systems for programming span over three last decades. System BIP (Barr 1976) teaching BASIC is developed at Stanford University. While previous systems presented course material independently of students' current knowledge, BIP is adaptable to each student regarding her or his current knowledge. BIP organizes course material in form of directed graphs, where nodes represent programming techniques, skills and tasks. Task nodes are connected to the skill nodes by directed arcs. The network allows individualized selection of tasks appropriate to given student model. When a task is accomplished correctly, BIP updates student model with skills and techniques linked to the task. The system evaluates program correctness performing automatic dynamic testing that is running program supplied by predefined inputs and comparing its outputs with those generated by program-model. Such kind of analysis is limited; it finds program correct or incorrect, but applied algorithm, program structure and its style remain hidden from the tutor.

LAURA (Adam 1980) automatically debugs students' FORTRAN programs. System developed at Caen University, France, represents program by directed graph avoiding syntax variations. Nodes are operations while directed arcs define program control flow. Semantic analysis is performed comparing graph of student's program against graph of program-model. It is well known that the same task may be solved using various algorithms, their variations and may be coded by different instructions. This nice programming feature puts in trouble system comparing two programs. In order to work around of this complication, LAURA normalizes both programs. Applying well defined rules, it transforms graphs to the form that shrinks searching space.

PROUST is developed at Yale University by W.L. Johnson and E. Soloway (1984) to help novices learn Pascal and adopt general problem solving skills. Authors find lack of deeply program understanding in previous systems. In their opinion, the key of solution is to establish relationship between programmer's intention and realized program. Using large library of programming plans, PROUST performs plan recognition in order to understand students' programs. Possible bugs are explained by authors' descriptive theory of learning to program.

Johnson and Soloway emphasize complication of ambiguity, common to all non-trivial programs, namely problem decomposition is not unique and program may be mapped to many problem decompositions.

PROUST is very effective in bug localization (94%). Still, it can not diagnose and explain precisely many bugs, possibly because it provides reflexive tutoring. Help to students with difficulties is too late and their programs accumulate many chained errors, putting PROUST in trouble to diagnose and explain all of them (Lane 2004).

J. R. Anderson and B. J. Reiser from Carnegie-Mellon University published LISP Tutor in 1985. It is based on ACT-R theory dealing with transfer of declarative to procedural knowledge. There is strong evidence by this theory, that novices perform better learning interactively with an immediate feedback.

The strength of LISP Tutor is based on expert system that is able to solve and code in LISP specified problems. In addition, it is extended by large library of bugs commonly found in students' programs. The system is supported by GRAPES, goal restricted system based on production rules. During tutoring session, work is switched from planning to coding mode. The system employs menu based dialog, asking students to announce their intentions. The tutor watches student's activity character by character as she or he types in text editor. When performed and predicted actions differ, the student's work is interrupted and help offered. Authors named this method of knowledge diagnoses Model Tracing.

Method was found very helpful for students with poor knowledge, while students performing well did not benefit too much. Evaluating LISP Tutor, students were unsatisfied with menus arising very often. The need for menus may be explained by top-down nature of model tracing.

INTELLITUTOR II, developed by Haruki Ueno (1994) and his team in period 1989-99, at Tokyo Denki University, supports teaching of Pascal and C languages. Students' programs are translated to common abstract language AL, and semantic analysis is based on such program representation.

While many systems focus on concrete programming languages, H.C. Lane and K. VanLehn (2004) authored PROPL at Pittsburg University. Their intelligent tutor conducts interactive dialog by natural language, guiding students in problem decomposition and constructing solution in pseudo code.

The BITS system (Butz 2006) developed at Regina University, Canada, is web oriented system adaptable to the current students' knowledge and skill. It recommends the learning goals and generates the best learning path in order to achieve these goals. Authors find impossible to determine students' knowledge exactly, and propose Bayesian network as well defined framework to make decisions based on probability. The BITS teaches subset of C++ programming language, representing related knowledge by Bayesian network. Based on students' answers to quiz questions, the student model is updated by probability of knowledge of each concept.

Developers of ViLLE (Laakso 2008) from Turku University, Finland, find very useful visualization of program execution and understanding of variables roles in the program. ViLLE, published in 2008, is unique in its support of different programming languages, including Java, C++ and Python.

OUR SYSTEM

Tutoring system may be seen as an intelligent agent with environment represented by students' knowledge. Perception of environmental states is provided analyzing students' behavior in problem solving, while system acts on their knowledge explaining concepts they haven't adopted yet. The agent utility is measured by students' achievement in solving programming tasks. The tutoring system has to provide two levels of feedback: strategic feedback finds differences between the target and current student's knowledge, while operational feedback focuses on a specific task, finding differences between expected and realized learners' doing.

Our system guides novices in learning syntax and semantics of programming language, problem decomposition, program design and testing. It is capable to teach different procedural languages. New language is introduced by grammar in Bachus-Naur form, while knowledge base is common, language independent, and system dynamically accommodates course material to the specific language, subject of each course.

Client: Server Architecture

Our system employs client-server architecture based on web services. Central knowledge base, implemented by semantic network holds concepts and their relationships. Courseware database is central, implemented by relational schema holding users, available courses, curriculums and links referring to concepts of knowledge base. The architecture supports usage of client processing power analyzing students' programs in real time, while system maintaining is easier due central knowledge base and tools configuration. Figure 1 shows the architecture of our system.

We identify three kinds of system actors and accordingly have designed user interfaces: domain expert, teacher and student.

Figure 1. Client: Server architecture of the system

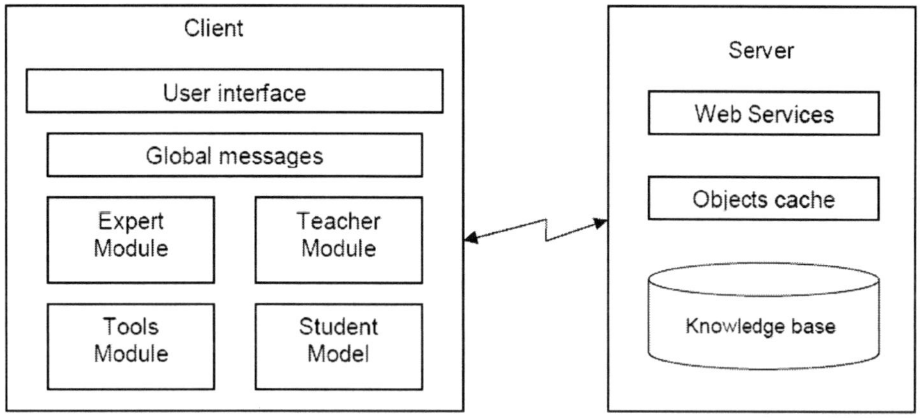

Expert's Use Case

Human expert defines concepts related to general knowledge of programming, as well as their relationships, using an interface shown on Figure 2. Constructs common to many or even all procedural programming languages are data types, variables, assignment statement, algebraic and logical expressions. All procedural languages support program flow control by selections and repetitive instructions, and program modularization based on procedures and functions. Procedural languages differ in syntax how these constructs are coded.

All languages don't share the same features, but we believe that it is possible to find superset of features that covers all procedural languages regularly used in real classrooms. Semantics of some language constructs may slightly differ as well. For example, if value 1 is added to a 16-bit-signed-integer variable, containing 32767, some languages produce new overlapped value -1, while others generate overflow exception. The principal source of problem in both cases is the same, but languages response to the problem differently.

With these facts in mind, human expert introduces principal concept, namely variable storage limitation and two kinds of responses, overlap and overflow. Later, when specific language is defined by grammar augmented with semantics rules, language is linked to one of these responses. An automatic lesson builder recognizes links between knowledge base and language grammar, and generates textual description relevant for specific language.

It is common to explain some language features by example of code. Our system is language independent, allowing human expert to code examples in one language, while lesson builder translates code to the syntax of teaching language.

Finally, expert defines stock of tasks. He describes requirement by natural language and attaches solution coded by special programming language we have developed for this purpose.

Figure 2. Expert's interface

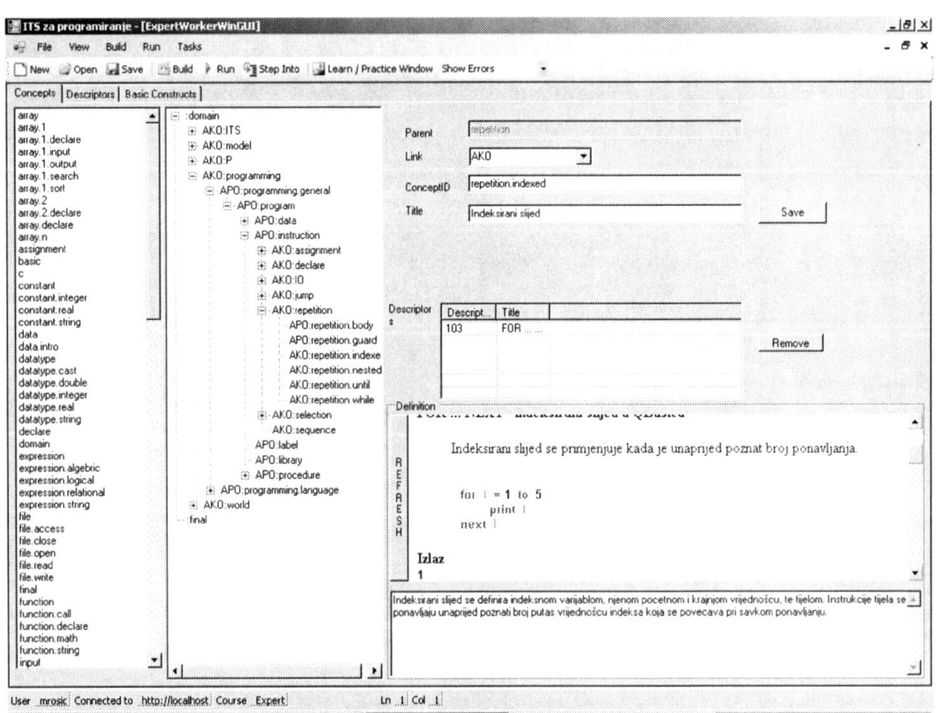

Teacher's Use Case

Human teacher creates course content using dedicated interface. He starts selecting language and creating course topics represented by tree. The tree serves as a base of menu generation during learning session. In the next step, teacher connects each topic with knowledge base concepts in order he wants them to appear on the lesson page. As mentioned earlier, the rest of job in lesson text generation is done automatically by lesson builder.

Teacher's responsibility is to tailor course appropriate for his students. For example, he may decide to omit pointers and recursion in course "Basics of C-Language". Teacher adds to the course not only concepts related to language features, but language independent algorithms, ensuring they are explained by course as well. The system automatically extends course by tasks selected from available stock. Task is selected only if set of implemented concepts is subset of concepts explained by the course. By phrase implemented concepts we mean instructions and algorithms needed to solve given problem. We have developed teacher's interface (Figure 3) that helps to accomplish course definition.

Student's Use Case

Student starts learning session logging on to the system. The interface (Figure 4) is restored to the state saved during user's last log out, so that learning always continues from the previous session. Typically student advances through the course clicking the button "Next", while system switches from textbook presentation to tasking mode. Student model is updated accordingly to user's behavior and success in tasks solving. The system helps to fix syntax errors and achieve correct program whenever finds student in trouble or when help is required explicitly. Course is completed when all concepts are marked by sign

Figure 3. Teacher's interface

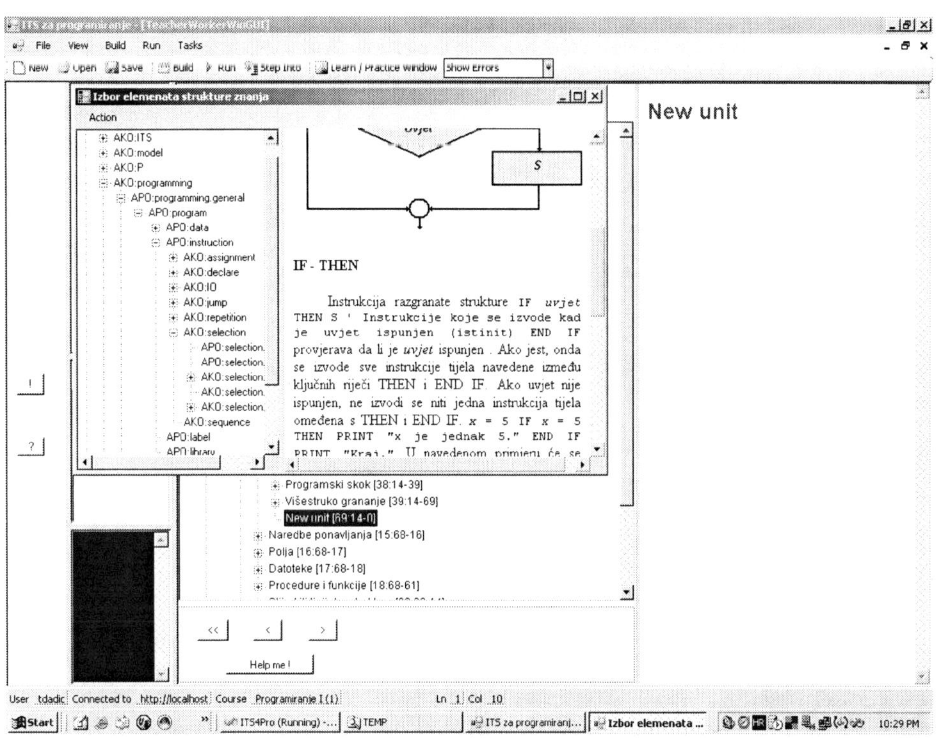

"+", meaning that student knows all concepts planned by course.

System Modules

Our system contains modules typical for an intelligent tutoring system, extended by Global messages unit and Tools module.

Global Messages Unit

The system modules cannot interact directly, but each module is restricted to its own objects. Communication between modules is supported by messages passing around the system. Global messages unit exposes a singleton queue to all parts of the system. A message addresses receiver, sender and identifies action requested by sender.

For example, when compiler built in Tools module detects a syntax error in the program, it sends error description to the Teacher module that requests student model object and makes conclusion about student's current knowledge and learning ability. Teacher module modulates help appropriate to student and request from User interface to display that message. Unit of global messages arise an event to addressed receiver and delivers message object to it. Receiver processes current message acknowledging success. The architecture supports multithreading, a technique supporting real time analysis of learners' activity.

Expert System

We precede two types of knowledge inherent to tutoring: declarative knowledge defines concepts and their relationship, while procedural knowledge plays role in solving given tasks.

Declarative knowledge of concepts and their relationship is represented by semantic network. Reasoning engine answers questions of type: what is super-class of concept, what parts it has, what

Figure 4. Student's interface

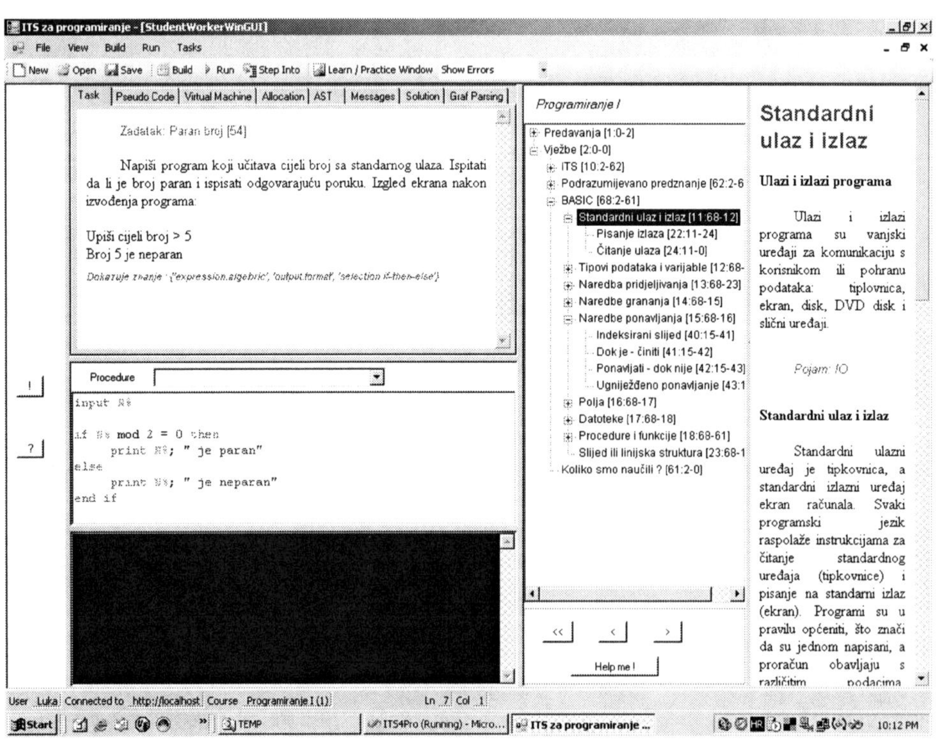

are its properties and what specific concept can do? For example, it finds that if-then instruction is a kind of selection, has conditional and two bodies. Instruction changes the path of program execution upon conditional satisfaction.

Very often students have lack of domain knowledge, and can start dialog with domain expert which assists them in problem solving. When students figure out steps and calculations needed to solve given task, they start to code program. Computerized expert for programming tries to understand their program, locate buggy code and diagnose the bug generators in students' thinking model. Expert analyzes students' source code and predicts possible paths to the final solution at each point of program.

Student Model

Student model identifies current status of student's knowledge, as well as his progress in concepts adoption over variety of tasks. In order to follow student's progress, the layout approach, traditionally used to diagnose student's knowledge is extended by sequences of error and help indicators. System updates student model database by data collected during his activity in tasks solving. This information is provided by syntax and semantic analyzers. Sample of student model shows progress in adoption of if – then statement (Table 1).

We interpret model of student identified by ID 101 as follows. Comparing time he spent to read if-instruction lesson with average time of the group, may be concluded that he skipped textual description. He started to code simple program identified by ID 11, and made a syntax error (leftmost sign minus of column Status). Student wasn't able to correct error on his own and system helped with a hint ("h" in column Status). Such advice wasn't helpful to the student, and system displayed syntactically correct instruction ("s" in column Status) that helped to achieve instruction without syntax errors (rightmost sign "+" in column Status). Student wrote correct program at first attempt, and then spent 3 minutes to run program step by step. After that, student studied textual explanation of nested if-then instructions for 6 minutes. Student had problem with logical errors in task 12, but pruned them out without system help, running program 3 times.

Detailed bookkeeping about students' behavior is useful for reasoning about their learning style and ability. It may be concluded that student in example tries to work around difficulties on his own, since asked for help only once. It is possible to rank each student within range of the group, comparing his total errors, help provided and timing with average numbers of the group.

Table 1. Student model sample

Student ID	*Concept ID*	*Task ID*	*Start-time*	*End-time*	*Status*
101	if-book	-	14:30:00	14:31:00	-
101	if-syntax	11	14:31:00	14:36:00	- h s +
101	if-semantics	11	14:36:00	14:36:00	+
101	step	11	14:36:00	14:39:00	*
101	if-nested-book	-	14:39:00	14:45:00	+
101	if-syntax	12	14:45:00	14:47:00	+
101	if-semantics	12	14:47:00	14:49:00	+
101	if-nested-syntax	12	14:45:00	14:47:00	- - +
101	run	12	14:45:00	14:47:00	***

Teacher Module

Computerized teacher guides students from one lesson to another, and selects programming tasks appropriate to their current knowledge, skill and learning ability. It observes students' work, interrupting if syntax or semantic errors are found.

Teaching Strategies

Students might differ widely not only in knowledge they bring to the course, but how they deal with difficulties. Perkins et al. (1989) identify two distinct learning styles: stoppers and movers. Stoppers tend to disengage from programming task at the first sign of trouble, whereas movers will begin tinkering with a partial solution. Perkins finds that stoppers can become movers if they are encouraged to decompose problem and focus on simpler sub-problem only.

The most important role of teacher expert is to classify each student by learning style. The classification determines the learning strategy applied to the student. Our system analyzes semantic correctness of students' programs performing distinct methods for stoppers and movers. Stoppers' programs are analyzed by model tracer, forcing student to write program in predefined order of steps. For example, if task requires reading input, do calculation and write output, stoppers have to follow these steps in program construction or get an error. In opposite, movers' programs are semantically analyzed by program recognizer that allows program writing in an arbitrary order of steps. Movers can start with output, and write input statement at the end. We assume program construction order, needless to say that input statement has to precede other statements in the program.

Right now we use rule of thumb to make decision about students' style in dealing with difficulties, that is: if student is found to be inactive during any problem solving more then 120 seconds or requires system help more than twice per task, then system identifies student as a stopper.

Identification of Concept Adoption

As we have described in previous section, student model holds data about students' behavior during adoption of each concept. Concatenating status indicators related to the same concept, we get a sequence of student's behavior in adoption of that concept during time (Table 2). Returning back to example, the overall status is shown by table.

The question is, when we can say that student knows some concept? If we say "knows the concept" then we assume that learner won't make an error dealing with that concept in the future. This question implies a new one: how many tasks implementing the concept have to be launched to the student? Right now we are not able to argue our answers. We make decision that student knows specific concept if overall status in student model ends with four pluses, and contains at least 50% pluses, meaning that related instruction has been applied successfully in four last tasks and in more then half of overall tasks.

Advancement through the Course

A course material is organized in chapters, sections and lesson units, where any unit may explain a number of concepts. The learning process is identified by current lesson student deals with, and his activity, which is textbook reading or task solving. Student starts with reading and clicks on the button "Next" when wishes to advance to the next stage of the course. The system responds displaying text of next lesson or switching student's activity to the task solving.

Table 2. Sequence of student's behavior in adoption of if statement

Student ID	*Concept ID*	*Overall Status*
101	if-syntax	- h s + +
101	if-semantics	+ - - +

Switch to the task solving triggers system process that selects task-candidates appropriate to the current status of student's knowledge. We describe each task by a set of concepts implemented by that task. The task is applicable candidate if all are true: task implements at least one concept explained in current lesson; task doesn't implement any concept that hasn't been explained in current or previous lessons; task implements at least one concept that student hasn't adopted yet by the student model.

The computer teacher chooses task by task from the list of task candidates and asks student to solve them. Tasking starts from the middle of list sorted by level of task complexity. If student's task solving ability is high, next task is picked from the middle of upper half of list. Task pointer is turned to the simplest task if student's performance is low. When an error in student's program is found system interrupts her or his work as we explain in section dealing with teaching scenario.

Computer teacher analyzes current status of student's knowledge and makes decision about his readiness to advance to the next lesson. As long as he hasn't adopted concepts explained by lesson, some more related tasks from the task-candidate list are presented.

Some students bring certain knowledge of programming to the course, and want to skip simpler lessons. They can select lesson of their interest from the menu of course content. Advancement is allowed if student model proves that student knows all required concepts. Required-concepts-set contains all concepts explained in lessons that precede the selected one.

If student hasn't proved knowledge of some concepts yet, computer teacher will find a list of tasks implementing those concepts. Students that are not able to solve these tasks may not advance to the lesson they selected. Advancement through the course implemented by our system insures that student possesses knowledge that can be activated in order to assimilate new information.

Tools Module

We have grouped all tools specific for the system to Tools module, containing units necessary to edit source code of program, translate it to intermediate representation, execute and analyze it semantically.

Compiler in Tutoring System

It is common to define programming language by grammar in Bachus-Naur form (Grune 2000). Syntax analyzer based on push-down automaton reads sequence of program tokens building abstract syntax tree. Standard parsers diagnose syntax errors and explain them in the form found – expected (Srbljic 2002).

Compiler employed in an environment of tutoring system for programming has to be adjusted in order to make information about student's syntax errors available to other modules. That is, student model is updated with concepts student uses correctly and incorrectly in his program by compiler provided information. In addition, today's compilers analyze program semantically independently of program requirements. For example, it is possible to detect dead code or endless loops statically, without program execution. Task dependent semantic analysis finds if program realizes requirement. Researchers in field invest significant effort exploring methods that might be useful, including program verification and validation methods, symbolic execution (King 1976) and logical assertions in specific program points (Manna 2007). Unfortunately, these methods are not applicable to learners, since they require additional knowledge and would make more complication to novices.

Apart of translating source code to executable, there are some additional requirements to compiler in environment of our system. First, compiler should be ready to compile new language as soon as it is defined by grammar. Second, we want detailed help delivered to student in case of syntax errors, which is a task dependent pattern of code that should be applied to get syntactically valid instruction. Standard compilers can-+not deliver such help, because they don't "know" the task and its solution. Third, we need to identify instructions that student codes with syntactic errors in order to update student model accordingly.

Obviously, we had to design compiler that meets this specific demands. We started by examination of features of languages commonly used in education: C-language, Pascal and Q-BASIC. Superset covering features of these languages defines requirement to our language independent system.

Since it is common in standard compilers to represent program by abstract syntax tree, we augment grammar by actions that build appropriate tree of specific program.

The tree nodes are universal, language independent and each node has attached output production rule that defines its source code representation. The output production rules are language dependent, and instruct system to write node in target programming language. When output production rules are called recursively, traversing the tree, source code of complete program is written by specific programming language.

Complication arises because languages don't support the same features, for example it isn't possible to use string in C-language, while Q-BASIC supports pointers indirectly by PEEK and POKE. Implication is that we have to define two solutions of the same programming task that, for example compares two strings for equality. Once for Pascal and Q-BASIC using equality operator, and second time for C-language, that needs to traverse two arrays of characters and compare one by one. We find such approach complicated and unacceptable for intelligent tutoring system intended to teach languages common in education. We solve problem designing special purpose programming language with features equal to superset of targeted languages. This language used to define model of program solution we call MODEL. It has keywords by which we can write single program that is sensitive to the expressiveness of target languages. For example, abstract syntax tree of model program contains node that forces lesson builder to check if target language supports string data type.

Request to make available detailed help showing complete instruction to the student, if she or he has problems with its syntax is satisfied by model tracer, explained later in this section. The key point is that compiler translates student's program to abstract syntax tree until first syntax error is found. Model tracer follows the tree of model program as long as it finds corresponding nodes in tree representing student's program. When there is a syntax error in student's program, nodes corresponding to invalid instruction miss, causing tracer to stop at node of model tree that is syntactically incorrect in student's program. Following output production rules of model tree it is easy to explain syntactically valid instruction based on pattern specific for current task.

Designing compiler we have to keep in mind that system actions depend on information about student's knowledge. For example, if student repeatedly commits syntax error of the same instruction, it is time to refresh knowledge about related syntax rules. Also, system needs to know instructions that student codes without error and those that hasn't used in his program. Since compiler is component dealing with students' source code, it has to make that information available to the rest of system. We satisfy requirement adding three sets of concepts to the compiler, namely: success, error and perturbation. Compiler inserts concept identifier of each correctly used instruction into set success, and those where syntax error is found to error set. Student can use some programming constructs in the wrong way. If he tries to multiply two strings, it is assumed that he perturbed meaning of strings, and its identifier is added to the last set. Finally, when student finishes with current task, student model is updated by concepts status appropriate to compiler findings.

In this section we have just shown techniques ready to offer detailed help. The usage of these capabilities in learning session depends of specific student's behavior and we deal with details in section describing syntax learning scenario.

Model Definition Language

It is common to analyze students' programs comparing with model programs, where model is represented by some language. We could code model by the language subject of learning, which is using the same language as student uses. Studying C-language books used in high school education in Croatia, we found that many or even all examples can be coded in Pascal or Q-BASIC. That sounds logical, since authors focus on fundamentals, rather then specifics of C –language. That suggests that we can save work, and represent examples and task solutions independently of course language. This assumption is valid not only when human expert codes model program, but when it is done by expert system automatically. Expert system needs knowledge to solve problem and code it by specific language. Work is saved if that knowledge is independent of spectrum of teaching languages.

Unfortunately, neither of standard languages can be used for this purpose, because language having features equal to superset of languages regularly used in classrooms doesn't exist. For example, C-language doesn't support strings; Pascal defines nested procedures and functions etc. Problem arises higher, because problem may be solved using various algorithms and their variations; an array may be sorted applying bubble-sort or quick-sort. In addition, an algorithm may be implemented by different instructions; repetition in C-language may be coded using while, do-while, for, or even by if and go-to. If we would use standard language to define model-program containing as many as possible variants of solution, then we would have to write many programs. Even if we are ready to accept that complication, how we can know that some solution is incorrect? May we say that solution is buggy, because it doesn't exist in model? Definitely we can not conclude that something is wrong, because isn't predicted by model-program.

In our opinion, the solution is a new language with features covering special demand to code model-program. We have developed such language and call it MODEL that stands for Model Definition Language. In addition, it supports all instructions that can be found in C –language, and nested procedures and functions definition as Pascal supports. Does it mean that student learning C may use features specific for Pascal? Answer is no, because C – grammar doesn't allow such instructions.

MODEL language is used to write source code of model-program that is by MODEL compiler translated to abstract syntax tree. The semantics of each node is defined by node type and parameters found in grammar augmented by tree-building-keywords. Semantic analyzer finds two programs semantically equivalent if tree of model-program contains all nodes existing in tree representing student's program. The approach to represent programs by abstract semantic tree is not new in our system, but inventive programming language makes easier to represent spectrum of possible solutions of given problem. We argue this statement by an example.

Task example: *Write program that reads an integer from standard input and writes to standard output message "odd" if integer is odd or "even" if integer is even or 0!*

It is possible to get at least two programs that realize requirements. We show programs by pseudo-code.

Program 1.

```
var n: integer;
begin
      raad(n);
      if even(n) thenwrite("{0}is
even", n);
```

```
      else
            write(«{0} is odd»,
n);
end.
Program 2:
var n: integer;
      s: string;
begin
      read(n);
      s:= "odd";
      if even(n) then
            s:= "even";
      write("{0} is {1}", n, s);
end.
```

Conditional even (n) may be implemented by one of expressions:

Expression 1:
even(n) is n % 2 == 0
Expression 2:
even(n) is (n / 2)*2 == n
Expression 3:
even(n) is n & 1 == 0 // & is bitwise operator

It is known from experience that students' may use inappropriate conditional expression to check even integer.

Buggy expression 4:
even(n) is n & 2 == 0

How many different programs students may construct, using above given patterns of code? Combination of two programs and four expressions makes eight possible programs. We don't need to say that this example is trivial, but still we have to consider at least eight programs. In order to explain to student why his solution is incorrect, the tutoring system has to recognize pattern of code used in program. Theoretically we need model covering all possible programs, including correct and incorrect solutions. Since number of possible errors is infinitive, we limit consideration to the bugs commonly found in novices' programs. Defining single program for each possible task solution we get explosion of programs. We prefer only one program for each task, and MODEL language helps here. Correct program solves given problem, in other words, it realizes goal required by programming task.

It is not easy to understand and solve non trivial problems at a glance, but programmers decompose complex problem to sub-problems (Simon 1980). The main goal is achieved if its sub-goals are achieved. Decomposition continues until remaining sub-problems can be easy solved applying instructions of programming language. If we want tutoring system to help novices to identify goal of the program and its decomposition to sub-goals, it needs knowledge about decomposition process. In addition, tutoring system should explain which sub-goal is realized by specific part of the program. Tutoring system has to stay silent if student decomposes his program as expected, and help if his decomposition is not found in model-program. The instruction GOAL is used to code into MODEL program such decomposition information. It contains identifier, hint and description in natural language of the current goal, while body of instruction represents plan. The plan is defined by intrinsic instructions, those that can be found in student's program. When appropriate, body of GOAL instruction may contain nested GOAL instructions. Semantic analyzer finds GOAL realized if all nested GOAL are realized and if mapping of intrinsic instructions between two programs exists.

Generally, single problem may be solved by spectrum of solutions. We say that model program contains variants of solution, and we code them by instruction SWITCH VARIANT. The body of instruction contains list of possible variants, where some are buggy solutions, marked by keyword BUG. Semantic analyzer finds sub-goal realized if student's program contains one of the variants present in the model program. If found variant is marked buggy, the system displays attached description to student, explaining why it is wrong.

Expressions may have variants as well, and we code them in MODEL by keywords ANYOF-EXPRESSION, referring to the list of possible expressions. Buggy expression is marked by keyword WRONG with attached textual explanation.

Program output is the same if some instructions or blocks of instructions change their order in source code. We call such instructions or blocks commutative, and code in MODEL by keyword INPARALLEL. Semantics analyzer finds student's program correct if instructions coded within INPARALLEL and END INPARALLEL exist in program in any arbitrary order.

Program 1 is rather simple running example, while MODEL language allows coding of model program of any complexity.

Semantic Analysis of Student's Program

Each programming task described by natural language has attached program model of possible solutions coded by Model Definition Language. Since MODEL and programming language subject of learning differs, we need two compilers, first to translate student's program, and second to translate MODEL program to the abstract semantic trees. Nodes of tree representing student's program are subset of nodes representing model program. Later tree contains some extra nodes needed to define sub-goals and possible variants of solution.

Abstract machine executes program translated to intermediate language, supports step by step execution and breakpoints. Comparer of abstract semantics trees performs semantics analysis of student's program, identifying its correctness and programming style. Comparer checks if student's program represented by tree follows any of variants existing in tree of model-program.

TEACHING SCENARIO

We have based the teaching scenario on facts that there exist distinguished categories of knowledge, and individual learners' ability. Programming requires language syntax knowledge, understanding of single instruction semantics, program design and testing skills.

Teaching Syntax

System watches source code editor character by character as student types. Delimiters (i.e. blank, new line) trigger syntax analysis of piece of code taken from the start of the procedure to the current cursor position. Whenever syntax error is found, student is interrupted with a message, for example: Syntax error found at row 3, column 12.

If student fixes error on his own, without future system help, it is assumed like typing error. While student is not able to get error free instruction, system provides three level help:

1. Found – expected: expected tokens instead of found one are shown.
2. Lesson launching: the lesson explaining syntax of statement is displayed.
3. Detailed help: syntactically valid instruction is shown.

System deals with syntax errors immediately, in computer coach manner, keeping student's focus on single problem at a time. Student is stopped at concept he doesn't know and has to learn. In opposite, error description delayed to compile time, could lead to accumulation of many errors and confuse novices.

Teaching Statement Semantics

Students' understanding of the statements semantics is assessed by three separated techniques:

Reformulation - source code of program is presented, asking student to do small modifications, for example change output messages or number of repetitions.

Transformation - student has to rewrite given code using different statements. For example, student can transform repetition implemented by if and unwanted go-to to while, if knows semantics of all these instructions.

Mental simulation of program execution - student is asked to predict the sequence of specific variable values or program output. Dialog is used to get student's answer and inform him about his findings. In case of incorrect answer, the new attempt with system directions is allowed. When correct answer is not achieved within three attempts, student may use programming language model, run program step by step and follow variable values.

Teaching Design Skills

Design skills are the group of techniques used to combine language features in order to form a program. These include knowledge of stereotypic patterns of code that perform complex functions such as sorting or an array traversal. Programmers decompose the problem into component parts and plan how to combine them into solution as a whole.

Our system helps to design program comparing student's and expert's solutions of given task. Expert's solution is organized in a tree of goals and plans, where root represents the program and leafs are plans. The goal is tuple of unique identifier, hint, description and list of statements – plan. The process of program recognition maps student's plan to expert's plan. Success of mapping means that student has accomplished the sub-goal. Unsuccessful mapping is assumed as a semantic error of specific sub-goal. We apply different approaches in recognition of stopper's and mover's programs. Stopper's program (syntactically correct) is analyzed immediately as he changes code. We call it early semantic analysis. Delay of student's action or semantic error interrupts his work and arises three level help: hint – system gives direction how to realize the goal, description – the goal is explained in details and plan – the code that accomplishes the goal is visible.

The system analyzes movers' program in the moment he calls compiler to translate program. We call it late semantic analysis. Program understanding is performed by application of constraint satisfaction problem (Woods 1998), where broken constraints diagnose semantic errors.

Early semantic analysis wakes up stoppers and keeps them on the path of correct solution. With late semantic analysis movers get opportunity to experiment with program finding correct solution on their own.

Notional Machine

DuBoulay et al. (1989) identify two basic approaches in learning to interact with a computer: the black box and the glass box. In the black box approach one puts in commands and data and gets the answer as if by magic. The mechanisms behind cover are hidden from the user, and the user is likely to assume that computers are just not understandable. Such users might memorize algorithms that solve one or other task, but are not able to understand what goes on inside the black box.

In glass box approach the user attempts to understand what is going on inside the computer running program. These actions can be described and understood. The important properties of model making hidden operations of language clearer to novices are: right level of details, simplicity and visibility.

Instructions of a program interact with memory locations – variables. Conditionals check variable values to make decision if some other instructions have to be executed, assignment changes variable values etc. Thus we implemented programming language model with properties:

Student may trace program running instructions step by step, while segment of memory allocated to variables is displayed. It is easy to change value of any variable and check effect on current step.

Authors (Bryant et al. 2008) explain fewer bugs in programs developed in pairs by driver's verbal explanation of each peace of code to the navigator. This finding suggests that student may better understand programming language if gets verbal description of instruction actions.

Our model is adaptable to the current status of student's knowledge. For example, if he knows scope and life time of variable, model shows appropriate information as well, and when it is identified that student has adopted instruction semantics, verbalization of program execution is omitted.

THE SYSTEM EVALUATION

During winter semester 2007/08 we have used our system in course of programming at Faculty of Natural Science and Mathematics. Three groups of 29 students in total have learnt concepts of programming using QBasic. They followed teaching scenario described earlier in this chapter. 16 (55%) of our students hadn't got any experience in programming before the course, while 13 (45%) had learnt programming in high school from ½ to 4 years. The later students had in average 3 semesters of experience in Pascal, C/C++ or QBasic.

Students' Evaluation Of The System

At the end of course students filled up a questionnaire based on 5 point Likert's scale concerning their motivation to learn programming, impression about system and it usefulness in learning.

We conclude that our system has achieved its main goal of usefulness in learning as 26 (89.7%) students found that system helped them to acquire the knowledge of programming.

Table 3. The system usefulness in learning

Point	*Answers*	*%*
1. Very Harmful	0	0.0
2. Harmful	0	0.0
3. Can't decide	3	10.3
4. Useful	4	13.8
5. Very Useful	22	75.9

Table 4. Graded usefulness

Item	*Median*	*Mean*	*Range*
Notional Model	7	6.2	4..7
Advancement	5	5.0	1..7
Syntax help	7	6.2	4..7
Semantic help	7	6.7	6..7

Students were asked to grade at 7 point Likert's scale how much each of components helped them in learning. (Point 1 is very harmful, 4 is neutral and 7 very useful.)

Some students found advancement is very harmful, because they would prefer to select lessons on their own and ignore planed sequence of concept adoption. As we expected, 20 students graded semantics help very useful and 9 useful.

Our Observation

During the course we tried to identify stoppers and movers, focusing on their behavior when weren't able to solve the problem on their own. From our experience we know that stoppers hesitate to ask the human teacher for help. Our system is capable to help stoppers, decomposing problem to simpler steps. We estimated that one third of our students were stoppers, while one third were movers. All students initially classified as stoppers, used opportunity to ask help from the system. Unfortunately, they very often asked for detailed help that is peace of code solving current step of program. This finding suggests that next version of the system should implement some kind of limitation in help.

RELATED WORK

Published intelligent tutoring systems for learning and teaching programming are dedicated to specific programming language. In our opinion, the principle of programming is language independent and acquisition of that knowledge should be the most important goal of introductory course. With this fact in mind, we have designed the system that teaches programming, and uses the specific programming language as necessary instrument to implement ideas solving given problem. We achieved the goal of language independent system, that is able to present solution of given problem in variety of languages for which the grammar is defined, introducing MODEL language for coding solution of problem. Due our best knowledge, this characteristic makes our system unique.

The LISP Tutor is found very effective in teaching students with low performance, but students doing well could not experiment with program and improve their skills (Anderson 1985). Seams like immediate feedback tend to stop movers. In our opinion, the movers will benefit if system applies different teaching methods, namely immediate feedback for stoppers and delayed for movers. Obviously, movers may need to implement some instructions that help to localize bugs and Model Tracing is not appropriate technique for students' program recognition in this case.

In opposite, PROUST (Johnson 1984) analyzes completed students' programs performing reflexive tutoring that may be too late for stoppers (Lane 2004). We propose the system that is able to teach stoppers applying the immediate feedback and movers analyzing their completed programs. Since movers programs may contain some additional instructions – it is analyzed mapping instructions to the model by application of Constraint Satisfaction Problem method (Woods 1998). Student's program is found correct as long as it maps to the model regardless of extra code.

Multilingual capability of our system differs from ViLLE (Laakso 2008), such that course material is language independent, automatically accommodated to the language, subject of each course. Our approach saves human work in course preparation, while it also processes programs independently of language as ViLLE does.

CONCLUSION

Our tutoring system for learning programming helps novices to understand what goes on behind "cover" of programming language. Notional machine provides program execution step by step, describes instruction actions and makes variable values accessible. Controlling advancement through the course material it encourages students to learn systematically, from simpler to more demanding lessons and supports meaningful learning connecting new information with present knowledge. Switching from declarative knowledge presentation to task generation, the system provides application of explained programming concepts in problem solving.

Our system distinguishes students' learning styles providing immediate feedback to stoppers and delayed to movers. The innovative programming language MODEL is used to define single model-program of problem solution including various algorithms and problem decomposition steps.

The evaluation of our system in real classroom argues its helpfulness in learning to program.

ACKNOWLEDGMENT

This work has been carried out within projects 177-0361994-1996 Design and evaluation of intelligent e-learning systems, funded by the Ministry of Science and Technology of the Republic of Croatia.

REFERENCES

Adam, A., & Laurent, J. P. (1980). LAURA, a System to Debug Student Programs. *Artificial Intelligence, 15*, 75–122. doi:10.1016/0004-3702(80)90023-5

Anderson, J. R., & Reiser, B. (1985). The LISP Tutor. *Byte, 10.*

Barr, A., Beard, M., & Atkinson, R. C. (1976). The computer as a tutorial laboratory: the Stanford BIP project. *Man-Machine Studies, 8*, 567–596. doi:10.1016/S0020-7373(76)80021-1

Brusilovsky, P. (1995). Intelligent Learning Environments for Programming. *Proceedings of AI-ED'95, 7th World Conference on Artifcial Intelligence in Education.* Washington, DC.

Brusilovsky, P. L. (1992). Intelligent Tutor: Environment and Manual for Introductory Programming. *Educational and Training Technology International.* 26-34.

Bryant, S., Romero, P., & DuBoulay, B. (2008). Pair programming and the mysterious role of the navigator. *International Journal of Human-Computer Studies, 66*(7), 519–529. doi:10.1016/j.ijhcs.2007.03.005

Budin, L. (2005). *Education in the Field of Information and Communication Technology in Elementary School.* Zagreb, Croatia: Croatian National Education Standard, Ministry of Science, Education and Sport.

Butz, C. J., Hua, S., & Maguire, R. B. (2006). A web-based Bayesian intelligent tutoring system for computer programming. *Web Intelligence and Agent System, 4*, 77–97.

Chee, Y. S., Tan, J. T., & Chan, T. (1993). Applying cognitive apprenticeship to the teaching of Smalltalk in a computer based learning environment. In *Proceedings of 7th International PEG Conference*, (pp. 569-588).

Dadic, T., Stankov, S., & Rosic, M. (2006).Prototype Model ofTutoring System for Programming. In *Proceedings of ITI Conference, Dubrovnik, Croatia.*

Dadic, T., Stankov, S., & Rosic, M. (2008). Meaningful learning in the Tutoring System for Programming. In *Proceedings of ITI Conference, Dubrovnik, Croatia.*

DuBoulay, B., O'Shea, T., & Monk, J. (1989). The Black Box Inside the Glass Box. In Soloway, E., & Spohrer, J. C. (Eds.), *Studying the Novice Programmer* (p. 431). Hillsdale, NJ: Lawrence Erlbaum Associates, Publishers.

Eisenberg, M. B., & Johnson, D. (2005). Learning and Teaching Information Technology Computer Skills in Context. *US Federal government.* Retrieved November, 20, 2009, from http://www.libraryinstruction.com/info-tech.html

Grune, D., Bal, H. E., Jacobs, C. J. H., & Langendoen, K. G. (2000). *Modern Compiler Design.* London: John Wiley & Sons, Ltd.

Guzdial, M. (2004). Programming Environments for Novices. In Fincher, S., & Petre, M. (Eds.), *Computer Science Education Research.* Springer-Verlag.

Hartman, J. (1991). Understanding natural programs using proper decomposition. In *Proceedings of the International Conference on Software Engineering* (pp 62-73). Austin, TX.

Hoare, C. A. R. (1969). An Axiomatic Basis for Computer Programming. *CACM, 12*(10), 576–583.

Johnson, W. L., & Soloway, E. (1984). PROUST: Knowledge based program understanding. In *Proceedings of the 7th international Conference on Software Engineering* (pp 369-380). Orlando, FL.

King, J. C. (1976). Symbolic Execution and Program Testing. *CACM, 19*(7), 385–394.

Laakso, Malmi, Korhonen, Rajala, Kaila, & Salakoski. (2008). Using Roles of Variables to Enhance Novice'sDebugging Work. *Issues in Informing Science and Information Technology, 5.*

Lane, H. C. (2004). *Natural Language Tutoring and the Novice Programmer*. (Unpublished doctoral dissertation), University of Pittsburgh, PA.

Lane, H. C., & VanLehn, K. (2003). Coached Program Planning: Dialogue-Based Support for Novice Program Design. In *Proceedings of the Thirty-Fourth Technical Symposium on Computer Science Education (SIGCSE)* (pp 148-152).

Lemut, Dettori, & Du Boulay. (1993). *Cognitive Models and Intelligent Environments for Learning Programming*. New York: Springer-Verlag.

Linn, M. C., & Dalbey, J. (1989). Cognitive Consequences of Programming Instruction. In Soloway, E., & Spohrer, J. C. (Eds.), *Studying the Novice Programmer* (pp. 57–81). Hillsdale, NJ: Lawrence Erlbaum Associates, Publishers.

Lister, R. (2004). A Multi-National Study of Reading and Tracing Skills in Novice Programmers. *SIGCSE Bulletin, 36*(4), 119–150. doi:10.1145/1041624.1041673

Manna, Z., & Bradley, A. R. (2007). *Lecture Notes on Verification CS156: Calculus of Computation*. Retrieved November, 13, 2007, from http://cs156.stanford.edu/notes/verify.pdf

Mayer, R. E. (1989). The Psychology of How Novices Learn Computer Programming. In Soloway, E., & Spohrer, J. C. (Eds.), *Studying the Novice Programmer* (pp. 129–141). Hillsdale, NJ: Lawrence Erlbaum Associates, Publishers.

Perkins, D. N., Hancock, C., Hobbs, R., Martin, F., & Simmons, R. (1989). Conditions of Learning. In Soloway, E., & Spohrer, J. C. (Eds.), *Studying the Novice Programmer* (pp. 261–280). Hillsdale, NJ: Lawrence Erlbaum Associates, Publishers.

Simon, H. A. (1980). Problem solving and education. In Tuma, D. T., & Reif, F. (Eds.), *Problem solving and education: Issues in teaching and research*. Hillsdale, NJ: Erlbaum.

Srbljic, S. (2002*). Language processors 2: analysis of source and synthesis of target language*. Zagreb, Croatia: Element (in Croatian language)

Stankov, S. (1997). *Isomorphic Model of the System as the Basis of Teaching Control Principles in an Intelligent Tutoring System*. (Unpublished doctoral dissertation), University of Split, Croatia. (in Croatian language).

Ueno, H. (1994). Integrated intelligent programming environment for learning programming. *IEICE Transactions on Information and Systems*, 68–79.

Woods, S. G., Quilici, A. E., & Yang, Q. (1998). *Constraint-Based Design Recovery for Software Reengineering: Theory and Experiments*. Norwell, MA: Kluwer Academic Publishers.

Chapter 10
Overlay Method in Testing Knowledge by Natural Language Dialogue

Branko Žitko
University of Split, Croatia

ABSTRACT

Irrespective how domain knowledge is well formalized, and irrespective of applying appropriate pedagogical techniques in Intelligent tutoring system, learning and teaching process can seem complex because of unfamiliar communication with computer tutor. Using even simplest NLP techniques makes benefits in computer's usage, not only in e-learning domain. Natural language generation is basic technique which can make learning and teaching process much more adaptable to the student. Presenting formal knowledge by natural language sentences, as well as testing in a form of dialogue are aims to be accomplished in new Intelligent Tutoring System based on Tutor-Expert System model. In making previous system more acceptable to the student, our first step is to perform natural language generation with Croatian localization for formalized domain knowledge following by problem generation and dialog based guidance to the problem solution.

INTRODUCTION

Intelligent tutoring system (ITS) is a kind of e-learning system which provides tutoring based on one-to-one scenario. Computer plays a role of tutor and guides student in assimilation of knowledge, skills and abilities. ITS modal architecture contains expert module which, as typical expert system, implements some domain knowledge using particular knowledge representation technique. Pedagogical module is responsible for applying teaching techniques over knowledge, and in doing so relays on the student model. Communication module is in relation with teacher module and provides interface for the student.

Applying natural language interface in communication module, even in a basic form, greatly improves learning and teaching process (Di Eugenio & Trolio, Can simple Natural Language Generation improve Intelligent Tutoring Systems, 2000)

DOI: 10.4018/978-1-61692-008-1.ch010

(Di Eugenio, Fossati, Yu, Haller, & Glass, 2005). Great influence on natural language processing (NLP) in ITS has domain knowledge representation. Usually ITS's are strictly specialized over some domain knowledge representations making NLP knowledge dependent. Besides, majority of natural language based ITS's incorporate dialogue exclusively as an only way of tutoring the student. Even so, these dialogues have different approaches depending on a knowledge representation. Today's most robust and fluent dialogue is probably utilized in AutoTutor (Wiemer-Hastings, Wiemer-Hastings, & Graesser, 1999). Robustness of AutoTutor is outcome of using statistical model of world knowledge containing large text corpora. Statistical approach to NLP in AutoTutor is based on latent semantic analysis of a large text corpora, and as every statistical approaches, has no ability to control outcome. Perhaps all that can be made better is to train computer tutor with specific examples, in the hope of enhancing results. CIRSCIM-Tutor (Glass, 2000) has finite state syntax approach where dialogue is generated using finite state transducers and is limited on a few simple words as an answer on tutor's question. Casual concept map in CIRSCIM-Tutor contains concepts described by a few words and relations for determining causalities. Simplicity of dialogue in this tutor is an effect of such knowledge representation. Frame-based semantic approach in Atlas-Andes (Rosé, 2000) can capture deeper meaning of natural language sentences presented or inputted by the student. On the other hand, semantic network with frames has basic inheritance mechanism which is insufficient for constructing complex logical expressions.

Aim of our research is to make model of Tutor-Expert System (TEx-Sys) (Stankov, 1997) more acceptable by students. Necessary step in doing so is appliance of NLP techniques. Frame-based semantic net is a backbone of all of learning and testing methodologies used in TEx-Sys and we believe that acceptability of the system will be significantly increased if this knowledge representation is going to be extended with logic formalism and if NLP is going to relay on it. Basic idea of applying natural language process in ITS is refitting TEx-Sys model by replacing semantic net with description logic and uniting previous testing methods (quiz and overlay) into natural language dialogue. Moreover, interface between student and ITS will be completely based on natural language.

Natural language generation is essential technique for producing sentences and questions in tutor dialogue. Specifics of approach described in this article greatly relays on description logic for defining structure of formal knowledge expressions as an basis for natural language sentences. These formalized expressions are inputs for generating questions and recognizing student's answers during test in form of a dialogue. Computer tutor takes role of a dialogue manager, and is responsible for guiding student during execution of dialogue. Besides generating questions and recognizing answers, computer tutor dictate updates of the student model. Proposed student modeling is relaying on basic overlay model (Carr & Goldstein, 1977), as well as, model presented in TEx-Sys. Enhancement of proposed student modeling are made because of new knowledge formalism applied and since different way of interaction is made with the student.

In the second chapter is given overview of TEx-Sys model with a focus on knowledge representation using semantic network and their influence on presenting the domain knowledge, as well as generating and evaluating tests to the students. Foundations presented in the second chapter are used to devise general framework of natural language dialogue in the third chapter which incorporates overlay model for testing student's knowledge. Semantic and syntax of natural language is depending on description logic, while morphology is based on a structure and standards used in a morphological lexicon.

In the fourth chapter is introduced a basic approach to natural language generation in ITS which is depending on knowledge representation formalism. In order to accomplish generation of grammatically correct sentences, essential syntactical and morphological structures are introduced in the same chapter. Furthermore, natural language techniques are applied in realization of the tutor dialogue, as shown in the fifth chapter. Initialization, execution and finalization of tutor dialogue are accompanied with previews of generated questions, scaffolding and realization of overlay model for finalizing mark of the knowledge.

BACKGROUND

Model of Tutor-Expert System (TEx-Sys) (Stankov, 1997) (Stankov, Rosić, Žitko, & Grubišić, 2008) is built on cybernetic-model which is used for control and measure student's achievement during learning and testing. Process of learning and testing in TEx-Sys is guided during presenting knowledge as well as execution of knowledge tests. Decisions made through guidance are based on domain knowledge representation, and student's acceptance of TEx-Sys model is greatly influenced by the same.

TEx-Sys relays its knowledge representation on semantic nets with frames. Nodes in semantic net are used to represent physical objects, concepts or situations, while links are used to signify different relations. Nodes are typified as generic and individual. Generic node describes class of concept, while individual node represents particular individual belonging to the concept.

Due to relationship, knowledge is a cohesive structure with ability of knowledge inference. Learning in this kind of domain knowledge representation is based on discovering concepts by following links. One problem of semantic net usage is there is no standard definition for link names. In some semantic nets IS-A is used for both generic and individual relations even though "a kind of" (AKO) relation is more appropriate for connecting generic nodes. Misinterpretation is made since IS-A is used in a sense of the common words "is a" for connecting individual to a class in natural language. Defining other properties of the nodes can be made by introducing other non-standard links. In such way semantic net may become unreadable and hard to infer. By focusing on the general properties of an object it is easier to reason about them. Enhancing semantic net with frames provides objects that are typical to a given situation. A frame is analogous to the record structure in high-level languages, in which slots and fillers correspond to the fields and values of a record. Common feature of knowledge described using semantic net with frames is that almost everything can be characterized using (Object, Attribute, Value) triplets (Figure 1). These triplets can be compared to simple natural language sentences using (Subject, Predicate, Object) triplets.

In TEx-Sys model there are two methods of knowledge testing. Testing by quiz and testing by

Figure 1. Representing semantic net with frames using triplets

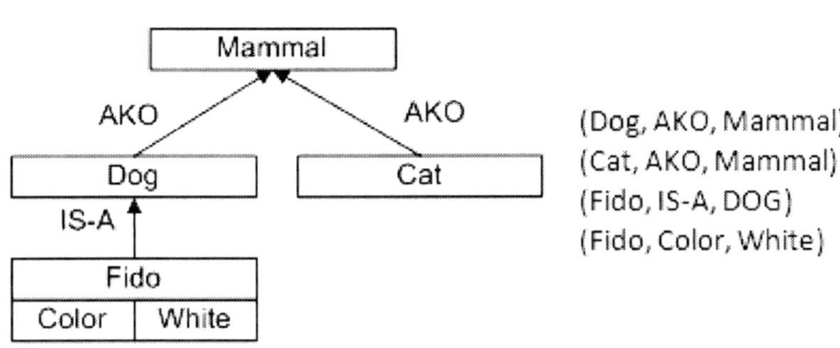

constructing knowledge is evaluated according to overlay student model. Both testing methods have automated problem definition made over semantic net with frames.

In quiz method, problem is represented using dynamically generated questions with attached answers where one or more of them can be correct (Stankov, Rosić, & Glavinić, 2001). Generating questions in TEx-Sys is a process of filling previously prepared question and answer templates with elements of semantic net with frames. If knowledge is assumed as an (Subject, Predicate, Object) triplet set, than one of the question and answer template can be interpreted as "Who (X, Predicate, Object)?" where X is a correct answer. Generally, question and answer templates are formed by removing one or two items from (Subject, Predicate, Object) triplet and proposing those items as an answer, as well as arbitrary incorrect answers. Only Yes/No typed question and answer template does not removes any item from (Subject, Predicate, Object). In Figure 1 first type of a question is a Yes/No, and there is no removed item from (Subject, Predicate, Object) triplet. However, in second, third, and forth question type, there is one item removed from a triplet. Only fifth question has two items removed.

Student's correct or incorrect answering on such questions displays misconceptions and missing conceptions which are used in overlay student modeling. If student has answered incorrectly for any question from example in Figure 2 then he or she is missing conception. Misconception will be made if student answers incorrectly on a question which is not in domain knowledge, for example "Is Fido a kind of Cat?" or "What is Mammal Color?".

In quiz method of knowledge testing (Stankov, Rosić, & Glavinić, 2001), correct answers are always served for each question. Answering correctly on them students' knowledge is oncoming experts' knowledge. Missing conception is made if student answers wrongly on a second and third question from example on Figure 2. Wrongly answering on fourth question, student is dealing with missing relation. Missing conception and missing relation is showed by wrongly answering on fifth question. Final mark is made by overlaying student knowledge with expert knowledge.

Other way of testing, used in the first version of TEx-Sys, is conceived according to constructivism theory. Through processes of accommodation and assimilation, students construct new knowledge from their experiences gained during learning. Students' achievement in testing can be measured using overlay method. In this method student model is inferred by calculating overlap between 3 layers of knowledge:

- Experts' knowledge (EK) which represents original knowledge built by the domain expert
- Problem knowledge (PK) is produced by eliminating elements in EK
- Student knowledge (SK) is constructed by students' effort to achieve EK starting from PK.

Figure 2. Dynamic question generation over semantic net with frames

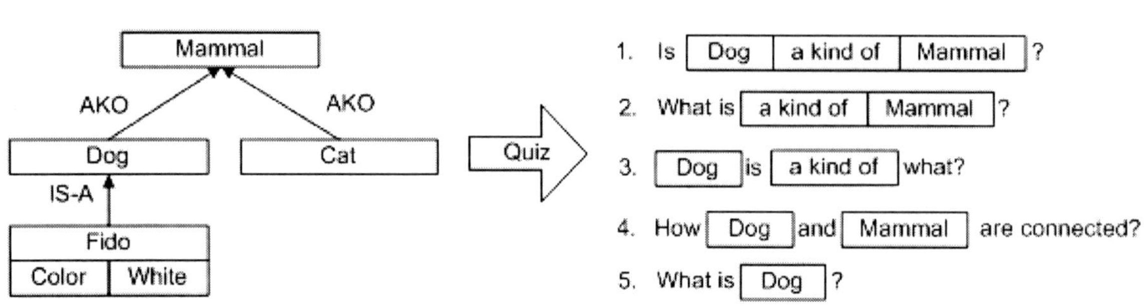

In the TEx-Sys model, EK is designed by expert and is assumed to be completed. ITS is generating PK by removing nodes, links and/or frames from experts knowledge. Thereafter, student can make correct and remove incorrect concepts and/or relations (See Figure 3).

Overlaying these three knowledge bases we can see that "Animal" and "Black" are misconceptions since they are not contained in EK, not in PK and are contained in SK. "Cat" is missing conception because it is contained in both EK and PK, but not in SK. Only correct conception is "Dog".

As a conclusion, both methods of knowledge testing in TEx-Sys model have lacks. In quiz method generating question is made by filling single template with no applied grammatical rules over words in question. Another lack is concerned on easiness of answering questions, because student can easily eliminate wrong answers. On the opposite, constructivist method is far harder way of testing knowledge because student can easily made spelling mistakes while adding missing knowledge in an aspiration to fulfill expert knowledge.

DIALOGUE FRAMEWORK

Although providing natural language generation over semantic net with frames is moderately simple, only simple sentences can be formed. Two connected nodes will produce simple sentence; if node A is connected using link B to another node C then simple sentence would have A as subject, B as predicate and C as object. For node A having slot S with filler F will also produce simple sentence having A as subject, B as predicate and C as object. Besides, all of these simple sentences can be connected using conjunction. Moreover, semantic net has no built-in abilities to make complement of concept or to construct disjunction of concepts.

These limitations can be solved firstly by providing knowledge representation which is based on logic, but can include expressiveness of semantic net. Description logic has both characteristics. OWL DL is a formal language having correspondence to description logic, and is our choice for expressing domain knowledge. Names of concepts and relations in OWL DL can have entries which are human readable. On this fact is based generation of natural language sentences. Moreover, words contained in names of concepts and relations have to be processable in order to

Figure 3. Overlay method in TEx-Sys model

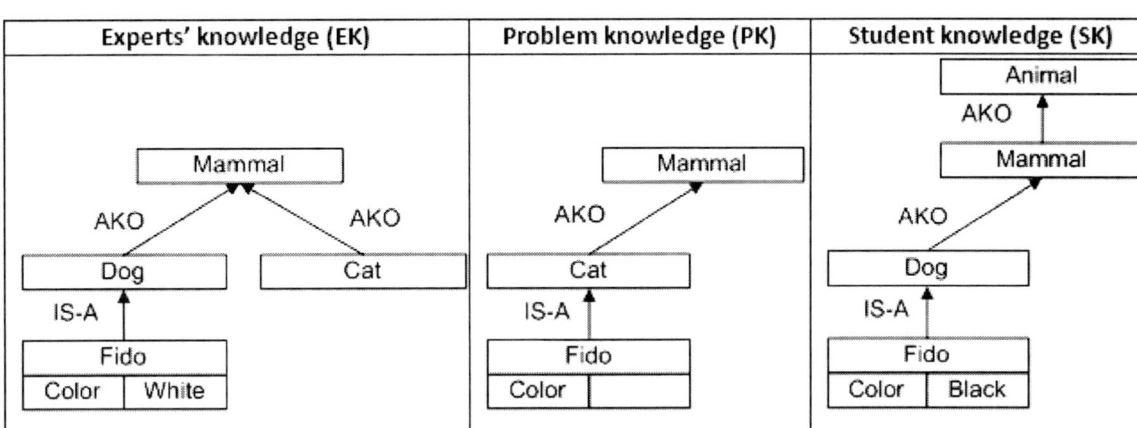

generate grammatically correct sentences. Processing of the words is made on morphological level and is supported by morphological lexicon. For Croatian language is used Hrvatski morfološki leksikon (HML) (Tadić & Fulgosi, 2003) whose morphology of words is described using Multext-East specification (Erjavec, Krstev, Petkevič, Simov, & Tadić, 2003). OWL DL and HML are retaining walls of NLP in our ITS. Additionally, teaching contents and student model are also based on OWL DL representation of domain knowledge. Inclusion of NLP pushes boundaries of previous testing methods towards tutor dialogue. In ITS, computer tutor manages dialogue accordingly to the domain knowledge and student model. It sends commands to communication module in order to generate natural language sentences or to wait for user input. On Figure 4 is given overview of dialogue framework in ITS.

Dialogue in ITS is a sequence of dialogue frames. In each frame question is asked, answered and evaluated. Depending on result of evaluation scaffolding may occur in a frame. After each frame student model is updated. These phases of dialogue frame are described in chapter 5. Finishing the dialogue student model is evaluated using overlay method and, as a result, is given mark of student's knowledge.

In following chapter is described appliance of description logic as a knowledge representation. As an outcome, besides graphical representation of related concepts, student will be dealing with sentences generated over same related concepts in knowledge. Applying natural language generation in process of learning will be also applied in process of testing knowledge by dialogue. Computer tutor will interface with student during process of testing by natural language dialogue and finally, evaluation of students' knowledge will be based on overlay model.

NATURAL LANGUAGE GENERATION IN ITS

Although semantic nets can be very useful in representing declarative knowledge, they have limitations, such as lack of name standards for nodes and links. Phrase is lexical unit intended for naming concept and relations in domain knowledge. In order to achieve proper grammatical structure of generated sentences, phrases are strictly specified and specification depends on morphosintatical description of contained words. Words included in phrases are mutually dependent and are utilizing morphological lexicon for finding proper word form.

Figure 4. Dialogue framework

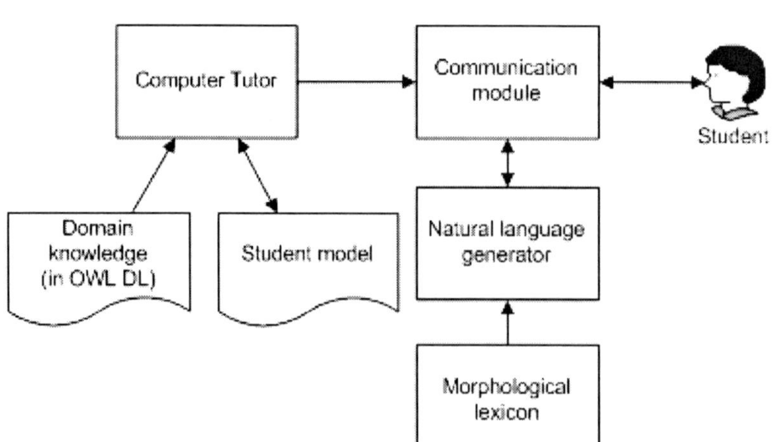

Generally, natural language generation recognizes and specifies phrases from domain knowledge, following by building sentence tree in order to change phrase specification. New phrase specification requires finding proper word form for some containing words, and after applying morphological lexicon, sentence tree is ready to be transformed to the list of words forming natural language sentence.

Process of natural language generation is usually decomposed (Reiter & Dale, 2000) and contains three main modules (Figure 5):

1. Document planner,
2. Micro-planner and
3. Surface realizator

Document planner produces content specification and structure of the test on the domain and application knowledge basis depending on communication goal and user model. This module is usually developed by the experts in domain knowledge. In some cases it is necessary to completely specify content and structure of the text. However, majority of NLG systems uses micro-planner to make decisions about the language. Micro planner is used to optimize information packaging into the sentences. As a result of this manner, micro planner decides relations between phrases in the sentence. For example, if two neighbor sentences describes the same meaning and begins with the same phrase, then it is common to use pronouns. Some NLG systems have text output from micro planner, but it is common to separate specific knowledge for generating grammatical structures in particular language. For example, micro-planner can produce abstract specification of text content, while surface realization will modify abstract text into the natural text. Micro planner can determine tense of the sentence, apropos if the sentence is in a past, present or a future, and leave to the surface realization decision of which morphological form of the word to use.

Language generation in ITS uses common NLG module architecture in order to produce sentences. Input to document planer is OWL ontology and resulting output is an abstract sentence three. Leafs of abstract sentence tree are specified phrases and micro-planner decides about relation and morphological form of those phrases. Phrase as a sequence of word makes input to surface realizator in order to give proper word form, and to end with natural language sentence.

Abstract Sentence Tree

Formal language specified by description logic and expressed by OWL ontology is input in a natural language generator. OWL ontology structure is represented as a set of expressions which can be generally categorized as axioms and facts. Axioms describe schema for a formalized knowledge, namely classes, object properties and datatype properties, while facts constructs individuals over schema. Expressions for identify classes, properties and individuals in OWL ontology are used in a NLG to produce abstract sentence tree. OWL abstract syntax helped in making production rules of the abstract sentence tree. Nodes of the abstract sentence tree can be:

- a simple sentence having subject, predicate and object branch,

Figure 5. Natural language generator overview

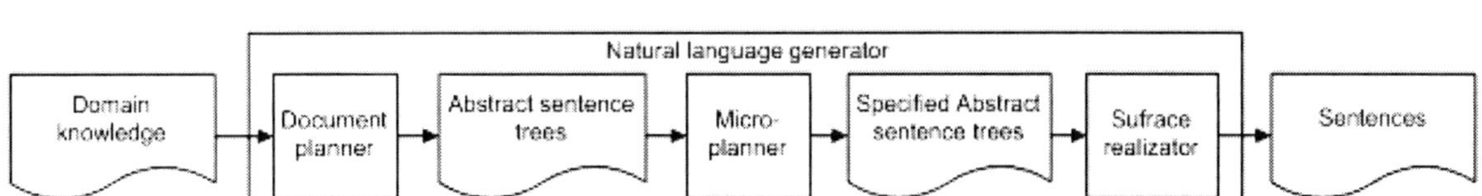

- a simple sentence having only predicate and object branch,
- logical expression nodes AND, OR and NOT,
- existential and universal quantifier expression node,
- numeric relation node (less than, greater than, exactly) and
- phrase node, which is used to identify concepts and relations in the OWL ontology.

Simple sentence node can have two or three branches, logic AND and OR can have more two or more branches. Only the phrase node is a leaf of the abstract sentence tree and is not having child nodes, while all other nodes can have exactly one child node.

Commonly phrase nodes are used to identify elements of OWL ontology, but there are some predefined phrases relaying on ontology abstract syntax constructors (Patel-Schneider, Hayes, & Horrocks, 2004).

Generally, phrases can be grouped as:

- Identifying phrase nodes for naming concepts and relations in ontology
- Structure constant phrase nodes which are predefined for realization of basic taxonomy constructors
- Other constant phrase nodes for realization of property quantifiers and cardinality.

Almost all directives in OWL ontology can be transferred to abstract sentence tree. Class axiom is one of them and is used to identify class as well as to describe it. For example,

Class(#RAM_memory #main_memory restriction(#can_read value(#data)) restriction(#can_write hasValue(#data)))

This expression contains phrases #RAM_memory, #main_memory, #can_read, #can_write and #data. In Figure 6 are listed some productions used for transforming OWL abstract syntax to abstract sentence tree for previous example.

Class axiom abstract syntax contains class identifier #RAM_memory and a set of descriptions. For connecting #RAM_memory with description is used constant predicate phrase #is_kind_of. In this example, first description is class identifier #main_memory following by two object property restrictions. First property restriction is value restriction on object property #can_read, while

Figure 6. Transforming OWL abstract syntaxt to abstract sentence tree

<table>
<tr><th>OWL abstract syntax</th><th>Abstract sentence tree</th></tr>
<tr><td>Class(#X description1 ... descriptionN)</td><td>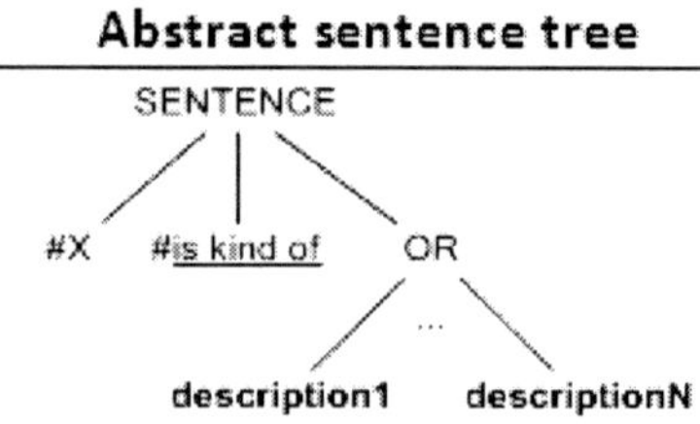
</td></tr>
<tr><td>#X</td><td>#X</td></tr>
<tr><td>restriction(#OP individualRestrictionComponent1 ... individualRestriscionComponentN)</td><td>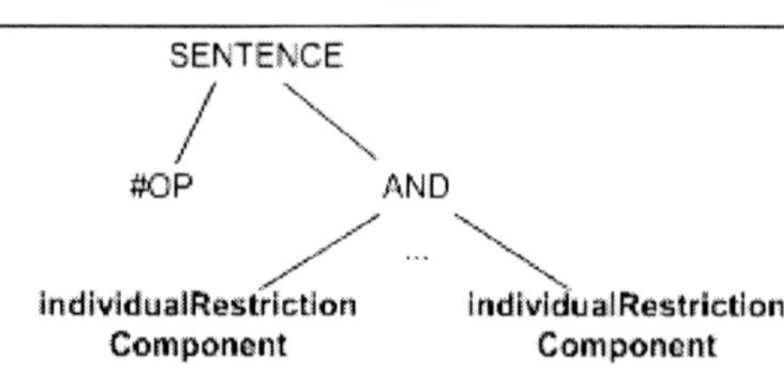
</td></tr>
<tr><td>value(#I)</td><td>#I</td></tr>
</table>

other is defined on property #can_write. Resulting abstract syntax tree is showed on Figure 7.

Afterward, abstract sentence tree is optimized in order to remove non necessary nodes. There are several algorithms involved in optimization. Basic tree traversal is used in order to find sufficient tree nodes and remove them, as well as for joining appropriate nodes. In this example, AND nodes are removed because they have only one child node (Figure 8).

For reducing the size and the shape of the abstract sentence tree several optimizing algorithms are used (Figure 9). First algorithm is removing logic AND or OR node if they have only one child node. Another optimization algorithm bubbles logic NOT node outside the object branch of the sentence and insert it into the predicate branch. If there are logic AND or OR nodes having the same parent node, next optimization joins them into only one logic node. Final optimization is joining sentence node where second sentence node is in object branch of first sentence node and both sentence nodes have same predicate node.

Abstract sentence tree is a result of document planning. Following NLG task is to identify lexical attributes of the phrases and put them in mutual correspondence, which is a task of micro-planner.

Figure 7. Abstract sentence tree

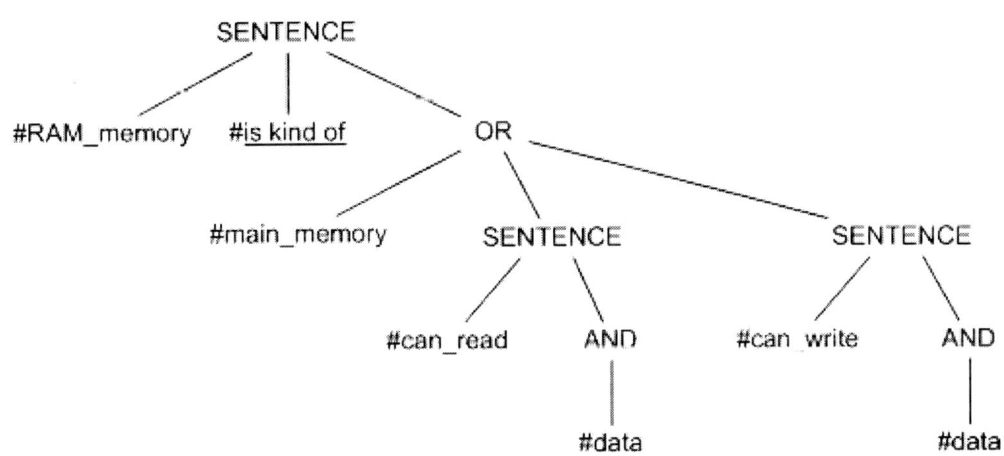

Figure 8. Optimized abstract sentence tree

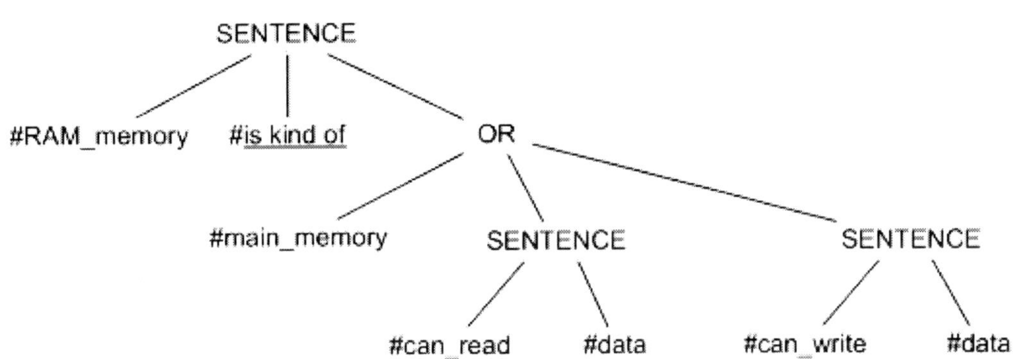

Figure 9. Optimization of abstract sentence tree

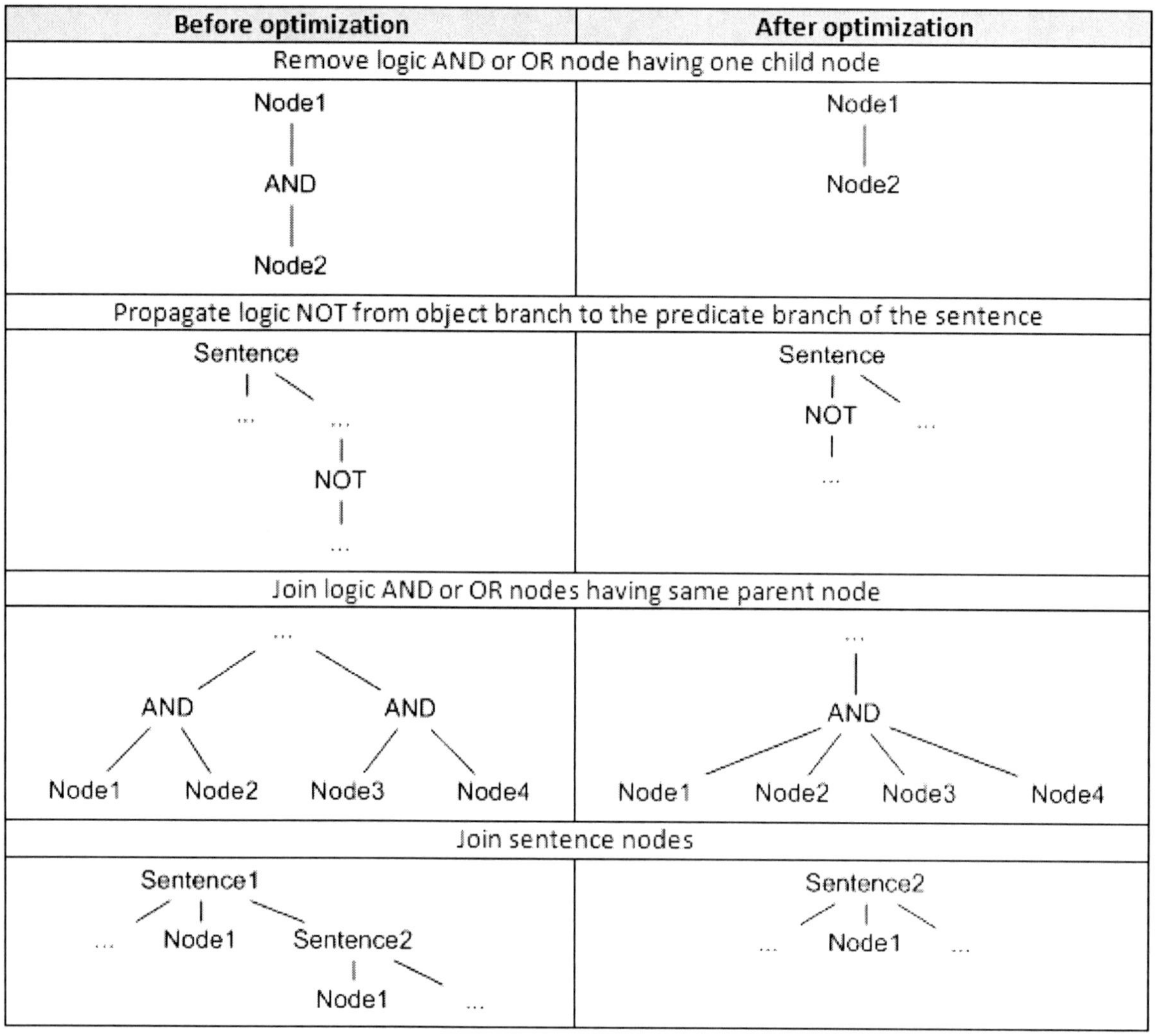

Phrase Specification

Leafs of abstract sentence tree are phrases. Some of them are selected from ontology, while others (underlined) are constant predicate phrases. From sentence viewpoint phrases can be categorized as subject, predicate and object phrases. Phrase is a sequence of words and if phrase identifies ontology element, that sequence of words is ontology element identifier. Subject and object phrase identifiers originate from class and individual identifiers of ontology. Their sequence of words is built-up around nouns, while predicate phrase identifier word sequence is built-up around verb. In Croatian language, morphological form of noun mainly depends on number and case attributes, so subject and object phrase is specified by the same morphological attributes. Another unchangeable attribute of noun is gender and has influence on micro-planning of the sentence. After all, subject and object phrase specification is specified using gender (G), number (N) and case (C). Specification of the predicate phrase as connector of the subject and object phrases has two set of attributes. First set of attributes depends on subject, while second set of attributes depends on object phrase(s) of sentence. Each set has gender and number attribute but, for some predicate phrases, they are not all required. Finally predicate phrase has case attribute which is used to mark case of the object phrase, as well as negative attribute which tells if the verb in predicate phrase is in negative form.

On Figure 10 #hard_disk is subject phrase having neutrino as gender (G=n), singular as number (N=s) and nominative as case (C=n). Because there is one subject phrase in the sentence, so number of the constant predicate phrase #is_kind_of is not going to be changed, but case of predicate phrase is going to change case of the object phrase. In general, all subject phrases have nominative case and singular number, gender does not have influence on predicate phrase. First number N1 of predicate phrase is going to be plural only if sentence has more than one subject phrases which are logically connected using AND or OR operator as showed on Figure 11.

After applying appropriate attribute values to the phrases, leafs of abstract sentence tree contains only phrase identifiers. Other words and characters needed to be put in sentence in-between phrases are correlative conjunctions. Those conjunctions are built-up around logical operators that have more than one parameter. In example from Figure 11 phrases #CD_ROM and #hard_disk are connected using AND operator, therefore micro-planner will insert word #and between those phrases. Resulting sequence of phrases is input to surface realization, as a final step in natural language generation. Surface realization takes care on finding proper morphological form of word using lexicon. There are two basic lexicon procedures; first is to find lemma for proper word form and another is to give all word forms for a given lemma.

Before abstract sentence tree is generated from ontology expressions, all phrases are recognized by finding all lemmas for all words in phrases used for identify concepts or relations. Morphological lexicon utilized for this function is able

Figure 10. Phrase specification and their interdependence

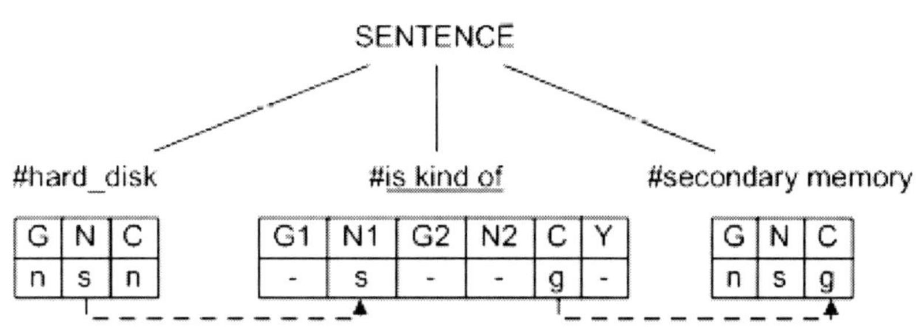

Figure 11. Phrase specification of sentence having more than one subject phrase

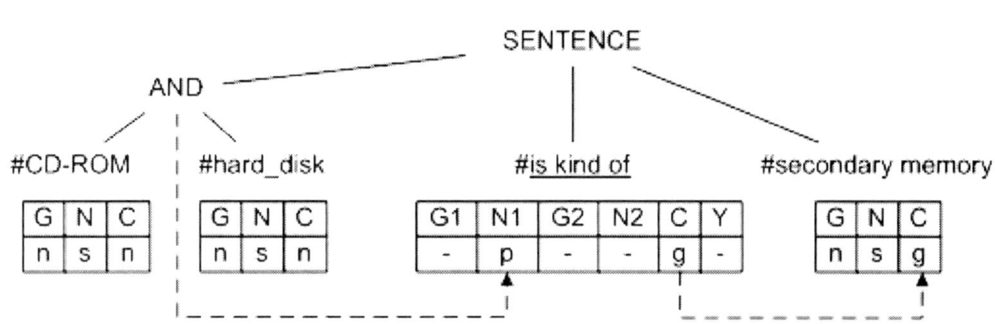

to classify and specify words. After generation of the abstract sentence tree, production of natural language sentence will also utilize lexicon for finding proper word form on a basis of a given lemma and word specification.

Word Specification

If sentence generated from ontology expression is going to be grammatically correct, prerequisite is set on adequate naming of a concepts and relations. Phrase is a name of a concept or a relation and is constrained by production rules. Linguistically speaking, phrase is a sequence of words where those words can depend on each other. Words dependence relay on attribute of a word. We use Multext-East morphosyntactic specification (Erjavec, Krstev, Petkevič, Simov, & Tadić, 2003) where each word has a part of speach attribute and an array of other attributes. For example, Croatian word "memorija" which is "memory" on English has "Ncfsn" as a morphosyntatic description (MSD) where:

- "N" is a noun as a part of speech,
- "c" stands for common noun as an type of word,
- "f" is feminine as gender,
- "s" is single as number and
- "n" is nominative as an case.

Croatian language is morphologically rich, having seven cases, two numbers and three genders. Mostly words in a phrase depend on case, number and/or gender. Nouns, verbs and adjectives are kind of words included in phrases in major. All of those words have gender, number and case attributes. Definition of phrase rules depends on sequence of words, as well as mutual dependence on attributes of the word. There are several rules for different phrase kind's definition.

Class in ontology is abstract concept where it can stand as a subject set or object set in a sentence. Main word in a class phrase is a common noun which usually can be preceded by adjectives and succeeded with adjectives of a personal noun. Full class phrase specification is

$$C\mathbf{g}_1\mathbf{n}_1\mathbf{c}_1{:}{==}\ \{As\text{--}\mathbf{n}_1 n\}\ \{Af\text{-}\mathbf{g}_1\mathbf{n}_1 n\}\ \{Rgp\}\ \underline{Nc\text{-}\mathbf{g}1\mathbf{n}1\mathbf{c}1}\ \{\{As\text{--}\mathbf{n}_2 g\}\ \{Af\text{-}\mathbf{g}_2\mathbf{n}_2 g\}\ \{Rgp\}\ \{Nc\text{-}\mathbf{g}_2\mathbf{n}_2 g\}\}\ \{Np\}$$

where g_1 is a variable attribute for a gender, n_1 is for number and c_1 stands for case of a common noun. If adjectives are present and are preceding the main word, then they need to have some corresponding attributes. Other words following the main word are not depending on a main word, but they have some other common attributes.

For example, "radna memorija" (engl. "main memory") is a class phrase containing adjective "radna" specified by Afpfsn and noun "memorija" specified by Ncfsn.

Phrase for individual specification includes class phrase specification and following rule

$$C\mathbf{g}_1\mathbf{n}_1\mathbf{c}_1{:}{==}\ \{As\text{--}\mathbf{n}_1 n\}\ \{Af\text{-}\mathbf{g}_1\mathbf{n}_1 n\}\ \{Rgp\}\ \underline{Np\text{-}\mathbf{g}1\mathbf{n}1\mathbf{c}1}\ \{\{As\text{--}\mathbf{n}_2 g\}\ \{Af\text{-}\mathbf{g}_2\mathbf{n}_2 g\}\ \{Rgp\}\ \{Nc\text{-}\mathbf{g}_2\mathbf{n}_2 g\}\}\ \{Np\}$$

where underlined main word is a personal noun.

Property phrase have several rules mainly depending on cases in Croatian language. Object property, which relates some class to another class, has role of a predicate in a sentence where subject class is relating to object class. For example, in a sentence "Računalo ima radnu memoriju" (engl. "Computer has main memory.") "ima" (engl. "has") is a object property phrase and is specified as accusative object property, meaning that object phrases is going to have same accusative case. Generally, object property phrase specification attributes includes gender and number of subject, gender, number and case of object and negation of predicate. Specification of object property phrase "ima" (engl. "has") is (-s--a-). Some of attributes are not required and are marked as dash.

When micro-planner sets attributes of the phrases, changed attributes affect attributes of containing word. For example, class phrase "radna memorija" is specified as

Cfsn:== Afpfsn Ncfsn

and changing attributes of the phrase will result in changing attributes of belonging words as follows:

Cfpa:== Afpfpa Ncpfa

After having lexical attributes of all words in each phrase properly changed, next step is sending list of pairs containing word lemmas and required MSD to the morphological lexicon. As a result, lexicon will return proper word form. In this example input would be ("radan", Afpfpa), ("memorija", Ncpfa) and lexicon output will be list of words "radnu", "memoriju".

In this final step, surface realization has a sequence of morphed words and joining them using whitespace as a separator will produce natural language sentence. Surface realization traverse abstract sentence tree and puts in a list all the phrases. Next step is creation of list of word forms in all phrases and concatenating them for producing natural language sentence.

NLG process is basic natural language technique used for presenting knowledge to the student. This same process is extensively used in creating test for the student. Test realization realized by natural language dialogue accompanies several phases, starting by problem generation and ending by knowledge evaluation.

TUTOR DIALOGUE

Natural language generation is one of NLP techniques used for presenting domain knowledge to the student. For testing knowledge, computer tutor leads the natural language dialogue with student. In tutor dialogue realization, computer generates problem knowledge by taking original domain knowledge and randomly taking out some concepts and relations. Dialogue is started by computer asking a question. Response to the student answer on that question could be to continue asking new question or to assist student by asking sub question or repeating the question. If student wrongly answer on particular question, as well as wrongly answers on all assisting question, computer skips that question and ask another.

This tutor centered dialogue can be generally described by tutoring frame showed on Figure 12. (Graesser, Person, & Magliano, 1995)

Example of generated sentences also with student answers is given in Figure 13.

Figure 12. Tutoring frame state diagram

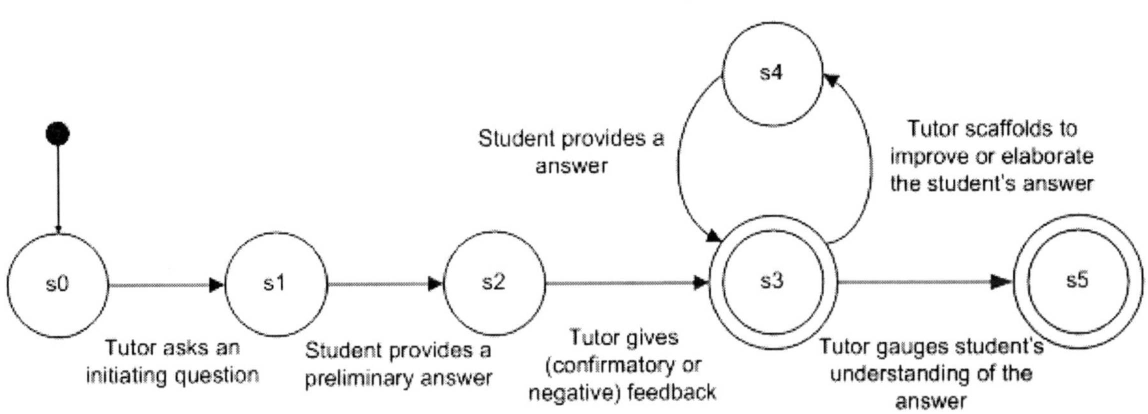

Figure 13. Example of tutoring frame

1	Tutor	RAM is kind of what?
2	Student	Memory
3	Tutor	Correct; RAM is kind of memory.
4	Tutor	Is RAM kind of main memory?
5	Student	Yes
6	Tutor	Correct.
7	Tutor	RAM is kind of main memory. Main memory is kind of memory

Question 1 is generated when tutoring frame is in state s1. After student's answer, tutoring frame makes transition from state s2 to s3 in which tutor generates feedback for this answer. In this example, student has provided particular answer to the main question, so tutor scaffolds with additional question 4 and switch to state s4. Student's answer to this question is correct and transition to the state s5 is made. In this state tutor gives explanation which includes correct answers of question 1 and question 4.

Providing mark to the student begins when dialogue is finished. Overlay student model is used to distinguish what student knows and what is not known. Balance between students' knowing and not knowing is going to be used for calculating final mark.

In following is described process of generating problem knowledge as well as NLP techniques used in asking and answering and finally, calculating mark of the knowledge.

Generating Problem Knowledge

Input to problem generator is OWL ontology. After each OWL directive is converted to abstract sentence tree, problem generator randomly chooses phrases for removing. For example, generator makes problem by removing phrases #main_memory and #can_write in abstract sentence tree from Figure 14.

Algorithm for choosing phrases for removing from abstract sentence tree analyses sentence nodes by discovering how many phrase identifiers are in subtree of sentence subject and sentence predicate, as well as how much subsentences are in subject or object branch of the sentence. Moreover discovered phrase identifiers are quali-

Figure 14. Generating problem over abstract sentence tree

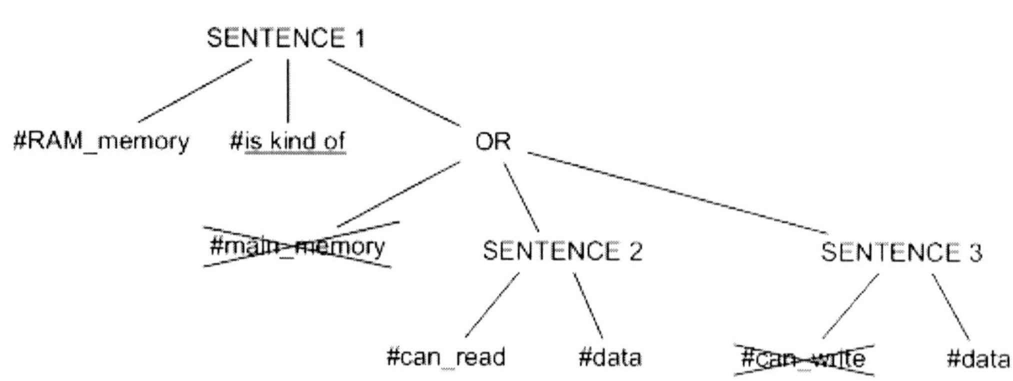

fied as simple if path from starting sentence node to discovered phrase node does not contain any sentence node, otherwise they are complex phrases (Figure 15).

In example from Figure 14 root sentence node contains 1 simple phrase for subject and 1 simple and 2 complex phrases in sentence object. Another qualifier is depth of the sentence, which is a count of sentence nodes contained in a path from starting sentence node to the root. Importance of the question is measured by its depth. Sentence is more important if it has less depth. Proposed algorithm for removing phrases is showed below (Figure 16).

After marking phrase nodes of abstract sentence tree as removed, following step is generation of a question. These questions are direct questions because they are generated from marked abstract sentence tree which is directly generated from domain knowledge. This type of questions are not answer dependent, unlike assisting questions which are used for helping student in case of incorrect answering on a direct question.

Asking and Answering Questions

Sentence is made of subject, predicate and object. Asking a question over some sentence firstly depends in which branch phrase node is removed from sentence node. If subject phrase node is removed than question will start with "Who" or "What". Form of asked question over

Figure 15. Qualifying abstract sentence tree

Qualifier	SENTENCE 1	SENTENCE 2	SENTENCE 3
Depth	0	1	1
Transitive predicate phrase identifier	Yes	No	No
Simple phrase count in subject branch	1	0	0
Simple phrase count in object branch	1	1	1
Complex phrase count in subject branch	0	0	0
Complex phrase count in object branch	2	0	0

Figure 16. Selecting and removing phrases during problem generation

```
Select sentence
if simple phrase count in subject branch > simple phrase count in object branch then
        remove random simple phrase in subject branch
else
        remove random simple phrase in object branch
if abstract sentence tree has only 1 sentence then
        if complex phrases count in subject branch > complex phrases count in object branch then
                remove random complex phrase in subject branch
        else
                remove random complex phrase in object branch
else
        choose random sentence with less importance than main sentence node
        if simple phrases count in subject branch > simple phrases count in object branch then
                remove random simple phrase in subject branch
        else
                remove random simple phrase in object branch
```

abstract sentence tree with removed object phrase depends on case attribute of the predicate phrase (see Figure 17).

For example, asking a question for a SENTENCE 1 in Figure 14 having removed common object phrase and having predicate phrase with genitive case will produce question "RAM memory is kind of what?".

If sentence has removed predicate phrase, generating question is going to be of type "yes or no". Generated question over SENTENCE 3 from Figure 14 will be "Is it true that RAM memory can write data?". Obviously "true" is correct answer for this question, so generator will occasionally select incorrect object phrase or negate predicate phrase to make "false" a correct answer. Algorithm for selecting incorrect object phrase depends on ontological type of phrase. If object' phrase identifies class in ontology, than it is possible that answer is correct for some other phrase. For example RAM memory is a kind of hardware, because RAM memory is a kind of main memory, which is a kind of memory, which is a kind of hardware. This is a case when predicate phrase is transitive and object phrase identifies class which is a superclass of selected class. Same case could happen if object phrase identifies ontology's' individual while predicate phrase identifies transitive object property. Reasoning over description logic will make a list of concepts in transitive relations in order to conclude correctness of the answer. Such process is used in tutor scaffolding in order to find all possible correct answers to the asked question.

Answer form on the generated question will depend on kind of location of removed phrase in the sentence node. If problem generator has removed subject or object phrase, expected answer will be that removed phrase. In a case of removing predicate phrase, generated question will be of yes/no type. Simple natural language understanding is used in the first case to recognize grammatical correctness of typed phrase. If recognition was successful, next step is decision if question was correctly answered, and if it is not than tutor assistance is needed.

Evaluating Answer and Simple Scaffolding

Every asked question is asked for each described concept in ontology. For some concepts computer tutor will ask at least one direct question. Direct question is question which is generated directly from abstract sentence tree made by problem generator. Correctness of answer on a tutor' question is graduated in scale from 0% to 100%. Yes and No answers are always graduated by 0% or 100%, while "phrase" answers can be in-between. Obviously, there is no assistance from the tutor side if the question type is yes/no. Otherwise assistance depends on transitivity of the predicate phrase's identifier and on possible other subsentence nodes in an abstract sentence tree which could generate full sentence.

One of most used built-in transitive property is "#is_kind_of". If ontology has several class phrase identifiers related by transitive property

Figure 17. Croatian words for questions in case of removed object phrase

	Croatian		English	
Case	**Object is personal**	**Object is common**	**Object is personal**	**Object is common**
genitive	koga	čega	of whom	of what
dative	komu	čemu	to who	to what
accusative	Koga	što	whom	what
locative	komu	čemu	to who	to what
instrumental	Kim	čim	with who	with what

phrase identifier "#is_kind_of" then all class phrase identifiers could represent correct answer, but only one is 100% correct. For example, RAM memory is a kind of memory, which is a kind of hardware. Asking question "RAM memory is a kind of what" computer tutor predicts and graduates all possible correct answers (see Figure 14). If student answer is "memory" than tutor evaluates it as 66% correct answer and helps student by directing her or him to the "main memory". Computer tutor tells that "RAM memory is a kind of memory. That is correct, but could you be more precise, it is a kind of?". If students' next answer is "main memory" than it is a 100% correct answer, and total correctness of asked question is (66% + 100%) / 2 or amount of graduated answers divided by number of tries.

Other types of questions are asked over sentences which are not having transitive predicate phrase identifier and have removed phrase node in subject or in object branch. In this case computer tutor tries to find all the sentence nodes in the abstract sentence tree which can be used for generating assistance question. Those sentence nodes must have at least one phrase in subject, object and in predicate branch, so simple sentence can be generated. Simple sentence nodes does not have subject branch, but they can be also used for generating assistance question if they have parent sentence node with at least one phrase node in a subject branch.

In abstract sentence tree from Figure 18 direct question generated for node SENTENCE3 would be "What CD-ROM cannot write?". If student answer to this question is incorrect, assisting question will be generated using sentence built-up from node SENTENCE2 because it is only sentence node having predicate and object phrase node. Computer assisting question will include SENTENCE2 and will repeat question for SENTENCE3 as follows: "CD-ROM can read data. What CD-ROM cannot write?". If the student still answers incorrectly, then answer correctness to this question is going to be 0%. In other case, when student answers correctly, answer correctness would be 100% divided by number of tries.

All of these correctness's of the answers would be involved in final determination of student's knowledge. Since direct questions are generated from domain knowledge elements, great deal in calculating overall mark will have importance in overlaying knowledge's included in dialogue instance.

Marking and Evaluating Knowledge

Final mark of student's knowledge is made by comparing knowledge layers. Generated problem is represented by test knowledge made from original expert's knowledge. By finishing the dialogue between computer tutor and student, test knowledge is expanded to solution knowl-

Figure 18. Abstract sentence tree with removed phrases

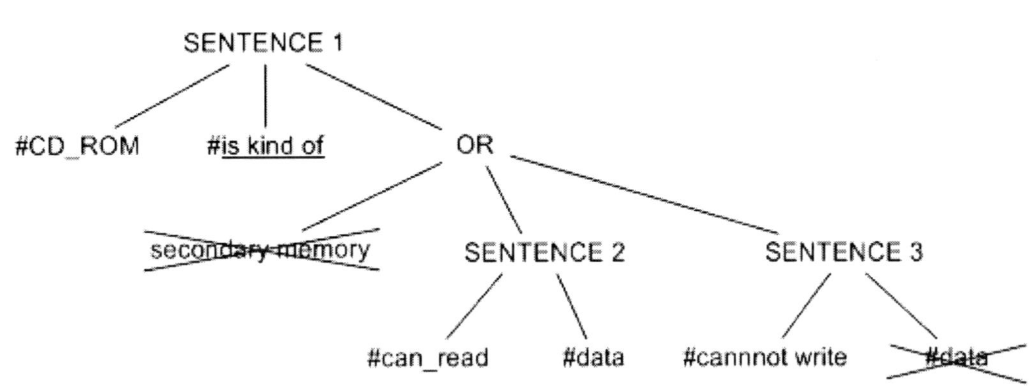

Figure 19. Depth and weight of concepts in knowledge taxonomy

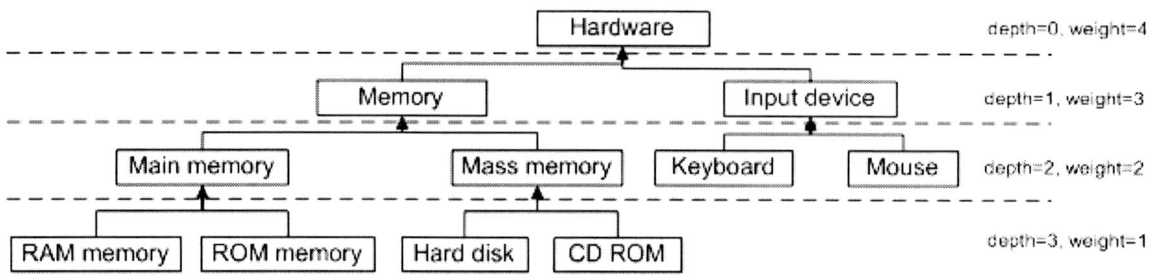

edge. Final mark is ratio of score of generated problem knowledge, gained score from solution knowledge, and score and maximum score from expert's knowledge. Knowledge score is sum of all weights for each concept and relation in knowledge, while weight of concept or relation is inverse proportional with depth of the concept or relation. In order to calculate weight, it is necessary to find deepest concept or relation in ontology taxonomy, so root concept will have weight equal to incremented depth of the deepest concept or relation. In taxonomy from Figure 19 "RAM" is one of the deepest concept having depth equal to 3, so weight of the "Memory" is 3 + 1, while depth of "RAM" is 1.

Calculating expert's knowledge and problem's score is simple process of summing weights of each concept and relation in it. Score of solution knowledge is influenced by correctness of answered questions. Since each concept in problem knowledge has one or more generated direct questions, average of correctness for each concept's question makes quantifier of weight of that concept. For example, there are 2 generated

Figure 20. Final Mark

$$FinalMark = \frac{Score(Student\ knowledge) - Score(Problem\ knowledge)}{Score(Expert\ knowledge) - Score(Problem\ knowledge)} \times 100$$

Figure 21. Overlay model

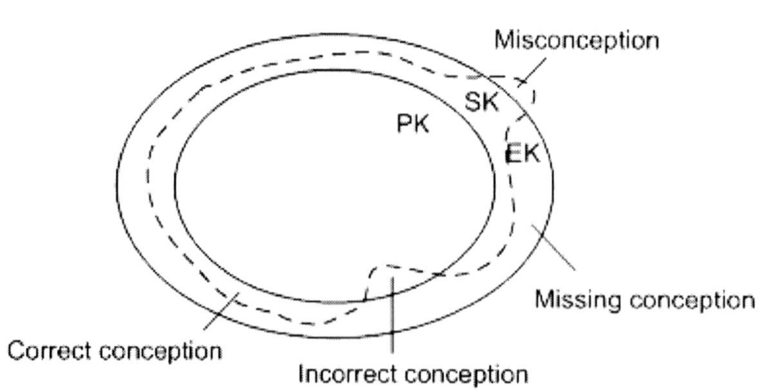

questions for concept #RAM memory represented by problem sentence in Figure 14. Weight of the sentence is equal to weight of concept for which is generated abstract sentence. If correctness of generated questions is 83% and 100% then overall correctness of the concept is their average, 91.5% respectively. Furthermore, determination of concept score in solution's knowledge is made by multiplying weight of the concept with the average of question's correctness. In this example, weight of #RAM memory is 1 so score will be 0.915.

Giving weight to each concept simulates importance of that concept. If student is not familiar with general concepts, final mark is going to be far more less than if student knows details represented by deepest concepts. Final mark represented to student is ratio of expert knowledge and solution knowledge.

Therefore for getting a passing grade student has to know almost all general concepts, and almost none of detailed concept.

Standard overlay model (Figure 21) is augmented by correctness of the answer for a specific concept. It also includes misconceptions which are made by answering on a question by concept which is not originally in expert's knowledge. However, misconception is in tutor dialogue evaluated as missing conception where answer correctness is 0%.

Incorrect conceptions are so far also evaluated as missing conceptions, but ongoing research will provide solution for giving sign to the correctness of the answers. Such research result will consider distance and position between asked and answered concept.

CONCLUSION

Building model of intelligent tutoring system based on natural language or upgrading existing ITS with some natural language components is expected task if ITS is going to improve learning and teaching process. Our approach does not upgrade existing TEx-Sys model because of the new approach to the domain knowledge representation which greatly infects natural language. Semantic network from TEx-Sys model is replaced with description logic realized through OWL ontology. Description logic can use full set of logic operators, as well as restriction over relations to specify concepts.

This ability of description logic has consequence in natural language representation; sentences and their parts can be conjugated, negated and quantified. Natural language generator is for each expression in ontology producing abstract sentence tree which contains phrases as a leaf nodes. Phrase's classification has influence on a containing words, so changing some word specification will have impact on a phrase's class, and vice versa.

Built abstract sentence trees are also used in execution of tutor dialogue. Marking phrase nodes of abstract sentence tree is first step before generation of the questions. Answering on a question is assisted by computer tutor, and can help student to be recalled on a correct answering. Importance of the concept or relation for asked question as well as correctness of the answer characterizes concept or relation in overlay model.

REFERENCES

Carr, B., & Goldstein, I. P. (1977). *Overlays: A Theory of Modelling for Computer Aided Instruction, AI Memo*. Cambridge, MA: Massachisetts Institute of Technology, Artificial Intelligence Lab.

Di Eugenio, B., Fossati, D., Yu, D., Haller, S., & Glass, M. (2005). Natural Language Generation for Intelligent Tutoring Systems: a case study. In Proceedings of *AIED 2005, the 12th International Conference on Artificial Intelligence in Education*. Amsterdam.

Di Eugenio, B., & Trolio, M. J. (2000). Can simple Natural Language Generation improve Intelligent Tutoring Systems. In *Proceedings of the AAAI 2000 Fall Symposium on Building Dialogue Systems for Tutorial Applications.* North Falmouth, MA.

Erjavec, T., Krstev, C., Petkevič, V., Simov, K., & Tadić, M. V. (2003). The MULTEXT-east morphosyntactic specifications for Slavic languages. In *Proceedings of the 2003 EACL Workshop on Morphological Processing of Slavic Languages*, (pp. 25-32). Budapest, Hungary.

Glass, M. (2000). Processing Language Input in the CIRCSIM-Tutor Intelligent Tutoring System. In *Proceedings of AAAI 2000 Fall Symposium on Building Dialogue Systems for Tutorial Applications* (pp. 74-80). San Antonio, TX: AAAI Press.

Graesser, A. C., Person, N. K., & Magliano, J. P. (1995). Collaborative dialog patterns in naturalistic one-on-one tutoring. *Applied Cognitive Psychology*, *9*, 495–552. doi:10.1002/acp.2350090604

Patel-Schneider, P. F., Hayes, P., & Horrocks, I. (2004). *Web Ontology Language (OWL) Abstract Syntax and Semantics.* Retrieved June 2, 2009, from W3C Recommendation: http://www.w3.org/TR/2004/REC-owl-semantics-20040210/

Reiter, E., & Dale, R. (2000). *Building Natural Language Generation Systems*. Cambridge, UK: Cambridge University. Press.

Rosé, C. P. (2000). Syntactic Framework for Semantic Interpretation. In *Proceedings of the Workshop on Linguistic Theory and Grammar Implementation 2000.* Birmingham, UK.

Stankov, S. (1997). *Isomorphic Model of the System as the Basis of Teaching Control Principles in an Intelligent Tutoring System.* (PhD Thesis (in Croatian)), Faculty of Electrical Engineering, Mechanical Engineering and Naval Architecture. Split, Croatia: University of Split.

Stankov, S., Rosić, M., & Glavinić, V. (2001). Using Quizzes in an Intelligent Tutoring System. In [Maribor, Slovenia.]. *Proceedings of International Summer School of Automation, CEEPUS CZ, 103*, 87–91.

Stankov, S., Rosić, M., Žitko, B., & Grubišić, A. (2008). TEx-Sys model for building intelligent tutoring systems. *Computers & Education, 51*, 1017–1036. doi:10.1016/j.compedu.2007.10.002

Tadić, M., & Fulgosi, S. (2003). Building the Croatian Morphological Lexicon. In *Proceedings of the EACL2003 Workshop on Morphological Processing of Slavic Languages*, (pp. 41-46). Budapest, Hungary.

Wiemer-Hastings, P., Wiemer-Hastings, K., & Graesser, A. C. (1999). *Improving an intelligent tutor's comprehension of students with Latent Semantic Analysis. Artificial Intelligence in Education* (pp. 535–542). Amsterdam: IOS Press.

Section 4
Personalized Advanced E-Learning Environments

Chapter 11
Student Modeling in an Intelligent Tutoring System

Mingyu Feng
SRI International, USA

Neil Heffernan
Worcester Polytechnic Institute, USA

Kenneth Koedinger
Carnegie Mellon University, USA

ABSTRACT

Student modeling and cognitively diagnostic assessment are important issues that need to be addressed for the development and successful application of intelligent tutoring systems (its). Its needs the construction of complex models to represent the skills that students are using and their knowledge states, and practitioners want cognitively diagnostic information at a finer grained level. This chapter reviews our effort on modeling student's knowledge in the ASSISTment project. Intelligent tutors have been mainly used to teach students. In the ASSISTment project, we have emphasized using the intelligent tutoring system as an assessment system that provides instructional assistance during the test. Usually it is believed that assessment get harder if students are allowed to learn during the test, as its then like try to hit a moving target. So our results are surprising that by providing tutoring to students while they are assessed we actually prove the assessment of students' knowledge. Additionally, in this article, we present encouraging results about a fine-grained skill model with that system that is able to predict state test scores. We conclude that using intelligent tutoring systems to do assessment seems like a reasonable way of dealing with the dilemma that every minute spent testing students takes time away from instruction.

INTRODUCTION

In the United States there are concerns about poor student performance on new high-stakes standards based tests required by the No Child Left Behind Act (NCLB, 2002) legislation. To address this issue, educational technologies, like intelligent tutoring systems (ITS) have been developed and proven to be useful helping students learn. For instance, the Cognitive Tutors leads to large learning gains (Koedinger et al, 1997). Recently, President Obama made a commitment

DOI: 10.4018/978-1-61692-008-1.ch011

to increase investment on educational software, saying that, "[W]e will devote more than 3 percent of our GDP to research and development. ... Just think what this will allow us to accomplish: solar cells as cheap as paint, ..., *learning software as effective as a personal tutor*...." [1] So, how do we build ITS that are as effective as a personal tutor? To create an effective piece of learning software, we need a good model of student learning. Assessment of an examinee's ability is the first step of student modeling in an ITS because student state is a prerequisite for creating a pedagogical strategy. The student model provides valuable information for the tutor to help build tutoring strategy (e.g., when to interrupt and what to say when interrupt), problem sequencing (e.g., what's the next appropriate task to give to a student so his learning gain is maximized), performance prediction (how a student will respond to a step associated with certain rules), etc.

Recently, in an interview with U.S. News & World Report (Ramírez & Clark, 2009), U.S. Secretary of Education Arne Duncan weighed in on the NCLB Act and called for continuous assessment. He said that he is concerned about over-testing, and feels that fewer, better tests would be more effective. He wants to develop better data management systems that will help teachers track individual student's progress in real-time, so teachers and parents can assess and monitor student strengths and weaknesses. To reflect on the "continuous assessment" idea, we think, one way that ITS research distinguishes itself from other educational software development is that it is concerned with modeling the knowledge of the learner in some computationally useful and inspectable way (McCalla & Greer, 1994). The modeling phase should involve understanding learner behavior in the rich context of the environment in which learning occurs, thus, obtaining a better understanding of each student's pre-existing, or current knowledge status and how that knowledge is changing over time.

Student models in ITS are constructive, especially cognitive models. Cognitive modeling involves a great deal of detailed protocol collection and task analysis. The models are not easy to construct and are difficult to verify. Yet, cognitive modeling is very important in an ITS as it is the basis of cognitively diagnostic assessment and teacher reporting. Wiliam (2006) describes an assessment as formative only if information about what is being assessed results in change that would otherwise not occur. Here the definition of formative assessment becomes more detailed to the utility for teachers to understand if and how students are learning. By giving teachers cognitively diagnostic data in a timely fashion, teachers can change their teaching in response to the data they collect about student understanding. The US Department of Education (2003) stated, "Research shows that teachers who use student test performance to guide and improve teaching are more effective than teachers who do not use such information" (p. 2). Therefore, if assessments are to move from assessments *of* learning to assessments *for* learning (c.f., Stiggins 2005) then we must continue to focus on the box that encompasses diagnostic modeling data and teachers as the end-users.

In this chapter, we will describe how various student modeling approaches have been applied in an online cognitively diagnostic assessment system, called the ASSISTment System that provides both assistance and assessment in an integrated fashion. In the second section, we focus on giving an overview of the ASSISTment System, including the structure of an ASSISTment, the problem sequencing, the teacher reports, the authoring tools, content development and usage and also the evidence showing the effectiveness of tutoring in ASSISTments. The third section of this chapter is devoted to student modeling in ITS. We first conduct a literature review of student modeling approaches, and then report our work in the ASSISTment System. We will describe how we improve the accuracy of assessment by measuring how much assistance students need and by tracking the change of student knowledge longitudinally. Furthermore, our fine-grained cognitive models that map each question to a few knowledge components allow us to more accurately predict these scores. We conclude the chapter with some general implications in the forth section.

BACKGROUND ON THE ASSISTMENT SYSTEM

There has been intense interest in using periodic benchmark tests to predict student performance on end-of-year accountability assessments (Olson, 2005). Some teachers make extensive use data from practice tests and released items from statewide assessments to target specific student knowledge needs and identify learning opportunities for individual students as well as the class as a whole so that their instruction could be data-driven. However, such formative assessments not only require great effort and dedication, but also take valuable time away from instruction. Limited classroom time in middle school classes compels teachers to choose between time spent assisting students' learning and time spent assessing students' abilities. Critics of NCLB are calling the bill "No Child Left Untested" emphasizing the negative side of assessment, in that every hour spent assessing students is an hour lost from instruction. But does it have to be? What if we better integrated assessment into the classroom and we allowed students to learn during the test? Noticing the situation, Dr. Heffernan at Worcester Polytechnic Institute and his colleagues at Carnegie Mellon University started to build a system ("ASSISTments"[2], http://www.assistment.org) to help resolve this dilemma.

Traditionally the two areas of testing (i.e., Psychometrics) and instruction (i.e., math educational research and instructional technology research) have been separate fields of research with their own goals. Therefore, in order to put them together the solution here must involve a way whereby students can take an assessment, but at the same time, make sure that students' time is spent primarily on learning. It should be able to provide an accurate prediction of student performance on the standardized tests so that teachers have an idea of how their students will perform on end-of-year assessment. Meanwhile, it will present a more fine-grained evaluation of student abilities so the teachers will be able to use this detailed feedback to tailor their instruction to focus on the particular difficulties identified by the system. The ASSISTment project's[3] goal is to provide cognitive-based assessment of students while providing tutoring content to students. The system aims to assist students in learning the different skills needed for the Massachusetts Comprehensive Assessment System (MCAS[4]) test or (other state tests) while at the same time assessing student knowledge to provide teachers with fine-grained assessment of their students' knowledge. The system tutors students in learning different skills using scaffolding questions, hints, and incorrect messages (or buggy messages) (Razzaq et al., 2005). Assessment of student performance is provided to teachers through real-time reports based on statistical analysis.

The system is primarily used by middle and high school[5] teachers and students throughout Massachusetts who are preparing for the MCAS test. Using the web-based ASSISTment System is free and only requires registration on the website; no software need be installed. The system started in the year 2004 by interviewing a few middle school math teachers about how they would tutor a problem. Then when the system was built and ready to be used, these teachers were willing to bring in their students to try it before the MCAS. Those were the first 60 students who worked in ASSISTments. Because the ASSISTment System was practical, easily-accessible, informative, and more importantly free, it was gradually accepted by more and more teachers and schools.

Things changed from Heffernan and colleagues running around schools to introduce the system to school administrators and teachers contact us to "join" the ASSISTment team. Currently, there are over 3000 students and 50 teachers using our system as part of their regular math classes. The ASSISTments is a collaborating project between researchers and teachers: now over 30 teachers have used the system to create contents and 17 teachers are participating in a workshop at WPI to learn how to make more effective use of diagnostic assessment data from ASSISTments. Heffernan and his colleagues including WPI graduate students still visit schools regularly to help with technical issues and on how to use ASSISTment data to drive classroom instructions. It is worth pointing out that both the ASSISTment System and its authoring tools are open, generic and not limited to any specific domain. The system was initially built to help 8th grade (13 to 14 year olds) students be better prepared for the MCAS. The subject content was mainly mathematics, as this was the subject on which students from Worcester, Massachusetts showed worst performance[6]. Later on, more content such as 6th grade and 10 grade mathematics materials were introduced into the system. More recently, a new program was launched in the ASSISTment project to tutor science inquiry skills (Sao Pedro, Gobert, Heffernan & Beck, 2009).

Though the ASSISTment System is a derivative of the Cognitive Tutor (Anderson et al., 1995), it is built for different classroom use than the Cognitive Tutor. Cognitive Tutor students are intended to use the tutor for two class periods a week. Students are expected to proceed at their own rate letting the mastery learning algorithm advance them through the curriculum. Some students will make steady progress while others will be stuck on early units. There is value in this in that it allows students to proceed at their own paces. One downside from the teachers' perspective could be that they might want to have their class all do the same material on the same day so they can assess their students simultaneously. The ASSISTment System was created with this classroom use in mind. The ASSISTment System was created with the idea that teachers would use it once every two weeks as part of their normal classroom instruction, meant more as a formative assessment system and less as the primary means of assessing students. Cognitive Tutor advances students only after they have mastered all of the skills in a unit. We know that some teachers use some features to automatically advance students to later lessons because they might want to make sure all the students get some practice on quadratics, for instance.

We think that no one system is "the answer" but that they have different strengths and weaknesses. If the student uses the computer less often there comes a point where mastery learning based program (i.e., the Cognitive Tutor) may be behind on what a student knows, and seem to move along too slowly to teachers and students. On the other hand, a weakness of ASSISTments is that does not offer mastery learning and adaptive activity selection, so if students struggle, it does not automatically adjust. It is assumed that the teacher (and not the computer system) will decide if a student needs to go back and look at a topic again.

The Structure of an ASSISTment

Koedinger et al. (2004) introduced pseudo-tutors which mimic cognitive tutors. The ASSISTment system uses a further simplified pseudo-tutor, called an ASSISTment, where only a linear progression through a problem is supported which makes content creation easier and more accessible to a general audience.

An ASSISTment consists of a single main question (a.k.a. original question) and a tutoring session for assistance. As students work in the system, the main question will be presented first and can be treated as an assessment task for which students need to submit an answer. In contrast to a traditional testing environment, students can request assistance if they don't know how to answer the question, though it is generally thought to be pedagogically more desirable that a student submits a thoughtful answer before accessing the tutoring. For any given problem, assistance to students is available either in the form of a hint sequence or a set of scaffolding questions. Hints are messages that provide insights and suggestions for solving a specific problem, and each hint sequence ends with a *bottom-out* hint that gives the student the answer. Scaffolding questions are designed to lead the student one-step-at-a-time to the solution and each step addresses specific skills needed to answer the original question. Students must answer each scaffolding question in order to proceed to the next scaffolding question. When students finish all of the scaffolding questions, they may be presented with the original question again to finish the problem. Each scaffolding question also has a hint sequence to help the students answer the question if they need extra help. Additionally, constructive feedback called *buggy* messages are provided to students if certain anticipated incorrect answers are selected or entered, otherwise a generic feedback message will be shown. For problems without scaffolding, a student will remain in a problem until the problem is answered correctly and can ask for hints that are presented one at a time. If scaffolding is available, the student will be programmatically advanced to the scaffolding questions in the event of an incorrect answer. The ASSISTments assume that students may know certain skills and rather than slowing them down by going through all of the scaffolding questions first, ASSISTment allowS students to try to answer questions without showing every step. This differs from Cognitive Tutors (Anderson et al., 1995) and Andes (VanLehn et al., 2005) which both ask the students to fill in many different steps in a typical problem.

Underlying Architecture

The system was built on the eXtensible Tutor Architecture (XTA) (Nuzzo-Jones et al., 2005), a framework that controls the interface and behaviors of our intelligent tutoring system via a collection of modular units. Each conceptual unit has an abstract and extensible implementation allowing for evolving tutor types and content delivery methods. Different from many other ITSs that are client-based such as the Cognitive Tutors and Andes, the ASSISTment System, is a web-based tutoring system that allows us to bypass the process of client software installation and administration, thus, drastically increases the accessibility and visibility of the system, as suggested by Ritter & Koedinger (1996) and Brusilovsky & Peylo (2003). It also provides great control over content distribution, server updates, and log data collection. Meanwhile, the server-centered structure also brings up scalability issue. Patvarczki et al. (2008) and Patvarczki, J., Politz J., Heffernan, N. (2009) addressed the scalability issue by introducing a load-balancing and fault- tolerance architecture. They proposed a symmetric clustered infrastructure to avoid single-points-of-failure, and, increase the fault- tolerance of ASSISTments. More over, a load-balancing algorithm was developed to distribute the load between the cluster members based on round-robin selection. These works build foundation for further expansion of the ASSISTment System for a broader adoption.

Authoring Tools

Hints, scaffolds, and buggy messages together help create ASSISTments that are structurally simple but can address complex student behavior and provide appropriate intervention. The structure and the supporting interface used to build ASSISTments (*the authoring tools* or sometimes referred to as *the builder*, Razzaq et al., 2009), shown in Figure 1, uses common web technologies such as

HTML and JavaScript, allowing it to be used on most modern browsers. The authoring tools are simple enough that users with little or no computer programming experience or cognitive psychology background can use it easily. Figure 1 shows an ASSISTment being built on the left and what the student sees is shown on the right. Content authors can easily enter question text, hints and buggy messages by clicking on the appropriate field and typing; formatting tools are also provided for easily bolding, italicizing, etc. Images and animations can also be uploaded in any of these fields. The builder also enables scaffolding within scaffold questions, although this feature has not been used often in our existing content.

Several studies (Heffernan et al., 2006; Turner et al., 2005) have been conducted to evaluate the authoring tools in terms of usability and decreased creation time of tutors. The builder was augmented to track how long it takes authors to create an ASSISTment[7]. Thus, once we know how many ASSISTments authors have created, we can estimate the amount of content tutoring time created by using the previously established number that students spend about 2 minutes per ASSISTment (Heffernan et al., 2006). This produced a ratio of development time to on-line instruction time of about 40:1, comparing against the literature suggesting a 200:1 ratio (Anderson et al., 1995). Therefore, our method for creating tutoring content was much more cost effectively. We did this by building a tool that reduces both the skills needed to create content as well as the time needed to do so. Our subject matter expert was satisfied with the quality of the contents. Additionally, as we will point out later in section 2.1.6, several studies showed that the ASSISTments created by the content authors produced significant learning.

Figure 1. The builder and the corresponding student screen

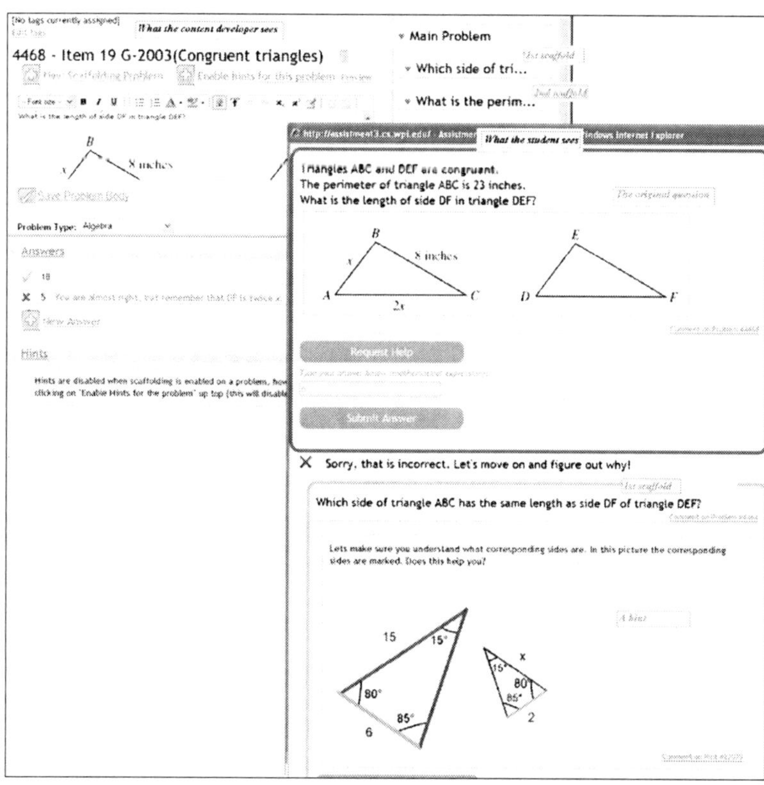

Reporting

Schools seek to use the yearly MCAS assessments in a data-driven manner to provide regular and ongoing feedback to teachers and students on progress towards instructional objectives. But teachers do not want to wait six months for the state to grade the exams. Teachers and parents also want better feedback than they currently receive. The reporting (Feng & Heffernan, 2007b) in the ASSISTment System has been built to identify the difficulties individual students - and the class as a whole – are having. It is intended that teachers will be able to use this detailed feedback to tailor their instruction to focus on the particular difficulties identified by the system.

The "Grade Book," shown in Figure 2, is the ASSISTment report used most frequently by teachers. Each row in the report represents information for one student, including our prediction of his MCAS score based on student response to the original questions. Besides presenting information on the item level, it also summarizes the student's actions in "ASSISTment metrics" that tells more about students' actions besides their performance. For example, it illuminates students' unusual behaviour, such as making far more attempts and requesting more hints than other students in the class. By clicking the link of the skill that the student has the lowest percent correct, the teacher can see what those questions were and what kind of errors the student made. Knowing students' reactions to questions helps teachers to improve their instruction and enable them to correct students' misunderstandings in a straightforward way. Finding out which knowledge components are difficult for students may also help us improve our item sequencing strategies.

The grade book report gives an overview of a student/a class's performance. Figure 3 shows an item report that is generated based on detailed, action-level logs of students. The report shows teachers how students are doing on individual problems. In particular, the item report in Figure 3 shows how three students from one class did on an assignment of eight problems focusing on Pythagorean Theorem, a skill that students need to acquire in the eighth grade. By presenting information in different colours and using different tags, the report helps teachers quickly tell if a student answered the question correctly (indicated by a "+" sign in the report), or incorrectly (indicated by an "x" sign) at their first attempt, or requested a hint (indicated by a message "Hint requested"). For instance, the three yellow-highlighted cells in the third row leap out at the first sight. Therefore, the teacher can tell at a glance that the student is asking for too many bottom-out hints. Actually, the student requested for hint messages 53 times, far more than others. Teachers can also see what students have answered for each question. As shown in the report, the correct answer of item #131 is "14" yet two of the three students gave the answer "192," which could be a warning signal to the teacher suggesting there are some common misunderstandings among students. Through providing the detailed information, we hope to help teachers inform their instructions and provide better remediation to students.

Figure 2. Grade book report

Student Name	Elapsed time(hh:mm)	Original Items				Scaffolding + Original Items			Most Difficult Learning Standard
		# Done	% Correct	MCAS Score*	Performance Level	# Done	% Correct	# Hint Req.	
Tom*	4:12	90	38%	214	Warning/Failing-High	228	44%	233	N.1.8 Understanding -number -representation
Dick*	4:01	98	66%	244	Pro./Adv.	158	59%	58	P.1.8 Understanding -patterns
Harry*	4:07	58	40%	219	Needs improv.-Low	154	38%	77	P.7.8 Setting-up-and-solving-equations

Figure 3. An item report tells teachers how students are doing on individual problems

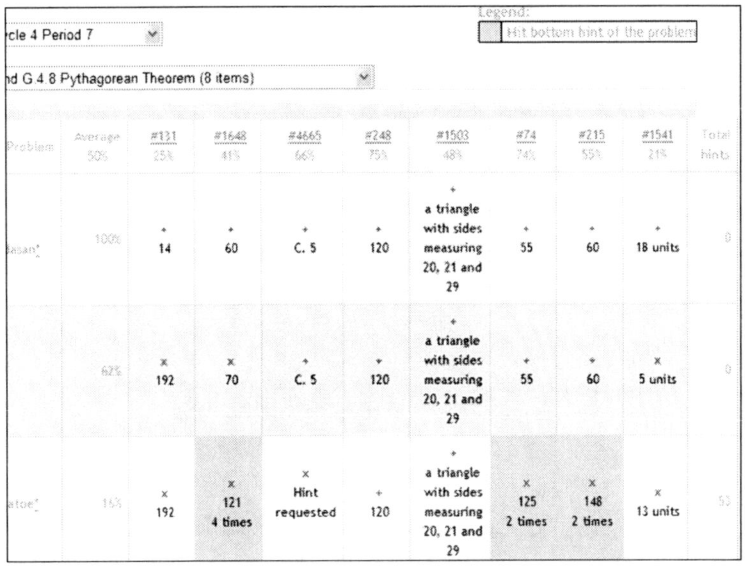

Teachers think highly of the ASSISTment System not only because their students can get instructional assistance in the form of scaffolding questions and hint messages while working on real MCAS items, but also because they can get online, live reports on students' progress while students are using the system in the classroom.

Content Development and Management

We are attempting to support the full life cycle of content authoring and management with the tools available in the ASSISTment system. Teachers can create problems with tutoring, map each question to the skills required to solve them, bundle problems together in sequences that students work on, view reports on students' work and use tools to maintain and refine their content over time.

Figure 4 shows how 1) students login, 2) get assignments to do that show up such as in the right hand side of Figure 1. Figure 2 also shows that our web-based system allows teachers access to 3) get reports, 4) manage classes, 5) get reports on students, 6a) create, edit and maintain content with the builder, 6b) find their own and others people's content (such as their students' content) 6c-e) bundling that content and assigning it to their students. We even have working reports (step 7) that automatically analyze the results of experiments that randomly assign students to conditions, which is the sort of analysis we need to determine if learning is happening.

Analyzing Learning Effectiveness in ASSISTments

We analyzed data within the ASSISTment System usage to determine whether the System effectively teaches. For the studies reported by Feng, Heffernan, & Koedinger (2006a, 2006b), we used the ASSISTment System to track student knowledge longitudinally over the course of a schools year, based upon each student using our system about a dozen times during the course of the year. This result confounded learning from the computer system with students learning from their sitting their normal class. To eliminate this confound, Feng, Heffernan, Beck & Koedinger (2008) looked to see if students were reliably learning from their time spent with the *computer in a single day*. We conducted a focused analysis of a subset

Figure 4. ASSISTment supports the full life cycle of content authoring

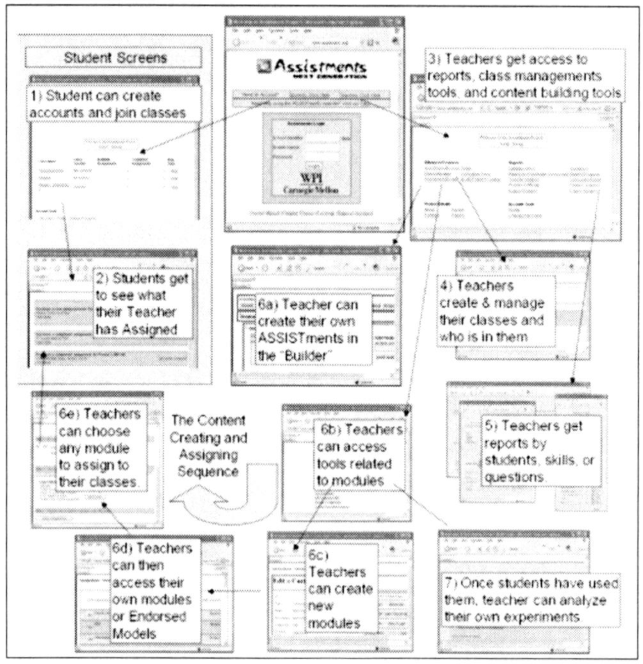

of items. Items that have the same deep features or knowledge requirements, like approximating square roots, but have different surface features, like cover stories, were organized into a Group of Learning OPportunity (GLOP). We assessed learning by comparing student performance the first time they were given one item from a GLOP with their performance when they were given more items (also more opportunities) from the same GLOP in the same day. If students tended to perform better on later opportunities of items in a GLOP, then they might have learned[8] from the instructional assistance provided on items by the ASSISTment system that they worked on earlier by answering the scaffolding questions or by reading hint messages. Our results suggested that students performed better later in the same computer session on similar skills, which indicated students learned from using ASSISTments. However, learning was rather uneven across groups of skills. We brought up a few hypotheses to explain this phenomenon and found out that students learned more from group of items that are more cohesive. Interestingly, human expert judgments were more predictive as to which groups of skills were learnable than the automated approaches. Following this work, Feng, Beck, & Heffernan (2009a, 2009b) and Pardos & Heffernan (2009a) reported our efforts on analyzing the relative effectiveness of items in a GLOP. More recently, Pardos et al. (2009) engaged in finding prerequisite relationship among problems in a GLOP using educational data mining approach. The results that have been validated through simulation studies provided an opportunity to improve overall learning from a GLOP and to inform content authors of item pairs of high transfer.

As seen from our student survey results, students complained that being forced into scaffolding questions was time consuming and frustrating. We were not sure if all of the time we invested into these "fancy" scaffolding questions was worth it. Luckily, the ASSISTment System provides a good platform to run randomized controlled experiments to find answers for such questions. Razzaq & Heffernan (2006) and Razzaq, Heffernan, & Lindeman (2007) reported the experiments comparing different tutoring strategies, hints vs. scaffolding. vs. delayed feedback[9]. The results showed that in general, scaffolding led to higher averages on a post-test, although it was not statistically significant. After a closer examination of the effect of math proficiency and the level of feedback on learning, they found out that honor students benefit more from delayed feedback and regular students did better in the scaffolding condition. One possible explanation was that less proficient students benefit from more interaction and coaching through each step to solve a problem while more proficient students benefit from seeing problems worked out and seeing the big picture. The fact that one strategy seems better than the other is an important research finding that potentially could improve the overall instructional efficacy of the system. However, that is not the main point. The point is that it is a future goal for the ASSISTment System to do this sort of analysis automatically for content creators, and based on the research results, pick the most suitable tutoring for the individual learners.

STUDENT MODELING

Literature Review of Student Modeling Approaches

An intelligent learning environment adapts the educational interaction to the specific needs of the individual student. Thus, student modeling is an essential component in such an environment and the learning effectiveness depends heavily on the understanding of student knowledge, difficulties, and misconceptions. Modeling student response data from intelligent tutoring systems has a long history (e.g. Corbett, Anderson, & O'Brien, 1995; Draney, Pirolli, & Wilson, 1995). One stream of modern educational research is on the modeling of student's individual problem-solving performance. Such analysis provides detailed assessments of student competence at different skills, and the results are usually used to guide the selection of next instructional actions in ITS. Corbett & Anderson (1995) proposed a process called knowledge tracing to model students' changing knowledge state during skill acquisition using a two-state Markov model. They showed the model was very successful in predicting test performance. Corbett, Anderson, & O'Brien (1995) further explored the quality of student modeling in the ACT programming tutor. Corbett, Anderson & O'Brien (1995) observed the power function might not hold for some complex skills thus there are blips in the learning curves. In addition, they found complex skills can be decomposed into subskills that result in smoother learning curve. This work led some cognitive scientists to look back at existing cognitive model and to bring up methods to improve cognitive models (e.g. learning factor analysis, Cen, Koedinger, & Junker, 2005, 2006).

Corbett and his colleagues employed a very detailed model of skills, but their system did not have questions tagged with more than one production rule (Anderson, 1993). Our collaborators (Ayers & Junker, 2006) were engaged in trying to allow multi-mapping[10] using a version of the fine grained model but reported their Linear Logistic Test Model (LLTM) does not fit well. Different from the approach we will report later in this chapter, the model they applied does not track student performance over time.

Bayesian networks are becoming an increasingly popular way of representing the state of a student's knowledge, skills, or abilities, especially in intelligent learning environments. Mislevy and colleagues (e.g. Mislevy, 1995; Mislevy & Gitomer, 1996; Mislevy, Steinberg, & Almond, 2003) focused on the role of probabilistic reasoning in ITS. They suggested evaluating students and providing feedback to students and teachers based on evidence. Almond et al. (2007) examined the application of Bayesian frameworks to Item Response Theory-based cognitive diagnostic modeling. Bayesian networks have also been used to investigate the results of skill hierarchies using real world data in intelligent tutoring systems (e.g., Ferguson et al., 2006) and simulated users (e.g., Collins, Greer, & Huang, 1996; Daniel et al., 2007). Conati & VanLehn (1997) used Bayesian networks to model student knowledge and updated the networks in real time. In addition to skill assessment and performance prediction, the model was also used to do plan recognition, and was used by the Help component of ANDES system to provide tailored support (VanLehn, 2005). The Bayesian network for a problem was automatically constructed from the solution graph produced by a problem solver. The display capability of Bayesian networks is designed to work with individual student one at a time. Yet, Almond et al. (2008) viewed the problem from a teacher's perspective, for example, how to make inferences about a group of students. To ease the complicated coding effort involved in the usage of Bayes nets, especially dynamic Bayes nets, Chang et al. (2006) introduced a Bayes Net Toolkit for Student Modeling (BNT-SM) that allows a researcher to describe causal relationships between student knowledge and observed behavior. Later on in Beck et al. (2008) dynamic Bayesian networks were trained up using the toolkit for evaluating the efficacy of assistance that was provided to students in an ITS that tutors reading.

Student modeling (or user modeling) is a distinctive feature of user-adaptive software systems, including adaptive hypermedia and other adaptive Web systems, and has caught attention of many researchers. For instance, Brusilovsky, Sosnovsky, & Shcherbinina (2005) addressed the issue of user modeling in a distributed learning architecture. They described a generic student modeling server and introduced a specific, topic-based knowledge modeling approach that was used in an adaptive system to help students to select the most relevant self-assessing quizzes. Brusilovsky & Millán (2007) focused on user modeling in adaptive systems. They explored the nature of the information being modeled in adaptive web (including users' knowledge, interests, goals and tasks, background, individual traits, and context of work), the overlay modeling approach, and uncertainty-based user modeling for adaptive systems.

Another stream of student modeling in learning environment has to do with the study of open learner models (Bull, 2004; Bull & Kay, 2007). Student models (or learner models) are usually not accessible to the students themselves. However, some work integrated the educational benefits of allowing students to access the learner model content, and even to negotiate with the system on the understanding of their knowledge proficiency. It was argued that this exposure will increase students' self-awareness of their knowledge and enhance learning (e.g. Kay, 1997; Bull & Nghiem, 2002). Certain amount of work has been done on application and evaluation of open learner models in various learning environments (e.g. Dimitrova, Self, & Brna, 2001; Mitrovic & Martin, 2002; Bull & McEvoy, 2003; Bull, et al., in press; Wongchokprasitti & Brusilovsky, 2007; Ahn et al., 2007).

There has also been a large interest in building cognitively diagnostic models. What we refer to as a "skill model" later in section 3.2 is referred to as "Q-Matrix" by some Artificial Intelligence researchers (Barnes, 2005) and psychometricians (Tatsuoka, 1990); Croteau, Heffernan, & Koedinger (2004) called it "transfer model"; while Cen, Koedinger & Junker (2005), and Griel, Wang, & Zhou (2008) used the term "cognitive model." In all cases, a skill model is a matrix that relates questions to the skills needed to solve the problem. Such a model provides an interpretative framework to guide test development and psychometric analyses so test performance can be linked to specific cognitive inferences about the examinees. Researchers in machine learning have been using automatic/semi-automatic techniques to search for skill models, including the rule space method (Tatsuoka, 1990), the Q-matrix method (Barnes, 2005), and Learning Factor Analysis (Cen, Koedinger, & Junker, 2005, 2006).

In the following section, we will describe our effort on modeling students in the context of ASSISTment System.

Student Modeling in ASSISTments

The ASSISTment System has two assessment goals: predicting student performance on end-of-year accountability exams, and cognitively assess student knowledge to help teachers target next instructional steps. These goals are complicated by two features of the system: assessment is ongoing throughout the school year as student proficiency develops, and the ASSISTment System itself as a tutoring system changes student proficiency. Nevertheless, prediction using simple student models and a number of "assistance metrics" (summaries of hint-seeking behavior, time spent on questions correctly vs. incorrectly answered, etc.) can be almost optimally effective at predicting end-of-year exam scores, as we will show below. Statistical uncertainty in teacher feedback reports based on more-detailed student models is sometimes surprisingly low, but even in cases where the per-student uncertainty is high, reports aggregated over groups of students can be quite reliable. These ideas will be considered both for the ASSISTment System and in the broader context of online assessment and learning systems.

Predicting Student End-of-Year Exam Score

The first assessment goal for ASSISTments is to make a prediction of student end-of-year exam scores. We have reported the results of several studies where we used log data collected via ASSISTments to try to predict scores of the MCAS high-stake tests required of all students in the state of Massachusetts. We will now review of a few of those results. All the participants of studies mentioned in this chapter were from Worcester Public Schools, Worcester, Massachusetts. They were all 8th grade students at the time they used ASSISTments. The students practiced problems within the ASSISTment System as a part of their regular math class. No selection processes based on student demographic information or personal traits have been conducted before the data analysis. In all of these studies we compared students actual MCAS test scores with the predicted to get calculate the Mean Absolute Deviation (MAD) which was then used as the measure to evaluate the student models.

As mentioned above, the ASSISTment System is not a pure assessment system but also provides instructional assistance when students have difficulties. Does providing assistance hurt the accuracy of the assessment? Surprisingly, these studies reported that the assistance provided actually improves the assessment. The idea is that by seeing how much help students needed allows a more sensitive measure of student knowledge then just whether they got a question correct.

Much work has been done in the past 10 years or so on developing "online testing metrics" for dynamic testing (or dynamic assessment) (Grigorenko & Sternberg, 1998) to supplement accuracy data (wrong/right scores) for characterizing student proficiency. Researchers have been interested in trying to get more assessment value by comparing traditional assessment (students getting an item marked wrong or even getting partial credit) with a measure that shows how much help they needed. Brown, Bryant, & Campione (1983) compared traditional testing paradigms against a dynamic testing paradigm. Grigorenko & Sternberg (1998) reviewed relevant literature on the topic and expressed enthusiasm for the idea. In the dynamic testing paradigm a student would be presented with an item and when the student appeared to not be making progress, would be given a prewritten hint. If the student was still not making progress, another prewritten hint was presented and the process was repeated. In this study they wanted to predict learning gains between pretest and posttest. They found that static testing prediction did not correlate ($R = 0.45$) with student learning data as well as the "dynamic testing" did (R = 0.60). Brown et al. (1983) suggested that this method could be effectively done by computer, but, as far as we know, their work was not continued. Luckily, the ASSISTment system provides an ideal test bed as it already provides a set of hints to students. So it is a natural way to extend and test this idea and see if we can replicate their finding of ASSISTment-style measures being better assessors. Our hypothesis was that we could achieve more accurate assessment by not only using data on whether students get test items right or wrong, but by also using data on the effort required for students to learn how to solve a test item.

We continued the dynamic testing approach (Feng, Heffernan & Koedinger, 2006a, 2006b, 2009; Feng, Beck, Heffernan, & Koedinger, 2008) and developed a group of "assistance" metrics that focused on student-system-interaction behaviors during the tutoring session (scaffoldings or hints). The metrics included accuracy (percent correct on scaffolding questions), speed (how many seconds a student needs to solve a problem), attempts (on average, how many attempts a student made to finally get the correct answer) and help-seeking behavior (on average how often a student asks for hint messages; how many times he/she reaches the bottom-out hint). These metrics were either not available or have largely been ignored in traditional assessment environments. But as a computer-based tutoring system, ASSISTments have the potential to use far more. We computed the metrics from our log data and found out that all these metrics were reliably correlated with students' real MCAS test scores. Then we built different students models to predict end-of-year MCAS scores. Our goal was to see if we can reliably predict students' test scores and to evaluate how well on-line use of the ASSISTment system can help in the prediction.

A number of different regression models were compared for measuring student knowledge during ASSISTments use, including a static model that was based only on accuracy on original questions, a dynamic assessment model that was built on all assistance metrics except the accuracy, and a mixed model that incorporates the static model and the dynamic model. The key contrast of interest was between a static model that mimicked paper practice tests by scoring students as either correct or incorrect on each main question, with the dynamic assessment model that leveraged the assistance metrics to take into account the amount of assistance students need before they get an item correct. We trained the models on two data sets from two school years. The data set we collected during the school year of 2004-2005 involved 417 students who practiced mathematics problems in the ASSISTment system since September 2004 till May 2005, for a mean length of 267 minutes (standard deviation = 79) across about 9 class sessions, finishing on average 147 items (standard deviation = 60). For this data set, the predicted score from the static model correlated with the MCAS test scores, with an R-value of 0.733 and the dynamic assistance model correlated with an R-value of 0.821, reliably higher than the correlation between the static prediction and MCAS scores. The second data set came from the usage of 616 8th grade students during 2005-2006 school year. These students on average worked in the ASSISTment system for 196 minutes (standard deviation = 76), and finished an average of 88 items (at least 39 items, standard deviation = 42). Again, we found the same trend in the data set that the dynamic assessment model did reliably better on predicting MCAS scores (R = 0.816) than the static model (R = 0.784). For both data sets, we could improve our prediction of MCAS score further by combining the assistance metrics with the static model. Additionally, we verified the validity of the combined model by cross-validating the combined model both inside same year's data and using data across two years. Thus, we can claim that the ASSISTment System did a better job of predicting student knowledge by being able to take into consideration metrics such as how much tutoring assistance was needed and how fast a student solves a problem.

We suspect that a better job of predicting MCAS scores could be done if students could be encouraged to take the system seriously and reduce "gaming behavior." One way to reduce gaming is to detect it and then to notify the teacher (in the teacher's reporting session) with evidence that the teacher can use to approach the student. Our preliminary work on gaming detection was presented in Walonoski & Heffernan (2006). It is assumed that teacher intervention will lead to reduced gaming behavior, and thereby affect more accurate assessment, and higher learning. Adding visual feedback, as one ongoing work in the ASSISTment System does, aims to help teachers quickly detect gaming behaviors.

Tracking Student Performance Longitudinally

In Razzaq et al. (2005) and Feng, Heffernan, Beck, & Koedinger (2008), we reported results that suggested students were learning directly during the assisting in ASSISTments. We did this by looking at groups of items that had the same skills and to see if performance later in the class period was associated with higher performance. The gain score over all of the learning opportunity pairs suggested that students were learning in the system. In this section, instead of discussing within-system learning, we focused on tracking student progress that results from both classroom instruction and ASSISTments tutoring over a long periods of time. To investigate this question, we did a longitudinal analysis (Singer & Willett, 2003; Fitzmaurice, Laird & Ware, 2004) by fitting mixed-effect models on the ASSISTment data to investigate if learning happens over time. We gradually introduced factors such as what school they are in, who their teacher is, or which class they are from, into our models. By doing so, we attempted to provide an answer to the question of what factors impact (or are correlated with) students' learning rate.

During the school year of 2004-2005, there were approximately 650 students using the system, with each student coming to the computer lab about 7 times. We created a table with 4550 rows, one row for each student for each day, with an average percent correct which itself is averaged over about 15 MCAS items done on a given day. In Figure 5, average student performance is plotted versus time. The y-axis is the average percent correct on the original item (student performance on the scaffolding questions is ignored in this analysis) in a given class. The x-axis represents time, where data is combined together into months, so some students who came to the lab twice in a month will have their numbers averaged. The fact that most of the class trajectories are generally rising suggests that most classes are learning between months. The result of statistical modeling confirms what we saw in the plot. Our fitted longitudinal model ended up with a statistically significant learning slope that indicates that student performance was reliably increasing during the school year. Additionally, our model was able to detect different rates of learning at different schools, but not among different teachers and classes.

Given that it was the first year of the ASSISTments project, new content is created each month, which introduces a potential confounder of item difficulty. It could be that some very hard items were selected to give to students in September, or students were not really learning but were being tested on easier items. In the future, this confound will be eliminated by sampling items randomly. Adding automated applied longitudinal data analysis is being pursued.

More work is needed to build models to better detect differences between teachers' effects on the learning rates of students that presumably exist. Besides this, other factors will be investigated about their possible impact on students' learning over time. Information from student profiles such as gender, race and ethnicity, special education status, free-lunch status, etc., is being added. During this analysis, we noticed the fact that

Figure 5. Average student performance is plotted over time

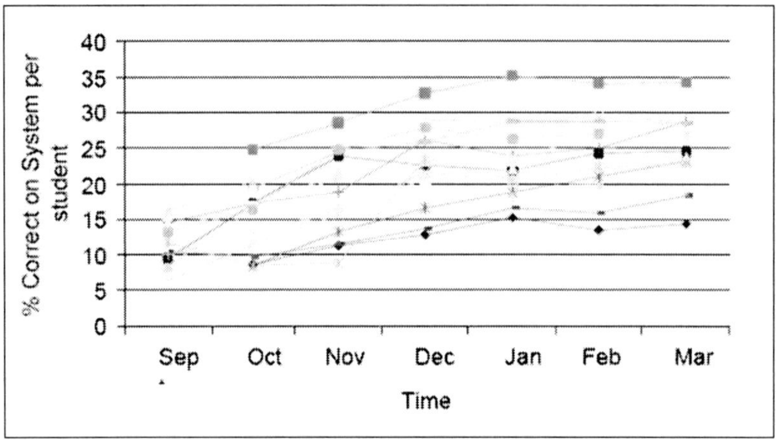

generally speaking, groups with higher estimated initial scores showed lower rates of learning. Our preliminary speculation on this fact is that 1) this may be attributed to the "ceiling effect": it is hard for top students to make fast progress; 2) good students were assigned to Algebra class and learning content that won't be tested until 10th grade and won't appear in the ASSISTment system. Further investigation needs to be done to explain this phenomenon.

Modeling Fine Grained Student Knowledge

Most large standardized tests are "unidimensional" in that they are analyzed as if all the questions are tapping a single underlying skill. However, cognitive scientists such as Anderson & Lebiere (1998) believe that students are learning individual skills. Among the reasons that psychometricians analyze large scale tests in a unidimensional manner is that students' performance on different skills are usually highly correlated, even if there is no necessary prerequisite relationship between these skills. Another reason is that students usually do a small number of items in a given setting (for instance, 39 items for the 8th grade math MCAS test), which makes it hard to acquire identifiability for each single skill, especially when the number of skills that need to be mastered is larger than the number of the items in the test. Such tests work pretty well at telling you which students are performing well but are not good at *informing educators* about which skills are causing difficulty and how to help students. However, the question of tagging items with learning standards is very important because schools seek to use the MCAS assessments in a data-driven manner to provide regular and ongoing feedback to teachers and students on progress towards instructional objectives. In this section, we describe our work on constructing fine-grained skill models. More precisely, our research question is what the right grain size of skill models and how model granularity impacts the effectiveness of a student's knowledge tracking. Tracking student skills at a very fine- grained level is not applicable in the traditional assessment environment because of limited testing time and test items where it is hard to determine which skill(s) to credit or blame, especially when a wrong answer is given. However, the special structure of the ASSISTment System gives teachers that very information. Original questions are always followed by scaffolding questions, each addressing a single piece of the student's knowledge. Therefore, when a student answered the original question wrong, we can rely on his responses to scaffolding questions to figure out exactly where the student has a misunderstanding and are able to track the specific knowledge component precisely. Moreover, students are using the ASSISTment System regularly in their normal math class during a school year, working on mathematic questions drawn from a pool of more than 1,400 questions. The continuous usage allows us to collect more evidence of student's performance on every skill.

Skill Models Development and Skill Mapping

The ASSISTments approach is task-centric (development of main questions and scaffolding materials starts from released state exam items) instead of skill-centric (tasks are developed based upon the skills to be focused) and it directly attributes individual differences to unobservable skills or other latent variables. In April 2005, we invited our subject matter expert to conduct cognitive task analysis over the released state test items. They set out to make up skills and tag the entire existing 8th grade MCAS items with these skills. There were about 300 released test item to code. Because we wanted to be able to track learning between items, we wanted to come up with a number of skills that were somewhat fine-grained but not too fine-grained such that each item had a different skill. We therefore imposed upon our subject-matter expert that no one item would be tagged with more than 3 skills. The subject manner expert was free to make up whatever skills she thought appropriate. Although we have English names for the skills, those names are just a handy tag; the real meaning of a skill must be divined by the questions with which it is associated. We ended up with a cognitive model of 106 skills that we refer to as WPI-106.

One aspect of the project is that the ASSISTment System must serve a variety of stakeholders, and not all of them need or want reports at the same level of granularity. Therefore, even though WPI-106 may be closer to optimal for providing teacher feedback, we built other cognitive models at coarser grain size[11]. We used the fine-grained model to guide us to create the coarse-grained models. We decided to use the same 5 strands that both the National Council of Teachers of Mathematics uses, as well as the Massachusetts Department of Education. These categories are named 1) "Patterns, Relations and Algebra," 2) "Geometry," 3) "Data Analysis, Statistics and Probability," 4) "Number Sense and Operations," and 5) "Measurement." The Massachusetts Department of Education actually tags each item with exactly one of the 5 categories, but our mapping was not necessarily the same as the State's. Furthermore, we allowed multi-mapping, i.e., allowing an item to be tagged with more than one skill. In addition to the model with 5 strands (i.e. the WPI-5), a middle-level model of 39 skills was also derived (the WPI-39) by nesting a group of skills from WPI-106 into the each one of the 39 learning standards from Massachusetts Curriculum Framework. We will refer the unidimensional model as WPI-1 where "math" is the only skill in it.

Figure 6 shows the hierarchal nature of the relationship among the three models of different grain size. We think we will be able to track student knowledge in the fine- grained model, partly because students usually finished many problems along the year (on average 100+ main problems, 200+ scaffolding questions) and partly because the strategy of scaffolding questions gives us the *identifiablity*. As mentioned before, when creating scaffolding questions for the tutoring session, the authors try to focus on one skill at a time, which makes the scaffolding questions as *cognitively diagnostic assessment* on top of tutoring therefore student response to scaffolding questions can be used to determine what are the skills students have mastered or have difficulty on.

A secondary purpose of the ASSISTments builder was to aid the mapping between skills and the questions. As they are building content, the authors use the builder to tag certain skills to specific problems to indicate that a problem requires knowledge of that skill.

Figure 6. Cognitive models in a hierarchy structure

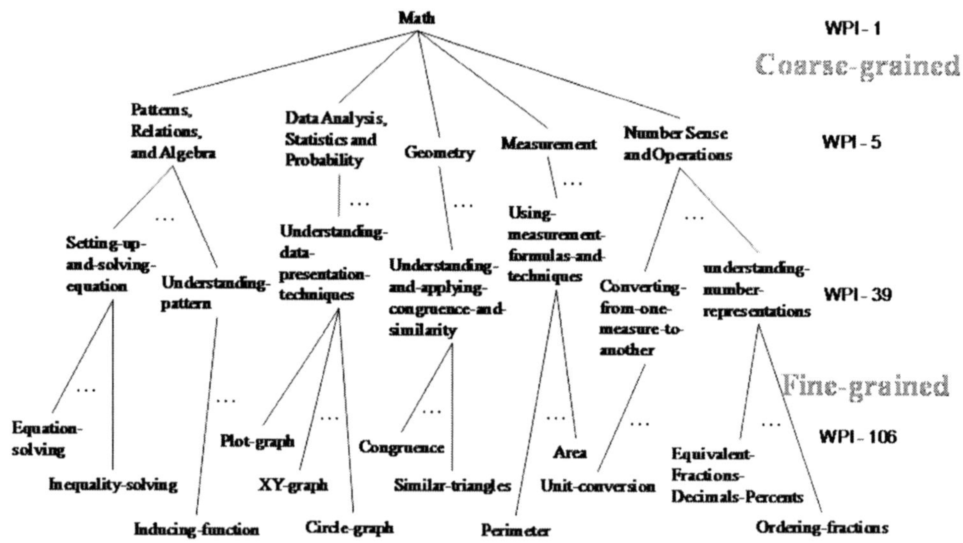

Inference of Skill Level and Reporting to Teachers

Mapping between skills and problems allows our reporting system to track student knowledge over time using longitudinal data analysis techniques (Singer & Willett, 2003; Fitzmaurice, Laird, & Ware, 2004) and make inference of student proficiency level on each skills based on their performance on the problems. In ASSISTments, the inference of student proficiency level is rather simple. Students get full credit for a skill when they correctly answer the questions tagged with the skill. In the case of a wrong answer to a question tagged with multiple skills, the system relies on response to scaffolding questions (typically tagged with only one skill) to determine which skill "to blame" (i.e., the cause of the wrong answer to the main question). If no scaffolding questions available, the most difficult skill will be blamed. Thus, connection between proficiencies and tasks is relatively loose and informal.

Turning to teacher feedback, Figure 7 shows the skill analysis report that informs teachers about the knowledge status of selected classes. Skills (labelled as Knowledge Components in the report) are ranked according to their correct rate—labelled "Rate" and displayed as "Skill Meter"—which is the percent correct rate at the items tagged with that skill model. Skills in the reports are organized hierarchically in three levels of grain sizes. Links in the column entitled "39 learning standards" will lead to the definition of a particular learning standard in Mathematics Curriculum Framework. Clicking the name of a skill in WPI-106 (labelled as "106-KC Transfer Model"), teachers will be redirected to another page showing the items tagged with that skill. In the new page, teachers are able to see the question text of each item and continue to preview or analyze the item if they want to know more about it. By presenting such a report, we hope we can help teachers to decide which skill and items should be focused on to maximize the gain of students' scores at a class level when instructional time is limited.

The Effect of Model Granularity on Student Performance Prediction

Model granularity is important because students seem to reason at many grain sizes, that is, students can have both deep and shallow knowledge (e.g., Koedinger & Nathan, 2004; Feng & Beck,

Figure 7. Class level skill analysis report

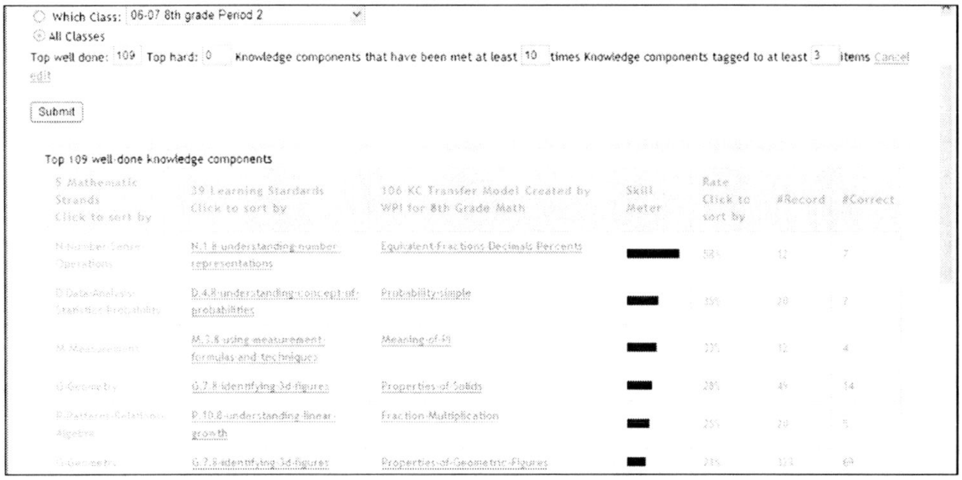

2009). The range of understanding the student has, from a deep mental model through a shallower strategy to surface code, encapsulates three simultaneously held perspectives on the problem's solution at three different grain sizes. Now that we constructed a hierarchical structure of cognitive models of various granularity, we engaged in an effort to investigate if we could do a better job of end-of-year standardized test by modeling individual skills in a finer grain size (Pardos et al., 2007; Pardos et al., 2006; Feng, Heffernan, Heffernan, & Mani, 2009) than coarser grain sizes. We considered the 4 different models: unidimensional, 5 skills, 39 skills, and 106 skills and analyzed usage data of 921 students from two school years (2004-2005, and 2005-2006). We fit mixed-effects logistic models to track student knowledge change longitudinally and then made a prediction of how a student would perform on each skill in the MCAS test[12] at the end of the year. The measure of model performance was the accuracy of the predicted MCAS test score based on the assessed skills of the students (%Error). We found out that the WPI-106 model was superior in terms of prediction accuracy of MCAS tests, followed by the model with 39 skills, and then the model with 5 skills. This suggested that finer-grained skill models were more helpful in tracking students' knowledge over time. In particular, for 2004-2005 data (shown in Figure 8.), the WPI-106 still did better than the WPI-39, but the difference was not reliable ($p=0.21$). Yet, they were both statistically significantly better than the WPI-5 and WPI-1. And the WPI-106 predicted MCAS scores marginally better ($p = 0.10$) than the Rasch model (van der Linden & Hamilton, 1997) that has been widely used in computer adaptive testing for assessment. For the 2005-2006 data, the WPI-106 model was statistically reliably better than the WPI-39, WPI-5 and WPI-1 ($p<0.001$ in all cases). Yet, the Rasch model produced a significant lower error than the WPI-106 model in the 2005-2006 data. We also tried to add item difficulty parameters obtained from a Rasch model into the mixed-effects logistic models as an additional covariate to account for the fact that questions tagged with the same skill may vary on difficulty, but the result suggested that the combination does not improve prediction (Feng & Heffernan, 2007a).

CONCLUSION, CONTRIBUTION & MORE DISCUSSION

In this chapter, we addressed the testing challenge in the ASSISTment system, a web-based e-learning

Figure 8. Comparing the prediction accuracy of different models on two years' data

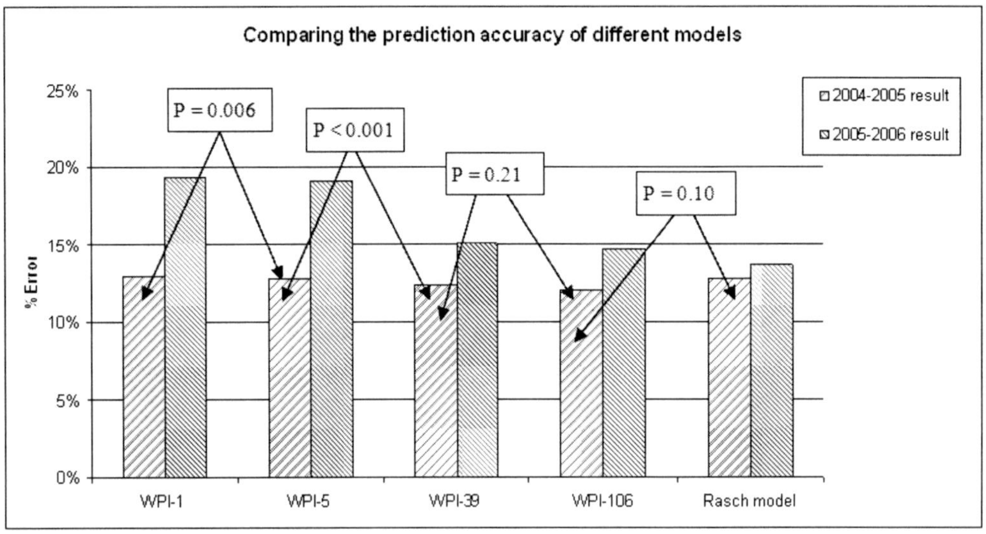

and e-assessment system. We concentrated on the assessment ability of the system. Some evidence was presented that the online assessment system did a better job of predicting student knowledge by being able to take into consideration how much tutoring assistance was needed. Promising evidence was also found that the online system was able to track students' learning during a year well, and fine-grained skill models can be used in ASSISTments to better track student knowledge than coarse grained models. Furthermore, we showed how individual skills were modeled in the ASSISTment System and being used to give feedback to teachers. The results presented in this paper further showed that not only can reliable assessment and instructional assistance be effectively blended in a tutoring system, but more importantly, such a system can provide teachers with useful fine-grained student-level knowledge they can reflect on and adjust their pedagogy.

This chapter's main contribution lies in two aspects. First, our work provides evidence for the value of assistance measures, like the percent correct for scaffolding, the use of help, hint requests, time to respond, and other factors for prediction of standardized test scores. Traditional assessment usually focuses on whether a student answered a question correctly or incorrectly, but ignores all other student behaviors during the test (e.g., response time). However, an ITS has the potential to use far more. In this work, we take advantage of ASSISTments to collect extensive and rich data while students interact with the system. While the combined model leads to the best predictions, the relative success of the assistance model over the lean model highlights the power of the assistance measures. Not only is it possible to get reliable test information while "teaching on the test," data from the teaching process actually improves reliability. While the nature and amount of help that a student is given appear to be of obvious value in judging a student's mastery of knowledge, we claim that operationalizing the idea and assessing whether this promise is achievable in an implemented system is an important contribution.

Second, we demonstrated the value of a very fine-grained versus more coarse-grained model within intelligent tutoring systems. While some prior research in the field of intelligent tutoring systems has looked at the value of coming up with accurate skills models (and has generated some automated methods for doing so, such as Barnes,

2005; Cen et al., 2005, 2006), our work is different in that we hand-coded the skill models and built the connection between skills and questions. This is similar to what Ferguson et al. (2006) did as they also associated problems with skills by hand, but they employed a different methodology. We are not the only ones who have been concerned with the question of granularity. Early in 1994 when speculating on long term research goals, McCalla & Greer (1994) pointed out that the ability to represent and reason about knowledge at various levels of detail is important for robust tutoring. As far as we know, our investigation is entirely unique in that it rigorously evaluates the effect of the level of details within the skill models using real student data from a tutoring system, going from very broad to very detailed. Since intelligent tutoring systems tend to use fine-grained skill models, the work validates a core underlying assumption. The only work we are aware of that shows that by building fine-grained skill models researchers could build better fitting models was by Yun, Willett & Murnane (2004). They developed an alternative curriculum framework and showed that the alternative framework fits data better suggesting the state's learning standards is subject to improvement. However, they did not try to answer the question regarding to the right grain size of skill models. Collins, Greer, & Huang (1996) investigated the results of skill hierarchies. Unlike us, they were using simulated users and have not applied their approach to real student data. Carmonal et al. (2005) also introduced hierarchy structure into their Bayesian models. Yet, they focused on prerequisite relations among skills but not the various granularities of skill models, as we did.

Currently we are beginning to focus statistical modeling work on improving student knowledge modeling in the ASSISTment System. For example, Cen, Koedinger & Junker (2006) model learning curves using ideas of Draney, Pirolli & Wilson (1995). Another approach as elaborated in the Evidence Centered Design (ECD, Mislevy, Steinburg, & Almond, 2003) framework gives special attention to the role of probability-based reasoning in accumulating evidence across task performances, in terms of belief about unobservable variables that characterize the knowledge, skills, and/or abilities of students. Another approach combines the knowledge tracing algorithm of Corbett, Anderson & O'Brien (1995) with Bayes Net (DINA) models (Junker & Sijtsma, 2001). The key criterion in determining which approach to pursue is how well a model predicts data and how interpretable the model is.

One idea upon which we can reflect is, "what is the right way to judge a project like this one, which tries to blend assessment and assisting (increasing student learning)?" The system does not have to be either the best assessment system in the world, or the best learning system in the world. It needs to be a good balance between the two. Fundamentally, there will always be tradeoffs between the accuracy of assessment data and increases in students' learning, due to the fact that schools have only a finite number of days in a year.

Many states are moving towards adopting "*value added*" assessments as a new way to measure teaching and learning, which allows the states to identify not only the progress made by individual students but also how much individual teachers, schools and districts have contributed to the progress. Using this approach, researchers can predict the amount of growth those students are likely to make in a given year, based on a review of students' test score gains from previous grades. Thus, value-added assessment can tell whether a student has made expected progress, or he/she achieves beyond the expected progress. Such systems could benefit from data collected every two weeks, instead of once a year, thereby allowing schools to more quickly figure out what works at increasing student learning. Because the ASSISTment System teaches while it assesses, it makes the testing more politically palatable. In fact, this article provides evidence that because the system teaches while it assesses, it does a better job of assessing (if you hold the number of items done constant, instead of time). In the future, states and school systems may benefit from implementing an assessment tracking system that offers continuous assessment every few weeks in addition to, or even or instead of, a test that happens once a year.

Last, we want to address again that student performance modeling and assessment is not the ultimate goal, but it can provide a compass for helping us get to the ultimate goal of better student achievement. Early findings of the national *Study of Education Data Systems and Decision Making* indicate that although there is dramatic increase in teacher access to student data systems, the data from these systems are having little effect on teachers' daily instructional decisions (Means, Padilla, DeBarger, & Bakia, 2009). Recently in a speech, Arne Duncan, the United States Secretary of Education, called for teachers to use data to drive instruction in order to improve student achievement. He has been critical of the fact that teachers are currently learning to use data to drive instruction *on the job*, instead of that being part of their teacher preparation program and in service. He pointed out that "one of our collective challenges is to talk about data and research in ways that people understand."[13] There is a lot of hard work to be done for teachers to change their teaching. In the education research area, new practices are being proposed to aid this change. For instance, the Diagnostic Geometry Assessment (Russell & Masters, 2009), an online assessment, provides a collection of lesson plans and instructional resources targeting common misconceptions. Teachers also have access to follow-up tests that can be administered to the student after instruction to measure whether the student has corrected the misconception. At WPI, we have a partnership program in Math and Science education (PIMSE[14]) that involves participants of teachers, graduate students, and an ASSISTment coach. The goal of the project is to help teachers figure out the best ways of integrating data-driven instruction into their own classroom practices. A workshop has been set up for 17 local teachers in the 2009-10 school year and a college seminar entitled *Using Advanced Educational Technology to Support Data-driven Decision Making*[15] is available for teachers. Though it is a challenging task, we believe in the power of the data. As Arne Duncan has suggested, we just need to be "much more thoughtful about how we look at assessments and create incentives so that every child is pushed to excel and pushed to reach their potential". [16]

ACKNOWLEDGMENT

This research was made possible by the U.S. Department of Education, Institute of Education Science (IES) grants, "Effective Mathematics Education Research" program grant #R305K03140 and "Making Longitudinal Web-based Assessments Give Cognitively Diagnostic Reports to Teachers, Parents, & Students while Employing Mastery learning" program grant #R305A070440, the Office of Naval Research grant #N00014-03-1-0221, NSF CAREER award to Neil Heffernan, and the Spencer Foundation. All the opinions, findings, and conclusions expressed in this article are those of the authors, and do not reflect the views of any of the funders. We would like to acknowledge Joseph Beck for his insightful comments on this research.

REFERENCES

Ahn, J., Brusilovsky, P., Grady, J., He, D., & Syn, S. Y. (2007). Open user profiles for adaptive news systems: help or harm? In *Proceedings of the 16th international conference on World Wide Web (WWW '07)* (pp 11-20), New York: ACM Press.

Aleven, V. A. W. M. M., & Koedinger, K. R. (2002). An effective metacognitive strategy: Learning by doing and explaining with a computer-based Cognitive Tutor. *Cognitive Science, 26*(2), PAGE NUMBERS.

Almond, R. G., DiBello, L. V., Moulder, B., & Zapata-Rivera, D. (2007). Modeling diagnostic assessment with Bayesian networks. *Journal of Educational Measurement, 44*(4), 341–359. doi:10.1111/j.1745-3984.2007.00043.x

Almond, R. G., Shute, V., Underwood, J., & Zapata-Rivera, D. (2009). Bayesian networks: A teacher's view. *International Journal of Approximate Reasoning, 50*, 450–460. doi:10.1016/j.ijar.2008.04.011

Anderson, J. R. (1993). *Rules of mind.* Hillsdale, NJ: Lawrence Erlbaum Associates.

Anderson, J. R., Corbett, A. T., Koedinger, K. R., & Pelletier, R. (1995). Cognitive tutors: Lessons learned. *Journal of the Learning Sciences, 4*(2), 167–207. doi:10.1207/s15327809jls0402_2

Anderson, J. R., & Lebiere, C. (1998). *The Atomic Components of Thought.* Hillsdale, NJ: Lawrence Erlbaum Associates.

Anderson, J. R., & Lebiere, C. (1998). *The Atomic Components of Thought.* Mahwah, NJ: Erlbaum: LEA.

Anozie, N. O., & Junker, B. W. (2006, July). *Predicting end-of-year accountability assessment scores from monthly student records in an online tutoring system.* Poster presented at the American Association for Artificial Intelligence Workshop on Educational Data Mining (AAAI-06), Boston.

Ayers, E., & Junker, B. W. (2006, July). *Do skills combine additively to predict task difficulty in eighth-grade mathematics?* Poster presented at the American Association for Artificial Intelligence Workshop on Educational Data Mining (AAAI-06), Boston, MA.

Barnes, T. (2005). Q-matrix Method: Mining Student Response Data for Knowledge. In Beck. J. (Ed), *Educational Data Mining: Papers from the 2005 AAAI Workshop.* Menlo Park, CA: AAAI Press.

Beck, J. E. (2006). Using learning decomposition to analyze student fluency development. In *Proceedings of the Workshop on Educational Data Mining at the 8th International Conference on Intelligent Tutoring Systems (pp 21-28).* Jhongli, Taiwan. eck, J. E., Chang, K., Mostow, J., & Corbett, A. (2008). Does help help? Introducing the Bayesian Evaluation and Assessment methodology. In *Proceedings of the 9th International Conference on Intelligent Tutoring Systems,* (pp 383-394).

Brown, A. L., Bryant, N. R., & Campione, J. C. (1983). *Preschool children's learning and transfer of matrices problems: Potential for improvement.* Paper presented at the Society for Research in Child Development meeting, Detroit, MI.

Brusilovsky, P., & Millán, E. (2007). User models for adaptive hypermedia and adaptive educational systems. In: P. Brusilovsky, A. Kobsa and W. Neidl (Eds.). *The Adaptive Web: Methods and Strategies of Web Personalization: Lecture Notes in Computer Science, 4321*, 3-53. Berlin Heidelberg New York: Springer-Verlag.

Brusilovsky, P., & Peylo, C. (2003). Adaptive and intelligent web-based educational systems. *Journal of Artificial Intelligence in Education, 13*(2-4), 159–172.

Brusilovsky, P., Sosnovsky, S., & Shcherbinina, O. (2005). User Modeling in a Distributed E-Learning Architecture. In: L. Ardissono, P. Brna and A. Mitrovic (Eds.) *Proceedings of 10th International User Modeling Conference: Lecture Notes in Artificial Intelligence*, vol. 3538. Berlin: Springer Verlag

Bull, S. (2004). Supporting Learning with Open Learner Models. In *Proceedings of 4th Hellenic Conference with International Participation: Information and Communication Technologies in Education*, Athens, Greece.

Bull, S., Gardner, P., Ahmad, N., Ting, J. & Clarke, B. (in press). Use and Trust of Simple Independent Open Learner Models to Support Learning Within and Across Courses. *User Modeling, Adaptation and Personalization,* Springer-Verlag, Berlin Heidelberg.

Bull, S., & Kay, J. (2007). Student Models that Invite the Learner In: The SMILI Open Learner Modelling Framework. *International Journal of Artificial Intelligence in Education, 17*(2), 89–120.

Bull, S., & McEvoy, A. T. (2003). An Intelligent Learning Environment with an Open Learner Model for the Desktop PC and Pocket PC. In Hoppe, U., Verdejo, F., & Kay, J. (Eds.), *Artificial Intelligence in Education* (pp. 389–391). Amsterdam: IOS Press.

Bull, S., & Nghiem, T. (2002). Helping Learners to Understand Themselves with a Learner Model Open to Students, Peers and Instructors. In P. Brna & V. Dimitrova (Eds.), *Proceedings of Workshop on Individual and Group Modeling Methods that Help Learners Understand Themselves, International Conference on Intelligent Tutoring Systems*, (pp. 5-13).

Campione, J. C., Brown, A. L., & Bryant, N. R. (1985). Individual differences in learning and memory. In Sternberg, R. J. (Ed.), *Human abilities: An information-processing approach* (pp. 103–126). New York: W.H. Freeman.

Carmonal, C., Millán, E., Pérez-de-la-Cruz, J. L., Trellal, M. & Conejo, R. (2005). Introducing Prerequisite Relations in a Multi-layered Bayesian Student Model. In Ardissono, Brna & Mitroivc (Eds.). *10th International Conference on User Modeling 2005,* (pp. 347-356), Berlin, Germany: Springer-Verlag

Cen, H., Koedinger, K., & Junker, B. (2005). Automating Cognitive Model Improvement by A*Search and Logistic Regression. In Beck. J (Eds). *Educational Data Mining: Papers from the 2005 AAAI Workshop*. Menlo Park, CA: AAAI Press.

Cen, H., Koedinger, K., & Junker, B. (2006, June). *Learning factors analysis: a general method for cognitive model evaluation and improvement.* Presented at the Eighth International Conference on Intelligent Tutoring Systems (ITS 2006), Jhongli, Taiwan.

Chang, K., Beck, J., Mostow, J., & Corbett, A. (2006, June). *A Bayes Net Toolkit for Student Modeling in Intelligent Tutoring Systems.* Presented at Eigth International Conference on Intelligent Tutoring Systems, Jhongli, Taiwan

Collins, J., Greer, J., & Huang, S. (1996). Adaptive assessment of using granularity hierarchies and Bayesien nets. In *Lecture Notes in Computer Science: Proceedings of the third Intelligent Tutoring Systems*, (pp. 569 -577), London: Springer-Verlag.

Computing Research Association. (2005). Cyber infrastructure for Education and Learning for the Future: a Vision and Research Agenda. *Final report of Cyber learning Workshop Series workshops held Fall 2004 - Spring 2005 by the Computing Research Association (CRA) and the International Society of the Learning Sciences (ISLS).* Retrieved from http://www.cra.org/reports/cyberinfrastructure.pdf

Conati, C., Gertner, A., VanLehn, K., & Druzdzel, M. (1997). On-Line Student Modeling for Coached Problem Solving Using Bayesian Networks. In Jameson A., Paris C., Tasso C., (Eds.), *Proceedings of the sixth International Conference on User Modeling (UM'97).* New York: Springer-Wien.

Corbett, A. T., & Anderson, J. R. (1995). Knowledge tracing: Modeling the acquisition of procedural knowledge. *User Modeling and User-Adapted Interaction*, *4*, 253–278. doi:10.1007/BF01099821

Corbett, A. T., Anderson, J. R., & O'Brien, A. T. (1995). Student modeling in the ACT programming tutor. In Nichols, P., Chipman, S., & Brennan, R. (Eds.), *Cognitively Diagnostic Assessment*. Hillsdale, NJ: Erlbaum.

Corbett, A. T., Koedinger, K. R., & Hadley, W. H. (2001). Cognitive Tutors: From the research classroom to all classrooms. In Goodman, P. S. (Ed.), *Technology Enhanced Learning: Opportunities for Change*. Mahwah, NJ: Lawrence Erlbaum Associates.

Dimitrova, V., Self, J., & Brna, P. (2001). Applying Interactive Open Learner Models to Learning Technical Terminology. In M. Bauer, P. J. Gmytrasiewicz & J. Vassileva (Eds.), *User Modeling 2001: 8th International Conference*, (pp. 148-157). Springer-Verlag, Berlin Heidelberg.

Draney, K. L., Pirolli, P., & Wilson, M. (1995). A measurement model for a complex cognitive skill. In Nichols, P., Chipman, S., & Brennan, R. (Eds.), *Cognitively Diagnostic Assessment*. Hillsdale, NJ: Erlbaum.

Feng, M., & Beck, J. (2009). Back to the future: a non-automated method of constructing transfer models. In Barnes & Desmarais (Eds.), *Proceedings of the 2nd International Conference on Educational Data Mining*. Cordoba, Spain, 2009.

Feng, M., Beck, J., & Heffernan, N. (2009a) Using learning decomposition to analyze instructional effectiveness in the ASSISTment system. In *Proceedings of the 14th International Conference on Artificial Intelligence in Education (AIED-2009)*. Brighton, UK: IOS Press.

Feng, M., Beck, J., Heffernan, N., & Koedinger, K. (2008). Can an Intelligent Tutoring System Predict Math Proficiency as Well as a Standardized Test? In Beck & Baker (Eds.). In *Proceedings of the 1st International Conference on Education Data Mining*. Montreal, Quebec.

Feng, M., Beck, J., & Heffernan, N. T. (2009b). Using Learning Decomposition and Bootstrapping with Randomization to Compare the Impact of Different Educational Interventions on Learning. In Barnes, Desmarais, Romero, & Ventura (Eds.), *Proceedings of the 2nd International Conference on Educational Data Mining* (pp. 51-60). Cordoba, Spain: Copisterias Don Folio, S.L.

Feng, M., & Heffernan, N. (2007b). Towards Live Informing and Automatic Analyzing of Student Learning: Reporting in ASSISTment System. *Journal of Interactive Learning Research*, *18*(2), 207–230.

Feng, M., Heffernan, N., Beck, J., & Koedinger, K. (2008). Can we predict which groups of questions students will learn from? In Beck & Baker (Eds.), *Proceedings of the 1st International Conference on Education Data Mining*. Montreal, Quebec.

Feng, M, Heffernan, N., Heffernan, C. & Mani, M. (2009). Using mixed-effects modeling to analyze different grain-sized skill models. *IEEE Transactions on Learning Technologies*, retrieved from/doi.ieeecomputersociety.org/10.1109/TLT.2009.17.

Feng, M., & Heffernan, N. T. (2007a). *Assessing Students' Performance: Item Difficulty Parameter vs. Skill Learning Tracking*. Paper presented at the National Council on Educational Measurement, Chicago.

Feng, M., Heffernan, N. T., & Koedinger, K. R. (2006a). Addressing the testing challenge with a web based E-assessment system that tutors as it assesses. In *Proceedings of the 15th Annual World Wide Web Conference*. New York: ACM Press.

Feng, M., Heffernan, N. T., & Koedinger, K. R. (2006b). Predicting state test scores better with intelligent tutoring systems: developing metrics to measure assistance required. In Ikeda, Ashley & Chan (Eds.), *Proceedings of the Eighth International Conference on Intelligent Tutoring Systems,* (pp 31–40). Springer-Verlag: Berlin.

Feng, M., Heffernan, N. T., & Koedinger, K. R. (2009). Addressing the assessment challenge in an online system that tutors as it assesses. *User Modeling and User-Adapted Interaction: The Journal of Personalization Research (UMUAI journal), 19.*

Ferguson, K., Arroyo, I., Mahadevan, S., Woolf, B., & Barto, A. (2006). Improving Intelligent Tutoring Systems: Using Expectation Maximization to Learn Student Skill Levels. In Ikeda, Ashley & Chan (Eds.), *Proceedings of the Eight International Conference on Intelligent Tutoring Systems*, (pp.453-462). Berlin: Springer-Verlag.

Fitzmaurice, G., Laird, N., & Ware, J. (2004). *Applied Longitudinal Analysis.* Hoboken, New Jersey: Wiley & Sons.

Gierl, M. J., Wang, C., & Zhou, J. (2008). Using the attribute hierarchy method to make diagnostic inferences about examinees' cognitive skills in Algebra on the SAT. Journal of Technology, Learning, and Assessment, *6*(6). Retrieved May 2008, from www.jtla.org.

Grigorenko, E. L., & Sternberg, R. J. (1998). Dynamic testing. *Psychological Bulletin, 124,* 75–111. doi:10.1037/0033-2909.124.1.75

Heffernan, N. T., Turner, T. E., Lourenco, A. L. N., Macasek, M. A., Nuzzo-Jones, G., & Koedinger, K. R. (2006). The ASSISTment Builder: Towards an Analysis of Cost Effectiveness of ITS creation. Presented at FLAIRS2006, Florida.

Junker, B. W., & Sijtsma, K. (2001). Cognitive assessment models with few assumptions, and connections with nonparametric item response theory. *Applied Psychological Measurement, 25,* 258–272. doi:10.1177/01466210122032064

Kay, J. (1997). Learner Know Thyself: Student Models to Give Learner Control and Responsibility. In Z. Halim, T. Ottomann & Z. Razak (Eds.), *Proceedings of International Conference on Computers in Education* (pp. 17-24), Association for the Advancement of Computing in Education (AACE).

Koedinger, K. R., & Aleven, V. Heffernan. N. T., McLaren, B., & Hockenberry, M. (2004). Opening the Door to Non-Programmers: Authoring Intelligent Tutor Behavior by Demonstration. In *Proceedings of the 7th International Conference on Intelligent Tutoring Systems*, Maceio, Brazil.

Koedinger, K. R., Anderson, J. R., Hadley, W. H., & Mark, M. A. (1997). Intelligent tutoring goes to school in the big city. *International Journal of Artificial Intelligence in Education*, *8*, 30–43.

Koedinger, K. R., & Mathan, S. (2004). Distinguishing qualitatively different kinds of learning using log files and learning curves. In the Working Notes of the ITS2004 Workshop on Analyzing Student-Tutor Interaction Logs to Improve Educational Outcomes. Maceiò, Alagoas, Brazil.

McCalla, G. I., & Greer, J. E. (1994). Granularity- based reasoning and belief revision in student models. In Greer, J. E., & McCalla, G. I. (Eds.), *Student Modeling: The Key to Individualized Knowledge-Based Instruction* (pp. 39–62). Berlin: Springer-Verlag.

Means, B., Padilla, C., DeBarger, A., & Bakia, M. (2009). *Implementing Data-Informed Decision Making in Schools--Teacher Access, Supports and Use. Report prepared for U.* Menlo Park, CA: S. Department of Education, Office of Planning, Evaluation and Policy Development. Prepared by SRI International.

Mislevy, R. J. (1995). Probability-based reasoning in cognitive diagnosis. In Nichols, P., Chipman, S., & Brennan, R. (Eds.), *Cognitively Diagnostic Assessment*. Hillsdale, NJ: Erlbaum.

Mislevy, R. J., & Gitomer, D. H. (1996). The role of probability-based inference in an intelligent tutoring system. *User Modeling and User-Adapted Interaction*, *5*, 253–282. doi:10.1007/BF01126112

Mislevy, R. J., Steinberg, L. S., & Almond, R. G. (2003). On the structure of educational assessments. *Measurement: Interdisciplinary Research and Perspectives*, *1*, 3–67. doi:10.1207/S15366359MEA0101_02

Mitrovic, A., & Martin, B. (2002). Evaluating the Effects of Open Student Models on Learning. In P. De Bra, P. Brusilovsky & R. Conejo (Eds.), *Adaptive Hypermedia and Adaptive Web-Based Systems, Proceedings of Second International Conference*. Berlin Heidelberg, Germany: Springer-Verlag.

No Child Left Behind Act of 2001, Pub. L. No. 107-110, 115 Stat. 1425. (2002). *No Child Left Behind Act of 2001*. Retrieved September 6, 2005, from www.ed.gov/legislation/ESEA02/

Nuzzo-Jones, G., Walonoski, J. A., Heffernan, N. T., & Livak, T. (2005). *The eXtensible tutor architecture: A new foundation for ITS.* Presented at the Workshop on Adaptive Systems for Web-Based Education: Tools and Reusability held at the 12th Annual Conference on Artificial Intelligence in Education. Amsterdam, Netherlands.

Olson, L. (2005). Special report: testing takes off. *Education Week, November 30*, 10–14.

Pardos, Z., & Heffernan, N. (2009a). Detecting the Learning Value of Items in a Randomized Problem Set. In *Proceedings of the 14th International Conference on Artificial Intelligence in Education (AIED-2009).* IOS Press. Brighton, UK.

Pardos, Z., & Heffernan, N. T. (2009b). Determining the Significance of Item Order In Randomized Problem Sets. In *Proceedings of the Second International Conference on Educational Data Mining*. Cordoba, Spain.

Pardos, Z. A., Feng, M., Heffernan, N. T., & Heffernan, C. L. (2007). Analyzing Fine-Grained Skill Models Using Bayesian and Mixed Effect Methods. In Luckin & Koedinger (Eds.). In *Proceedings of the 13th Conference on Artificial Intelligence in Education*. pp. 626-628. Amsterdam, Netherlands: IOS Press

Pardos, Z. A., Heffernan, N. T., Anderson, B., & Heffernan, C. L. (2006). *Using Fine Grained Skill Models to Fit Student Performance with Bayesian Networks.* Workshop in Educational Data Mining held at the Eighth International Conference on Intelligent Tutoring Systems. Taiwan.

Patvarczki, J., Almeida, S., Beck, J., & Heffernan, N. T. (2008). Lessons Learned from Scaling Up a Web-Based Intelligent Tutoring System. In Woolf & Aimeur (Eds.), *Proceeding of the 9th International Conference on Intelligent Tutoring Systems.* Berlin, Germany: Springer-Verlag.

Patvarczki, J., Politz, J., & Heffernan, N. (2009). *Scalability and Robustness in the Domain of Web Based Tutoring. Scalability issues.* Presented at AIED Workshop at the 14th International Conference on Artificial Intelligence in Education. Brighton, UK.

Ramírez, E., & Clark, K. (2009, Feb/). *What Arne Duncan Thinks of No Child Left Behind: The new education secretary talks about the controversial law and financial aid forms.* Retrieved on March 8, 2009, from http://www.usnews.com/articles/education/2009/02/05/what-arne-duncan-thinks-of-no-child-left-behind.html

Rasch, G. (1960/1980). *Probabilistic models for some intelligence and attainment tests. (Copenhagen, Danish Institute for Educational Research), expanded edition (1980) with foreword and afterword by B. D. Wright.* Chicago: The University of Chicago Press.

Razzaq, L., Feng, M., Nuzzo-Jones, G., Heffernan, N. T., Koedinger, K. R., Junker, B., et al. Upalekar. R, Walonoski, J. A., Macasek. M. A., & Rasmussen, K. P. (2005). The Assistment Project: Blending Assessment and Assisting. In C.K. Looi, G.McCalla, B. Bredeweg, & J. Breuker (Eds.) *Proceedings of the 12th Artificial Intelligence In Education,* (pp 555–562). Amsterdam: ISO Press.

Razzaq, L., & Heffernan, N. T. (2006). Scaffolding vs. hints in the Assistment System. In Ikeda, Ashley & Chan (Eds.), *Proceedings of the 8th International Conference on Intelligent Tutoring Systems*, (pp. 635-644. Springer-Verlag: Berlin.

Razzaq, L., Heffernan, N. T., & Lindeman, R. W. (2007). What level of tutor interaction is best? In Luckin & Koedinger (Eds.), *Proceedings of the 13th Conference on Artificial Intelligence in Education*. Amsterdam: IOS Press.

Razzaq, L., Parvarczki, J., Almeida, S. F., Vartak, M., Feng, M., Heffernan, N. T., & Koedinger, K. (2009). *The ASSISTment builder: Supporting the Life-cycle of ITS Content Creation*. IEEE Transactions on Learning Technologies.

Renkl, A. (1997). Learning from worked-out examples: A study on individual differences. *Cognitive Science*, *21*, 1–29. doi:10.1207/s15516709cog2101_1

Ritter, S., & Koedinger, K. (1996). An architecture for plug-in tutor agents. *Journal of Artificial Intelligence in Education*, *7*(3-4), 315–347.

Rothman, S. (2001). *2001 MCAS Reporting Workshop: The second generation of MCAS results. Massachusetts Department of Education.* Retrieved November 2006, from www.doe.mass.edu/mcas/2001/news/reporting wkshp.pps

Russell, M., & Masters, J. (2009). *Formative Assessment Tools for Algebra and Geometry.* Presentation at Technology Supports for Formative Assessment Symposium of 2009 American Educational Research Association (AERA) Annual Meeting. San Diego, CA.

Sao Pedro, M., Gobert, J., Heffernan, N., & Beck, J. (2009). Comparing Pedagogical Approaches for Teaching the Control of Variables Strategy. In *Proceedings of the Cognitive Science Society Annual 2009 Conference*. Amsterdam.

Singer, J. D., & Willett, J. B. (2003). *Applied longitudinal data analysis: Modeling change and occurrence*. New York: Oxford University Press. doi:10.1093/acprof:oso/9780195152968.001.0001

Stiggins, R. (2005). From formative assessment to assessment FOR learning: A path to success in standards-based schools. *Phi Delta Kappan*, *87*(4), 324–328.

Tatsuoka, K. K. (1990). Toward an Integration of Item Response Theory and Cognitive Error Diagnosis. In Frederiksen, N., Glaser, R., Lesgold, A., & Shafto, M. G. (Eds.), *Diagnostic monitoring of skill and knowledge acquisition* (pp. 453–488). Hillsdale, NJ: Lawrence Erlbaum Associates.

Turner, T. E., Macasek, M. A., Nuzzo-Jones, G., & Heffernan, N. T. (2005). The ASSISTment Builder: A Rapid Development Tool for ITS. In *Proceedings of the 12th Annual Conference on Artificial Intelligence in Education.* (pp. 929-231). Amsterdam: IOS Press.

United States Department of Education. (2003). *Using data to influence classroom decisions*. Washington, DC. Retrieved November 2008, from http://www.ed.gov/teachers/nclbguide/datadriven.pdf van der Linden, W. J., & Hambleton, R. K. (Eds.) (1997). *Handbook of Modern Item Response Theory*. New York: Springer-Verlag.

VanLehn, K., Lynch, C., Schulze, K., Shapiro, J. A., Shelby, R., & Taylor, L. (2005). The Andes Physics Tutoring System: Lessons Learned. *International Journal of Artificial Intelligence in Education*, *15*(3), 1–47.

Walonoski, J., & Heffernan, N. T. (2006). Detection and Analysis of Off-Task Gaming Behavior in Intelligent Tutoring Systems. In Ikeda, Ashley & Chan (Eds.), *Proceedings of the 8th International Conference on Intelligent Tutoring Systems* (pp. 382-391). Springer-Verlag: Berlin.

Wiliam, D. (2006). Formative Assessment: Getting the focus right. *Educational Assessment*, *11*(3&4), 283–289. doi:10.1207/s15326977ea1103&4_7

Wongchokprasitti, C., & Brusilovsky, P. (2007). NewsMe: A Case Study for Adaptive News Systems with Open User Model. In *Proceedings of The Third International Conference on Autonomic and Autonomous Systems, ICAS*, IEEE Press.

Yun, J. T. Willet. J., & Murnane, R. (2004) *Accountability-Based Reforms and Instruction: Testing Curricular Alignment for Instruction Using the Massachusetts Comprehensive Assessment System.* Paper presented at the Annual American Educational Research Association Meeting. San Diego, California.

KEY TERMS AND DEFINITIONS

ASSISTment: A collaborative project among Worcester Polytechnic Institute, Carnegie Mellon University and local public schools. The website www.assistment.org provides free accounts to teachers and students. It allows students to practice math problems as well as getting tutoring from the computer tutor. It also informs teachers of their students' progress frequently online. The term "ASSISTment" was coined by Kenneth Koedinger from Carnegie Mellon University to blend assess**ment** and **assist**ing.

Cognitive Diagnostic Assessment: Usually designed to measure student's mastery states of specific knowledge and their cognitive processing skills in a given domain. It provides detailed information about strength and weakness of students' cognitive skills. Results from cognitive diagnostic assessment have great potential to inform instruction to help student learning.

Dynamic Assessment (or Dynamic Testing): A kind of interactive testing process. During dynamic assessment, students are provided with assistance when they are having difficulty with test items. The amount of help needed is then used to supplement accuracy data (wrong/right scores) for characterizing student proficiency. Dynamic assessment allows differentiating of student capability at intermediate level between unaided success or failure.

Formative Assessment: Different from summative assessment, formative assessment refers to the assessment items or tests that are administered to students along with instruction, instead of at the end of a period of instruction. Formative assessment differs from summative assessment on the information it seeks and how the information will be used as well. It aims at providing feedback for teachers and students to adapt the teaching/learning process in order to meet learners' need.

Longitudinal Modeling: Refers to the process of tracking learner's progress over a long period of time and then building a learning trajectory by applying statistical model approaches. The longitudinal models can then be used to analyze the trend of learning progress, predict later performance, to detect impact of certain factors on learning, etc.

Student Modeling: Refers to the process of constructing student models that contains description of students' knowledge, skills or behaviors based on their responses, which can then be used to predict their performance, errors, or learning time, etc. The process of student modeling is crucial for an intelligent learning environment to be able to adapt to the needs and knowledge of individual students

ENDNOTES

1 http://my.barackobama.com/page/community/post/amyhamblin/gGxW3n.

2 The term "ASSISTment" was coined by Kenneth Koedinger and blends Assess*ment* and *Assist*ing.

3 The ASSISTment project is funded by grants from the U.S. Department of Education, the National Science Foundation, and the Office of Naval Research.

4 All students in the tested grades who are educated with Massachusetts public funds MCAS tests are mandated to participate in MCAS. The Massachusetts Education Reform Law of 1993 requires that all students who are seeking to earn a high school diploma must earn certain scores on the MCAS English Language Arts (ELA) and Mathematics tests, in addition to meeting all local graduation requirements. http://www.doe.mass.edu/mcas/overview.html

5 In the United States, students enrolled in middle school are around ages from 11 to 14, and students in high schools are usually from the age of 14 or 15 to 17 or 18.

6 http://www.doe.mass.edu/mcas/2002/results/

7 This does ignore the time it takes authors to plan the ASSISTment, work with their subject-matter expert, and any time spent making images and animated gifs. All of this time can be substantial, so we cannot claim to have tracked all time associated with creating content.

8 There is controversy over whether same-day learning opportunities should be used as evidence of learning. For example, Beck (2006) thought repeated trials were not indicative of learning, but just retrievals from short-term memory.

9 Delayed feedback is similar to worked-out examples (Renkl, 1997) in that it shows the solution to a problem all at once. The difference is that students are administered problems first, but get no feedback until they complete a problem set. After finishing each problem, students will be told "we will give feedback at the end of the problem set."

10 A "multi-mapping" skill model, in contrast to a "single-mapping" model, allows one item to be tagged with more than one skill.

11 As the ASSISTment system is considered in multiple states and other jurisdictions, additional transfer models will be needed, that are aligned to those states' learning standards.

12 All items in the MCAS tests are tagged in all the four models before this analysis by our subject manner expert.

13 http://www.ed.gov/news/speeches/2009/06/06082009.html

14 http://teacherwiki.assistment.org/PIMSE_Schedule_2009-2010

15 http://nth.wpi.edu/MME562.htm

16 http://ies.ed.gov/director/conferences/09ies_conference/duncan_transcript.asp

Chapter 12
Using Effect Size for Group Modeling in E-Learning Systems

Divna Krpan
University of Split, Croatia

Suzana Tomaš
University of Split, Croatia

Roko Vladušić
University of Split, Croatia

ABSTRACT

There is great need for collaboration in education and e-learning systems which imply the necessity for group modeling. Since Bloom's experiment, which produced effect size of 2-sigma, there were many attempts to repeat those results with intelligent tutoring systems. Our experiments show effectiveness of xTEx-Sys in measure of effect size. The goal of our research and development is to get as close as possible to effect size of 2-sigma. There is greater need for collaboration in e-learning systems and there are some indications that collaboration could increase effectiveness. Since collaboration is closely coupled with groups, directions for future development and exploration of e-learning systems lay in field of group modeling. Group modeling also implies creation of stereotype models.

INTRODUCTION

There is a gap between knowledge and skills that students acquire in school and those required in business. To bridge that gap, additional learning is required. Development of industry and business imply lifelong learning and teaching process. Since traditional instruction is expensive and dependant on specific restraints, for example, time, place and location, it is necessary to search for easier solutions. E-learning could be the answer. With increasing availability of the Internet, high speed and bandwidth, and rapid development of computer technology, it is more convenient to deliver content to students at distance.

Some authors define e-learning as an interactive learning in which learning content is available online and provides automatic feedback to the student's learning activities, but online communication between participants (students and teachers, or between students) doesn't have to be included, so the main focus is on learning content (Paulsen, 2002).

DOI: 10.4018/978-1-61692-008-1.ch012

The e-learning includes different ways of delivering educational content: via Internet (LAN and WAN), audio and video tape, CD-ROM, interactive TV, satellite broadcasting. It covers applications and processes such as computer-based learning, virtual classrooms, Web-based learning and digital collaboration.

E-learning can be delivered in two ways: synchronously and asynchronously (IsoDynamic, 2006). Synchronous e-learning (Erudium, 2001) takes place in virtual classroom. It is based on a simultaneous access of instructors and all other participants to content, in real time; it may include Web-based videoconferencing, audio conferencing and online chat. In synchronous mode, e-learning has no space constraints, but time constraints are present because learning is done at precise appointments between instructors and students. Asynchronous e-learning may take place at any time, and is self paced, it refers to learning methods in which student and teacher interact with each other one at a time, in turn. Asynchronous e-learning is probably more interesting because of its lower cost of development and reusable components and it eliminates all time and location related constraints. In asynchronous e-learning teacher and student are not active or online at same time (examples of activities are: e-mail, forums, newsgroups, etc.) (Erudium, 2001).

Advances in Internet access speed and availability of personal computing platforms have increased opportunities for use of e-learning technologies (Collier, 2002). The technology infrastructure must support users and network and provide open environment to support interoperability between components, and also security to protect distributed users and content.

A special class of asynchronous e-learning systems are Intelligent Tutoring Systems (ITSs) that represent an advanced learning and teaching environment adaptable to individual student's characteristics (Stankov, et al., 2008). The ITSs are intended to emulate one teacher interacting with one student more directly (IsoDynamic, 2001). They model how a teacher would teach in the class and also keep track of student's performance (Jain, 2008). The intelligent tutoring system (ITS) can be defined as a learning technology that dynamically adapts learning content to needs and preferences of the student and learning (Erudium, 2001).

Rickel (1989) presents the following components of the ITS: (i) learning scenario, (ii) domain knowledge representation, (iii) student modeling, (iv) pedagogical knowledge, and (v) user interface. Those components are sometimes different, according to different authors. For example, Shute and Psotka (1995) point out that the ITS must have: (i) knowledge of the domain (expert model), (ii) knowledge of the learner (student model), and (iii) knowledge of the teaching strategies (tutor).

In 1982, Sleeman and Brown (1982) reviewed the state of the art in computer aided instruction and first coined the term Intelligent Tutoring System. They used the term student model for describing an abstract representation of the student or learner, within the computer program. Student modeling is the process of collecting and representing information about the student. Student learns from the ITS while solving problems tailored according to student abilities (previously recorded by the ITS in "student model"). System must behave intelligently or, more specifically, it must be able to accurately diagnose students' knowledge and skills, decide what to do next and adapt instruction (Shute & Psotka, 1995). Intelligence in the ITS is based on artificial intelligence (AI) techniques. The process of student modeling includes diagnosis of student's knowledge, but different ITSs use different student modeling techniques. Based on the input and structural properties of student model, it can be classified using three dimensions (VanLehn, 1998):

1. Bandwidth – represents categorization of the amount and quality of student's input or approximation of student's mental states while solving problem;

2. Target knowledge type – there are two common types of knowledge: procedural and declarative knowledge;
3. Differences between the student and expert– while learning, student should move from initial state to expert model which represents mastery of the domain knowledge, and it is important for diagnosis to check whether the goal is reached or not.

Student model may include different information, based on specific ITS, and there is no general agreement on that. It could include knowledge about domain, learning preferences, progress in the current course, goals, etc. The ITS makes diagnosis based on current state of the student model, and then adapts instruction accordingly.

There are different approaches to student modeling or process of collecting information about student's knowledge. Student modeling is conducted through observing student's behavior. During that process, a lot of information, that is useful for diagnosing individual student's knowledge, may be collected. While comparing individual students' knowledge, it is obvious that some students share common characteristics, for example learning style. If we group students based on those characteristics, then we could compare knowledge and progress of whole group to determine if one group of students learns better than the other and why. This leads us to discuss different type of problem which is called group modeling.

In the mid 1980's ITSs began to attract critical reactions (Du Boulay & Luckin, 2001). At the beginning, some of the critics were that the majority of ITS references are from computing literature and have limited range and adaptability when compared to human teachers. Bloom and others (Bloom, 1984) have presented evidence that individualized tutoring is more efficient than traditional classroom based instruction. The goal is to achieve two standard deviation improvements with tutoring over traditional instruction methods in classroom. That experiment was inspiration for further research because results were impressive. The intention was to reach that success with ITSs, or at least to get close.

Bloom's experiment in 1984 showed that there was two standard deviations difference, which is also called 2-sigma difference, between traditional instruction and tutoring instruction. The 2-sigma or two standard deviations difference is actually effect size of some experimental treatment. Effect size of two standard deviations in favor of experimental group, tells us that average student from experimental group was better than average student in control group for two standard deviations. That average student can be observed as representative of his group and that is also the reason why it is not unusual to say that experimental group outperformed control group. Since that experiment showed advantages of tutoring instruction, and after computers were emerged into learning and teaching process enriched with artificial intelligence, a vision of computerized tutor appeared. It is impossible to have human tutor for each student, but the ITS could be the solution for that problem.

Bloom's experiment was encouragement for our research and development in the area of ITSs. We have been intensively developing a web oriented authoring shell for building intelligent tutoring systems, called eXtended Tutor–Expert System (xTEx-Sys) (Stankov et al, 2008), trying to achieve the best results as possible, and also aiming for that magic 2-sigma difference. Our experiments on the xTEx-Sys show improvement over traditional instruction. Effect size and the way it is used for comparing group's performance, encouraged us to wonder if effect size could be used as adequate tool for group modeling.

The paper is organized as follows: the second section we will give a review of literature considering forms of group modeling related to existence of collaboration in a learning and teaching process; the third section briefly describes some experiments conducted on the xTEx-Sys and gives a short overview of measured results in a form of effect size; the fourth section presents conclusions and gives directions of our future research related to a group modeling as a approach of improving our system and get it closer to 2-sigma difference.

FROM STUDENT MODELING TO GROUP MODELING

E-learning systems are becoming more collaborative because more individuals need to work together on different tasks. Some types of e-leaning systems, like Intelligent Learning Management System (iLMS), may also provide unrestricted user interactions, including natural language communication, which is more difficult to track in student model, so it also requires modeling of groups (Yacef, 2003). Students and teachers are often geographically isolated and don't have face to face communication so there is obviously a growing need for more support in their online collaboration because they also form groups (Baghaei, 2007). Computer can be a powerful tool for improving students' achievements in combination with collaborative learning (McCullough, 2000).

Sometimes, collaboration and cooperation are used as synonyms, but there is a difference (Dillenbourg, 1999). In cooperation, members of group working on a same project split work and do their part individually and independently from others. Later they assemble everything together as final solution. On the other hand, in collaboration, group members must work together and interact with each other during whole project. Group members are usually at similar level of competence or abilities and can perform similar actions and have same goals. In this paper, we are going to focus on collaboration.

Nevertheless, since ITSs are one class of the e-learning systems, we should also consider social aspects and organizational settings into which they are embedded, without forgetting that the focus of the ITSs is on individual learning.

Collaborative Learning

Collaboration discussed here is specific because it concerns collaboration while learning. We can use widely accepted term collaborative learning. According to (Dillenbourg, 1999), researchers do not always agree about definition of collaborative learning, because the use is different in each academic field. The broadest definition is that collaborative learning is "a situation in which two or more people learn or attempt to learn something together." Some interaction between participants in that situation is expected, and it may trigger learning, but that is not certain. Peers also learn because they perform additional activities which are not common with individual students. According to Vygotsky all learning is social in nature which leads to group work (McCullough, 2000).

Collaborative learning could help in keeping students' interest and motivation and encourage students to work together, explain their actions and opinions, be more responsible for their learning, etc. In one to one tutoring, system interacts with one student and adapts instruction to his/her individual characteristics. Collaborative learning can be described as one to many learning environment where system must interact with group of students, and instruction is adapted accordingly.

Researchers should observe interactions that occur in collaborative learning more closely to understand its mechanisms and how they affect learning process. While discussing collaborative learning, we can't avoid term group because it is active entity in collaborative learning and should be observed as a whole. Teachers may have the need to monitor performance and progress of group of students with common characteristics, for example nationality, age range, class, etc. (Kosba, 2004). They can be informed of common problems that some group of students may encounter. That is also useful for future work with different group of students with same characteristics in order to predict their behavior, or to examine how problems may be connected with those common characteristics of specific group. Teachers in traditional classroom also use some common characteristics like misconceptions to start discussions with students. In collaborative learning, teachers can monitor and regulate interactions, setup initial conditions, specify scenario, etc. We could say that teacher facilitates interaction, and that is why teachers in collaborative learning are often named facilitators instead tutors.

Group Modeling Techniques

Student modeling is problem studied since 1970's, but group modeling is not that well researched (Winter, 2004). Review of literature shows that group modeling problem exists, and there are researches about it, some suggested techniques and systems which are described as being able to model groups, but actual group modeling techniques are not explained in detail.

There are two different approaches while observing problem of group modeling: (i) build group model from all individual models in that group and (ii) ignore individual attributes and monitors group behavior as entity and actions specific for collaboration and communication. The optimal approach for group modeling is probably something in between. Group modeling creates more problems that could be harder to master than with student modeling. For example, if we have a group which consists of one excellent programmer and two poor programmers, can we state that programming skills for that group are excellent, average or poor?

Probably the simplest way to implement the first approach is to compute averages of the corresponding data in individual student models and then compute grade averages for student groups and whole classes (for example in Moodle, www.moodle.org). Teachers in traditional classroom also calculate average grades for their class. Han (2001) in his thesis used that approach to build group model, and also suggested that data from existing group model can be used to initialize individual models of a similar new group of students. Initialization of student model or problem of "new student" is important issue. System developers must decide what their system should initially know about new student.

Initial data can be collected by using questionnaires and tests. Some researchers (Vasilyeva et al., 2007) suggested use of stereotype model which can be based on data from group of people with similar characteristics. According to Lock (2005), stereotype and group models are different, although stereotype is also considered as form of group model. In group model, student usually belongs to one group, but in stereotype model student may belong to multiple groups. Stereotype model is created from individual student models, and is used mostly for initialization of student models, and group actions are not considered. Stereotype model is useful if a quick assessment of user's background is required. That kind of assessment doesn't have to be accurate, which can also be used in learning environments for initial student models.

Kosba (2004) in his thesis uses fuzzy techniques along with certainty factor theory to build models of individual students, and group model is derived from aggregation of individual student models. Each domain concept is represented in student model with measures of belief and disbelief a student may have about concept. Initially those values are equal to zero which means that system does not know anything about student's understanding of that concept.

Group modeling is generalization of student modeling. Singley et al. (1999) attempted to model groups in Algebra Jam system by gathering information from student models about domain knowledge and their collaborative activities, and also overall group. Algebra Jam guides group of students through solving algebra word problems. Domain knowledge of each student is modeled with traditional tutoring system. Evidences about collaboration activities are observed through events triggered by student, and those events determine that student is taking one of five defined roles (Observer, Apprentice, Specialist, Leader, Coach), and then those evidences are used to update beliefs about knowledge states. Roles reflect different collaborative activities. For example, Coach will respond to help request, offer help, etc. If Student A asks for help about specific domain concept from Student B, then Student B is taking a role which is recognized as Coach. It is also observed that Student A does not know that domain concept and belief about student's knowledge is decreased. Singley et al. (2000) used Bayesian inference networks for inferences about student's knowledge states.

Generating group model from individual models is difficult process because there are characteristic factors that affect group performance (Winter, 2004). For example, group members have communication inside their group, task division and conflict resolution, but as individuals they do not have those issues. On the other hand, group is consisted of individuals and their individual abilities affect group performance as whole. Another problem is to decide whether to measure the whole process of group activity while working together or only outcome of that group activity which may disregard functioning of a group. Assessment of group performance based only on final result or outcome in real life settings (uncontrolled situations), is not appropriate, because there are many factors that may contribute to group's success, but they are not part of group's knowledge and skills. It is not possible to determine how much group members and their collaboration contributed to overall success. It is more complicated to observe process of group activity and there is no generally accepted formal theory that supports correlation of group behavior and group effectiveness. Specific group behavior may have different effect on group success in different situations.

Hoppe (1995) suggested three basic assumptions for group learning situations:

1. the complementary criterion – student with good knowledge encourages student with low knowledge;
2. the competitiveness criterion – two students with similar knowledge encourage each other to achieve better results through competition;
3. the problem-selection criterion – the group should solve problem that can't be solved by individual student in group.

Multiple individual student models can be analyzed and then used to combine students into some kind of peer groups. The intention is to trigger initial interactions between students in group. Those interactions can be the trigger for "pairing" students or determining potential collaborators, because while students learn or solve problems, at certain point they may encounter some difficulties and then ask for assistance. Instead of giving help or advice, information from individual student models is analyzed and then they are paired with peer helpers (Hoppe, 1995). Peer helpers are students which are members of that group and they can help others, based on criterions described above. Also, when group is given specific task, individuals can be grouped together based on analysis of their individual models. Group is able to complete specific task if each sub-task can be completed by one or more group members. Beliefs about student's knowledge or competence are extracted from individual student model. This approach may be good place to start, although it ignores some aspects of group interactions and it is based on questionable criterions which may be analyzed and refined through practical experiments. Hoppe has developed heuristics for translating the knowledge from individual models to group model. (Quignard & Baker, 1999) extend Hoppe's work by developing an algorithm to pair two group members with purpose of encouraging argumentation.

Another approach of using individual models, besides identification of collaborators, is providing specific support during collaboration (Jameson et al., 2003). For example, Jameson et al. (2003) suggested generative models of individual group members that should be able to interact with other members. Basic idea concerns with problems of asynchronous communication. While group members communicate synchronously (video conference), they can reach an agreement about some issue based on their beliefs. But, when some members are not present, there is a computational model of that member which contains his/her beliefs, preferences and other properties. Computational model could possess certain authority to make decision instead of group member.

From Paiva (1997), a group model is considered as "a way of capturing the aspects that identify a group as a whole" and it may include group beliefs, group actions, group goals, group misconceptions, differences between individuals and group conflicts. Researchers building group model must decide which characteristics from individual student models can be used for group modeling. On the other hand, there is a problem on how to use collaborative interactions to build student models. Usual student modeling techniques used for developing student models must be adapted to support collaborative situations. Students as members of group besides beliefs about domain concepts also have beliefs about other students and interactions. For example, if student doesn't participate in communication and has poor results, then the system can characterize him/her as "weak and uncommunicative student" and report that to the teacher (Kosba, 2004). Same conclusions can be drawn for group of students. Communication is important characteristic for collaborative learning. Diagnostic capabilities used for student modeling, may be adapted for group modeling and are less problematic because human intervention may correct wrong assumptions.

There has been some research what factors make groups successful in order to determine what should be incorporated in group model (Winter & McCalla, 2003). Those factors are more significant if group members are working together on specific project or task. The four factors are:

1. Functional knowledge and skills – knowledge and skills required by each individual for specific task;
2. Teamwork skills and social intelligence – skills that are required for efficient collaboration with other group members, based on roles that each member might have (for example, coordinator, implementer, etc.);
3. Task type – task should be selected in the way that individual members must work together and can not solve it alone;
4. Context and situation – contextual factors are about project deadlines and availability of resources for the project, and situational factors include physical location, availability of group members, student workload and use of educational resources.

Last factor is more difficult to observe because it involves a lot of information that is not closely related to the group and specific project.

There are also other approaches for group modeling, based on Psychological theories (Tedesco & & Rosatelli, 2004). It is difficult to translate psychological models into information that can be processed by the computer. There are some AI techniques used for that purpose:

- Logic – Logic-based student models consist of the set of beliefs. The most common representations of student model are: propositional calculus, first order predicate calculus, and other specific formalisms like semantic networks and frames. It is important to note that complex logic-based models are hard to maintain and not very efficient.
- Machine learning – Machine learning techniques are used in applications that encompass large domains which are difficult to specify. These techniques don't require complicated domain knowledge acquisition processes commonly used for making predictions about students. Data about

the user behavior generate a set of training examples. System uses those examples to predict student's future actions. However, direct application of machine learning techniques is difficult because student's model characteristics (large data sets, computational complexity…).

- Plan recognition – It is important for student modeling to determine student's future plans and objectives. At the start of plan inference process there is a set of objectives which might be pursued by an agent. Agent's actions are then observed in order to determine how those actions contribute to specific objectives. All changes in plan recognition process produce multiple hypotheses about agent's plan. There is a great deal of uncertainty in plans inference. We already mentioned Bayesian networks which are commonly used as a solution for that problem if enough data can be collected. But, plan recognition is also difficult to apply especially in ITSs because new student is also unqualified in domain and makes unknown errors.
- Uncertainty and probabilistic reasoning – When there is incomplete information available, there is a problem of dealing with uncertainty. Machine learning and reasoning under uncertainty form predictive statistical models (e.g., Decision Trees, Neural Networks, Markov Models, Bayesian Networks …)

In order to choose the adequate AI technique it is important to consider different factors, such as: purpose of the system, system architecture, mode of interaction, goals of collaboration and resources.

Tedesco & Rosatelli (2004) recommend hybrid student and group model. In Web-based systems there is huge amount of available data appropriate for machine learning and uncertainty and probabilistic reasoning. Those techniques may be combined with logic-based models.

EXPERIMENTAL RESEARCH

The significance of collaboration in e-learning systems was described in previous section. The existence of collaboration among students implies that those students cannot longer be observed as individuals, but rather as a group of individuals. Therefore, we have to take into consideration social aspects of ITSs and define an approach to group modeling that bases itself on the effectiveness of a group of the individuals.

In this section we are going to describe experiments conducted with students in elementary and secondary school and university, in order to reveal the effectiveness of the xTEx-Sys system. Future research and development will be focused on checking whether or not effect sizes can be used for group modeling in ITSs. In this paper we present preliminary research which might clarify group modeling approaches in ITSs.

Effect size gives us information about size of experimental effect. Effect size is positive when experimental group performs better then control group in experiment, and it is negative when control group is better. Effect size in our experiments is measured as the standardized difference between two means.

If the results of students' achievements are distributed normally, then they can be represented graphically in the form of Gauss curve or normal curve. Sometimes that curve is called bell because of its shape. At the peak of curve there is mean of all results. In normal distribution, results are grouped around mean. Shape is determined by standard deviation of the results and mean.

For example, if we try to represent graphically two groups of results that differ for two standard deviations (Bloom's experiment (Bloom, 1984)), then we would have two curves as shown in Figure 1. Effect size is represented as distance between means in units of standard deviation. In this example, curve for experimental group is more on the right side or shifted into positive direction of the axis, when compared to control group. It is possible to interpret results graphically in such way, because it is obvious which group performed better, but it is not obvious if that difference is statistically significant or not.

All experiments described in this paper were conducted in order to evaluate the same environment: eXtended Tutor–Expert System (xTEx-Sys) – a web oriented authoring shell for building intelligent tutoring systems. The first implementation of that system was on site version Tex-Sys which enabled learning and teaching for students and teachers. Teachers were able to develop learning content, and also test and evaluate students' knowledge. On site version was followed by Distributed Tutor–Expert System (DTEx-Sys) which was based on dynamic Web documents. Finally, xTEx-Sys, which is based on Web services, was developed (from 2003. to 2005.) (Stankov et al, 2008). Web services facilitate communication and cooperation between different Web oriented learning systems. Web oriented intelligent authoring shell xTEx-Sys is environment adapted for experts, teachers and students. Experts develop domain knowledge bases, teachers prepare courses for students from available domain knowledge, and students learn individually. Knowledge is represented in form of semantic networks. Teacher makes hierarchical organization of domain knowledge into units, lessons, topics and instructional items, and also quizzes for knowledge evaluation (Božičević & Stankov, 2006).

Introducing computers in education enables solving of different kind of problems for students, and accomplishment of educational objectives for teachers (Mužić & Rodek, 1987). Considering that, we conducted experiments in elementary school, secondary school and university. In those experiments we used different domain knowledge: Nature and society, Chemistry, Computer architecture and Introduction to computer science. Summary of experimental components is shown in Table 1. After each experiment, results will be presented graphically with Gauss curve.

Experimental research is very common in psychology and education (Mark & Greer, 1993). There are different experimental designs that can be used to evaluate educational influence of an e-learning system. All experiments described here are based on pre-and-post test control group experimental design with surveys before and after

Figure 1. Graphical representation of 2-sigma difference

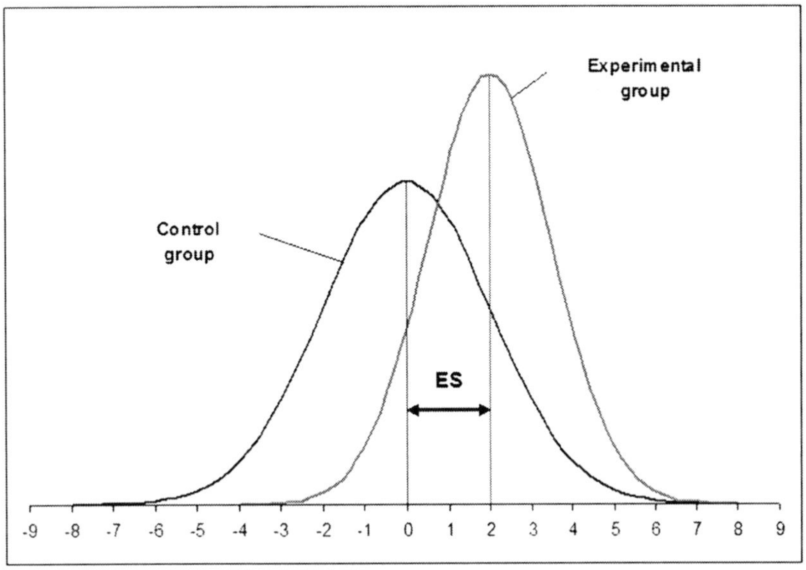

Table 1. Experimental components

	Elementary school	Elementary school	Secondary school	University
Sample Population	136 students: • 48 students, 2nd grade (age: 8) • 48 students, 3rd grade (age: 9) • 40 students, 4th grade (age: 10)	89 students: • 48 students, 7th grade (age: 13) • 41 students, 8th grade (age: 14)	60 students: • 1st grade (age: 15-16)	80 students: • 2nd academic year (age: 19-20)
Time And Location	• school "Spinut", Split (2005/06) • 6 weeks	• school "oca Petra Perice", Makarska (2005/06) • 10 weeks	• III Gymnasium, Split (2006/07) • 3 weeks	• Faculty of Natural Sciences, Mathematics and Kinesiology (2005/06) • 14 weeks
Goal	What is the educational influence of an e-learning system on students?			
Research Instruments	• survey • pre-test • post test	• initial survey • abilities tests • pre-test • post-test • final survey	• survey • pre-test • post test	• pre-test • post-test
Domain Knowledge	Nature and society	Chemistry	Computer architecture	Introduction to computer science
Experimental Factor	xTEx-Sys			

experimental treatment. Experimental group was exposed to independent variable (treatment), and control group was not. Independent variable or experimental factor in all experiment was xTEx-Sys. Students were tested before and after the intervention, so the influence of independent variable could be examined based on difference in results of control and experimental group (Milas, 2005). Effect size is used to determine the size of experimental effect.

However, each experiment is specific and in next section we are going to describe them separately.

Experiment: Elementary School 1

This research was conducted in elementary school "Spinut" in Split (Croatia) with purpose of determining if xTEx-Sys could be used as an adequate support for teacher in nature and society course in the 2nd, 3rd and 4th elementary school grade (Tomaš, 2007). It included: initial tests with Task Objective Items (TOI) (Gronlund, 1985), learning and teaching in each grade and the final survey which was conducted on randomly selected sample of students. The control and experimental groups were equalized on the basis of data collected through survey and applied TOI test (TOI-1, or pre-test). The control group learned with traditional type of instruction, and experimental group learned with the support of xTEx-Sys. Finally, students were tested with second TOI test (TOI-2, or post test).

Results of surveys were a good foundation and encouragement for conducting the experiment. Based on survey responses, we made the following conclusions:

- Students grow up surrounded with modern information and communication technologies. Computers have important impact on students, regardless if they are used with or without Internet connection. Intense development of computer technology offers many educational programs and wide range of nonviolent, creative and educational computer games, and all that makes the use of computers in education inevitable.

- Providing guidelines for self-learning to students when they are very young, with constant supervision of parents and teachers, offers different opportunities for their future professions. Students, although most of them use computer for playing games (33%), think that computer helps them while learning at school (40%) and at home (47%).
- Information and communication technologies have significant influence on the observed sample of students in this study, because 80% of them have a computer at home.

The standardized mean difference is calculated by dividing the difference between the experimental and the control group means of gains (TOI-1, TOI-2) by the standard deviation of the control group. The analysis of the results of Task Objective Items (TOI-1 and TOI-2) for students of second, third and fourth grade, showed statistically significant differences in acquired knowledge between control and experimental groups. Accepted level of significance is $p = 0.05$. Based on results and p-value, we rejected all null hypotheses:

- H1: "There is no statistically significant difference in the effectiveness of learning and teaching contents of Nature and society between the control and experimental groups in the other Class section."
- H2: "There is no statistically significant difference in the effectiveness of learning and teaching contents of Nature and society between the control and experimental groups in the Third Class section."
- H3: "There is no statistically significant difference in the effectiveness of learning and teaching contents of Nature and society between the control and experimental groups in the fourth Class section."

We accepted following conclusion: "learning and teaching of students in the second, third and fourth grade of elementary school with the aid of intelligent tutoring system contributes to acquiring more knowledge from Nature and society than traditional instruction."

We calculated effect size for each grade. Students in experimental group for 3rd grade showed the largest improvement with effect size of 1,47 σ. Effect size for 2nd grade was 0,97 σ, and for 4th grade 1,11 σ. Students in all experimental groups accepted learning and teaching with computers and accessed all modules of xTEx-Sys. Graphical representation of difference between experimental and control group for 2nd, 3rd and 4th grade is shown on Figure 2.

Experiment: Elementary School 2

This research was conducted in elementary school "oca Petra Perice" in Makarska (Croatia) with purpose of determining if xTEx-Sys could be used as an adequate support for teacher in traditional teaching of chemistry course in 7th and 8th elementary school grades (Vladušić, 2006). It was important to determine if the xTEx-Sys is efficient in learning and teaching of basic chemistry concepts and in what extent the students are content with that strategy of learning, and also to find out if their motivation and interest in chemistry had increased.

Based on our goal, we stated a hypothesis: Learning and teaching of Chemistry with the aid of "computerized teacher" contributes to knowledge acquisition more than traditional instruction, it contributes to motivation increase and results in overall content. Because this hypothesis consists of three parts, it was divided into three null-hypotheses (for each grade separately):

- H1: "There is no difference in achievement between Control and Experimental group."
- H2: "There is no difference in content between learning and teaching in xTEx-Sys and traditional learning and teaching."

Figure 2. Graphical representation of difference between experimental and control group (Elementary school)

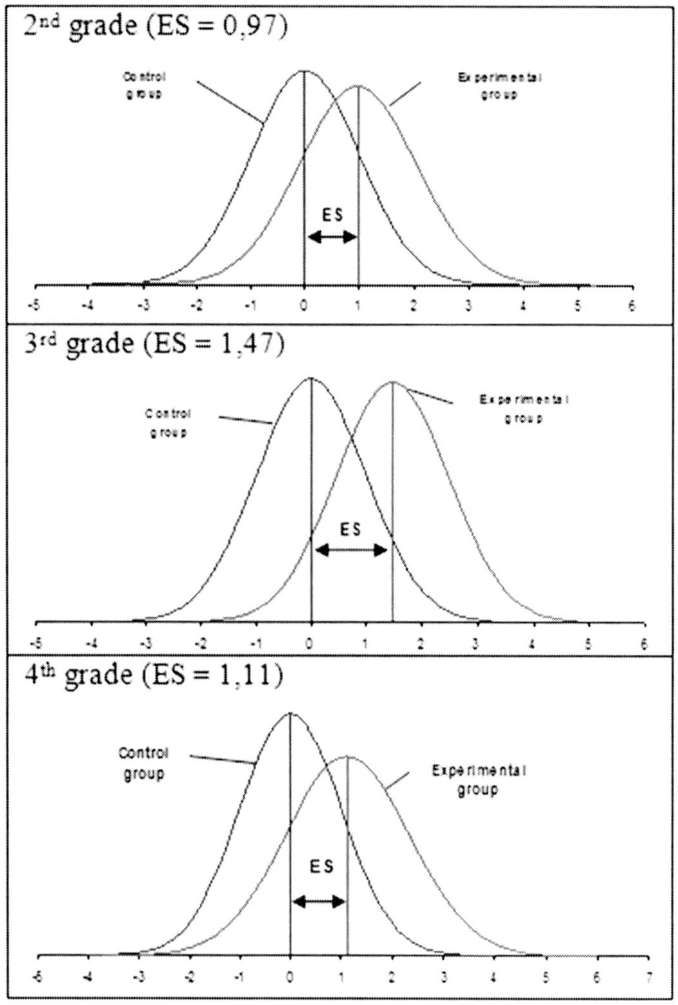

- H3: "Learning Chemistry in xTEx-Sys does not increase interest for that subject."

Psychologist conducted abilities test with purpose of equalization of groups. Based on results, students were divided into two experimental and two control groups (one experimental and one control group for each grade). Students in experimental group learned in computer lab with aid of intelligent tutoring system xTEx-Sys and students in control group had traditional instruction.

There were two surveys for 7th grade and two for 8th grade. First survey was conducted for all students before introducing experimental factors, and other only for experimental group after experiment was finished. After introducing experimental factor, all students (experimental and control group) had regular checkpoint tests using Task Objective Items (TOI): TOI-2, TOI-3, TOI-4 and finally TOI-5 (post test). Students in experimental group were also tested on computer while using the xTEx-Sys.

Effect size calculated from results of control and experimental groups in 7th grade is: 0.36 σ (sigma) and that is approximately close to the value of 0.32 σ observed by Kulik (1994) in meta-analysis based on 97 studies of computer aided learning. If we compare that effect size with Fletcher's (2003) results, then we can conclude that our effect size is far from his 1.05 σ, achieved in recent ITS, but it is close to the results of learning in simple user interface (0.39 σ). Students in control and experimental group achieved relatively good results, but the difference was not statistically significant and we accept null-hypothesis H1.

Effect size calculated from results of control and experimental groups in 8th grade is: 0.70 σ (sigma) which is much closer to Fletcher's result of 1.05 σ. Since experimental group achieved better results which are statistically significant, we reject null-hypothesis H1 for 8th grade.

Based on survey responses, we concluded that majority of students in 7th and 8th grade (91.67% and 88%) consider learning of chemistry with xTEx-Sys more interesting than traditional instruction, and they would like to continue learning chemistry in that environment. 75% of students in 7th grade and 64% students in 8th grade had increase of interest for learning chemistry. Based on results of control and experimental group, null-hypotheses H2 and H3 were rejected for both grades. Graphical representations and comparison of the results for control and experimental group in 7th and 8th grade are shown on Figure 3.

Experiment: Secondary School

This research was conducted in secondary school "III Gymnasium" in Split (Croatia) with purpose of determining if xTEx-Sys could be used as an adequate support for teacher in traditional teaching of computer architecture course in 1st secondary school grade.

Figure 3. Graphical representation of difference between experimental and control group (Elementary school)

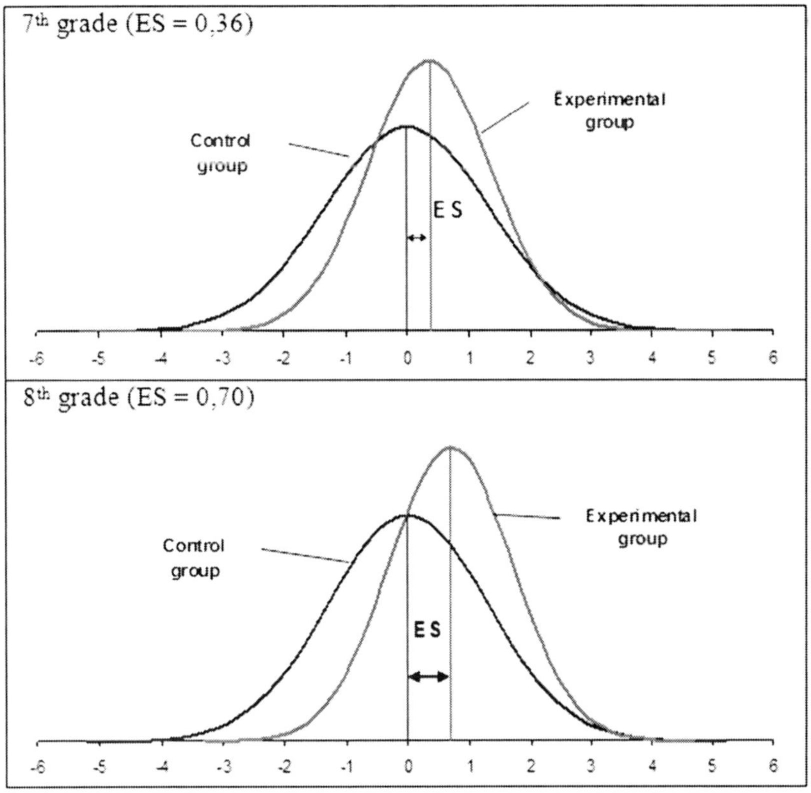

First, all students had to take pre-test which was announced but students were not informed about domain knowledge. Based on results of pre-test, they were divided into two groups: control and experimental with equal number of 30 students. Control group learned in traditional manner, and experimental group used the xTEx-Sys. Students also took initial survey in order to determine their skills in using computers and Internet. All students had to take final test (post-test) and also final survey. After final survey was analyzed, it was determined how many students used the xTEx-Sys at home and for how long, in what extent they understood subject matter they learned, etc.

Results were analyzed by system EVEDIN (EValuation of EDucational INfluence) (Grubišić, 2006). In order to determine difference between groups, t-test was used and t-value for pre-test was -0.35. As calculated by EVEDIN, groups were statistically equivalent (there was no statistically significant difference between groups).

Null-hypothesis was stated: "There is no statistically significant difference between Experimental and Control group with the results of final test." T-value was 0.28, and null-hypothesis was accepted, which means that difference was not statistically significant.

Analysis of results of final test shows that control group is better than experimental, but results are not statistically significant. Effect size in this experiment is negative -0.04σ.

After analyzing surveys, we can make conclusion that students are open for new technologies, but also very critic, and they generally accepted the xTEx-Sys very well. We can also observe graphical representation of the results in Figure 4. Control group performed better then experimental group and effect size was negative.

Experiment: University

This research was conducted with first year students at the University of Split (Croatia) with purpose of determining if xTEx-Sys could be an adequate support for teacher in traditional teaching introduction to computer science course (Grubišić, 2006).

At the beginning of the experiment, students which participated in experiment had to take 45-minute pre-test to determine starting level of their knowledge. It is important to establish the existence of statistically significant differences between the groups. Based on the results of pre-test, students were divided into two groups: control and experimental (equalization of groups). As in previous experiments, control group was involved in traditional learning and teaching process, and experimental used the xTEx-Sys. Both groups had to take final tests.

Figure 4. Graphical representation of difference between experimental and control group (Secondary school)

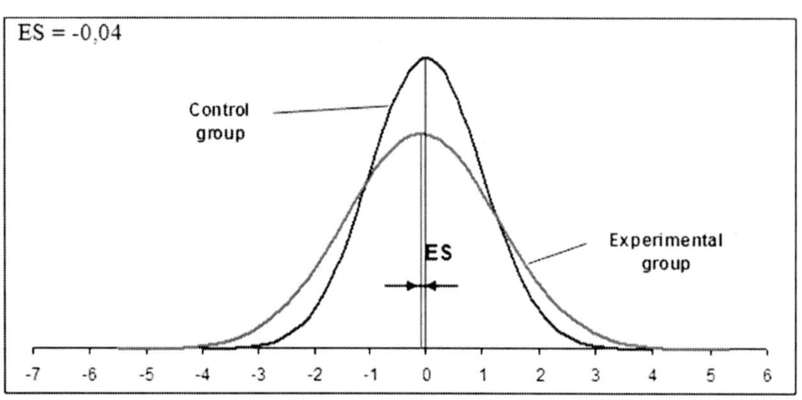

Null-hypothesis is: "There is no significant difference between the Control and the Experimental group." Then, the means of gains for both groups were calculated, and also t-values to determine if there is statistically significant difference between two groups.

Analysis of results was conducted with system EVEDIN. Effect size for post-test was 0.81σ. Difference between control and experimental group for experiment conducted in university is shown on Figure 5.

Data Analysis and Interpretation

Means and standard deviations for all experiments are presented in Table 2. There is a graph in Figure 6. which summarizes all effect sizes for previously described experiments.

Students in experimental group in third grade of elementary school achieved the best results. These students participated in a similar experiment in the school year 2004/2005 (Tomaš, 2005), a year before this experiment. Because of that, the experimental group had advantage of previous experience with ITSs and they could focus more on learning content and not the environment.

There are more ways for interpretation of effect size in one experiment. Cohen (Cohen, 1969) considered the effect size value of 0.2 σ as small, the effect size of 0.5 σ is considered to be moderate, and the effect size of 0.8 σ is considered to be large. Respecting Cohen's interpretation of effect size, in this experiment we concluded that effect size for experimental group is large. While analyzing responses from final survey, we observed that students participating in the experiment accepted

Figure 5. Graphical representation of difference between experimental and control group (University)

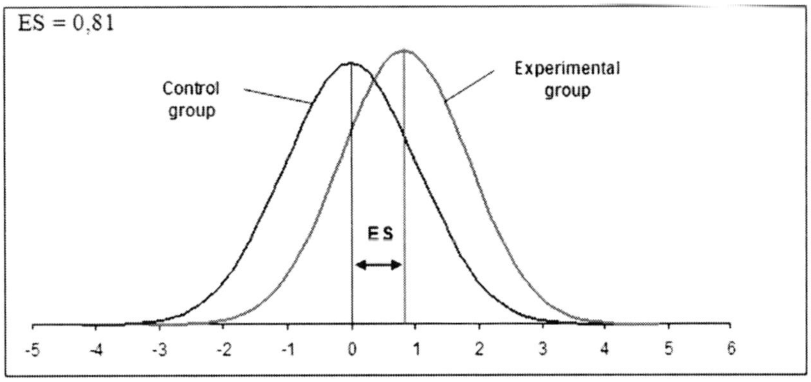

Table 2. Means and standard deviations for all experiments

Grade	Age	Mean		Standard deviation	
		Control	Experimental	Control	Experimental
2nd	8	2,29	3,71	1,78	1,92
3rd	9	2,81	4,31	1,80	1,82
4th	10	3,25	5,45	1,97	2,39
7th	13	23,48	25,70	7,00	5,28
8th	14	26,24	30,94	7,61	5,86
1st	15/16	31,86	30,90	11,13	15,03
2nd ac. year	19/20	-12,53	-1,09	14,32	13,66

Figure 6. Effect sizes for all experiments

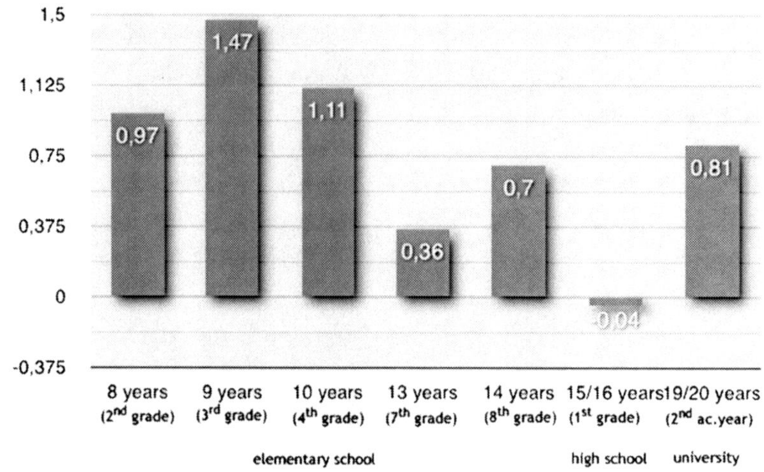

this method of instruction very well. Students were learning in positive atmosphere, didn't even object taking tests after school hours.

There are several reasons that might have influenced on effect size in 7th and 8th elementary school grades:

- Students in each class were divided in two groups, so the number of those learning chemistry in traditional manner was cut in half. In that situation, with only half of students (about 12), it is easier to have more individual approach and to achieve educational objectives.
- Because there was only one computer lab in school, students in experimental group had to attend chemistry classes out of their usual schedule, and that was early in the morning, before first class and sometimes late in the afternoon when they are more tired. That probably influenced the results, because it was observed that students are more ready for work during second and third class in the morning.
- It was assumed that students in experimental group are able to use computers and its resources as well as they use their textbooks. After analysis of survey responses related to computer skills, 40% of students in 7th grade stated that their skills are excellent, 50% good, and 10% superficial, which implies that significant number of students had to learn how to use computer instead of learning chemistry.
- Because of all previously described limitations of equipment and skills, students in experimental group were introduced to the xTEx-Sys shortly before testing, and they have never used it before. In that relatively short time period they had to understand concept of semantic network and special rules of formal language used in xTEx-Sys. Also, xTEx-Sys is web oriented, which requires Internet connection, but connection speed was also limited. That made learning more difficult and slower. Students were losing their patience and getting restless while content was slowly loading.
- Population sample was relatively small. T-test is affected by the sample size. We calculated that increase of population sample on 122 students would be enough for statistical proof of independent variable effect.

Experiment conducted in secondary school showed opposite results then other experiments described in this paper, because students in control group achieved better results, but statistical analysis showed that difference was not statistically significant. Analysis of the survey responses showed that only 20% of students used Internet for learning. When students had to evaluate their computer skills, 28% of students considered that their skills were excellent, 53% considered them good, and 18% poor. Only 18% of students considered computer science as simple and easy, 55% of students considered it as medium difficult, and 27% of students think that it is very complex and difficult. Most of the students stated that they also had problems with formal knowledge representation in xTEx-Sys.

In previously described experiments which were conducted in elementary school, students learned topics in computer lab which are not related to computer science. Learning content in unusual environment made that content more interesting and different. They usually use computer labs only for computer science related courses.

Instructional strategies based on learning and teaching supported by ITS offer new possibilities for organization of educational process. There is a change in the approach to learning process and also the teacher's role. Student-centered learning is focusing on the needs, abilities, interests, and learning styles of the students. Teacher is facilitator of learning. Work with the xTEx-Sys is based on constructivist principles of learning and teaching. Students individually explore domain knowledge and discover correlation with previously acquired concepts. Use of systems like xTEx-Sys, with well designed knowledge bases brings positive results for students in learning and teaching process.

Although there are some similarities or common characteristics between all experiments, generally, their results are completely different. Younger students, especially in elementary school seem to be more interested and open for new methods of learning and consider them as a challenge instead an obstacle. Is it because of their age (which is one of their common characteristics), subject matter, or something else? Well, we can not speculate, but based on previous literature review about groups and group modeling, we can conclude it is worth of further discussion and also planning of future directions for our research.

CONCLUSION

While researching and developing the e-learning systems, at a certain point, researchers attempt to evaluate or measure effect of their systems, as described in previous section. There are many experiments on xTEx-Sys which show good results, but since we still haven't reached goal of 2-sigma, further work is necessary.

In order to measure and enable comparison of the effect of some intervention or treatment on student achievement, a standardized measure is introduced: effect size (WWC, 2002). It represents the change in an average student's outcome which can be expected with given treatment or intervention. Effect sizes can be compared across studies because they are standardized. Effect size tells us how much the average student from one group is better than average student from the other group. Average student may be considered as representative for his group. Based on average student's belonging to specific group, a stereotype user may be created. When new student attempts to access the system, there is a problem, because system knows nothing about him. There is similar situation when we are being introduced to new person or coworker. It takes time to get acquainted with that person, and sometimes it would be a lot easier if we had more information ahead. New student could be identified as a member of existing group with specific characteristics which are contained in stereotype model, and system would adapt learning and teaching process accordingly.

There is a growing need for collaboration among online users and especially students which are in the focus of our interest. Effects of collaborative learning must be assessed. That is usually performed through assessment of individual performance, but there are group specific interactions which don't occur if students work independently and do not collaborate. While evaluating group performance, it can be verified if performance of specific group increased, or maybe group members have some useful ability that could be reused in other groups. Individuals are pool drawn for experiments, so if researchers aim to examine reasons why one group is more or less successful then the other, they sometimes focus on collaboration of individuals or teamwork skills. However, both individual knowledge and skills must be considered. Group cannot be successful if group members do not possess necessary knowledge and skills to perform joint projects. While students work in team on project, some of them may lag because there are always some hard-working students that may do all work. If that is the case, then individual student model should also be updated considering student's performance as a group member. Automatic assessment of individual student performance in group settings is limited because doing plan recognition for groups of human students may be very complex. The challenge of adapting the system to the group is an open research question in group modeling (Tedesco & Rosatelli, 2004). When a student behaves in a similar way to other students, he can then be assigned to that group, and data from such group of students can be used for predictions about other individual students in order to determine where they belong. Similar idea is also used in online shopping when web site makes suggestions for the buyer with the list of additional products. It is based on data analysis of previous buyers' preferences.

Development of the e-learning systems with support for natural language dialog offers possibilities to give advices tailored not only to individual students, but also to whole group. One of the aspects that make tutoring more efficient is the fact that tutor offers enough interactions and feedback to keep student busy, but not confused or frustrated.

According to Lane (2006) there are several traditional areas of research for ITSs: (i) student or learner modeling, (ii) authoring systems, (iii) group, collaborative and online learning and (iv) natural language dialog.

Some benefits of collaborative learning were expected but not reached, for example: increase of motivation and participation. There are also low communication rates. It is important to focus on peer tutoring and intelligent pairing of students and also group members.

Considering all previously discussed issues, we suggest some directions for future development:

- Exploring collaborative aspects of learning in e-learning systems in general.
- Determining how to design individual student model in order to reflect group interactions.
- Determining and applying group modeling techniques for extraction group model from individual student models.
- Researching student's characteristics with purpose of designing stereotype student model by using measure of effect size.

Review of the experiments shows our experience with research methodology and effect of our ITS with students of different age and domain knowledge. Since at present time our system does not support extensive collaboration one of our future directions is also developing support for collaboration and group modeling. Literature review shows that group modeling is still uncharted territory with many opportunities for research and future development.

Finally, after describing the significance of collaboration in e-learning systems and different approaches to group modeling, we draw important conclusions. We are observing students as group of individuals who work together and collaborate, therefore must consider social aspects of ITSs, as well as, individual characteristics of group members. Effect size, as measure of effectiveness, will help us to determine the differences between groups, and to observe common individual characteristics of group members that will help us to find out which of them improve students' learning and teaching process.

REFERENCES

Baghaei, N. (2007). *A collaborative constraint-based intelligent system for learning object-oriented analysis and design using UML.* (Unpublished Ph.D. Thesis) (Partial fulfilment), Canterbury, UK: University of Canterbury.

Bloom, B. S. (1984). The 2 Sigma Problem: The Search for Methods of Group Instruction as Effective as One-to-One Tutoring. *Educational Researcher*, *13*, 4–16.

Božičević, J., & Stankov, S. (2006). Continuous Innovation And Evolution Of The Intelligent Tutoring System TEx-Sys. In *Proceedings of the 1st International Conference 2006 - Future Challenges and Current Issues in Business Information, Organization and Process Management.* (pp. 191-197), London, United Kingdom: Center for Business Information, Organization and Process Management, Westminster Business School.

Cohen, J. (1969). *Statistical Power Analysis for the Behavioral Sciences*. New York: Academic Press.

Collier, G. (2002). e-Learning Application Infrastructure. *SUN Microsystems White Paper*.

Dillenbourg, P. (1999). What do you mean by collaborative learning? In Dillenbourg, P. (Ed.), *Collaborative-learning: Cognitive and Computational Approaches* (pp. 1–19). Oxford: Elsevier.

Du Boulay, B., & Luckin, R. (2001). Modelling Human Teaching Tactics and Strategies for Tutoring Systems. *International Journal of Artificial Intelligence in Education*, *12*, 235–256.

Erudium. (2001). *Erudium online glossary*. Retrieved February 20, 2009, from http://www.erudium.polymtl.ca/html-eng/home.php

Fletcher, J. D. (2003). Evidence for learning From Technology-Assisted Instruction. In O'Neil, H. F., & Perez, R. S. (Eds.), *Technology Application in Education – A learning View*. Mahwab, NJ: Lawrence Erlbaum Ass. Publishers.

Gronlund, N. E. (1985). *Measurement and Evaluation in Teaching* (5 ed.). New York: Macmillan Publishing Company.

Grubišić, A. (2007). *Evaluating Educational Influence of Intelligent E-learning Systems.* (Unpublished MS Thesis), Zagreb, Croatia: Faculty of Electrical Engineering and Computing(in Croatian).

Grubišić, A., Stankov, S., & Žitko, B. (2006). An Approach to Automatic Evaluation of Educational Influence. In *Proceedings of the 6th WSEAS International Conference on DISTANCE LEARNING and WEB ENGINEERING (DIWEB '06)*, (pp. 20-25), Lisbon, Portugal.

Han, B. (2001). *Student modelling and adaptivity in web based learning systems.* (Unpublished Masters Thesis), New Zealand: Massey University.

Hoppe, U. (1995). The Use of Multiple Student Modeling to Parameterize Group Learning. In J. Greer (Ed.), *Proceedings of AI-ED '95, 7th World Conference on Artificial Intelligence in Education*, (pp. 234-249), Washington, DC: AACE.

IsoDynamic. (2001). *E-Learning - A White Paper from IsoDynamic*. Retrieved February 16, 2009, from http://www.isodynamic.com/web/pdf/IsoDynamic_elearning_white_paper.pdf

IsoDynamic. (2006). *What is E-Learning?* Retrieved February 20, 2009, from http://www.isodynamic.com/web/e_learn.htm

Jain, M. (2008). *Generalized Knowledge Representation Architecture for Intelligent Tutoring System.* (Unpublished MS Thesis), Kharagpur, India: Indian Institute of Technology, Jameson, A., Baldes, S., & Kleinbauer, T. (2003). Generative Models of Group Members as Support for Group Collaboration. In *UM'03 9th International Conference on User Modeling*, (pp. 1-14), Johnstown, PA.

Kosba, E. M. A. M. (2004). *Generating Computer-Based Advice In Web-Based Distance Education Environments.* (Unpublished Ph.D. Thesis), Leeds, UK: University of Leeds

Kulik, J. A. (1994). Meta-Analytic studies of findings on computer-based instruction. In Baker, E. L., & O'Neil, H. F. (Eds.), *Technology Assessment in Education and Training* (pp. 9–33). Hillsdale, NJ: Lawrence Erlbaum Associates.

Lane, H. C. (2006). Prospects for Guided Practice and Efficient Learning. In *Whitepaper for the Army's Science of Learning Workshop*. Hampton, VA: Intelligent Tutoring Systems.

Lock, Z. (2005). *Performance and Flexibility of Stereotype-based User Models.* (Unpublished Ph.D. Thesis) (Partial fulfilment), Heslington, York: University of York.

Mark, M. A., & Greer, J. E. (1993). Evaluation methodologies for intelligent tutoring systems. *Journal of Artificial Intelligence in Education, 4*(2/3), 129–153.

McCullough, L. E. (2000). *The Effect of Introducing Computers into Introductory Physics Problem-Solving Laboratories.* (Unpublished PhD Thesis), University of Minnesota.

Milas, G. (2005). *Research methods in psychology and other social sciences*. Jastrebarsko, Croatia: Naklada Slap. (in Croatian)

Mužić, V., & Rodek, S. (1987). *Computers in school transformation*. Zagreb, Croatia: Školska knjiga, (in Croatian).

Paiva, A. (1997). Learner Modelling for Collaborative Learning Environments. In B. de_Boulay & R. Mizoguchi (Eds.), *Proceedings of the International Conference on Artificial Intelligence in Education (AI-ED 97)*, (pp. 215-222), Kobe, Japan: IOS Press.

Paulsen, M. F. (2002). *Online Education Systems: Discussion and definition of terms*. Retrieved February 10, 2009, from http://www.nettskolen.com/forskning/Definition%20of%20Terms.pdf

Quignard, M., & Baker, M. (1999). Favouring modellable computer-mediated argumentative dialogue in collaborative problem-solving situations. In Lajoie, S. P., & Vivet, M. (Eds.), *Artificial Intelligence in Education*. IOS Press.

Rickel, J. W. (1989). Intelligent Computer-Aided Instruction: A Survey Organized Around System Components. *IEEE Transactions on Systems, Man, and Cybernetics, 19*(1), 40–57. doi:10.1109/21.24530

Shute, V. J., & Psotka, J. (1995). Intelligent Tutoring Systems: Past, Present, and Future. In Jonassen, D. (Ed.), *Handbook of Research on Educational Communication and Technology*.

Singley, M. K., Singh, M., Fairweather, P., Farrell, R., & Swerling, S. (2000). Algebra jam: supporting teamwork and managing roles in a collaborative learning environment. In *Proceedings of the 2000 ACM conference on Computer supported cooperative work*, Philadelphia, PA: ACM.

Sleeman, D., & Brown, J. S. (1982). *Intelligent Tutoring Systems*. New York: Academic Press.

Stankov, S., Rosić, M., Žitko, B., & Grubišić, A. (2008). TEx-Sys model for building intelligent tutoring systems. *Computers & Education, 51*, 1017–1036. doi:10.1016/j.compedu.2007.10.002

Tatsuoka, M. (1993). Effect size. In Keren, G., & Lewis, C. (Eds.), *A Handbook for Data Analysis in the Behavioral Sciences* (pp. 461–481). Mahwah, NJ: Lawrence Erlbaum Associates.

Tedesco, P. A., & Rosatelli, M. C. (2004). Helping Groups Become Teams: Techniques for Acquiring and Maintaining Group Models. In J. Mostow & P. Tedesco (Eds.), *Designing Computational Models of Collaborative Learning Interaction.).* Paper presented at the ITS 2004 Workshop, Maceio-Alagoas, Brazil.

Tomaš, S. (2005). E-learning in primary education. In *Workshop: Intelligent e-learning systems, Consulting: Computers in school IX, Croatian Association for the Promotion of Computer Education (HDPIO)*, Šibenik, Croatia (in Croatian).

Tomaš, S. (2007). *Learning and teaching in primary education using tutoring systems.* (Unpublished MS Thesis), Falcuty of Philosophy, Zagreb.

Vasilyeva, E., Pechenizkiy, M., & Bra, P. D. (2007). Adaptation of Feedback in e-learning System at Individual and Group Level. In P. Brusilovsky, M. Grigoriadou & K. Papanikolaou (Eds.), *Proceedings of Workshop on Personalisation in E-Learning Environments at Individual and Group Level, 11th International Conference on User Modeling*, (pp. 49-56).

Vladušić, R. (2006). *The intelligent tutoring systems in chemistry in primary education.* (Unpublished MS Thesis), Faculty of Natural Sciences, Mathematics and Kinesiology, Split, Croatia, (in Croatian).

Winter, M. (2004). *Developing A Group Model For Student Software Engineering Teams.* (Unpublished MS Thesis). Saskatoon, Saskatchewan: University of Saskatchewan

Winter, M., & McCalla, G. (2003). An Analysis of Group Performance in Terms of the Functional Knowledge and Teamwork Skills of Group Members. In *UM'03 9th International Conference on User Modeling*, (pp. 35-44), Johnstown, PA.

WWC. (2002). *IES What Works Clearinghouse (WWC) Glossary of Terms.* Retrieved February 20, 2009, from http://ies.ed.gov/ncee/wwc/help/glossary/

Yacef, K. (2003). Some thoughts about the synergetic effects of integrating ITS and LMS Technologies Together to the Service of Education. In *11th International Conference on Artificial Intelligence in Education*, Sydney, Australia.

Chapter 13
A Personalized Learning System Based on Semantic Web Technologies

Funda Dağ
University of Kocaeli, Turkey

Kadir Erkan
University of Kocaeli, Turkey

ABSTRACT

In this study, a personalized learning system framework that is KOULearn (Kocaeli University Learning System) has been proposed. It is based on learning object and produces a personalized learning content according to learning style and cognitive knowledge level of an individual. The proposed framework is situated in advanced learning technologies according to educational perspective and is a semantic web application according to development technologies. The proposed framework is aimed to form a personalized learning environment. Three models are included in this system: domain model, user model and adaptation model, respectively. Components of the system have been realized by ontology based knowledge modeling approach. Execution of the personalized learning content structure and learning environment of the system, related to electric education, has been examined by resonance learning module which is constituted considering personalization requirements of the system.

INTRODUCTION

Today's Web is an important learning technology platform. Its' underlying technologies that is named as e-learning technologies has made it a successful environment in particular for the creation and presentation of learning resources. Especially, today's e-learning technologies are aimed at creation of searchable, reusable learning resources on the web. However, an e-learning application should recommend students learning resources that are easily understandable according to their level of the knowledge and interesting enough to keep the students' attention. So, adaptivity or personalization is key characteristic of today's-learning applications and e-learning researches.

Currently, the Semantic Web can be exploited as a very suitable platform for implementing a personalized e-learning system. Semantic Web is based on ontology technology. Ontology is a

DOI: 10.4018/978-1-61692-008-1.ch013

knowledge representation framework (Pahl & Holohan, 2004). It is a collection of formal explicit definition of some concepts about any domain to represent the knowledge of the domain (Oguejiofor et all, 2004). It provides more advantages and flexibility to develop e-learning system that is has personalization or adaptability. For example; learning ontology development, ontology-based annotation of learning resources, ontology-based composition in learning content and delivery of the learning resources through e-learning portals are some application and research areas of the ontology based personalized or adaptive e-learning.

The potential of ontology technology for the development personalized or adaptive e-learning system can assist developers, instructors and the learners to discover, generate and compose learning resources and also to organize and publish of knowledge both for learning content but also the metadata level on the e-learning system.

The personalized management of the learning content means the set of rules and mechanisms that are used to select learning resources based on the student's characteristics, the educational objectives, the teaching model, and the available media (Wenying & Deren, 2006). Many e-learning communities have combined and integrated these three factors in e-learning systems, leading to some ontology based standardization projects. These projects have focused on determining the standard architecture and format for learning environments, such as IEEE Learning Technology Systems Architecture (LTSC), Instructional Management Systems (IMS), and Sharable Content Object Reference Model (SCORM). IMS and SCORM define and deliver XML-based interoperable specifications for exchanging and sequencing learning contents, i.e., learning objects, among many heterogeneous e-learning systems. They mainly focus on the standardization of learning and teaching methods as well as on the modeling of how the systems manage interoperating educational data relevant to the educational process (Bick, Adelsberger, & Pawlowski, 2000).

Besides, personalized or adaptive e-learning systems are a research area for AI-Education. Researchers work to improve instructional planning practices for presentation of learning objects by using course sequencing techniques of ITS and adaptation techniques of AHS (Hatzilygeroudis, Prentzas & Garofalakis, 2005). In recent years, researchers work to integrate between instructional design theories, learning objects and e-learning environments by using ontological design approaches (Mohan, Greer & McCalla, 2003).

The chapter is organized as follows. Section 2, gives an overview of ontology and semantic web technologies. E-learning specifications for metadata of learning objects and content models of learning objects and relations among the learning object specifications, the learning object content models and ontology technology are discussed. In addition, ontology based personalized e-learning systems are discussed on the most interesting projects in this field in the literature. Section 3, describes general architecture a personalized e-learning system that is named as Kou-Learn. Section 4, describes to implementation of important components of the proposed system and explains results of the application study of Kou-Learn. Section 5, gives an overall discussion and some conclusion remarks as well as guidelines for the future work.

BACKGROUND

This section gives an overview of Semantic Web technologies and current state of personalized e-learning. Relations among Semantic Web, e-learning, e-learning standards, learning objects, learning object content models and personalization issues in the literature are discussed. Some ontology based personalized e-learning researches in the literature are presented. This section focuses on presenting a set of visions for the Semantic Web and ontology technology and also application and development of personalized e-learning applications based on the Semantic Web and ontology technology.

Semantic Web Technologies and Ontology

The Semantic Web aims to represent web content in a form that is more easily machine process able and to use intelligent techniques searching and retrieving suitable information from the web content. (Berners-Lee et. all, 2001). To describe the content on the web explicitly interpretable by software processes, semantic annotations are added to descriptions of web resources or documents. At this point, ontology technology is used to specify meaning of semantic annotations and also to support commonly shared understanding for the semantic description of the web content.

Ontology is central notion for the Semantic Web. In general definition, ontology is an explicit and formal specification of conceptualization (Gruber, 1993). In general, ontology is a formal description or specification of a certain domain. In typical, ontology consists of a list of terms and relationships between these terms (Antoniou & Van Harmelen, 2008). The terms denote important concepts (classes of objects) of the domain. For example, at a course ontology, chapter, lesson, topic are important concepts of this ontology. The relationships include typical hierarchies of classes (e.g. lesson and topic are subclasses of chapter). In addition, the ontology may include some information are related to properties, restrictions and attributes of classes (e.g. a topic is part of only a lesson, a course must include at least one chapter, each course has a title). In this format, ontology describes each concept's crucial properties within the domain. Thus, ontology encodes knowledge in the domain. It makes that knowledge reusable (Choe, 2006). So, ontology supports to generate shared vocabulary to overcome differences in terminology for a certain domain like in e-learning standardization projects. So it provides a shared understanding for the domain. In addition, by defining direct mappings between different ontologies that is supported to form a common terminology in among similar domains. So, ontologies support semantic interoperability (Antoniou & Van Harmelen, 2008).

Semantic Web technologies are based on the XML (Extensible Markup Language). It comprises a layered framework. There are three layers in this framework. First layer of the framework is "metadata layer" offers an extensible framework in order to express the web content by simple semantic assertions (e.g., vocabularies or taxonomies). This conceptual model can be use to attach metadata (data about data) to each Web resource.

Second layer of the framework is "schema layer" offer to specify simple ontologies in order to define a hierarchical description of the concepts and properties for a given resource. In this layer, there are different languages specifically designed to represent ontology. These are Extensible Markup Language (XML) based languages. XML is a universal meta-language for defining markup but does not provide semantic meaning of data. Resource Description Framework (RDF) is primitive ontology modeling language in the Semantic Web. Essentially, RDF is a "data model" not a "language". It inherits the benefits associated with XML. Some limitations of the expressivity of RDF, The Web Ontology Working Group of W3C identified the need for more powerful ontology modeling language that is OWL (Web Ontology Language). The OWL Web Ontology Language facilitates greater machine interpretability of Web content than that supported by XML, RDF, and RDF Schema (RDF-S) by providing additional expressive power along with a formal semantics.

Third layer of the framework is "the logical layer". The logical layer of the Semantic Web is not fully developed yet. Its implementation will offer proof and trust mechanism for the Semantic Web. To model complex ontologies with more expressivity and to infer new knowledge from existing ontology can be able to usage of logical principles. OWL language is based on Description Logics.

From knowledge representation viewpoint, DLs support ontology design; offer well defined semantics for interpretation of ontology and offer reasoning support (Baader et. all, 2003). However, some expressivity limitations of Owl, rule-based formalisms grounded in logic programming have repeatedly been proposed as a possible solution to overcome design and reasoning limitations of the Semantic Web applications (O'Connor et al., 2005). In the future, different reasoning services will exist to be used by the applications oriented to Semantic Web.

Current approaches to support to development of more personalized e-learning application is related to Semantic Web technologies and ontology. Semantic Web technologies offer more advantages and flexibility to develop applications for e-learning domain. In e-learning context, the Semantic Web offer technology for effective information storage and retrieval (Aroyo & Dicheva, 2004). It supports / can support that

- to describe a learning object with metadata and to extend this description by use of similar specifications,
- semantic conceptualization of a learning domain, to develop learning and teaching ontologies for different learning domains and to define mapping between learning ontologies,
- to develop reasoning services for personalization of learning content for any different learning scenario or individual needs of specific learners through processing the learning and information retrieval by web services or software agents.

In following chapter, these issues are discussed.

Learning Objects and Metadata

E-learning systems enable people to find very kinds of learning materials on various courses and to access to the learning materials at anytime and from anywhere. At this point, essential problem is how to find required learning resources. So, to define a formal description framework for learning resources on the Web is very important. "Metadata" is used to describe these learning materials and "metadata schemas" are used to group learning materials.

Metadata is defined as *"information about an object; be it physical or digital"* (LTSC, 2002), which are effective in the description of learning resources. According to that, a learning resource is semantically annotated by metadata. A number of metadata models have been proposed for the Web information management by e-learning communities. Dublin Core Metadata Initiative and IEEE LTSC Learning Object Metadata (LOM) Working Group (http://ltsc.ieee.org/wg12/) provide metadata standards which are effective in the description of learning resources. Learning Object Metadata (LOM) is essentially a cataloging scheme for learning resources and defines the descriptive, structural and semantic features of a learning object with 9 categories of metadata elements as general, life cycle, meta-metadata, educational, technical, educational, rights, relation, annotation, and classification. The SCORM (Sharable Content Object Reference Model) (http://www.adlnet.gov/Technologies/scorm/) extends these standards by further specifying the runtime environment of LMSs (Learning Management Systems), including APIs and data elements needed to launch the SCOs (Sharable Content Objects).

These efforts of e-learning communities mainly focus on information sharing in e-learning environments. They use the term of "learning object" to define learning resources which are annotated with metadata and are shared and used for repurposed in e-learning environments. Therefore, instances of learning objects can be used by e-learning environments such as Learning Content Management System (LCMS), Learning Management System (LMS), Virtual Learning Environments (VLE), etc. to manage, locate, evaluate or exchange learning objects. E-learning environments should be designed in a way that they provide easy access to all levels of learning objects from atomic to the most complex structures in the learning process. To perform this and to find appropriate learning objects and to produce personalized learning content that match the learner's learning objectives and the level of the study, metadata and searching of the learning objects and learning resources by using metadata should be facilitated.

On the other hand, learning object is important for todays' learning researches and applications but, the complete and common definition of it is still rather vague, as different organizations view learning objects differently in terms of "physical size, terminology and focus" (Chrysostomou & Papadopoulos, 2005).

IEEE LTSC defines a learning object as *"any entity, digital or non digital, which can be used, reused or referenced during technology-supported learning"* (LTSC, 2002). Although according to this definition a learning object is defined as digital or non digital, apperantly learning objects are commonly accepted as an object-oriented component of the technology dominating current and future of e-learning researches. Therefore, a learning object designed as context-independent chunks in an object-oriented programming environment can be shared with other users, recombined with other learning objects or redesigned by other instructional developers (Merrill, 1998).

However, there is a number of learning object content models. They define learning objects according to instructional features and also extremely physical size which is defined as "granularity" (Verbert & Duval, et al., 2004). Scorm Content Aggregation Model (Dodds, 2001) and the Cisco RLO/RIO Model (Barrit, Lewis, & Wieseler, 1999) are featured of these models. These content models have been used to describe a learning object in the domain ontology of our proposed work.

Scorm Content Aggregation Model is a part of Scorm Reference Model. Scorm defines the learning object according to the implementation technology and clearly defines granularity of the learning object from the point of technical aspects. The last version of the SCORM content aggregation model (known as Scorm 2004) (ADL, 2002) contains four components: These are Assets, Sharable Content Asset (SCA) and Sharable Content Objects (SCO) and Content Aggregations, respectively. Assets are an electronic representation of media, text, images, audio, web pages or other data that can be presented in a web client. A Sharable Content Asset (SCA) represents a collection of one or more assets. A Sharable Object (SCO) represents a collection of one or more assets and SCAs. Also, to improve the reusability, a SCO should be independent of its learning context. A SCO can for example be reused in different learning experiences to fulfill different learning objectives. SCOs are meant to be small units, such that reusability in more learning objectives is feasible. A Content Aggregation is a map (content structure) that can be used to aggregate learning resources in a well integrated unit of education (for example course, chapter, module, etc.).

Cisco content model which has more pedagogical sound defines the learning object according to pedagogical methodology perspectives and defines granularity of the learning object clearly from the point of pedagogical aspects (Cisco, 2003). A Reusable Learning Object (RLO) is a collection of seven or nine Reusable Information Objects (RIOs). To make a complete learning experience or lesson from a collection of RIOs, an Overview, Summary and Assessment are added to the packet. Reusable Information Objects (RIOs) are pieces of information that are built around a single learning objective. Each RIO is composed of three components: content items, practice items and assessment items. A practice item is an activity that gives the learner the ability to apply its knowledge and skills, like a case study or a practice test. An assessment item is a question or measurable activity used to determine if the learner has mastered the learning objective for a given RIO.

We used Cisco Content Model to describe and classification of learning objects that is another part of the domain ontology of our work.

Learning object metadata standards (such as IEEE LOM, Scorm) aim to support the common description of learning objects in terms of reusability and granularity. The learning object is created once in a different granularity afterwards it can be reused in different e-learning environments and learning context numbers of times. The learning object metadata standarts and learning object content models address means of this sentence. Granularity is a qualitative value for the learning object (Sampson & Karagiannidis, 2002; Duncan, 2003). There is a connection between reusability and granularity of the learning object. According to that, if a learning object is to be more granular than it can be more reusable for any learning context. Reusability of learning object requires that they are described in a common format (metadata standarts) for the construction of the courses (Chrysostomou & Papadopoulos, 2005). But, technical descriptions of these standards are inadequate for defining of the granularity degree and instructional qualifications and quality of learning objects efficiently. (Wiley, 2000; Duval & Hodgins, 2007). Therefore, learning object content models identify more clearly kinds of learning objects and their components according to granularity degree and instructional qualifications and quality of the learning object than descriptions of metadata standarts. But, there are content models and some other principles and guidelines that can be use to aid as principles and guidelines in the design process. These principles and guidelines suggest how to determine the size and instructional content of learning objects, ways they might be given context within an instructional track, and how they should be stored in a repository for future use (Hamel & Ryan-Jones, 2002). According to above descriptions of learning objects, we say that, learning object definition of Scorm is adequate to describe metadata structure and properties of the learning object as a software component. In addition, the learning object definition of Cisco is more adequate to describe instructional qualifications and quality of the learning object. We used Scorm Content Aggregation Model to describe and classification of digital learning materials that is a part of the domain ontology of our work. In addition to that, in our view, learning objects and digital learning materials should be considered separately from each other. A learning object is composed of digital learning materials and it should be small but pedagogically complete segments of instructional content that can be assembled as needed to create larger units of instruction, such as lessons, modules and courses. So, we used Cisco Content Model to classify of learning objects according to instructional qualifications and quality characteristics of learning objects.

According to personalization context of e-learning researches; granularity, reusability and instructional qualifications and quality characteristics of learning objects are effective to produce a personalized learning content which is composed of learning object(s) due to learning goals, cognitive knowledge level, learning requirements and preferences of the learner. So, compositon of learning objects is important. Compositon of learning objects should be learner centered, the personalization and intelligent services should be provided based on learners individual difference, Semantic web technologies allow us to enhance existing learning objects specifications using classes of objects with common attributes (Mohan, Greer & McCalla, 2003). Although the standardization efforts offer mainly information sharing in e-learning environments, they are not brought into effect. The reason is there is lacking of standard terms in e-learning resources. Since the semantic heterogeneous, descriptions to the same discipline among different teachers are different. Obviously, these factors result in that the e- Learning resources and learning objects couldn't be shared within different platforms and different systems, in the real sense. To deal with these problems, the domain ontology should be imported into e-Learning system. (Hendler, 2001) In following chapter, why and how ontology based modeling aspects are included in learning objects and personalized e-learning researches are explained.

Ontology Based Approaches in E-Learning

In AI – Education research area, various techniques were used in several educational systems in order to adapt to individual user needs and characteristics since middle nineties. These educational systems are named as Adaptive Educational Hypermedia Systems (AEHS). AEHS integrates several technologies from both hypermedia and Intelligent Tutoring Systems (ITS). First examples of the AEHS are mostly domain dependent systems. They have application-specific models of the user and the domain, and a limited, predefined set of adaptation rules (Koesling et al, 2008). In contrast according to some non-adaptive systems, AEHS are often systems that are used by a small audience (Paramythis & Loidl-Reisinger, 2004). The content–dependent problems of AEHS has caused not to find wide application area (Mizoguchi & Bourdeu, 2000).

There are some AI-ED researches they claimed that ontology based modeling approach and semantic web technologies can be solution for the content related problems of the AEHS. They are aimed to create and sequence LO by using instructional planning approach of ITS and adaptation approaches of AEHS (Mohan, Greer & McCalla, 2003) These researches are inherited their architectural model from AEHS and ITS. They are aimed to combine their aggregations in these areas with learning objects and Semantic Web technologies (Dicheva, Sosnovsky, Gavrilova & Brusilovsky, 2005; Aroya&Dicheva, 2004; Dvedžić, 2004; Mizoguchi & Bourdeau, 2000).

Current researches about personalized or adaptive e-learning mainly focus on two technologies: adaptive hypermedia technology and semantic web technology. Adaptive hypermedia systems can provide adaptive presentation and adaptive navigation for users. Ontology technology of Semantic Web brings a new way to represent domain knowledge concepts on which application can process reasoning rules for some specific adaptation purposes.

As well as most current adaptive e-learning systems aim to support adaptive or dynamic course generation with in e-learning (Karampiperis & Sampson, 2004). In this context, adaptive or dynamic course generation is required instructional planning (Brusilovsky & Vassileva, 2003). Instructional planning is related to pedagogical decision making. Pedagogical decision making is concerned with both the content and the delivery of instruction (Vassileva & Wasson, 1996; Karampiperis & Sampson, 2004). Adaptive course generation which is concerned with delivery of instruction supports to sequencing of course content according to specific learning goals and initial cognitive knowledge level of the learner. Dynamic course generation which is concerned with content of instruction aims to provide adaptive course content that is dynamically changes by interactions of the learner with the course according to learners' specific needs and requirements (Brusilovsky & Vassileva, 2003). In this direction, recent researches have been maintained to combine instructional planning approaches with learning object.

Karampiperis and Sampson (2004) presented an approach for adaptive sequencing of learning objects in learning environment. They used domain ontologies and metadata for learning objects. They defined an optimization criterion which is learning time for each learning object and used a shortest path algorithm to produce the learning path. Ullrich (2005) presented a hierarchical planner approach. He used HTN planning to represent the pedagogical objectives and tasks in order to obtain a course structure. The one of the most recent works is presented in (Kontopoulos et al., 2008). They presented a system that provides personalized curricula to the learner by using learning objects. The presented system complies with an ontology concerning both learning objectives and prerequisites and a planning mechanism which is recognized by machine learning techniques.

All of these approaches, especially, depend on domain model and domain ontology. The domain ontology specifies the domain concepts and the relations among them, which represent the instructional knowledge in specific subject. In instructional perspective, domain concepts are not sufficient to constitute an instruction. So, learning goals based instructional design, including taxonomic classifications of learning goals and domain concepts and prerequisites analysis of domain concepts could be used to planning domain ontology (Onaindía, Sapena & Garrido, 2007). In addition to that, all of these approaches use an instructional planning mechanism is performed by an instructional planner or an adaptation Module, for interpretation of the domain ontology.

As described under the heading of Semantic Web and Ontology, the Semantic Web technologies can be used to construct a personalized e-learning application. In design process, primarily, ontology based modeling approach should be used to realize domain ontology which is represent the instructional knowledge of the learning system and user ontology which is represent parameters of the user model to produce an personalized learning path for the learner. So, semantic conceptualization of the learning domain can be implemented and to reasoning process, mapping can be defined between domain ontology and user ontology. In addition to that, a reasoning service for personalization of learning content for any different learning scenario or individual needs of specific learners through processing the learning should be developed. For that, in our proposed system, the adaptation model was developed by DL based reasoning and rule based reasoning technologies. We used these technologies to inference knowledge which is related to the a selected course of the system and cognitive level and learning style about the user from the domain and user ontologies of the system. Protégé 2000 OWL tool is used to main development tool for this work (Gennari et al., 2003). All ontologies were realized by Owl Web Ontology Language. Adaptation rules which are related to the adaptation model were written by Swrl Semantic Web Rule Language that provides a convenient starting point for integrating rule systems to work with the Semantic Web. Swrl can provide a rich rule based reasoning facility for the Semantic Web (Horrocks et al., 2004). These rules are similar to the teaching model of AEHS which includes the set of some generic and specific pedagogic rules. This approach enabled to construct adaptation process of the proposed system. So, rule-based reasoning was used to generate learning paths. Moreover, new learning goal and contents are adjusted according to learner's learning history and performance during his/her learning process. In addition, Semantic Query-Enhanced Web Rule Language (Sqwrl) was used to query generation of the adaptive learning objects in the system.

THE COMPONENTS OF KOULEARN

KouLearn is a personalized learning environment framework. The proposed system is aimed to form a personalized learning environment. Three models are included in this system: domain model, user model and adaptation model, respectively. Components of the system have been realized by ontology based knowledge modelling approach.

In the proposed system, learning content is defined as LO (such as course, module, lesson, topic) and also educational material is defined as digital resource (ppt, pdf, doc, etc. files). Each LO has a structure that is composed of different digital resources. Metadata which is used to define LO was developed according to Cisco content model. Also, metadata which is used to define digital resource was developed according to Scorm Content Aggregation Model and LOM Metadata Schema.

Additionally, a new domain ontology which is suitable to produce personalized learning content was developed by integrating two main LO content models that have different approaches to compose a LO and domain model structure that is used in Intelligent Tutoring System (ITS) and Adaptive Educational Hypermedia System (AEHS) with ontology based knowledge modelling.

The Domain Ontology

In the domain ontology of the proposed system is composed of concepts are related to each other thus forming a kind of semantic network. We used the domain model structure which is explained in AHAM reference model. AHAM is an important reference model for AHS (Wu et al., 2001). But, domain model structure in AHAM has strong limitations for describing concepts and relationships between them (Madhour & Forte, 2006). The limitations whihch are related to the descriptions of domain concepts according to the AHAM, ontology based conceptualization of the concepts was used in this work. Therefore, each concept and relationships between concepts in description of the knowledge base was defined through a series of arguments that were grouped to constitute presentation chain of a learning content.

There are three layers were defined in the domain ontology as in Figure 1. Each layer of the information model is represented by a semantic network. These are conceptual layer, learning content layer and learning material layer, respectively.

According to the Figure 1, in the domain ontology, conceptual layer is composed from two directed a cyclic graph (DAG)s. One of these graphs is learning goal network of a subject domain (course).The other is concept network of the course. To build a model of an instructional goal is a very useful feature of AHS that extends its adaptivity and flexibility. In this approach, a teacher can be assign different instructional goals to a learner. Goal based design of the domain model was inherited by educational AHS from earlier works in the field of ITS (Brusilovsky, 2003). There are different approaches which are used in AEHS to design instructional goal based domain model. For example, (Papanikolaou et al., 2002) lets a student to pick up a structured educational goal for learning. This structured goal can be composed of a sequence of elementary sub-goals called layers each one composed as a set of concepts to be learned. This approach was a fountain head for to compose instructional goal structure in our system.

In the conceptual layers of the domain ontology, learning objectives of a course are detailed in three levels in the learning goal network. Therefore, two node types are used to describe learning objectives of the course. These are general learning goals and sub-learning goals, respectively. First level nodes of the learning goal network (general learning goals) are used to describe general objectives of the course. A course may be one or more general learning objectives. Second and third level nodes of the learning goal network (sub-learning goals)

Figure 1. Layered structure of the domain ontology

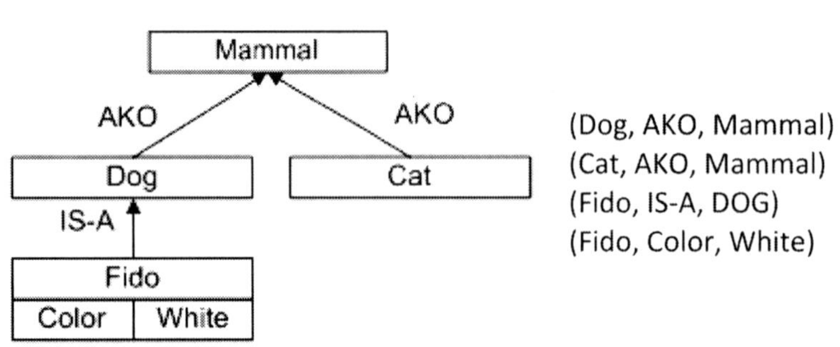

are used to describe the objectives are covered more specific objectives of the course. By some specific learning objectives is formed a general learning objective of the course. For description of this expression, some relations are constructed to associate nodes of the goal network. For example, a general learning goal consists of only one or more general learning goals or only some sub-learning goals. Also, a relation is used to make order among same type nodes of the goal network.

The concept network of the course has been described by domain model structure of AHAM reference model (Wu et al., 2001). Two nodes types were defined in this network. These are respectively, composite concept node and atomic concept node. A composite concept consists of only one or more composite concepts or only some atomic concepts. Atomic concept is the smallest concept of the network, does not consist of any concept. There is a prerequisite relation between same type concepts of the concept network. This relationship has been used to sort nodes of the concept network according to pre-conditions of learning.

There is a relation among nodes of the goal network and the concept network. So, each one composed as a set of nodes to be learned. For example each general learning goal is related to a composite concept and it has a set of nodes that consist of this composite concept. Reverse is true in relations between the two network.

According to the Figure 1, the content is described as a learning object in the domain ontology. The learning object is created to teach specific knowledge about a concept or a learning objective of the course. Therefore, each learning object of the content layer is related to the nodes of the networks of the conceptual layer. In proposed model, a learning content has been constituted according to instruction oriented knowledge representation that is Cisco Learning Object Content Model (Cisco, 2003). According to that, in the learning content layer, four type learning objects were defined due to instructional granularity. These are Course, Module, Lesson and Topic, respectively.

In the domain ontology, each knowledge base is related to Course type learning object. The course covers all general learning objectives of a subject domain and explained a set of composite concepts of the subject domain. A module is composed of lessons and a lesson is composed of one or more topics. The module covers one general learning objective of the course and is explained by a composite concept or set of atomic concepts of that composite concept. The lesson covers one or more sub-learning objective of the course and is explained by a composite concept or set of some atomic concepts. Topic is the smallest learning object in the model. Each goal or domain concept of the knowledge base could be presented by one or more learning object. For example, the course is presented to the learner by different sub learning objects such as Module, Lesson or Topic. In addition, according to the personalization criteria of the system, only a part of the course like as a lesson is presented with sub learning objects that is compose one or more Topic(s). What will be presented to learners of learning objects is determined by adaptation rules.

In addition to that, each learning object is defined as media independent in the domain model. It is composed from digital learning materials. According to the Figure 1, in the learning material layer, learning materials are grouped according to the granularity and instructional properties. Granularity is referred to size of the digital learning materials. Also, the digital learning materials are classified by their instructional properties such as explanation materials, evaluation materials and application materials. Instructional properties and granularity degree of the learning materials has been facilitated of classification and query of the digital learning materials, when they are used to build up learning object.

Scorm Content Aggregation Model (v1.3) was used to define granularity definitions of the digital learning materials. For that, there are three types concepts are detailed according to granularity in this layer. These are Sharable content object (sco), sharable content asset (sca) and asset. Asset is the least granular digital learning material. An asset can be a pdf file, an image file or a word file. Each asset has been classified due to instructional functions also. Sca is composed of assets or other Sca. One type or different type assets has been gathered to form a Sca. Each Sco is a meaningful learning content that has one or more learning goals, one or more learning materials and (or) assessment items. Sco is a set of some assets and Sca. Sco is content equivalent of a *"Topic"* type learning object.

The domain ontology and also the user ontology of the system were realized by OWL Web Ontology Language and in the Protégé OWL Tool (Gennari et al., 2003). In the domain ontology, some classes were used to define nodes of the networks for the layers. Some descriptions which create the structure in the Figure 2 were made in the domain ontology. Each class has been described and defined by some restrictions which are written in OWL Language. Then, the components of a course (such as objectives, important concepts, and learning materials) are created as concrete examples (individuals) of these classes by the author and thereby a knowledge base is cerated for the course. The content of individualized instruction is provided to produce in the form of learning objects with the logical inferences that is made on this knowledge base according to various criteria.

As shown in Figure 2, each layer of the domain ontology has been defined by a parent class. Each parent class has one or more sub classes. A sub class can be a parent class or a child class. A child class has not a sub class such as a parent class or a child class. For example, "*DomainKonwedge*" class and *"DomainKonowledgeBase"* class are parent classes. Also, *"DomainConcept"* class is a parent class and sub class of the *"Domain-Knowledge"* class.

In the ontology, a subject domain or course is defined as an individual of *"DomainKnowledge"* class. Also, each subject domain is defined as an individual of *"DomainKnowledge base"* class. According to layered structure of the ontology, the learning content layer was defined by *"LearningObject"* class as you can see from Figure 2. A relation has been defined between *"DomainKnowledge base"* class and a subclass of the *"LearningObject"* class. This relation has been formed by *"Course"* class. Because of this definition, each Course LO has a knowledge base which is constructed learning objectives (goals) and concepts of this course. So, desired learning path can be produced from the knowledge base of the course. According to this structure, the domain ontology and also the proposed personalized learning system can be used to constitue knowledge bases for different subject domains (or courses),

Figure 2. Class hierarchy of the Domain Ontology

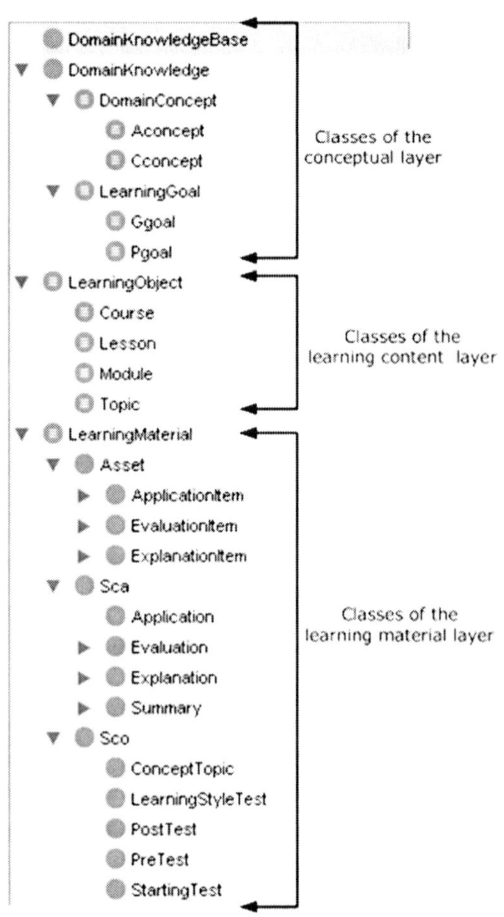

synchronically. *"Course"* class, "*Module*" class, "*Lesson*" class and "*Topic*" class are subclasses of "*LearningObject*" class. Some properties have been defined for the classes to form hierarchical arrangement of these learning object types.

According to layered structure of the domain ontology, learning material layer has been defined by *"LearningMaterial"* class. As known that, digital learning materials are classified by according to granularity and instructional properties in the layered structure of the domain ontology. So, we created some sub classes for *"LearningMaterial"* class. For example, we used five types subclass for *"Sco"* class. These are, *"ConceptTopic"* class, *"PostTest"* class, "*PreTest*" class, "*StartingTest*" class and *"LearningStyleTest"* class, respectively. Individuals of "ConceptTopic" class are used to compose content of *Topic* type learning object. Individuals of "PostTest", "StartingTest" and "PreTest" classes are used to compose an evaluation part of Course, Module or Lesson type learning objects.

However, in the domain ontology, some interrelations are defined among the layers of the domain ontology. The relations between the conceptual layer and the learning material layer, relations between the conceptual layer and the learning object layer and relations between the learning object layer and the learning material layer are used to make logical inferences from the ontology. Therefore, in the domain ontology, not only class taxonomy but also properties of classes and relationships among classes were built. The relationships among layers of the ontology were built. For this reason, some properties (object properties and data properties) were used to describe interrelations between nodes and characteristics of the nodes. Personalized learning content that is in form of learning objects are produced by querying of object and data type properties of the classes in the ontology and the content structure of a learning object is produced by KouLearn like as shown in Figure 3.

In the domain ontology, some data type properties have been defined for each class. The data type property is a data type. Data type property is a similar (may be same) thing with metadata element of the learning object metadata. In the ontology, metadata descriptions of IEEE LOM were mostly used. According to that, some classes have data type properties, such as "hasDifficulty" is difficulty metadata of a learning object and "hasTypicalLearningTime" is proposed time to study for a learning object. Furthermore, some object properties have been used in the ontology. The object property is a link that connects two individuals of some classes. It is a same thing with a link that is a binding between two nodes of a semantic network. For example, each learning goal is related to one or more domain concepts in the ontology. Description of this situation "relates" and "relatedTo" object properties have been used to match "LearningGoal" class and "DomainConcept" class of the ontology. In ad-

Figure 3. The content structure of "Lesson" type learning object

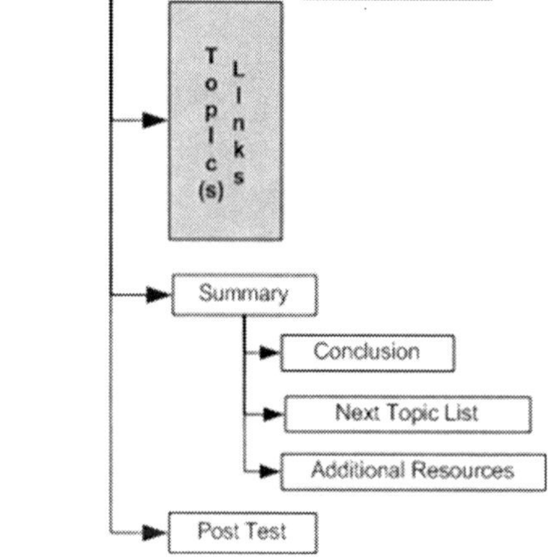

dition, each individual of "Pgoal" or "Aconcept" classes are related to a learning content such as Topic or Lesson. This relation is described by "explainedBy" and "explains" object properties.

The User Ontology

The user ontology is second ontology of the system. We designated a limited user model and its ontology. The user ontology of the proposed system is performed to create a user profile contains the the user's cognitive level information and learning style information This information can be used to the selection of learning objects and the selection of digital resources which compose learning objects.

According to the Figure 4, IMS LIP standart attributes was used to describe the learner type user. There are two types metadata in the user ontology. These are standart information metadata which is used to describe the learner by identifier number, name, surname, email, education department and etc. This metadata group was defined and described by "User" class and its subclasses. The other metadata type is preferences metadata which used to define cognitive knowledge level, learning style of the learner and preferred content types of the learner such as difficulty level, representation types, and abstractness of the content. This metadata group was defined and described by "Preferences" class and its subclasses. Classes of the user ontology and sample individuals of the user ontology are shown in Figure 4.

All of the individuals of the user ontology in the proposed system include static data and this data defined when the user login to the system, and then keep going learning process. This data are used to select suitable interaction mode in the learning environment and to compose personalized learning objects which is formed some learning materials are selected preferences parameters of the user ontology and combined with other related learning objects to produce a personalized learning content for the learner.

Adaptation Rules and the Adaptation Engine

To support the logical inference capability of KouLearn, adaptation rules and an adaptation engine have been developed. The adaptation mechanism of KouLearn can be explained according to the Figure 5. In the Figure 5, digital learning materials and user data are described by the domain ontol-

Figure 4. The User ontology of the system

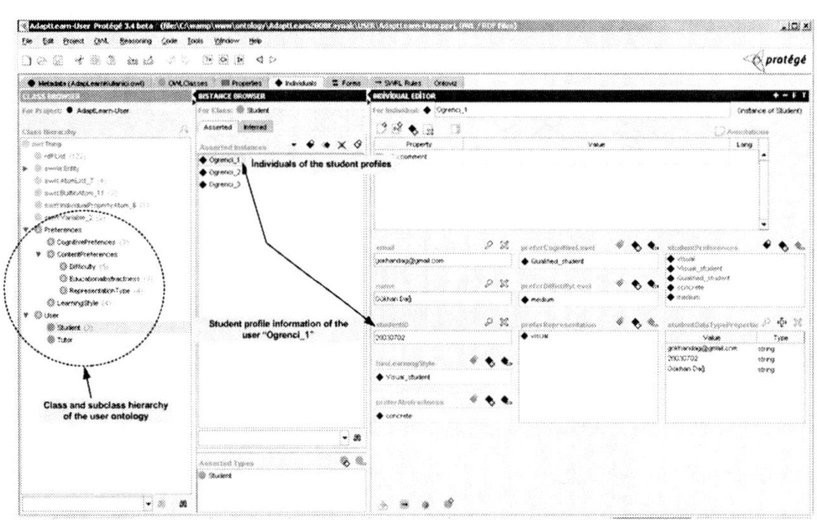

ogy and the user ontology are stored in databases. These are asserted individuals of the ontologies. In adaptation process; firstly, the inference process is realized on the asserted individuals of the ontologies and so, inferred course knowledge base and inferred user knowledge base have been created. The inferred course knowledge base is an Owl file. Then, some software agents that constitute the adaptation engine of the system; produce the learning objects for personalized learning content by using personalization criterias (learning style, knowledge level, etc.) on the inferred course knowledge base. Then, the produced personalized content is presented to the learner in the user interface of the system.

Adaptation rules are important in the system. There are two main functions of these rules. One of the functions of these rules is to perform the concept selection process by using the knowledge about the conceptual layer of the course knowledge base. The other function of them is to perform content selection process by using the knowledge about the learning object and the learning material layers of the course knowledge base.

Adaptation rules of the system are collected in three groups due to their properties. The first rule group is written to facilitate inference of some knowledge about the data type and object type properties of the classes that are parts of the conceptual layer of the domain ontology. The second rule group is written to facilitate inference of some knowledge about the data type and object type properties of the classes that are parts of learning object layer of the domain ontology

Figure 5. The adaptation mechanism of KouLearn

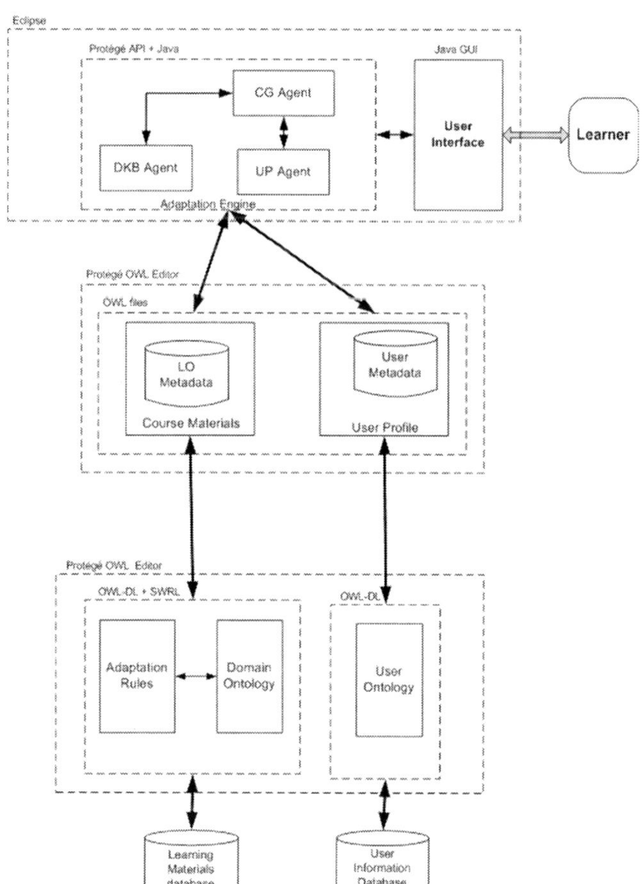

according to asserted relationships between the conceptual layer and the learning object layer of the domain ontology. And, third rule group is written to facilitate some knowledge about the data type and object type properties of the classes that are parts of the learning material layer of the domain ontology according to asserted relationships between the learning object and the learning material layer of the domain ontology. First rule group is written to facilitate achievement of the concept selection process. The second and third rule groups are written to facilitate the achievement of the content selection proccess.

All adaptation rules were written by Swrl Semantic Web Rule Language. Swrl is Description Logic based rule language. It can provide a rich rule based reasoning facility for the Semantic Web applications (Horrocks et al., 2004). Swrl rules are written as antecedent-consequent pairs. The antecedent is referred to as the body of a rule and the consequent is referred to as the head of the rule. Both the head and the body consist of a conjunction of one or more atoms. Swrl rules reason about Owl individuals which are instances of ontology, primarily in terms of Owl classes and properties. At present, although Swrl is an important rule language that can be used to infer new knowledge from existing Owl knowledge base, some expressivity problems have been presently. Swrl does not support more complex logical combinations (O'Connor et al., 2005). In addition, Swrl itself has no inference capabilities. So, we used a reasoning mechanism to provide this functionality. In this work, we used Jess rule engine is integrated in Swrl to support inferencing mechanism of Swrl. In our proposed model, to overcome expressivity problems of adaptation rules of the system, we used some Owl axioms and Swrl rules together. So, we brought to successful conclusion to manipulation of our proposed model.

For example, we wrote a Swrl rule to provide truly the property of the domain independency. It can be seen in Figure 6. In this rule, we aim to infer the knowledge is means that *"if a general goal is belongs to a knowledgebase (a course) all learning goals that are parts of this general goal should be belongs to same knowledgebase."* By this expression we can support domain independency of the domain ontology. So, the ontology can be used to describe concepts of one or more subject domains (or courses) in an e-learning environment and concepts can be grouped according to which one belongs to the knowledge bases (or the courses).

Conceptual layer and Learning Objects matching rules are executed to complete content structure of a learning object of the course. These rules are used to fulfill some property or metadata fields of the learning object.

For example, according to the rule that can be seen in Figure 7, *"If the contents of a Module type learning object is composed of some lessons and these lessons are consisted of the content list of the module, the module and te lessons are related to composite concepts, the lessons should be a part of this module and they should be composed of outline list of the module."* When this rule is executed, it fulfills property fields of a Module type learning object such as "*hasOutline*" and "*hasPartLo*" and *"isPartOfLo"*, automatically. This situation can be seen in Figure 8. It is shown that an example of the individual of the Learning Object of the "Resonance" course.

Learning objects and learning materials matching rules are executed to complete some educational metadata relations between an educational learning object and the learning materials. In addition, these rules are written to facilitate connection

Figure 6. An example of the conceptual layer matching rules

```
Ggoal(?x) ∧Pgoal(?y) ∧ Pgoal(?z) ∧
DomainKnowledgeBase(?dkb) ∧
hasPartDk(?x, ?y) ∧ hasPartDk(?y, ?z) ∧
belongsToDkb(?x, ?dkb)
|
 → belongsToDkb(?y, ?dkb) ∧belongsToDkb(?z, ?dkb)
```

Figure 7. One of the conceptual layer and learning objects matching rules

```
Module(?m) ∧ Lesson(?l) ∧
Cconcept(?a) ∧ Cconcept(?b) ∧
hasPartDk(?a, ?b) ∧ explainedBy(?a, ?m) ∧
explains(?m, ?a) ∧ explainedBy(?b, ?l) ∧
explains(?l, ?b) →
hasOutline(?m, ?l) ∧ hasPartLo(?m, ?l) ∧ isPartOfLo(?l, ?m)
```

Figure 8. An example of the individual of the Learning Object of the "Resonance" course

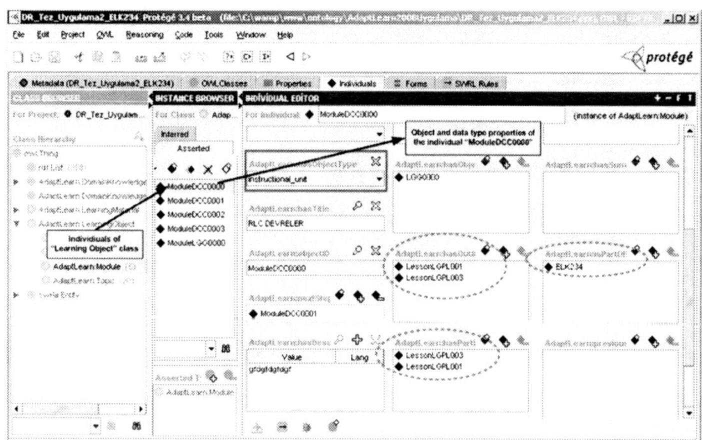

of suitable learning materials to an educational learning object for constitution of the content of the educational learning object.When these rule groups are executed, they are fulfill the suitable properties of the individuals of the *"LearningMaterial"* class and subclasses automatically like in the individuals of the *"LearningObject"* class and subclasses as described above.

The other part of the inference mechanism of the KouLearn is the adaptation engine. The adaptation engine interprets the adaptation rules which both of the concept selection process and the content selection process are related and then it creates a ranking for learning content is in the form of learning object such as a Course or a module or a lesson or a list of topic(s).It is composed of three software agents. These are DKB (Domain Knowledge base) agent, UP (User Profile) agent and CG (Content Generation) agent, respectively. These agents have been used to make inference from the domain ontology, the user ontology and adaptation rules. Some methods of the Protege Reasoning API and SQWRLQuery API have been used to construct the adaptation engine.

DKB agent decodes relations about conceptual graphs which represent learning goals and concepts of a course in the domain ontology and compose learning goal list and concept list of the course for using goal based and concept based learning modes. This list is presented to the user on the system's user interfaces as in Figure 9. DKB agent realizes the concept selection process of the system. This process is the selection of the concept(s) that are related to the learning objective(s) of the user about the course from the domain ontology according to preference of the user or interests of the system. Then the selected concepts are extracted by comparison with the student's known cognitive knowledge level and by using these extracted concepts, a last concept

Figure 9. Production of the course concept list

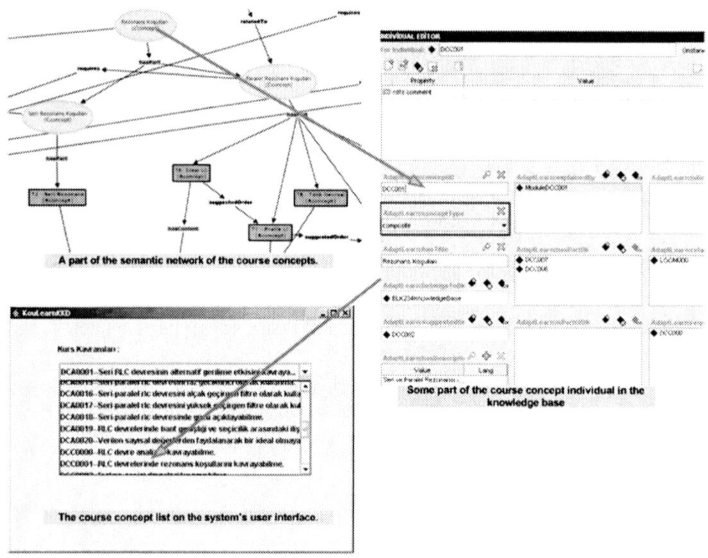

list is created by the concepts of not knowing the student's need to learn.

UP agent is used to query user data about learning style and cognitive knowledge level of the user from the user ontology and used on the system's user interface as in Figure 10. Lastly, CG agent produces personalized learning objects that are related to inferred unknown course concepts from the DKB agent and the learning style knowledge for the user from the UP agent.

LEARNING ENVIRONMENT OF KOULEARN

In the learning environment of KouLearn; the learner is active substituted for the instructor. The learner decides his (her) own learning preferences. The learner can be learn in an environment that is controlled by the system or can be designate his (her) own learning environment according to own learning preferences. For this purpose, in

Figure 10. A part of the user interface of KouLearn

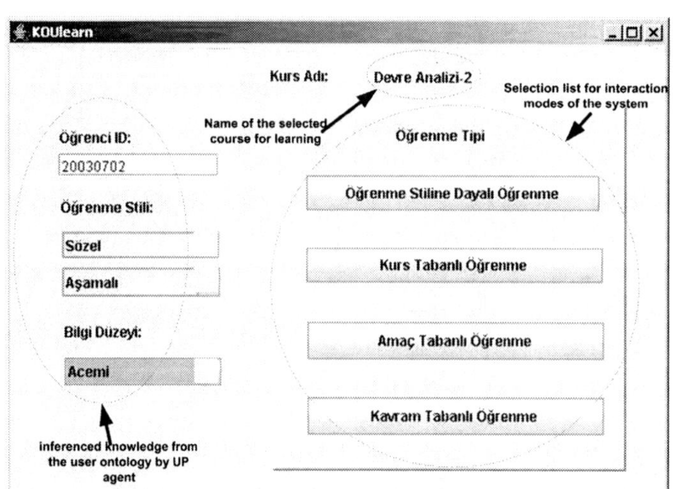

the learning environment, four interaction modes are presented to the learner. These are *"Learning style based learning"*, *"Goal based learning"*, *"Concept based learning"* and *"Course based learning"*, respectively. The learner can be select one of these interaction modes, and then the system produces a personalized learning content according to selected interaction mode by the learner and also cognitive knowledge level and learning style of the learner. The algorithm of the interaction modes of the learning environment is sawn in Figure 11. Interaction modes have been used to determine adaptation processes of the system. So, the algorithm of the interaction modes summarizes running of the adaptation processes.

According to Figure 11, if *"course based learning adaptation"*.mode is selected by the learner or determined by the system for the learner, a selected course is presented to the learner by Modules, Lessons and Topic type learning objects due to link adaptation techniques in addition to curriculum sequencing technique. If *"concept based learning adaptation"*is selected, a set of Topic type learning objects that explains specific knowledge for a selected concept of the course is presented to the learner. If *"goal based adaptation"* mode is selected, a part of the course such as a set of Lessons of the course or a set of modules of the course is presented to the learner due to type of the selected learning goals by the learner or determined by the system. However, "Learning Style Based Learning" interaction mode is not has its own adaptation process. It is only used to choose one of the other interaction modes that are suitable for the learner according to the user characteristics like as user's learning style. Properties of this interaction mode is explained in the title of "How to use Learning Style in Learning Environment Design of KouLearn" in detail.

After any interaction mode is selected by the learner, learning content is presented by learning objects in the learning environment. KouLearn presents learning objects to the learner by different formats such as a course that is composed of some modules or a set of modules which are composed of some specific lessons, a set of lessons which are composed of some special topics or a set of specific topics. In the learning environment, presentation of which learning objects has been specified according to algorithm of the selected interaction mode. In addition, each learning object is presented by a standard content structure which is sawn in Figure 12.

How to Use Learning Style in Learning Environment Design of KouLearn

As described in Figure 11; the learning content is produced based on descriptions of a course on the domain ontology of KouLearn and is adapted according to cognitive learning level of the learner

Figure 11. The algorithm of the interaction modes

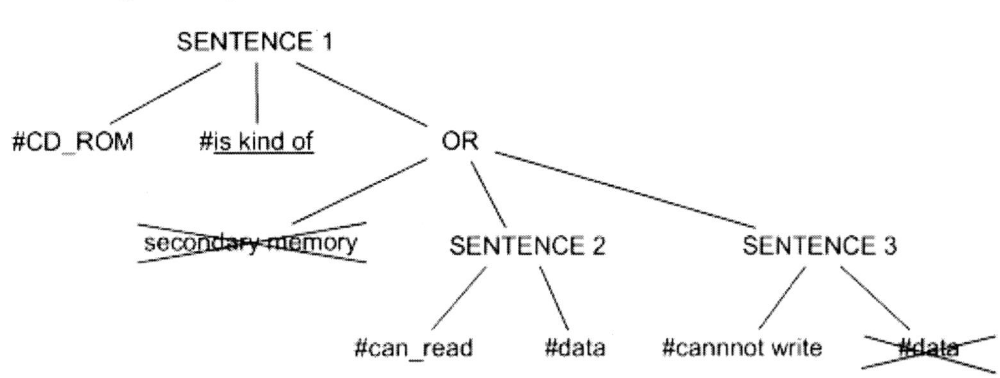

Figure 12. Standard content structure of educational learning objects in KouLearn

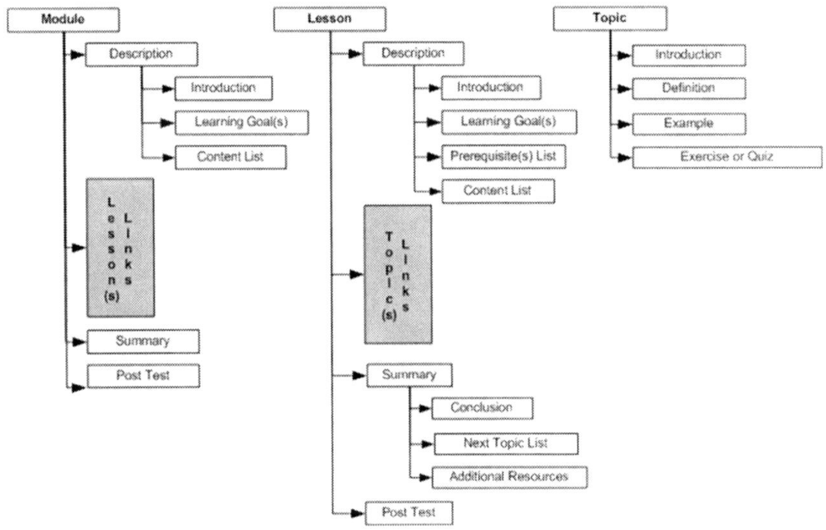

and the learning style which is identified to knowledge acquisition way of the learner like as visual or verbal, if the learner "Course based learning", "Concept based learning" or "Goal based learning" modes of interaction chooses. In addition, the system will guide to the learner to choose "course based learning" or "goal based learning" modes of interaction due to using the learning style of the learner which is identified considering two dimensions are knowledge acquisition way of the learner like as visual or verbal and understanding form of the learner like as sequential or global. If the learner, "Learning Style based learning" mode of interaction will choose, the system redirects the learner "course based learning" or "goal based learning" modes of interaction. Thus, learning style information is used by the system to determine teaching method which used to guide to the learner in the learning environment and to determine learning material types which is used to compose educational learning objects.

We used learning style knowledge for two purposes in the system. One of them is selection of the learning material types which are used to compose learning objects. For example if the learner has visual learning style, the system compose the learning object by mainly visual learning materials such as images, demonstrations. The other purpose is determination of the teching method.We used Felder and Silverman Learning Style Model (Felder & Silverman, 1988) in the system. This learning style model is selected because of that it is meaningful in terms of educational perspective and is suitable for web based learning environment (Carver, Howard & Lavelle, 1996). Also, this model is used as an adaptation source in early adaptive learning systems (Triantafillou, Georgiadou, & Economides, 2006; Aase & Kurfess, 2004; Hong & Kinshuk, 2004).

Felder and Silverman Learning Style Model describe the learning styles of an individual in four dimensions. In this study we used only two dimensions of the model. These dimensions are knowledge acquisition way of the indivual (visual or verbal) and understanding form of the individual (sequential or global).

We used understanding form of the individual to determine a teaching method which is used to guide for the learner in the learning environment. According to that, if an individual is sequential learner tend to gain understanding in linear steps with each step following logically from the previous one. So this type learner is guided to course based learning for learning of the learning materials is logically sorted. On the other hand, if an individual is global learner tend to realize that he (she) need the big picture of a subject before he (she) can master details. So this type learner is guided to goal based learning for seeing all learning goals of a subject and selecting individual subjects by him (her) self.

We used knowledge acquisition way of the indivual to determine learning material types which is used to compose educational learning objects. According to that, if an individual is visual learner tend to learn mostly visual materials such as pictures, diagrams, films, demonstrations. So, an educational learning object is composed by using mostly visual materials for this type learner. If an individual is verbal learner tend to learn mostly verbal materials such as textbooks, lecture notes, explanations. So, an educational learning object is composed by using mostly verbal materials for this type learner.

IMPLEMENTATION OF KOULEARN: A LEARNING MODULE FOR TEACHING OF RESONANCE SUBJECT

In this chapter we explain working of the components of KouLearn. For this purpose, we created a learning module for teaching of Resonance subject by using the components of KouLearn and evaluated running of the system.

Firstly, we identified important concepts of the example learning module. In addition, the conceptual graphs for learning goals and course concepts of the learning module were created by a tutor and an instructional technology expert. In addition, we created some learning materials for this learning module. Then, important concepts used in creating DAG type conceptual graphs are entered to the domain ontology as individuals of the classes. By this way, first form of the course knowledge base has been created. After that, adaptation rules have been working on this knowledge base by through Jess Rule Engine. The adaptation rules that are running, the knowledge base are renewed again.

For experimantal tests, we tested the knowledge base of the example learning module by some queries to show how the learning object produced by KouLearn. Firstly, we tested that after a learning goal or a domain concept from the knowledge base of the learning module is selected by the learner, the system how learning objects produced. At the query in Figure 13, learning objects that are explains the selected concept (DCC0001) of the learning module are queried, we saw that the system can produce the list of the learning objects (Module "Rezonans Koşulları" and lessons of the module that are Lesson "Paralel Rezonans" and Lesson "Seri Rezonans Koşulları" and topics of the lesssons that are Topic "Tank Devresi", Topic "İdeal LC", etc.) are listed according to the structure of the semantic networks that are defined in the domain ontology of the system are listed correctly. The query result of this example query can be seen in Figure 14. So we tested that the queries of the adaptation engine is working and the information requested in the correct format can make inferences from the knowledge base of the Resonance Learning Module.

In addition to the query based evaluation of the system, we evaluate the learning environment of KouLearn. For this purpose, we reviewed running of the interaction modes in the learning environment. In the learning environment, the learner login to the system by identifier number. And then the learner selects one of the courses. After the course selection, the learner selects one of the interaction modes. Lastly, KouLearn present a learning content to the learner by using the knowledge base of the selected course which has been described by the domain ontlogy, preferenced interaction mode of the learner and user model data has been queried from the user ontology. In the Figure 15, presented learning content can be

Figure 13. The example query is show that the production of learning objects according to the selected concept or goal of the knowledge base of the learning module

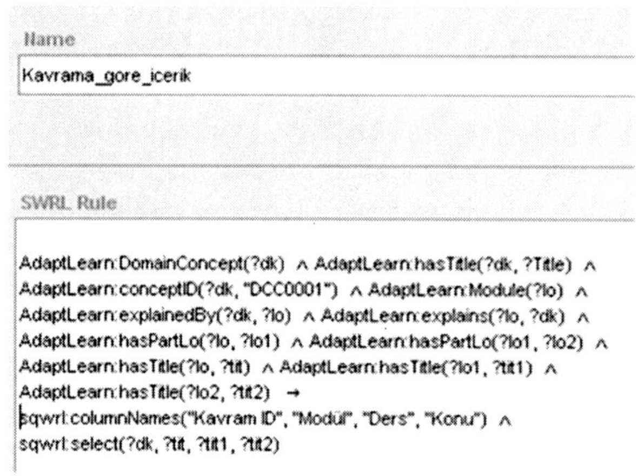

Figure 14. The result of the example query in the Figure 13

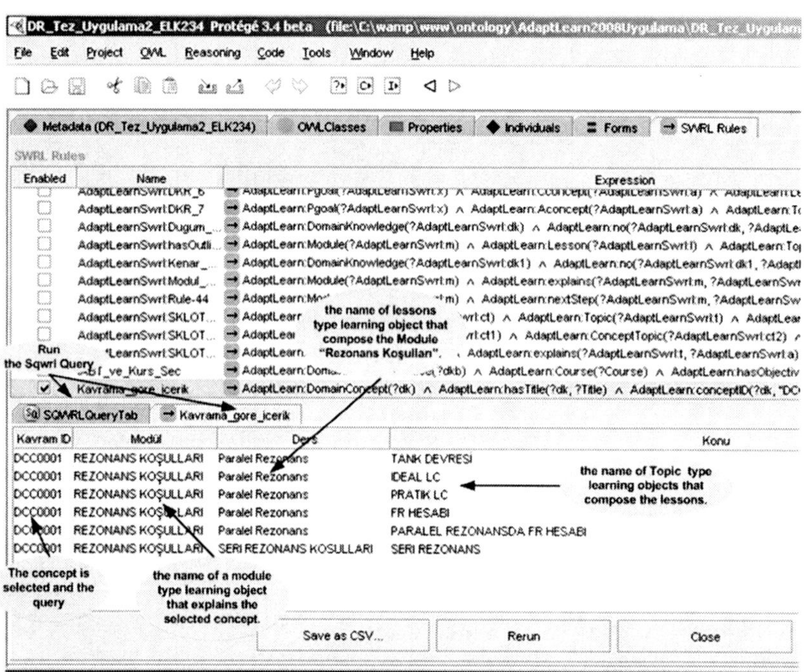

seen in the learning environment. Learning content is presented in educational learning object format and by a standard content structure such as explained in Figure 12.

Also, we test some additional queries to show reusability of both learning objects and learning materials in KouLearn. In the Figure 16, we show that a Sqwrl query is used to explain the reusability of learning objects. In this query, content of the module type learning objects of the learning module have been queried. The query result that is in cvs file format is presented in Figure 17. The marked fields are examined, as seen in Figure 17, *"LessonLGPL001-Paralel RLC"* lesson and sub

Figure 15. Educational learning objects in the learning environment

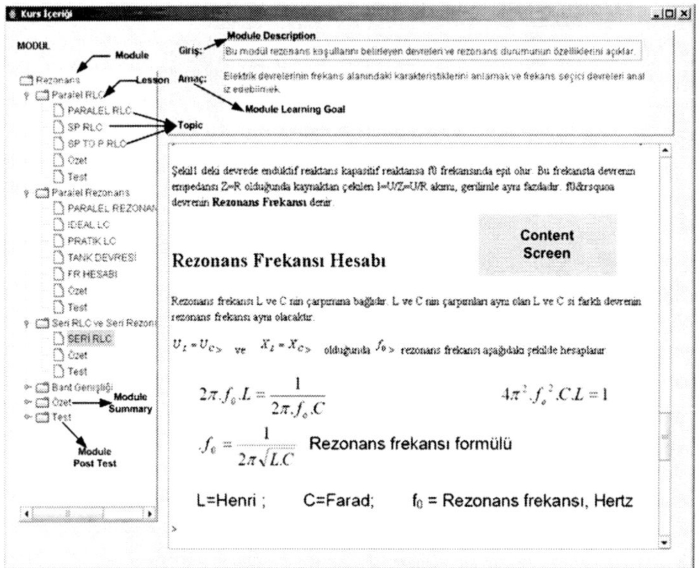

topics of this lesson are used to content parts of both different Module type learning objects that are *"ModuleDCC0000-RLC Devreler"* module and *"ModuleLGG0000-Rezonans"*module of same course. This situation is showed that, same lessons can be used to compose different modules for the learning module. In conclusion, we can say that learning objects or learning materials of a course that are defined in KouLearn can be use once and again in same course or different courses are existed in KouLearn.

FUTURE WORKS

Ontology based modeling approach is most appropriate implementation approach for the personalized learning systems and supports a new sight to solve content related design problems of them. By using ontologies, domain model and user model of the system have been recognized quite easily and in a flexible manner. But, today, there are some problems in inference mechanism and expressivity of the Semantic Web Tools. Because of that especially, methods or ways should be investigated to make more applicable the adaptation model of the personalized learning systems according to ontology based modeling paradigms. So, roadmaps of the personalized learning systems are specified according to researches and developments in the areas of DL based reasoning techniques and Semantic Web rule languages. Therefore, if more expressive rules have been written by rule languages, adaptation capabilities

Figure 16. A query for expressing of reusability of learning objects

Module(?m) ∧ Lesson(?l) ∧ Topic(?t) ∧ hasTitle(?m,?tit1)∧
hasTitle(?l,?tit2) ∧ hasTitle(?t,?tit3) ∧ hasOutline(?m,?l) →
hasOutline(?l,?t) ∧ sqwrl: select(?m,?tit1,?l,?tit2,?t,?tit3) ∧
sqwrl: orderBy(?m) ∧ sqwrl: orderBy(?l)∧ sqwrl: orderBy(?t)

Figure 17. List of "Module" type educational learning objects of the Resonance Learning Module

```
?ModulID,      ?ModulAdı,    ?ModuleAitDersID,?DersAdı,  ?DerseAitKonuID,?KonuAdı
ModuleDCC0000, "RLC DEVRELER", LessonLGPL001, "Paralel RLC", Topic3, "PARALEL RLC"
ModuleDCC0000, "RLC DEVRELER", LessonLGPL001, "Paralel RLC", Topic4, "SP RLC"
ModuleDCC0000, "RLC DEVRELER", LessonLGPL001, "Paralel RLC", Topic5, "SP TO P RLC"
ModuleDCC0000, "RLC DEVRELER", LessonLGPL003, "Seri RLC ve Seri Rezonans", Topic1, "SERÝ RLC"
ModuleDCC0001, "REZONANS KOÞULLARI", LessonDCC0006, "SERI REZONANS KOSULLARI", Topic2, "SERI REZONANS"
ModuleDCC0001, "REZONANS KOÞULLARI", LessonLGPL002, "Paralel Rezonans", Topic20, "PARALEL REZONANSDA FR HESABI"
ModuleDCC0001, "REZONANS KOÞULLARI", LessonLGPL002, "Paralel Rezonans", Topic6, "IDEAL LC"
ModuleDCC0001, "REZONANS KOÞULLARI", LessonLGPL002, "Paralel Rezonans", Topic7, "PRATIK LC"
ModuleDCC0001, "REZONANS KOÞULLARI", LessonLGPL002, "Paralel Rezonans", Topic8, "TANK DEVRESÝ"
ModuleDCC0001, "REZONANS KOÞULLARI", LessonLGPL002, "Paralel Rezonans", Topic9, "FR HESABI"
ModuleDCC0002, "FREKANS SEÇÝCÝ DEVRELER", LessonDCC0008, "FAZ ARTTIRICI DEVRELER", Topic14, "FAZ ARTTIRICI DEVRELER"
ModuleDCC0002, "FREKANS SEÇÝCÝ DEVRELER", LessonDCC0008, "FAZ ARTTIRICI DEVRELER", Topic15, "FAZ GECIKTIRICI DEVRELER"
ModuleDCC0002, "FREKANS SEÇÝCÝ DEVRELER", LessonDCC0009, "FÝLTRE DEVRELERÝ", Topic16, "ALÇAK GEÇÝRGEN FÝLTRE"
ModuleDCC0002, "FREKANS SEÇÝCÝ DEVRELER", LessonDCC0009, "FÝLTRE DEVRELERÝ", Topic17, "YUKSEK GECIRGEN FILTRE"
ModuleDCC0002, "FREKANS SEÇÝCÝ DEVRELER", LessonDCC0010, "RLC DEVRELERDE GÜÇ", Topic18, "SP RLC DEVREDE GUC"
ModuleDCC0003, "BG ve SEÇÝCÝLÝK", LessonDCC0011, "BANT GENÝÞLÝÐÝ", Topic10, "SERI DEVRELERDE BG"
ModuleDCC0003, "BG ve SEÇÝCÝLÝK", LessonDCC0011, "BANT GENÝÞLÝÐÝ", Topic11, "PARALEL DEVRELERDE BG"
ModuleDCC0003, "BG ve SEÇÝCÝLÝK", LessonDCC0013, "KALÝTE FAKTÖRÜ", Topic13, "KALITE FAKTORU"
ModuleDCC0003, "BG ve SEÇÝCÝLÝK", LessonDCC0014, "SECICILIK", Topic19, "BG VE SECICILIK ILISKISI"
ModuleDCC0003, "BG ve SEÇÝCÝLÝK", LessonLGPL004, "Bant Geniþliði", Topic10, "SERI DEVRELERDE BG"
ModuleDCC0003, "BG ve SEÇÝCÝLÝK", LessonLGPL004, "Bant Geniþliði", Topic11, "PARALEL DEVRELERDE BG"
ModuleDCC0003, "BG ve SEÇÝCÝLÝK", LessonLGPL004, "Bant Geniþliði", Topic12, "BG VE KALITE FAKTORU ILISKISI"
ModuleDCC0003, "BG ve SEÇÝCÝLÝK", LessonLGPL004, "Bant Geniþliði", Topic13, "KALITE FAKTORU"
ModuleDCC0003, "BG ve SEÇÝCÝLÝK", LessonLGPL004, "Bant Geniþliði", Topic14, "FAZ ARTTIRICI DEVRELER"
ModuleDCC0003, "BG ve SEÇÝCÝLÝK", LessonLGPL004, "Bant Geniþliði", Topic19, "BG VE SECICILIK ILISKISI"
ModuleLGG0000, "Rezonans", LessonLGPL001, "Paralel RLC", Topic3, "PARALEL RLC"
ModuleLGG0000, "Rezonans", LessonLGPL001, "Paralel RLC", Topic4, "SP RLC"
ModuleLGG0000, "Rezonans", LessonLGPL001, "Paralel RLC", Topic5, "SP TO P RLC"
ModuleLGG0000, "Rezonans", LessonLGPL002, "Paralel Rezonans", Topic20, "PARALEL REZONANSDA FR HESABI"
ModuleLGG0000, "Rezonans", LessonLGPL002, "Paralel Rezonans", Topic6, "IDEAL LC"
ModuleLGG0000, "Rezonans", LessonLGPL002, "Paralel Rezonans", Topic7, "PRATIK LC"
ModuleLGG0000, "Rezonans", LessonLGPL002, "Paralel Rezonans", Topic8, "TANK DEVRESÝ"
ModuleLGG0000, "Rezonans", LessonLGPL002, "Paralel Rezonans", Topic9, "FR HESABI"
ModuleLGG0000, "Rezonans", LessonLGPL003, "Seri RLC ve Seri Rezonans", Topic1, "SERÝ RLC"
ModuleLGG0000, "Rezonans", LessonLGPL004, "Bant Geniþliði", Topic10, "SERI DEVRELERDE BG"
ModuleLGG0000, "Rezonans", LessonLGPL004, "Bant Geniþliði", Topic11, "PARALEL DEVRELERDE BG"
ModuleLGG0000, "Rezonans", LessonLGPL004, "Bant Geniþliði", Topic12, "BG VE KALITE FAKTORU ILISKISI"
ModuleLGG0000, "Rezonans", LessonLGPL004, "Bant Geniþliði", Topic13, "KALITE FAKTORU"
ModuleLGG0000, "Rezonans", LessonLGPL004, "Bant Geniþliði", Topic14, "FAZ ARTTIRICI DEVRELER"
ModuleLGG0000, "Rezonans", LessonLGPL004, "Bant Geniþliði", Topic19, "BG VE SECICILIK ILISKISI"
```

of the learning systems have been enhanced. In addition, if we see that the personalized learning system is a semantic web application, DL based reasoning engines should be designed to handle large-scale knowledge bases. So, efficient and effective analyses of large ontologies such as the learning ontology are being possible. Also, web services are important research and implementation areas for semantic web applications which can be designed distributed systems.

In this work, we prove that user ontology can be developed based on ontological approach. But, this subject should be depthly examined. Also, subject of learning content personalization due to learning styles should be improved.

As a future work, adaptation capabilities of personalized learning systems should be improved. Especially, adaptation rules which are about teaching strategies should be added for creation of personalized content in the e-learning environment.

CONCLUSION

In this study, a personalized learning system that is KOULearn (Kocaeli University Learning System) has been proposed. It is based on learning object and produces a personalized learning content according to learning style and cognitive knowledge level of an individual. The proposed system is situated in advanced learning technologies according to educational perspective and is a semantic web application according to development technologies. The proposed system is aimed to form a personalized learning environment. Three models are included in this system: domain model, user model and adaptation model, respectively. Components of the system have been realized by ontology based knowledge modeling approach.

In the proposed system, learning material has been represented by learning object and also, educational content has been represented by digital resource. Each learning object has a structure that is composed of different digital resources. Metadata which is used to define learning object has been developed according to Cisco content model. Metadata which is used to define digital resource has been developed according to content model of Scorm Reference Model. In KouLearn, we proposed a new domain ontology which is suitable to produce personalized learning content has been developed by integrating two main learning object standards and domain model structure that is used in Intelligent Tutoring System (ITS) and Adaptive Educational Hypermedia System (AEHS) with ontology based knowledge modeling.

Adaptation model of the proposed system has been developed by DL based reasoning and rule based reasoning technologies which are used to inference from the domain ontology and knowledge is about the user in accordance with interaction modes of the system. Adaptation model is composed of two main parts. One part of it is adaptation rules which are used to contsruct relations are among the layers of domain model which are represented by definitions and descriptions of classes in the domain ontology. The other part of it is the adaptation engine. It is composed of three software agents. These agents have been realized to make inference according to DL based reasoning techniques. Some methods of the Protege Reasoning API and SQWRLQuery API have been used to construct the adaptation engine.

User model of the proposed system is static that is used to determine cognitive knowledge level and learning style of the individual. For learning style based personalization, Felder and Silverman Learning Style Model has been used.

Execution of the personalized learning content structure and learning environment of the system, related to electric education, has been examined by resonance learning module which is constituted considering personalization requirements of the system.

This work is proved that ontology based modelling approach is applicaple method to recognize designing of the personalized learning systems. By using ontologies and semantic web reasoning techniques models of the personalized learning system can be implemented quite easily and in a flexible manner.

REFERENCES

Aase, M., & Kurfess, F. J. (2004, August). *Utilizing Learning Styles for Interactive Tutorials*. Paper presented at the IEEE International Conference on Advanced Learning Technologies (ICALT 2004), Joensuu, Finland, (2004).

ADL. (2002). Advanced Distributed Learning Sharable Content Object Reference Model Version 1.3, Application Profile Working Draft 0.9, *Advanced Distributed Learning Network*, Retrieved May 06, 2009, from http://xml.coverpages.org/SCORMV13-SeqAppProfile.pdf

Antoniou, G., & Van Harmelen, F. (2008). *A semantic web primer* (2nd ed.). Cambridge, MA: The MIT Press.

Aroya, L., & Dicheva, D. (2004). The new challenges for e-learning: the educational semantic web. *Journal of Educational Technology & Society*, *7*(4), 59–69.

Baader, F., Calvanese, D., McGuinness, D. L., Nardi, D., & Patel-Schneider, P. F. (Eds.). (2003). *The Description Logic Handbook: Theory, Implementation, and Applications*. New York, NY, USA: Cambridge University Press.

Barrit, C., Lewis, D., & Wieseler, W. (1999). CISCO Systems Reusable Information Object Strategy Version 3.0. *Cisco Systems*. Retrieved May 06, 2008, from http://www.cisco.com/warp/public/779/ibs/solutions/learning/whitepapers/el_cisco_rio.pdf

Berners-Lee, T., Hendler, J., & Lassila, O. (2001). The Semantic Web. *Scientific American*, *184*(5), 34–43. doi:10.1038/scientificamerican0501-34

Bick, M., Adelsberger, H., & Pawlowski, J. (2000). The Essen Learning Model A Step Towards a Standard Model of Learning Processes. In J. Bourdeau & R. Heller (Ed.), *Proceedings of World Conference on Educational Multimedia, Hypermedia and Telecommunications 2000* (pp. 118-123). Chesapeake, VA: AACE.

Brusilovsky, P. (2003). Developing adaptive educational hypermedia systems: From design models to authoring tools. In: T. Murray, S. Blessing and S. Ainsworth (Ed.), *Authoring Tools for Advanced Technology Learning Environment (*377-409). Dordrecht, The Netherlands: Kluwer Academic Publishers.

Brusilovsky, P., & Vassileva, J. (2003). Course sequencing techniques for large-scale web-based education. *International Journal of Continuing Engineering Education and Lifelong Learning, 13*(1-2), 75–94.

Carver, C. A., Howard, R. A., & Lavelle, E. (1996). Enhancing student learning by incorporating student learning styles into adaptive hypermedia. In *Proceedings of EDMEDIA 96 - World Conference on EducationalMultimedia and Hypermedia* (118-123). Boston.

Choe, H. (2006). Ontology based e-learning Authoring System. *Asian Journal of Information Technology*, *5*(12), 1319–1322.

Chrysostomou, C. P., & Papadopoulos, G. A. (2005, May). *An Evaluation of E-Learning Technologies and Trends: Establishing and Object-Oriented Approach to Learning Object Design and Development*. Paper presented at *the First International Conference on E-Business and E-learning (EBEL'05),* 88-96. Amman, Jordan. Retrieved May 06, 2008, from http://www.psut.edu.jo/EBEL/pdf/16.pdf

Cisco Systems Inc. (2003). Reusable Learning Object Authoring Guidelines: How to Build Modules, Lessons, Topics Version 4.5. Retrieved May 06, 2008, from http://db.formez.it/fontinor.nsf/c658e3224c300556c1256ae90036d38e/DF95A2799A3D7085C1256E59003B33F5/$file/Cisco%20Reusable%20LO%20Authoring%20Guidelines%2007-2003.pdf

Dicheva, D., Sosnovsky, S., Gavrilova, T., & Brusilovsky, P. (2005, July). *Ontological web portal for educational ontologies*. Paper presented at International Workshop on Applications of Semantic Web Technologies for E-Learning (*SWEL*) AIED'*05*. Amsterdam.

Dodds, P. (2001). Advanced Distributed Learning Sharable Content Object Reference Model Version 1.2, *The SCORM Content Aggregation Model*, Retrieved May 06, 2009, from http://coco.ccu.uniovi.es/e-learning/scorm/overview/organiza/ContentAM.pdf

Duncan, C. (2003). Granularization. In Littlejohn, A. (Ed.), *Reusing online resources: a sustainable approach to eLearning* (pp. 12–19). London: Kogan Page.

Duval, E., & Hodgins, W. (2007). Learning objects revisited. In McGreal, R. (Ed.), *Online Education Using Learning Objects* (pp. 71–82). London: Routledge/Falmer.

Dvedžić, V. B. (2004). Web intelligence and artificial intelligence in education. *Journal of Educational Technology & Society*, *7*(4), 29–39.

Felder, R. M., & Silverman, L. K. (1988). Learning and Teaching Styles in Engineering Education. *English Education*, *78*(7), 674–681.

Gennari, J. H., Musen, M. A., Fergerson, R. W., Grosso, W. E., Crubézy, M., & Eriksson, H. (2003). The evolution of Protégé: an environment for knowledge-based systems development. I*nt. J. Hum.-* [IJMMS]. *Comput. Stud.*, *58*(1), 89–123.

Gruber, T. (1993). A translation approach to portable ontology specifications. *Knowledge acquisition*, 5(2), 199-220. Retrieved May 06, 2008, from http://ksl-web.stanford.edu/knowledge-sharing/papers/README.html#ontolingua-intro

Hamel, C. J., & Ryan-Jones, D. (2002). Designing Instruction with Learning Objects. *International Journal of Educational Technology*, *3*(1).

Hatzilygeroudis, I., Prentzas, J., & Garofalakis, J. (2005, July). *Personalized learning in web-based intelligent educational systems: technologies and techniques*. Paper presented at the 11th International Conference on Human-Computer Interaction (HCII-2005), Las Vegas, Nevada, USA.

Hendler, J. (2001). Agents and the Semantic Web. *IEEE Intelligent Systems*, *16*(2), 30–37. doi:10.1109/5254.920597

Hong H. & Kinshuk, (2004). Adaptation to student learning styles in web based educational systems. In L.Cantoni & C. McLoughlin (Ed.), *Proceedings of ED-MEDIA 2004 - World Conference on Educational Multimedia, Hypermedia & Telecommunications* (pp. 491-496). Lugano, Switzerland: AACE.

Horrocks, I., Patel-Schneider, P. F., Boley, H., Tabet, S., Grosof, B., & Dean, M. (2004). SWRL: A Semantic Web Rule Language Combining OWL and RuleML. *W3C Member Submission*. Retrieved May 6, 2009, from http://www.w3.org/Submission/SWRL/

IEEE LTSC. (2002). Draft Standard for Learning Object Metadata, IEEE Learning Technology Standards Committee, IEEE 1484.12.1-2002. *IEEE LTSC Working Group*, Retrieved May 06, 2008, from http://ltsc.ieee.org/wg12/files/LOM_1484_12_1_v1_Final_Draft.pdf

Karampiperis, P., & Sampson, D. (2004, August). *Adaptive instructional planning using ontologies*. Paper presented at the IEEE International Conference on Advanced Learning Technologies (ICALT'2004), Joensuu, Finland.

Koesling, A. W., Krause, D., & Herder, E. (2008). Flexible Adaptivity in AEHS Using Policies. In Nejdl, W. (Eds.), *AH 2008, LNCS 5149* (pp. 410–415). Heidelberg: Springer.

Kontopoulos, E., Vrakas, D., Kokkoras, F., Bassiliades, N., & Vlahavas, I. (2008). An ontology-based planning system for e-course generation. *Expert Systems with Applications*, *35*(1-2), 398–406. doi:10.1016/j.eswa.2007.07.034

Madhour, H. Forte, M.,W. (2006). *Semantic Learning Model and eXtended Student Model: Towards an AHAM-based adaptive system*. Paper presented at WBE 2006, Puerto Vallarta, Mexico.

Merrill, M. (1998). Knowledge analysis for effective instruction. *CBT Solutions* (pp.1-11). Retrieved May 09, 2009 from http://id2.usu.edu/Papers/KnowledgeObjects.PDF

Mizoguchi, R., & Bourdeu, J. (2000). Using Ontological Engineering to Overcome AI-ED Problems. *International Journal of Artificial Intelligence in Education*, *11*(2), 107–121.

Mohan, P., Greer, J., & McCalla, G. (2003, August). Instructional planning with learning objects. Paper presented at the 18th International Joint Conference on AI Workshop on Knowledge Representation and Automated Reasoning for E-Learning System (KRR-5), Acapulco, Mexico.

O'Connor, M., Knublauch, H., & Tu, S. (2005). Supporting Rule System Interoperability on the Semantic Web with SWRL. In *Proceedings. 4th International Semantic Web Conference (ISWC-2005)* (pp.974-986). Held Galway, Ireland.

Oguejiofor, E., Kicinger, R., Popovici, E., Arciszewski, T., & De Jong, K. (2004). Intelligent Tutoring Systems: an ontology-based approach. *International Journal of IT in Architecture. Engineering and Construction*, *2*(2), 115–128.

Onaindía, E., & Sapena, O. Garrido. A. (2007, October). *An AI planning-based approach for automated design of learning routes*. Paper presented at the ECEL 2007, 6th European Conference on e-Learning, Copenhagen, Denmark.

Pahl, C., & Holohan, E. (2004). Ontology Technology for the Development and Deployment of Learning Technology Systems - a Survey. In L. Cantoni & C. McLoughlin (Ed.), *Proceedings of World Conference on Educational Multimedia, Hypermedia and Telecommunications 2004* (pp. 2077-2084). Chesapeake, VA: AACE.

Papanikolaou, K. A., Grigoriadou, M., Kornilakis, H., & Magoulas, G. D. (2002). INSPIRE: An INtelligent System for Personalized Instruction in a Remote Environment. In *Revised Papers From the Nternational Workshops Ohs-7, Sc-3, and Ah-3 on Hypermedia: Openness, Structural Awareness, and Adaptivity* (August 14 - 18, 2001). S. Reich, M. Tzagarakis, and P. D. Bra (Ed), Lecture Notes In Computer Science, 2266, 215-225.

Paramythis, A., & Loidl-Reisinger, S. (2004). Adaptive Learning Environments and e-Learning Standards. *Electronic Journal of e-Learning 2(2)*. Retrieved May 09, 2009 from http://www.ejel.org/volume-2/vol2-issue1/issue1-art11.htm

Sampson, D., & Karagiannidis, C. (2002). From Content Objects to Learning Objects: Adding Instructional Information to Educational Metadata. In *Proceedings of the IEEE International Conference on Advanced Learning Technologies (ICALT 02)* (pp. 513-518).

SQWRL (Semantic Query-Enhanced Web Rule Language). *Protege Wiki Home Page*. Retrieved May 6, 2009, from http://protege.cim3.net/cgi-bin/wiki.pl?SQWRL

Triantafillou, E., Georgiadou, E., & Economides, A. A. (2006). Adaptive Hypermedia Systems: A Review of Adaptivity Variables. In *Proceedings of the Fifth Panhellenic Conference–Information and Communication Technologies in Education* (pp.75-82). Thessaloniki, Greece.

Ullrich, C. (2005). Course generation based on HTN planning. In A. Jedlitschka & B. Brandherm (Ed.), *Proceedings of 13th Annual Workshop of the SIG Adaptivity and User Modeling in Interactive Systems*, (pp.74-79).

Vassileva, J., & Wasson, B. (1996, September). *Instructional planning approaches: from tutoring towards free learning*. Paper presented at the Proceedings of Euro-AIED'96, Lisbon.

Verbert, K., Klerkx, J., Meire, M., Najjar, J., & Duval, E. (2004). Towards global component architecture for learning objects: An ontology based approach. *Lecture Notes in Computer Science*, *3292*, 713–722.

Wenying, G., & Deren, C. (2006). Semantic Approach for e-learning System. *In Proceedings of First International Multi-Symposiums on Computer and Computational Sciences (IMSCCS 2006)*, (vol.2, pp.442-446). Hangzhou, Zhejiang, China.

Wiley, D. A. (2000). *Learning object design and sequencing theory*. (Unpublished doctoral dissertation), Brigham Young University.

Wu, H. Kort.E., De Bra,P. (2001). Design Issue for General Purpose Adaptive Hypermedia Systems. *In Proceedings of the ACM Conference on Hypertext and Hypermedia* (pp.141-150), Aarhus, Denmark.

Chapter 14
A Survey of Optimized Learning Pathway Planning and Assessment Paper Generation with Swarm Intelligence

Lung-Hsiang Wong
National Institute of Education, Singapore

Chee-Kit Looi
National Institute of Education, Singapore

ABSTRACT

One major direction in research on technology-enabled learning systems revolves round the notion of generating optimal learning pathways. Two examples of the application areas that could be presented as search and optimization problem in the context of Artificial Intelligence are:- (1) Adaptive selection and sequencing of learning objects based on the learning profiles, preferences and abilities of individual learners; (2) Automatic composition of assessment or examination papers based on instructors' specifications. In this chapter, we present a critical discussion of the research which is concerned with the application of the paradigm of "swarm intelligence" in these two areas. The main aim of this survey is to highlight the new trends and key research achievements that have been realised in the last few years. We will also outline a range of relevant research issues and challenges that have been generated by this body of work.

INTRODUCTION

Since the early years of research in Intelligent Tutoring System (ITS), researchers in the educational technology field has been deploying Artificial Intelligence (AI) to resolve the difficulties in automating decision making or data processing for various educational application systems. However, classic AI techniques like rule-based systems which have been used by earlier ITSs have been gradually losing their edge due to their limitations in dealing with the complex and uncertain nature of learning activities. The knowledge that is incorporated into such systems may be inadequate to take account of the different contexts of use, and the different goals and perspectives of end

DOI: 10.4018/978-1-61692-008-1.ch014

users. This is probably one of the reasons that the research activities in conventional single-machine ITS's have been "saturated" and declining since late 1990s.

We observe that in the past decade, what we have learned in ITS research has not been translated to the design of recent networked learning systems in a significant way yet. The design of such new systems may not directly adhere with the conventional ITS framework as a whole as they do not consist all four typical ITS modules – interface, domain knowledge, tutoring and student modeling. Instead they adopt and refine individual existing ITS techniques that belong only to specific components of the ITS, say, the content sequencing technique (one classic ITS technique under the tutoring module) or the overlay model (a classic ITS student modeling technique), in the context of a broader learning environment (e.g., Shang & Shi, 2000).

Meanwhile, researchers and designers of learning technologies have been exploring the use and application of techniques in soft computing, an umbrella term in AI that encompasses neural networks, fuzzy systems, genetic algorithms, and so on, into education-oriented systems. Being tolerant of imprecision, uncertainty, partial truth and approximation in solving NP-hard problems, soft computing offers the potential for feasible solutions to such potentially complex data processing and decision making processes in the new generation of learning systems.

In this paper, we survey the educational applications of yet another set of soft computing techniques – swarm intelligence (Bonabeau, Dorigo & Theraulaz, 1999). This set of algorithms is inspired by and simulates natural phenomena like the swarms of insects, birds or fishes in the form of multi-agent systems (MAS) – hence the alternative name "self-organizing agents." Typically, individual agents in such MAS possess low-level intelligence. But at the aggregate level, through some evolutionary mechanisms, high-level intelligence and adaptability could emerge from swarms of such agents. These algorithms are known to be good for solving NP-hard problems (Zhang & Lu, 2007).

In the educational technology field, swarm intelligence has been applied in various optimization tasks like curriculum planning, intelligent assessment paper generation, computer adaptive testing, student group forming, and class/exam scheduling. Except for scheduling, a common characteristic of these applications is that they emphasize the monitoring of the background, learning behaviors and performances of individuals or groups of students in order to improve their intelligence, somewhat resembling the student modeling functionality of typical ITS. Such applications are about "learning about learners" (Chen, 2008).

To date, however, no comprehensive literature survey has been conducted in this area. In this paper, we present a critical discussion of the applications of swarm intelligence in two particular areas: (1) adaptive learning object selection and sequencing according to the learner profile, preferences and ability of individual students (which are essentially state-of-the-art solutions to the classic ITS problem of curriculum sequencing); (2) automatic composition of assessment or examination papers based on the instructors' specifications (which may offer potential add-on solutions to the student modeling process of typical ITS). As functionalities in learning systems, they bear some resemblance in their computational processes as they are both relevant to optimized selections of certain objects. The main aim of this survey is to highlight the new trends and key research achievements that have been carried out in the last few years. We will also outline a range of relevant research issues and challenges that have been generated by this body of work.

SWARM INTELLIGENCE

A common feature of swarm intelligence and the "conventional" multi-agent systems (MAS) is that both constructs do not rely on centralized control of individual agents' behaviors; each agent has limited, local knowledge of the environment that it is situated in. In contrast, individual agents in a conventional MAS usually possess the intelligence of a "mini expert system" (e.g., pedagogical agents (Johnson, 1998) or virtual students (Chan & Baskin, 1990). The intelligence of the agents in a swarm intelligence system is typically as low as the insects or birds that they are simulating. Furthermore, swarm agents do not directly communicate; instead, they exchange information through leaving marks in the environment or observing the locations of their peers nearby. Through individual agents' reactions to such indirectly transferred information, the entire swarm will gradually self-organize, thus leading to the emergence of collective behaviors that demonstrate high intelligence.

The key feature of swarm intelligence is "to balance exploitation (of the known best solution) and exploration (of the unknown solutions)" (Dagli & Kilicay, 2006). Such a feature facilitates adaptability in such swarm systems in dynamic or unstable environments, e.g., the best solution in the present may become invalid in the next moment (Holland, 1992; Di Marzo, Gleizes & Karageorgos, 2006).

Next, we will give a brief introduction to the two sets of swarm intelligence algorithms, namely, Ant Colony Systems and Particle Swarm Optimizations, which have been applied to educational applications.

Ant Colony System or Ant Colony Optimization (ACO)

In the natural phenomenon of Ant Colony Optimization, ants construct networks of paths to link their nests with available food sources. These networks form minimum spanning trees, minimizing the energy ants expend in bringing food into the nest. This globally optimal structure emerges from the simple actions of the individual ants (Parunak, 1997; Dorigo & Stützle, 2004). The ants generated scent markers called "pheromones" to mark the paths that they have passed through for their peers to follow. The initial path will not be straight, but the tendency of the ants to wander even in the absence of pheromones will generate shortcuts across initial meanders. As pheromone paths have some breadth, they tend to merge together to a trace that becomes straighter the more it is used.

The method could not perform well without pheromone decay, or it would lead to the amplification of the initial random fluctuations, which probably would not be optimal. Therefore, the quantity of the pheromone that was "deposited" earlier should be decayed with time.

The ACO has inspired algorithms (e.g., Dorigo, 1992; Bonabeau, Dorigo & Theraulaz, 1999) for planning routes in the Traveling Salesman Problem (TSP – to find a tour of minimal length connecting n cities; each city must be visited once and only once). In the case where the number of cities is huge, soft computing techniques like genetic algorithms or ACO become better alternatives than conventional AI search techniques in solving such a problem.

In an algorithm proposed by Dorigo (1992), for example, a huge set of ant-like agents is moving on the problem graph until each of them completes a tour. Initially, each agent selects the next connected city randomly when it reaches one city and maintains a memory of the cities it has visited and the distance of each edge. After completing a tour, it lays a quantity of pheromone Q/L on each edge that it has used, where Q is a parameter and L the total length of the tour.

With the pheromones being accumulated one each edge, each of the subsequent agents' selection of the next city to visit when it reaches one city will be influenced by the pheromone of each corresponding edge. There is a probability factor here – the greater the value of a particular edge's pheromone, the higher the probability the agent selects the edge. This is the key mechanism to "balance exploitation and exploration".

ACO has been applied to many practical areas like telecommunication network routing, robot control, scheduling and constraint satisfactions, automatic material sorting, and program optimization, among others.

Particle Swarm Optimization (PSO)

Proposed by Eberhart & Kennedy (1995), Particle Swarm Optimization (PSO) simulates flocking birds or schooling fish where these animals could stay in their moving swarm without crashing with each other. Each bird or fish's behavior is governed by the following rules: (1) Maintain the minimum distance with the peers nearby; (2) Maintain the same velocity with the peers nearby; (3) Keep close to the center of the swarm. In other words, the birds or fish must stay observant and react to, as well as influence, the dynamics of the swarm and strive for balance in complying with the three rules (Dorigo & Stützle, 2004).

Similarly, PSO maintains a swarm of particles that are "flying" within an N-dimensional solution space. The coordinate of each particle in the solution space represents a solution to the optimization problem that the algorithm is trying to solve. Each particle adjusts its velocity by "observing" the velocities of the neighboring particles and the currently known best solution, determined by a fitness function, in the swarm. With more iterations of swarming, the swarm will gradually move toward the direction of the globally optimal solution – this is the process of evolution of the particles. When the swarming process satisfies some termination condition, the system will choose the best solution among the particles as the output solution.

As PSO is good for any functional optimization problem, it has become a powerful "rival" of the genetic algorithms. Although both techniques do not guarantee the generation of the genuine globally optimal solution, they are able to discover better solutions in a shorter time than conventional AI techniques. Major application areas of PSO include engineering optimization, scheduling, fine-tuning of neural networks, and personalized recommender systems.

SWARM INTELLIGENCE FOR CONTENT PLANNING & ASSESSMENT PAPER GENERATION

In this section, we will survey prior studies on the applications of swarm intelligence in content planning and assessment paper generation. As this chapter is positioned as an overview survey and due to the space constraint, we will focus only on text-based explanations of the mechanisms without going into the engineering and algorithmic details. Readers who are interested in the software engineering details of individual techniques are advised to refer to the relevant literature.

Content Planning I (ACO-Based)

As a key component of conventional ITS's, content planning, also known as curriculum planning or course planning, refers to the process of selecting of the content for instructional goal that places the student on an appropriate learning path (Wasson, 1990). Most of the early ITS content planning mechanisms rely on rule-based systems who search for the suitable learning paths on a content network represented as a state-space.

Typically, a content network comprises a set of interconnected learning objects. The edge or arc that connects two given learning objects represents the relationship between the two, e.g., learning object A is the "prerequisite knowledge" of B, or "specialization" of C. Such relationships are metadata to facilitate the firing of the "prescriptive (content planning) rules", e.g., "choose prerequisite A before B". Examples of earlier works in this area are Barr, Beard & Alkinson (1976), Peachey & McCalla (1986), and Arshard (1989).

However, prescriptive rules are typically designed based on commonsense or expert notions of how a learning path should be chosen, which are not always valid and could still be relatively rigid. Brookfield (1985) suggests an alternative approach, "successful self-directed learners... place their learning within a social setting in which the advice, information, and skill modelling provided by other learners are crucial conditions for successful learning." The argument finds echoes in the information navigation literature, where the term "social navigation" (Höök & Benyon, 2003) has been coined to describe research reflecting that "navigation is a social and frequently a collaborative process." (Dieberger, Höök, Svensson & Lönnqvist, 2001) In particular, "indirect social navigation" exploits traces of interactions left by others and can be used as the basis of a recommendation system (Shipman, Furuta, Bremer, Chung & Hsieh, 2000).

In the light of the alternative notion, e-learning technology facilitates convenient collection and analysis of the activity logs, the performances and the results of a large pool of learners, a task that is obviously tedious for standalone ITS's. That opens the door for recent studies on data mining-like, constructivist induction mechanisms where the historical data of previous learners' learning paths and/or actual performances can serve as a basis in selecting learning paths for new learners.

Some examples of such e-learning technologies are Hidden Markov Model-based Tutorlet Agents (Niemczyk, 2000), Time Spent Reading algorithm-based Knowledge Sea (Farzan & Bruisilovsky, 2005), and FP-Tree-based cross-level frequent pattern mining for web-based instruction (Huang, Chen & Cheng, 2007). The common feature of these technologies is that they are all statistically inducing the learning paths that most of the previous learners have passed through, and then recommend "the next learning object" after the present learner has completed studying the current object. In this paper, we refer to the learner who is presently accepting the system's recommendation of learning paths as "target learner."

Nevertheless, as Tang & McCalla (2005) argue, making recommendations in e-learning is different from that in other domains (e.g., movie recommendations), as "items liked by learners might not be pedagogically appropriate for them." In other words, the recommended learning paths that are simply "induced" from the most travelled paths by the past learners may not be the genuine optimal paths. To achieve effectively personalized learning path recommendation, there are two issues to consider. First, such mechanisms should select a set of past learners whose characteristics such as the background, learning styles and learning objectives are similar to the given target learner, instead of recommending the most travelled paths and falling into the pitfall of the sheep flock effect or "the rich get richer, the poor get poorer" (Dron, 2006). The greater amount of the past learners are, the more heterogeneous the past learner group is, which will result in greater inaccuracy in the recommended learning paths. Second, apart from the past learners' learning paths, their learning performances should be incorporated into the computation as well. This is because "the road most traveled" is not necessarily the most effective path.

The above-mentioned statistical technologies do not deal with the two issues. Although these technologies could further incorporate some student clustering mechanism to resolve the first issue, the Hidden Markov Model, Time Spent Reading algorithm and FP-Tree which these technologies are based on could only be used to discover usage patterns but not to analyze student performances.

Therefore, some researchers have started to look into adopting ACO to resolve the second issue. Such content planning techniques treat past learners as ant-like agents. Each of the agents traverses the learning paths that its corresponding past learner has gone through, and deposit pheromones on the way. The amounts of the deposited pheromones are either some constant (i.e., merely computing the frequencies of the individual arcs being traversed) or determined by the learner performances. In general, such techniques comprise of two major processes: (1) Computation of the pheromones in the entire content network; (2) Recommendation of a learning path for the target learner.

In recommending a learning path, some systems straightaway display the complete path to a new target learner. Others operate along with the learner's learning progress, that is, the system recommends the next learning object when a learner has completed his/her current learning object. No matter which approach is adopted, when the system "reaches" a learning object, it constructs a roulette wheel to select one from the set of "outgoing" arcs from the current learning object – the roulette wheel works in the way that the more pheromone it is deposited on an outgoing arc as compared with the others, the higher probability that the next object that the arc points to will be selected.

However, there are some significant differences in the detailed designs of the relevant techniques. Seven such techniques, which do not constitute entire learning systems but are incorporated as components of bigger learning systems, are introduced and compared as below. First of all, Gutiérrez, Pardo & Kloos's (2006) approach makes use of both the ex-learners' learning paths and performances to compute the recommended path. In their approach, sequencing (state-space) graphs simply record the numbers of "successful" and "failed" learners of various paths. The information is presented to the target learner every time she finishes a learning unit (a "node" in our context), so she could choose the next unit by referring to how all her peers performed in the same situation.

Van den Berg *et al.*'s (2005) approach applies a highly simplified ACO algorithm which only keeps the records of the paths selected by the learners who have "successfully completed the course", determined by a post-course 5-question multiple-choice quiz, by maintaining a transition matrix that records the number of learner transitions between individual pairs of nodes on such paths. The full path will then be recommended to the next learner with the roulette wheel mechanism. Janssen *et al.* (2007) applied this approach on an e-learning portal with more than 800 students who used or did not use the recommendation mechanism as target users. The finding was that the approach managed to increase the learning effectiveness but not necessarily the efficiency (i.e., students' time spent to complete the course).

Similarly, in developing Experience Matrix System (EMS), Ho, Tsai, Yang & Chuang (2004) incorporate a modified ACO algorithm that is modelled after TSP – the pheromone computation is based merely on the frequency of each arc being visited. To determine the "goodness" of individual learning paths, two factors are taken into consideration, namely, the frequency of each complete path being visited (the higher the better) and the number of learning nodes (the more the better).

The Paraschool System (Semet, Lutton & Collet, 2003; Valigiani *et al.*, 2005) makes use of another modified ACO algorithm. In computing the pheromones, the course designers are required to assign weights to individual arcs within the course network to reflect the "goodness" of the learners following particular outgoing arcs upon completion of a learning node. The weights, which could be considered as a form of "prescriptive preferences", will be adjusted by real learners' performances later. Paraschool deposits two types of pheromones, namely, "success pheromones" and "failure pheromones", on the arcs for future fitness function-based (a concept from Genetic Algorithms) computations and recommendations.

Utilizing the ACO technique as well, the Style-based Ant Colony System (SACS) (Wang, Wang & Huang, 2008) simply categorizes alumni into four learning styles (visual, audio, text or kinesthetic). In recommending the next node, the pheromones deposited by the alumni who fall into the same category with the current learner are favored in the computations. Furthermore, the pheromone computation is not based on alumni's performances but merely the number of times the alumni have traveled.

Similar to but more complex than SACS, the AACS (Attribute-based Ant Colony System) (Yang & Wu, 2009) requires course designers to tag each learning object with two attributes – object type (graphs, videos, text or XML) and object level (initial, introductory, advance, professional). Similarly, the instructors need to tag each learner with two attributes – learning style (corresponding to object type) and knowledge level (corresponding to object level). When each ant-like agent deposits the pheromones along their ways, the amount of the pheromones depend on the similarity level between the attributes of the learner that the agent represents and the attributes of the learning objects that the agent passes through.

Some other researchers have proposed the complementary combination of prerequisite rules and social navigation in content planning. For example, both CoFind (Dron, Siviter, Boyne & Mitchell, 2000) and PRS (Hummel *et al.*, 2007) incorporate metadata and direct recommendations by the members of the learning community (by rating individual learning objects) to recommend learning paths. However, both techniques' direct recommendation mechanisms make use of relatively simple statistical method, not ACO.

On the contrary, Wong & Looi's (2002; 2009) earlier work, DYLPA (DYnamic Learning Path Advisor), was probably the first learning path recommendation technique that combines "prescriptive rules" and ACO-based "social navigation". DYLPA requires the instructor to specify the "DYLPA training size" with an amount of *N*. At the early stage after a DYLPA-based e-learning system is launched and before the number of learners (or ex-learners) hits *N*, the learning path recommendation mechanism relies solely on the prescriptive rules. This is to prevent inaccurate recommendation by the ACO algorithm due to low training size.

When the number of ex-learners grows beyond *N*, the ACO-based mechanism is triggered. The system selects up to *N* ex-learners with high similarity levels with the target learner, and computes and deposits the pheromones according to their traveled paths and performances. If the number of the selected "similar" ex-learners is less than *N*, say, *K*, the system will generate a "prescriptive agent" that traverses the content network according to the prescriptive rules. The pheromones that are deposited by the prescriptive agent are multiplied by *(N-K)*. In other words, even if there are ant-like agents who deposit pheromones, the "prescriptive path" still carries a weight in the computation; however, the latter's weight will be gradually reduced as the number of ex-learner grows.

A notable issue is that whether the pheromones generated by such ACO-based techniques should be time decaying (evaporating). We argue that such a feature is important due to the following reasons: (1) when a greater set of historical data is accumulated, the number of learners that are more "similar" to the current learner tends to increase, resulting in more "accurate" pheromones/recommendations; (2) possible updates of the course content such as changes of network topology, addition or deletion of learning nodes, and amendments of the contents might affect the overall performances of the "similar" ex-learners who were enrolled at different period of time, making the previously deposited pheromones less accurate in predicting the performances of the new learners. The first two techniques introduced above do not incorporate time decaying. The rest of the techniques implement such a mechanism in different manner but each of them has been able to fit into the needs of the overall design of the respective technique.

Figure 1 summarizes the features of the seven techniques.

Figure 1 shows that most of the techniques reviewed in this section only make use of infor-

Figure 1. Comparison of the features of six ACO-based learning path recommendation techniques

	Gutiérrez *et al.* (2006)	Van den Berg *et al.*(2005)	Ho, Tsai, Yang & Chuang (2004)	Semet, Lutton & Collet (2003)	Wang, Wang & Huang (2008)	Yang & Wu (2009)	Wong & Looi (2002; 2009)
Pheromone computation based on ex-learners' paths or performances ?	paths	paths	paths	Paths + performance	paths	paths	paths + performance
Pheromones are time decaying?	no	no	no	yes	yes	yes	yes
Computation based on whose data?	All ex-learners	Only ex-learners who have " successfully " completed the course	All ex-learners	All ex-learners	Categorizing ex-learners according to their learning styles; only learners who fall into the same category with the target learner are selected	All ex-learners; but the pheromone "thickness" is adjusted according to the similarity level between each ex-learner and the target learner	Computing the similarity level between the attributes of the target learner and individual alumni; only alumni who have high similarity levels with the target learners are selected
Combining prescriptive and induction planning?	no	no	no	no; but human course designers are to annotate weights on each arc in the content network as "prescribed preferences"	no	no	yes

mation about ex-learners' learning paths but not their performances in computing the pheromones. These techniques conform to the notion of social navigation where collective opinions are prioritized. However, in order to achieve truly personalized learning path recommendations, three of the techniques indeed recognize the importance of matching target and ex-learners' attributes. The above-stated research group of Gutiérrez & co. has even "reverse-engineered" their ACO-based learning path recommendation technique to develop a tool for evaluating, based on ex-learners' performances, the courses designed by human instructors (Gutiérrez, Valigiani, Jamont, Collet & Kloos, 2007). Similarly, Wong & Looi (2002) proposed the use of such a technique to data-mine and identify new prescriptive rules for content planning.

A somewhat related study was carried out by Koper (2004) who made use of NetLogo (Wilensky, 1999), a simulation tool, to develop a simulated learning network based on a "drop-out model" (e.g., Ryan & Deci, 2000). Education psychologists developed drop-out models to simulate and study the motivational factors of the drop-outs of learning networks. For example, a learner's learning motivation may decline due to external interferences, the perception of low curriculum quality or the selections of unsuitable learning objects; when her learning motivation drops to zero, she will quit the learning network.

Koper's study aimed to find out whether the ACO-based learning path recommendation could raise the learners' learning motivation, thus the decrease of the drop-out rate of the entire learning network. In his simulation environment, a group of ant-like agents representing individual learners traverse the learning object network, select learning objects to learn according to the path recommendation mechanism, store their performances in the form of pheromones, and therefore influence their peers' learning paths.

The simulation results showed that the ACO algorithm did successfully decrease the drop-out rate. However, as the simulation did not incorporate empirical data but merely relied on the theoretical drop-out models for computations, it is doubtful whether the findings could be applied to real-life situations.

Content Planning II (ACO-Based)

Unlike the systems described in the previous section where ex-learners' learning paths and performances are used to induce and recommend learning paths, Chang, Tsai & Chu (2008) and Huang, Huang & Cheng (2008) employed PSO to "compose" a set of learning materials that are tailored to individual students' needs. Chang, Tsai & Chu's PCCPSO (Personalized Course Composition approach based on PSO) algorithm focuses on composing suitable "formal" learning materials to generate a "formal" course. On the other hand, Huang, Huang & Cheng's SBACPSO (Serial Blog Article Composition PSO) algorithm is specialized in selecting course-related blog articles written by the instructors, the course designers and the learners as learning references. As the application of PSO in content planning is a relatively new research direction in the field, we only managed to discover two related systems in the prior literature to date, as compared to seven ACO-based systems discussed above.

The learning materials or blog entries retrieved and stored by both mechanisms must be tagged on their respective attributes like difficulty levels and related learning points. Furthermore, SBACPSO tracks the individual blog entries' number of replies/comments and number of trackbacks (i.e., different bloggers' blog articles which comment on or refer to a given blog article).

The two PSO-based algorithms are governed by different sets of fitness functions. For PCCPSO, the fitness functions are: (1) The learning points (known as "concepts" in the literature) of the composed course to match the learning objectives of the learner; (2) The average difficulty level of the course to match the learner's knowledge level; (3) The estimated learning time of the course to match the learning time specified by the learner. For SBACPSO, the fitness functions are:- (1) The overall difficulty level of the chosen set of blog articles to match the learner's knowledge level; (2) The blog article contents to match the learner's learning objectives; (3) The higher the number of the blog articles' "backtracks" the better; (4) the higher the number of the blog articles' replies the better.

The two algorithms work in a similar manner. At first, the technique generates an initial set of particles, each represents a combination of learning materials or blog articles. More precisely, each particle makes use of a set of binary numbers to represent the selections or no selections of individual materials or articles say, if there are five materials/articles called a, b, c, d, e stored in the database, then particle 11001 represents the combination of a, b, e being selected while c, d not.

After being initialized, the particle swarm starts to "fly" (swarm) within the solution space. The system makes use of the above-mentioned fitness functions to assess the "goodness" of each particle in order to adjust the "swarming velocities" of the particles, i.e., to strike a balance between "maintaining the same velocity with neighboring particles" and "flying toward the particle with the 'best' solution so far." When each particle reaches its new location, it will adjust the solution that it "carries" according to the new coordinate, thus producing a new generation of particles. The particle swarm continues to evolve in the same manner until the best particle reaches an expected fitness value or the computation process satisfies a stop condition, e.g., at most 500 rounds of swarming.

A potential pitfall of both algorithms is that they are only composing courses or blog article sets but not ordering them. The sequencing of the learning content would affect the performances of the learners. Therefore, we argue that both systems could at least incorporate some above-mentioned prescriptive rules in order to recommend ordered sets of learning materials or blog articles to their target learners.

Intelligent Assessment Paper Generation (PSO-Based)

Intelligent assessment paper generation refers to automated selection and composition of assessment papers from an assessment question database satisfying various constraints pre-specified by the instructor, e.g., number of questions, average difficulty level, proportions of relevant chapters, etc. Examples of the techniques that have been used in intelligent assessment paper generation are random functions (e.g., Ying & Hu, 2000), Expert System (e.g., Tian, Chen & Xu, 2000), Constraint Satisfaction Programming (Dai & Li, 1995), Genetic Algorithms (e.g., Quan & Fan, 1999), Quantitative Model (e.g., Wang & Hou, 2003), and Fuzzy Arithmetic (e.g., Lu & Wang, 2001), etc.

Among those, the random function method is relatively simple and fast in the selections of individual items but the papers generated eventually are often far from being optimal. The genetic algorithm-based solutions might also suffer inaccuracy in the search process due to way too many parameters to adjust (Wang & Chu, 2008). Therefore, the PSO algorithms which are able to elegantly adjust multiple parameters become a plausible alternative for the stated applications.

There are five studies in PSO-based assessment paper generation. In Huang's (2006) system, each assessment question stored in the database is assigned a difficulty coefficient. The PSO algorithm begins with generating the initial set of particles to swarm in the solution space, in order to find the optimal combination of assessment questions (i.e., the number or ratio of the questions with various difficulty coefficients) that matches the desired average difficulty level of the entire paper as pre-set by the instructor.

Chen & Jiang (2007) refer to the algorithm that they adopted for their assessment paper generation technique as "artificial fish schooling algorithm", but it is essentially PSO. Their algorithm strongly resembles Chang, Tsai & Chu's (2008) PCCPSO as described above except that one is for selecting assessment questions while another for selecting teaching materials. Chen & Jiang's algorithm is governed by three sets of control variables pre-specified by the instructors, namely, the learning points to cover, the ratios of the questions with various difficulty levels, and the total marks of the entire paper. The system generates a fitness function that incorporates these control variables, followed by generating an initial set of "artificial fish" (particles) in the form of *binary* number strings to represent whether or not to select individual assessment questions in the database. The system makes use of the fitness function to evaluate the "goodness" of individual particles, and let the particles swarm toward the direction of the optimal solution, until a certain stopping condition is satisfied.

Yin, Chang, Hwang, Hwang & Chen's (2006) technique works in almost the same way as Chen & Jiang's technique. The underlying difference is the set of control parameters to be pre-specified by the instructor, namely, the difficulty level, the knowledge points to cover, the assessment time limit, and the number of repeatedly chosen items in the previously generated papers.

On the other hand, Wang & Chu (2008) incorporate the genetic algorithm-inspired operations of crossover and mutation in their PSO-based technique. Each assessment item in the database carries several attributes like question type and difficulty level, all of which are coded as binary numbers, e.g., [1 1 0 1 0 1 1]. The binary string is known as "question model". The control parameters pre-specified by t, and so on. The computation process is, (1) randomly selects an initial set of items and generates a question model for each of them (to become a particle); (2) performs mutation (selects some particles and changes their swarming velocities) and crossover (selects a pair of particles and exchanges one or a few corresponding binary numbers held by certain positions in the question models; the new pair of particles will replace the weakest pair in the current particle swarm); (3) evaluate the particle swarm which has undergone mutation and crossover operations to see whether a stopping condition is satisfied; if not, go back to (2); (4) when a stopping condition is satisfied, searches for a set of assessment items that match individual question models represented by the particle swarm.

Finally, Lü's (2008) modified PSO-based system models the optimizing assessment paper in terms of a two-dimensional matrix S_{mn}, where m is the required number of items in the assessment paper while n is the number of attributes of each assessment item. In other word, an assessment paper model, as represented by each particle, specifies the attributes of the assessment item set to be optimized. The control parameters consist of the total marks of the entire paper, the total marks of each learning point, the overall difficulty level, the number of each type of questions, and the estimated time to complete the paper. Nevertheless, what makes this approach unique is the integration of another optimization technique called Grey Relational Analysis that avoids a common pitfall of PSO-based algorithms, that is, manual (either by the programmer or the end users – for assessment paper generation, they are the instructors) assignment of *ad-hoc* weights to the conditions or control parameters.

Figure 2 summarizes the characteristics of these techniques.

According to Figure 2, although the five techniques adopt PSO to solve the same optimization

Figure 2. Comparison of four PSO-based assessment paper generation techniques

		Huang (2006)	Chen & Jiang (2007)	Yin, *et al.* (2006)	Wang & Chu (2008)	Lu (2008)
Instructor's control parameters	Difficulty level	Overall difficulty level of the paper	Ratios of items of different difficulty levels	Overall difficulty level of the paper	Overall difficulty level of the paper	Overall difficulty level of the paper
	Learning points covered	–	Learning points covered (and minimum percentage of each point)	Learning points covered	Ratios of different learning points covered	Total marks of individual learning points
	Repeated questions	–	–	Maximum numbers of questions appeared in previous papers	–	–
	Assessment time	–	–	Minimum & maximum time limits	–	Estimated time to complete the paper
	Question types	–	–	–	Ratios of different question types	Numbers of different question types
	Number of questions or total marks	Number of questions	Total marks	–	Number of questions	Total marks
Particle model (What each particle represents?)		Overall paper structure (amounts of questions of different difficulty levels)	Selections or non-selections of individual questions in the database	Selections or non-selections of individual questions in the database	The model of a question (values of various attributes)	The attributes of the assessment question set to be optimized
Algorithm		Typical PSO	Typical PSO	Typical PSO	PSO + Genetic Algorithm	PSO + Grey Relational Analysis

problem (assessment paper generation), the flexibility of the soft computing paradigm is obvious. For example, different techniques require the instructors to pre-specify different sets of control parameters – of course, the more parameters the instructor is to specify, the longer computing time a system will take, and the harder the globally optimal solution will be discovered.

Apart from the control parameters, the forms of the optimal solutions to be generated by the algorithms as reflected by the particle models vary. In Wang & Chu's algorithm, each particle represents the model of an assessment question; the technique will eventually make use of all the evolved particles to pick their corresponding assessment questions. The rest of the algorithms have only one particle in the swarm to represent the overall solution.

Furthermore, as compared to Chen & Jiang's algorithm that makes "the ratios of the questions with various difficulty levels" as a control parameter to be pre-specified by the teachers, Huang's algorithm aims for optimizing the ratios instead.

CONCLUSION

Swarm intelligence has become a field of its own less than two decades ago. In recent years, we witness such a technology being gradually explored and experimented by researchers and designers of educational technologies. As a powerful tool for stochastic analysis, it has been repeatedly proven efficient and effective in solving highly complex optimization problems or pattern recognition. It has provided a class of approaches for the educational technology field which thrives for improving the adaptability of certain "conventional" functionalities of the educational software (e.g., assessment paper generation) and for developing new functionalities (e.g., social navigation-based content planning, computer-based evaluation of human-designed curriculum).

The systems developed by the surveyed work may not be full-fledged ITSs in the conventional sense. However, the ways the AI techniques that are used in such systems are undoubtedly influenced by the ITS paradigm such as applying them to provide or guide curriculum sequencing or the automatic composition of examination paper motivated in prior research work in student modeling and tutoring modules. We predict that with the rise of e-learning and online collaborative learning, swarm intelligence will become a key technology for the development of a new generation of intelligent learning applications. Furthermore, we advocate that researchers and developers of future ITS's should look into these soft computing techniques in order to keep the traditionally single machine-based paradigm current and relevant to the new century of e-, mobile, and community-based/collaborative learning.

REFERENCES

Arshard, F. N. (1989). Knowledge based learning advisors. In *Proceedings of International Conference on Technology and Education* (pp.213-217), Orlando, FL.

Barr, A., Beard, M., & Alkinson, R. C. (1976). The computer as a tutorial laboratory: The Stanford BIP project. *Man-Machine Studies*, *8*, 567–596. doi:10.1016/S0020-7373(76)80021-1

Bonabeau, E., Dorigo, M., & Theraulaz, G. (1999). *Swarm Intelligence: From Natural to Artificial Systems*. New York: Oxford University Press.

Brookfield, S. (1985). Self-directed learning: A critical review of research. In Brookfield, S. (Ed.), *Self-Directed Learning From Theory to Practice* (pp. 5–16). San Francisco: Jossey-Bass.

Chan, T.-W., & Baskin, A. (1990). Learning companion systems. In Frasson, C., & Gauthier, G. (Eds.), *Intelligent Tutoring Systems: At the Crossroads of Artificial Intelligence and Education*. New York: Ablex.

Chang, Y.-J., Tsai, C.-C., & Chu, C.-P. (2008). A personalized course composition mechanism based on PSO. *Presented at: TWELF'08*. Retrieved 7 June 2008, from: http://itech.ntcu.edu.tw/twelf2008/papers/F/F1.pdf

Chen, L., & Jiang, W. (2007). The design and implementation of a general examination system [In Chinese]. *Computer Engineering and Design*, *28*(17), 4285–4289.

Chen, Z. (2008). Learning about learners: system learning in virtual learning environment. *Computers. Communications and Control*, *3*(1), 33–40.

Dagli, C., & Kilicay, N. (2006). Understanding behavior of system of systems through computational intelligence techniques. *IEEE Systems Conference'06* (pp.1-7), Honolulu, USA.

Dai, Y., & Li, X. (1995). An analysis on computer-based automatic assessment paper generation algorithms [In Chinese]. *Mini & Micro Computer Systems*, *16*(9), 51–55.

Di Marzo, G., Gleizes, M.-P., & Karageorgos, A. (2006). Self-organisation and emergence in MAS: An overview. *Informatica*, *30*, 45–54.

Dieberger, A., Höök, K., Svensson, M., & Lönnqvist, P. (2001). Social navigation research agenda. *Presented at Conference on Human Factors in Computing Systems'01*, Seattle, USA.

Dorigo, M. (1992). *Ottimizzazione, apprendimento automatico, ed algoritmi basati su metafora natural*. (Unpublished doctoral dissertation) Politecnico di Milano, Italy.

Dorigo, M., & Stützle, T. (2004). *Ant Colony Optimization*. Cambridge, MA: MIT Press.

Dron, J. (2006). Social software and the emergence of control. *Proceedings of the 6th IEEE International conference on Advanced Learning Technologies '06* (pp.904-908), Kerkrade, Netherlands.

Dron, J., Siviter, P., Boyne, C., & Mitchell, R. (2000). CoFIND: Step towards a self-organising learning environment. In [San Antonio, USA.]. *Proceedings of WebNet*, *2000*, 146–151.

Eberhart, E., & Kennedy, J. (1995). A new optimizer using particle swarm theory. In [Nagoya, Japan.]. *Proceedings of International Symposium on Micro Machine & Human Science*, *1995*, 39–43.

Farzan, R., & Brusilovsky, P. (2005). Social navigation support in e-learning: What are the real footprints? In *Proceedings of ITWP'05*. Edinburgh, UK.

Gutiérrez, S., Pardo, A., & Kloos, C. D. (2006). Finding a learning path: toward a swarm intelligence approach. In [Puerto Vallarta, Mexico.]. *Proceedings of International Conference on Web-based Education*, *06*, 94–99.

Gutiérrez, S., Valigiani, G., Jamont, Y., Collet, P., & Kloos, C. D. (2007). A swarm approach for automatic auditing of pedagogical planning. [Nigata, Japan.]. *Proceedings of IEEE International Conference on Advanced Learning Technologies*, *07*, 136–138.

Ho, J.-H., Tsai, C.-W., Yang, C.-S., & Chuang, C.-Y. (2004). Applying data mining and evolutionary algorithm to the analysis of digital learning paths *(In Chinese)*. In *Proceedings of Workshop on Digital Archives Technologies* (pp.155-161), Taipei, Taiwan.

Holland, J. H. (1992). *Adaptation in Natural and Artificial Systems*. Cambridge, MA: MIT Press.

Höök, K., & Benyon, D. (2003). *Designing Information Spaces: The Social Navigation Approach*. London: Springer.

Huang, L. (2006). The application of PSO in intelligent assessment paper generation [In Chinese]. *Zhenjiang Institute Journal*, *19*(3), 53–56.

Huang, T.-C., Huang, Y.-M., & Cheng, S.-C. (2008). Automatic and interactive e-Learning auxiliary material generation utilizing particle swarm optimization. *Expert Systems with Applications*, *35*(4), 2113–2122. doi:10.1016/j.eswa.2007.09.039

Huang, Y.-M., Chen, J.-N., & Cheng, S.-C. (2007). A method of cross-level frequent pattern mining for web-based instruction. *Journal of Educational Technology & Society*, *10*(3), 305–319.

Hummel, H. G. K., Van den Berg, B., Berlanga, A. J., Drachsler, H., Janssen, J., Nadolski, R., & Koper, R. (2007). Combining social-based and information-based approaches for personalised recommendation on sequencing learning activities. *Learning Technology*, *3*(2), 152–167. doi:10.1504/IJLT.2007.014842

Janssen, J., Tattersall, C., Waterink, W., Van den Berg, B., Van Es, R., Bolman, C., & Koper, R. (2007). Self-organizing navigational support in lifelong learning: How predecessors can lead the way. *Computers & Education*, *49*, 781–793. doi:10.1016/j.compedu.2005.11.022

Johnson, W. L. (1998). Pedagogical agents. In [Beijing, Cina.]. *Proceedings of International Conference on Computers in Education*, *98*, 13–22.

Koper, R. (2004). Increasing learner retention in a simulated learning network using indirect social interaction. *Learning Networks PrePrints Open University of the Netherlands*. Retrieved June 9, 2008, from: http://dspace.ou.nl/bitstream/1820/249/4/preprint-LNsimulation.pdf

Lü, J. (2008). Application of improved PSO in intelligent test paper auto-generation system *(In Chinese). Modern Computer, 2008*(7), 109-111.

Lu, P., & Wang, M. (2001). A study on a strategy for automatic assessment paper generation [In Chinese]. *Computer Development & Applications*, *14*(2), 9–11.

Niemczyk, S. (2000). *On pedagogical-aware navigation of educational media through virtual tutors*. Internal Document, Department of Civil & Environmental Engineering, Massachusetts Inst. of Technology.

Parunak, H. V. D. (1997). "Go to the ant": Engineering principles from natural multi-agent systems. *Annals of Operations Research*, *75*, 69–101. doi:10.1023/A:1018980001403

Peachey, D. R., & McCalla, G. I. (1986). Using planning techniques in intelligent tutoring systems. *Man-Machine Studies*, *24*, 79–98.

Quan, H., & Fan, G. (1999). The study in an intelligent assessment paper generation system based on Genetic Algorithms [In Chinese]. *Journal of Wuhan University: Natural Science Edition*, *45*(5), 758–760.

Ryan, R. M., & Deci, E. L. (2000). Self-determination theory and the facilitation of intrinsic motivation, social developments and well being. *The American Psychologist*, *55*, 68–78. doi:10.1037/0003-066X.55.1.68

Semet, Y., Lutton, E., & Collet, P. (2003). Ant colony optimization for e-learning: observing the emergence of pedagogic suggestions [Indianapolis, IN.]. *Proceedings of IEEE Swarm Intelligence Symposium*, *03*, 46–52.

Shipman, F., Furuta, R., Brenner, D., Chung, C., & Hsieh, H. (2000). Guided paths through web-based collections: Design, experiences, and adaptations. *Journal of the American Society for Information Science American Society for Information Science*, *51*, 260–272. doi:10.1002/(SICI)1097-4571(2000)51:3<260::AID-ASI5>3.0.CO;2-J

Tang, T., & McCalla, G. (2005). Smart Recommendation for an evolving e-learning system: Architecture and experiment. *e-Learning, 4*(1), 105-129.

Tian, X., Chen, G., & Xu, L. (2000). The design and implementation of an expert system for self-assessment paper generation for Guangdong Province [In Chinese] [Singapore.]. *Proceedings of Global Chinese Conference on Computers in Education, 2000*, 475–480.

Valigiani, G., Biojout, R., Jamont, Y., Lutton, E., Bourgeois, C., & Collet, P. (2005). Experimenting with a real-size man-hill to optimize pedagogical paths. *Proceedings of the ACM Symposium on Applied computing '05* (pp.4-8), Santa Fe, NM.

Van den Berg, B., Van Es, R., Tattersall, C., Janssen, J., Manderveld, J., & Brouns, F. (2005). Swarm-based sequencing recommendations in e-learning. [Wroclaw, Poland.]. *Proceedings of International Conference on Intelligence Systems Design and Applications, 05*, 488–493.

Wang, Q., & Chu, L. (2008). The application of PSO in intelligent assessment paper generation *(In Chinese). Neijiang Technology, 2008*(1), 134-135.

Wang, T. I., Wang, K.-T., & Huang, Y.-M. (2008). Using a style-based ant colony system for adaptive learning. *Expert Systems with Applications, 34*(4), 2449–2464. doi:10.1016/j.eswa.2007.04.014

Wang, Y., & Hou, S. (2003). A study on an algorithm for automatic assessment paper generation [In Chinese]. *Harbin Technological University, 35*(3), 342–346.

Wasson, B. (1990). *Determining the focus of Instruction: Content planning for intelligent tutoring systems*. (Unpublished Doctoral Thesis), Department of Computational Science, University of Saskatchewan, Canada.

Wilensky, U. (1999). *NetLogo (and NetLogo User Manual). Center for Connected Learning and Computer-based Modeling*. Northwestern University.

Wong, L. H., & Looi, C. K. (2002). *Learning pathways & intelligent software agents. (Unpublished internal document)*. Institute of Systems Science, National University of Singapore.

Wong, L. H., & Looi, C. K. (2009). Adaptable learning pathway generation with ant colony optimization. *Journal of Educational Technology & Society, 12*(3), 309–326.

Wong, L. H., Looi, C. K., Lai, T. W., Lee, P., Chong, C., & Ong, P. Y. (2004). Adaptable learning pathway planning with self-organizing agents. *Proceedings of International Conference on Intelligent Agents, Web Technologies and Internet Commerce '04*, Gold Coast, Australia.

Yang, Y. J., & Wu, C. (2009). An attribute-based ant colony system for adaptive learning. *Expert Systems with Applications, 36*(2), Part 2, 3034-3047.

Yin, P.-Y., Chang, K.-C., Hwang, G.-J., Hwang, G.-H., & Chan, Y. (2006). A particle swarm optimization approach to composing serial test sheets for multiple assessment criteria. *Journal of Educational Technology & Society, 9*(3), 3–15.

Ying, J., & Hu, L. (2000). The construction and realization of a mathematical model for random assessment question selections [In Chinese]. *Computer Applications, 20*(1), 46–47.

Zhang, T., & Lu, X. (2007). Research progress of Swarm Intelligence algorithms. *Shanxi Architecture, 33*(1), 14–16.

ADDITIONAL READING

Anderson, C., & McShea, D. W. (2001). Intermediate-level parts in insect societies: Adaptive structures that ants build away from the nest. *Insectes Sociaux, 48*(4), 291–301. doi:10.1007/PL00001781

Bruisilovsky, P., & Marybury, M. T. (2002). From adaptive hypermedia to adaptive web. *Communications of the ACM, 45*(5), 31–33.

Cheng, S. C., Lin, Y. T., & Huang, Y. M. (2009). Dynamic question generation system for web-based testing using particle swarm optimization. *Expert Systems with Applications, 36*(1), 616–624. doi:10.1016/j.eswa.2007.09.064

Christodoulopoulos, C. E., & Papanikolaou, K. A. (2007). A group formation tool in an e-learning context. In [Patras, Greece.]. *Proceedings of IEEE Conference on Tools with Artificial Intelligence, 07*, 117–123.

Costello, R., & Mundy, D. P. (2009). The adaptive intelligent personalised learning environment. In [Riga, Latvia.]. *Proceedings of ICALT, 09*, 606–610.

Dorigo, M., & Birattari, M. (2007). Swarm intelligence. *Scholarpedia, 2*(9), 1462. doi:10.4249/scholarpedia.1462

Frick, T. (1992). Computerized adaptive mastery tests as expert systems. *Educational Computing Research, 8*, 187–213.

Garnier, S., Gautrais, J., & Theraulaz, G. (2007). The biological principles of swarm intelligence. *Swarm Intelligence, 1*(1), 3–31. doi:10.1007/s11721-007-0004-y

Graf, S., & Bekele, R. (2006). Forming heterogeneous groups for intelligent collaborative learning systems with ant colony optimization. In [Jhongli, Taiwan.]. *Proceedings of the International Conference on Intelligent Tutoring Systems, 06*, 217–226.

Hassan, R., Cohanim, B., de Weck, O., & Venter, G. (2005). A comparison of particle swarm optimization and the genetic algorithm. In [Austin, TX.]. *Proceedings of AIAA Multidisciplinary Design Optimization Specialist Conference, 05*, 1138–1150.

Huang, M.-J., Huang, H.-S., & Chen, M.-Y. (2007). Constructing a personalized e-learning system based on genetic algorithm and case-based reasoning approach. *Expert Systems with Applications, 33*(3), 551–564. doi:10.1016/j.eswa.2006.05.019

Poli, R. (2007). An analysis of publications on Particle Swarm Optimization Applications. Retrieved 6 June, 2008, from http://cswww.essex.ac.uk/technical-reports/2007/tr-csm469.pdf

Riedmiller, M. (1994). Advanced supervised learning in multi-layer perceptions – from backpropagation to adaptive learning algorithms. *Computer Standards & Interfaces, 16*(5), 265–278. doi:10.1016/0920-5489(94)90017-5

Scalise, K., Bernbaum, D. J., Timms, M., Harrell, S. V., Burmester, K., & Kennedy, C. A. (2007). Adaptive technology for e-learning: principles and case studies of an emerging field. *American Society for Information Science & Technology, 58*(14), 2295–2309. doi:10.1002/asi.20701

Sedlacek, W. E. (2003). Alternative admissions and scholarship selection measures in higher education. *Measurement & Evaluation in Counseling & Development, 35*, 263–272.

Shang, Y., & Shi, H. (2000). IDEAL: An integrated distributed environment for asynchronous learning. In *Proceedings of International Workshop on Distributed Communities on the Web 2000* (pp.182-191), Quebec, Canada.

Triantafillou, E., Georgiadou, E., & Economides, A. A. (2008). The design and evaluation of a computerized adaptive test on mobile devices. *Computers & Education, 50*(4), 1319–1330. doi:10.1016/j.compedu.2006.12.005

Wang, T. I., Tsai, K. H., Lee, M. C., & Chiu, T. K. (2007). Personalized learning objects recommendation based on the semantic aware discovery and the learner preference pattern. *Journal of Educational Technology & Society, 10*(3), 84–105.

Wang, Y.-K., & Yang, T.-W. (2005). The application of ant-like mobile agents in the search of the distributed learning resources *(In Chinese)*. Retrieved 29 May, 2008, from http://www.ee.fju.edu.tw/new1/centerFrame/eemprrc/paper/2005ann/paper2005/papers/oral/02.pdf

Weiss, D. J., & Kingsbury, G. G. (1984). Application of computerized adaptive testing to educational problems. *Educational Measurement: Issues and Practice*, *21*, 361–375.

Zäıane, O. R. (2001). Web usage mining for a better web-based learning environment. *Proceedings of Conference on Advanced Technology for Education*. (pp.60-64), Banff.

Zhang, Y.-W. (2002). *Item selection strategies for distant assessments based on knowledge map* (In Chinese). Master Dissertation, Taiwan: Chung-Yuan University. Retrieved June 1, 2008, from: http://thesis.lib.cycu.edu.tw/ETD-db/ETD-search/getfile?urn=etd-0821103-095255&&filename=8977014.pdf

KEY TERMS AND DEFINITIONS

Ant Colony Optimization (ACO): The Ant Colony Optimization is a special form of Swarm Intelligence that models after natural ants finding good paths through graph traversing in solving optimization problems.

Content Planning: Content planning is a key component of conventional Intelligent Tutoring Systenms that aims to select the content for instructional goal that places the student on an appropriate learning path.

Fitness Functions: A fitness function is a mathematical function that quantifies the optimality of a solution in a Particle Swarm Optimization or genetic algorithm.

Multi-Agent Systems (MAS): A multi-angent system refers to a system composed of multiple intelligent agents that can be used to solve problems which are tedious for an individual agent to handle.

Particle Swarm Optimization (PSO): The Particle Swarm Optimization is a special form of Swarm Intelligence that models after the social behaviors of flocking birds or a school of fish in solving optimization problems.

Pheromones: A pheromone refers to a chemical marker generated by animals to trigger a natural response in other members of the same species. In the context of Ant Colony Optimization, pheromones are "simulated" in the form of constantly updated parameters for stochastic computation.

Social Navigation: Social navigation is a group navigational activity in an information space where information received from other people in the space can be shared and used in one's process of identifying the correct or optimal path.

Swarm Intelligence: Swarm Intelligence is a set of soft computing-based of algorithms that is inspired by and simulates natural phenomena like the swarms of insects, birds or fishes in the form of multi-agent systems (MAS). With the guidance of some evolutionary mechanisms, high-level intelligence and adaptability could emerge from swarms of such agents.

Traveling Salesman Problem (TSP): The Traveling Salesman Problem is a classic problem in Artificial Intelligence whose objective is to find the shortest possible path that visits each of a given list of cities (and their pair-wise distances) exactly once.

Section 5
E-Learning Systems Effectiveness

Chapter 15
Factors Determining the Overall Effectiveness of E-Learning Systems Used in Higher Education

Benedict du Boulay
University of Sussex, UK

Julie Coultas
University of Sussex, UK

Rosemary Luckin
London Knowledge Laboratory, UK

Fred Garnett
London Knowledge Laboratory, UK

ABSTRACT

This chapter examines part of the broad question: "How compelling is the evidence for the effectiveness of e-Learning in the post-16 sector? It concentrates, largely from a UK perspective, on higher education and on policy issues. In the first section the UK Higher Education Funding Council for England (HEFCE) e-Learning strategy is outlined and previous, partial reviews of e-Learning in higher education are examined. The evidence on the effectiveness of e-Learning in higher education is presented using Kirkpatrick's (1998) levels of evaluation, under the following questions: What are the learners' reactions to e-Learning? What is the student experience of e-Learning? What is the quality of the learning? Does e-Learning in higher education alter the behaviour of the learner? What is the impact of e-Learning on the organisation. In the final section recommendations for policy and future research are outlined.

DOI: 10.4018/978-1-61692-008-1.ch015

INTRODUCTION

This chapter is very closely based on part of an unpublished monograph, prepared largely by Julie Coultas, for Eduserv under the title "How compelling is the evidence for the effectiveness of e-Learning in the post-16 sector? A review of the literature in higher education, the health sector and work-based learning and a post-review stakeholder consultation". The chapter has a narrower scope than the monograph and concentrates, largely from a UK perspective, on higher education and outlines policy issues and further research.

The original monograph was informed by a number of seminars with experts who pointed us towards relevant literature. They emphasised that E-learning is a dynamic concept that has been both complex and ever-changing, so to measure how effective it has been in itself is a challenge. The review identified definitional elements, key factors in e-learning, how to measure effectiveness within the literature, but also raised the question of whether the research was examining the right issues, which was born out in the review process. Relevance to institutions, work-based learning and health were also reviewed in the original monograph but not included here.

Definitions were identified as containing three components; skills, computer technology and style of learning. Key factors in effective e-learning were identified as being learner confidence, prior knowledge (both operational and conceptual), the presence and involvement of the Teacher, communication (the dialogues between teachers and learners) and the cultural issues relating to managing change. This range of categories in itself identifies the complexity of the field under review, even so both the complexity of the definitions, and the number of key factors, were added to through the expert review process. In the end we adopted the following definition of e-learning:

E-Learning is a portmanteau term covering:

- A **style of learning** with a particular focus on technology-mediated interactivity and collaboration.
- The **use of computer technology** in leaning with a particular focus on internet technology.
- The **set of skills** that enables learners to exploit technology in order to develop understanding or capability.

E-learning requires a different mode of learning, which was characterised as "independent learning", and critically changes the combinations of Space, Time and Money necessary for learning to take place. Teachers are beginning to get insights in how to use "timely interventions" to deal with a learning mix of "theorising and socialising". Institutions, however, are not yet equipped to modify the ways that they deal with these combinations not least because key performance indicators (KPI's) map to traditional learning outcomes.

E-learning is no longer a subset of learning used in distance learning but has evolved into "learning in technology-rich environments" which occurs in multiple contexts both within and beyond the institution. With technology and learning both developing rapidly, but independently, we now have the capability for the co-creation of learning through the integration of the range of technologies available for learning. Institutions however need to move away from the use of simple KPI outcome measures and begin to focus on quality improvement. This has a number of repercussions for an ITS perspective on the field.

In the first section of the chapter, on Higher Education, the HEFCE e-Learning strategy is outlined and previous, partial reviews of e-Learning in higher education are examined. The evidence on the effectiveness of e-Learning in higher education is presented using Kirkpatrick's (1998) levels of evaluation, as follows:

(1) What are the learners' reactions to e-Learning? What is the student experience of e-Learning?
(2) What is the quality of the learning?
  - Effective e-Learning and learning styles
  - Comparing the quality of the learning
  - Studies of students' motivation and self-efficacy in e-Learning environments
(3) Does e-Learning in higher education alter the behaviour of the learner?
(4) What is the impact of e-Learning on the organisation

The Conclusion section looks at policy and research implications.

HIGHER EDUCATION

The Higher Education Funding Council for England (HEFCE) in embedding their e-Learning strategy '...want to ensure that there is confident use of the full range of pedagogic opportunities provided by ICT. For HE this encompasses flexible learning as well as distance learning, and the use of ICT as a communications and delivery tool between individuals and groups, to support students and improve the management of learning' (HEFCE, 2005). They see the HE sector moving towards

- Meeting the greater diversity of student needs
- Increasing flexibility of provision
- Enhancing the capacity for integrating study with work and leisure through work-based and home-based learning
- Developing approaches to individualised support for planning and recording achievements.

In order to do this HEFCE work closely with the Higher Education Academy and the Joint Information Systems Committee (JISC).

HEFCE consider the measures of success and the acceptance of e-Learning to be when:

1. ICT is commonly accepted into all aspects of the student experience of higher education, with innovation for enhancement and flexible learning, connecting areas of HE with other aspects of life and work.
2. Due to more coherence and collaboration, technical issues have been addressed to give better value for money.
3. Students are able to access information, tutor support, expertise and guidance, and communicate with each other effectively wherever they are. They are able to check and record their achievement in a form designed for multiple uses to enable personal and professional development.
4. Tutors have tools for course design to enable better communication between them and their students, giving feedback and targeted support. Individual teachers have access to information about the materials available, and support for continuous improvement of them.
5. Subject communities are able to share materials in ways that enhance their ability to produce customised high quality courses. They are supported to work collaboratively in designing materials, which are effectively quality assured and widely disseminated. They have access to research information to inform curriculum development and research-based teaching.
6. Institutions are able to build appropriate infrastructure and resources support for integrating registration and learning functions. They have links with regional networks of institutions to support progression and community involvement.

7. Lifelong learning networks support connectivity between institutions to provide seamless access for students and staff.
8. Staff are supported at all stages to develop appropriate skills in e-Learning, and these skills are recognised in their roles and responsibilities and in reward structures. They have access to accreditation for their level of skills and professional practice in linking learning technology with teaching. (HEFCE Strategy for e-Learning, 2005)

Systematic Reviews of e-Learning in Higher Education

Despite a plethora of studies that have looked at specific e-Learning interventions, large-scale reviews of the evidence for the effectiveness of e-Learning in higher education are few and far between. Analysis of the Evidence for Policy and Practice Information and Co-ordinating Centre's (EPPI) list of systematic reviews conducted in the post-16 sector up to early 2006 produced one review that has relevance to the research question that this present review addresses. The review (Hassan, Hauger, Nye & Smith, 2005) looked at the use and effectiveness of synchronous audiographic conferencing (SAC) in modern language teaching and learning (online language tuition). In order to be included in Hassan et al.'s in-depth review, studies not only needed to meet all the criteria for inclusion but also to be primary reports of experimental studies testing the effect of a language learning intervention against another intervention, or standard practice or no intervention. The researchers found 14 descriptive intervention studies conducted since 1990. Four of the studies considered both learners and teachers while another three studies focused primarily on the teachers but also gave information on the learners. The studies varied in their design from experimental to the more naturalistic and observational. The majority of the studies were in the secondary or post-secondary sectors and were carried out in Australia, the UK, USA, and Canada. Not all these studies would be relevant to this present review of e-Learning in the post-16 sector. Hassan et al's review concluded that although the studies reported positive findings for synchronous audiographic conferencing no study was used in the in-depth review as they did not meet the inclusion criteria. The authors of this review recommended that larger scale, robust studies looking at the effectiveness of SAC in relation to various outcomes were undertaken.

In a meta-analytic review comparing the performance of students in distance education and students in traditional classes, Allen, Mabry, Mattrey, Bourhis et al. (2004) found that distance education students slightly outperformed traditional students on exams and course grades. They argued that their results demonstrated 'no clear decline in educational effectiveness when using distance education technology' (p 402). The overall number in their sample was 71,731 however it should be noted that 63,516 were on a Tanzanian Teacher Training Programme. At first sight there seemed to be no decline in educational effectiveness when using distance education. When the results were examined more closely they showed that for military-related instruction the distance learning environment lowered performance while for the natural sciences and education courses the effect was practically zero. However, Allen et al. did find that foreign language instruction was more effective when technology was used. They also noted that there did not seem to be support for the notion that synchronous interactive technologies increase performance compared to traditional classes.

In a UK review of the literature on implementing e-Learning programmes for higher education, O'Neill, Singh & O'Donoghue, (2004) acknowledged that technology can enhance the learning process but not replace the lecturer or tutor. They list the implications of e-Learning for universities who need quality and flexibility to meet the diversity of students' needs:

- Tailoring courses to suit differing educational needs and aspirations
- Lecturers will be forced to fundamentally change their approach to teaching to accommodate the shift in student learning styles.
- Increased workload requires proactive and effective management. This has implications for the fundamental structure of the university itself.
- Universities must change to accommodate demand and in response to new competition from global, giant corporate and virtual universities. However the problems associated with the change must be fully recognised prior to the transition taking place.
- Many e-Learning implementations in the UK university sector are costly and yet superficial, in terms of learner engagement and activity. They provide a content repository and in many cases limited active learner participation.
- When staff are 'forced' down the e-Learning route as a consequence of management dirctives and mission statements the creation of sound pedagogic practice is often flawed or missing completely and the activities constructed service the technology rather than student or learner progression or association.

While this review focused largely on the technology and its implementation, O'Neill et al. (2004) argued that the critical factors for success will change with the implementation of e-Learning programmes and asserted that the new key elements in the success of the e-Learning experience are:

- Prior experience of using technology
- The technological infrastructure
- The lecturer

On a practical level they suggested that HE institutions can help students to achieve success by providing three elements:

- A face-to-face session familiarising students with the courseware. This will help to overcome the issue of prior experience.
- The functionality of the technological infrastructure should be ensured before the course is implemented. This should be backed up by technical support from either the lecturer or a course facilitator.
- Human resources should be committed to the project at an early stage and lecturers should be selected based on their attitude towards technology, teaching style and ability to control to technology.

Another UK review of the literature looked at the student experience of e-Learning in higher education (Sharpe & Benfield, 2005). This review acknowledged the impact of e-Learning on institutions, practitioners and students and pointed to a gap in the research exploring the experience of the e-Learner. They focused on blended learning (a combination of face-to-face and e-Learning) putting distance learning at one end of the continuum. They looked for literature that illustrated the key features of the student experience and speculated on what had an impact on the student experiences. It was noted that most of the research on student experience of e-Learning focused on very specific and often narrow aspects, for example, asynchronous computer mediated communication. Sharpe and Benfield found that when e-Learning created new or unusual pedagogies the learners reported 'an intensely emotional experience and a major concern with time and time management' (p 6). They argued that e-Learning is often presented as providing flexibility in time and pace of study and that time is a primary concern for students engaging in e-Learning. Their review highlighted some factors:

- Students appreciate having access to course materials and key contacts online
- There is a need to provide induction into e-Learning environments that engage the learners
- Intense emotions are elicited during the learning process ranging from inspiration to frustration
- Students are concerned with time
- Online collaboration or a significant change in the role of the tutor produced the most inconsistencies in student perceptions
- There is a need for tutors to give more explicit explanations of the purposes of online work

HOW COMPELLING IS THE EVIDENCE FOR THE EFFECTIVENESS OF E-LEARNING IN HIGHER EDUCATION?

What are the Learners' Reactions to E-Learning? What is the Student Experience of E-Learning?

Following the Kirkpatrick methodology, we ask what do students think about e-Learning? Are they satisfied with their learning experience? These are measures of the effectiveness of e-Learning and are often assessed by the use of questionnaires and course evaluation forms.

Positive Attitudes

In a study where preferences were compared using two types of online presentation of course materials, Evans, Gibbons, Shah and Griffin (2004) explored student reactions and performance in different types learning environments. In one study 67 final year students were given the material as web pages and another cohort (n = 48) were given the material as a virtual lecture. Questionnaire analysis demonstrated a preference for a virtual lecture approach. In another study, positive attitudes to a hybrid course format (part online, part face to face) compared to a traditional course were reported by 55 students who thought that the quality of interaction with the tutor was good, that they read text more often, and that they studied in groups more frequently (Riffel and Sibley, 2005). Preferences about the way that learning takes place were expressed in a Japanese study of 333 female students learning English vocabulary via mobile phones. Seventy one per cent of students preferred receiving their lessons via mobile phones and 93% felt that it was a valuable teaching method (Thornton and Houser, 2005).

Attitudes to e-Learning can be influenced by both personal and situational factors. The role of individual attitudes toward the web as a survey tool based on theories and personal perceptions was explored by Huang and Liaw (2005). They used a survey to assess 279 information management students' attitudes to the web in relation to self-efficacy (a student's judgment of their own capabilities to achieve a specific learning goal), anxiety, usefulness, liking, and the intention to use web surveys. The results indicated that perceived usefulness had a significant impact on intention to use the web. The respondents in this survey with high self efficacy used web surveys. These findings are relevant to issues linked to computer confidence.

Student reactions to e-Learning will inevitably change over time with later cohorts entering higher education with greater computer literacy and confidence in their skills. This was demonstrated by a longitudinal UK study of student experience by Garland and Noyes (2004) which reported that students in later cohorts had more years of computer use and greater confidence. In another study Braak (2004) used a self perceived computer confidence and competence scale and found that there was a significant difference between cohorts across even one year (between 2001 and 2002) on both computer experience and computer use. The later cohort (2002) of students reported more confidence with computers and also more knowledge of distinct computer applications. Both experience and intensity of computer use predicted computer competence. It is also useful to note that the measure is a self-perceived computer competence and that 95% of students in the sample had a computer at home.

Do students value increased access to computers? And does increased access lead to greater academic success? A US qualitative study explored 25 student reactions to a campus-wide laptop initiative at a small liberal arts institution (Demb, Erickson and Hawkins-Wilding, 2004). The value of the laptop to the student was explored through their perceptions of: academic success, study habits, faculty utilisation, development of a learning community, personal use, future plans, and cost. A significant relationship was found between student perception of the effectiveness of faculty members' classroom use of technology and their own perceptions of the value of the laptop to their learning and success.

Negative Attitudes

Students' negative reactions to some types of e-Learning tools were voiced in a study of 36 students in a project design class in civil engineering which implemented two different technologies: a groupware (shared workspace) and shared wireless laptop computers (Nicol and MacLeod, 2005). It seems that although management group folders (a shared resource) were an effective tool, the students' perceptions of assessment requirements and their negative attitudes to resource sharing limited the use of the folders. Laptops and shared workspace supported quite different types of collaborative learning. This study also pointed to the individual needs of students in terms of assessment requirements thwarting some collaboration.

Mixed Attitudes

It is essential to provide students with experiences in online collaboration (Reisslein, Seeling and Reisslein, 2005). However in Reisslein et al's study they found that although the students (33 on-campus students and 4 distance learners split into 8 teams) had very positive attitudes toward the project they were indifferent to the online aspect of the project. Nearly half of the students indicated that what they liked least about the project was that it was all online and over a third indicated that having some project work face to face would improve it. This is an argument for a blended approach to learning that takes into account the students' need for some face to face interaction. How social interaction can be achieved in a virtual environment is one of the foci of social presence research.

Social presence is linked to communication and collaboration and can be defined in a number of ways (1) The ability to define social relationships with reference to the environmental context, divorced from pre-existing relationships (2) The social presence of a virtual tutor mediated by verbal written information, by written information and various personal views, by written and spoken information, by text, by views and spoken language (3) The sense of being together created by the use of telecommunications systems (4) The disappearance of the computer interface in an interaction.

Nowak and Walther (2005) studied the effects of synchrony and the number of cues on the person perception process in computer-mediated communication. 142 students randomly assigned to 39 groups collaborated over a 5 week period to produce oral reports using alternative versions of communication systems or meeting face to face. It had been claimed that the lack of social context cues means that leaner media (e.g. text based systems) induce people to focus more on the task as these systems are not well suited to social interactions. The results of the study showed that those using low cue media felt more certain (more comfortable about their ability to predict other groups members' values, attitudes, feelings and emotions) than those using high cue media. The students also reported that their conversations were more effective but this only happened in low cue groups. These results make a contribution to the discussion of the effectiveness of an online learning environment because they showed that those using low cue media (text only) were more positive about their partners.

What is the Quality of the Learning? Are Students Learning the Material?

In this section we look at Kirkpatrick's (1998) second level and the wide variety of proposed measures of learning and factors affecting how well e-Learning works. Learning/cognitive style is proposed as a factor that influences learner performance.

Effective E-Learning and Learning Styles

Hypertext has been used in a number of studies to explore how students learn effectively. This has relevance to the development of learning skills and also to learning styles. Bromme and Stahl (2005) described how 40 psychology students with no previous experience of hypertext construction were given introductory explanations on the text format 'hypertext' based on either a book (linear) or space (non linear) metaphor. The focus topic was linking nodes about the internet and a 'prior knowledge of the internet' test was given before the task was undertaken. The book metaphor produced a more linear way of viewing hypertexts and this conflicted with the complexity of the content to be processed. The 20 students in the space metaphor group created significantly more links than the 20 students in the book metaphor group. Based on these findings it was claimed that the book (linear) and space (non-linear) metaphors had significantly different effects on the constructed hypertext, the construction process, and knowledge acquisition. The space metaphor is more useful for preparing learners to deal with the complexity of content structures and hypertext structures. However it was acknowledged that performance on a knowledge test showed that metaphorical knowledge does not ensure deeper learning processes i.e. the space (non-linear) metaphor students did not gain more knowledge about semantic relations and more transfer knowledge than the book (linear) metaphor group. Therefore it would seem in this study that the hypertext did not facilitate deep learning processes.

Another study using hypertext questioned the link between an individual's preferred cognitive style (this can be understood as learning style) and the manner in which they access information (Calcaterra, Alessandro & Underwood, 2005). This study looked at the influence of cognitive style (analytical-sequential (linear) *vs* holistic-intuitive (non-linear)), spatial orientation and computer expertise on hypertext navigation patterns and learning outcomes when 40 undergraduates interacted with a hypermedia presentation. Calcaterra et al. referred to the argument that hypermedia should facilitate learning because of its similarity to human associative memory. This is related to the schemata theory of learning where meaningful learning occurs when students integrate fresh information into an existing schema or when a new schemata is created by acknowledging similarity to existing schemata. However the researchers found that hypermedia navigation was linked to computer skills rather than to cognitive styles and that neither cognitive styles nor abilities affected learning outcomes (as measured by a post test). Higher performance was associated with re-visiting hypermedia sections and visiting overview sections in early stages of hypermedia browsing. This type of behaviour is related to self-explanation and deep learning and is related to a constructivist approach to learning.

So are prior knowledge and also computer skills more important than learning style in computer environments? Mitchell, Chen & Macredie (2005) stated that it is a student's prior knowledge that makes a difference in terms of their learning and argued that hypermedia allows for less knowledgeable students to make greater improvement than knowledgeable students. This means that an understanding of a student's prior knowledge can increase the effectiveness of the learning environment (hypermedia) and lead to greater learning gains. In Mitchell et al.'s view hypermedia forces students to make their own decisions on navigation strategies as these systems present course material in a non-linear structure. Two types of prior knowledge were proposed: domain expertise and system expertise. The results showed that out of 74 computer science undergraduate students, those with lower domain knowledge gained more from the hypermedia environment than students with higher prior knowledge i.e. they showed greater improvement in learning performance. The findings also indicated that examples were useful to students with low levels of domain knowledge.

Of course, it does depend on how the cognitive or learning styles are defined.

Lee, Cheng, Rai & Depickere (2005) took a different approach to cognitive style by labeling the dimensions as either field dependent (linear) or field independent (non-linear). They then argued that their results indicate that non-linear learning is the primary dimension that determines students' cognitive style. Out of 217 undergraduates on an information technology course, those individuals who preferred a linear learning approach in a hypermedia environment were categorised as field dependent and 'Such individuals generally demonstrate greater social orientation that means that they enjoy working in groups' (p 4). Here the authors are making a number of not necessarily firm links between what they categorised as cognitive/learning style and social orientation. They also argued that based on their findings field dependent (linear) individuals are less capable of controlling their own learning experience. Field independent individuals, however, were more likely to perform better in a hypermedia learning environment as they tended to need less navigational support. The field dependent linear style of learning would seem to be related to the analytical-sequential style of learning mentioned by Calcaterra et al. (2005) and the field independent non-linear style of learning to the holistic-intuitive. However, whereas Lee et al. (2005) found that field independent (non-linear) students were more likely to perform better in a hypermedia environment, Calcaterra et al. (2005) found that it was computer expertise and not cognitive/learning style that affected learning performance. But none of these studies tell us very much about learning at a deeper level.

So does information such as suggested paths through a learning environment facilitate learning? Dunser and Jirasko (2005) examined the effect of structural aid (suggested path through the learning environment) on the learning achievement of 86 students with global (non-linear) and sequential (linear) learning styles, using hypertext. The sequential (linear) learners showed poorer results when learning without the suggested path whilst the global (non-linear) learners achieved the same results in both conditions. Students with global learning styles did not show significantly better learning results when learning with hypertext. Nor did students learning with hypertext with an additional path through the document achieve better learning results when learning with hypertext. However sequential learners learned significantly less when no additional path through the document was provided. It is argued that the findings suggest that hypermedia learning environments with additional navigational aids such as a suggested path should be created in order to help students with different learning preferences.

These different learning preferences or styles would seem to be fixed according to the studies presented so far. In fact, Dunser and Jirasko cite Ramsden (1988) who stated 'Learning styles can be described as the habitual use of a set of similar strategies. Thus they indicate a learner's learning behavior, which is more or less stable'. This would seem to be the general opinion of researchers designing experiments using hypermedia/hypertext. This notion of a fixed and immutable learning style possessed by each learner allows for experiments to be designed on the basis of this being a stable variable. However, the lack of consensus across these studies would seem to have brought the stability (and description) of this variable into question. This is also confirmed by Coffield et al., 2004 who point out that almost all learning styles in the models that they evaluated were assessed using self-report methods. This seemingly simple task (assessing learning styles) is complex as so many learning styles models and instruments are being developed.

Comparing the Quality of the Learning

There are not many direct comparisons between traditional and online learning partly because, as the DfES in the UK argue, 'Traditional teaching methods and e-Learning can and should complement each other' (DfES, 2005). However one proposed method of gauging the learning gain (effectiveness) is through the comparison of online learning with pen and paper, traditional lecture, and face-to-face (F2F) learning. Some studies have compared the proposed learning gains of online learning with those of traditional learning (see e.g. du Boulay, 2000, for a review of evaluations of intelligent learning environments). Morris (2001) described the design and evaluation of a computer assisted learning tool to help 50 psychology students to review their understanding of correlation. It was concluded that both computer assisted and paper-based instructional materials equally contribute to the student's understanding of correlation. However the student's prior knowledge needs to be taken into account in the design of the tool. It was argued that computer assisted learning could provide additional and alternative instruction for students to acquire statistical concepts.

Blended learning (the combination of online and F2F) is an approach to e-Learning that is advocated by many (see DfES above). Riffel and Sibley (2005) reported on a hybrid course format (part online, part F2F) that was developed to deliver a biology course to undergraduates. The hybrid course consisted of bi-weekly online assignments and weekly F2F meetings. The hybrid course (55 students) was taught in parallel with a traditional course (74 students) in which passive lectures covered the same material as the online assignments. Performance on the post course test indicated that the hybrid course was better or equivalent to the traditional course. Online assignments were perceived as equivalent or better than passive lectures and active-Learning was more effective when combined with online activities. It is suggested that online assignments may have improved students' problem solving skills which could have improved the effectiveness of the active learning exercises. This reinforces the argument for a blended approach to learning.

Does the presence of a tutor or instructor in different learning environments have an effect on the quality of the learning? In a qualitative approach to learning Heckman and Annabi (2005) described the similarities and differences in the learning processes that occurred within a face to face (FTF) environment and in an asynchronous learning environment (ALN) with 120 students in four groups. Using discourse analysis they measured the content-relevant communication between learners and instructors. The results were analysed in terms of the discourse process where it was found that the number of utterances in the average FTF were greater than the average in the ALN. The teacher presence was more evident in the FTF compared to ALN. The FTF discussions were more question driven whilst there was more indication of continuing the thread in the ALN. In terms of the teaching process – there were more examples of traditional teaching in the FTF with 125 instances of direct instruction in FTF and only 18 in ALN. Cognitive processes were separated into exploration, analysis and integration. In FTF discussions there were more low level (exploration) categories (70%) compared to ALN (17%). It would seem that the presence of a tutor was more evident and the cognitive processes were more low level in the FTF. This would be an argument for the ALN environment facilitating more analysis and integration through interaction between the students rather than being guided by the tutor.

In addition, are there elements other than the presence (or lack) of a tutor in the virtual environment that can affect learning? Wastlund, Reinikka, Norlander and Archer (2005) examined the effects of video display terminal (VDT) and paper presentation on performance of a reading comprehension task. They also tested students for both perceptions of workload and stress, using a number of scales. After the test the students completed another stress, tiredness and hunger test (STH) test. In study one (n = 72) the paper condition produced more correct answers on the reading comprehension test. The students in the VDT condition reported significantly higher levels of stress and tiredness. In a second study (n = 72), a verbal creativity test was used. A greater number of alternative answers were produced in the paper than the VDT condition. However there were no significant effects of stress, tiredness or hunger in the second study. These two studies demonstrated that students performed better (achieved more learning gains) with a paper and pencil task and that a comprehension test but not a creativity task caused students to experience more stress online. This is an illustration of how contextual variables (the different levels of stress dependent on task) can affect performance in learning environments.

When comparing different learning environments it is also important to acknowledge that the behaviour of the student can have an effect on whether the learning is successful. Scheines, Leinhardt, Smith & Kwangsu (2005) pointed to an interesting practical issue that can have an effect on learning outcomes and the effectiveness of an online course. They described a series of 5 experiments where over 650 students completed a course on causal and statistical reasoning in either traditional lecture/hour long class or online/hour long class format (blended learning). Online students did as well as the traditionally taught students but the face to face contact during the class (the blended learning element) played a part. For those in the traditional lecture/class condition, attendance in class was 4 times more predictive of exam score than attendance at lecture. The students in the online environment could work through voluntary comprehension checks but only 50% took advantage of this. Students could print out the modules stripped of the comprehension checks and all interactive material. There was an indication that performance on final exams suffered because of the omission of the interactive aspect of the online course. The results of this study again presented the case for blended learning. Scheines et al. make a valid point in terms of the potential effectiveness of any e-Learning environment - it is important to build online learning environments that support students not only with content and interactivity but also with *advice* as to how best to exploit the resources available.

Motivation, Self-Efficacy and Assessment

Before looking at the studies of motivation and self-efficacy in e-Learning it is important to state what we mean by these terms. A standard definition of motivation is as follows:

A construct that is used to explain the initiation, direction, intensity, and persistence of an individual's behavior in a particular situation (see e.g., Byrnes, 2001)

The concept of motivation can be discussed under three main headings; (1) goals - what someone wants in the future, (2) knowledge - knowing how to achieve goals using procedures and strategies, and (3) metacognitive processes – which include monitoring progress, use of beliefs to appraise actions, evaluating outcomes, and explaining why outcomes occur (Byrnes, 2001). In addition, intrinsic motivation - when people engage in a task as an end in itself, and extrinsic motivation - where people are motivated to engage in a task as a means to an end need to be taken into account.

Dweck (1999) developed a model of achievement motivation and argued that the theories that students develop about their own intelligence guides the goals that they pursue. She suggested that the concept of self-esteem and its role in motivation needs to be rethought. The four common assumptions about successful individuals who love learning, seek challenges, value effort and persist in the face of obstacles, are that (1) students with high ability are more likely to display mastery-oriented qualities (2) success in school fosters mastery-oriented qualities (3) praising students' intelligence encourages mastery-oriented qualities (4) students' confidence in their own intelligence is integral to mastery-oriented qualities. Self-efficacy is a related term which essentially means a students' judgment of their own capabilities to achieve a specific learning goal or outcome.

In a study mentioned in a previous section, Riffel and Sibley (2005) examined the motivation and performance of students (n = 55) in a hybrid course which consisted of online assignments and F2F meetings. They found that significantly more hybrid cohort students than traditional cohort students reported studying or working in groups several times during the semester. They suggested that online assignments may have improved students' problem solving skills which could have improved the effectiveness of the active learning exercises. In terms of motivation, the hybrid cohort students may have been more focused and motivated to work on active learning exercises when they came to class. Perhaps this is because they had more control over their own learning.

Assessment is another motivator that can drive student learning. In a qualitative study, Macdonald and Twining (2002) looked at student (n = 200) and tutor (n = 12) perspectives on the assessment of an innovative undergraduate course that employed an activity-based approach in a networked environment. They pointed out that assessment plays a major role in driving student learning appropriately. This means that assessment must be intimately linked to effectiveness and motivation. Their study explored (1) the extent to which assessment supports student learning and participation (2) the factors influencing the effective design of assessment for activity-based learning in networked environments. The issue of participation (which can be seen as a measure of effectiveness) is crucial for an activity-based course. Macdonald and Twining argued that when the activities involve online communication the issue of participation is even more important as non-participation by one student can have an impact on other students on the course.

In terms of participation in online conferencing and internet searching with fellow students it was found that success was related to a variety of factors, most notably the skill and moderation style of the tutor. However the greatest barrier to successful participation was the lack of integration of assessment with the collaborative task. Macdonald and Twining pointed out that the effects of assessment on student learning are common knowledge within conventional university courses. They explained the lack use of a learning portfolio during the course in terms the importance of integrating learning activities closely with assessment and also making clear the penalties for not fulfilling the assessment criteria.

The three key issues for the assessment of activity-based learning, according to Macdonald and Twining, are that (1) Assessment must reflect course philosophy. For example, if the course is activity based, the assessment must reflect the type, or types of activities in which students are expected to engage. (2) Assessment is essential in creating learning opportunities at critical points. In order to ensure the student's participation there needs to be a close integration of learning activities with assessment. (3) Assessment provides an opportunity for feedback. Assessment can provide a vehicle through which online distance students receive feedback. Macdonald and Twining pointed out that assessment plays a major role in driving student learning appropriately. This means that assessment must be intimately linked to effectiveness and motivation.

But does intrinsic motivation, where students engage in a task as an end in itself, always lead to better performance? Martens, Gulikers and Bastiaens (2004) state that students with high intrinsic motivation, where the activity is performed for the inherent satisfaction of the activity itself, often perform better than students with low intrinsic motivation. They investigated the behaviour of students in an electronic learning environment (ELP) that was designed as a game-like realistic simulation in which students played the role of a junior consultant. The results showed that although there was no significant relationship between intrinsic motivation and the number of pages visited in the learning environment, intrinsically motivated participants were more explorative. However performance measures (multiple choice test and content statements) showed that intrinsically motivated students did not acquire more knowledge of the content.

Learner control seems to be a factor in Marten et al.'s findings and certainly individual differences in students' learning preferences in online learning environments play a part. Lee et al. (2005) point out that students' preferences within learning dimensions such as linear/non-linear, level of learner control and multiple tool usage need to be taken into account as a means of motivating the student's acquisition of subject matter through individualised instruction. This is supporting the argument that there are individual differences in approaches and performance within hypermedia. But the context, which includes the learning environment itself, is also important.

Do authentic online learning environments, which reflect the way knowledge and skills will be used in real life, result in higher performance and an improvement in intrinsic motivation of students? Gulikers, Bastiaens and Martens (2005) reported the effects of an authentic learning environment on student performance and experiences (n = 34). It was shown that the students in the authentic learning environment did not perform better than the students in the less authentic environment and that students in the non authentic learning environment used more content statements and more words in their report. The reported experience of learning also did not differ between the two groups. It is suggested that the non-authentic condition might have been less distracting – it did not contain as many multimedia features – though this opens questions about the meanings of "authentic" and "non-authentic". This leads to the conclusion that the multimedia environment did not motivate students more than the non authentic learning environment. Gulikers et al. seriously question the effectiveness and efficiency of many of the multimedia features and add-ons that are all too often in 'modern' electronic learning environments.

However, the environment and its design are considered to be important in motivating students (McAlister, Ravenscroft and Scanlon, 2004). McAlister et al. suggested that educational dialogue can be used to support learners in the development of critical thinking, reasoning and argumentation in a synchronous online peer discussion. The tool can guide students' dialogue in ways that improve argumentation and collaborative knowledge development i.e. it provides sentence openers organized by intention 'I think' 'I disagree because'. They claimed that students (n = 22) engaged more with each others' positions and produce deeper and more extended argumentation when using the tool. The claims are tempered by the statement that these are preliminary findings and that the improved dialectic was not necessarily significant.

One indicator of motivation is when students choose, voluntarily, to engage in learning outside the compulsory requirements of a course. Grabe

(2005) looked at the voluntary use of online lecture notes to explore issues of student effectiveness and motivation (n = 183). Notes can be provided on the web but tutors are reluctant to provide them as they worry that this will lead to non-attendance at lectures. Grabe used log files and questionnaires to examine the voluntary use of online lecture notes, look at patterns of note use and the use of notes as an alternative to class attendance. The conscientious use of online notes was associated with higher examination scores. However there were no difference in examination scores between those note users who skipped class and those who did not.

If students are given a choice in the way that they can navigate learning environments does this motivate them to learn? Dunser and Jirasko (2005) suggested that hypermedia learning environments with additional navigational aids should be created in order to help students with different learning preferences. They further claimed that the opportunity to choose the learning environment can also improve student's motivation for and interest in learning. Perhaps confidence in the learning environment is also a factor when considering choice? Garland and Noyes (2004) in one of the few longitudinal studies in this review, reported two studies with 235 undergraduates looking at undergraduate use, confidence toward and expectations of learning from computers. They found that students in later cohorts reported more years of computer use and greater confidence. They further demonstrated that higher levels of computer use and confidence were associated with higher levels of learning as measured by correct scores on the recall test. They argued that it would seem that the learning expectations from computers are improving and are now at similar levels to print media. 'Multimedia presentations may be differentially beneficial to less literate people, even in a group with low overall formal education' (p 268).

Does E-Learning Change the Behaviour of the Students?

In this section the evidence for proposed changes in the behaviour or performance of the learner due to e-Learning is examined? Monitoring interaction with and through technology is one way of assessing any change in the behaviour of the learner. The importance of assessing learners' skills is linked to the engagement of the workforce. Engaging learners through interaction with the medium can support deep learning and familiarity with the internet will enable those users to exploit interactive features (Ford & Murphy, 2002).

Interaction and Collaboration

One type of collaboration is learning through the sharing and exchanging of information among a peer group and this can be mediated through computers. Measures of this type of collaboration would be the manner in which the tools are used, the relative contributions of the collaborators, and the logs of the interactions. One study that gave an interesting insight into how tools are used collaboratively for individual ends was Wilson's (2004) investigation of how the use of an asynchronous learning environment can affect students' attitude and performance. The asynchronous learning environment was meant to augment a traditional lecture/lab course by allowing 86 students to devise, critique and revise questions which then contributed to end of course exams. The posted questions in the learning environment could be challenged but prior to being challenged questions could be deleted by team members. High grades were achieved by students who made numerous challenges (this was assessed by the logs) and who accessed the exam question database frequently. This is in contrast to the claim that it was collaborative learning as such. Wilson pointed out that 'High levels of participation were gained in the present study simply by setting up structural incentives and social pressures, e.g. automated public notices of laggardly performance. Students realised quickly that posting their questions ahead of schedule gave them a wider range of material to choose from, and once they accessed ExamNet [the learning environment] to earn participation credits many students found it interesting and game-like to review their peers' questions and consequently become internally motivated to continue' (p 101). This illustrates the point that although this paper purports to be about collaborative learning it has more to say about individual motivation and changes in behaviour in response to the learning environment.

In another study which looked at resource sharing and collaboration in a project design class in civil engineering (n = 36), two different technologies: a groupware (a shared workspace) and shared wireless laptop computers were implemented (Nicol and MacLeod, 2005). The focus of the study was on way the two technologies supported resource sharing within and across project groups and the forms of group collaboration that resulted. There was a difference in the way that the two technologies were used. The shared workspace was used as a location-independent central repository of resources and group activities were coordinated around it. The laptops were used as a focal point for F2F discussion of these resources. This means that different types of learner collaboration could be afforded by the different technologies. Management group folders (a shared resource) were an effective tool but the students' perceptions of assessment requirements and their negative attitudes to resource sharing limited the use of the folders. Laptops and shared workspace supported quite different types of collaborative learning. This study also points to the individual needs of students in terms of assessment requirements thwarting some collaboration. In this sense this paper also addresses issues of motivation.

Another type of collaboration would be a discursive process where the measure of its effectiveness would be gauged through the analysis of the discourse. Heckman and Annabi (2005) used discourse analysis to measure the content-relevant communication between 120 learners (in four groups) and instructors. Their study has been described in the section on learning where they look at the similarities and differences in the learning processes that occur within FTF environment and in an asynchronous learning environment (ALN). They proposed that responses from learners to learners differ from those responses from learners to instructors. The results indicated that teacher presence was more evident in the FTF (average141 utterances) compared to ALN (average 11). The FTF discussions were more question-driven whilst there was more indication of continuing the thread in the ALN. Students played a greater role in creating a social environment in ALN. This paper addressed questions about the type of interactions and learning that took place in the two environments and pointed to a difference in behaviour dependent upon whether the interaction is FTF or asynchronous.

In a recent approach to the facilitation of collaborative learning at the process level, learners were provided with cooperation scripts that specified and sequenced their collaborative learning activities (Makitalo, Weinberger, Paivi, Jarvela & Fischer, 2005). This study investigated the effects of an epistemic cooperation script (which gave guidance in the form of prompts) on the amount of discourse, information seeking and individual learning outcomes in collaborative learning in an online learning environment (a website where the learners can post messages). The results showed that the amount of discourse was higher in the epistemic script condition. It was reported that learners sought information less often in the epistemic condition but this was not significant. Individual learning outcomes were higher in the unscripted (uncertain) condition. It was argued that learning environments should provide a degree of uncertainty. Uncertainty reduction theory proposes that as the amount of verbal communication in initial interaction situations increases, the level of uncertainty decreases. It was claimed that in this study it was the unscripted uncertainty condition that improved learning outcomes. Participants in the unscripted group sought information more directly by clearly indicating their lack of understanding. The unscripted (uncertain) environment elicited the type of behaviour (communicating a lack of understanding) that led to improved learning outcomes.

Does communication in electronic discussion groups have an impact on cognitive processing? Schellens and Valcke (2005) asked whether collaborative learning in discussion groups could result in enhanced academic discourse and knowledge construction. They predicted that (1) that proportion of task oriented communication would be greater than the proportion of non-task-oriented communication (2) the more discussion activities in groups, the more phases of higher knowledge construction would appear. Of the 1428 messages analysed, 1095 were task oriented. Communication in the groups did not become more task oriented over time and more communication reflecting higher phases (for instance, co-construction) of knowledge construction was not observed at the end of the research period. However more discussion activity in the groups did mean that more phases of higher knowledge construction appeared. By higher knowledge they mean the knowledge as categorised by the 5 phase model of; sharing/comparing, dissonance/inconsistency, negotiating/co-construction, testing tentative constructions, statement/application of new knowledge. This was a study of collaborative learning based on a proportion of data taken from a massive data set using 23 groups of 10 students over 4 months. This study highlighted the fact that immense amounts of data can be available from virtual interactions.

Collaboration in most studies is seen as a 'good' outcome or process even if the motives of the students are more individual and competitive than collaborative. Reisslein, Seeling and Reisslein (2005) argued that it is essential to provide students with experiences in online collaboration. The study focused on an online team design project in which students (33 on-campus students and 4 distance learners split into 8 teams) collaborated via a team website on a design project related to an emerging communications network topic. It was found from analysis of online interactions on the team websites that online team communication was to a large extent concentrated on managing the team and the project. Both the students with higher prior knowledge and lower prior knowledge achieved approximately the same learning gain. However the students were indifferent to the online aspect of the project. Nearly half of the students indicated that what they liked least about the project was that it was all online and over a third indicated that having some project work face to face would have improved the experience.

Another study of behaviour and technology was a campus-wide laptop initiative studied by Demb, Erickson and Hawkins-Wilding (2004). They found that laptops impacted on the study habits of 73 students in that they were used for convenience, typing and research. However there was little mention of interaction online. For two thirds of students the laptops made a difference to their study habits, academic and social lives. It is important to note that student perception of the value of the laptop to their academic success was tightly correlated with their perception of the success of faculty in integrating the laptop into teaching and classroom activity. There was a negative response to the creation of online communities with 62% not using chat rooms. It would seem that behaviour can change with the introduction of technology (e.g. laptops) but other behavioural variables, such as the success of the tutors in integrating the technology into the classroom and teaching, has an impact.

Another study of online communities also pointed to the behaviour of the students being influenced by contextual variables (Erlich, Erlich-Philip and Gal-Ezer, 2005). The study with 153 computer mediated communication

(CMC) course students demonstrated that the use of CMC was minimal and that the use of the technologies depended on the levels of expertise of the individuals using them. Erlich et al. came to this conclusion after examining whether taking a computer literacy and applications (CLA) course before a CMC course had an impact on students' participation in the CMC course and on the effective use of the tools. The implication from this study is that prior computer literacy can influence the level of usage of a computer mediated communication environment. Perhaps this is because the level of computer skills of an individual could be gauged by their fellow students if they were interacting in a shared environment? This could lead to decreased motivation, fear of failure (to communicate), low self esteem, and anxiety. A shared environment could be perceived as more threatening to the less computer literate.

What are the Organisational Effects Resulting from the Learner's Performance?

In this review of the evidence of the effectiveness of e-Learning in higher education there was very little research that looked at the organisational effects resulting from e-Learning. Twigg (2003), in an extensive USA study made strong claims about the improvement of quality and the reduction of costs linked to e-Learning. The study monitored the progress of a programme whose purpose was to encourage colleges to 'redesign their instructional approaches using technology to achieve cost savings as well as quality enhancements' (p 1). The first round of projects involved ten institutions over two years from 1999 to 2001. It was set up as the pilot project for the overall program and redesigned courses included sociology, statistics, mathematics, computer literacy, American government, astronomy, psychology, chemistry and algebra. Five of the ten projects reported improved learning outcomes, four reported significant difference and one was inconclusive. Most of the learning outcomes were based on tests/grades. Seven of the ten projects showed improvement in course completion/retention rate. All ten projects made significant shifts to a more active learner-centred enterprise. The most effective quality improvement techniques as reported by the ten projects included: continuous assessment and feedback, increased interaction among students, online tutorials, and undergraduate learning assistants (ULAs).

In terms of cost reduction strategies and successes, Twigg reported that the approach most favoured (7 out of 10 of the projects) was to keep student enrolments the same while reducing instructional resources. Seven of the ten projects showed a decrease in drop/failure/withdrawal (DFW) rates. The most effective cost savings techniques, taking into account that the single most costly item was personnel, were reducing faculty time and transferring some tasks to technology assisted activities. The main techniques used by the projects included: online course management systems, online automated assessment of exercises, online tutorials, shared resources, staffing substitutions, and reduction of space requirements. This program encouraged colleges to redesign their instructional approaches in order to use technology to achieve cost savings as well as quality enhancements. The learning outcomes however were less clearly defined. The courses were diverse (e.g. sociology, algebra) and there was no insight into any differences between the courses in terms of measurement of learning outcomes and students response to the learning.

CONCLUSION AND RECOMMENDATIONS

The straightforward comparison between traditional and online learning is not reported extensively but it has been found, for instance, that both a computer assisted learning tool and traditional paper–based materials can contribute to a student's understanding of correlation. Online students often do as well as the traditionally taught students but again context can play a part.

There are many studies that compare a blended approach (a mixture of online and face-to-face) to traditional face-to-face (FTF) approaches, but their results are conflicting and often depend on the type of task and environment in use,

Assessment is a powerful driver of student learning in higher education and can contribute to motivation in learning. To ensure participation there needs to be a close integration of learning activities with assessment in a networked learning environment. We note that e-learning has enabled a greater use of formative assessment, which in its turn has improved learners performance.

Some of the factors affecting the quality of the learning of students, detailed in this chapter, concur with previous reviews. For instance, previous reviews indicated that high ability students could benefit from an individualised expert teaching system, computer expertise of the students contributed to the success of an e-Learning experience, and tutors' attitudes towards technology, their teaching style, and their ability to control the technology influenced students' performance in an e-Learning environment. This relates to the findings in this review that teacher presence (virtual as well as physical) and the students' understanding of the potential of the learning environment are both factors that can have an impact on the success of e-Learning. So it is the human factor that makes a difference to learning in virtual environments.

Collaboration is seen as the sharing and exchanging information and high levels of participation can be gained by setting up structural incentives and social pressures. Different environments encourage different types of collaborative behaviour. A shared workspace can be used as a location-independent central repository of resources whereas laptops can be used as a focal point for face to face discussion of these resources. Discourse analysis has shown that students can play a greater role in creating a social environment in an asynchronous learning environment rather than in a face to face interaction. A degree of uncertainty facilitates learning in an environment where students needed to ask more questions improved learning outcomes. However it has also been shown that more discussion activity in groups does not always lead to increase in knowledge. Communication in groups is sometimes about management of the teams rather than about the learning itself and the provision of computers does not always lead to collaboration but rather more individual activities. In online communities students can also be influenced by contextual variables such as levels of expertise of the individuals using them.

Previous reviews have shown that there is very little evidence available on the effect of e-Learning on the behaviour of undergraduate students. The gaps in the literature lead us to recommend that more research is undertaken that includes:

- Studies that look at the impact of the integration of learning activities with assessment in a networked learning environment
- Studies that look at different types of assessment and their effect on the motivation of students
- More exploration of students and tutors' use of handheld devices.
- Observational studies of student behaviour in coordination with self-report methods.
- Studies looking at the impact of a shared learning environment on the less computer literate.
- Studies that look at the impact of online learning on attendance at parallel face to face sessions.

If we move away from an approach that attempts to categorise the student (learning styles) and towards an exploration of the e-Learning environment (which includes other students) then an understanding of when collaboration works and when it breaks down is essential if students are going to communicate effectively with each other and with their tutor.

The issues as they stand at the end of the review in the previous section can be summarised as follows:

- "e-learning" has evolved into "learning in technology-rich environments": how these environments are resourced and managed is key, and so a driver in the post-16 New Build.
- Definitions, key factors and learning are all constantly evolving and learning should not be seen as stopping at institutional boundaries; learning occurs in multiple contexts and learning across all relevant contexts needs to be designed for.
- The learner changes their mode of learning in different learning contexts, but in what way and how this can be supported needs to be investigated
- Research needs to look at the transformational nature of e-learning and how it affects the process and "discourses of learning";
- New measures of effectiveness are needed as Key Performance Indicators tend to map to traditional outcome measures;
- Identifying the change roles of practitioners and learners is critical and "Designing for Learning" may be the best way of integrating these developing roles to support a co-creation model.
- Learning, Technology and Institutions are all developing in differing ways so "Integration rather than standards" is a key issue as "we don't know what people do to support their learning outside the institution". How can we best measure this?

In many of the papers that we reviewed, the learning theory that guided the planning of an intervention and its implementation was not made explicit. In the original review we produced an overview of theories that inform research on e-Learning. We do not claim that they are exhaustive but they are a starting point in a process where we need to become more explicit about how we think that students, trainees and practitioners learn.

Recommendations for Evaluation and Methodology in E-Learning

Evidence about how well e-Learning is performing was found in a whole host of different journals, websites, conference papers and presentations emanating from a wide range of disciplines. The review of evidence for the effectiveness of e-Learning spanned a large number of disciplines within higher education e.g. cognitive science, computer science, management studies, and psychology. In medical education the review covered the learning of both students and medical practitioners. Bearing in mind this diversity we outlined some of the underlying theories and approaches to e-Learning that guided and supported both the practice and the evaluations.

At the end of this review, in addition to specific recommendations about studies that should be undertaken, we believe that there is a need for an open discussion of the types of research methods used in the field of e-Learning. To a certain extent this discussion has already been opened up by Coffield et al. (2004) in their review of learning styles. The diversity of approaches to the collection of evidence for the effectiveness of e-Learning is considerable and needs to be brought together in a book that is focused on research methods in e-Learning. This book would be both an interdisciplinary and 'inter-sector' textbook. This seems like a simple solution but could alleviate the problems inherent in a field where we are trying to compare studies and interventions, which at first sight seem comparable e.g. two studies of students' attitudes to blended learning. In the field of e-Learning where there are as many attitudinal scales as there are students' attitudes, comparison is not always easy. There can be no comparative measure of students'/learners' attitudes until we know that we are using the same scale. In addition, a large number of studies use 'partial scales'. That is, attitudinal scales that have used a small number of items from a larger scale.

Rather than exclude studies on the basis of quality we have included studies where the research questions and methodology were interesting and the findings were of potential relevance to the review question. For future research in e-Learning there needs to be more coherence in how the questions in studies are asked (hypotheses are developed) and about the tools that are used to answer these questions. This is one of our strong recommendations stemming from this review of the evidence for the effectiveness of e-Learning. Scales used to measure, for example attitudes or learning styles, need to be standardised across the e-Learning field. This would help when trying to compare studies where outcome measures (e.g. learning gains) and attitudes were used. More studies need to use more than one type of research method e.g. combining observational method with a self report/questionnaire design. It is not sufficient to present the learners' attitudes assessed through a short questionnaire containing few items. The validity of these questionnaires is doubtful and therefore the validity of the studies is also a problem. Without other measures including; interview data, focus group studies, observational studies, to reinforce the findings of the surveys we cannot be sure that we are really looking at evidence.

However some of the studies that have used 'incomplete' research tools do have value. Examples of studies from our review and suggestions from previous reviews that open up new ways of looking at e-Learning include:

- A study in the work-based e-Learning review that looked at people's behaviour when using an automated banking system. This, of course, does not tell us about deep learning but it did give insight into potential variables involved in e-Learning from a user perspective e.g. age and gender. Also much of the ground of e-learning is being shifted by the rise of social media. So much so that the HEA when reviewing University e-learning use identified the rise of "Hidden Learning Environments" as the practical use of e-learning tools was effectively under the institutional radar.
- Suggestions that observation of students accessing remote learning facilities is needed
- Involvement of tutors in both face to face and virtual interactions between students. This can be beneficial or detrimental to learning depending on the type of involvement and at what level.
- Interactions using different technologies. The use of instant messaging in conjunction with other technologies was an example of behavioural change in an organisation. Again, it possibly does not tell us about deep learning but it does give us an insight into types of collaboration and co-operation facilitated by technology.

Finally, a fifth level of evaluation, the societal implications of e-Learning has only been touched on in this review. This is because there is very little evidence and our focus was on higher education *per se* where the social implications were less relevant than if we had included, for example, a review of informal learning. In terms of methodology, the diffusion of innovation literature that divides the intervention into the type of attributes of an innovation (e-Learning) would be useful in developing research methods both at the organisational and the societal level. For instance, is e-Learning better than what was available before? Is it compatible with what is already happening? Can we see that it is better? Can we make it easy to use so adoption is not a problem?

REFERENCES

Allen, M., Mabry, E., Mattrey, M., Bourhuis, J., Titsworth, S., & Burrell, N. (2004). Evaluating the effectiveness of distance learning: A comparison using meta-analysis. *The Journal of Communication*, *54*(3), 402–420. doi:10.1111/j.1460-2466.2004.tb02636.x

Braak, J. P. (2004). Domains and determinants of university students' self-perceived computer competence. *Computers & Education*, *43*(4), 299–312.

Bromme, R., & Stahl, E. (2005). Is hypertext a book or a space? The impact of different introductory metaphors on a hypertext construction. *Computers & Education*, *44*, 115–133. doi:10.1016/j.compedu.2004.01.003

Byrnes, J. P. (2001). *Cognitive Development and Learning in Instructional Contexts*. Boston: Allyn and Bacon.

Calcaterra, A., Alessandro, A., & Underwood, J. (2005). Cognitive style, hypermedia navigation and learning. *Computers & Education*, *44*, 441–457. doi:10.1016/j.compedu.2004.04.007

Coffield, F., Moseley, D., Hall, E., & Ecclestone, K. (2004). *Learning styles and pedagogy in post-16 learning?*Learning and Skills Research Centre LSDA.

Demb, A., Erickson, D., & Hawkins-Wilding, S. (2004). The laptop alternative: Student reactions and strategic implications. *Computers & Education*, *42*(3), 383–401.

Department for Education and Skills. (2005) *The e-Strategy - Harnessing Technology: Transforming learning and children's services*. Retrieved from http://www.dfes.gov.uk/publications/e-strategy/

du Boulay, B. (2000). Can we learn from ITSs? In Gilles Gauthier, Claude Frasson, and Kurt VanLehn (Editors), *Intelligent Tutoring Systems: Proceedings of 5th International Conference, ITS 2000,* Montreal, number 1839 in Lectures Notes in Computer Science, 9-17. Berlin-Heidelberg, Germany: Springer-Verlag.

Dunser, A., & Jirasko, M. (2005). Interaction of hypertext forms and global versus sequential learning styles. *Journal of Educational Computing Research*, *32*(1), 79–91. doi:10.2190/1J25-LWQF-PQ3W-LABM

Dweck, C. S. (1999). *Self Theories: Their Role in Motivation, Personality, and Development.* Boca Raton, FL: Taylor Francis.

Erlich, Z., Erlich-Philip, I., & Gal-Ezer, J. (2005). Skills required for participating in CMC courses: An empirical study. *Computers & Education*, *44*(3), 477–487. doi:10.1016/j.compedu.2004.04.010

Evans, C., Gibbons, N. J., Shah, K., & Griffin, D. K. (2004). Virtual learning in the biological sciences: pitfalls of simply "putting notes on the web". *Computers & Education*, *43*, 49–61. doi:10.1016/j.compedu.2003.12.004

Ford, N., & Murpy, G. (2002). The development and piloting of a training web site for health and safety enforcement officers. *British Journal of Educational Technology*, *33*(1), 65–76. doi:10.1111/1467-8535.00239

Garland, K., & Noyes, J. (2004). Changes in learning expectations and confidence toward computers: a study of five successive years of undergraduates. *Journal of Educational Computing Research*, *31*(3), 273–279. doi:10.2190/NQWC-WTVR-VUUE-CXW4

Grabe, M. (2005). Voluntary use of online lecture notes: correlates of note use and note use as an alternative to class attendance. *Computers & Education*, *44*, 409–421. doi:10.1016/j.compedu.2004.04.005

Gulikers, J. T. M., Bastiaens, T. J., & Martens, R. L. (2005). The surplus value of an authentic learning environment. *Computers in Human Behavior*, *21*, 509–521. doi:10.1016/j.chb.2004.10.028

Hassan, X., Hauger, D., Nye, G., & Smith, P. (2005). *The use and effectiveness of synchronous audiographic conferencing in modern language teaching and learning (online language tuition): a systematic review of available research*. Retrieved from http://eppi.ioe.ac.uk/EPPIWeb/home.aspx?page=/reel/review_groups/MFL/review_three_abstract.htm

Heckman, R., & Annabi, H. (2005). A content analysis comparison of learning processes in online and face-to-face case study discussion. *Journal of Computer-Mediated Communication & Education*, *42*(3), 87–107.

Higher Education Funding Council for England. (2005). *HEFCE Strategy for e-Learning*. Retrieved from http://www.hefce.ac.uk/pubs/hefce/2005/05_12/05_12.pdf

Huang, H. M., & Liaw, S. S. (2005). Exploring users' attitudes and intentions toward the web as a survey tool. *Computers in Human Behavior*, *21*, 729–743. doi:10.1016/j.chb.2004.02.020

Kirkpatrick, D. L. (1998). *Evaluating Training Programs: The Four Levels* (2nd ed.). San Francisco: Berrett-Koehler.

Lee, C. H. M., Cheng, Y. W., & Rai, S., & Depickere. (2005). What affect student cognitive style in the development of hypermedia system? *Computers & Education*, *45*, 1–19. doi:10.1016/j.compedu.2004.04.006

Macdonald, J., & Twining, P. (2002). Assessing activity-based learning for a networked course. *British Journal of Educational Technology*, *33*(5), 603–618. doi:10.1111/1467-8535.00295

Makitalo, K., Weinberger, A., Paivi, H., Jarvela, S., & Fischer, F. (2005). Epistemic cooperation scripts in online learning environments: fostering learning by reducing uncertainty. *Computers in Human Behavior*, *21*, 603–622. doi:10.1016/j.chb.2004.10.033

Martens, R. L., Gulikers, J., & Bastiaens, T. (2004). The impact of intrinsic motivation on e-learning in authentic computer tasks. *Journal of Computer Assisted Learning*, *20*, 368–376. doi:10.1111/j.1365-2729.2004.00096.x

McAlister, S., Ravenscroft, A., & Scanlon, E. (2004). Combining interaction and context design to support collaborative argumentation using a toll for synchronous. *Computer Mediated Communication*, *20*, 194–204.

Mitchell, T. J., Chen, S. Y., & Macredie, R. D. (2005). Hypermedia learning and prior knowledge: domain expertise vs. system expertise. *Journal of Computer Assisted Learning*, *21*, 53–64. doi:10.1111/j.1365-2729.2005.00113.x

Morris, E. (2001). The design and evaluation of Link: A computer-based learning system for correlation. *British Journal of Educational Technology*, *32*(1), 39–52. doi:10.1111/1467-8535.00175

Nicol, D. J., & MacLeod, I. A. (2005). Using shared workspace and wireless laptops to improve collaborative project learning in an engineering design class. *Computers & Education*, *44*, 477–487. doi:10.1016/j.compedu.2004.04.008

Nowak, K. L., Watt, J., & Walther, J. B. (2005). The influence of synchrony and sensory modality on the person perception process in computer-mediated groups. *Journal of Computer-mediated Communication, 10*(3), Article 3.

O'Neill, K., Singh, G., & O'Donoghue, J. (2004). Implementing eLearning Programmes for Higher Education: A Review of the Literature. *Journal of Information Technology Education*, *3*, 313–323.

Pintrich, P. (2003). Motivation and classroom learning. *Handbook of Psychology: Educational Psychology, 7*, 103-122.

Ramsden, P. (1988). *Improving learning: New perspectives*. London: Kogan Page.

Reisslein, J., & Seeling, P., & Reisslein. (2005). Integrating emerging topics through online team design in a hybrid communication networks course: Interaction patterns and impact of prior knowledge. *The Internet and Higher Education, 8*, 145–165. doi:10.1016/j.iheduc.2005.03.004

Riffel, S., & Sibley, D. (2005). Using web-based instruction to improve large undergraduate biology courses: An evaluation of a hybrid course. *Computers & Education, 44*(3), 217–235. doi:10.1016/j.compedu.2004.01.005

Scheines, R., Leinhardt, G., & Smith, J., & Cho, Kwangsu. (2005). Replacing lecture with web-based course materials. *Journal of Educational Computing Research, 32*(1), 1–26. doi:10.2190/F59B-382T-E785-E4J4

Schellens, T., & Valcke, M. (2005). Collaborative learning in asynchronous discussion groups: what about the impact on cognitive processing? *Computers in Human Behavior, 21*, 957–975. doi:10.1016/j.chb.2004.02.025

Sharpe, R., & Benfield, G. (2005). The student experience of e-Learning in higher education: A review of the literature. *Brookes eJournal of Learning and Teaching, 1*(3), 1-22.

Thornton, P., & Houser, C. (2005). Using mobile phones in English education. *Journal of Computer Assisted Learning, 21*(3), 217–228. doi:10.1111/j.1365-2729.2005.00129.x

Twigg, C. A. (2003). *Improving learning and reducing costs: lessons learned from round 1 of the Pew Grant Program in Course*. Redesign Center for Academic Transformation, Rensselaer Polytechnic Institute. Retrieved from http://www.center.rpi.edu/PewGrant/Rd1intro.html

Wastlund, E., Reinikka, H., Norlander, T., & Archer, T. (2005). Effects of VDT and paper presentation on consumption and production of information: Psychological and physiological factors. *Computers in Human Behavior, 21*, 377–394. doi:10.1016/j.chb.2004.02.007

Wilson, E., V. (2004). ExamNet asynchronous learning network: augmenting face-to-face courses with student-developed exam questions. *Computers & Education, 42*(3), 87–107. doi:10.1016/S0360-1315(03)00066-6

KEY TERMS AND DEFINITIONS

Assessment: The mechanism by which providers of educational experiences determine the degree to which the consumers of those experiences have understood the material and acquired the skills.

Blended Learning: The combined use of both e-learning and non-technology-enhanced learning methodologies.

Collaboration: A methodology for learning that involves two or more learners working together to achieve understanding or master skills.

E-Learning: A portmanteau term covering: A style of learning with a particular focus on technology-mediated interactivity and collaboration, the use of computer technology in leaning with a particular focus on internet technology, and the set of skills that enables learners to exploit technology in order to develop understanding or capability.

Kirkpatrick's (1998) "Levels": A methodology for evaluating e-Learning under hierarchical general questions: (1) What are the learners' reactions to e-Learning? What is the student experience of e-Learning? (2) What is the quality of the learning? (3) How does e-Learning alter the behaviour of the learner? (4) What is the impact of e-Learning on the organisation

Learning Style: A predisposition to approach a new learning task in a particular manner, for instance in terms of the order in which the material is understood, or in terms of the particular activities undertaken to support learning, or in terms of a particular focus or perspective.

Motivation: The reason why a learner expends effort on the learning process and is a conjunction of factors around her values, expectations and feelings (following Pintrich, 2003).

Chapter 16

A Meta-Analytic Estimation of a Common Effect Size from a Series of Experiments Related to an E-Learning System Effectiveness Evaluation

Ani Grubišić
University of Split, Croatia

ABSTRACT

As the acquisition of knowledge is often an expensive and time-consuming process, it is important to know whether it actually improves the student performance. The e-learning is a revolutionary paradigm that has lately been significantly evolving and it is closely related to the intelligent tutoring systems. Methodology for evaluating the educational influence of learning and teaching process, questions whether and in what amount, students learn effectively. Our contribution to this compulsive field of research is a meta-analysis of a series of experiments based on the same two-group methodology that reveals a more precise effect size of one particular e-learning system - eXtended Tutor-Expert System, a representative of web-based authoring shells for building intelligent tutoring systems.

INTRODUCTION

Today, e-learning is commonly used in everyday life and it enables students to quality participate in learning and teaching process even when distance, schedule and similar circumstances makes that practically impossible. E-learning is enabled in e-learning systems which present a "personal teacher" for each student.

An evaluation offers information to make decision about using the product or not (Phillips & Gilding, 2003). One special form of e-learning system evaluation is evaluation of effectiveness designed to answer one specific research question: "What is the educational influence of an e-learning system on students?". The main result gained through effectiveness evaluation is presented in a form of an effect size.

DOI: 10.4018/978-1-61692-008-1.ch016

The most important effect size in literature comes from one of the most stimulating studies in the field of educational psychology. That is a Bloom's (Bloom, 1984) statement of the 2-sigma problem. Bloom reviewed the results of published meta-analyses and conducted one experiment, which showed that students who received individualized tutoring displayed an effect size of 2.0 compared with those who received normal instruction. In other words, students who received individualized tutoring scored an average of two standard deviations above others on achievement tests. Consequently, this gain of two standard deviations became the ideal toward which normal, group oriented instruction should strive. So, the 2-sigma problem became the quest for the ways how to get the quality of group instruction closer to individualized tutoring. Many researchers have taken up this search.

One possible solution for the 2-sigma problem is the usage of such e-learning systems which provide each student with a learning experience similar to the ideal one-to-one tutoring. The best representative of such e-learning systems are intelligent tutoring systems (ITS) that apply their learning and teaching process to each student individually. Intelligent tutoring systems are computer systems that support and improve the learning and teaching processes in a variety of knowledge domains, while respecting the individuality of the learner (Sleeman & Brown, 1982; Wenger, 1987; Burns & Capps, 1988). The major problem associated with ITS, is their expensive and time consuming development process. In order to overcome these problems we chose an approach of creating a particular ITS from flexible shells acting as program generators.

As scientists have known for a long time that only one experiment cannot solve a major issue (Hunter & Schmidt, 2004), in order to determine effect size of e-learning systems in general, as well as, different categories of e-learning systems, a different, more complex approach has to be used – a meta-analytic approach.

A meta-analysis (Glass, 1976) integrates the results of a set of experiments without losing relevant information and is used for assessing a quality of quantitative results. It is usually conducted to increase the internal and the external validity of the conclusions that can be drawn from those experimental studies, giving us far more definitive statistical conclusions. It is necessary to emphasize that meta-analysis can only be applied on researches that have empirical results, that is, only on those researches that use quantitative measures to produce quantitative results (Lipsey & Wilson, 2001).

The researchers should be familiar with meta-analysis process and should report their results in a way that is appropriate for meta-analyzing, in order to speed up a process of determining how close or distant we are from solving a 2-sigma problem with present state-of-the-art e-learning systems.

A paper providing a referent point for everyone who wants to evaluate the effectiveness of e-learning systems is Fletcher's research (Fletcher, 2003) where he summarized some research findings for technology-based instruction: computer-based instruction 0.39 sigma (233 studies), interactive multimedia instruction 0.50 sigma (47 studies), "intelligent" tutoring systems 0.84 sigma (11 studies), recent intelligent tutoring systems 1.05 sigma (5 studies). These results suggest steady progress in learning outcomes.

Our contribution to this compulsive field is a meta-analysis of a series of experiments based on the same two-group methodology (Figure 1.), that reveals a more precise effect size of one particular e-learning system - eXtended Tutor-Expert System (xTEx-Sys) (Stankov, 2003), a representative of web-based authoring shells for building intelligent tutoring systems (ITS).

Before presenting the results of the meta-analysis, we reviewed the fifteen-year long research and development of the Tutor-Expert System (TEx-Sys) model (Stankov, 1997), and we gave an overview of the evaluation methodol-

Figure 1. Classical two-group experimental design

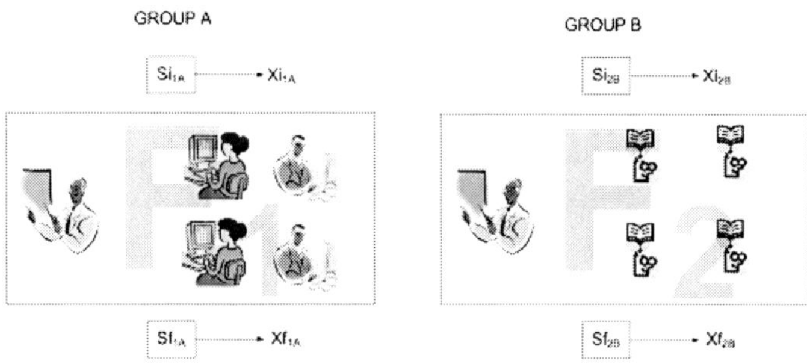

ogy that has been used in these researches. In the third chapter we present four different types of effect size estimators, their confidence intervals and homogeneity testing, as well as estimations of effect sizes based on a series of experiments. Finally, we present the results of meta-analysis conducted in order to determine the overall xTEx-Sys's effectiveness. It included 11 experiments that were carried out in academic years 2005/2006 and 2006/2007 and included 499 students.

BACKGROUND

The first implementation of an intelligent authoring shell model called the TEx-Sys was the on-site TEx-Sys (1992-2001) (Stankov, 1997). It has enabled the realization of the learning and teaching process for a student and a teacher, enabling them their basic functionalities respectively: (i) designing learning contents related to any domain of knowledge and (ii) learning and teaching as well as testing and evaluating knowledge. After that followed the web-based intelligent authoring shell (1999-2003, Distributed Tutor-Expert System, DTEx-Sys) (Rosić, 2000), the system based on the dynamic web documents. This web-oriented ITS has been developed by keeping in mind issues like (i) accessibility for a large number of potential users and (ii) learning and teaching in arbitrary domains. Finally, the system based on web services (2003-2005, xTEx-Sys) (Stankov, 2003) was implemented where we strictly differentiate the functionalities between experts and teachers.

The xTEx-Sys system is a web-based authoring shell with an environment that can be utilized by the following users: an expert who designs the domain knowledge base, a teacher who designs courseware for the student learning and teaching process (as well as tests for the student knowledge evaluation), a student who selects a course and navigates through the domain knowledge content using didactically prepared course content, and finally, an administrator who supervises the system.

The xTEx-Sys system is not only a quiz-administering tool, but it also provides a practice venue for students. In addition, questions that xTEx-Sys administers are not predefined, but rather generated by the system based on the predefined semantic network structures related to the domain of interest.

In the past decade, there were numerous applications of the TEx-Sys model in the learning and teaching process that involved students on all educational levels, from primary to tertiary. In the period from 2001 to 2007, 1692 students took 5976 content knowledge tests in one of the TEx-Sys model versions in order to evaluate their understanding of different knowledge domains.

Questionnaires about the students' impressions were given to the students after finishing the courses that were supported by the TEx-Sys model. The qualitative analysis of the results of questionnaires revealed that most students expressed positive attitudes toward using the model, and they were open to the idea of embracing that kind of learning and teaching support. The qualitative analysis alone was not sufficient to determine the utility of the TEx-Sys system. Therefore, we conducted 11 quantitative experiments in order to evaluate the educational influence of the TEx-Sys model (Stankov, Rosic, Žitko & Grubišić, 2008).

Eleven quantitative experiments previously mentioned used a modification of a classical two-group experimental design with pre-and-post tests (Grubišić, 2007). The majority of them (8 experiments) involved primary school pupils. It is very interesting to note that primary school pupils have embraced the learning and teaching process with the xTEx-Sys system more readily than university students, what can be seen while observing calculated effect sizes and survey results. Results gained through the conducted experiments have shown a need for adding some extended functions for courseware development and learning management in the xTEx-Sys system in order to get it as close as possible to the Bloom's 2-sigma target (Bloom, 1984).

ESTIMATIONS OF EFFECT SIZES

The effect size measurement tells us the size of experimental effect and it is used to synthesize experimental results. It is a standard way to compare the results of two experiments. Effect size is positive when the experimental group in the study outperforms the control group, and is negative when the control group is better.

By examining the effect sizes from several experiments, it has to be determined whether, with all of these effect sizes combined, the impact of this experimental factor (treatment) causes the difference that is big enough to recommend changes in educational practices (Lipsey & Wilson, 2001).

Different Types of Effect Size Estimators

Effect sizes are often interpreted as the standardized score (z score) or correlation coefficient. In this section we discuss several alternative estimators of the effect size from a classical two-group experiment, as presented by Hedges and Olkin (Hedges & Olkin, 1985).

Glass suggested estimator based on arithmetic means (Glass, 1976). If $\bar{Y}^E$ and $\bar{Y}^C$ are experimental and control group means respectively, and s^* is standard deviation, then standardized mean difference is:

$$\delta = \frac{\bar{Y}^E - \bar{Y}^{C^*}}{s^*} \quad (1)$$

We can use different standard deviations in this formula, such as standard deviation of control group s^C, or standard deviation of experimental group s^E, or even pooled standard deviation s that combines s^E and s^C. Glass (Glass, 1976) suggests the usage of s^C:

$$g' = \frac{\bar{Y}^E - \bar{Y}^C}{s^C} \quad (2)$$

The value g' is in literature commonly known as *Glass's Δ*.

If the assumption of equal population variance is reasonable, a pooled standard deviation can be used:

$$g = \frac{\bar{Y}^E - \bar{Y}^C}{s} \quad (3)$$

Where s is pooled standard deviation calculated using the following formula:

$$s = \sqrt{\frac{\left(n^E - 1\right)\left(s^E\right)^2 + \left(n^C - 1\right)\left(s^C\right)^2}{n^E + n^C - 2}} \tag{4}$$

where n^E and n^C are sample sizes of experimental and control group respectively. The bias and variance of g are smaller than the ones of g'. The value g is in literature commonly known as *Hedges's g*.

Since g has small sample bias, it can be removed by defining a new *unbiased estimator d*:

$$d = J(N-2)g, \tag{5}$$

where the constant $J(m)$ is approximated by

$$J\left(m\right) = 1 - \frac{3}{4m - 1} \tag{6}$$

or approximately:

$$d \cong \left(1 - \frac{3}{4N - 9}\right) g \tag{7}$$

The bias and variance of d are smaller than the ones of g.

The *maximum likelihood estimator* $\hat{\delta}$ of effect size δ is given by

$$\hat{\delta} = \sqrt{\frac{N}{N-2}} \frac{\bar{Y}^E - \bar{Y}^C}{s} = \sqrt{\frac{N}{N-2}} g \tag{8}$$

The bias of $\hat{\delta}$ is larger than the bias of Glass's estimator g'. Also, the variance of $\hat{\delta}$ is larger than the variance of d. Since all three estimators $\hat{\delta}$, g and d have the same asymptotic distribution, they are equivalent in large samples.

The last type of effect size estimator is *shrunken estimator* $\tilde{g}$:

$$\tilde{g} = \frac{N-4}{N-2} \frac{g}{J\left(N-2\right)} = \frac{N-4}{N-2} \frac{d}{\left[J\left(N-2\right)\right]^2} \tag{9}$$

It has smaller mean-square error than d, regardless of the value of the parameter δ.

To conclude, the following four effect size estimators are commonly used in theory and practice (Hedges & Olkin, 1985):

$$g = \frac{\bar{Y}^E - \bar{Y}^C}{s}, \quad d = J\left(N-2\right) g, \quad \hat{\delta} = \sqrt{\frac{N}{N-2}} g, \quad \tilde{g} = \frac{N-4}{N-2} \frac{g}{J\left(N-2\right)} \tag{10}$$

Because of the constants in their definitions, mentioned effect size estimators approach the same value as sample sizes become larger. Therefore, they have the same large sample distributions and large sample properties. All four methods are based on calculating pooled standard deviation, because in order to calculate d, $\hat{\delta}$ and $\tilde{g}$, first we have to calculate g that depends on that pooled standard deviation. The four estimators of δ are ordered like (Hedges & Olkin, 1985):

$$\hat{\delta}^2 \geq g^2 \geq d^2 \geq \tilde{g}^2 \tag{11}$$

as well as their variances:

$$Var\left(\hat{\delta}\right) \geq Var\left(g\right) \geq Var\left(d\right) \geq Var\left(\tilde{g}\right) \tag{12}$$

Effect Sizes Confidence Intervals

In order to estimate an effect size, we need to know its distribution and its confidence interval. Here we will present an approximation of the effect size estimator distribution, as its exact calculation has rather complicated analytic form.

The large sample distribution of d is normal with mean δ and estimated variance $\hat{\sigma}^2(d)$ (Hedges & Olkin, 1985):

$$\hat{\sigma}^2(d) = \frac{n^E + n^C}{n^E n^C} + \frac{d^2}{2(n^E + n^C)} \quad (13)$$

In literature, $\hat{\sigma}(d)$ is also called *standard error of effect size (SE)* (Hedges & Olkin, 1985).

A 100(1-α) -percent confidence interval (δ_L, δ_U) for δ is given by

$$\delta_L = d - C_{\frac{\alpha}{2}}\hat{\sigma}(d), \quad \delta_U = d + C_{\frac{\alpha}{2}}\hat{\sigma}(d) \quad (14)$$

where $C_{\frac{\alpha}{2}}$ is two-tailed critical value of the standard normal distribution (Hedges & Olkin, 1985). In our research we are interested in calculating 95-percent confidence interval (for α-0.05).

The effect size estimator distribution approximation is correct for sample sizes that are larger than 10, when absolute values of effect sizes are between 0.25 and 1.50 (Hedges & Olkin, 1985).

Estimations of Effect Sizes Based On a Series of Experiments

If a series of k experiments is expected to share a common effect size δ, then a combined estimate of δ should be pooled from all experiments. Here we present one method for obtaining pooled estimates of δ, based on using weight.

Each experiment result calculation is based on a specific sample. The size of samples used in different experiments varies, and different effect sizes are based on a different sample sizes. Generally speaking, larger sample sizes present the population better and therefore produce more precise effect sizes. It means that larger sample sizes have smaller *sampling error*. In estimation of *total effect size* in meta-analysis, we have to use effect sizes with different sampling errors. It would be wrong just to calculate their arithmetic mean, because in that way each effect size contributes to mean effect size equally, regardless of their sampling error (Lipsey & Wilson, 2001).

This problem can be solved by *weighting effect sizes* to determine their precision based on sample size (Lipsey & Wilson, 2001). Hedges and Olkin have proved that the best weighting measure is based on standard error of effect size (Hedges & Olkin, 1985), because it depends on a sample size. Less precise effect size has higher standard error, and, therefore effect size is weighted using inverse standard error square, that is, inverse variance. Effect size weight w is calculated using the following formula (Lipsey & Wilson, 2001):

$$w_i = \frac{1}{\sigma^2(d_i)} = \frac{1}{SE_i^2} \quad (15)$$

Hedges and Olkin (Hedges & Olkin, 1985) make weight calculation more precise by dividing inverse variance of a single experiment with a sum of inverse variances of all experiments:

$$w_i = \frac{\frac{1}{\sigma^2(d_i)}}{\sum_{j=1}^{k} \frac{1}{\sigma^2(d_j)}} \quad (16)$$

where $\sigma^2(d_i)$ is a variance of d_i.

Therefore, the most commonly used method for estimating effect size from a series of experiments is a method based on determining weighted linear combination of effect size estimates. As a result, estimation of effect sizes based on a series of experiments is given by the following formula (Hedges & Olkin, 1985):

$$d_W = w_1 s_1 + \ldots + w_k d_k \qquad (17)$$

Where $w_1, \ldots, w_k$ are nonnegative weighting factors. This estimator is based on finding weights that minimize its variance.

If experiments have different sample sizes, then effect size estimates from experiments with larger sample sizes are more precise than the ones from experiments with smaller sample sizes. Therefore, larger weights are given to more precise effect size estimates.

Since weight i depends on variance d_i, that depends on an unknown parameter δ, it is necessary to use weights that are based on variance and do not depend on δ. In that way, approximate weight is given by (Hedges & Olkin, 1985):

$$w_i \cong \frac{\tilde{n}_i}{\sum_{j=1}^{k} \tilde{n}_j} \qquad (18)$$

where $\tilde{n} = \dfrac{n^E n^C}{n^E + n^C}$.

The weighted estimator of δ based on sample estimate can be calculated using the following formula (Hedges & Olkin, 1985):

$$d_+ = \frac{\sum_{i=1}^{k} \frac{d_i}{\hat{\sigma}^2(d_i)}}{\sum_{i=1}^{k} \frac{1}{\hat{\sigma}^2(d_i)}} \qquad (19)$$

where $\hat{\sigma}^2(d)$ is defined in (13). The weights in estimator d_+ are attained using d_i to estimate δ_i. Eventhough d_i is unbiased, d_+ has a small bias in large samples and tends to zero as the samples become larger (Hedges & Olkin, 1985).

Testing for Homogeneity of Effect Sizes

Before estimating a total effect size from a series of k experiments, it is essential to find out do those experiments really share a common effect size. A statistical test for the homogeneity of effect sizes is, in fact, a test of the hypothesis stating that all k experiments have the same effect size, against the alternative hypothesis stating that at least one of the effect sizes differs from the remainder (Hedges & Olkin, 1985).

Large sample test is based on the Q statistic (Hedges & Olkin, 1985):

$$Q = \sum_{i=1}^{k} \frac{\left(d_i - d_+\right)^2}{\hat{\sigma}^2\left(d_i\right)} \qquad (20)$$

where d_+ is the weighted estimator of the effect size given in (19) and $\hat{\sigma}^2(d)$ is defined in (13).

When each experiment has a large sample size, the asymptotic distribution of Q can be used for testing the homogeneity of the δ_i. If all k experiments have the same effect size, then Q has asymptotic χ^2 distribution with k–1 degrees of freedom (Hedges, according to Hedges & Olkin, 1985). For that reason, if Q exceeds the 100(1-α)-percent critical value of x^2 distribution with k–1 degrees of freedom, we reject the hypothesis that the δ_i are equal. If this hypothesis is rejected, it is advisable not to estimate the total effect size, as they do not estimate the same parameter (Hedges & Olkin, 1985).

Test for the homogeneity of effect sizes on a small sample depends on the accuracy of the asymptotic distribution of Q in finite samples. In the simulation studies (Hedges, according to Hedges & Olkin, 1985) two thousand replications were generated for each sample size configuration and for each effect size $\delta = 0.25$, 0.50, 1.00 and

1.50. The homogeneity statistics Q was computed for each replication and the proportion of the test statistics exceeding various critical values was tabulated. Results for $k = 2$ and 5, and for the combinations of the sample sizes $n^E = n^C = 10, 20, 30, 40$ and 50, are given in the Figure 2.

A computational formula for the homogeneity statistic Q is (Hedges & Olkin, 1985):

$$Q = \sum_{i=1}^{k} \frac{d_i^2}{\hat{\sigma}^2\left(d_i\right)} - \frac{\left(\sum_{i=1}^{k} \frac{d_i}{\hat{\sigma}^2\left(d_i\right)}\right)^2}{\sum_{i=1}^{k} \frac{1}{\hat{\sigma}^2\left(d_i\right)}} \qquad (21)$$

Now, after giving a theoretical background, we can approach to the estimation of a total effect size from a series of 11 experiments related to the xTEx-Sys system effectiveness.

ESTIMATION OF A TOTAL EFFECT SIZE FROM A SERIES OF EXPERIMENTS RELATED TO THE XTEX-SYS SYSTEM EFFECTIVENESS

In this paper we will present how a meta-analysis related to xTEx-Sys system effectiveness was

Figure 2. The Q calculation based on 2000 simulations (Hedges according to Hedges & Olkin, 1985)

Sample sizes	δ	Mean of Q	Variance of Q	Proportion of test statistics exceeding the nominal significance value					
				0.40	0.30	0.20	0.10	0.05	0.01
				$k = 2$					
(10, 10)	0.25	0.988	2.241	0.380	0.286	0.195	0.100	0.052	0.011
(10, 20)	0.25	0.992	2.154	0.402	0.290	0.194	0.090	0.044	0.011
(10, 50)	0.25	0.980	2.086	0.389	0.284	0.190	0.102	0.051	0.009
(50, 50)	0.25	0.951	1.937	0.383	0.274	0.184	0.089	0.048	0.012
(10, 10)	0.50	0.954	1.825	0.386	0.289	0.186	0.092	0.045	0.008
(10, 20)	0.50	0.907	1.756	0.366	0.262	0.178	0.083	0.041	0.007
(10, 50)	0.50	0.915	1.742	0.369	0.271	0.179	0.094	0.045	0.008
(50, 50)	0.50	1.043	2.130	0.412	0.305	0.199	0.114	0.058	0.012
(10, 10)	1.00	1.006	2.205	0.393	0.302	0.199	0.098	0.049	0.013
(10, 20)	1.00	0.953	1.730	0.389	0.291	0.192	0.090	0.042	0.008
(10, 50)	1.00	1.015	1.956	0.418	0.313	0.201	0.093	0.051	0.011
(50, 50)	1.00	0.990	2.056	0.390	0.288	0.194	0.099	0.055	0.007
(10, 10)	1.50	1.034	2.107	0.403	0.311	0.208	0.104	0.056	0.010
(10, 20)	1.50	0.992	1.944	0.394	0.304	0.202	0.095	0.046	0.010
(10, 50)	1.50	0.992	1.841	0.400	0.301	0.206	0.098	0.043	0.006
(50, 50)	1.50	1.059	2.383	0.402	0.295	0.211	0.109	0.058	0.011
				$k = 5$					
(10, 10, 10, 10, 10)	0.25	3.828	7.327	0.378	0.282	0.184	0.085	0.040	0.009
(10, 10, 10, 50, 50)	0.25	3.788	7.602	0.377	0.274	0.179	0.079	0.042	0.010
(20, 20, 20, 20, 20)	0.25	3.896	8.199	0.392	0.285	0.184	0.091	0.048	0.011
(50, 50, 50, 50, 50)	0.25	3.858	7.297	0.397	0.298	0.191	0.092	0.035	0.005
(10, 10, 10, 10, 10)	0.50	3.846	7.490	0.377	0.287	0.177	0.090	0.048	0.008
(10, 10, 10, 50, 50)	0.50	3.900	7.883	0.389	0.290	0.189	0.095	0.045	0.009
(20, 20, 20, 20, 20)	0.50	3.900	7.320	0.395	0.288	0.190	0.093	0.048	0.007
(50, 50, 50, 50, 50)	0.50	3.992	8.078	0.394	0.299	0.198	0.097	0.045	0.012
(10, 10, 10, 10, 10)	1.00	3.933	8.035	0.397	0.293	0.192	0.087	0.044	0.013
(10, 10, 10, 50, 50)	1.00	3.950	7.807	0.394	0.295	0.187	0.092	0.047	0.011
(20, 20, 20, 20, 20)	1.00	3.821	7.489	0.361	0.268	0.183	0.091	0.050	0.007
(50, 50, 50, 50, 50)	1.00	3.926	7.729	0.395	0.289	0.195	0.086	0.043	0.010
(10, 10, 10, 10, 10)	1.50	3.932	7.292	0.396	0.300	0.205	0.093	0.041	0.009
(10, 10, 10, 50, 50)	1.50	4.068	8.362	0.412	0.308	0.211	0.106	0.057	0.010
(20, 20, 20, 20, 20)	1.50	4.019	8.024	0.400	0.304	0.195	0.099	0.054	0.009
(50, 50, 50, 50, 50)	1.50	4.121	8.784	0.412	0.316	0.222	0.112	0.054	0.013

conducted and what are her results. This meta-analysis includes experiments that took place in the academic years 2005/2006 and 2006/2007 and involved 499 students that enrolled several courses: Introduction to Computer Science, QBASIC Programming, Chemistry, Physics – optics, Nature and Society and Mathematics. These experiments are briefly presented in Figure 3.

We will show, in what manner, were the methods for estimating effect sizes in each experiment used, determine effect sizes confidence intervals, check the homogeneity of effect sizes, and accordingly, apply a method weighted linear combination of effect size estimates in order to estimate a total effect size of the xTEx-Sys. Also, we have checked if there was any correlation between duration of experiment, sample size, sample age and estimated effect size.

Estimation of Effect Size for Each Experiment

The first experiment has sample size $n^E = n^C = 40$ and s_{pooled}=13,99. Using Formulas (3), (4), (7), (8) and (9) we have calculated effect size estimators for the first experiment:

$$g = \frac{\overline{X}^E - \overline{X}^C}{s_{pooled}} = \frac{-1,09-(-12,53)}{13,99} = \frac{11,44}{13,99} = 0,8175 \tag{22}$$

an unbiased estimator of effect size:

$$d = \left(1 - \frac{3}{4(N-2)-1}\right) * g = \left(1 - \frac{3}{4\left(80-2\right)-1}\right) * 0,8175 = \\ = 0,9904 * 0,8175 = 0,8096, \tag{23}$$

the maximum likelihood estimator of effect size:

$$\hat{\delta} = \sqrt{\frac{N}{N-2}} g = \sqrt{\frac{80}{80-2}} * 0,8175 = 0,8279 \tag{24}$$

and shrunken estimator of effect size:

Figure 3. Experiments used in meta-analysis

No.	Course	Sample size	Sample age	Duration	Statistically sig. difference	Gain score means and st.dev.	Pooled st.dev.
1	Introduction to computer science	Exp. group 40 1st year students Ctrl. group 40 1st year students	19	14 weeks	α=0,05, df=78 t=-3,62, p=0,0005 YES	cg: $\overline{X}$=-12,53, sd=14,32 eg: $\overline{X}$=-1,09, sd=13,66	13,99
2	Introduction to computer science	Exp. group 20 1st year students Ctrl. group 19 1st year students	19	14 weeks	α=0,05, df=37 t=-3,77, p=0,0006 YES	cg: $\overline{X}$=-0,21, sd=11,79 eg: $\overline{X}$=14,26, sd=12,14	11,97
3	QBASIC programming	Exp. group 20 1st year students Ctrl. group 19 1st year students	19	14 weeks	α=0,05, df=37 t=-1,83, p=0,0753 YES	cg: $\overline{X}$=21,76, sd=15,23 eg: $\overline{X}$=32,60, sd=21,67	18,70
4	Chemistry	Exp. group 20 8th grade primary school pupils Ctrl. group 21 8th grade primary school pupils	14	10 weeks	α=0,05, df=39 t=-1,81, p=0,0780 YES	cg: $\overline{X}$=-9,53, sd=7,95 eg: $\overline{X}$=-4,63, sd=6,71	7,37
5	Physics – optics	Exp. group 40 8th grade primary school pupils Ctrl. group 40 8th grade primary school pupils	14	7 weeks	α=0,05, df=78 t=-3,67, p=0,0004 YES	cg: $\overline{X}$=0,16, sd=0,24 eg: $\overline{X}$=0,34, sd=0,20	0,22
6	Nature and society	Exp. group 24 2nd grade primary school pupils Ctrl. group 24 2nd grade primary school pupils	8	6 weeks	α=0,05, df=46 t=-2,88, p=0,0060 YES	cg: $\overline{X}$=8,17, sd=8,30 eg: $\overline{X}$=14,83, sd=7,69	8,00
7	Nature and society	Exp. group 24 3rd grade primary school pupils Ctrl. group 24 3rd grade primary school pupils	9	6 weeks	α=0,05, df=46 t=-3,08, p=0,0035 YES	cg: $\overline{X}$=8,67, sd=7,24 eg: $\overline{X}$=15,17, sd=7,36	7,30
8	Nature and society	Exp. group 20 4th grade primary school pupils Control group 20 4th grade primary school pupils	10	6 weeks	α=0,05, df=38 t=-3,48, p=0,0012 YES	cg: $\overline{X}$=10,83, sd=6,57 eg: $\overline{X}$=18,17, sd=7,98	7,31
9	Mathematics	Exp. group 9 6th grade primary school pupils Ctrl. group 9 6th grade primary school pupils	12	7 weeks	α=0,05, df=16 t=-2,33, p=0,0331 YES	cg: $\overline{X}$=-42,00, sd=13,93 eg: $\overline{X}$=-24,00, sd=20,11	17,30
10	Mathematics	Exp. group 9 8th grade primary school pupils Ctrl. group 9 8th grade primary school pupils	14	7 weeks	α=0,05, df=16 t=-0,24, p=0,8134 NO	cg: $\overline{X}$=17,22, sd=14,12 eg: $\overline{X}$=19,56, sd=25,56	20,65
11	Mathematics	Exp. group 24 5th grade primary school pupils Ctrl. group 24 5th grade primary school pupils	11	5 weeks	α=0,05, df=46 t=-1,03, p=0,3096 NO	cg: $\overline{X}$=-5,65, sd=12,87 eg: $\overline{X}$=-1,29, sd=14,26	12,64

$$\tilde{g} = \frac{N-4}{N-2} * \frac{g}{1 - \frac{3}{4(N-2)-1}} = \frac{80-4}{80-2} * \frac{0,8175}{1 - \frac{3}{4(80-2)-1}} =$$
$$= 0,9744 * 0,8256 = 0,8043. \quad (25)$$

In this experiment, values of four different effect size estimators g= 0,8175, d= 0,8096, $\hat{\delta}$ = 0,8279 and $\tilde{g}$ =0,8043 are very similar. Therefore, effect size estimations are reliable as $\hat{\delta}^2 \geq g^2 \geq d^2 \geq \tilde{g}^2$ and

$$Var(\hat{\delta}) \geq Var(g) \geq Var(d) \geq Var(\tilde{g}).$$

In this way, we have calculated estimators g, d, $\hat{\delta}$ and $\tilde{g}$ for every experiment. The results are presented in Figure 4.

For all experiments effect size estimations are reliable as $\hat{\delta}^2 \geq g^2 \geq d^2 \geq \tilde{g}^2$, as well as $Var(\hat{\delta}) \geq Var(g) \geq Var(d) \geq Var(\tilde{g})$.

Effect Sizes Confidence Intervals

The first experiment has an unbiased estimator of effect size d=0,8096 and sample size $n^E = n^C = 40$. Using Formula (13) and (15) we have determined 95% confidence interval:

$$\hat{\sigma}(d) = \sqrt{\frac{n^E + n^C}{n^E n^C} + \frac{d^2}{2(n^E + n^C)}} = \sqrt{\frac{40+40}{40*40} + \frac{0,8096^2}{2(40+40)}} = 0,2326$$

$$\delta_L = d - C_{\frac{\alpha}{2}} \hat{\sigma}(d) = 0,8096 - 1,96 * 0,2326 = 0,3537$$

$$\delta_U = d + C_{\frac{\alpha}{2}} \hat{\sigma}(d) = 0,8096 + 1,96 * 0,2326 = 1,2655$$

to be exact, confidence interval for δ is 0,3537 $\leq \delta \leq$ 1,2655.

In this way, we have calculated confidence intervals for each experiment. The results are presented in the Figure 5.

Hedges (Hedges & Olkin, 1985) says that the effect size estimation for samples larger than 10 participants in each group is correct if that effect size is between 0,25 and 1,50. In our case it would mean that experiments 1, 5 and 7 have a correct effect size estimator, and experiments 2, 6 and 8 have an effect size estimator that is on a border line of correctness. Experiments 3, 4, 9, 10 and 11 have incorrect effect size estimator.

Experiments that have statistically significant (confidence level α=0,05) results are those whose confidence intervals do not contain zero. Those experiments are all but 3, 4, 10 and 11 for which we have already established that their effect size estimators are incorrect. The only difference is experiment 9 that has incorrect effect size estimator, but its lower confidence interval boundary is very close to zero.

Testing for Homogeneity of Effect Sizes

If the effect sizes have homogenous distribution, then their dispersion around their average is not larger than expected sample error. That is, in homogenous distribution, each effect size differs

Figure 4. Single effect size estimators

No.	Domain knowledge	$\hat{\delta}$	$\hat{\delta}^2$	g	g^2	d	d^2	$\tilde{g}$	$\tilde{g}^2$
1.	Introduction to computer science	0,8175	0,6683	0,8096	0,6555	0,8279	0,6854	0,8043	0,6469
2.	Introduction to computer science	1,2079	1,4591	1,1833	1,4001	1,2401	1,5379	1,1664	1,3606
3.	QBASIC programming	0,5809	0,3374	0,5690	0,3238	0,5964	0,3556	0,5609	0,3146
4.	Chemistry	0,1623	0,0263	0,1596	0,0255	0,1669	0,0279	0,1575	0,0248
5.	Physics – optics	0,8145	0,6639	0,8070	0,6512	0,8252	0,6810	0,8017	0,6427
6.	Nature and society	0,8324	0,6929	0,8155	0,6704	0,8503	0,7230	0,8095	0,6553
7.		0,8904	0,7928	0,8758	0,7670	0,9095	0,8272	0,8659	0,7497
8.		1,0042	1,0085	0,9845	0,9693	1,0303	1,0616	0,9707	0,9422
9.	Mathematics	1,0984	1,2064	1,0461	1,0943	1,1650	1,3572	1,0091	1,0184
10.		0,1128	0,0127	0,1075	0,0115	0,1197	0,0143	0,1037	0,0107
11.		0,3198	0,1022	0,3145	0,0989	0,3266	0,1067	0,3110	0,0967

Figure 5. Confidence intervals

No.	Domain knowledge	d	$\hat{\sigma}(d)$	Confidence interval	Correct	Statistically significant
1.	Introduction to computer science	0,5096	0,2326	$0,3537 \le \delta \le 1,2655$	yes	yes
2.	Introduction to computer science	1,1963	0,3472	$0,5027 \le \delta \le 1,8639$	yes	yes
3.	QBASIC programming	0,5753	0,3268	$-0,0715 \le \delta \le 1,2095$	no	no
4.	Chemistry	0,1612	0,3129	$-0,4537 \le \delta \le 0,7730$	no	no
5.	Physics – optics	0,8070	0,2325	$0,3512 \le \delta \le 1,2627$	yes	yes
6.	Nature and society	0,8244	0,3005	$0,2297 \le \delta \le 1,4078$	yes	yes
7.		0,8818	0,3022	$0,2835 \le \delta \le 1,4681$	yes	yes
8.		0,9945	0,3348	$0,3280 \le \delta \le 1,6405$	yes	yes
9.	Mathematics	1,0878	0,5026	$0,0610 \le \delta \le 2,0312$	no	yes
10.		0,1118	0,4717	$-0,8171 \le \delta \le 1,0321$	no	no
11.		0,3167	0,2905	$-0,2548 \le \delta \le 0,8838$	no	no

from the average effect size only by that error. We test homogeneity of effect sizes by calculating Q using Formula (21) and $1/\hat{\sigma}^2(d)$, $d/\hat{\sigma}^2(d)$ and $d^2/\hat{\sigma}^2(d)$ given in Figure 7:

$$Q = 69{,}0828 - \frac{82{,}4492^2}{116{,}0970} = 10{,}5295\,.$$

Gained Q value is not larger than critical value 19.66 of χ^2 for 11 degrees of freedom ($\alpha = 0.05$) (StatSoft, 2008). Hence, we accept homogeneity null-hypothesis. That means that variability of effect sizes is not larger than a sample error.

Weighted Linear Combination of Effect Size Estimates

Weighted linear combinations of effect size estimations can be expressed using the formula $d_W = w_1 d_1 + \ldots + w_k d_k$. Therefore, we have to calculate nonnegative unbiased weights w_i using the Formula (16). The Figure 6 contains values of the parameters needed for the calculation of common effect size δ*using previously mentioned formula. Weighted linear combinations of effect size estimations, that is, a common effect size estimation is $d_W = 0{,}7230$.

We will calculate weighted linear combinations of effect size estimations using variance of d_i in order to calculate d_+ using the Formula (19). Therefore, we calculated $\hat{\sigma}^2(d_i)$, $1/\hat{\sigma}^2(d_i)$ and $d/\hat{\sigma}^2(d_i)$ for each experiment and results were presented in the Figure 7.

The weighted mean is

$$d_+ = \frac{\sum_{i=1}^{k} \frac{d_i}{\hat{\sigma}^2(d_i)}}{\sum_{i=1}^{k} \frac{1}{\hat{\sigma}^2(d_i)}} = \frac{82,4492}{116,0970} = 0,7102,$$

Figure 6. Parameters needed for the calculation of the common effect size estimation

No.	Domain knowledge	n^E	n^C	$\tilde{n}$	w	d	wd
1.	Introduction to computer science	40	40	20	0,1603	0,5096	0,1298
2.	Introduction to computer science	20	19	9,74	0,0781	1,1533	0,0924
3.	QBASIC programming	20	19	9,74	0,0781	0,5690	0,0444
4.	Chemistry	20	21	10,24	0,0821	0,1596	0,0131
5.	Physics – optics	40	40	20	0,1603	0,8070	0,1294
6.	Nature and society	24	24	12	0,0962	0,8188	0,0788
7.		24	24	12	0,0962	0,8758	0,0843
8.		20	20	10	0,0802	0,9945	0,0799
9.	Mathematics	9	9	4,5	0,0361	1,0461	0,0377
10.		9	9	4,5	0,0361	0,1075	0,0039
11.		24	24	12	0,0962	0,3145	0,0303

Figure 7. Parameters needed for the calculation of d_+

No.	Domain knowledge	n^E	n^C	d	$\hat{\sigma}^2(d)$	$1/\hat{\sigma}^2(d)$	$d/\hat{\sigma}^2(d)$	$d^2/\hat{\sigma}^2(d)$
1.	Introduction to computer science	40	40	0,8096	0,0541	18,4854	14,9660	12,1167
2.	Introduction to computer science	20	19	1,1833	0,1206	8,2931	9,8130	11,6114
3.	QBASIC programming	20	19	0,5690	0,1068	9,3648	5,3287	3,0321
4.	Chemistry	20	21	0,1596	0,0979	10,2114	1,6300	0,2602
5.	Physics – optics	40	40	0,8070	0,0541	18,4946	14,9244	12,0434
6.	Nature and society	24	24	0,8188	0,0903	11,0722	9,0656	7,4226
7.		24	24	0,8758	0,0913	10,9502	9,5900	8,3988
8.		20	20	0,9843	0,1121	8,9198	8,7796	8,6416
9.	Mathematics	9	9	1,0461	0,2526	3,9585	4,1409	4,3317
10.		9	9	0,1075	0,2225	4,4935	0,4829	0,0519
11.		24	24	0,3145	0,0844	11,8534	3,7281	1,1725
Sum						116,0970	82,4492	69,0828

with estimated variance

$$\hat{\sigma}^2(d_+) = \left(\sum_{1=1}^{k} \frac{1}{\hat{\sigma}^2(d_i)}\right)^{-1} = \frac{1}{116,0970} = 0,0086$$

$$\hat{\sigma}(d_+) = \sqrt{0,0086} = 0,0928$$

A 95% confidence interval (δ_L, δ_U) for δ^*, according to the Formula (14) is:

$$\delta_L = d_+ - C_{\frac{\alpha}{2}} \hat{\sigma}\left(d_+\right) = 0,7102 - 1,96 * 0,0928 = 0,5283$$

$$\delta_U = d_+ + C_{\frac{\alpha}{2}} \hat{\sigma}\left(d_+\right) = 0,7102 + 1,96 * 0,0928 = 0,8921$$

that is, confidence interval for δ^* is $0.5283 \leq \delta^* \leq 0.8921$. According to Hedges & Olkin, 1985, this common effect size estimation is correct. As this interval does not include zero, we can conclude that the result is statistically significant (confidence level $\alpha = 0.05$).

Beyond Effect Size Calculation

We have checked if there was any correlation between duration of experiment, sample size, sample age and estimated effect size. The correlation coefficients are presented in Figure 8.

As we can see from the above table, sample age and experiment duration are highly correlated. Other combinations yielded very small correlation coefficients, and, therefore, we can conclude that neither sample size, nor sample age, nor duration of the experiment are in any correlation with the estimated effect size of experiment.

Analysis of Meta-Analysis Results

For the purpose of this meta-analysis, we have calculated different estimates of effect size for each included experiment. Those effect size estimates slightly differ. Furthermore, we have determined effect size confidence interval for each experiment and found out which experiments have statistically significant effect sizes (significance level is $\alpha = 0.05$). The most dispuTable results are related to experiments in relation to domain knowledge areas QBASIC programming, Chemistry and Mathematics. Finally, we have estimated total effect size. Homogeneity test Q was affirmative and we were able to estimate a total effect size. The total effect size estimate was calculated using

Figure 8. Correlation coefficients

	Sample size	Sample age	Duration	Estimated effect size
Sample size	-	0,1834	0,1861	0,1729
Sample age	0,1834	-	0,9250	0,0023
Duration	0,1861	0,9250	-	0,1413
Estimated effect size	0,1729	0,0023	0,1413	-

unbiased effect size estimator d and we got the total effect size $d_+ = 0.71$ sigma.

The xTEx-Sys system had the highest effect size 1,18 in the second experiment related to Introduction to computer science domain knowledge. The second best effect size 1,04 appeared in the ninth experiment related to Mathematics. The lowest effect size 0.10 was found in the tenth experiment related to Mathematics as well. That reveals a question concerning the existence of a relation between a domain knowledge thought in experiment and the effect size gained for that experiment. That question should be explored in another meta-analysis and would include a much larger number of experiments and also a much larger sample size in each experiment.

Despite the fact that this meta-analysis included only eleven experiments, the xTEx-Sys proved to be efficient because, according to Cohen (Cohen, 1988), an effect size of 0,71 sigma is a large effect size.

CONCLUSION

This paper briefly explains differences between different effect size estimators, it describes how effect size confidence intervals are calculated, how do we test homogeneity of effect sizes and, finally, how do we estimate a total effect size. Explained meta-analysis approach was applied on a series of experiments related to the xTEx-Sys effectiveness calculation. This meta-analysis includes eleven experiments and 499 students that enrolled several courses: Introduction to computer science, QBASIC programming, Chemistry, Physics – optics, Nature and society and Mathematics. Gained estimate of total effect size is 0,71.

Although the ITSs are less effective than human tutors, they certainly influence positively learning and teaching process of students that use them. One of the advantages of ITSs is a reduction of learning time needed and enhancement of motivation. These systems enable students to learn in their own pace, give them immediate feedback and correction.

Anyway, the ITSs cannot replace teachers and they are not intended to do so, but they can ease and improve their work. They would significantly smooth the progress of learning and teaching and the teachers could spend some more time on quality communication with students. The ITSs should be included in education as one method for learning and teaching, and meta-analysis, like this one, can give directions for their selection and improvements.

A meta-analysis conducted using results gained through valid experiments based on the same methodology is a key issue in resolving a problem of making conclusions about overall e-learning systems effectiveness. Therefore, a replication of experiments related to e-learning systems' effectiveness calculation, is a first step in meta-analysis.

What should be done in the future to validate findings of the meta-analysis related to the xTEx-Sys effectiveness evaluation? One proposal certainly comprises conducting more experiments in included domain knowledge areas to see if domain knowledge influences effect size estimations. A new meta-analysis should be done for each domain knowledge separately and include a much larger number of experiments and a much larger sample size as well. In that way, we would be able to make some conclusions if there are domain knowledge areas that are more appropriate for learning and teaching using the xTEx-Sys.

REFERENCES

Bloom, B. S. (1984). The Two-Sigma Problem: The Search for Methods of Group Instruction as Effective as One-to-One Tutoring. *Educational Researcher*, *13*, 4–16.

Burns, H. L., & Capps, C. G. (1988). Foundations of intelligent tutoring systems: an introduction. In Poison, M. C., & Richardson, J. J. (Eds.), *Foundations of intelligent tutoring systems* (pp. 1–19). Hillsdale, NJ: Lawrence Erlbaum.

Cohen, J. (1988). *Statistical Power Analysis for the Behavioral Sciences*. Hillsdale, NJ: Lawrence Erlbaum.

Cohen, P. A., Kulik, J. A., & Kulik, C. L. C. (1982). Educational outcomes of tutoring: A meta-analysis of findings. *American Educational Research Journal*, *19*(2), 237–248.

Fletcher, J. D. (2003). Evidence for Learning from Technology-Assisted Instruction. In O'Neal, H. F., & Perez, R. S. (Eds.), *Technology applications in education: a learning view* (pp. 79–99). Mahwah, NJ: Lawrence Erlbaum.

Glass, G. V. (1976). Primary, secondary, and meta-analysis of research. *Educational Researcher*, *5*, 3–8.

Grubisic, A. (2007). *Evaluating Educational Influence of Intelligent E-learning Systems*. Faculty of Electrical Engineering and Computing, Zagreb, Croatia, (MS Thesis), (in Croatian).

Hedges, L. V., & Olkin, I. (1985). *Statistical methods for meta-analysis*. New York: Academic Press.

Hunter, J. E., & Schmidt, F. L. (2004). *Methods of meta-analysis: Correcting error and bias in research findings*. Thousand Oaks, CA: Sage Publications, Inc.

Lipsey, M. W., & Wilson, D. B. (2001). *Practical meta-analysis*. Thousand Oaks, CA: Sage Publications, Inc.

Phillips, R., & Gilding, T. (2003). *Approaches to evaluating the effect of ICT on student learning*. ALT Starter Guide 8.

Rosić, M. (2000). *Establishing of Distance Education Systems within the Information Infrastructure*, Faculty of Electrical Engineering and Computing, Zagreb, Croatia, (MS Thesis), (in Croatian)

Sleeman, D. H., & Brown, J. S. (1982). Introduction - Intelligent Systems. In D. H. Sleeman & J. S. Brown (Eds.), *Intelligent Tutoring Systems* (pp. 1-10). London: Academic Press, Inc (Ltd).

Stankov, S. (1997). *Isomorphic Model of the System as the Basis of Teaching Control Principles in an Intelligent Tutoring System*, Faculty of Electrical Engineering, Mechanical Engineering and Naval Architecture, Croatia, (PhD Thesis), (in Croatian)

Stankov, S. (2003). Project TP-02/0177-01 Web oriented intelligent hypermedial authoring shell, Croatia: Ministry of Science and Technology, (2003-2005).

Stankov, S., Rosic, M., Žitko, B., & Grubišić, A. (2008). TEx-Sys model for building intelligent tutoring systems. *Computers & Education*, *51*(3), 1017–1036. doi:10.1016/j.compedu.2007.10.002

StatSoft. (2008). *Chi-square table*. Retrieved November 09, 2009, from http://www.statsoft.com/textbook/ sttable.html#chi

Wenger, E. (1987). *Artificial Intelligence and Tutoring Systems: Computational and Cognitive approaches to the Communication of Knowledge*. Los Altos, CA: Morgan Kaufmann.

KEY TERMS AND DEFINITIONS

Authoring Shell: program generators used to overcome expensive and time consuming development process of ITSs

Effect Size: is a quantitative measurement that tells us the size of experimental effect and it is used to synthesize experimental results

Effectiveness Evaluation: answers what is the educational influence of an e-learning system on students

E-Learning: is commonly used in everyday life, it enables students to quality participate in learning and teaching process even when a distance, schedule and similar circumstances makes that practically impossible.

Evaluation: offers information to make decision about using the product or not

Intelligent Tutoring System: computer systems that support and improve the learning and teaching processes in a variety of knowledge domains, while respecting the individuality of the learner

Meta-Analysis: integrates the results of a set of experiments without losing relevant information and for assessing a quantitative results quality

Chapter 17
Assessment of the Effectiveness of Distance Learning Courses and of Interactive Processes in Virtual Learning Environments

Francisco Villa Ulhôa Botelho
Universidade Católica de Brasília, Brasil

Rosa Maria Vicari
Universidade Federal do Rio Grande do Sul, Brasil

ABSTRACT

The general objectives of this study are: to analyze significant indicators for assessment of the effectiveness of Distance Learning (DL) courses; to check the extent to which such effectiveness is related to the quality of interactive processes; to examine characteristic elements of individuals' conversations while they interact in study groups within virtual environments, with a view to contributing toward the effectiveness of DL courses; the development of a methodology for assessing the effectiveness of distance learning courses. Results confirm the importance of the context, the teacher, and learning-group variables for the effectiveness of distance courses. They also illustrate the relevance of certain speech features of students and teachers in virtual learning environments that generate conversational dynamics and contribute toward meeting the goals of DL courses.

INTRODUCTION

Use of information and communications technologies (ICT) and large-scale access to the worldwide web have required paradigmatic changes in the education sector. The possibility of researching an array of digital sources, of instant communication and of collaborative work, of electronic publication and of simulation is radically changing approaches to teaching and learning.

It is not simply the adding of new technical media to the traditional and well-known pedagogical structure, as was the case during the audiovisual era of the 1960s and 1970s, when the pedagogical structure was altered only temporarily and superficially. Rather, it represents such a great

DOI: 10.4018/978-1-61692-008-1.ch017

impact on both teachers and pupils that they must re-plan both teaching and learning. As we take stock of the unexpected consequences of such upcoming changes, we are in for a shock (Petters, 2003, p. 58).

It is in this context that DL is fulfilling an important role. Often, it is presented as just another modality of formal education, however, the current configuration of society requires certain specificities from educational actions that are greatly in consonance with DL. The need for continuing education, for permanent updating of information and for production of new knowledge requires flexible and dynamic educational processes that breach the difficulties imposed by barriers of time and space. This is the field of DL, and the learning/teaching methodologies of DL seamlessly fulfill the needs of contemporary society.

Learning processes are the kernel of education, and learning is related to the way in which people relate among themselves and with their environment. Beyond the elementary sensorial perceptions and reflexes, learning is a component of higher mental processes that are mediated by tools and signals.

Thus, to comprehend the dynamics of learning processes we must first obtain an understanding of their components: individuals, environment or context, and mediation. We realize that DL has a characteristic distinctiveness in relation to the mediation component. In view of the need to overcome barriers of time and distance, DL makes intensive use of ICT resources to promote interactive processes.

The building of effective learning environments is a matter of human relations. It also depends upon the emotional input invested in such relations. Thus, knowing how to perform in virtual environments with the aim of creating the necessary climate for stimulating learning processes is of utmost importance.

All these challenges motivated this research. We need to deepen our knowledge on characteristics that DL has assumed with the advent of the information age and the emergence of networks. Developing knowledge on the effective use of DL courses represents yet another step along this path.

Evaluation of the effectiveness of distance learning courses and the dynamics of interactive learning processes are the issues stated in the title of this chapter. They convey efforts to comprehend the phenomenon and seek to identify a methodology that combines both evaluation of processes and of results.

This study is concerned with the relationship between objectives and results of distance education processes and seeks to identify indicators for effecting permanent evaluation of actions. Thus, beginning with the question of quality in DL, we limited our theme to evaluation of the effectiveness of distance-learning courses. In this context, our research was guided by the following general objectives:

- analyze indicators that could be useful for evaluation of the effectiveness of distance-learning courses;
- verify to what extent the effectiveness of DL courses is correlated with the quality of interactive processes;[1]
- seek characteristics of conversations among individuals in interaction within study groups formed within virtual environments that contribute toward the effectiveness of distance-learning courses;
- develop a methodology for evaluating the effectiveness of distance-learning courses.

SCIENTIFIC LITERATURE ON EVALUATION OF THE EFFECTIVENESS OF DISTANCE-LEARNING COURSES

Over time, publications on distance learning have accompanied the dissemination of DL practices throughout the world. Such studies have sought to deal with the various dimensions involved in this modality of education. Most are papers that describe case studies and present models, development of theories, etc.

For the purposes of thematic synthesis, such publications can be grouped as follows:

a) studies on planning and production of teaching materials;
b) studies on technological support for DL;
c) studies on DL scenarios, the evolution of models, legislation and trends;
d) studies on distance learning/teaching processes, interactive systems, didactics for DL, and evaluation of learning resulting from DL processes; and studies on DL management: e-learning, e-training, quality evaluation, impact and effectiveness of programs and courses.

Status of the Theme in Specialized Congresses

To assess the state-of-the-art of evaluation studies on effectiveness of distance-learning courses, we conducted a survey of publications from the most recent congresses of the Brazilian Distance Education Association (*Associação Brasileira de Educação a Distância -ABED*), the main scientific organization dealing with DL in Brazil. We also examined papers presented at the 22nd World Conference of the International Council for Open and Distance Education (ICDE), one of the main international scientific organizations in the field.

We sought to identify works that addressed evaluation of DL courses and programs, and separated those that assessed results, impacts, or effectiveness of courses. The theme or sub-theme of evaluation of results appeared only at the 11th and 12th ABED Congresses (as shown in Figure 1).

Figure 1. Thematic organization of works presented at recent ABED congresses (http://www2.abed.org.br/congressos.asp[2])

EVENT	THEME	SUB-THEMES	TOTAL NUMBER OF PAPERS	NUMBER OF PAPERS ON EVALUATION OF RESULTS (IMPACT OR EFFECTIVENESS)
8th Congress 2001	From the information society to the knowledge society: challenges for Distance Education	DL in education systems Planning, preparation and evaluation of teaching materials for DL Systems management for DL Professional training for DL	55	0
9th Congress 2002	Rethinking learning by Distance Education	Best practices in DL; New techniques and technologies to enhance quality of learning. The future of learning.	60	0
10th Congress 2003	Achieving Quality through Competent Planning	Training of Professionals for Distance Education; Planning, Preparation and Evaluation of teaching materials for Distance Education; Management of Distance Education Systems; Distance Education in Education Systems.	115	0
11th Congress 2004	Evaluation – commitment to quality and results	Training of Professionals for Distance Education; Planning, Preparation and Evaluation of teaching materials for Distance Education; Management of Distance Education Systems, and Distance Education in Education Systems	119	3
12th Congress 2005	Distance Education and Integration of the Americas	Strategies and Policies Content and Skills Methods and Technologies Support and Services Management and Logistics Research and Evaluation	206	2

It was at these same events that the first studies on the theme were discussed but, even then, they represented only a very small number in relation to the total of papers presented.

In Figure 1, we can clearly perceive the emergence of two issues: firstly, growing concern on the part of researchers with quality evaluation or results of courses and programs, since the subject arises as one of the themes for discussion at the congresses; secondly, that the theme remains underexploited, as is reflected in the small number of articles presented.

As observed at the ABED congresses, concern with evaluation of results of programs and courses was also discussed at the 22nd ICDE World Conference, the theme of which was "Promoting Quality in Distance Education, Flexible and ICT Based Education".[3] As Figure 2 shows, the entire conference was structured around the guiding theme of quality in Distance Education (DL). At this event, held in September 2006 in Rio de Janeiro, 347 articles were selected from throughout the world. However, only two of these directly addressed the theme of effectiveness evaluation. One of these articles was by Botelho & Vicari (2006), who presented considerations of possible paths for evaluation of the effectiveness of distance-learning courses; and the other, by a Chinese author (LUYI 2006) who describes in general lines a Chinese Government evaluation program that aims to ensure the quality of distance education. Once again, one is left with the impression that very little research has been dedicated to the subject.

The theme of evaluation also appears in books. However, the aspect that receives the most attention is learning, i.e., the main focus is evaluation of learning through distance-learning courses. In 2006, for example, a book entitled *Avaliação da aprendizagem em educação online* (Evaluation of learning in online education) was published in Brazil, reflecting this focus.[4]

Studies on Interactive Processes in Virtual Learning Environments

With the development of telematics, so-called virtual learning environments have become the spaces of choice for establishment of communities and for the holding of distance-learning courses.

Figure 2. Thematic organization of papers presented at the 22nd ICDE World Conference (www.icde22.org.br/portugues/theme.htm)

THEME	SUB-THEMES
1. Value of Distance Education, Flexible and ICT Based Education in relation to:	1.1. Requisites for National Development 1.2. Education for "Capacity Building" 1.3. Continuing Education and Education at the Workplace 1.4. International Collaboration
2. Promotion of Quality in Education with a view to:	2.1. Teachers (recruitment, accreditation, training and evaluation) 2.2. Pedagogy (methods for delivery and communication, role of students, etc.) 2.3. Evaluation of Results of Learning 2.4. Technology and Delivery 2.5. Cultural and Linguistic Diversity
3. Questions of Institutional Quality Referent to:	3.1. Development of Quality Standards 3.2. Development Methods for Promoting Quality (evaluation, benchmarking, incentive systems, involvement of users, international collaboration etc.) 3.3. Questions Relating to Accreditation and Regulation across Borders 3.4. The Costs of Quality: Economic Questions 3.5. Facing the Challenge of Poor Quality (ghost-universities, false on-line diplomas etc.)
4. Research and New Paths Referent to:	4.1. Methods of Evaluation and Quality Assurance 4.2. Pedagogy 4.3. Technology and Communications 4.4. Service

According to Silvio (2000, p.23), "virtual communities are groupings that reproduce the sociability of human beings at a virtual level, and that perceive cyberspace and its technologies as instruments for communication and life in social groups".

The development of virtual learning communities is an essential strategy in distance-learning courses, which are intensive users of ICTs. From this perspective, the design of distance-learning courses has harnessed current communications tools in these spaces, placing them at the service of students and teachers for use in interactive processes.

Studies on these processes exploit the various angles of the phenomenon. Examples of the different ways of approaching interactive processes in virtual learning environments can be examined through the work of three researchers: Torres (2004), Beiler (2004), and Araújo (2004).

Torres (2004) carried out research on manifestations of emotion in written communications within virtual environments. He assesses "speech", i.e., written interventions in the activities of forums during two courses: Informatics in Education I, and Education and Multimedia. According to the author:

Analysis of speech demonstrated that certain individuals possess similar mechanisms for emotional manifestation and for expressing the status of their consciousness by means of written language. As a consequence, contrary to what common sense might indicate, computers do not impede development of affection among persons (Torres, 2004, p. 13).

Beiler (2004) examined the formation of conversation networks in accordance with Humberto Maturana's approach, and produced interesting mapping and evaluations of the processes of consensual coordination of actions for promoting learning. To this end, he also examined records of conversations at discussion forums, with the aim of developing a methodology that could assist teachers to diagnose the quality of interactions. This author concluded that:

[...] conversation networks open up possibilities that envisage not only cognitive but, more especially, relational sharing and enable configuration of concepts expressed in conversation flows, within this space of coexistence, in the interlaced flows of consensual coordination of language and emotion. It is learning that arises from coexistence, learning from living (Beiler, 2004, p. 17).

The last of the three authors mentioned, Araújo (2004), based his research on information in the record of written communications of forums of a distance-learning course at The Catholic University of Brasilia (*Universidade Católica de Brasília - UCB*) in the field of Tourism. The objective was to study the effectiveness of practices for production of knowledge at asynchronous meetings in DL courses. He also studied the conversational competencies necessary to engage in such interactions with competence and quality in. Araújo (2004) used as one of his theoretical premises the Meta Learning model, which is also one of the focuses of this present research.

These three research papers were developed based upon similar objects (conversations or interactive processes in virtual learning environments) and worked with the same information sources, i.e., interventions in discussion forums. In this respect, this present work shares some similarities, however, the aims are different, as are also the theoretical and methodological references.

REQUISITES FOR A STUDY ON INTERACTIVE PROCESSES, LEARNING, AND EVALUATION OF THE EFFECTIVENESS OF DISTANCE-LEARNING COURSES

Three issues are of strategic importance in this study: distance learning; learning and interaction;

and evaluation of effectiveness. If we consider evaluation of the effectiveness of courses as a question of methodology, as will be discussed in another section, it remains only for us to ponder the two other issues in order to fulfill the theoretical requisites of our research goals.

Distance education or distance learning is a modality of education; and education, essentially, entails learning. Thus, learning and interactive processes are the most comprehensive themes, and the ones that require reflection on theoretical inputs that underpin our research approach.

We seek these essentials through two approaches that may complement each other in guiding our studies on the effectiveness of interactive processes in virtual learning environments, namely: Vygotsky's historical-cultural theory; and the bases of complex thought.

An initial explanation for these theoretical approaches is an understanding that learning should be assessed without reducing it to an outcome of a formal act of teaching, in which the individual is passive and the phenomenon may be isolated from its context. Rather, learning should be treated as an action in which people interact with others and with their environment in the process of production, conservation, and changing of their lives. In this case, the phenomenon encompasses most elements of interaction, comprising a complex reality.

Through Vygotsky's historical-cultural approach, we sought to understand the importance of interactive processes in human learning, i.e., how people learn and develop. From complex thought, we extracted the guidance that learning does not abide by a linear cause-and-effect logic, but rather, that it constitutes a dynamic process, as a result and factor of multiple interactions, and as part of a process of self-organization of people and of society.

From among these approaches we sought a definition of learning and an understanding of its processes. We explored theoretical inputs to assist us in the process of evaluation of the effectiveness of DL courses. We therefore extracted from these approaches lessons that not only shed light upon components of the human learning system to be evaluated, but also on their interconnections, movements and self-organization.

Human learning encompasses multiple dimensions, ranging from psycho-social to historical. Such dimensions make up complex phenomena. To study this in the light of complex thought, we sought a methodology capable of guiding analysis of the interactive processes within a virtual environment. We found this in the Meta Learning model, proposed by Losada.

The Meta Learning Model

Losada is a Chilean researcher who spent a major portion of his life in the United States, where he carried out extensive research on the performance of work groups. Meta Learning consists of a model that he developed as a theoretical reference, with collaborating researchers from the Santa Fé Institute (complex adaptive systems), Maturana and Varela (biology of cognition).

The Meta Learning model is defined as a process of learning in which people, in their groups, manage to dissolve limiting dynamics such as point attractors and limit cycles that impede effective action (Figure 3, provides a graphic representation of the fixed-point and limit-cycle attractors) and to develop attractors that open up possibilities for effective action (Figure 3: chaotic attractor or complexor, to use the terminology employed by Losada)[5]. It is thus an explicative model of the dynamics of the workings of teams and of interaction among the persons that comprise them. It is focused on an understanding of factors that contribute toward creating and maintaining the dynamics of high performance groups.

After testing and analyzing a set of variables, Losada's research arrived at three bipolar variables of great significance for explaining the dynamics of interaction. Depending upon these dynamics, the performance of groups is either marked by

Figure 3. Graphic representation of attractors (LOSADA, 1997)

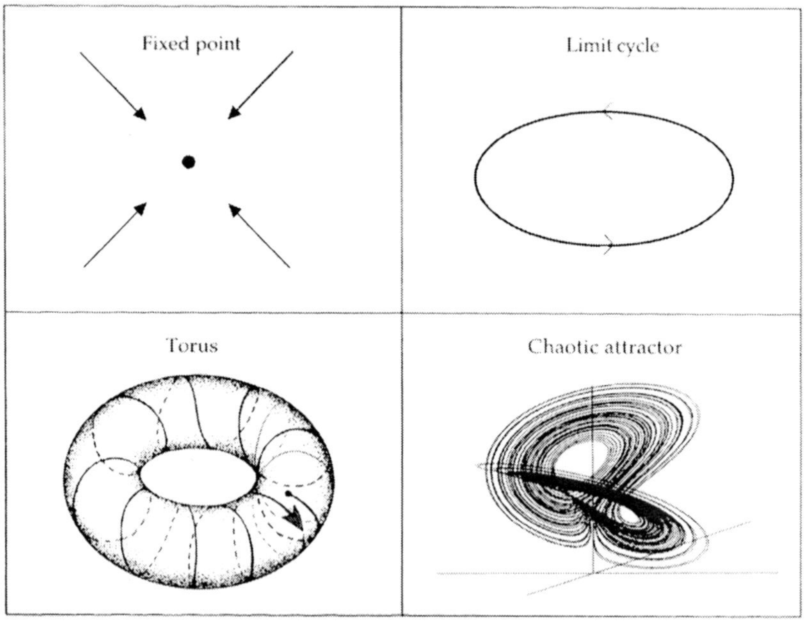

creativity and innovation, or by common sense and repetition. They are descriptive variables of the postures of persons in interactive processes, and are indicative of the quality of the positions assumed by persons in relation to the "speech" of others and in relation to positivity or negativity of characteristics, of questioning or proposition, or of forcing oneself upon the other (Figure 4).

Interaction is treated as connectivity. Connectivity is indicated by the quantity of connections, understood as being nexuses. According to Losada & Heaphy (2004), nexuses are strongly inter-related standards of conduct, sustained over time among members of a team and that indicate a process of mutual influence. According to the model, what defines a high-performance team is its capacity for connectivity, related to three bipolar variables.[6]

The connectivity of a high-performance team corresponds to an average of 32 nexuses; for medium-performance teams the average is 22 nexuses; and for low-performance teams 18 nexuses.

Among the bipolar variables, positivity/negativity is central to interactive processes, as it operates as a powerful feedback system for generating different emotional spaces. These spaces are represented in the Meta Learning model (Figure 5) by P/N rates (total of positive interventions divided

Figure 4. Team performance matrix (Losada & Heaphy, 2004)

Performance	Dynamics	Connectivity	Bipolar Variables		
			Questioning/ Proposition	The other/ Oneself	Positivity/ Negativity (Emotional Space)
High	Complexor	High	Balanced	Balanced	Expansive P>>N
Medium	Limit cycle	Medium	Tendency to unbalance in the direction of proposition	Unbalanced oriented to oneself	Restrictive P>N
Low	Fixed point	Low	Unbalanced in the direction of proposition	Entirely unbalanced oriented to oneself	Highly restrictive N>P

by the total of negative interventions). When this rate is within an adequate band, the persons are creating expansive emotional spaces that enhance connectivity and induce better performance on the part of the group. If they lie outside this band, it means that the actions are resulting in restrictive emotional spaces that hamper performance.

The P/N rate is calculated and set within a reference band known as the Losada Line, in which positivity varies from 2.9013 or over (but not greater than 11.6153) to 1 of negativity. This means that, for each negative intervention in the interactions of a team, there should be at least three positive interventions.

In view of the importance of the positivity/negativity variable, Losada reached the conclusion that it is sufficient to know the P/N rate to calculate connectivity.[7] Therefore, to determine the performance of a team, it is sufficient to observe conversation during the dynamics of interaction, to codify the acts of speech identified as positive and negative, to calculate the P/N rate, and thus obtain the resultant connectivity.

By observing the development of organizations and the role of work groups in this process, Losada & Heaphy (2004: 20) indicated how important it is that the actions of persons be guided by creation of expansive conversational dynamics:

We need organizations in which there is polarity of the other and of oneself, of you and of I, integrated in the sense of we; in which the polarity of questioning and of proposition, of questions and of answers can direct a positive and fortifying dialog; in which the abundance of positivity, supported by constructive negative responses can generate a state of realistic enthusiasm that enables organizations to achieve heights of excellence.

Figure 5. Losada's Meta Learning model (Source: Losada & Heaphy (2004)

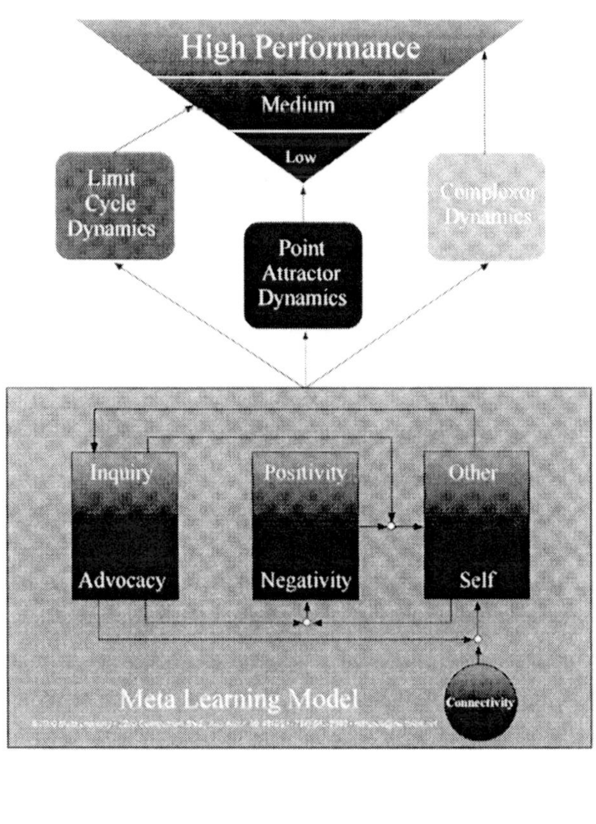

Losada developed his model by studying teams engaged in activities that affected the economic-financial performance of their organizations. This same model is being used in research relating to the dynamics of teams focused on other activities, such as education and production of knowledge.

Impact Evaluation: A Contribution to Organizational Psychology

In the field of Organizational Psychology there is an array of research papers on evaluation of Training and Development (T&D) programs.[8] Studies focusing on DL, however, are incipient.

Abbad (2000) summarized a traditional approach of Kirkpatrick (1976) and Hamblin (1978), under which evaluation of the efficacy of training was built upon five levels: reaction (degree of satisfaction with the training); learning (performance measurements of students in the course); behavior in the position or impact of the training (application of knowledge acquired to the work); organizational change (effect on the learner's behavior); and final value (improvement in the quality of products and services). Under the traditional approach, there is a positive relationship among these levels, i.e., the greater the level of satisfaction, the better the prospects for learning, the greater the applicability to the work, the greater the positive effects on the groups and on the organization and, possibly, the better the quality of products and services.

In the search for an explanation of the relations between the levels of evaluation, Abbad (2000) examined the correlation between reaction and learning, on the one hand and, on the other, the impact of training on the work. She argues that the literature on evaluation of training does not demonstrate any necessary relationship between favorable reactions of trainees to training, and learning of the content taught and application of new contents to the work. This gap calls into question the validity of traditional training-evaluation approaches and suggests a need to include other variables, such as the environment or organizational context, to explain the impact of training on the work.

Having examined papers on evaluation of training, Sallas & Cannon-Bowers (2001) stated that theories, models, empirical results, analysis and meta-analysis have never been so readily available. Whether such research has had a practical effect on training, i.e., a significant impact on how organizations are conducting training, is open to debate. In other words, from the authors' standpoint, while realizing that companies are indeed nowadays concerned about their human capital and evaluation of the effectiveness of training, it cannot be stated that the results examined are being used to enhance training practices.

DESCRIPTION OF A POSSIBLE APPROACH FOR EVALUATING THE EFFECTIVENESS OF DISTANCE-LEARNING COURSES

One of the main difficulties in studies on evaluation of the effectiveness of courses or educational programs is monitoring of each phase, which entails examination of the beginning of the action, the process, its end and subsequent checking of results. Certain components of distance education, such as the wide area that the action includes and the size and heterogeneity of the target-public, tend to make such evaluation even more difficult. Such difficulties may explain the scarcity of studies on the effectiveness of DE.

Characteristics of the Case Study

With a view to overcoming the challenge of assessing the effectiveness of DL courses, we selected an on-going DL experience, i.e., a course that, since its inception, had been planned to contain a project-evaluation component. This course, and the data-collection instruments used, was set up by *Universidade Católica de Brasília Virtual* (UCB VIRTUAL).

Courses were offered in Portuguese and Spanish by the Salesian Higher Education Institutions (*Instituições Salesianas de Educação Superior - IUS*) for residents of countries of the Americas and of Europe. There are currently 17 participating institutions in 10 countries and approximately 1,500 students[9]. IUS considers the course a strategic initiative and perceives it as a step in the process of consolidating its identity at its many university institutions throughout the world.

The objective of the course is to develop values, knowledge, skills and attitudes and enable professors to construct effective practices during the process of teaching and learning using new communication and information technologies, with a view to structuring cooperative learning environments, in line with the Salesian style of education[10]. In this manner, the training aims to develop and/or consolidate a set of teaching practices, based upon a posture of care for students, through the creation of welcoming environments and learning situations that stimulate autonomy and student participation.

The course takes place in a virtual environment (UCB VIRTUAL) accessed by the Internet. The teaching material is structured in Autonomous Study Units. Each of these units is comprised of contents formatted as hypertexts, case studies and exercises, with references to the literature and websites, and digitalized conventional texts for supplementary reading. There are five units, equivalent to 240 hours of study, and maximum course duration is seven months.

All monitoring of the learning process is conducted by professors, by means of a tutorial system comprised of two presential meetings and interactive processes carried out in the virtual environment. The most commonly used interactive tools are chat rooms and discussion forums.

Evaluation of learning is carried out in a formative and summative manner, through participation in virtual debates and submission of written work with systematizations of the learning. Among the significant evaluative actions is comparison of the participants' teaching plans. At the beginning of the course, each participant submits a plan to be used during his practice as a teacher and, at the end of the course when the work is being finalized, delivers a modified teaching plan designed to incorporate new learning.

The students participating in the course that we examined were professors of higher education that work at Salesian Higher Education Institutions (IUS) who had concluded the course more than six months earlier and had undergone a final evaluation.

Procedures for Gathering and Organizing Information/Data

Most information on the research database relates to the impact of distance-learning courses and the quality of interactive processes. There follows an account of procedures for establishing this database and analysis of the information it contains.

Distance-Learning Outcome/ Impact Indicator

The main sources of research information were the course participants (university professors), their peers, the coordinators in each area, and students of the subjects they teach in their respective institutions.

The information is gathered by means of electronic questionnaires containing both open and closed questions. The data-gathering process is carried out according to the model described in Figure 6.

The information obtained in this model consists of:

1. Profiles of the participants: demographic data (sex, age, schooling level, etc), occupational data (institution where they work, position, weekly workload, etc.), data

Figure 6. Evaluation model (based on the five-stage model developed by Abbad (2000)

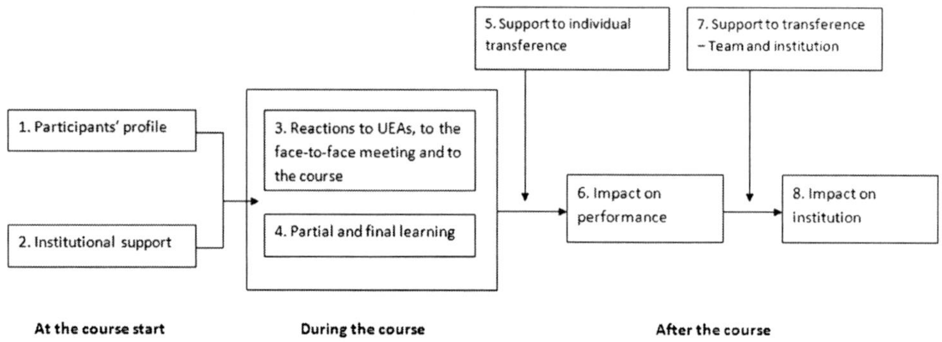

relating to investment in the course (type of enrolment, interest in its proceedings, expectations, etc.), culture of autonomous study (independent searches for information, time management, etc.).

2. Institutional support: for the holding of the course (equipment available, regard for the course on the part of coordinators and peers, course-load availability for participating in the course at work, adequate venue for holding the course at the institution etc.).
3. Reaction: satisfaction of the participants with regard to media used to distribute course material, quality and depth of course materials, interactive processes (tutor-learner, learner-learner, learner-academic secretary, learner-technological support), course methodology, and presential meetings etc.
4. Learning: grades (final scores) obtained by learners in course activities[11].
5. Support for individual transfers (level of professional performance of the participants): institutional support to ensure impact at the performance level (material and technological support necessary for application of knowledge, competencies and skills acquired through the course in the area of professional activity, support of the coordination and of peers for application, regard for the course on the part of the coordination and of peers, etc.).
6. Impact on performance: change in professional performance as a consequence of the course (changes in aspects relating strictly to the objectives of the course – impact on depth, changes in aspects not directly related to such objectives – impact on the scope).
7. Support for transfers at the group and institution level (institutional level): institutional support to ensure impact at the institutional level (joint survey of indicators with institutional managers, specialists in evaluation of the requesting institution, etc.).
8. Impact on the institution: changes at the institution as a consequence of the course (joint survey of indicators with institutional managers, specialists in evaluation of the requesting institution etc.)

This model was developed by Abbad (2000) from the traditional approach of Kirkpatrick (1976) and Hamblin (1978). Using it, we can gather information for studies on the reaction of students to training, learning, behavior of students at their posts/work or impact of training, on organizational change, and on the final value measured in terms of improved quality of products and services of organizations (the three final levels were assessed during training provided, based on a given institutional demand).

Although this process of analysis utilizes practically all the information collected according to the model described, the indicators - that are the main objective of our study - focus on results. These indicators are comprised of information described in item 6 of Figure 6 above, namely: change in professional performance as a consequence of the course (changes in aspects relating to course objectives or in-depth impact).

Questions relating to impact, to be found in the evaluation questionnaires, attempt to capture changes in performance of the participants and in their teaching activities, in relation to the objectives of the course. Questions contained in the questionnaires responded by course participants bear a correspondence to those responded by their students, regularly enrolled in one of the subjects taught at their institution of origin.

Interactive Process Quality Indicators

Reference to the historical-cultural approach and to complex thought appears clearly in two expressions: dynamics of the interactive processes; conversational dynamics. An examination of interactive processes as a path for understanding the quality of DL courses finds support in Vygotsky's concept of learning. The theoretical references mentioned also guide the focus toward the dynamics of interactive processes, in that they view the phenomenon of human learning as an open system that establishes relations with the socio-historical context.

This being so, when we seek to assess the quality of interactive processes, we are constructing a response to the following question: what type of intervention should be sought, and how can we combine interventions within the contexts of groups to generate a positive conversational dynamic for learning and for ensuring the effectiveness of courses (a dynamic that Losada calls a "complexor")? This issue is crucial for construction of indicators and for the development of an analysis capable of describing this dynamic and its attractors.

In any communication among persons, we know that, when certain "speeches' are proffered, the conversation may come to an end or be reduced to repetitions. On the other hand, they may generate animation, capable of ensuring the opening of persons to continuity of the conversation, or its resumption at another time. This also occurs in conversations within a family group, among groups of friends, or in a classroom. Teachers know when a class has attained a dynamic of strong participation and interest, or when they appear to be speaking to the walls. What interventions induce each of these dynamics?

In the classification/codification of each participation in the forum, interventions are considered as units of verbal communication or enunciations. According to Bakhtin (2000: 319), an enunciation is:

[...] a link in the chain of verbal communication. It has clear limits, determined by alternation of speaking subjects (speakers) but, within these limits, the enunciated, like Leibniz's mónade, reflects the verbal process, the enunciations of others and, above all, earlier links (sometimes the closest, but often more distant ones, in areas of cultural communication).

In the study of discussion forums during the course, two pairs of bipolar variables were adapted and presented within the Meta Learning model. This adaptation was carried out through suppression of one of the three pairs of variables in the model and reformulation of the description of the other two pairs. The need to eliminate one of the pairs of variables is justified by the fact that Losada's research was carried out through observation of people/teams, in a manner that enabled observation of the body language of participants engaged in conversation, thus providing information on reception variables. On our case, observation of the variables was taken from the discussion-forum records. Thus, written verbal communication impeded us from observing body-language aspects of the participants.

Figure 7 shows that we redefined the inquiry/proposition and positivity/negativity variables in the Meta Learning model. In the first case we chose inquiry/proposition and, in the second, approval/disapproval.

For a better understanding of the way in which enunciations recorded from the discussion forums of the course were interpreted, the following Figure 8 to Figure 11, provide a representative data set.

Each of the texts of records of conversations in the discussion forums was interpreted by two analysts, i.e., two separate readings were carried out, and later the compatibility of the results was checked. When there was a divergence in the classifications of the analysts, it was resolved under the guidance of a supervisor[12].

Structure and Consistency of the Database

The research database was structured on an Excel spreadsheet, and the information organized with a line per student. As is shown in Figure 12, the initial database had 1,494 lines-students. This is

Figure 7. Definition of variables in the analysis of interactive processes

VARIABLES (classification of forum interventions)	DEFINITIONS
QUESTIONING	• (investigation) • Questioning on the theme • Question to qualify or deepen interaction • Question to start interaction • Expression of curiosity
PERSUASION	(argumentation) • Defense of standpoints and polemic/debate resources, which may include: • Questions as a resource for defense or contraposition of ideas • Experience reports as a defense resource of thesis contestation • Introduction of a new thesis
APPROVAL	• (agreement/acceptance/confirmation) • Being in favor (acceptance of another person's thesis or standpoint) • Affirmation by repeating the thesis or proposition of others (confirmation)
DISAPPROVAL	• (disagreement/rejection/denial) • Contrary standpoint (rejection of another person's thesis or standpoint) • Opposition to a proposition (opposition)

Figure 8. Examples of the classification of interventions in discussion forums, Variables: Approval and Persuasion

VARIABLE	INTERVENTION
APPROVAL PERSUASION	**From: STUDENT Y 02/11/02** Dear colleagues, I fully agree with the statement that Planning is a "crucial point in the "teaching-learning" process. I also agree with the statement that video is an "extra" resource. However I ask: what resource is not an "extra"? As an English Language teacher I use (but do not abuse) video quite frequently. I comment on one of the activities that my students most enjoy. We watch a small part of a film (that they have not seen before, but that I, of course, have previewed during the PLANNING of the class) and I stop the tape. I ask questions such as: how would you resolve this problem if you were in X's position? If you were Y, would you act in the same way she did? How do you imagine this issue was solved? We then watch the rest of the film or the part that answers the questions raised, and continue our class with discussions. I would also like to remark that the students enjoy making their own films. Indeed, they are very creative and film our quality interviews! STUDENT Y

Figure 9. Examples of classification of interventions in discussion forums, Variables: Approval, Persuasion and Questioning

VARIABLE	INTERVENTION
	From: STUDENT Z 26/10/02 Dear teachers,
APPROVAL	Like Teacher Q, I also use a lot of video in the classroom. I teach English Language and English and North-American Literature and the use of video has become indispensible in both subjects.
PERSUASION	In English Language classes, for example, students can work on pronunciation, intonation and colloquial language in an entertaining way. They can also create subtitles for certain films. In my literature classes I love to present literary adaptations so that we can discuss them after the film has finished. The results have been most encouraging!
QUESTIONING	I am curious to learn new techniques for the use of video in the classroom. A happy Saturday evening to you all and enjoy the election tomorrow. STUDENT Z.

Figure 10. Examples of classification of interventions during discussion forums, Variables: Persuasion and Disapproval

VARIABLE	INTERVENTION
	From: STUDENT X 25/10/02 Dear colleagues.
PERSUASION	I think that one good reason for using audio-visual resources is the question of " didactic intentionality ". If there is planning, based on specific objectives for the lesson, the resource merely provides a more effective means of achieving said objectives.
DISAPPROVAL	But audio-visual resources can actually "miss the target " when they are regarded as being more important than the content that is to be transmitted in the classroom. Sometimes the non-use of such resources is a good educational strategy, or alternation of such resources can produce good educational results. STUDENT X.

Figure 11. Examples of classification of interventions in discussion forums, Variable: Questioning

VARIABLE	INTERVENTION
QUESTIONING	**From: TUTOR 3 25/10/02** Dear teachers, Currently, the use of audio-visual media within the educational context has undergone considerable growth. How can we use video to improve the quality of educational processes? A friendly embrace, TUTOR 3.

information from 17 higher-education institutions in 10 countries.

In the columns, there is information on the origin and characteristics of the students, professors/tutors, classes, learning evaluation results, responses to impact evaluation questionnaires, and bipolar variables (Meta Learning adapted model) gathered from the discussion forums.

Filtering of the data in the database was carried out in view of the need to have only individuals/students who had concluded the course and had been evaluated by their respective learners in their institutions, i.e., which had undergone impact evaluation. Thus, the following categories of students were eliminated:

a) students who had not undergone impact evaluation (carried out six months after conclusion of the course);
b) students of classes in which rates of return of questionnaires was very low (as shown in Figure 13, all institutions with over 50% return of impact-evaluation questionnaires were accepted).

After these cuts, the database was reduced to 267 students from 6 institutions in various countries.

Figure 12. Distribution of students enrolled in the course by institution and country of origin

INSTITUTION	STUDENTS ENROLLED
UCDB - BRAZIL	70
UCB - BRAZIL	223
FSV - BRAZIL	45
UNISAL - BRAZIL	97
FASNE - BRAZIL	14
FSDB - BRAZIL	17
FDB - BRAZIL	35
USB - BOLIVIA	391
SAL - ARGENTINA*	30
UCSH - CHILE	70
ISS - PERU	62
UPS - EQUADOR	248
IUSPO - VENEZUELA	23
UDB - EL SALVADOR	61
UMG - GUATEMALA	80
CESDB - SPAIN	17
EUSS - SPAIN	11
General Total	1494

Procedures for Analysis of the Correlation between Impact Results and Characteristics of Interactive Processes

The procedure for preparation of the analysis entailed comparison of the results of two analytical processes, structured by means of the five-stage model and the adapted Meta Learning model. The impact-evaluation results of the five-stage model (cf. Figure 6) were utilized. Based on the Meta Learning model, an adaptation of the best codification of verbal written communication was conducted, forums were analyzed, and codification starting with such bipolar variables as inquiry/persuasion and approval/disapproval (cf. Figure 7) carried out. The reference for these variables was application of the Meta Learning model, however, its content was redefined for a better standardization of the codification of forum texts, as shown in Figure 14.

Analysis of the forums, along with results that express the incidence of each variable of "speech" or intervention by students and teachers, was compared with the impact evaluation averages obtained

Figure 13. Percentage of students that submitted impact-evaluation questionnaires, by institution of origin

INSTITUTION	% OF STUDENTS
A	53,5
B	87,5
C	65,8
D	85,7
E	86,7
F	89,5
Total	60,1

Figure 14. Effectiveness evaluation model applied to this research

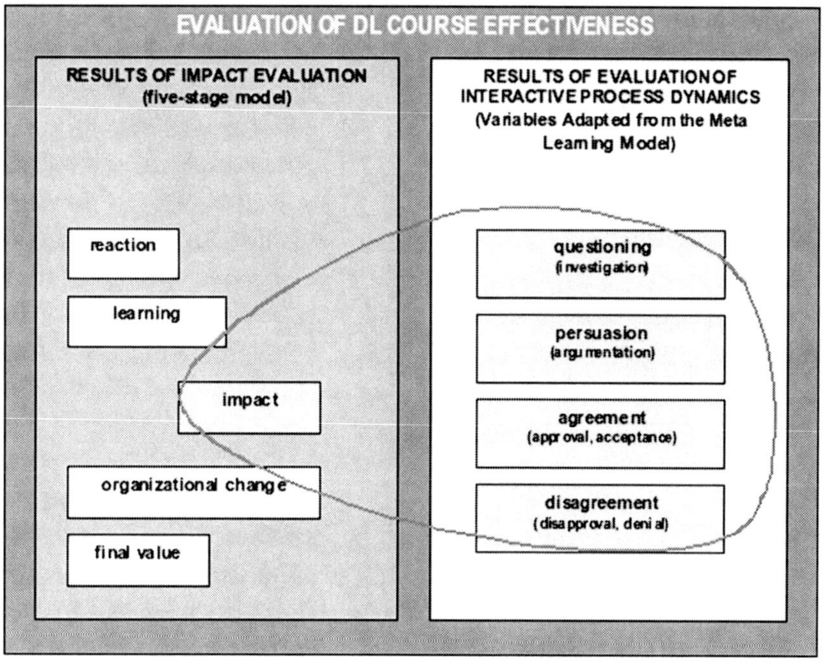

by students. It was thus possible to characterize the "speech" of the participants in the forums, and to rank the groups according to higher or lower concentrations in the impact evaluation.

For these same groups, classified by impact-evaluation quality, the dynamics in the forums were assessed by analysis of the evolution of the configuration of "speech", from the first to the last forums in the course.

In synthesis, the itinerary for analytical processing of information complied with the following steps:

a. identify, using impact indicators, persons with the highest or lowest evaluation scores;
b. verify in which group/class these people belong, if there was hegemony in relation to impact evaluation, i.e., whether or not there were groups with greater concentrations of people with high or low impact evaluation.

If groups with high or low impact were identified:

c. identify, within such groups, distinctive conversational characteristics in discussion forums, by means of the two bipolar variables of the adapted Meta Learning model, and by observing distinctive characteristics relating to the number of interventions;
d. verify the (dynamic) evolution of these conversational characteristics by comparing results of the first and last forums of the course.

To analyze the information and synthesize results, the following descriptive statistical resources were used:

a. descriptive graphics and tables;
b. a parametric description in which the values of certain parameters were estimated, to facilitate description of the data set: central-tendency and statistical-dispersion measures;[13]
c. correlations among variables.[14]

The realization that statistical results are merely a support for understanding the phenomena oriented this analysis. Although the correlation among different variables has been exhaustively explored, only those that significantly contribute information for an understanding of research issues were utilized.

SUMMARY OF OUTCOMES

The main results of the analysis of the data collected correspond to the general objectives of the research, which were: analysis of indicators of significance for evaluation of the effectiveness of DL; verification of to what measure the effectiveness of courses is correlated with the quality of interactive processes; identification of characteristics of individuals' conversations in interactions in study groups formed within virtual environments that may contribute toward the effectiveness of DL courses. These findings can be summarized as follows:

a. participants in the course gave it a positive evaluation;
b. the final grades of the evaluation of participants in the course and their self-evaluations after the course do not appear to be good indicators of course effectiveness, as no correlation could be established between the final grade, the self-evaluation, and the impact evaluation;
c. the context proved to be an important factor for course effectiveness;
d. the group, and the dynamics of interaction among its components, were considered important factors for course effectiveness;
e. the teacher's performance was also deemed relevant for course effectiveness, as his presence, with constant interventions throughout the entire course (initial and final forums) and the quality and equilibrium (bipolar variables) of his/her interventions during the course, proved to have a significant impact on the groups;
f. with respect to characteristics of interventions in the internal conversations of learning groups, it was observed that persuasion stood out as a significant feature in the conversations of both (high and low impact) groups; there was an imbalance in relation to persuasion in the inquiry/persuasion bipolar variable in both groups; only in the high impact groups could compatibility be perceived in relation to the variables approval/disapproval on the Losada Line (high impact group– in the 1 P/N forum = 7.9 and in the 2 P/N forum = 3.9, low impact group – in the 1 P/N forum = 12.5, and in the 2 P/N forum = 13.3); thus, the study asserted the Meta Learning model and indicated the importance of expansive emotional space (Losada Line band) for positive dynamics of the groups;
g. non-correlation of final grades in the evaluation of course participants and impact on participant performance, and the importance of the context for such impact, also confirmed outcomes of previous Organizational Psychology research on the impact of training in presential courses (Abbad, 2000).

In brief, the importance of the variables - context, teacher, and group - were identified as important for course effectiveness. Likewise, the relevance of certain characteristics of "speech" by students and teachers for generation of conversational dynamics that result in better course effectiveness was also confirmed.

Certain other aspects of these results are also worthy of mention. First of all, the influence of the context. In DL, the student is at a distance and has greater flexibility in scheduling his studies; nonetheless, institutional support for this process is crucial. This support needs to be available in various aspects, e.g., when the course is at a corporation - through incentives from coordinators and classmates, learning to apply what is learned, though support materials and technology etc.; and when the course is targeted at the general public - with support infrastructure at the locations where students live, thus the importance of DL hubs.

A second element to be underscored is the importance of the teacher as a mediator in learning processes. This theme has had a strong impact on DL models being used throughout the world. In general, three broad tendencies orient the structuring of the role of the teacher in the principal DE systems:

a. The teacher, as a subject coordinator, orients a set of tutors who interact with the students. In this case, it is the tutors (usually new graduates or even undergraduates) who established direct relations with the students;
b. The teacher/tutor, who coordinates the subject matter and interacts directly with the students (as in presential courses and model adopted in the courses in this research);
c. Courses with no teacher or tutor interactions, with a strong self-instructional component and no human interaction, where students are guided by the teaching materials.

Distance Education is constantly facing the challenges of conciliating particular and universal issues in its pursuit of training outcomes. This, to some degree, is also a general dilemma in all education: a universal curriculum that must be relevant to an array of particular knowledge, constituted by a variety of identities.

Within Distance Education, particularly, there are a number of specificities: on the one hand, there is the heterogeneity of the target public to be reached. DL is an educational modality generally used to cover extensive geographical areas and reach large populations. On the other hand, there is a need for a certain standardization of learning instruments to enable management of the system. This adds complexity to the educational system, thereby redoubling the challenge.

These issues can be addressed by adding flexibility to course outlines, in order to reconcile curricular content with local cultures and students' prior knowledge. In this sense, the secret for achieving effectiveness of the process lies in actions of the teacher, as has been demonstrated in this research.

FINAL CONSIDERATIONS

Within a context of belated capitalism that enhances extremes, a world of the network society, of ubiquitous Internet, on a planet marked by social exclusion, in which education is regarded as a source of hope, teachers continue to play an essential role. On the role of the teacher, we appeal to classical authors, the "ancients", to enlighten us. It is their works that merit the sobriquet "classics" because they are, at the same time, timeless and eternally current, and of significance to our searches and endeavors to encounter transitory answers and to couch new questions.

Many people think that the new pedagogical system attributes an insignificant role to the teacher, that it is pedagogy without a pedagogue, or a school without teachers. Imagining that in the school of the future the teacher will have nothing to do is like believing that man's participation in mechanical production will be reduced to the point where he simply does nothing. It may appear that, in the new school, the teacher will be transformed into a mechanical mannequin. In reality, the teacher's role will be infinitely increased, and will require that he be well prepared for life, so that he can transform education into preparation for life (VYGOTSKY, 2004: 457).

This work contains a series of incompleteness. We would like to underscore two of them, as they head the list of our future research agenda. The first such incompleteness, in dealing with ongoing research, is the long evolutionary path of the impact-evaluation models and interactive processes. There is also the question of the continuity of the DL course that was studied, and a consequent need for new gathering of information and analysis. The second incompleteness resides in the need to explore, in greater depth, the influence of variables of context or environment, i,e., learning groups and actions of the teacher to promote effectiveness of the course, and to better understand the particular behavior of each of these variables and the specificities of their interactions within DL courses.

To complete our agenda for future research and development, we list the following topics:

a) gathering, in discussion forums, the third bipolar variable (The other/Oneself) of the Meta Learning model so as to analyze its importance for conversational dynamics in learning groups within a virtual environment;
b) development of contents and methodologies for training of teachers to perform in a virtual environment, based on the results of this research;
c) development of software (intelligent tutoring systems) that assist the actions of teachers and students in communication within virtual environments; the results on characterization of conversations (bipolar variables) may constitute significant parameters for the development of such systems.

Finally, we consider the development of an evaluation process for assessing the effectiveness of distance-learning courses, taking as a reference the Meta Learning model adapted to the virtual learning environment, as the most important contribution of this work. Thus, we have presented a methodology that seeks to reflect the (non-linear) dynamics of interactive processes, as a methodology that comprehends learning not as a deterministic (cause-effect) process, but rather, as a complex phenomenon.

Evaluation respecting the other. Evaluating to learn and modify our own views and actions. Such phrases are more than mere affirmations; they are the guiding principles of our research and, most certainly, will underlie its continuity.

REFERENCES

Abbad, G. (2000). *Um modelo integrado de avaliação do impacto do treinamento no trabalho – IMPACT* (Doctoral Thesis). Brasília: Universidade de Brasília.

Araujo, L. H. de L. (2004). *Uma aplicação da dinâmica não-linear para a avaliação de desempenho de comunidades virtuais de aprendizagem: além da tela do computador: linguagem, emocionalidade e corporalidade* (Master's Dissertation). Brasília: Universidade Católica de Brasília.

Bakhtin, M. (2000). *Estética da criação verbal* (3ª ed.). São Paulo: Martins Fontes. [Translation. Maria Ermantina Galvão; Rev. Marina Appenzeller]

Beiler, A. (2004). *A produção de redes de conversação como base à aprendizagem*. (Doctoral Thesis). Porto Alegre: Universidade Federal do Rio Grande do Sul.

Borges-andrade, J. E. (2002). Desenvolvimento de medidas em avaliação de treinamento. *Estudos de Psicologia, 7*(Número Especial), 31-43.

Botelho, F. V. U., & Vicari, R. (2006). Course evaluation and program evaluation in distance learning – The effectiveness of interactive processes in learning virtual environment. In *Anais da 22ª Conferência do ICDE (CD-ROM)*. Rio de Janeiro.

Losada, M. (2000). *Meta Learning*. Conference proffered at the course on Art of Business Coaching. Brasília, Manuscript.

Losada, M., & Heaphy, E. (2004). The role of positivity and connectivity in the performance of business teams: a nonlinear dynamics model. In Cameron, K. S & Caza, A. (eds.), *Contributions to positive organizational scholarship. American Behavioral Scientist, 47*(6): 740-765.

Luyi, S. (2006). Evaluation: a principle method to promote quality of distance education. In *Anais da 22ª Conferência do ICDE (CD-ROM)*, Rio de Janeiro.

Paulista, G. (2005). *O impacto da conectividade e da positividade/negatividade na gestão do conhecimento: Uma intervenção baseada nas teorias do caos e da complexidade e dinâmica não-linear* (Master's Dissertation). Brasília: Universidade Católica de Brasília.

Petters, O. (2001). *Didática do ensino a distância*. São Leopoldo, RS: Editora Unisinos.

Rocha, I. (n.d.). *Uma análise do caos na dinâmica do espaço emocional*. (In Press)

Sallas, E., & Cannon-Bowers, J. (2001). The science of training: a decade of progress. *Annual Review of Psychology, 52*, 471–499. doi:10.1146/annurev.psych.52.1.471

Silva, M., & Santos, E. (2006). *Avaliação de aprendizagem em educação online*. São Paulo: Loyola.

Silvio, J. (2000). *La virtualización de la universidad: cómo podemos transformar la educación superior com la tecnología?* Caracas: IESALC/UNESCO.

Torres, V. S. (2004). *Significações emocionais e cognitivas na aprendizagem em ambiente informatizado: Uma relação necessária à superação da modernidade* (Doctoral Thesis). Porto Alegre: Universidade Federal do Rio Grande do Sul.

Vygotsky, L. S. (1998). *A formação social da mente: O desenvolvimento dos processos psicológicos superiores*. São Paulo: Martins Fontes. [Translation. José Cipolla Neto et alli]

Vygotsky, L. S. (2004). *Psicologia pedagógica*. São Paulo: Martins Fontes. [Translation. Paulo Bezerra]

Vygotsky, L. S. (2005). *Pensamento e linguagem*. São Paulo: Martins Fontes. [Translation. Jefferson Luiz Camargo; Rev. José Cipolla Neto]

ADDITIONAL READING

Aretio, L. G. (2005). *Rizando el rizo de la calidad de la educación a distancia*. Espanha. Editorial

Bened (n.d.). *Boletín Electrónico de Noticias de Educación a Distancia (BENED)*. Retrieved August 1, 2006, from http://www.uned.es/cued/boletin.html

Bonniol, J. J., & Vial, M. (2001). *Modelos de avaliação*. Porto Alegre: Editora Artmed.

Botelho, F. V. U., & Vicari, R. (2009) A qualidade dos processos interativos como chave para a avaliação da efetividade de cursos a distância. *Revista Brasileira de Informática na Educação*, v., *17*, 6-19.

Botelho, F. V. U., & Vicari, R. (2009). Evaluation of distance course effectiveness - exploring the quality of interactive processes. In Arthur Tatnall; Anthony Jones. (Eds.), *Education and technology for a better world* (1 ed.). Berlin Heidelberg New York: Springer.

Castells, M. (1999). *A era da informação: economia, sociedade e cultura* (Vol. 1, 2 e 3). São Paulo: Paz e Terra.

de Oliveira, M. K. (1997). *Vygotsky: Aprendizado e desenvolvimento, um processo sócio-histórico*. São Paulo: Editora Scipione.

Hamblin, A. C. (1978). *Avaliação e controle de treinamento*. São Paulo: McGraw- Hill do Brasil.

Hoffmann, J. (2000). *Avaliação: mito e desafio*. Porto Alegre: Editora Mediação.

Kirkpatrick, D. L. (1976). Evaluation of training. In Craig, R. L. (Ed.), *Training and development handbook (2ª edição)* (pp. 18.1–18.27). New York: McGraw-Hill.

Lester, J. C., Vicari, R. M., & Paraguaçu, F. (orgs.) (2004). Intelligent tutoring systems. In *Proceedings of the 7th International Conference*. Berlim: Springer.

Maturana, H. R., & Varela, F. J. (2001). *A árvore do conhecimento: As bases biológicas da compreensão humana*. São Paulo: Editora Palas Athena. [Trad. Humberto Mariotti e Lia Diskin]

Moore, M. G., & Anderson, W. G. (2003). *Handbook of distance education*. Mahwah, NJ: Lawrence Erlbaum Associates.

Morin, E. (2001). *Os sete saberes necessários à educação do futuro*. 3ª edição, São Paulo: Cortez; Brasília, DF: UNESCO. [Trad. Catarina Eleonora F. da Silva e Jeanne Sawaya; Rev.: Edgard de Assis Carvalho]

Morin, E. (2005). *Introdução ao pensamento complexo*. Porto Alegre, RS: Editora Sulina. [Trad. Eliane Lisboa]

Morisson, G. R., Steven, M. R., & Kemp, J. E. (2001). *Designing effective instruction (3ª edição)*. New York: John Wiley & Sons.

Nicholson, P., Ruohonen, M., Thompson, J. B., & Multisilta, J. (2005). *E-training practices for professional organizations (IFIP TC3 2003)*. Dordrecht: Kluwer Academic Publishers. doi:10.1007/b101890

Nussenzveig, H. M. (org) (2003). *Complexidade e caos* (2ª. Edição). Rio de Janeiro: Editora UFTJ/COPEA.

Pallof, R. M., & Pratt, K. (2002). *Construindo comunidades de aprendizagem no ciberespaço*. Porto Alegre: Editora Artmed. [Trad. Vinícius Figueira]

Palloff, R. M., & Pratt, K. (2004). *O aluno virtual: Um guia para trabalhar com estudantes on-line*. Porto Alegre: Editora Artmed. [Trad. Vinícius Figueira]

Peters, O. (2003). *A educação a distância em transição*. São Leopoldo, RS: Editora Unisinos.

Schreiber, D. A., & Berge, Z. L. (orgs.) (1998). *Distance training: How innovative organizations are using technology to maximize learning and meet business objectives*. San Francisco, CA: Jossey-Bass Publishers.

Van der Veer, R., & Valsiner, J. (2001). *Vygotsky: Uma síntese*. São Paulo: Edições Loyola. [Trad. Cecília C. Bartalotti]

Vygotsky, L. S. (2004). *Teoría de las emociones: Estudio histórico-psicológico*. Madrid: Akal Ediciones. [Trad. Judith Viaplana]

Warr, P., & Downing, J. (2000). Learning strategies, learning anxiety and knowledge acquisition. *The British Journal of Psychology*, *91*, 311–333. doi:10.1348/000712600161853

KEY TERMS AND DEFINITIONS

Connectivity: In the Meta Learning model, interaction is considered as connectivity, made of behavior patterns that are strongly inter-related and that support each other through time. It indicates a process of mutual influence among the members of a group.

Distance Learning (DL) or Distance Education: Is an educational modality which is characterized by the flexibility of its action in time and space dimensions. It involves the intensive use of technology to support its activities and communication among people that can be studying in different moments and places.

Effectiveness Evaluation: The search for information and knowledge construction about the relation between the objectives and the results of a certain educational process; learning about the effect or achievement of the purposes of an educational process.

Interactive Processes: In general terms, interaction is the action that is mutually established between two or more people or things; therefore, it's a reciprocal action. In this work, we use the concept of interaction processes as relations established by men amongst each other and with the environment or relations between parts of a system or different systems.

Learning Process: The process of acquisition of information, skills, attitudes, values and competences that is achieved by the individual through the interaction with others and the environment.

Meta Learning Model: The process of learning in which people, in their groups, are capable of dissolving the attractors that limit the possibilities of action and, on the other hand, develop attractors that open possibilities to effective action; it is a model that explains the dynamics of group functioning and interaction among people in their groups. It is focused in the understanding of the factors that contribute to create and maintain a high level of effectiveness in the groups' dynamics.

Virtual Communities: Relation among people that meet in the cyberspace; human groups that develop social interaction in virtual environments supported by technology of communication and information.

ENDNOTES

1 In general terms, interaction is action that takes place between two or more things, or two or more persons; reciprocal action. In this work we employ the concept of interactive processes as relations established by men amongst themselves and with the environment or relations among parts of a system or relations between systems. The concepts of interaction and of learning, that underlie this study will be developed more fully in chapter 4, that deals with theoretical references.

2 The number of papers refers to those on the programs of the congresses mentioned herein. They were obtained from the ABED website and the count conducted by the present authors.

3 Source: http://www.icde22.org.br/portugues/tema.htm.

4 Silva & Santos (2006).

5 The characteristics of the attractors can be thus defined (PAULISTA, 2005): fixed point, when the trajectory tends to be a fixed point; cycle limit, when a system shows dynamics of regular periodicity; torus, when a system shows dynamics of regular periodicity, in more than one dimension; chaotic, strange or complexor, a system that displays dynamics where the trajectory is never repeated, but has a finite geometric structure within the space of the phase.

6 Verification of the connectivity performance relationship among the groups was carried out using connectivity indicators (obtained by means of observation and codification of the activities of groups during work meetings) and the economic-financial outcomes of these teams.

7 Rocha (in preparation) points to the need for at least three processes to obtain a complex dynamic.

8 Organizational Psychology is focused upon T&D processes. According to Borges-Andrade (2002), T&D are used as a method for acquiring new information and motor or intellectual skills for development of cognitive strategies and attitudes. In this context, T presupposes a greater organizational intentionality and a more systematic u3se of instructional technology, whereas D is based on self-management of learning. In the author's view, however, organizational demands for continuous growth and diversified competencies have eliminated the

differences between T&D, since training, when formulated to address the performance problems of some, may constitute a development opportunity for others.

9 This course is managed by a management committee with representatives of the following institutions: Universidade Católica Cardenal Silva Henríquez – Chile, Universidade Católica de Brasília – DF, Universidade Católica Dom Bosco – Campo Grande/MS, Centro Universitário Salesiano de São Paulo – SP, Faculdade Salesiana de Vitória – ES, Dicastério da Formação and the Youth Pastorate of the Steering Committee of the Society of St Francis of Sales – Rome/Italy.

10 In general terms, the Salesian way of educating implies a posture on the part of the teacher in relation to the student characterized by respect, care, shelter and affection; and by the development of learning situations that strengthen autonomy and participation.

11 In the five-level model, the second is called learning (and likewise the forth item is gathering of information) and is based upon evaluations of activities carried out during the course. As we work with different learning concepts, and aiming at clarity of conclusions, we refer to the results of this level of evaluation as "participants performance in the course".

12 Codification was carried out by two pairs of analysts and a supervisor. The pairs were comprised of one person trained in Letters and the other in Psychology. The supervisor held a doctorate in Linguistics.

13 Measures of central trends: We generally respond to the first challenge by using the arithmetical average, median, or mode. At times, we select specific values of the function of accumulated distribution, known as quartiles. Measures of dispersion: The most common measures of variability for quantitative data are variance; square root, standard deviation; total amplitude, interquartile distance, and absolute deviation.

14 In descriptive statistics the coefficient of the Pearson ratio, also known as the "coefficient of the product-moment ratio" or simply the "Pearson r", measures the degree of correlation (and the direction of said correlation – whether positive or negative) between two variables on a metric scale (interval or ratio). This coefficient, normally represented by the letter "r", assumes only values between -1 and 1.

15 $r = 1$ means a perfect positive correlation between the two variables.

16 $r = -1$ means a perfect negative correlation between the two variables; i.e.., if one rises, the other always declines.

17 $r = 0$ means that the two variables do not depend linearly upon each other.

18 However, there may be another dependence that is "non-linear". Thus, the result $r = 0$ must be investigated by other means.

Afterword

Different authors come from different research and development environments as well as different interest groups. Evaluating this unique mixture of contributors', personal view on the future and new directions on intelligent tutoring system design, implementation and evaluation is presented in this section. The future of intelligent tutoring system will depend on innovative academic and industrial contributions to this evolving area. Since authors have been involved in development of cutting edge intelligent tutoring systems technologies for variety of uses and functions their contribution is valuable on global scale. Individual and group opinion is presented in alphabetic order of presenting author/authors. Finally, it is important to understand that this section present different point of view on the same domain. Opinions of contributors are their personal point of view and perceptions of the intelligent tutoring system field without any reviewers' and editors intervention. We leave the reader to evaluate and choose the most valuable contribution that will serve as an inspiration for their research of the ever enchanting world of intelligent tutoring systems.

Julie Coultas

One very clear message that we can take from past experience with any information and communications technology is that users are getting younger and younger. On this basis can we make any predictions about the future? From my study of young children using electronic learning devices it seems that they are at ease with the technology (Coultas, 2008).

There are some research factions in developmental psychology (see Psychologist, 2007) who believe that young children do not need contact with educational technology – a cardboard box and some material is enough to stimulate imagination. But does this type of thinking really take into account how the cultural environment affects the child? Young children see their parents using handheld devices (e.g. Blackberry, iPhone), deeply engrossed in communication, downloading information and more often than not focusing their attention on these devices. Is it surprising that young children take an interest their parent's devices? They are following their parent's direction of gaze.

In an impromptu study with my 8 months old young granddaughter, we gave her the choice of two communication devices. These devices were placed on the floor within crawling distance of the 8 month old. No matter how many times we repeated this experiment (moving her away from the two devices, moving the devices around, placing them screen down) she invariably chose one over the other. One reason, I propose, for this behavior is that her father uses the preferred device. She has watched her father and mother using a mobile and also a laptop computer. Children, even very young ones, imitate the people around them (Lightfoot, Cole and Cole, 2009; Berk, 2009). They observe their parents behavior and copy it (Bandura, 1977)

Infants enter their social world predisposed to copy and interact with the people around them. Nowadays a large part of our interaction and learning comes from our electronic devices. These are cultural tools. These tools not only change the way we interact and learn they also facilitate learning (Carr and Yuill, 2009). Is there an argument for delaying contact with these devices until the child is at a certain age? Perhaps delaying contact until the child has started full time formal education? The answers to these questions depend on whether we believe that children are disadvantaged or advantaged through contact with electronic learning devices. Do they stifle a child's imagination and creativity? There is still plenty of debate in this area and more research needs to be undertaken to illuminate particular aspects of the technology that can facilitate children's learning.

Tonći Dadić

Power of computerized expert of an intelligent tutoring system is based on teaching domain knowledge. Definition of such knowledge requires significant human expert effort, estimated to 100 – 200 hours of human work for each teaching hour. Authoring shells supporting knowledge representation by controlled natural language will make building of tutoring systems easier in acceptable period of time. Diagnoses of student's program correctness and bug localization is an essential functionality of intelligent systems for teaching programming. Traditionally, it is provided comparing student's program against model program. Complication arises because single programming task may be solved by various algorithms, and coded by different instructions, while algebraic and logical expressions may differ as well. Student's program is semantically equivalent with model as long as both produce the same sequence of outputs for the same sequence of inputs. Diagnoses techniques that compare computational sequences of programs require complete models, predicting possible variations. Lack of model completeness implies false alarms that are considered very harmful in educational process. We believe that comparison based on semantics equivalence of programs would improve diagnoses, and simplify modeling of correct solution.

Benedict du Boulay

Various researchers are building educational systems that attempt to take the learner's motivational, metacognitive and/or affective state dynamically into account (see e.g., Paiva, Prada, & Picard, 2007). For example, AutoTutor (Graesser, et al., 2008) has been instrumented to observe the facial expression and posture of the learner in an attempt to move the learner towards (or maintain the learner in) a positive learning state such as "engaged", and also to move the learner away from negative learning states such as "bored". In a similar vein, Kapoor and others (2007) have developed a system that is able to make a good estimate of when a learner is "frustrated" based on a number of features such as hand pressure by the learner on the mouse. These technologies are also now finding their way into mainstream education (Arroyo, Cooper, et al., 2009) and the more general issue of the affective dimension of human computer interaction is well established (Picard, 2000).

These kinds of system raise a number of theoretical and practical questions: What kinds of data are available on which to make inferences about the motivational, metacognitive affective states of the learner? What is the nature of the theory that links such data to inferred motivational, metacognitive and affective states? What kinds of motivational states are to be distinguished, one from another? What are the relationships between learning and either relatively stable personality traits or relatively transient motivational states and feelings, or less transient affective states such as moods? What are the predictable trajectories between affective states over the duration of a lesson or of a course? And what is the nature of the theory that determines how a caring system might best assist the learner to move away from trajectories or states that might inhibit learning towards those that might enhance it? In other words, what is the nature of the theory that helps the learner follow a trajectory of states that enhances and opens new possibilities (see e.g., Kort & Reilly, 2002), even if there are individual negative episodes along the way, as opposed to a trajectory that limits possibilities and is dysfunctional or maladaptive, even if there are individual positive states along the way?

Curilem G.M., Vizcarra, B., Poo, A.M. Huenteman, D., Brasil, L.M.

Intelligent Tutoring Systems (ITS) stand in the intersection of education, cognitive science, artificial intelligence and human-computer interaction. They also are influenced by many pedagogical paradigms, like constructivism, behaviorism, collaborative learning, affective states, etc. These knowledge areas influence its modules implementations. Although, most of the systems developed until now have privileged some of the modules and some of the paradigms, it seems important to synthesize the different knowledge areas and develop more integral systems. However, in our opinion, cognitive sciences are the most important knowledge that ITS require to be more effectives, as it brings reliable information about how the learning process occurs. We consider that ITS can be used to evaluate cognitive hypothesis about learning and thus, may contribute to improve cognitive science knowledge. In our work we propose a methodology to develop an adaptive interface to some learning styles of the students. The system can be used to assess whether learning styles influence the learning process and even which styles are more relevant. This is why we believe that ITS are in an insipient stage of their development and they may have an enormous impact in education, not only to support learning but also to understand it.

Funda Dag, Kadir Erkan

Ontology based modeling approach is most appropriate implementation approach for the personalized e-learning systems. It supports a new sight to solve content related design problems of ITS and AEHS. By using ontologies, domain model and user model of the systems such as ITS have been recognized quite easily and in a flexible manner. But, today, there are some problems in inference mechanism and expressivity of the Semantic Web Tools. Because of that especially, methods or ways should be investigated to make more applicable the adaptation model of the personalized learning systems according to ontology based modeling paradigms. So, roadmaps of the personalized learning systems are specified according to researches and developments in the areas of DL based reasoning techniques and Semantic Web rule languages. Therefore, if more expressive rules have been written by rule languages, adaptation capabilities of the learning systems have been enhanced. In addition, if we see that the personalized learning system is a semantic web application, DL based reasoning engines should be designed to handle large-scale knowledge bases. So, efficient and effective analyses of large ontologies such as the learning ontology are being possible. Also, web services are important research and implementation areas for semantic web applications which can be designed distributed systems.

Jeroen Geuze, Egon L. van den Broek

In the early 70s, the idea of computer-based instruction emerged. With the human teacher as educational model, artificial intelligence (AI) were applied to achieve this goal. As became apparent in the next decades, ITS are a typical AI challenge. With ITS, their major challenge is threefold, it requires understanding of: 1) the behavior of human teachers, 2) the student's behavior, and 3) their interaction. However, human teachers and their students are no homogeneous groups, they vary substantially in all possible aspects. Consequently, their interaction is highly complex. So far, true, flexible, generic ITS are far beyond science's current research. A substantially deeper (multi-level) understanding of human beings is required. Perhaps then, decades from now, ITS will appear future instead of fiction.

Ani Grubišić

Although the ITSs are less effective than human tutors, they certainly influence positively learning and teaching process of students that use them. Anyway, the ITSs cannot replace teachers and they are not intended to do so, but they can ease and improve their work. The ITSs should be included in education as one method for learning and teaching, and results of meta-analysis can give directions for their selection and improvements.

In the future, more experiments with different ITSs in different domain knowledge areas should be conducted to see if domain knowledge influences effect size estimations. A new meta-analysis should be done for each domain knowledge and for each ITS separately, and include a larger number of experiments and a larger sample size, as well. In that way, it would be possible to make some conclusions about domain knowledge areas that are more appropriate for learning and teaching using particular ITS, as well as, how much are those ITS effective in general.

Divna Krpan, Suzana Tomaš, Roko Vladušić

Intelligent Tutoring Systems (ITS) provide the benefits of one-to-one instruction. There is a challenge on transferring to computers the skills of human teacher while overcoming space and time restrictions. There are studies that show that one-to-one human tutoring is more effective than other modes of instruction. ITSs support on line tutoring in different domains. They must be capable to accurately diagnose students' knowledge, skills, and learning styles and then decide how to adapt instruction and provide feedback. The advances in computer technologies facilitated the development of ITSs. With advances of new technologies such as Web 2.0 there are new ways in which students learn. For example, social networking invokes collaboration of students. There are discussions if learners should interact with ITS individually or collaboratively. Collaborative learning imposes team or group work, which then implies group modeling. Group modeling requires different design techniques then student modeling, and it is not researched in same extent. ITSs should incorporate different learning strategies which also include group modeling support.

The interoperability of ITSs is a great advantage for sharing learning content, but it cannot be achieved without standardization. The most emphasized standard is SCORM. There is a problem because many of Web 2.0 technologies are not addressed in SCORM, and also there is not adequate support for all aspects of group modeling. The omissions of SCORM will hopefully be covered with work of the International Federation for Learning, Education, and Training Systems Interoperability (LETSI).

Evaluation of existing intelligent tutoring systems shows that such systems are often more effective than traditional learning and teaching. "Freedom" provided by this method of student's learning requires more motivation, discipline and personal organization to fulfill given tasks on time. This method of learning and teaching can keep parents involved in the activities of their children. Although these systems can never fully replace live teacher, they can be great help in teaching.

Alke Martens, Andreas Harrer

Traditionally, the development of intelligent tutoring systems has been driven mainly by the knowledge engineering task to produce powerful and elaborate domain representations. As every complex system, ITSs tend to be hard to maintain over a longer time of usage and cannot be extended easily if not carefully designed also from a software engineering perspective. Thus, we observed increasing discussion and efforts to create ITS not from scratch, but by using framework systems (Aleven, McLaren et al. 2006), extensible knowledge representations (constraint-based tutors as of Mitrovic et al. 2007), and lightweight authoring techniques (e.g. the example tracing tutors (Aleven et al., in press) used in the Pittsburgh Science of Learning Center).

We expect that these lines of actions will gain increasing importance to create ITS faster, more efficient, and more flexible by adoption of established practice from the field of software engineering: *ITS middleware* approaches are called for, as well as sharing of design knowledge (in the form of patterns for software architecture, software design and pedagogical design) and of opening codebases to the field in open source initiatives (one first example is the encore community: www.encorewiki.org).

Abdolhossein Sarrafzadeh, Jamshid Shanbehzadeh, Scott Overmyer

Today's intelligent tutoring systems are able to adapt their teaching strategies to the knowledge and abilities of individual learners. They have been demonstrated to be effective, with better learning outcomes than simple programmed instruction. Studies have shown that ITSs can even outperform traditional classroom instruction: they are always available, non-judgmental and can provide tailored feedback. Even so, we assert that one-to-one human tutoring is superior to intelligent tutoring systems. What we believe is missing in intelligent tutoring systems is the ability that human tutors have to adapt to the affective state of the learner. Existing tutoring systems, with few notable exceptions, such as Eve, are not able to do that. The authors believe that future intelligent tutoring systems will be able to adapt to perceived nonverbal behavior of the learner bringing them much closer in effectiveness to best human tutors.

Lung-Hsiang Wong, Chee-Kit Looi

With the rise of e-learning, online collaborative learning and mobile/ubiquitous learning, the ITS paradigm has been gradually shifting from a classic, single-machine setting to a modern, distributed and social construct which may be leveraging more on soft-computing techniques as feasible solutions to such potentially complex data processing and decision making processes in the new generation of learning systems.

Marija Zelić

The next generation of e-learning systems, and especially the intelligent tutoring systems, has to put even more emphasis on intelligence, adaptively, knowledge sharing issues, as well as reusability and interoperability. The latest research and development efforts, such as the Semantic Web and AI, provide means for semantic representation and organization of data - hence enabling semantic search, reasoning and integration of heterogeneous data, as well as creation of semantic web services for promoting reusability and interoperability of the e-learning systems. Intelligent agents can be deployed to perform automated discovery, composition and invocation of the services based on the learner profile and the current learning context. The agents, services as well as data can be distributed all over the world and offered by different organizations and universities. From this perspective, the e-learning system is envisioned as a collection of distributed components assembled on-the-fly for a specific purpose.

Branko Žitko

Even so intelligent tutoring systems (ITS) are converging to human tutor and possess many benefits that human tutor doesn't; there are still three global challenges. Those challenges can be characterized as ITS thinks, acts and reacts as a human tutor. Overall challenges lay on artificial intelligence and cognitive science, and are tending to mimic the way of how tutor brain works. Acting and reacting are also depending on ITS abilities to process large scale of information gained from and expressed to the student. Those two characteristics are based on accomplishment in a field of human computer interaction. It is proved that natural language processing has great impact on effectiveness of ITS, but other kinds of interaction with students, like virtual reality and other ways of expressing subject matter are procurable and successfully implemented today. On the other, tutor has to measure and react on student's behavior, so biometric is a promising field specialized for collecting physical and behavioral data from the individuals.

REFERENCES

Aleven, V., McLaren, B. M., Sewall, J., & Koedinger, K. R. (2006). The Cognitive Tutor Authoring Tools (CTAT): Preliminary evaluation of efficiency gains. In M. Ikeda, K.D. Ashley, & T-W. Chan (Eds.), *Proceedings of the 8th International Conference on Intelligent Tutoring Systems* (ITS-2006), Lecture Notes in Computer Science, 4053 (pp. 61-70). Berlin, Germany: Springer.

Aleven, V., McLaren, B. M., Sewall, J., & Koedinger, K. R. (in press). A New Paradigm for Intelligent Tutoring Systems: Example-Tracing Tutors. *International Journal of Artificial Intelligence in Education* (IJAIED), (Special Issue on "Authoring Systems for Intelligent Tutoring Systems)."

Arroyo, I., Cooper, D. G., Burleson, W., Woolf, B. P., Muldner, K., & Christopherson, R. (2009). Emotion Sensors Go to School. In V. Dimitrova, R. Mizoguchi, B. du Boulay & A. Grasser (Eds.), *Artificial Intelligence in Education. Building Learning Systems that Care: from Knowledge Representation to Affective Modelling* (Vol. Frontiers in Artificial Intelligence and Applications 200, pp. 17-24) Amsterdam: IOS Press.

Bandura, A. (1977). *Social Learning Theory*. Englewood Cliffs, NJ: Prentice Hall

Berk, L. E. (2009). *Child Development* (8th edition). Upper Saddle River, NJ: Pearson. USA

Carr, A., & Yuill, N. (2009, September). How interactive tabletops affect self-regulation and joint attention in children's collaborative problem-solving. In *Proceedings of the BPS Developmental Section Conference.* , Nottingham, UK.September 2009

Coultas, J. (2008). *Creating Baby Einsteins? A longitudinal study of infants using an interactive educational learning toy.* Presentation to the Human Centred Technology Group University of Sussex (February 2009).

Graesser, A., D'Mello, S., Craig, S., Witherspoon, A., Sullins, J., McDaniel, B., et al. (2008). The Relationship Between Affective States and Dialog Patterns During Interactions With Auto Tutor. *Journal of Interactive Learning Research, 19*(2), 293.

Kapoor, A., Burleson, W., & Picard, R. (2007). Automatic prediction of frustration. *International Journal of Human-Computer Studies, 65*(8), 724-736.

Kort, B., & Reilly, B. (2002). An Affective Module for an Intelligent Tutoring System. In S. A. Cerri, G. Guy & F. Paraguacu (Eds.), *Proceedings of the 6th International Conference on Intelligent Tutoring Systems* . 6th International Conference(, ITS2002), Biarritz, France and San Sebastian, Spain , Proceedings (Vol. Lecture Notes in Computer Science 2363, pp. 955-962) Biarritz, France and San Sebastian, Spain: Springer.

Lightfoot, C., Cole, M., & Cole, S. R. (2009). *The Development of Children* (6th edition). New York: Worth Publishers. USA

Mitrovic, A., Martin, B., & Suraweera, P. (2007). : Intelligent Tutors for All: The Constraint-Based Approach. *IEEE Intelligent Systems, 22*(4), : 38-45.

Paiva, A., Prada, R., & Picard, R. W. (Eds.). (2007). Affective Computing and Intelligent Interaction. In *Proceedings of the : Second International Conference* , (ACII 2007), Lisbon, Portugal, Proceedings (Vol. Lecture Notes in Computer Science 4738) Lisbon, Portugal: Springer.

Picard, R. W. (2000). *Affective Computing.* Cambridge, MAassachusetts: MIT Press.

Psychologist (2007, May). Does TV harm young children? *Psychologist.*May 2007

Compilation of References

Aase, M., & Kurfess, F. J. (2004, August). *Utilizing Learning Styles for Interactive Tutorials*. Paper presented at the IEEE International Conference on Advanced Learning Technologies (ICALT 2004), Joensuu, Finland, (2004).

Abbad, G. (2000). *Um modelo integrado de avaliação do impacto do treinamento no trabalho – IMPACT* (Doctoral Thesis). Brasília: Universidade de Brasília.

Adam, A., & Laurent, J. P. (1980). LAURA, a System to Debug Student Programs. *Artificial Intelligence, 15*, 75–122. doi:10.1016/0004-3702(80)90023-5

ADL. (2002). Advanced Distributed Learning Sharable Content Object Reference Model Version 1.3, Application Profile Working Draft 0.9, *Advanced Distributed Learning Network*, Retrieved May 06, 2009, from http://xml.coverpages.org/SCORMV13-SeqAppProfile.pdf

Agent Management Specification, F. I. P. A. (2004). *FIPA Standard SC00023K*. Reterieved from http://www.fipa.org/specs/fipa00023/index.html

Aguilera, M., & M'endiz, A. (2003). Video games in education. *Computers in Entertainment, 1*(1), 1–14.

Ahn, J., Brusilovsky, P., Grady, J., He, D., & Syn, S. Y. (2007). Open user profiles for adaptive news systems: help or harm? In *Proceedings of the 16th international conference on World Wide Web (WWW '07)* (pp 11-20), New York: ACM Press.

Albirini, A. (2007). The crisis of educational technology, and the prospect of reinventing education. *Journal of Educational Technology & Society, 10*(1), 227–236.

Alcalde, S., Ravenna, A., & Guala, M. (1998). *Mediación en la Escuela: Convivir y Aprender*. Argentina: Editorial Homo Sapiens.

Aleven, V. A. W. M. M., & Koedinger, K. R. (2002). An effective metacognitive strategy: Learning by doing and explaining with a computer-based Cognitive Tutor. *Cognitive Science, 26*(2), PAGE NUMBERS.

Aleven, V., & Koedinger, K. R. (2000). Limitations of student control: Do students know when they need help? In *Proceedings of ITS'2000*.

Aleven, V., Koedinger, K. R., et al. (1999). Tutoring Answer Explanation Fosters Learning with Understanding. In *Proceedings of AIED'99*.

Alexander, S., Sarrafzadeh, A., & Hill, S. (2008). Foundation of an Affective Tutoring System: Learning How Human Tutors Adapt to Student Emotion. *International Journal of Intelligent Systems Technologies and Applications, 4*(4). doi:10.1504/IJISTA.2008.017278

Alexander, C., Ishikawa, S., & Silverstein, M. (1977). *A Pattern Language – Towns Buildings Construction*, Vol. 2 of Center for Environmental Structure Series. New York: Oxford University Press.

Allen, M., Mabry, E., Mattrey, M., Bourhuis, J., Titsworth, S., & Burrell, N. (2004). Evaluating the effectiveness of distance learning: A comparison using meta-analysis. *The Journal of Communication, 54*(3), 402–420. doi:10.1111/j.1460-2466.2004.tb02636.x

Almond, R. G., DiBello, L. V., Moulder, B., & Zapata-Rivera, D. (2007). Modeling diagnostic assessment with Bayesian networks. *Journal of Educational Measurement, 44*(4), 341–359. doi:10.1111/j.1745-3984.2007.00043.x

Almond, R. G., Shute, V., Underwood, J., & Zapata-Rivera, D. (2009). Bayesian networks: A teacher's view. *International Journal of Approximate Reasoning, 50*, 450–460. doi:10.1016/j.ijar.2008.04.011

Alonso, C., Gallego, D., & Honey, P. (1999). *Los estilos de aprendizaje procedimientos de diagnostico y mejora. España* (Mensajero, B., Ed.).

Alpert, S. R., Singley, M. K., & Fairweather, P. G. (1999). Deploying intelligent tutors on the web: an architecture and an example. *International Journal of Artificial Intelligence in Education*, *10*(2), 183–197.

Alsop, G., & Tompsett, C. (2007). From effect to effectiveness: The missing research questions. *Journal of Educational Technology & Society*, *10*(1), 28–39.

American Society for Training and Development. (2001). *A Vision of E-Learning for America's Workforce*. Report of the Commission on Technology and Adult Learning.

Anderson, J. R. (1983). *The architecture of cognition*. Cambridge, MA: Harvard University Press.

Anderson, J. R. (1993). *Rules of the Mind*. Mahwah, NJ: Lawrence Erlbaum.

Anderson, J. R., Boyle, C. F., Corbett, A. T., & Lewis, M. W. (1990). Cognitive Modeling and Intelligent Tutoring. *Artificial Intelligence*, *42*, 17–49. doi:10.1016/0004-3702(90)90093-F

Anderson, J. R., Corbett, A. T., Koedinger, K. R., & Pelletier, R. (1995). Cognitive tutors: Lessons learned. *Journal of the Learning Sciences*, *4*(2), 167–207. doi:10.1207/s15327809jls0402_2

Anderson, J. R., & Lebiere, C. (1998). *The Atomic Components of Thought*. Hillsdale, NJ: Lawrence Erlbaum Associates.

Anderson, J. R., & Reiser, B. (1985). The LISP Tutor. *Byte, 10*.

Anozie, N. O., & Junker, B. W. (2006, July). *Predicting end-of-year accountability assessment scores from monthly student records in an online tutoring system*. Poster presented at the American Association for Artificial Intelligence Workshop on Educational Data Mining (AAAI-06), Boston.

Antoniou, G., & Van Harmelen, F. (2008). *A semantic web primer* (2nd ed.). Cambridge, MA: The MIT Press.

Antunez, S. (2000). *Disciplina y convivencia en la institución escolar*. Barcelona: Editorial Laboratorio Educativo.

Araujo, L. H. de L. (2004). *Uma aplicação da dinâmica não-linear para a avaliação de desempenho de comunidades virtuais de aprendizagem: além da tela do computador: linguagem, emocionalidade e corporalidade* (Master's Dissertation). Brasília: Universidade Católica de Brasília.

Arón, A. M. (2000). Un Programa de Educación para la No-Violencia. *Psykhe Revista de la Escuela de Psicología. Facultad de Ciencias Sociales Pontificia Universidad Católica de Chile*, *9*(2), 25–39.

Aroya, L., & Dicheva, D. (2004). The new challenges for e-learning: the educational semantic web. *Journal of Educational Technology & Society*, *7*(4), 59–69.

Arroyo, I., & Woolf, B. (2005). Inferring learning and attitudes from a Bayesian network of log file data. In *Proceedings of AIED 05, The 12th international conference on artificial intelligence in education.*

Arshard, F. N. (1989). Knowledge based learning advisors. In *Proceedings of International Conference on Technology and Education* (pp.213-217), Orlando, FL.

Ashby, W. R. (1956). *An introduction to cybernetics*. London: Chapman & Hall.

Atolagbe, T., Hlupic, V., & Taylor, S. J. E. (2001). GENISA: A Web based interactive learning environment for teaching simulation modelling. In *Proceedings of the 2001 winter simulation conference.*

Attewell, J. (2005). From Research and Development to Mobile Learning: Tools for Education and Training Providers and their Learners. In *Proceedings of mLearn 2005*. Retrieved December 20, 2005, from http://www.mlearn.org.za/papersfull.html

Ayers, E., & Junker, B. W. (2006, July). *Do skills combine additively to predict task difficulty in eighth-grade mathematics?* Poster presented at the American Association for Artificial Intelligence Workshop on Educational Data Mining (AAAI-06), Boston, MA.

Baader, F., Calvanese, D., McGuinness, D. L., Nardi, D., & Patel-Schneider, P. F. (Eds.). (2003). *The Description Logic Handbook: Theory, Implementation, and Applications*. New York, NY, USA: Cambridge University Press.

Baghaei, N. (2007). *A collaborative constraint-based intelligent system for learning object-oriented analysis and design using UML.* (Unpublished Ph.D. Thesis) (Partial fulfilment), Canterbury, UK: University of Canterbury.

Bai, X., Black, J. B., Vikaros, L., Vitale, J., Li, D., & Xia, Q. (2007). *Learning in One's Own Imaginary World.* Chicago: American Educational Research Association.

Bai, X., Black, J. B., & Vitale, J. (2007). REAL: Learn with the Assistance of a Reflective Agent. *Agent-Based Systems for Human Learning Conference*, Hawaii.

Bakhtin, M. (2000). *Estética da criação verbal* (3ª ed.). São Paulo: Martins Fontes. [Translation. Maria Ermantina Galvão; Rev. Marina Appenzeller]

Barnes, T. (2005). Q-matrix Method: Mining Student Response Data for Knowledge. In Beck. J. (Ed), *Educational Data Mining: Papers from the 2005 AAAI Workshop*. Menlo Park, CA: AAAI Press.

Barr, A., & Feigenbaum, E. A. (1982). *The Handbook of Artificial Intelligence* (*Vol. 2*). Los Altos, CA: Kaufmann.

Barr, A., Beard, M., & Atkinson, R. C. (1976). The computer as a tutorial laboratory: the Stanford BIP project. *Man-Machine Studies*, *8*, 567–596. doi:10.1016/S0020-7373(76)80021-1

Barrit, C., Lewis, D., & Wieseler, W. (1999). CISCO Systems Reusable Information Object Strategy Version 3.0. *Cisco Systems*. Retrieved May 06, 2008, from http://www.cisco.com/warp/public/779/ibs/solutions/learning/whitepapers/el_cisco_rio.pdf

Baylor, A. L. (2001). Permutations of control: Cognitive considerations for agent-based learning environments. *Journal of Interactive Learning Research*, *12*(4), 403–425.

Bazerman, M. H., Curhan, J. R., Moore, D. A., & Valley, K. L. (2000). Negotiation. *Annual Review of Psychology*, *51*, 279–314. doi:10.1146/annurev.psych.51.1.279

Beal, C. R., Beck, J., & Woolf, B. (1998). Impact of intelligent computer instruction on girls' math self concept and beliefs in the value of math. *Paper presented at the annual meeting of the American Educational Research Association.*

Beck, J. E. (2006). Using learning decomposition to analyze student fluency development. In *Proceedings of the Workshop on Educational Data Mining at the 8th International Conference on Intelligent Tutoring Systems (pp 21-28).*

Beck, J., & Woolf, B. P. (2000). High-Level Student Modeling with Machine Learning. In *Intelligent Tutoring Systems* (pp. 584-593).

Beiler, A. (2004). *A produção de redes de conversação como base à aprendizagem.* (Doctoral Thesis). Porto Alegre: Universidade Federal do Rio Grande do Sul.

Bellifemine, F., Poggi, A., & Rimassa, G. (2001). JADE: a FIPA2000 compliant agent development environment. In *Proceedings of the 5th International Conference on Autonomous Agents (Agents 2001)* (pp. 216-217). Montreal, Canada.

Berge, C. (1976). *Graphs and hypergraphs*. Amsterdam: North-Holland Pub. Co.

Bergin, R. A., & Fors, U. G. H. (2003). Interactive Simulated Patient - An Advanced Tool for Student-activated Learning in Medicine and Healthcare. *Computers & Education*, *40*(4), 361–376. doi:10.1016/S0360-1315(02)00167-7

Berners-Lee, T., Hendler, J., & Lassila, O. (2001). The Semantic Web. *Scientific American*, *184*(5), 34–43. doi:10.1038/scientificamerican0501-34

Bertalanffy, L. (1968). *General System Theory: Foundations. Development, Applications*. New York: George Braziller.

Berz, M., Erdelyi, B., & Hoefkens, J. (1999). Experiences with interactive remote graduate instruction in beam physics. *Journal of Interactive Learning Research*, *10*(1), 49–58.

Bick, M., Adelsberger, H., & Pawlowski, J. (2000). The Essen Learning Model A Step Towards a Standard Model of Learning Processes. In J. Bourdeau & R. Heller (Ed.), *Proceedings of World Conference on Educational Multimedia, Hypermedia and Telecommunications 2000* (pp. 118-123). Chesapeake, VA: AACE.

Bickmore, T. (2003). *Relational Agents: Effecting Change through Human-Computer Relationships*. (Ph.D. Thesis). Cambridge, MA: Massachusetts Institute of Technology.

Biswas, G., Schwartz, D. L., & Bransford, J. D.The Teachable Agents Group at Vanderbilt. (2001). *Technology support for complex problem solving: From SAD Environments to AI*. Menlo Park, CA: AAAI/MIT Press.

Biswas, G., Schwartz, D. L., Leelawong, K., & Vye, N., & TAG-V. (2005). Learning by teaching: A new agent paradigm for educational software. *Applied Artificial Intelligence*, *19*, 363–392. doi:10.1080/08839510590910200

Black, J. B. (1992). *Types of Knowledge Representation CCT Report*. New York: Teachers College, Columbia University.

Black, J. B. (2007). Imaginary Worlds. In Gluck, M. A., Anderson, J. R., & Kosslyn, S. M. (Eds.), *Memory and Mind: A Festschrift for Gordon H. Bower*. Mahwah, NJ: Lawrence Erlbaum Associates.

Black, J. B., & Bower, G. H. (1980). Story understanding as problem-solving. *Poetics*, *9*, 223–250. doi:10.1016/0304-422X(80)90021-2

Blandford, A. E. (1994). Teaching through collaborative problem solving. *Journal of Artificial Intelligence in Education*, *5*(1), 51–84.

Blankeney, C. D., & Blankeney, R. A. (1991). Understanding and reforming misbehavior among behaviorally disordered adolescents. *Behavioral Disorders*, *16*(2), 120–126.

Bloom, B. S. (1984). The 2 Sigma Problem: The Search for Methods of Group Instruction as Effective as One-to-One Tutoring. *Educational Researcher*, *13*, 4–16.

Bonabeau, E., Dorigo, M., & Theraulaz, G. (1999). *Swarm Intelligence: From Natural to Artificial Systems*. New York: Oxford University Press.

Bonnet, A. (1985). *Artificial Intelligence: Promise and Performance*. London: Prentice Hall.

Boole, G. (1854). *An investigation of the laws of thought on which are founded the mathematical theories of logic andprobabilities, Macmillan, 1854/1958*. New York, NY: Dover Publications.

Borges-andrade, J. E. (2002). Desenvolvimento de medidas em avaliação de treinamento. *Estudos de Psicologia*, *7*(Número Especial), 31-43.

Botelho, F. V. U., & Vicari, R. (2006). Course evaluation and program evaluation in distance learning – The effectiveness of interactive processes in learning virtual environment. In *Anais da 22ª Conferência do ICDE (CD-ROM)*. Rio de Janeiro.

Boven, L. V., & Thompson, L. (2003). A Look into the Mind of the Negotiator: Mental Models in Negotiation. *Group Processes & Intergroup Relations*, *6*, 387–404. doi:10.1177/13684302030064005

Božičević, J., & Stankov, S. (2006). Continuous Innovation And Evolution Of The Intelligent Tutoring System TEx-Sys. In *Proceedings of the 1st International Conference 2006 - Future Challenges and Current Issues in Business Information, Organization and Process Management*. (pp. 191-197), London, United Kingdom: Center for Business Information, Organization and Process Management, Westminster Business School.

Braak, J. P. (2004). Domains and determinants of university students' self-perceived computer competence. *Computers & Education*, *43*(4), 299–312.

Bratman, M. E. (1999). *Intention, Plans, and Practical Reason*. CSLI Publications.

Braubach, L., Lamersdorf, W., & Pokahr, A. (2003). Jadex: Implementing a BDI-Infrastructure for JADE Agents. *EXP - in search of innovation, 3*, 76-85.

Bromme, R., & Stahl, E. (2005). Is hypertext a book or a space? The impact of different introductory metaphors on a hypertext construction. *Computers & Education*, *44*, 115–133. doi:10.1016/j.compedu.2004.01.003

Brookfield, S. (1985). Self-directed learning: A critical review of research. In Brookfield, S. (Ed.), *Self-Directed Learning From Theory to Practice* (pp. 5–16). San Francisco: Jossey-Bass.

Brown, J. S., & Burton, R. R. (1978). Diagnostic models for procedural bugs in basic mathematical skills. *Cognitive Science, 2*, 155–192. doi:10.1207/s15516709cog0202_4

Brown, A. L., Bryant, N. R., & Campione, J. C. (1983). *Preschool children's learning and transfer of matrices problems: Potential for improvement.* Paper presented at the Society for Research in Child Development meeting, Detroit, MI.

Bruillard, E. (1997). *Les Machines a Enseigner*. Paris: Editions Hermes.

Brusilovsky, P., & Peylo, C. (2003). Adaptive and intelligent web-based educational systems. *International Journal of Artificial Intelligence in Education, 13*(2–4), 159–172.

Brusilovsky, P., & Vassileva, J. (2003). Course sequencing techniques for large-scale web-based education. *International Journal of Continuing Engineering Education and Lifelong Learning, 13*(1-2), 75–94.

Brusilovsky, P. (1998). Methods and techniques of adaptive hypermedia. In Brusilovsky, P., Kobsa, A., & Vassileva, J. (Eds.), *Adaptive hypertext and hypermedia* (pp. 1–43). Dordrecht, The Netherlands: Kluwer Academic Publishers.

Brusilovsky, P. (1995). Intelligent Learning Environments for Programming. *Proceedings of AI-ED'95, 7th World Conference on Artifcial Intelligence in Education.* Washington, DC.

Brusilovsky, P. (2003). Developing adaptive educational hypermedia systems: From design models to authoring tools. In: T. Murray, S. Blessing and S. Ainsworth (Ed.), *Authoring Tools for Advanced Technology Learning Environment (*377-409). Dordrecht, The Netherlands: Kluwer Academic Publishers.

Brusilovsky, P. L. (1992). Intelligent Tutor: Environment and Manual for Introductory Programming. *Educational and Training Technology International.* 26-34.

Brusilovsky, P., & Millán, E. (2007). User models for adaptive hypermedia and adaptive educational systems. In: P. Brusilovsky, A. Kobsa and W. Neidl (Eds.). *The Adaptive Web: Methods and Strategies of Web Personalization*: *Lecture Notes in Computer Science, 4321*, 3-53. Berlin Heidelberg New York: Springer-Verlag.

Brusilovsky, P., Schwarz, E., & Weber, G. (1996). ELM–ART: An intelligent tutoring system on World Wide Web. *3rd international conference on intelligent tutoring systems ITS 96*, 261–269.

Brusilovsky, P., Sosnovsky, S., & Shcherbinina, O. (2005). User Modeling in a Distributed E-Learning Architecture. In: L. Ardissono, P. Brna and A. Mitrovic (Eds.) *Proceedings of 10th International User Modeling Conference: Lecture Notes in Artificial Intelligence*, vol. 3538. Berlin: Springer Verlag

Bryant, S., Romero, P., & DuBoulay, B. (2008). Pair programming and the mysterious role of the navigator. *International Journal of Human-Computer Studies, 66*(7), 519–529. doi:10.1016/j.ijhcs.2007.03.005

Budin, L. (2005). *Education in the Field of Information and Communication Technology in Elementary School.* Zagreb, Croatia: Croatian National Education Standard, Ministry of Science, Education and Sport.

Bull, S., & Kay, J. (2007). Student Models that Invite the Learner In: The SMILI Open Learner Modelling Framework. *International Journal of Artificial Intelligence in Education, 17*(2), 89–120.

Bull, S., & McEvoy, A. T. (2003). An Intelligent Learning Environment with an Open Learner Model for the Desktop PC and Pocket PC. In Hoppe, U., Verdejo, F., & Kay, J. (Eds.), *Artificial Intelligence in Education* (pp. 389–391). Amsterdam: IOS Press.

Bull, S. (2004). Supporting Learning with Open Learner Models. In *Proceedings of 4th Hellenic Conference with International Participation: Information and Communication Technologies in Education*, Athens, Greece.

Bull, S., & Nghiem, T. (2002). Helping Learners to Understand Themselves with a Learner Model Open to Students, Peers and Instructors. In P. Brna & V. Dimitrova (Eds.), *Proceedings of Workshop on Individual and Group Modeling Methods that Help Learners Understand Themselves, International Conference on Intelligent Tutoring Systems*, (pp. 5-13).

Bull, S., Gardner, P., Ahmad, N., Ting, J. & Clarke, B. (in press). Use and Trust of Simple Independent Open Learner Models to Support Learning Within and Across Courses. *User Modeling, Adaptation and Personalization,* Springer-Verlag, Berlin Heidelberg.

Burger, T. (2003). Percepcija i stavovi studenata prema" u enju putem Interneta. *EDUpoint časopis o informacijskim tehologijama u obrazovanju, III*(16). Retrieved from http://edupoint.carnet.hr/casopis/broj-16/clanak-01/sazetak.html

Burleson, W. *(2006, September)* Affective Learning Companions: Strategies for Empathetic Agents with Real-Time Multimodal Affective Sensing to Foster Meta-Cognitive and Meta-Affective Approaches to Learning, Motivation, and Perseverance, *MIT PhD Thesis.*

Burns, H. L., & Capps, C. G. (1988). Foundations of intelligent tutoring systems: an introduction. In Poison, M. C., & Richardson, J. J. (Eds.), *Foundations of intelligent tutoring systems* (pp. 1–19). Hillsdale, NJ: Lawrence Erlbaum.

Buschmann, F., Meunier, R., Rohnert, H., Sommerlad, P., & Stal, M. A. (1996). *System of Patterns.* Chichester, UK: John Wiley & Sons.

Butz, C. J., Hua, S., & Maguire, R. B. (2006). A web-based Bayesian intelligent tutoring system for computer programming. *Web Intelligence and Agent System, 4,* 77–97.

Byrnes, J. P. (2001). *Cognitive Development and Learning in Instructional Contexts.* Boston: Allyn and Bacon.

Calcaterra, A., Alessandro, A., & Underwood, J. (2005). Cognitive style, hypermedia navigation and learning. *Computers & Education, 44,* 441–457. doi:10.1016/j.compedu.2004.04.007

Campione, J. C., Brown, A. L., & Bryant, N. R. (1985). Individual differences in learning and memory. In Sternberg, R. J. (Ed.), *Human abilities: An information-processing approach* (pp. 103–126). New York: W.H. Freeman.

Canfield, W. (2001, Spring). ALEKS: A Web-based intelligent tutoring system [ProQuest Education Journals.]. *Mathematics and Computer Education, 35*(2), 152.

Cap, C., & Martens, A. (2009). Patterns for eLearning Systems. In Hambach, S., Martens, A., Urban, B. (eds.) *Proc. of the eLBa 2009 e-Learning Baltics International Scientific Conference* (pp. 115-124) Stuttgart, Germany: Fraunhofer IRB Verlag.

Capuano, N., Marsella, M., & Salerno, S. (2004). ABITIS. An Agent Based Intelligent Tutoring System for Distance Learning. In *Proceedings of the International Workshop in Adaptive and Intelligent Web-basedEducational Systems.*

Carbonell, J. R. (1970). artificial intelligence in CAI: An artificial intelligence approach to computer-aided instruction. *IEEE Transactions on Man-Machine Systems, 4*(11), 190–202. doi:10.1109/TMMS.1970.299942

Carmona1, C., Millán, E., Pérez-de-la-Cruz, J. L., Trella1, M. & Conejo, R. (2005). Introducing Prerequisite Relations in a Multi-layered Bayesian Student Model. In Ardissono, Brna & Mitroivc (Eds.). *10th International Conference on User Modeling 2005,* (pp. 347-356), Berlin, Germany: Springer-Verlag

Carr, B., & Goldstein, I. P. (1977). *Overlays: A Theory of Modelling for Computer Aided Instruction, AI Memo.* Cambridge, MA: Massachisetts Institute of Technology, Artificial Intelligence Lab.

Carver, C. A., Howard, R. A., & Lavelle, E. (1996). Enhancing student learning by incorporating student learning styles into adaptive hypermedia. In *Proceedings of EDMEDIA 96 - World Conference on Educational Multimedia and Hypermedia* (118-123). Boston.

Carver, C., Howard, R., & Lavelle, E. (1996). Enhancing student learning by incorporating learning styles into adaptive hypermedia. In *Proceedings 1996 EDMEDIA world conference on educational multimedia and hypermedia* (pp. 118–123). Boston.

Casamayor, G. (2000). *Disciplina y Convivencia en la Institución Escolar.* Venezuela: Editorial Laboratorio Educativo.

Cen, H., Koedinger, K., & Junker, B. (2005). Automating Cognitive Model Improvement by A*Search and Logistic Regression. In Beck. J (Eds). *Educational Data Mining: Papers from the 2005 AAAI Workshop.* Menlo Park, CA: AAAI Press.

Cen, H., Koedinger, K., & Junker, B. (2006, June). *Learning factors analysis: a general method for cognitive model evaluation and improvement.* Presented at the Eighth International Conference on Intelligent Tutoring Systems (ITS 2006), Jhongli, Taiwan.

Chan, T.-W., & Baskin, A. (1990). Learning companion systems. In Frasson, C., & Gauthier, G. (Eds.), *Intelligent Tutoring Systems: At the Crossroads of Artificial Intelligence and Education.* New York: Ablex.

Chang, K., Beck, J., Mostow, J., & Corbett, A. (2006, June). *A Bayes Net Toolkit for Student Modeling in Intelligent Tutoring Systems.* Presented at Eigth International Conference on Intelligent Tutoring Systems, Jhongli, Taiwan

Chang, Y.-J., Tsai, C.-C., & Chu, C.-P. (2008). A personalized course composition mechanism based on PSO. *Presented at: TWELF'08.* Retrieved 7 June 2008, from: http://itech.ntcu.edu.tw/twelf2008/papers/F/F1.pdf

Chee, Y. S., Tan, J. T., & Chan, T. (1993). Applying cognitive apprenticeship to the teaching of Smalltalk in a computer based learning environment. In *Proceedings of 7th International PEG Conference,* (pp. 569-588).

Chen, L., & Jiang, W. (2007). The design and implementation of a general examination system [In Chinese]. *Computer Engineering and Design, 28*(17), 4285–4289.

Chen, Z. (2008). Learning about learners: system learning in virtual learning environment. *Computers. Communications and Control, 3*(1), 33–40.

Cheung, B., Hui, L., Zhang, J., & Yiu, S. M. (2003). SmartTutor: An intelligent tutoring system in web-based adult education. *Journal of Systems and Software, 68,* 11–25. doi:10.1016/S0164-1212(02)00133-4

Choe, H. (2006). Ontology based e-learning Authoring System. *Asian Journal of Information Technology, 5*(12), 1319–1322.

Chou, C. (1999). Developing CLUE: a formative evaluation system for computer network learning courseware. *Journal of Interactive Learning Research, 10*(2), 179–193.

Chrysostomou, C. P., & Papadopoulos, G. A. (2005, May). *An Evaluation of E-Learning Technologies and Trends: Establishing and Object-Oriented Approach to Learning Object Design and Development.* Paper presented at *the First International Conference on E-Business and E-learning (EBEL'05),*88-96. Amman, Jordan. Retrieved May 06, 2008, from http://www.psut.edu.jo/EBEL/pdf/16.pdf

Cisco Systems Inc. (2003). Reusable Learning Object Authoring Guidelines: How to Build Modules, Lessons, Topics Version 4.5. Retrieved May 06, 2008, from http://db.formez.it/fontinor.nsf/c658e3224c-300556c1256ae90036d38e/DF95A2799A3D7085C1256E59003B33F5/$file/Cisco%20Reusable%20LO%20Authoring%20Guidelines%2007-2003.pdf

Clancey, W. J. (1982). Tutoring rules for guiding a case method dialogue. In D. H. Sleeman et & J. S. Brown (Ed.), *Intelligent tutoring systems* (pp. 201–225). London: Academic Press.

Clancey, W. J. (1984). Methodology for Building an Intelligent Tutoring System. In Kintsch, W., Miller, J. R., & Polson, P. G. (Eds.), *Methods and Tactics in Cognitive Sciences* (pp. 51–84). Hillsdale, NJ: Lawrence Erlbaum Associates.

Clancey, W. J. (1987). Methodology for Building an Intelligent Tutoring System. In: Kearsley (ed.): *Artificial Intelligence and Instruction.* Reading, MA: Addison Wesley.

Cobcroft, R., Towers, S., Smith, J., & Bruns, A. (2006). *Literature review into mobile learning in the university context.* Brisbane, Australia: Queensland University of Technology, Creative Industries faculty.

Cobcroft, R., Towers, S., Smith, J., & Bruns, A. (2006). Mobile learning in review: Opportunities and challenges for learners, teachers, and institutions. In *Proceedings of the Online Learning and Teaching Conference 2006 (OLT'06)* (pp. 21-30). Brisbane, Australia.

Coffield, F., Moseley, D., Hall, E., & Ecclestone, K. (2004). *Learning styles and pedagogy in post-16 learning?*Learning and Skills Research Centre LSDA.

Cohen, J. (1988). *Statistical Power Analysis for the Behavioral Sciences.* Hillsdale, NJ: Lawrence Erlbaum.

Cohen, P. A., Kulik, J. A., & Kulik, C. L. C. (1982). Educational outcomes of tutoring: A meta-analysis of findings. *American Educational Research Journal, 19*(2), 237–248.

Coie, J. D., Underwood, M., & Lochman, J. E. (1991). Programmatic intervention with aggressive children in the school setting. In Pepler, D. J., & Rubin, K. H. (Eds.), *The development and treatment of childhood aggression* (pp. 389–410). Hillsdale, NJ: Erlbaum.

Coleman, J. (1967). Learning Through Games. *Play, its Role in Development and Evolution*, 460-463.

Collier, G. (2002). e-Learning Application Infrastructure. *SUN Microsystems White Paper*.

Collins, A. M., & Loftus, E. F. (1975). A spreading-activation theory of semantic processing. *Psychological Review, 82*, 407–428. doi:10.1037/0033-295X.82.6.407

Collins, A. M. (1976). Processing in acquiring knowledge. In Anderson, R. C. (Ed.), *Schooling and the acquisition of knowledge*. Hillsdale, NJ: Lawrence Erlbaum Associates.

Collins, J., Greer, J., & Huang, S. (1996). Adaptive assessment of using granularity hierarchies and Bayesien nets. In *Lecture Notes in Computer Science: Proceedings of the third Intelligent Tutoring Systems*, (pp. 569 -577), London: Springer-Verlag.

Computing Research Association. (2005). Cyber infrastructure for Education and Learning for the Future: a Vision and Research Agenda. *Final report of Cyber learning Workshop Series workshops held Fall 2004 - Spring 2005 by the Computing Research Association (CRA) and the International Society of the Learning Sciences (ISLS)*. Retrieved from http://www.cra.org/reports/cyberinfrastructure.pdf

Conati, C., Gertner, A., & VanLehn, K. (2002). Using Bayesian networks to manage uncertainty in student modeling. *Journal of User Modeling and User Adapted Interaction, 12*(4), 371–417. doi:10.1023/A:1021258506583

Conati, C., & VanLehn, K. (2001). *Providing adaptive support to the understanding of instructional material*. Santa Fe, New Mexico: Proceedings Intelligent User Interfaces.

Conati, C., & Maclare, H. (2004). *Evaluating a Probabilistic Model of Student Affect*. Paper presented at the VII International Conference on Intelligent Tutoring Systems. Lecture Notes in Computer Science. Springer-Verlag Heidelberg, 55-66.

Conati, C., & Zhao, X. (2004). Building and Evaluating an Intelligent Pedagogical Agent to Improve the Effectiveness of an Educational Game. In *Proceedings of IUI '04, International Conference on Intelligent User Interfaces*, (pp. 6-13). Island of Madeira, Portugal.

Conati, C., Gertner, A., VanLehn, K., & Druzdzel, M. (1997). On-Line Student Modeling for Coached Problem Solving Using Bayesian Networks. In Jameson A., Paris C., Tasso C., (Eds.), *Proceedings of the sixth International Conference on User Modeling (UM'97)*. New York: Springer-Wien.

Connolly, T.M. and Stansfield, M.H. (2007) From eLearning to Games-based eLearning, International *Journal of Information Technology and Management, 26*(2/3/4), 188-208.

Corbett, A. T., & Anderson, J. R. (1995). Knowledge tracing: Modeling the acquisition of procedural knowledge. *User Modeling and User-Adapted Interaction, 4*, 253–278. doi:10.1007/BF01099821

Corbett, A. T., Koedinger, K. R., & Hadley, W. H. (2001). Cognitive Tutors: From the research classroom to all classrooms. In Goodman, P. S. (Ed.), *Technology Enhanced Learning: Opportunities for Change*. Mahwah, NJ: Lawrence Erlbaum Associates.

Corbett, A. T., Anderson, J. R., & O'Brien, A. T. (1995). Student modeling in the ACT programming tutor. In Nichols, P., Chipman, S., & Brennan, R. (Eds.), *Cognitively Diagnostic Assessment*. Hillsdale, NJ: Erlbaum.

Corbett, A. T., Koedinger, K. R., & Anderson, J. R. (1997). Intelligent Tutoring Systems. In M. Helander, T. K. & Landauer, P., & Prabuh (Eds.), *Handbook of Human-Computer Interaction*. Elsevier Science B.V., 2nd completely revised edition (pp. 849-874).

Cost, R. S., Finin, T., Joshi, A., Peng, Y., Nicholas, C., Chen, H., et al. (2001). Ittalks: A case study in the semantic web and daml. In *Proceedings of the 1st International Semantic Web Working Symposium (SWWS'01)* (pp. 477-494). Stanford, CA.

Craighead, J. (2008). Distributed, game-based, intelligent tutoring systems — The next step in computer based training? *Collaborative Technologies and Systems, 2008. CTS 2008. International Symposium on*, (pp. 247-256). Irvine, CA.

Curilem, S. G., Barbosa, A. R., & de Azevedo, F. M. (2007). Intelligent tutoring systems: Formalization as automata and interface design using neural networks. *Computers & Education*, *49*(3), 545–561. doi:10.1016/j.compedu.2005.10.005

Curilem, G. M. S., & de Azevedo, F. (2003). Didactic Ergonomy for the Interface of Intelligent Tutoring Systems. In Llamas-Nistal, M., Fernandez-Iglesias, M. J., & Anido-Rifon, L. (Eds.), *Computers and Education: Towards a Lifelong Learning Society* (pp. 75–88). The Netherlands: Kluwer Academic Publishers.

Dadic, T., Stankov, S., & Rosic, M. (2006).Prototype Model of Tutoring System for Programming. In *Proceedings of ITI Conference, Dubrovnik, Croatia.*

Dadic, T., Stankov, S., & Rosic, M. (2008). Meaningful learning in the Tutoring System for Programming. In *Proceedings of ITI Conference, Dubrovnik, Croatia.*

Dagli, C., & Kilicay, N. (2006). Understanding behavior of system of systems through computational intelligence techniques. *IEEE Systems Conference'06* (pp.1-7), Honolulu, USA.

Dai, Y., & Li, X. (1995). An analysis on computer-based automatic assessment paper generation algorithms [In Chinese]. *Mini & Micro Computer Systems*, *16*(9), 51–55.

Darino, S., & Gómez, M. (2000). *Resolución de Conflictos en las Escuelas. Proyectos y Ejercitación.* Argentina: Editorial Espacio.

Davidovic, A., Warren, J., & Trichina, E. (2003). Learning benefits of structural example based adaptive tutoring systems. *IEEE Transactions on Education*, *46*(2), 241–251. doi:10.1109/TE.2002.808240

de Azevedo, F. M. (1993). *Contribution to the Study of Neural Networks in Dynamical Expert System.* Unpublished Doctoral Dissertation. Facultés Universitaires Notre-Dame de la Paix (FUNDP), Namur, Belgium.

de Jong, T., & van Joolingen, W. (1998). Discovery learning with computer simulations of conceptual domains. *Review of Educational Research*, *68*, 179–201.

Demb, A., Erickson, D., & Hawkins-Wilding, S. (2004). The laptop alternative: Student reactions and strategic implications. *Computers & Education*, *42*(3), 383–401.

Demetriou, A. (1993). *The architecture and dynamics of developing mind.* Chicago: University of Chicago Press.

Denegri, M. (2004). *La construcción del conocimiento social en la infancia: reflexiones para la investigación y acción educativa.* Chile: Revista de Estudios y Experiencias en Educación. Universidad de Concepción.

Department for Education and Skills. (2005) *The e-Strategy - Harnessing Technology: Transforming learning and children's services.* Retrieved from http://www.dfes.gov.uk/publications/e-strategy/

Deutsch, M. (1991). *Koch, S. & Girard, K. (1997). Resolución de Conflictos en las Escuelas.* Argentina: Editorial Granica.

Devedžić, V. (1999). Using design patterns in ITS development. In: S.P. Lajoie, & M. Vivet, (Eds.) Artificial IntelligeNce in Education (pp. 657-659). Amsterdam: IOS Press / Tokyo: OHM Ohmsha.

Di Eugenio, B., & Trolio, M. J. (2000). Can simple Natural Language Generation improve Intelligent Tutoring Systems. In *Proceedings of the AAAI 2000 Fall Symposium on Building Dialogue Systems for Tutorial Applications.* North Falmouth, MA.

Di Eugenio, B., Fossati, D., Yu, D., Haller, S., & Glass, M. (2005). Natural Language Generation for Intelligent Tutoring Systems: a case study. In Proceedings of *AIED 2005, the 12th International Conference on Artificial Intelligence in Education.* Amsterdam.

Di Marzo, G., Gleizes, M.-P., & Karageorgos, A. (2006). Self-organisation and emergence in MAS: An overview. *Informatica*, *30*, 45–54.

Dicheva, D., Sosnovsky, S., Gavrilova, T., & Brusilovsky, P. (2005, July). *Ontological web portal for educational ontologies*. Paper presented at International Workshop on Applications of Semantic Web Technologies for E-Learning (*SWEL*) AIED'*05*. Amsterdam.

Dieberger, A., Höök, K., Svensson, M., & Lönnqvist, P. (2001). Social navigation research agenda. *Presented at Conference on Human Factors in Computing Systems '01*, Seattle, USA.

Dillenbourg, P., & Self, J. A. (1992). A computational approach to socially distributed cognition. *European Journal of Psychology of Education*, *3*(4), 353–372. doi:10.1007/BF03172899

Dillenbourg, P. (1999). What do you mean by collaborative learning? In Dillenbourg, P. (Ed.), *Collaborative-learning: Cognitive and Computational Approaches* (pp. 1–19). Oxford: Elsevier.

Dillenbourg, P., & Mendelsohn, P. (1991). Le Developpement de l'enseignement Intelligemment Assiste par Ordinateur. *Natural and Artificial Intelligence Symposium* (pp. 23–25). Rome.

Dillenbourg, P., & Schneider, D. (1995). *ICCAI 95 article*. Retrieved October 27, 2009, from http://tecfa.unige.ch/tecfa/research/CMC/colla/iccai95_1.html

Dimitrova, V., Self, J., & Brna, P. (2001). Applying Interactive Open Learner Models to Learning Technical Terminology. In M. Bauer, P. J. Gmytrasiewicz & J. Vassileva (Eds.), *User Modeling 2001: 8th International Conference*, (pp. 148-157). Springer-Verlag, Berlin Heidelberg.

DiNucci, D. (1999). Design & New Media: Fragmented Future-Web development faces a process of mitosis, mutation, and natural selection. *PRINT-NEW YORK*, *53*, 32–35.

Dodds, P. (2001). Advanced Distributed Learning Sharable Content Object Reference Model Version 1.2, *The SCORM Content Aggregation Model*, Retrieved May 06, 2009, from http://coco.ccu.uniovi.es/e-learning/scorm/overview/organiza/ContentAM.pdf

Doesburg, W. A., Heuvelink, A., & van den Broek, E. L. (2005). TACOP: A Cognitive Agent for a Naval Training Simulation Environment. In M. Pechoucek, D. Steiner, & S. ThompsonM. Pechoucek, D. Steiner, S. Thompson (Eds.), *Proceedings of the Industry Track of the Fourth International Joint Conference on Autonomous Agents and Multi-Agent Systems* (pp. 34-41). ACM.

Dorigo, M., & Stützle, T. (2004). *Ant Colony Optimization*. Cambridge, MA: MIT Press.

Dorigo, M. (1992). *Ottimizzazione, apprendimento automatico, ed algoritmi basati su metafora natural*. (Unpublished doctoral dissertation) Politecnico di Milano, Italy.

Draney, K. L., Pirolli, P., & Wilson, M. (1995). A measurement model for a complex cognitive skill. In Nichols, P., Chipman, S., & Brennan, R. (Eds.), *Cognitively Diagnostic Assessment*. Hillsdale, NJ: Erlbaum.

Dron, J., Siviter, P., Boyne, C., & Mitchell, R. (2000). CoFIND: Step towards a self-organising learning environment. In [San Antonio, USA.]. *Proceedings of WebNet, 2000*, 146–151.

Dron, J. (2006). Social software and the emergence of control. *Proceedings of the 6th IEEE International conference on Advanced Learning Technologies '06* (pp.904-908), Kerkrade, Netherlands.

Druckman, D., Harris, R., & Ramberg, B. (2002). Computer-Assisted International Negotiation: A Tool for Research and Practice. *Group Decision and Negotiation*, *11*, 231–256. doi:10.1023/A:1015281906202

Du Boulay, B., & Luckin, R. (2001). Modelling Human Teaching Tactics and Strategies for Tutoring Systems. *International Journal of Artificial Intelligence in Education, 12*, 235–256.

du Boulay, B. (2000). Can we learn from ITSs? In Gilles Gauthier, Claude Frasson, and Kurt VanLehn (Editors), *Intelligent Tutoring Systems: Proceedings of 5th International Conference, ITS 2000,* Montreal, number 1839 in Lectures Notes in Computer Science, 9-17. Berlin-Heidelberg, Germany: Springer-Verlag.

DuBoulay, B., O'Shea, T., & Monk, J. (1989). The Black Box Inside the Glass Box. In Soloway, E., & Spohrer, J. C. (Eds.), *Studying the Novice Programmer* (p. 431). Hillsdale, NJ: Lawrence Erlbaum Associates, Publishers.

Duncan, C. (2003). Granularization. In Littlejohn, A. (Ed.), *Reusing online resources: a sustainable approach to eLearning* (pp. 12–19). London: Kogan Page.

Dunser, A., & Jirasko, M. (2005). Interaction of hypertext forms and global versus sequential learning styles. *Journal of Educational Computing Research*, *32*(1), 79–91. doi:10.2190/1J25-LWQF-PQ3W-LABM

Duval, E., & Hodgins, W. (2007). Learning objects revisited. In McGreal, R. (Ed.), *Online Education Using Learning Objects* (pp. 71–82). London: Routledge/Falmer.

Dvedžić, V. B. (2004). Web intelligence and artificial intelligence in education. *Journal of Educational Technology & Society*, *7*(4), 29–39.

Dweck, C. S. (1999). *Self Theories: Their Role in Motivation, Personality, and Development*. Boca Raton, FL: Taylor Francis.

Eberhart, E., & Kennedy, J. (1995). A new optimizer using particle swarm theory. In [Nagoya, Japan.]. *Proceedings of International Symposium on Micro Machine & Human Science*, *1995*, 39–43.

Eisenberg, M. B., & Johnson, D. (2005). Learning and Teaching Information Technology Computer Skills in Context. *US Federal government*. Retrieved November, 20, 2009, from http://www.libraryinstruction.com/info-tech.html

Ekman, P., & Davidson, R. J. (1993). Voluntary smiling changes regional brain activity. *Psychological Science* 4: 342-345. Ekman, P. and W. V. Friesen (1978). *Facial Action Coding System*. Consulting Psychologists Press.

Eliot, C., & Woolf, B. (1994). Reasoning about the user within a simulation-based real-time training system. In *Proceedings of the fourth international conference on user modeling*, 121-126.

Eliot, C., Neiman, D., & Lamar, M. (1997). Medtec: a web-based intelligent tutor for basic anatomy. In S. Lobodzinski, & I. Tomek (Ed.), *Proceedings of WebNet '97, World Conference of the WWW, Internet and Intranet* (pp. 161–165). Charlottesville, VA: AACE.

Elsom-Cook, M. (1987). *Intelligent computer-aided instruction research at the Open University* (Tech. Rep. No. 63). Computer-Assisted Learning Research Group, The Open University, Milton Keynes.

Erjavec, T., Krstev, C., Petkevič, V., Simov, K., & Tadić, M. V. (2003). The MULTEXT-east morphosyntactic specifications for Slavic languages. In *Proceedings of the 2003 EACL Workshop on Morphological Processing of Slavic Languages*, (pp. 25-32). Budapest, Hungary.

Erlich, Z., Erlich-Philip, I., & Gal-Ezer, J. (2005). Skills required for participating in CMC courses: An empirical study. *Computers & Education*, *44*(3), 477–487. doi:10.1016/j.compedu.2004.04.010

Erudium. (2001). *Erudium online glossary*. Retrieved February 20, 2009, from http://www.erudium.polymtl.ca/html-eng/home.php

Evans, C., Gibbons, N. J., Shah, K., & Griffin, D. K. (2004). Virtual learning in the biological sciences: pitfalls of simply "putting notes on the web". *Computers & Education*, *43*, 49–61. doi:10.1016/j.compedu.2003.12.004

Evens, M., Brandle, S., Chang, R., Freedman, R., Glass, M., Lee, Y., et al. (2001). CIRCSIM-Tutor: An intelligent tutoring system using natural language dialogue. In *Proceedings of the 12th Midwest AI and cognitive science conference (MAICS 2001)*, pp. 16–23.

Farzan, R., & Brusilovsky, P. (2005). Social navigation support in e-learning: What are the real footprints? In *Proceedings of ITWP'05*. Edinburgh, UK.

Fasel, B., & Luettin, J. (2003). Automatic Facial Expression Analysis: A Survey. *Pattern Recognition*, *36*(1), 259–275. doi:10.1016/S0031-3203(02)00052-3

Felder, R. M. (1996). Matters of Styles. [December.]. *ASEE Prism*, *6*(4), 18–23.

Felder, R. M., & Silverman, L. K. (1988). Learning and Teaching Styles in Engineering Education. *English Education*, *78*(7), 674–681.

Feng, M., & Heffernan, N. (2007b). Towards Live Informing and Automatic Analyzing of Student Learning: Reporting in ASSISTment System. *Journal of Interactive Learning Research*, *18*(2), 207–230.

Feng, M, Heffernan, N., Heffernan, C. & Mani, M. (2009). Using mixed-effects modeling to analyze different grain-sized skill models. *IEEE Transactions on Learning Technologies*, retrieved from/doi.ieeecomputersociety.org/10.1109/TLT.2009.17.

Feng, M., & Beck, J. (2009). Back to the future: a non-automated method of constructing transfer models. In Barnes & Desmarais (Eds.), *Proceedings of the 2nd International Conference on Educational Data Mining*. Cordoba, Spain, 2009.

Feng, M., & Heffernan, N. T. (2007a). *Assessing Students' Performance: Item Difficulty Parameter vs. Skill Learning Tracking.* Paper presented at the National Council on Educational Measurement, Chicago.

Feng, M., Beck, J., & Heffernan, N. (2009a) Using learning decomposition to analyze instructional effectiveness in the ASSISTment system. In *Proceedings of the 14th International Conference on Artificial Intelligence in Education (AIED-2009).* Brighton, UK: IOS Press.

Feng, M., Beck, J., & Heffernan, N. T. (2009b). Using Learning Decomposition and Bootstrapping with Randomization to Compare the Impact of Different Educational Interventions on Learning. In Barnes, Desmarais, Romero, & Ventura (Eds.), *Proceedings of the 2nd International Conference on Educational Data Mining* (pp. 51-60). Cordoba, Spain: Copisterias Don Folio, S.L.

Feng, M., Beck, J., Heffernan, N., & Koedinger, K. (2008). Can an Intelligent Tutoring System Predict Math Proficiency as Well as a Standardized Test? In Beck & Baker (Eds.). In *Proceedings of the 1st International Conference on Education Data Mining.* Montreal, Quebec.

Feng, M., Heffernan, N. T., & Koedinger, K. R. (2006a). Addressing the testing challenge with a web based E-assessment system that tutors as it assesses. In *Proceedings of the 15th Annual World Wide Web Conference.* New York: ACM Press.

Feng, M., Heffernan, N. T., & Koedinger, K. R. (2006b). Predicting state test scores better with intelligent tutoring systems: developing metrics to measure assistance required. In Ikeda, Ashley & Chan (Eds.), *Proceedings of the Eighth International Conference on Intelligent Tutoring Systems,* (pp 31–40). Springer-Verlag: Berlin.

Feng, M., Heffernan, N. T., & Koedinger, K. R. (2009). Addressing the assessment challenge in an online system that tutors as it assesses. *User Modeling and User-Adapted Interaction: The Journal of Personalization Research (UMUAI journal), 19.*

Feng, M., Heffernan, N., Beck, J., & Koedinger, K. (2008). Can we predict which groups of questions students will learn from? In Beck & Baker (Eds.), *Proceedings of the 1st International Conference on Education Data Mining.* Montreal, Quebec.

Ferguson, K., Arroyo, I., Mahadevan, S., Woolf, B., & Barto, A. (2006). Improving Intelligent Tutoring Systems: Using Expectation Maximization to Learn Student Skill Levels. In Ikeda, Ashley & Chan (Eds.), *Proceedings of the Eight International Conference on Intelligent Tutoring Systems*, (pp.453-462). Berlin: Springer-Verlag.

Fitzmaurice, G., Laird, N., & Ware, J. (2004). *Applied Longitudinal Analysis*. Hoboken, New Jersey: Wiley & Sons.

Flamand, F., & Gervais, A. (2004). Les objets d'apprentissage: au-delà de la technologie, la pédagogie. *Bulletin Collegial des Technologies de l'Information et des Communications CLIC, 54*, 1–5.

Fletcher, J. D. (2003). Evidence for Learning from Technology-Assisted Instruction. In O'Neal, H. F., & Perez, R. S. (Eds.), *Technology applications in education: a learning view* (pp. 79–99). Mahwah, NJ: Lawrence Erlbaum.

Foote, R. (2007). Mathematics and Complex Systems. *Science, 318*(5849), 410–412. doi:10.1126/science.1141754

Forbes-Riley, K., Litman, D., & Rotaru, M. (2008). *Responding to student uncertainty during computer tutoring: A preliminary evaluation. 9th international conference on intelligent tutoring systems*. Montreal, Canada: ITS.

Ford, N., & Murpy, G. (2002). The development and piloting of a training web site for health and safety enforcement officers. *British Journal of Educational Technology, 33*(1), 65–76. doi:10.1111/1467-8535.00239

Forte, E., Haenni, F., Warkentyne, K., Duval, E., Cardinaels, K., & Vervaet, E. (1999). Semantic and Pedagogic Interoperability Mechanisms in the ARIADNE Educational Repository. [SIGMOD]. *SIGMOD Record, 28*(1), 20–25. doi:10.1145/309844.309870

Fossati, D. (2003). DIAG-NLP: Improving Intelligent Tutoring System with Natural Language Generation Technology. (Master's Thesis), *University of Illinois at Chicago*. (pg. 25).

Frand, J. (2000). The information age mindset: Changes in students and implications for higher education. *EDUCAUSE Review*, *35*(5), 15–24.

Friedman, S. L. (1986). *The brain, cognition, and education*. Orlando: Academic Press.

Friedman-Hill, E. (2003). *Jess in Action: Rule-Based Systems in Java*. Greenwich, CT: Manning Publications.

Gagne, R. M., Briggs, L. J., & Wagner, W. W. (1988). *Principles of instructional design* (3rd ed.). New York: Holt Rinehart and Winston.

Gamboa, H., & Fred, A. (2001). Designing intelligent tutoring systems: A bayesian approach. In *Proceedings ICEIS 01, 3rd international conference on enterprise information systems.*

Gamma, E., Helm, R., Johnson, R., & Vlissides, J. (1995). *Design Patterns: Elements of Reusable Object-Oriented Software*. Reading, MA: Addison-Wesley.

Gardner, H. (1993). *Multiple Intelligences: The Theory in Practice*. NY: Basic Books.

Garland, K., & Noyes, J. (2004). Changes in learning expectations and confidence toward computers: a study of five successive years of undergraduates. *Journal of Educational Computing Research*, *31*(3), 273–279. doi:10.2190/NQWC-WTVR-VUUE-CXW4

Gee, J. P. (2003). *What video games have to teach us about learning*. New York: Pal grave.

Gennari, J. H., Musen, M. A., Fergerson, R. W., Grosso, W. E., Crubézy, M., & Eriksson, H. (2003). The evolution of Protégé: an environment for knowledge-based systems development. I*nt. J. Hum.-* [IJMMS]. *Comput. Stud.*, *58*(1), 89–123.

Gertner, A., & VanLehn, K. (2000). Andes: A coached problem solving environment for physics. In *Proceedings ITS 2000, intelligent tutoring systems*, (pp. 131–142).

Ghezzi, C., Jazayeri, M., & Mandrioli, D. (2003). *Fundamentals of Software Engineering* (2nd ed.). Prentice Hall, Pearson Education.

Gierl, M. J., Wang, C., & Zhou, J. (2008). Using the attribute hierarchy method to make diagnostic inferences about examinees' cognitive skills in Algebra on the SAT. Journal of Technology, Learning, and Assessment, *6*(6). Retrieved May 2008, from www.jtla.org.

Giesbers, B., Van Bruggen, J., Hermans, H., Joosten-Ten Brinke, D., Burgers, J., & Koper, R. (2007). Towards a methodology for educational modelling: A case in educational assessment. *Journal of Educational Technology & Society*, *10*(1), 237–247.

Gilbert, J., & Han, C. (1999). Adapting instruction in search of a significant difference. *Journal of Network and Computer Applications*, 22.

Gillespie, J. J., Thompson, L. L., Loewenstein, J., & Gentner, D. (1999). Lessons from Analogical Reasoning in the Teaching of Negotiation. *Negotiation Journal*, *15*, 363–371. doi:10.1111/j.1571-9979.1999.tb00734.x

Girard, K., Rifkin, J., & Townley, A. (1985). *Peaceful persuasión: A guide to creating mediation dispute resolution programs on college campuses*. Washington, DC: National Institute for Disputes Resolution.

Glass, G. V. (1976). Primary, secondary, and meta-analysis of research. *Educational Researcher*, *5*, 3–8.

Glass, M. (2000). Processing Language Input in the CIRCSIM-Tutor Intelligent Tutoring System. In *Proceedings of AAAI 2000 Fall Symposium on Building Dialogue Systems for Tutorial Applications* (pp. 74-80). San Antonio, TX: AAAI Press.

Glavinić, V., Rosić, M., & Zelić, M. (2007). Agents in m-Learning Systems Based on Intelligent Tutoring. In C. Stephanidis (Ed.), *Universal Access in Human-Computer Interaction. Applications and Services: Vol. 4556. Programming and Software Engineering* (pp. 578-587). Berlin: Springer.

Glavinić, V., Rosić, M., & Zelić, M. (2008). Analysis of an Agent-based m-Learning System. In *Proceedings of the 14th IEEE Mediterranean Electrotechnical Conference (MELECON'08)* (CD-ROM Proceedings pp. 1-6). Ajaccio, France.

Gobet, F., Voogt, A., & Retschitzki, J. (2004). *Moves in mind: The psychology of board games*. New York: Psychology Press.

Grabe, M. (2005). Voluntary use of online lecture notes: correlates of note use and note use as an alternative to class attendance. *Computers & Education*, *44*, 409–421. doi:10.1016/j.compedu.2004.04.005

Graesser, A.C., Wiemer-Hastings, K., Wiemer-Hastings, P., & Kreuz, R., & TRG. (1999). AutoTutor: A simulation of a human tutor. *Journal of Cognitive Systems Research*, *1*, 35–51. doi:10.1016/S1389-0417(99)00005-4

Graesser, A. C., Person, N. K., & Magliano, J. P. (1995). Collaborative dialog patterns in naturalistic one-on-one tutoring. *Applied Cognitive Psychology*, *9*, 495–552. doi:10.1002/acp.2350090604

Grigorenko, E. L., & Sternberg, R. J. (1998). Dynamic testing. *Psychological Bulletin*, *124*, 75–111. doi:10.1037/0033-2909.124.1.75

Gronlund, N. E. (1985). *Measurement and Evaluation in Teaching* (5 ed.). New York: Macmillan Publishing Company.

Gruber, T. (1993). A translation approach to portable ontology specifications. *Knowledge acquisition*, 5(2), 199-220. Retrieved May 06, 2008, from http://ksl-web.stanford.edu/knowledge-sharing/papers/README.html#ontolingua-intro

Grubišić, A., Stankov, S., & Žitko, B. (2007). EVEDIN: A System for Automatic Evaluation of Educational Influence. *International Journal WSEAS Transactions on Computers*, *6*(1), 1109–2750.

Grubišić, A. (2007). *Evaluating Educational Influence of Intelligent E-learning Systems*. (Unpublished MS Thesis), Zagreb, Croatia: Faculty of Electrical Engineering and Computing(in Croatian).

Grubišić, A., Stankov, S., & Žitko, B. (2006). An Approach to Automatic Evaluation of Educational Influence. In *Proceedings of the 6th WSEAS International Conference on DISTANCE LEARNING and WEB ENGINEERING (DIWEB '06)*, (pp. 20-25), Lisbon, Portugal.

Grune, D., Bal, H. E., Jacobs, C. J. H., & Langendoen, K. G. (2000). *Modern Compiler Design*. London: John Wiley & Sons, Ltd.

Guerra, N. G., Nucci, L., & Huesmann, R. L. (1994). Moral cognition and childhood aggression. In Huesmann, L. R. (Ed.), *Aggressive behavior: Current perspectives* (pp. 13–33). New York: Plenum.

Gulikers, J. T. M., Bastiaens, T. J., & Martens, R. L. (2005). The surplus value of an authentic learning environment. *Computers in Human Behavior*, *21*, 509–521. doi:10.1016/j.chb.2004.10.028

Gulz, A., & Haake, M. (2006). Design of animated pedagogical agents-A look at their look. *International Journal of Human-Computer Studies*, *64*, 322–339. doi:10.1016/j.ijhcs.2005.08.006

Gutiérrez, S., Pardo, A., & Kloos, C. D. (2006). Finding a learning path: toward a swarm intelligence approach. In [Puerto Vallarta, Mexico.]. *Proceedings of International Conference on Web-based Education*, *06*, 94–99.

Gutiérrez, S., Valigiani, G., Jamont, Y., Collet, P., & Kloos, C. D. (2007). A swarm approach for automatic auditing of pedagogical planning. [Nigata, Japan.]. *Proceedings of IEEE International Conference on Advanced Learning Technologies*, *07*, 136–138.

Guzdial, M. (2004). Programming Environments for Novices. In Fincher, S., & Petre, M. (Eds.), *Computer Science Education Research*. Springer-Verlag.

Hahne, M. N., & de Azevedo, F. M. (2008). Study on IAC networks models: learning and stability. *Neural Computing & Applications*, *17*(1), 65–74. doi:10.1007/s00521-007-0112-z

Halcartegaray, M. A. (1991). Reflexión en torno a la disciplina y el entorno moral. Corporación de Promoción Universitaria (CPU), 9-19, Santiago. Chile.

Hamel, C. J., & Ryan-Jones, D. (2002). Designing Instruction with Learning Objects. *International Journal of Educational Technology*, *3*(1).

Han, B. (2001). *Student modelling and adaptivity in web based learning systems*. (Unpublished Masters Thesis), New Zealand: Massey University.

Hansen, T. (1997). Development of Successful Object-Oriented Frameworks. in Proc. of the OOPSLA 97, Addendum to the 1997 ACM SIGPLAN conference on Object-Oriented Programming Systems, Languages, and Applications. New York: ACM Press, 115-119.

Harrer, A. (2003). Software Engineering Methods for re-use of Components and Design in Educational Systems. *International Journal of Computers & Applications, Special Issue on Intelligence and Technology in Educational Applications, Anaheim, CA, 25*, 1.

Harrer, A., Malzahn, N., & Roth, B. (2006). The remote control approach - how to apply scaffolds to existing collaborative learning environments. In Dimitriadis, Y., Zigurs, I., & Gomez-Sanchez, E. (Eds.), *Groupware: design, implementation, and use; proc. of CRIWG, Vol. LNCS 4154* (pp. 118–131). Berlin: Springer. doi:10.1007/11853862_10

Harrer, A., & Martens, A. (2006). Towards a Pattern Language for Intelligent Teaching and Training Systems. In T.-W. Chan & M. Ikeda & K. D. Ashley (Eds.): Proc. of the 8th International Conference on Intelligent Tutoring Systems. Lecture Notes in Computer Science LNCS 4053, Springer. 298-307.

Harrer, A., & Martens, A. (2007). An Integrated Approach for Teaching/Tutoring Process Models using Meta-Models. In Proceedings of the International Conference CELDA.

Hartman, J. (1991). Understanding natural programs using proper decomposition. In *Proceedings of the International Conference on Software Engineering* (pp 62-73). Austin, TX.

Hassan, X., Hauger, D., Nye, G., & Smith, P. (2005). *The use and effectiveness of synchronous audiographic conferencing in modern language teaching and learning (online language tuition): a systematic review of available research*. Retrieved from http://eppi.ioe.ac.uk/EPPIWeb/home.aspx?page=/reel/review_groups/MFL/review_three_abstract.htm

Hatzilygeroudis, I., & Prentzas, J. (2004). Knowledge Representation Requirements for Intelligent Tutoring Systems. *7th International Conference on Intelligent Tutoring Systems,* (pp. 87-97.). Maceio, Alagoas, Brazil: Springer.

Hatzilygeroudis, I., Prentzas, J., & Garofalakis, J. (2005, July). *Personalized learning in web-based intelligent educational systems: technologies and techniques*. Paper presented at the 11th International Conference on Human-Computer Interaction (HCII-2005), Las Vegas, Nevada, USA.

Hayes, B. G. (2001). Where's the data: Is Multimedia Instruction Effective in Training Counselors? *Journal of Technology in Counseling, 1*(1).

Heckman, R., & Annabi, H. (2005). A content analysis comparison of learning processes in online and face-to-face case study discussion. *Journal of Computer-Mediated Communication & Education, 42*(3), 87–107.

Hedges, L. V., & Olkin, I. (1985). *Statistical methods for meta-analysis*. New York: Academic Press.

Heffernan, N. T., Turner, T. E., Lourenco, A. L. N., Macasek, M. A., Nuzzo-Jones, G., & Koedinger, K. R. (2006). The ASSISTment Builder: Towards an Analysis of Cost Effectiveness of ITS creation. Presented at FLAIRS2006, Florida.

Heift, T., & Nicholson, D. (2001). Web delivery of adaptive and interactive language tutoring. *International Journal of Artificial Intelligence in Education, 12*(4), 310–324.

Heilman, M., Collins-Thompson, K., Callan, J., & Eskenazi, M. (2006). Classroom success of an intelligent tutoring system for lexical practice and reading comprehension. In *Proc. of the Ninth International Conference on Spoken Language Processing.*

Hendler, J. (2001). Agents and the Semantic Web. *IEEE Intelligent Systems, 16*(2), 30–37. doi:10.1109/5254.920597

Hendler, J., & Feigenbaum, E. A. (2001). Knowledge is power: the semantic web vision. In N. Zhong, Y. Yao, Liu, & S. Ohsuga (Ed.), *Web Intelligence: Research and Development, Proceedings of the First Asia-Pacific Conference, WI 2001*, lecture notes in artificial intelligence, vol. 2198 (pp. 18–29). Springer: Berlin.

Henze, N., & Nejdl, W. (2001). Adaptation in open corpus hypermedia. *International Journal of Artificial Intelligence in Education, 12*(4), 325–350.

Hewitt, A., & Forte, A. (2006). Crossing boundaries: Identity management and student/faculty relationships on the Facebook. *Poster presented at CSCW, Banff, Alberta.*

Higher Education Funding Council for England. (2005). *HEFCE Strategy for e-Learning*. Retrieved from http://www.hefce.ac.uk/pubs/hefce/2005/05_12/05_12.pdf

Hill, W. E. (1997). *Learning: A Survey of Psychological Interpretations*. Reading, MA: Addison-Wesley Educational Publishers Inc.

Himmelspach, J., & Uhrmacher, A. M. (2007). Plug'n simulate. In *Proceedings of the 40th Annual Simulation Symposium*. IEEE Computer Society. (pp. 137-143).

Hmelo-Silver, Merav, G. (2004). Comparing expert and novice understanding of a compex system from the perspective of structures, behaviors and functions. *Cognitive Science*, *28*, 127–138. doi:10.1207/s15516709cog2801_7

Ho, J.-H., Tsai, C.-W., Yang, C.-S., & Chuang, C.-Y. (2004). Applying data mining and evolutionary algorithm to the analysis of digital learning paths *(In Chinese)*. In *Proceedings of Workshop on Digital Archives Technologies* (pp.155-161), Taipei, Taiwan.

Hoare, C. A. R. (1969). An Axiomatic Basis for Computer Programming. *CACM*, *12*(10), 576–583.

Hobbs, L. J., & Yan, Z. (2008). Cracking the walnut: Using a computer game to impact cognition, emotion, and behavior of highly aggressive fifth grade students. *Computers in Human Behavior*, *24*(2), 421–438. doi:10.1016/j.chb.2007.01.031

Hocker, J., & Wilmont, W. (1991). *Koch, S. & Girard, K. (1997). Resolución de Conflictos en la Escuelas*. Argentina: Editorial Granica.

Holland, J. (1998). *Emergence: from chaos to order*. Reading, MA: Addison-Wesley.

Holland, J. H. (1992). *Adaptation in Natural and Artificial Systems*. Cambridge, MA: MIT Press.

Holt, P., & Dubs, S. (1994). Student Modeling: The Key to Individualized Knowledge-based Instruction. In Greer, J. E., & McCalla, G. I. (Eds.), *The State of Student Modeling*. Berlin, Germany: Springer-Verlag.

Honey, P., & Mumford, A. (1992). *The manual of learning styles* (3rd Ed.). Maidenhead.

Hong H. & Kinshuk, (2004). Adaptation to student learning styles in web based educational systems. In L.Cantoni & C. McLoughlin (Ed.), *Proceedings of ED-MEDIA 2004 - World Conference on Educational Multimedia, Hypermedia & Telecommunications* (pp. 491-496). Lugano, Switzerland: AACE.

Höök, K., & Benyon, D. (2003). *Designing Information Spaces: The Social Navigation Approach*. London: Springer.

Hoppe, U. (1995). The Use of Multiple Student Modeling to Parameterize Group Learning. In J. Greer (Ed.), *Proceedings of AI-ED '95, 7th World Conference on Artificial Intelligence in Education*, (pp. 234-249), Washington, DC: AACE.

Horrocks, I., Patel-Schneider, P. F., Boley, H., Tabet, S., Grosof, B., & Dean, M. (2004). SWRL: A Semantic Web Rule Language Combining OWL and RuleML. *W3C Member Submi*ssion. Retrieved May 6, 2009, from http://www.w3.org/Submission/SWRL/

Hu, S., & Wu, Y. (2006). Student diagnosing model based on neuro-fuzzy for web-based educational systems. *Journal of Computer Information Systems*, *2*(1), 377–382.

Huang, L. (2006). The application of PSO in intelligent assessment paper generation [In Chinese]. *Zhenjiang Institute Journal*, *19*(3), 53–56.

Huang, T.-C., Huang, Y.-M., & Cheng, S.-C. (2008). Automatic and interactive e-Learning auxiliary material generation utilizing particle swarm optimization. *Expert Systems with Applications*, *35*(4), 2113–2122. doi:10.1016/j.eswa.2007.09.039

Huang, Y.-M., Chen, J.-N., & Cheng, S.-C. (2007). A method of cross-level frequent pattern mining for web-based instruction. *Journal of Educational Technology & Society*, *10*(3), 305–319.

Huang, H. M., & Liaw, S. S. (2005). Exploring users' attitudes and intentions toward the web as a survey tool. *Computers in Human Behavior*, *21*, 729–743. doi:10.1016/j.chb.2004.02.020

Hummel, H. G. K., Van den Berg, B., Berlanga, A. J., Drachsler, H., Janssen, J., Nadolski, R., & Koper, R. (2007). Combining social-based and information-based approaches for personalised recommendation on sequencing learning activities. *Learning Technology*, *3*(2), 152–167. doi:10.1504/IJLT.2007.014842

Hunter, J. E., & Schmidt, F. L. (2004). *Methods of meta-analysis: Correcting error and bias in research findings*. Thousand Oaks, CA: Sage Publications, Inc.

Hyacinth, S. N. (1990). Intelligent Tutoring Systems: an overview. *Artificial Intelligence Review*, *4*, 251–277.

IEEE LTSC. (2002). Draft Standard for Learning Object Metadata, IEEE Learning Technology Standards Committee, IEEE 1484.12.1-2002. *IEEE LTSC Working Group*, Retrieved May 06, 2008, from http://ltsc.ieee.org/wg12/files/LOM_1484_12_1_v1_Final_Draft.pdf

Illmann, T., Weber, M., Martens, A., & Seitz, A. (2000). A Pattern-Oriented Design of a Web-Based and Case-Oriented Multimedia Training System in Medicine. 4th World Conference on Integrated Design and Process Technology, Dallas, US.

IsoDynamic. (2001). *E-Learning - A White Paper from IsoDynamic*. Retrieved February 16, 2009, from http://www.isodynamic.com/web/pdf/IsoDynamic_elearning_white_paper.pdf

IsoDynamic. (2006). *What is E-Learning?* Retrieved February 20, 2009, from http://www.isodynamic.com/web/e_learn.htm

Jackson, G. B. (2002, Janurary-March). Intelligent Tutoring Systems, *Technologies Today, TechKnowLogia*, Knowledge Enterprise, Inc. (pp 73-74).

Jacobson, M. J., & Kozma, R. B. (2000). *Innovations in science and mathematics education: Advanced designs for technologies of learning*. Mahwah, NJ: Erlbaum.

Jain, M. (2008). *Generalized Knowledge Representation Architecture for Intelligent Tutoring System.* (Unpublished MS Thesis), Kharagpur, India: Indian Institute of Technology, Jameson, A., Baldes, S., & Kleinbauer, T. (2003). Generative Models of Group Members as Support for Group Collaboration. In *UM'03 9th International Conference on User Modeling*, (pp. 1-14), Johnstown, PA.

Jansen, M. (2003). Matchmaker - a Framework to Support Collaborative Java Applications. In U. Hoppe, F. Verdejo & J. Kay (Eds.), Proc. of the 11th Int. Conf. on Artificial Intelligence in Education AIED. Amsterdam: IOS Press. 529-530.

Janssen, J., Tattersall, C., Waterink, W., Van den Berg, B., Van Es, R., Bolman, C., & Koper, R. (2007). Self-organizing navigational support in lifelong learning: How predecessors can lead the way. *Computers & Education*, *49*, 781–793. doi:10.1016/j.compedu.2005.11.022

Jaques, P. A., & Vicari, R. M. (2007). A BDI approach to infer student's emotions in an intelligent learning environment. *Computers & Education*, *49*(2), 360–384. doi:10.1016/j.compedu.2005.09.002

Jeremic, Z., & Deyedzic, V. (2004). Design patters ITS: Student model implementation. *In IEEE international conference on advanced learning technologies.*

Jhongli, Taiwan. eck, J. E., Chang, K., Mostow, J., & Corbett, A. (2008). Does help help? Introducing the Bayesian Evaluation and Assessment methodology. In *Proceedings of the 9th International Conference on Intelligent Tutoring Systems,* (pp 383-394).

John, K. O. (1988). *Schoolworlds/Microworlds: Computers and the culture of the classroom.* Oxford: Pergamon Press.

Johnson, W. L. (1986). *Intention-based diagnosis of errors in Novice programs*. Los Altos, CA: Morgan Kaufmann Publishers.

Johnson, J. (2006). Can Complexity Help Us Better Understand Risk? *RISK MANAGEMENT-LEICESTER*, *8*(4), 227. doi:10.1057/palgrave.rm.8250023

Johnson, W. L., Rickel, J. W., & Lester, J. C. (2000). Animated pedagogical agents: Face-to-face interaction in interactive learning environments. *International Journal of Artificial Intelligence in Education*, *11*, 47–78.

Johnson, W. L. (1998). Pedagogical agents. In [Beijing, Cina.]. *Proceedings of International Conference on Computers in Education*, *98*, 13–22.

Johnson, W. L., & Soloway, E. (1984). PROUST: Knowledge based program understanding. In *Proceedings of the 7th international Conference on Software Engineering* (pp 369-380). Orlando, FL.

Johnson, W. L., Shaw, E., et al. (2003). Evolution of user interaction: the case of Agent Adele. In *Proceedings Intelligent User Interfaces*.

Jonker, C. M., Robu, V., & Treur, J. (2007). An agent architecture for multi-attribute negotiation using incomplete preference information. *Autonomous Agents and Multi-Agent Systems*, *15*, 221–252. doi:10.1007/s10458-006-9009-y

Juan, T., Pierce, A., & Sterling, L. (2002). Roadmap: Extending the Gaia methodology for complex open systems. In *Proceedings of the 1st ACM Joint Conference on Autonomous Agents and Multi-Agent Systems (AAMAS 2002)* (pp. 3-10). Bologna, Italy.

Junker, B. W., & Sijtsma, K. (2001). Cognitive assessment models with few assumptions, and connections with nonparametric item response theory. *Applied Psychological Measurement*, *25*, 258–272. doi:10.1177/01466210122032064

Kaczmarek, J., & Landowska, K. (2006). Model of Distributed Learning Objects Repository for a Heterogenic Internet Environment. *Interactive Learning Environments*, *14*(1), 1–15. doi:10.1080/10494820600566312

Kagal, L., Perich, F., Chen, H., Tolia, S., Zou, Y., Finin, T., et al. (2002). Agents making sense of the Semantic Web. In *Proceedings of the Innovative Concepts for Agent-Based Systems: 1st International Workshop on Radical Agent Concepts (WRAC 2002)* (pp. 417-433). McLean, VA.

Karampiperis, P., & Sampson, D. (2005). Adaptive learning resources sequencing in educational hypermedia systems. *Journal of Educational Technology & Society*, *8*(4), 128–147.

Karampiperis, P., & Sampson, D. (2004, August). *Adaptive instructional planning using ontologies*. Paper presented at the IEEE International Conference on Advanced Learning Technologies (ICALT'2004), Joensuu, Finland.

Kay, J. (1997). Learner Know Thyself: Student Models to Give Learner Control and Responsibility. In Z. Halim, T. Ottomann & Z. Razak (Eds.), *Proceedings of International Conference on Computers in Education* (pp. 17-24), Association for the Advancement of Computing in Education (AACE).

Kearsley, G. (1987). *Artificial intelligence and instruction-Applications and methods* (p. 158). Reading, MA: Addison-Wesley Publishing.

Keles, A., Ocak, R., Keles, A., & Gülcü, A. (2009). ZOSMAT: Web-based Intelligent Tutoring System for Teaching-Learning Process. [Elsevier.]. *Expert Systems with Applications*, *36*, 1229–1239. doi:10.1016/j.eswa.2007.11.064

Kelly, H. (2005). Games, Cookies, and the Future of Education. *Issues in Science and Technology*, *21*, 33–40.

Kelly, D., & Tangney, B. (2004). *Predicting Learning Characteristics in a Multiple Intelligence Beased Tutoring System*. Paper presented at the VII International Conference on Intelligent Tutoring Systems. Lecture Notes in Computer Science. Springer-Verlag Heidelberg. 678–688.

Kemp, Z., & Lee, H. (2000). A Multidimensional Model for Exploratory Spatiotemporal Analysis. In *Proceedings of the 5th International Conference on GeoComputation*.

King, J. C. (1976). Symbolic Execution and Program Testing. *CACM*, *19*(7), 385–394.

Kinshuk Patel, A. (1997). A Conceptual Framework for Internet Based Intelligent Tutoring Systems. In A. Behrooz (Ed.), *Knowledge Transfer* (pp. 1). London, UK, pp117-124 (ISBN -900427-015-X)

Kintsch, W. (1988). The role of knowledge in discourse comprehension: A construction–integration model. *Psychological Review*, *95*, 163–182. doi:10.1037/0033-295X.95.2.163

Kirkpatrick, D. L. (1998). *Evaluating Training Programs: The Four Levels* (2nd ed.). San Francisco: Berrett-Koehler.

Klawe, M. (1998). When Does The Use Of Computer Games And Other Interactive Multimedia Software Help Students Learn Mathematics? *NCTM Standards 2000 Technology Conference*.

Klir, G. J. (1991). *Facets of systems science*. Springer.

Kodaganallur, V., Weitz, R. R., & Rosenthal, D. (2004). VersaTutor–Architecture for a constraint based intelligent tutor generator. *WWW 2004*. New York.

Koedinger, K. R., Anderson, J. R., Hadley, W. H., & Mark, M. (1997). Intelligent tutoring goes to school in the big city. *International Journal of Artificial Intelligence in Education*, *8*, 30–43.

Koedinger, K. R., & Aleven, V. Heffernan. N. T., McLaren, B., & Hockenberry, M. (2004). Opening the Door to Non-Programmers: Authoring Intelligent Tutor Behavior by Demonstration. In *Proceedings of the 7th International Conference on Intelligent Tutoring Systems*, Maceio, Brazil.

Koedinger, K. R., & Mathan, S. (2004). Distinguishing qualitatively different kinds of learning using log files and learning curves. In the Working Notes of the ITS2004 Workshop on Analyzing Student-Tutor Interaction Logs to Improve Educational Outcomes. Maceiò, Alagoas, Brazil.

Koesling, A. W., Krause, D., & Herder, E. (2008). Flexible Adaptivity in AEHS Using Policies. In Nejdl, W. (Eds.), *AH2008, LNCS 5149* (pp. 410–415). Heidelberg: Springer.

Kontopoulos, E., Vrakas, D., Kokkoras, F., Bassiliades, N., & Vlahavas, I. (2008). An ontology-based planning system for e-course generation. *Expert Systems with Applications*, *35*(1-2), 398–406. doi:10.1016/j.eswa.2007.07.034

Koper, R. (2006). Current research in learning design. *Journal of Educational Technology & Society*, *9*(1), 13–22.

Koper, R. (2004). Increasing learner retention in a simulated learning network using indirect social interaction. *Learning Networks PrePrints Open University of the Netherlands*. Retrieved June 9, 2008, from: http://dspace.ou.nl/bitstream/1820/249/4/preprint-LNsimulation.pdf

Kopf, D. (2007*). E-Learning Market to hit $52.6B by 2010.* Retrieved June 27, 2008, from http://www.thejournal.com/articles/21046

Kosba, E. M. A. M. (2004). *Generating Computer-Based Advice In Web-Based Distance Education Environments.* (Unpublished Ph.D. Thesis), Leeds, UK: University of Leeds

Kriz, W. C., Pushert, M., Karl, J., & Dufter-Weis, A. (2004). Effective *Learning through Gaming Simulation Design.* In: R. Shiratory, K. Arai & F. Kato & (Eds.), Simulation & Gaming (pp. 217-227)

Kuflik, T., & Shoval, P. (2000). User profile generation for intelligent information agents. In *Proceedings of the 2nd International Workshop on Agent-Oriented Information Systems (AOIS 2000)* (pp. 63-72). Stockholm, Sweden.

Kukulska-Hulme, A., & Traxler, J. (Eds.). (2005). *Mobile Learning: A Handbook for Educators and Trainers*. London: Routledge.

Kulik, J. A. (1994). Meta-Analytic studies of findings on computer-based instruction. In Baker, E. L., & O'Neil, H. F. (Eds.), *Technology Assessment in Education and Training* (pp. 9–33). Hillsdale, NJ: Lawrence Erlbaum Associates.

Kumar, S., Kunjithapatham, A., Sheshagiri, M., Finin, T., Joshi, A., Peng, Y., & Cost, R. S. (2002). A personal agent application for the semantic web. In *Proceedings of the 2002 AAAI Fall Symposia on Personalized Agents*. North Falmouth, MA.

Künzel, J. & Hämmer, V. (2003). Simulation in University Education: The Artificial Agent PSI as a Teaching Tool. *Simulation - Special Issue on Modeling and Simulation in Teaching and Training, 82, 11*. 761–767.

Laakso, Malmi, Korhonen, Rajala, Kaila, & Salakoski. (2008). Using Roles of Variables to Enhance Novice'sDebugging Work. *Issues in Informing Science and Information Technology, 5.*

Laird, J., Newell, Allen and Rosenbloom, Paul. (1987). SOAR: An architecture for general intelligence. *Artificial Intelligence*, *33*, 1–64. doi:10.1016/0004-3702(87)90050-6

Lajoie, S. F., & Lesgold, A. (1989). Apprenticeship training in the workplace: Computer-coached practice environment as a new form of apprenticeship. *Machine-Mediated Learning*, *3*, 7–28.

Lajoie, S. P., & Lesgold, A. (1989). Apprenticeship training in the workplace: Computer coached practice environment as a new form of apprenticeship. *Machine-Mediated Learning*, *3*, 7–28.

Lane, H. C. (2006). Prospects for Guided Practice and Efficient Learning. In *Whitepaper for the Army's Science of Learning Workshop*. Hampton, VA: Intelligent Tutoring Systems.

Lane, H. C. (2004). *Natural Language Tutoring and the Novice Programmer*. (Unpublished doctoral dissertation), University of Pittsburgh, PA.

Lane, H. C., & VanLehn, K. (2003). Coached Program Planning: Dialogue-Based Support for Novice Program Design. In *Proceedings of the Thirty-Fourth Technical Symposium on Computer Science Education (SIGCSE)* (pp 148-152).

Laningham, S. (2006, August 22). *Developerworks Interviews: Tim Berners-Lee*, CT316. Retrieved September 16, 2009, from http://www.ibm.com/developerworks/podcast/dwi/cm-int082206txt.html

Laouris, Y., & Eteokleous, N. (2005). We need an educationally relevant definition of mobile learning. In *Proceedings of mLearn 2005*. Retrieved December 20, 2005, from http://www.mlearn.org.za/papers-full.html

Leaf, P., & Keys, S. (2005). Collaborating for Violence Training Health Professionals. American *Journal of Preventive Medicine 29*(5S2):279–287.

Lee, J. S. (1983). Digital image smoothing and the sigma filter. *Computer Vision Graphics and Image Processing*, *24*, 255–269. doi:10.1016/0734-189X(83)90047-6

Lee, C. H. M., Cheng, Y. W., & Rai, S., & Depickere. (2005). What affect student cognitive style in the development of hypermedia system? *Computers & Education*, *45*, 1–19. doi:10.1016/j.compedu.2004.04.006

Lelouche, R. (1999). Intelligent Tutoring Systems from Birth to Now. In: KI-*Künstliche Intelligenz, 4,* 5-11.

Lemut, Dettori, & Du Boulay. (1993). *Cognitive Models and Intelligent Environments for Learning Programming*. New York: Springer-Verlag.

Leutner, D. (1993). Guided Discovery Learning with Computer-based Simulation Games: Effects of Adaptive and Non-adaptive Instructional Support. *Learning and Instruction*, *3*, 113–132. doi:10.1016/0959-4752(93)90011-N

Likert, R. (1932). A Technique for the Measurement of Attitudes. *Archives de Psychologie*, *140*, 5–53.

Linn, M. C., & Dalbey, J. (1989). Cognitive Consequences of Programming Instruction. In Soloway, E., & Spohrer, J. C. (Eds.), *Studying the Novice Programmer* (pp. 57–81). Hillsdale, NJ: Lawrence Erlbaum Associates, Publishers.

Lipsey, M. W., & Wilson, D. B. (2001). *Practical meta-analysis*. Thousand Oaks, CA: Sage Publications, Inc.

Lister, R. (2004). A Multi-National Study of Reading and Tracing Skills in Novice Programmers. *SIGCSE Bulletin*, *36*(4), 119–150. doi:10.1145/1041624.1041673

Lock, Z. (2005). *Performance and Flexibility of Stereotype-based User Models*. (Unpublished Ph.D. Thesis) (Partial fulfilment), Heslington, York: University of York.

Losada, M. (2000). *Meta Learning*. Conference proffered at the course on Art of Business Coaching. Brasília, Manuscript.

Losada, M., & Heaphy, E. (2004). The role of positivity and connectivity in the performance of business teams: a nonlinear dynamics model. In Cameron, K. S & Caza, A. (eds.), *Contributions to positive organizational scholarship. American Behavioral Scientist, 47*(6): 740-765.

Lourenço, O., & Machado, A. (1996). In Defense of Piaget's Theory: A reply to ten common criticisms. *Psychological Review*, *103*, 143–164. doi:10.1037/0033-295X.103.1.143

Lu, P., & Wang, M. (2001). A study on a strategy for automatic assessment paper generation [In Chinese]. *Computer Development & Applications*, *14*(2), 9–11.

Lü, J. (2008). Application of improved PSO in intelligent test paper auto-generation system *(In Chinese). Modern Computer, 2008*(7), 109-111.

Luck, M., Ashri, R., & d'Inverno, M. (2004). *Agent-Based Software Development*. Norwood, MA: Artech House Publishers.

Luyi, S. (2006). Evaluation: a principle method to promote quality of distance education. In *Anais da 22ª Conferência do ICDE (CD-ROM)*, Rio de Janeiro.

Macdonald, J., & Twining, P. (2002). Assessing activity-based learning for a networked course. *British Journal of Educational Technology*, *33*(5), 603–618. doi:10.1111/1467-8535.00295

Madhour, H. Forte, M.,W. (2006). *Semantic Learning Model and eXtended Student Model: Towards an AHAM-based adaptive system*. Paper presented at WBE 2006, Puerto Vallarta, Mexico.

Madsen, K. (2003). Five Years of Framework Building - Lessons Learned. In *Proc. of the OOPSLA Conference*, Anaheim, CA: ACM Press. (pp. 345-352).

Major, N. (1995). How Generic can Authoring Shells Become? In *Proceedings of the Workshop on Authoring Shells for Intelligent Tutoring Systems (AI-ED-95)* (pp. 75-82). Washington, DC.

Makitalo, K., Weinberger, A., Paivi, H., Jarvela, S., & Fischer, F. (2005). Epistemic cooperation scripts in online learning environments: fostering learning by reducing uncertainty. *Computers in Human Behavior*, *21*, 603–622. doi:10.1016/j.chb.2004.10.033

Malone, T. (1983). Guidelines for Designing Educational Computer Programs. *Childhood Education*, *59*, 241–247.

Mandl, H., & Lesgold, A. (Eds.). (1988). *Learning Issues for Intelligent Tutoring Systems*. London: Springer-Verlag.

Manna, Z., & Bradley, A. R. (2007). *Lecture Notes on Verification CS156: Calculus of Computation*. Retrieved November, 13, 2007, from http://cs156.stanford.edu/notes/verify.pdf

Mark, M. A., & Greer, J. E. (1993). Evaluation methodologies for intelligent tutoring systems. *Journal of Artificial Intelligence in Education*, *4*(2/3), 129–153.

Mark, M. A., & Greer, J. E. (1991). The VCR tutor: Evaluating instructional effectiveness. InHammond, K.J. and Gentner, D.Q. (Eds.): Proceedings of *13thAnnual Conference of the Cognitive Science Society*, Hillsdale, NJ: Lawrence Erlbaum Associates.

Martens, R. L., Gulikers, J., & Bastiaens, T. (2004). The impact of intrinsic motivation on e-learning in authentic computer tasks. *Journal of Computer Assisted Learning*, *20*, 368–376. doi:10.1111/j.1365-2729.2004.00096.x

Martens, A. (2004). *Ein Tutoring Prozess Modell für fallbasierte Intelligente Tutoring Systeme*. AKA Verlag infix.

Martens, A., & Himmelspach, J. (2005). Combining Intelligent Tutoring and Simulation Systems. In *Proc. of the Internat. Conference on Simulation in Human Computer Interfaces, SIMCHI, Part of the Western Multi Conference WMC '05*. New Orleans, LA. (pp. 65-70).

Martens, A., Hambach, S., & Lucke, U. (2009). Multiperspective Cooperation based on Boundary Objects. In: In *Proc. of the ICALT 2009, pp. 476-488, The 9th IEEE International Conference on Advanced Learning Technologies.*

Martins, W., & de Carvalho, S. D. (2004). *An Intelligent Tutoring System Based on Self-Organizing Maps. Design, Implementation and Evaluation*. Paper presented at the VII International Conference on Intelligent Tutoring Systems. Lecture Notes in Computer Science. Springer-Verlag Heidelberg 573-579.

Mayer, R. E., Johnson, W. L., Shaw, E., & Sandhu, S. (2006). Constructing computer-based tutors that are socially sensitive: Politeness in educational software. *International Journal of Human-Computer Studies*, *64*(1), 36–42. doi:10.1016/j.ijhcs.2005.07.001

Mayer, R. E. (1989). The Psychology of How Novices Learn Computer Programming. In Soloway, E., & Spohrer, J. C. (Eds.), *Studying the Novice Programmer* (pp. 129–141). Hillsdale, NJ: Lawrence Erlbaum Associates, Publishers.

Mayo, M., Mitrovic, A., & McKenzie, J. (2000). An Intelligent Tutoring System for Capitalization and Punctuation. In *Proc. of the Int. Workshop for Advanced Learning Technologies IWALT* (pp. 151–157). CAPIT.

McAlister, S., Ravenscroft, A., & Scanlon, E. (2004). Combining interaction and context design to support collaborative argumentation using a toll for synchronous. *Computer Mediated Communication*, *20*, 194–204.

McCalla, G. I., & Greer, J. E. (1994). Granularity- based reasoning and belief revision in student models. In Greer, J. E., & McCalla, G. I. (Eds.), *Student Modeling: The Key to Individualized Knowledge-Based Instruction* (pp. 39–62). Berlin: Springer-Verlag.

McCullough, L. E. (2000). *The Effect of Introducing Computers into Introductory Physics Problem-Solving Laboratories.* (Unpublished PhD Thesis), University of Minnesota.

McGovern, J., & Gray, K. (2005). Directions for organisation and management of university learning: Implications from a qualitative survey of student e-learning. In *Proceedings of ASCILITE 2005*. Retrieved January 12, 2006, from http://www.ascilite.org.au/conferences/brisbane05/proceedings.shtml

McLean, N. (2003). *The M-Learning Paradigm: an Overview* (A Report for the Royal Academy of Engineering and the Vodafone Group Foundation). Sydney, Australia: Macquarie University, IMS Australia.

McQuiggan, S. W., Mott, B. W., & Lester, J. C. (2008). Modeling self-efficacy in intelligent tutoring systems: An inductive approach. *User Modeling and User-Adapted Interaction, 18*, 81–123. doi:10.1007/s11257-007-9040-y

McQuiggan, S. W., Robison, J. L., Phillips, R., & Lester, J. C. (2008) Modelling parallel and reactive empathy in virtual agents: an inductive approach. In *Proceedings of the 7th international Joint Conference on Autonomous Agents and Multiagent Systems - Volume 1*. International Conference on Autonomous Agents. International Foundation for Autonomous Agents and Multiagent Systems, (pp. 167-174).

Means, B., Padilla, C., DeBarger, A., & Bakia, M. (2009). *Implementing Data-Informed Decision Making in Schools--Teacher Access, Supports and Use. Report prepared for U.* Menlo Park, CA: S. Department of Education, Office of Planning, Evaluation and Policy Development. Prepared by SRI International.

Mehrabian, A. (1971). *Silent messages*. Belmont, CA: Wadsworth.

Melis, E., & Siekmann, J. (2004). Activemath: An Intelligent Tutoring System for Mathematics. In R. Tadeusiewicz, L.A. Zadeh, L. Rutkowski, J. Siekmann, (Eds.), *7th International Conference 'Artificial Intelligence and Soft Computing' (ICAISC) Lecture Notes in AI LNAI 3070*. Springer-Verlag 91-101.

Menken, M. (n.d.). *JCLIPS - CLIPS for Java*. Retrieved on July 28, 2010, from http://sourceforge.net/projects/jclips/

Merrill, M. (1998). Knowledge analysis for effective instruction. *CBT Solutions* (pp.1-11). Retrieved May 09, 2009 from http://id2.usu.edu/Papers/KnowledgeObjects.PDF

Michel, P., & El Kaliouby, R. (2003). Real time facial expression recognition in video using support vector machines. In *Proceedings of the 5th international Conference on Multimodal interfaces* (ICMI '03), (pp. 258-264). New York: ACM.

Milas, G. (2005). *Research methods in psychology and other social sciences*. Jastrebarsko, Croatia: Naklada Slap. (in Croatian)

MINEDUC. (1996). La Reforma en Marcha. Jornada Escolar Completa Diurna para Todos. Santiago de Chile. Retrieved from http://www.mineduc.cl

MINEDUC. (2001). *Convivencia Escolar: Conclusiones de la Comisión sobre Reflexión y Compromiso por el Derecho a la Educación y la Convivencia Escolar*. Retrieved 2001, from http://www.mineduc.cl

Mishra, P., & Koehler, M. J. (2006). Technological pedagogical content knowledge: A framework for teacher knowledge. *Teachers College Record, 108*(6), 1017–1054. doi:10.1111/j.1467-9620.2006.00684.x

Mislevy, R. J., & Gitomer, D. H. (1996). The role of probability-based inference in an intelligent tutoring system. *User Modeling and User-Adapted Interaction, 5*, 253–282. doi:10.1007/BF01126112

Mislevy, R. J., Steinberg, L. S., & Almond, R. G. (2003). On the structure of educational assessments. *Measurement: Interdisciplinary Research and Perspectives, 1*, 3–67. doi:10.1207/S15366359MEA0101_02

Mislevy, R. J. (1995). Probability-based reasoning in cognitive diagnosis. In Nichols, P., Chipman, S., & Brennan, R. (Eds.), *Cognitively Diagnostic Assessment*. Hillsdale, NJ: Erlbaum.

Mitchell, T. J., Chen, S. Y., & Macredie, R. D. (2005). Hypermedia learning and prior knowledge: domain expertise vs. system expertise. *Journal of Computer Assisted Learning, 21*, 53–64. doi:10.1111/j.1365-2729.2005.00113.x

Mitrovic, A. (2003). An intelligent SQL tutor on the web. *International Journal of Artificial Intelligence in Education, 13*(2–4), 171–195.

Mitrovic, A., & Martin, B. (2002). Using evaluation to shape ITS design: results and experiences with sql-tutor. *International Journal of User Modeling and User-Adapted Interaction, 12*(2-3), 243–379. doi:10.1023/A:1015022619307

Mitrovic, A., & Martin, B. (2002). Evaluating the Effects of Open Student Models on Learning. In P. De Bra, P. Brusilovsky & R. Conejo (Eds.), *Adaptive Hypermedia and Adaptive Web-Based Systems, Proceedings of Second International Conference*. Berlin Heidelberg, Germany: Springer-Verlag.

Mizoguchi, R., & Bourdeu, J. (2000). Using Ontological Engineering to Overcome AI-ED Problems. *International Journal of Artificial Intelligence in Education, 11*(2), 107–121.

Mobilearn (2003). *The Mobilearn Project Vision*. Available at http://www.mobilearn.org/vision/visiton.htm

Mohan, P., Greer, J., & McCalla, G. (2003, August). Instructional planning with learning objects. Paper presented at the 18th International Joint Conference on AI Workshop on Knowledge Representation and Automated Reasoning for E-Learning System (KRR-5), Acapulco, Mexico.

Morris, E. (2001). The design and evaluation of Link: A computer-based learning system for correlation. *British Journal of Educational Technology, 32*(1), 39–52. doi:10.1111/1467-8535.00175

Munro, A. (1994) Authoring interactive graphical models. In De Jong, T.; Towne, D. M.; and Spada, H., eds., *The Use of Computer Models for Explication, Analysis and Experiential Learning Sciences 5*(1), 49-94.

Murray, T. (1999). Authoring intelligent tutoring systems: An analysis of the state of the art. *International Journal of Artificial Intelligence in Education, 10*, 98–129.

Murray, C. D., Fox, J., & Pettifer, S. (2007). Absorption, dissociation, locus of control and presence in virtual reality. *Computers in Human Behavior, 23*, 1347–1354. doi:10.1016/j.chb.2004.12.010

Mužić, V., & Rodek, S. (1987). *Computers in school transformation*. Zagreb, Croatia: Školska knjiga, (in Croatian).

Nadler, J., Thompson, L., & Boven, L. (2003). Learning Negotiation Skills: Four Models of Knowledge Creation and Transfer. *Management Science, 49*, 529–540. doi:10.1287/mnsc.49.4.529.14431

Naismith, L., Lonsdale, P., Vavoula, G., & Sharples, M. (2004). *NESTA Futurelab Report 11: Literature Review in Mobile Technologies and Learning*. Bristol, UK: NESTA Futurelab. Retrieved December 27, 2005, from http://www.nestafuturelab.org/research/reviews/reviews_11_and12/11_01.htm

Newell, A. (1990). *Unified theories of cognition*. Cambridge, MA: Harvard University Press.

Newell, A., & Simon, H. (1972). *Human Problem Solving*. Englewood Cliffs, NJ: Prentice-Hall.

Nicol, D. J., & MacLeod, I. A. (2005). Using shared workspace and wireless laptops to improve collaborative project learning in an engineering design class. *Computers & Education, 44*, 477–487. doi:10.1016/j.compedu.2004.04.008

Niemczyk, S. (2000). *On pedagogical-aware navigation of educational media through virtual tutors*. Internal Document, Department of Civil & Environmental Engineering, Massachusetts Inst. of Technology.

Nikraz, M., Caire, G., & Bahri, P. A. (2006). A methodology for the analysis and design of multi-agent systems using JADE. *International Journal of Computer Systems Science and Engineering, 21*, 99–116.

No Child Left Behind Act of 2001, Pub. L. No. 107-110, 115 Stat. 1425. (2002). *No Child Left Behind Act of 2001*. Retrieved September 6, 2005, from www.ed.gov/legislation/ESEA02/

Noble, J. (1998) Towards a pattern language for object oriented design. In Proceedings of Technology of Object-Oriented Languages. *TOOLS 28*, 2-13.

Novak, J. D. (1998). *Learning, creating, and using knowledge: Concept maps as facilitative tools in schools and corporations*. Mahwah, NJ: Lawrence Erlbaum Associates.

Nowak, K. L., Watt, J., & Walther, J. B. (2005). The influence of synchrony and sensory modality on the person perception process in computer- mediated groups. *Journal of Computer-mediated Communication, 10*(3), Article 3.

Nuzzo-Jones, G., Walonoski, J. A., Heffernan, N. T., & Livak, T. (2005). *The eXtensible tutor architecture: A new foundation for ITS.* Presented at theWorkshop on Adaptive Systems for Web-Based Education: Tools and Reusability held at the 12th Annual Conference on Artificial Intelligence in Education. Amsterdam, Netherlands.

Nwana, H., Ndumu, D., Lee, L., & Collis, J. (1999). ZEUS: A Tool-Kit for Building Distributed Multi-Agent Systems. *Applied Artificial Intelligence Journal, 13*, 129–186. doi:10.1080/088395199117513

O'Connor, M., Knublauch, H., & Tu, S. (2005). Supporting Rule System Interoperability on the Semantic Web with SWRL. In *Proceedings. 4th International Semantic Web Conference (ISWC-2005)* (pp.974-986). Held Galway, Ireland.

O'Neill, K., Singh, G., & O'Donoghue, J. (2004). Implementing eLearning Programmes for Higher Education: A Review of the Literature. *Journal of Information Technology Education, 3*, 313–323.

O'Reilly, T. (2006, October 12). Web 2.0 compact definition: Trying again. *O'Reilly radar*. Retrieved September 15, 2009, from http://radar.oreilly.com/2006/12/web-20-compact-definition-tryi.html

Oblinger, D. G. (2003). *Boomers & gen-Xers, millennials: Understanding the "new students"*. EDUCAUSE Review.

Oblinger, D. G. (2004). The Next Generation of Educational Engagement. *Journal of Interactive Media in Education*, 2004(8). Retrieved January 16, 2006, from http://www-jime.open.ac.uk/2004/8/oblinger-2004-8-disc-paper.html

Oertel, M. (2007). *Entwicklung eines Frameworks für intelligente Lehr-/Lernsysteme. (Masterthesis)*. Germany: University of Rostock.

Oertel, M., Martens, A., & Himmelspach, J. (2008). Teaching and Training System Plus Modeling and Simulation - A Component Based Approach. to appear in: Proc. of the EUROSIM.

Oguejiofor, E., Kicinger, R., Popovici, E., Arciszewski, T., & De Jong, K. (2004). Intelligent Tutoring Systems: an ontology-based approach. *International Journal of IT in Architecture. Engineering and Construction, 2*(2), 115–128.

Olson, L. (2005). Special report: testing takes off. *Education Week, November 30*, 10–14.

Omicini, A. (2001). SODA: Societies and infrastructures in the analysis and design of agent-based systems. In *Proceedings of the 1st International Workshop on Agent-Oriented Software Engineering (AOSE'01)* (pp. 185-193). Montreal, Canada.

Onaindía, E., & Sapena, O. Garrido. A. (2007, October). *An AI planning-based approach for automated design of learning routes*. Paper presented at the ECEL 2007, 6th European Conference on e-Learning, Copenhagen, Denmark.

Oreilly, T. (2007). What Is Web 2.0: Design Patterns and Business Models for the Next Generation of Software. *SSRN eLibrary*, Communications & Strategies, (65), 17-37.

Overmyer, S. P. (1999). If only my intelligent pedagogical agent could! *Journal of Educational Technology & Society, 2*(1).

OWL. (2007). *Web Ontology Language OWL*. Retrieved from http://www.w3.org/2004/OWL

Pahl, C., & Holohan, E. (2004). Ontology Technology for the Development and Deployment of Learning Technology Systems - a Survey. In L. Cantoni & C. McLoughlin (Ed.), *Proceedings of World Conference on Educational Multimedia, Hypermedia and Telecommunications 2004* (pp. 2077-2084). Chesapeake, VA: AACE.

Paiva, A. (1997). Learner Modelling for Collaborative Learning Environments. In B. de_Boulay & R. Mizoguchi (Eds.), *Proceedings of the International Conference on Artificial Intelligence in Education (AI-ED 97)*, (pp. 215-222), Kobe, Japan: IOS Press.

Palmer, J. A. (2001). *Fifty Modern Thinkers on Education: From Piaget to the Present Day* (1 ed.). London, UK: Routledge.

Pantic, M., & Rothkrantz, L. J. M. (1999). An Expert System for Multiple Emotional Classification of Facial Expressions. *IEEE International Conference on Tools with Artificial Intelligence*, Chicago.

Papanikolaou, K., Grigoriadou, M., Knornilakis, H., & Magoulas, G. (2003). Personalizing the interaction in a web-based educational hypermedia system: The case of INSPIRE. *User Modeling and User-Adapted Interaction, 13*, 213–267. doi:10.1023/A:1024746731130

Papanikolaou, K. A., Grigoriadou, M., Kornilakis, H., & Magoulas, G. D. (2002). INSPIRE: An INtelligent System for Personalized Instruction in a Remote Environment. In *Revised Papers From the Nternational Workshops Ohs-7, Sc-3, and Ah-3 on Hypermedia: Openness, Structural Awareness, and Adaptivity* (August 14 - 18, 2001). S. Reich, M. Tzagarakis, and P. D. Bra (Ed), Lecture Notes In Computer Science, 2266, 215-225.

Paramythis, A., & Loidl-Reisinger, S. (2004). Adaptive Learning Environments and e-Learning Standards. *Electronic Journal of e-Learning 2(2)*. Retrieved May 09, 2009 from http://www.ejel.org/volume-2/vol2-issue1/issue1-art11.htm

Pardos, Z. A., Feng, M., Heffernan, N. T., & Heffernan, C. L. (2007). Analyzing Fine-Grained Skill Models Using Bayesian and Mixed Effect Methods. In Luckin & Koedinger (Eds.). In *Proceedings of the 13th Conference on Artificial Intelligence in Education*. pp. 626-628. Amsterdam, Netherlands: IOS Press

Pardos, Z. A., Heffernan, N. T., Anderson, B., & Heffernan, C. L. (2006). *Using Fine Grained Skill Models to Fit Student Performance with Bayesian Networks.* Workshop in Educational Data Mining held at the Eighth International Conference on Intelligent Tutoring Systems. Taiwan.

Pardos, Z., & Heffernan, N. (2009a). Detecting the Learning Value of Items in a Randomized Problem Set. In *Proceedings of the 14th International Conference on Artificial Intelligence in Education (AIED-2009).* IOS Press. Brighton, UK.

Pardos, Z., & Heffernan, N. T. (2009b). Determining the Significance of Item Order In Randomized Problem Sets. In *Proceedings of the Second International Conference on Educational Data Mining*. Cordoba, Spain.

Parunak, H. V. D. (1997). "Go to the ant": Engineering principles from natural multi-agent systems. *Annals of Operations Research, 75*, 69–101. doi:10.1023/A:1018980001403

Patel, A. Kinshuk, Russell, D., & Oppermann, R. (2001). Intelligent Tutoring Systems: Confluence of Information Science and Cognitive Science. In *Proceedings of the 2001 Informing Science Conference* (pp. 392-397). Krakow, Poland.

Patel-Schneider, P. F., Hayes, P., & Horrocks, I. (2004). *Web Ontology Language (OWL) Abstract Syntax and Semantics*. Retrieved June 2, 2009, from W3C Recommendation: http://www.w3.org/TR/2004/REC-owl-semantics-20040210/

Patvarczki, J., Almeida, S., Beck, J., & Heffernan, N. T. (2008). Lessons Learned from Scaling Up a Web-Based Intelligent Tutoring System. In Woolf & Aimeur (Eds.), *Proceeding of the 9th International Conference on Intelligent Tutoring Systems*. Berlin, Germany: Springer-Verlag.

Patvarczki, J., Politz, J., & Heffernan, N. (2009). *Scalability and Robustness in the Domain of Web Based Tutoring. Scalability issues.* Presented at AIED Workshop at the 14th International Conference on Artificial Intelligence in Education. Brighton, UK.

Paulista, G. (2005). *O impacto da conectividade e da positividade/negatividade na gestão do conhecimento: Uma intervenção baseada nas teorias do caos e da complexidade e dinâmica não-linear* (Master's Dissertation). Brasília: Universidade Católica de Brasília.

Paulsen, M. F. (2002). *Online Education Systems: Discussion and definition of terms*. Retrieved February 10, 2009, from http://www.nettskolen.com/forskning/Definition%20of%20Terms.pdf

Peachey, D. R., & McCalla, G. I. (1986). Using planning techniques in intelligent tutoring systems. *Man-Machine Studies, 24*, 79–98.

Pearl, J. (1988). *Probabilistic Reasoning in Intelligent Systems: Networks of Plausible Inference*. San Francisco: Morgan Kaufmann.

Peña, C., Marzo, J., de la Rosa, J., & Fabregat, R. (2002). *Un sistema de tutoría inteligente adaptativo considerando estilos de aprendizaje*. In IE.

Peraya, D., Piguet, A., & Joye, F. (1999). *Rapport d'information sur les mondes virtuels. Rapport rédigé pour l» office fédéral de la formation professionnelle et le la technique*. Suisse: Berne.

Pérez, J. J. (2001). *Programación Neurolinguística y sus estilos de aprendizaje*. Retrieved October 2006, from http://www.aldeaeducativa.com/aldea/tareas2.asp?which=1683

Perkins, D. N., Hancock, C., Hobbs, R., Martin, F., & Simmons, R. (1989). Conditions of Learning. In Soloway, E., & Spohrer, J. C. (Eds.), *Studying the Novice Programmer* (pp. 261–280). Hillsdale, NJ: Lawrence Erlbaum Associates, Publishers.

Person, N. K., & Graesser, A. C. (2003). Fourteen Facts About Human Tutoring: Food for Thought for ITS Developers. In C. P. Rosé, & V. Aleven, (Ed.), *Supplementary Proceedings of the 11th International Conference on Artificial Intelligence in Education (AIED2003), VI: Workshop on Tutorial Dialogue Systems: with a view on the classroom*, (pp. 335-344).

Petters, O. (2001). *Didática do ensino a distância*. São Leopoldo, RS: Editora Unisinos.

Peylo, C., Thelen, T., Rollinger, C., & Gust, H. (2000). A Web-based intelligent educational system for PROLOG. In Peylo, C. (Ed.), *Proceedings of the International Workshop on Adaptive and Intelligent Web-based Educational Systems* (held in Conjunction with ITS 2000), Technical Report of the Institute for Semantic Information Processing, Osnabru¨ ck, (pp. 85–96).

Phillips, R., & Gilding, T. (2003). *Approaches to evaluating the effect of ICT on student learning*. ALT Starter Guide 8.

Piaget, J. (1967). *A psicologia da Inteligência*. Lisboa: Editora Fundo de Cultura S.A.

Picard, R. W. (1998). Towards Agents that Recognize Emotion. In *Proceedings of IMAGINA*, Monaco.

Pintrich, P. (2003). Motivation and classroom learning. *Handbook of Psychology: Educational Psychology, 7*, 103-122.

Poli, R. (1996). Ontology for Knowledge Organization. In Green, R. (Ed.), *Knowledge organization and change* (pp. 313–319). Frankfurt: Indeks.

Polsani, P. R. (2003). Use and Abuse of Reusable Learning Objects. *Journal of Digital Information, 3*(4), 11–21.

Prensky, M. (2001). Digital natives, digital immigrants. *Horizon, 9*(5), 1–6. doi:10.1108/10748120110424816

Quan, H., & Fan, G. (1999). The study in an intelligent assessment paper generation system based on Genetic Algorithms [In Chinese]. *Journal of Wuhan University: Natural Science Edition, 45*(5), 758–760.

Quignard, M., & Baker, M. (1999). Favouring modellable computer-mediated argumentative dialogue in collaborative problem-solving situations. In Lajoie, S. P., & Vivet, M. (Eds.), *Artificial Intelligence in Education*. IOS Press.

Quinn, C. (2000). M-Learning. Mobile, Wireless, In-Your-Pocket Learning. *Linezine, Fall 2000*. Available at http://www.linezine.com/2.1/features/cqmmwiyp.htm

Ramírez, E., & Clark, K. (2009, Feb/). *What Arne Duncan Thinks of No Child Left Behind: The new education secretary talks about the controversial law and financial aid forms*. Retrieved on March 8, 2009, from http://www.usnews.com/articles/education/2009/02/05/what-arne-duncan-thinks-of-no-child-left-behind.html

Ramsden, P. (1988). *Improving learning: New perspectives*. London: Kogan Page.

Rasch, G. (1960/1980). *Probabilistic models for some intelligence and attainment tests. (Copenhagen, Danish Institute for Educational Research), expanded edition (1980) with foreword and afterword by B. D. Wright.* Chicago: The University of Chicago Press.

Razzaq, L., Parvarczki, J., Almeida, S. F., Vartak, M., Feng, M., Heffernan, N. T., & Koedinger, K. (2009). *The ASSISTment builder: Supporting the Life-cycle of ITS Content Creation*. IEEE Transactions on Learning Technologies.

Razzaq, L., & Heffernan, N. T. (2006). Scaffolding vs. hints in the Assistment System. In Ikeda, Ashley & Chan (Eds.), *Proceedings of the 8th International Conference on Intelligent Tutoring Systems*, (pp. 635-644. Springer-Verlag: Berlin.

Razzaq, L., Feng, M., Nuzzo-Jones, G., Heffernan, N. T., Koedinger, K. R., Junker, B., et al. Upalekar. R, Walonoski, J. A., Macasek. M. A., & Rasmussen, K. P. (2005). The Assistment Project: Blending Assessment and Assisting. In C.K. Looi, G.McCalla, B. Bredeweg, & J. Breuker (Eds.) *Proceedings of the 12th Artificial Intelligence In Education,*(pp 555–562). Amsterdam: ISO Press.

Razzaq, L., Heffernan, N. T., & Lindeman, R. W. (2007). What level of tutor interaction is best? In Luckin & Koedinger (Eds.), *Proceedings of the 13th Conference on Artificial Intelligence in Education*. Amsterdam: IOS Press.

Reisslein, J., & Seeling, P., & Reisslein. (2005). Integrating emerging topics through online team design in a hybrid communication networks course: Interaction patterns and impact of prior knowledge. *The Internet and Higher Education*, *8*, 145–165. doi:10.1016/j.iheduc.2005.03.004

Reiter, E., & Dale, R. (2000). *Building Natural Language Generation Systems*. Cambridge, UK: Cambridge University. Press.

Renkl, A. (1997). Learning from worked-out examples: A study on individual differences. *Cognitive Science*, *21*, 1–29. doi:10.1207/s15516709cog2101_1

Rickel, J. W. (1989). Intelligent Computer-Aided Instruction: A Survey Organized Around System Components. *IEEE Transactions on Systems, Man, and Cybernetics*, *19*(1), 40–57. doi:10.1109/21.24530

Riffel, S., & Sibley, D. (2005). Using web-based instruction to improve large undergraduate biology courses: An evaluation of a hybrid course. *Computers & Education*, *44*(3), 217–235. doi:10.1016/j.compedu.2004.01.005

Riley, G. (n.d.). *CLIPS: A Tool for Building Expert Systems*. Retrieved July 28, 2010, from http://clipsrules.sourceforge.net/

Ritter, S., & Koedinger, K. (1996). An architecture for plug-in tutor agents. *Journal of Artificial Intelligence in Education*, *7*(3-4), 315–347.

Ritter, S. (1997). PAT Online: A model-tracing tutor on the world-wide web. In P. Brusilovsky, K. Nakabayashi, & S. Ritter (Ed.), *Proceedings of Workshop Intelligent Educational Systems on the World Wide Web at 8th World Conference on Artificial Intelligence in Education* (pp. 11–17). Kobe, Japan: ISIR.

Roberts, J. M., & Sutton-Smith, B. (1962). Child Training and Game Involvement. *Ethnology*, *1*, 166–185. doi:10.2307/3772873

Rocha, I. (n.d.). *Uma análise do caos na dinâmica do espaço emocional*. (In Press)

Rodrigues, M., Novais, P., & Santos, M. F. (2005). *Future Challenges in Intelligent Tutoring Systems – A Framework*. Recent Research Developments in Learning Technologies.

Rodrigues, L. M. L., & Carvalho, M. (2004). *Emotional and motivational ITS architecture*. Paper presented at the IEEE International Conference on Advanced Learning Technologies, ICALT 276-280.

Rogers, T. J., Ross, R., & Subrahmanian, V. S. (2000). IMPACT: A system for building agent applications. *Journal of Intelligent Information Systems*, *14*, 95–113. doi:10.1023/A:1008727601100

Romero, C., & Ventura, S. (2007). Educational data mining: A survey from 1995 to 2005. *Expert Systems with Applications*, *33*, 135–146. doi:10.1016/j.eswa.2006.04.005

Rosé, C. P. (2000). Syntactic Framework for Semantic Interpretation. In *Proceedings of the Workshop on Linguistic Theory and Grammar Implementation 2000*. Birmingham, UK.

Rose, D. H., & Strangman, N. (2007). Universal design for learning: Meeting the challenge of individual learning differences through a neurocognitive perspective. *Universal Access in the Information Society*, *5*(4), 381-391.

Rosenberg, E. L., & Ekman, P. (1994). Coherence between expressive and experiential systems in emotion. *Cognition and Emotion*, *8*, 201–229. doi:10.1080/02699939408408938

Rosić, M. (2000). *Establishing of Distance Education Systems within the Information Infrastructure*, Faculty of Electrical Engineering and Computing, Zagreb, Croatia, (MS Thesis), (in Croatian)

Rosić, M., Glavinić, V., & Stankov, S. (2001). DTEx-Sys – A Web Oriented Intelligent Tutoring System. In *Proceedings of the International Conference on Trends in Communications (EUROCON'01)* (pp. 255-258). Bratislava, Slovakia.

Rossano, V., Joy, M., Roselli, T., & Sutinen, E. (2005). A taxonomy for definitions and applications of learning objects: A meta-analysis of ICALT papers. *Journal of Educational Technology & Society*, *8*(4), 148–160.

Rothman, S. (2001). *2001 MCAS Reporting Workshop: The second generation of MCAS results. Massachusetts Department of Education.* Retrieved November 2006, from www.doe.mass.edu/mcas/2001/news/reporting wkshp.pps

Ruch, W. (1995). Will the real relationship between facial expression and affective experience please stand up: the case of exhilaration. *Cognition and Emotion*, *9*, 33–58. doi:10.1080/02699939508408964

Rumelhart, D. E., & McClelland, J. L. (1989). *Explorations in Distributed Processing. A Handbook of Models, Programs and Exercises* (Book, B., Ed.). Massachusetts Institute of Technology.

Russell, M., & Masters, J. (2009). *Formative Assessment Tools for Algebra and Geometry*. Presentation at Technology Supports for Formative Assessment Symposium of 2009 American Educational Research Association (AERA) Annual Meeting. San Diego, CA.

Ryan, R. M., & Deci, E. L. (2000). Self-determination theory and the facilitation of intrinsic motivation, social developments and well being. *The American Psychologist*, *55*, 68–78. doi:10.1037/0003-066X.55.1.68

Sahbi, H., & Geman, D. (2006). A Hierarchy of Support Vector Machines for Pattern Detection. *Journal of Machine Learning Research*, *7*, 2087–2123.

Salen, K., & Zimmerman, E. (2004). *Rules of Play*. Cambridge, MA: MIT Press.

Sallas, E., & Cannon-Bowers, J. (2001). The science of training: a decade of progress. *Annual Review of Psychology*, *52*, 471–499. doi:10.1146/annurev.psych.52.1.471

Sampson, D., & Karagiannidis, C. (2002). From Content Objects to Learning Objects: Adding Instructional Information to Educational Metadata. In *Proceedings of the IEEE International Conference on Advanced Learning Technologies (ICALT 02)* (pp. 513-518).

Saner, R. (2008). *The expert negotiator: Strategy, tactics, motivation, behaviour, leadership* (3rd ed.). Leiden, The Netherlands: Koninklijke Brill NV.

Sao Pedro, M., Gobert, J., Heffernan, N., & Beck, J. (2009). Comparing Pedagogical Approaches for Teaching the Control of Variables Strategy. In *Proceedings of the Cognitive Science Society Annual 2009 Conference*. Amsterdam.

Sarrafzadeh, A., Alexander, S., Dadgostar, F., Fan, C., & Bigdeli, A. (2008). How do you know that I don't understand? A look at the future of intelligent tutoring systems. *Elsevier Journal-. Computers in Human Behavior*, *24*(4), 1342–1363. doi:10.1016/j.chb.2007.07.008

Savery, J. R., & Duffy, T. M. (1995). Problem Based Learning: An instructivist model and its constructivist framework. *Educational Technology*, *35*(5), 31–38.

Schank, R. C., & Abelson, R. P. (1977). *Scripts, plans, goals, and understanding: An inquiry into human knowledge structures*. Hillsdale, NJ: Erlbaum.

Scheines, R., Leinhardt, G., & Smith, J., & Cho, Kwangsu. (2005). Replacing lecture with web-based course materials. *Journal of Educational Computing Research*, *32*(1), 1–26. doi:10.2190/F59B-382T-E785-E4J4

Schellens, T., & Valcke, M. (2005). Collaborative learning in asynchronous discussion groups: what about the impact on cognitive processing? *Computers in Human Behavior*, *21*, 957–975. doi:10.1016/j.chb.2004.02.025

Schiaffino, S., Garcia, P., & Amandi, A. (2008). eTeacher: Providing personalized assistance to e-learning students. *Computers & Education*, *51*, 1744–1754. doi:10.1016/j.compedu.2008.05.008

Schreiber, G., Akkermans, H., Anjewierden, A., Hoog, R., Shadbolt, N., & Velde, W. (2000). *Knowledge Engineering and Management, The CommonKADS Methodology*. Cambridge, MA: MIT Press.

Schümmer, T., & Lukosch, S. (2007). *Patterns for Computer-Mediated Interaction, Wiley Software Patterns*. New York: Wiley & Sons.

Self, J. (1999). The defining characteristics of intelligent tutoring systems research: ITSs care, precisely. *International Journal of Artificial Intelligence in Education*, (10): 350–364.

Self, J. A. (1990). Theoretical foundations for intelligent tutoring systems. *International Journal of Artificial Intelligence in Education*, *1*(4), 3–14.

Semet, Y., Lutton, E., & Collet, P. (2003). Ant colony optimization for e-learning: observing the emergence of pedagogic suggestions [Indianapolis, IN.]. *Proceedings of IEEE Swarm Intelligence Symposium*, *03*, 46–52.

Shaffer, D. W., Squire, K. D., Halverson, R., & Gee, J. P. (2005). Video Games and the Future of Learning. *Phi Delta Kappan*, *87*(2), 104–111.

Shang, Y., Shi, H., & Chen, S. (2001). An intelligent distributed environment for active learning. In *WWW 01*.

Sharma, S. K., & Kitchens, F. L. (2004). Web Services Architecture for M-Learning. *Electronic Journal on e-Learning, 2*(1), 203-216.

Sharpe, R., & Benfield, G. (2005). The student experience of e-Learning in higher education: A review of the literature. *Brookes eJournal of Learning and Teaching, 1*(3), 1-22.

Shell, G. R. (1995). Computer-Assisted Negotiation and Mediation: Where We Are and Where We Are Going. *Negotiation Journal*, *11*, 117–121. doi:10.1111/j.1571-9979.1995.tb00052.x

Shipman, F., Furuta, R., Brenner, D., Chung, C., & Hsieh, H. (2000). Guided paths through web-based collections: Design, experiences, and adaptations. *Journal of the American Society for Information Science American Society for Information Science*, *51*, 260–272. doi:10.1002/(SICI)1097-4571(2000)51:3<260::AID-ASI5>3.0.CO;2-J

Shoham, Y., Powers, R., & Grenager, T. (2007). If multi-agent learning is the answer, what is the question? *Artificial Intelligence*, *171*, 365–377. doi:10.1016/j.artint.2006.02.006

Shute, V. J., & Psotka, J. (1995). Intelligent Tutoring Systems: Past, Present, and Future. In Jonassen, D. (Ed.), *Handbook of Research on Educational Communication and Technology*.

Siemer, J., & Angelides, M. (1995). Evaluating intelligent tutoring with gaming-simulations. In *WSC '95: Proceedings of the 27th conference on Winter simulation* (pp. 1376-1383). Arlington, VA: ACM Press.

Silva, M., & Santos, E. (2006). *Avaliação de aprendizagem em educação online*. São Paulo: Loyola.

Silvio, J. (2000). *La virtualización de la universidad: cómo podemos transformar la educación superior com la tecnología?*Caracas: IESALC/UNESCO.

Simon, H. A. (1996). *The sciences of the artificial*. Cambridge, MA: The MIT Press.

Simon, H. A. (1980). Problem solving and education. In Tuma, D. T., & Reif, F. (Eds.), *Problem solving and education: Issues in teaching and research*. Hillsdale, NJ: Erlbaum.

Singer, J. D., & Willett, J. B. (2003). *Applied longitudinal data analysis: Modeling change and occurrence*. New York: Oxford University Press. doi:10.1093/acprof:oso/9780195152968.001.0001

Singh, H. (2003). Leveraging Mobile and Wireless Internet. *Learning Circuits, September 2003*. Available at http://www.learningcircuits.com/2003/sep2003/singh.htm

Singley, M. K., Singh, M., Fairweather, P., Farrell, R., & Swerling, S. (2000). Algebra jam: supporting teamwork and managing roles in a collaborative learning environment. In *Proceedings of the 2000 ACM conference on Computer supported cooperative work*, Philadelphia, PA: ACM.

Singular Inversions, Inc. (2009). *The FaceGen Modeler User Manual*. Retrieved January 8, 2009 from http://www.facegen.com/modeller_help.htm

Sklar, E., & Richards, D. (2006). The Use of Agents in Human Learning Systems. In *Proceedings of the 5th International Joint Conference on Autonomous Agents and Multiagent Systems (AAMAS 2006)* (pp. 767-774). Hakodate, Japan.

Sleeman, D. H., & Brown, J. S. (1982). Introduction - Intelligent Systems. In D. H. Sleeman & J. S. Brown (Eds.), *Intelligent Tutoring Systems* (pp. 1-10). London: Academic Press, Inc (Ltd).

Smith, A. S. G., & Blandford, A. (2003). MLTutor: An application of machine learning algorithms for an adaptive web-based information system. *International Journal of Artificial Intelligence in Education*, *13*(2–4), 233–260.

Spector, L. (2006). Evolution of artificial intelligence. *Artificial Intelligence*, *170*, 1251–1253. doi:10.1016/j.artint.2006.10.009

Squire, K., & Jenkins, H. (2003). Harnessing the power of games in education. *Insight (American Society of Ophthalmic Registered Nurses)*, *3*, 5–33.

SQWRL (Semantic Query-Enhanced Web Rule Language). *Protege Wiki Home Page*. Retrieved May 6, 2009, from http://protege.cim3.net/cgi-bin/wiki.pl?SQWRL

Srbljic, S. (2002*). Language processors 2: analysis of source and synthesis of target language*. Zagreb, Croatia: Element (in Croatian language)

Stankov, S., Rosić, M., & Glavinić, V. (2001). Using Quizzes in an Intelligent Tutoring System. In [Maribor, Slovenia.]. *Proceedings of International Summer School of Automation, CEEPUS CZ, 103*, 87–91.

Stankov, S., Rosic, M., Žitko, B., & Grubišić, A. (2008). TEx-Sys model for building intelligent tutoring systems. *Computers & Education*, *51*(3), 1017–1036. doi:10.1016/j.compedu.2007.10.002

Stankov, S. (1997). *Isomorphic Model of the System as the Basis of Teaching Control Principles in an Intelligent Tutoring System*, Faculty of Electrical Engineering, Mechanical Engineering and Naval Architecture, Croatia, (PhD Thesis), (in Croatian)

Stankov, S. (2003). Project TP-02/0177-01 Web oriented intelligent hypermedial authoring shell, Croatia: Ministry of Science and Technology, (2003-2005).

Stathacopoulou, R., Magoulas, G. D., Grigoriadou, M., & Samarakou, M. (2005). Neuro-fuzzy knowledge processing in intelligent learning environments for improved student diagnosis. *Information Sciences*, *170*(2-4), 273–307. doi:10.1016/j.ins.2004.02.026

StatSoft. (2008). *Chi-square table*. Retrieved November 09, 2009, from http://www.statsoft.com/textbook/ sttable.html#chi

Stiggins, R. (2005). From formative assessment to assessment FOR learning: A path to success in standards-based schools. *Phi Delta Kappan*, *87*(4), 324–328.

Suebnukarn, S., & Haddawy, P. (2006). Modeling individual and collaborative problem-solving in medical problem-based learning. *User Modeling and User-Adapted Interaction*, *16*(3-4), 211–248. doi:10.1007/s11257-006-9011-8

Suebnukarn, S., & Haddawy, P. (2004). A collaborative intelligent tutoring system for medical problem based learning. *In IUI_04*, Madeira, Funchal, Portugal.

Suraweera, P., & Mitrovi, C. A. (2002). A constraint-based tutor for database modeling. In *Proceedings 6th international conference on intelligent tutoring systems ITS*. Kermit.

Sycara, K., Giampapa, J. A., Langley, B. K., & Paolucci, M. (2003). The RETSINA MAS, a Case Study. In Garcia, A. (Ed.), *Software Engineering for Large-Scale Multi-Agent Systems: Research Issues and Practical Applications* (*Vol. 2603*, pp. 232–250). Berlin: Springer. doi:10.1007/3-540-35828-5_15

Szyperski, C. (2002). *Component Software. Addison Wesley, Component Software Series*. New York: ACM Press.

Tadić, M., & Fulgosi, S. (2003). Building the Croatian Morphological Lexicon. In *Proceedings of the EACL2003 Workshop on Morphological Processing of Slavic Languages*, (pp. 41-46). Budapest, Hungary.

Takatalo, J., Nymana, G., & Laaksonen, L. (2008). Components of human experience in virtual environments. *Computers in Human Behavior*, *24*, 1–15. doi:10.1016/j.chb.2006.11.003

Tang, T., & McCalla, G. (2005). Smart Recommendation for an evolving e-learning system: Architecture and experiment. *e-Learning, 4*(1), 105-129.

Tatsuoka, K. K. (1990). Toward an Integration of Item Response Theory and Cognitive Error Diagnosis. In Frederiksen, N., Glaser, R., Lesgold, A., & Shafto, M. G. (Eds.), *Diagnostic monitoring of skill and knowledge acquisition* (pp. 453–488). Hillsdale, NJ: Lawrence Erlbaum Associates.

Tatsuoka, M. (1993). Effect size. In Keren, G., & Lewis, C. (Eds.), *A Handbook for Data Analysis in the Behavioral Sciences* (pp. 461–481). Mahwah, NJ: Lawrence Erlbaum Associates.

Tedesco, P. A., & Rosatelli, M. C. (2004). Helping Groups Become Teams: Techniques for Acquiring and Maintaining Group Models. In J. Mostow & P. Tedesco (Eds.), *Designing Computational Models of Collaborative Learning Interaction.).* Paper presented at the ITS 2004 Workshop, Maceio-Alagoas, Brazil.

Thalmann, D., Noser, H., & Huang, Z. (1997). Autonomous virtual actors based on virtual sensors, in: Creating Personalities (Ed. R.Trappl, P. Petta), *Lecture Notes in Computer Science*, Springer Verlag, (pp. 25-42).

Thomas, S. (2005). Pervasive, persuasive eLearning: modeling the pervasive learning space. In *Proceedings of the 3rd International Conference on Pervasive Computing and Communications Workshops (PERCOMW'05)* (pp. 332-336). Kauai Island, Hawai'i: IEEE Computer Society.

Thompson, L., & Hastie, R. (1990). Judgement tasks and biases in negotiation. *Research on Negotiation in Organizations*, *2*, 31–54.

Thornton, P., & Houser, C. (2005). Using mobile phones in English education. *Journal of Computer Assisted Learning*, *21*(3), 217–228. doi:10.1111/j.1365-2729.2005.00129.x

Tian, X., Chen, G., & Xu, L. (2000). The design and implementation of an expert system for self-assessment paper generation for Guangdong Province [In Chinese] [Singapore.]. *Proceedings of Global Chinese Conference on Computers in Education*, *2000*, 475–480.

Tomaš, S. (2005). E-learning in primary education. In *Workshop: Intelligent e-learning systems, Consulting: Computers in school IX, Croatian Association for the Promotion of Computer Education (HDPIO)*, Šibenik, Croatia (in Croatian).

Tomaš, S. (2007). *Learning and teaching in primary education using tutoring systems.* (Unpublished MS Thesis), Falcuty of Philosophy, Zagreb.

Torres, V. S. (2004). *Significações emocionais e cognitivas na aprendizagem em ambiente informatizado: Uma relação necessária à superação da modernidade* (Doctoral Thesis). Porto Alegre: Universidade Federal do Rio Grande do Sul.

Towne, D. M. (1997a). Approximate reasoning techniques for intelligent diagnostic instruction. *International Journal of Artificial Intelligence in Education*, *8*, 262–283.

Towne, D. M. (1997b). Intelligent diagnostic tutoring using qualitative symptom information. In *AAAI97 Fall Symposium on ITS Authoring Tools*.

Triantafillou, E., Georgiadou, E., & Economides, A. A. (2006). Adaptive Hypermedia Systems: A Review of Adaptivity Variables. In *Proceedings of the Fifth Panhellenic Conference–Information and Communication Technologies in Education* (pp.75-82). Thessaloniki, Greece.

Tsovaltzi, D., Rummel, N., Pinkwart, N., Harrer, A., Scheuer, O., Braun, I., & McLaren, B. M. (2008). Cochemex: Supporting conceptual chemistry learning via computer-mediated collaboration scripts. In *Proceedings of the European Conference on Technology Enhanced Learning.*

Turner, T. E., Macasek, M. A., Nuzzo-Jones, G., & Heffernan, N. T. (2005). The ASSISTment Builder: A Rapid Development Tool for ITS. In *Proceedings of the 12th Annual Conference on Artificial Intelligence in Education.* (pp. 929-231). Amsterdam: IOS Press.

Twigg, C. A. (2003). *Improving learning and reducing costs: lessons learned from round 1 of the Pew Grant Program in Course.* Redesign Center for Academic Transformation, Rensselaer Polytechnic Institute. Retrieved from http://www.center.rpi.edu/PewGrant/Rd1intro.html

Ueno, H. (1994). Integrated intelligent programming environment for learning programming. *IEICE Transactions on Information and Systems*, 68–79.

Ullrich, C. (2005). Course generation based on HTN planning. In A. Jedlitschka & B. Brandherm (Ed.), *Proceedings of 13th Annual Workshop of the SIG Adaptivity and User Modeling in Interactive Systems*, (pp.74-79).

UNESCO. (2001). *UNESCO y la Cultura para la Paz*. Retrieved in 2001 from http://www.unesco.cl

United States Department of Education. (2003). *Using data to influence classroom decisions*. Washington, DC. Retrieved November 2008, from http://www.ed.gov/teachers/nclbguide/datadriven.pdf van der Linden, W. J., & Hambleton, R. K. (Eds.) (1997). *Handbook of Modern Item Response Theory*. New York: Springer-Verlag.

Urban-Lurain, M. (2003). An Historic Review in the Context of the Development of Artificial Intelligence and Educational Psychology. Retrieved October 24, 2009, from http://www.cse.msu.edu /rgroups/cse101/ITS/its.htm

Valigiani, G., Biojout, R., Jamont, Y., Lutton, E., Bourgeois, C., & Collet, P. (2005). Experimenting with a real-size man-hill to optimize pedagogical paths. *Proceedings of the ACM Symposium on Applied computing '05* (pp.4-8), Santa Fe, NM.

Van den Berg, B., Van Es, R., Tattersall, C., Janssen, J., Manderveld, J., & Brouns, F. (2005). Swarm-based sequencing recommendations in e-learning. [Wroclaw, Poland.]. *Proceedings of International Conference on Intelligence Systems Design and Applications*, *05*, 488–493.

van den Broek, E. (2004). Emotional Prosody Measurement (EPM): A voice-based evaluation method for psychological therapy effectiveness. [Medical and Care Compunetics]. *Studies in Health Technology and Informatics*, *103*, 118–125.

van Mulken, S., André, E., & Muller, J. (1998). The persona effect: How substantial is it? In *Proceedings of Human Computer Interaction*. Berlin.

van Rosmalen, P., Sloep, P., Kester, L., Brouns, F., de Croock, M., & Pannekeet, K. (2008). A learner support model based on peer tutor selection. *Journal of Computer Assisted Learning*, *24*, 74–86. doi:10.1111/j.1365-2729.2007.00245.x

VanLehn, K., Jordan, P. W., Ros'e, C., Bhembe, D., B¨ottner, M., & Gaydos, A. (2002). The architecture of Why2-Atlas: A coach for qualitative physics essay writing. *ITS 2002*. *LNCS*, *2363*, 158–167.

VanLehn, K., Lynch, C., Schulze, K., Shapiro, J. A., Shelby, R., & Taylor, L. (2005). The Andes Physics Tutoring System: Lessons Learned. *International Journal of Artificial Intelligence in Education*, *15*(3), 1–47.

Vanlehn, K. (1996). Conceptual and meta-learning during coached problem solving. In *Proceedings of the third international conference on intelligent tutoring systems (ITS96)*, (pp. 29–47).

Vasilyeva, E., Pechenizkiy, M., & Bra, P. D. (2007). Adaptation of Feedback in e-learning System at Individual and Group Level. In P. Brusilovsky, M. Grigoriadou & K. Papanikolaou (Eds.), *Proceedings of Workshop on Personalisation in E-Learning Environments at Individual and Group Level, 11th International Conference on User Modeling*, (pp. 49-56).

Vassileva, J., & Wasson, B. (1996, September). *Instructional planning approaches: from tutoring towards free learning*. Paper presented at the Proceedings of Euro-AIED'96, Lisbon.

Vavoula, G. N., & Sharples, M. (2002). KLeOS: a personal, mobile, knowledge and learning organisation system. In *Proceedings of the IEEE International Workshop on Wireless and Mobile Technologies in Education (WMTE'02)* (pp. 152-156). Vaxjo, Sweden: IEEE Computer Society.

Verbert, K., Klerkx, J., Meire, M., Najjar, J., & Duval, E. (2004). Towards global component architecture for learning objects: An ontology based approach. *Lecture Notes in Computer Science*, *3292*, 713–722.

Vladušić, R. (2006). *The intelligent tutoring systems in chemistry in primary education.* (Unpublished MS Thesis), Faculty of Natural Sciences, Mathematics and Kinesiology, Split, Croatia, (in Croatian).

Vugt, H. C., Konijn, E. A., Hoorn, J. F., Keur, I., & Eliëns, A. (2007). Realism is not all! User engagement with task-related interface characters. *Interacting with Computers*, *19*, 267–280. doi:10.1016/j.intcom.2006.08.005

Vygotsky, L. S. (1998). *A formação social da mente: O desenvolvimento dos processos psicológicos superiores*. São Paulo: Martins Fontes. [Translation. José Cipolla Neto et alli]

Vygotsky, L. S. (2004). *Psicologia pedagógica*. São Paulo: Martins Fontes. [Translation. Paulo Bezerra]

Vygotsky, L. S. (2005). *Pensamento e linguagem.* São Paulo: Martins Fontes. [Translation. Jefferson Luiz Camargo; Rev. José Cipolla Neto]

Wagner, E. D. (2005). Enabling Mobile Learning. *EDUCAUSE Review, 40*(3), 40–53.

Walonoski, J., & Heffernan, N. T. (2006). Detection and Analysis of Off-Task Gaming Behavior in Intelligent Tutoring Systems. In Ikeda, Ashley & Chan (Eds.), *Proceedings of the 8th International Conference on Intelligent Tutoring Systems* (pp. 382-391). Springer-Verlag: Berlin.

Wang, Q., & Woo, H. L. (2007). Systematic planning for ICT integration in topic learning. *Journal of Educational Technology & Society, 10*(1), 148–156.

Wang, Q., & Yang, J. (2006). Eye Detection in Facial Images with Unconstrained Background. *Journal of Pattern Recognition Research, 1*, 55–62.

Wang, N., Johnson, W. L., Mayer, R. E., Rizzo, P., Shaw, E., & Collins, H. (2008). The politeness effect: Pedagogical agents and learning outcomes. *International Journal of Human-Computer Studies, 66*, 98–112. doi:10.1016/j.ijhcs.2007.09.003

Wang, T.-I., Wang, K.-T., & Huang, Y.-M. (2008). Using a style-based ant colony system for adaptive learning. *Expert Systems with Applications, 34*(4), 2449–2464. doi:10.1016/j.eswa.2007.04.014

Wang, Y., & Hou, S. (2003). A study on an algorithm for automatic assessment paper generation [In Chinese]. *Harbin Technological University, 35*(3), 342–346.

Wang, Q., & Chu, L. (2008). The application of PSO in intelligent assessment paper generation *(In Chinese). Neijiang Technology, 2008*(1), 134-135.

Wasserman, S., & Faust, K. (1994). *Social network analysis: Methods and applications.* Cambridge, UK: Cambridge Univ Pr.

Wasson, B. (1990). *Determining the focus of Instruction: Content planning for intelligent tutoring systems.* (Unpublished Doctoral Thesis), Department of Computational Science, University of Saskatchewan, Canada.

Wastlund, E., Reinikka, H., Norlander, T., & Archer, T. (2005). Effects of VDT and paper presentation on consumption and production of information: Psychological and physiological factors. *Computers in Human Behavior, 21*, 377–394. doi:10.1016/j.chb.2004.02.007

Watson, J., & Hardaker, G. (2005). Steps towards personalised learner management system (LMS): SCORM implementation. *Campus-Wide Information Systems, 22*(2), 56–70. doi:10.1108/10650740510587074

Wenger, E. (1987). *Artificial Intelligence and Tutoring Systems: Computational and Cognitive approaches to the Communication of Knowledge.* Los Altos, CA: Morgan Kaufmann.

Wentzel, P., van Lammeren, R., Molendrijk, M., de Bruin, S., & Wagtendonk, A. (2005). *Using Mobile Technology to Enhance Students' Educational Experiences.* Boulder, CA: EDUCAUSE Center for Applied Research.

Wenying, G., & Deren, C. (2006). Semantic Approach for e-learning System. *In Proceedings of First International Multi-Symposiums on Computer and Computational Sciences (IMSCCS 2006)*, (vol.2, pp.442-446). Hangzhou, Zhejiang, China.

Westerink, J. M., & Ouwerkerk, M. overbeek, T., Pasveer, W. F., & Ruyter, B. (2008). *Probing Experiences: From Academic Research to Commercial Propositions.* Dordrecht, The Netherlands: Springer.

Whitehurst, R. A., Powell, C. L., et al. (1998). Utilizing the student model in distance learning. In *Proceedings of ITiCSE'98*. Dublin, Ireland.

Wiemer-Hastings, P., Wiemer-Hastings, K., & Graesser, A. C. (1999). *Improving an intelligent tutor's comprehension of students with Latent Semantic Analysis. Artificial Intelligence in Education* (pp. 535–542). Amsterdam: IOS Press.

Wilensky, U. (1999). *NetLogo (and NetLogo User Manual). Center for Connected Learning and Computer-based Modeling.* Northwestern University.

Wiley, D. A. (2000). *Learning object design and sequencing theory*. (Unpublished doctoral dissertation), Brigham Young University.

Wiliam, D. (2006). Formative Assessment: Getting the focus right. *Educational Assessment, 11*(3&4), 283–289. doi:10.1207/s15326977ea1103&4_7

Wilson, E., V. (2004). ExamNet asynchronous learning network: augmenting face-to-face courses with student-developed exam questions. *Computers & Education, 42*(3), 87–107. doi:10.1016/S0360-1315(03)00066-6

Winter, M. (2004). *Developing A Group Model For Student Software Engineering Teams.* (Unpublished MS Thesis). Saskatoon, Saskatchewan: University of Saskatchewan

Winter, M., & McCalla, G. (2003). An Analysis of Group Performance in Terms of the Functional Knowledge and Teamwork Skills of Group Members. In *UM'03 9th International Conference on User Modeling*, (pp. 35-44), Johnstown, PA.

Wolfe, C. J., & Murthy, U. S. (2006). Negotiation Support Systems in Budget Negotiations: An Experimental Analysis. *Journal of Management Information Systems, 22*, 351–381. doi:10.2753/MIS0742-1222220312

Wong, L. H., & Looi, C. K. (2002). *Learning pathways & intelligent software agents. (Unpublished internal document).* Institute of Systems Science, National University of Singapore.

Wong, L. H., & Looi, C. K. (2009). Adaptable learning pathway generation with ant colony optimization. *Journal of Educational Technology & Society, 12*(3), 309–326.

Wong, L. H., Looi, C. K., Lai, T. W., Lee, P., Chong, C., & Ong, P. Y. (2004). Adaptable learning pathway planning with self-organizing agents. *Proceedings of International Conference on Intelligent Agents, Web Technologies and Internet Commerce '04*, Gold Coast, Australia.

Wongchokprasitti, C., & Brusilovsky, P. (2007). NewsMe: A Case Study for Adaptive News Systems with Open User Model. In *Proceedings of The Third International Conference on Autonomic and Autonomous Systems, ICAS*, IEEE Press.

Woods, S. G., Quilici, A. E., & Yang, Q. (1998). *Constraint-Based Design Recovery for Software Reengineering: Theory and Experiments*. Norwell, MA: Kluwer Academic Publishers.

Wooldridge, M., Jennings, N. R., & Kinny, D. (2000). The Gaia methodology for agent-oriented analysis and design. *Journal of Autonomous Agents and Multi-Agent Systems, 3*, 285–312. doi:10.1023/A:1010071910869

Wooldridge, M. J., & Jennings, N. R. (1995). Intelligent Agents: Theory and Practice. *The Knowledge Engineering Review, 10*(2), 115–152. doi:10.1017/S0269888900008122

Woolf, B. P., & McDonald, D. D. (1984). *Building a Computer Tutor: Design Issues* (pp. 61–73). IEEE Computer.

Wu, H. Kort.E., De Bra,P. (2001). Design Issue for General Purpose Adaptive Hypermedia Systems. *In Proceedings of the ACM Conference on Hypertext and Hypermedia* (pp.141-150), Aarhus, Denmark.

WWC. (2002). *IES What Works Clearinghouse (WWC) Glossary of Terms.* Retrieved February 20, 2009, from http://ies.ed.gov/ncee/wwc/help/glossary/

Xenos, M. (2004). Prediction and assessment of student behavior in open and distance education in computers using Bayesian networks. *Computers & Education, 43*(4), 345–359.

Xu, Y., & Aliaga, D. G. (2007). Efficient multi-viewpoint acquisition of 3D objects undergoing repetitive motions. In *Proceedings of the 2007 Symposium on interactive 3D Graphics and Games, I3D '07.* (pp. 113-120). New York: ACM.

Yacef, K. (2003). Some thoughts about the synergetic effects of integrating ITS and LMS Technologies Together to the Service of Education. In *11th International Conference on Artificial Intelligence in Education*, Sydney, Australia.

Yang, Y. J., & Wu, C. (2009). An attribute-based ant colony system for adaptive learning. *Expert Systems with Applications, 36*(2), Part 2, 3034-3047.

Yannibelli, V., Godoy, D., & Amandi, A. (2006). A Genetic Algorithm Approach to Recognise Students' Learning Styles. *Interactive Learning Environments, 14*(1), 55–78. doi:10.1080/10494820600733565

Yaron, D., Cuadros, J., Leinhardt, G., Evans, K. L., & Karabinos, M. (2005). Virtual Laboratories and Scenes to Support Chemistry Instruction, in About Invention and Impact: Building Excellence in Undergraduate STEM (Science, Technology, Engineering, and Mathematics) Education. In *Proceedings from National Science Foundation Course, Curriculum, and Laboratory Improvement (NSF-CCLI) program conference*. Arlington, VA, 2004, edited and prepared by NSF.

Yazdani, M. (1986). Intelligent tutoring systems survey. *Artificial Intelligence Review*, *1*, 43–52. doi:10.1007/BF01988527

Yazdani, M. (1987). Intelligent tutoring systems: an overview. In Lawler, R., & Yazdani, M. (Eds.), *In Artificial Intelligence and Education* (pp. 182–201). Norwood: Ablex.

Yin, P.-Y., Chang, K.-C., Hwang, G.-J., Hwang, G.-H., & Chan, Y. (2006). A particle swarm optimization approach to composing serial test sheets for multiple assessment criteria. *Journal of Educational Technology & Society*, *9*(3), 3–15.

Ying, J., & Hu, L. (2000). The construction and realization of a mathematical model for random assessment question selections [In Chinese]. *Computer Applications*, *20*(1), 46–47.

Yun, J. T. Willet. J., & Murnane, R. (2004) *Accountability-Based Reforms and Instruction: Testing Curricular Alignment for Instruction Using the Massachusetts Comprehensive Assessment System.* Paper presented at the Annual American Educational Research Association Meeting. San Diego, California.

Zhang, D. (2007). Web Content Adaptation for Mobile Handheld Devices. *Communications of the ACM*, *50*, 75–79. doi:10.1145/1216016.1216024

Zhang, T., & Lu, X. (2007). Research progress of Swarm Intelligence algorithms. *Shanxi Architecture*, *33*(1), 14–16.

Zhu, X. (2007). Extending the SCORM specification for references to the open content object. *Journal of Educational Technology & Society*, *10*(1), 248–264.

Zywno, M. S., & Stewart, M. F. (2005). *Learning styles of engineering students, online learning objects and achievement.* Paper presented at the ASEE Annual Conference and Exposition, Conference Proceedings. (pp. 9615-9623).

About the Contributors

Slavomir Stankov is a professor of computer science at the Faculty of Science University of Split, Croatia. Since 1996 he has been heading three scientific and one technological project. He has participated on some projects related to the information and communication technology applications in education, in particular the intelligent tutoring systems and authoring shells for their design, implementation and deployment. He has authored or co-authored more than seventy scientific and expert papers.

Vlado Glavinić is a professor of computer science and engineering at the Faculty of Electrical Engineering and Computing, University of Zagreb, Croatia. His main research interests are in the areas of computer networks, user interfaces and digital systems design, and particularly in modeling and development of intelligent distributed applications and services for the information infrastructure here including distributed educational systems. He has collaborated in and led a number of research and industrial R&D projects, and has authored or co-authored more than 100 research and professional papers in journals, conferences and books, along with several educational texts.

Marko Rosić is an associate professor of computer science at the Faculty of Science University of Split, Croatia. His scientific work is related to the information and communication technology applications in the distance learning systems. Researching possibilities of using agents and the semantic Web technologies for developing the distance learning systems based on the intelligent tutoring systems is in the centre of his interest. He participates in many scientific and technological projects related to the field of his scientific interest. He has authored or co-authored about twenty scientific papers.

* * *

Xin Bai is an assistant professor of Educational Technology in Department of Teacher Education at York College, City University of New York (CUNY). She earned her doctorate in Instructional Technology & Media from Teachers College at Columbia University. Her study focuses on educational games, simulations, intelligent tutoring systems, self-paced e-learning, and ubiquitous learning through mobile devices. Her work is built on the research done on cognitive science, artificial intelligence, and educational technologies. Xin taught several graduate core courses at Teachers College at Columbia, including Cognition and Computers and Intelligent Computer-Assisted Instruction before joining CUNY. She was a Project Director of the REAL (REflective Agent Learning environment) Project at the Institute for Learning Technologies at Columbia University. She also worked as a Chief Learning Architect at a company in charge of facilitating adult e-learning and designing Learning Management Systems.

John B. Black is the Cleveland E. Dodge Professor at Teachers College, Columbia University in the Departments of Human Development, and Mathematics, Science, and Technology. He is Chair of the Department of Human Development, Coordinates the Program in Cognitive Studies and is the Director of the Institute for Learning Technologies. He has a BS in Math form MIT and a PhD in Cognitive Psychology from Stanford. He was an Assistant and Associate Professor in Psychology and Computer Science at Yale University. He is the author of over 100 journal articles and four books. His current research focuses on basic research in cognition, especially grounded/embodied approaches to cognition, and its application to improving learning, memory, understanding, problem solving and motivation. He is especially interested in using technologies like multi-user virtual environments, video games, TV/videos, intelligent tutoring systems and robots to improve learning, memory, understanding, problem solving and motivation.

Francisco Villa Ulhôa Botelho, Doctor in Informatics in Education by the Federal University of Rio Grande do Sul (UFRGS); Professor and General Director of the Virtual Catholic University of Brasília (UCBV); Member of the Gestor Committee of the Catholic Institutions of Superior Education Web (RICESU); General Coordinator of the International Group for Distance Education of the Salesian University Institutions (UNIVERS-IUS); member of the Scientific Committee of the Brazilian Distance Education Association (ABED); member of the Editorial Council of the Colabor@ journal; evaluator of Distance Education of the Brazilian Ministry of Education (MEC).

Lourdes Mattos Brasil is a professor/ researcher and head of Electronic Course and Lato Sensu in Clinical Engineering Course at the University of Brasília, Gama Faculty. She has a D.Sc. in Electrical Engineering/Biomedical Engineering from University of Santa Catarina, Brazil, (1999), a Sandwich Doctorate in Mathematical Applied from *Facultés Universitaires Notre-Dame de La Paix* (FUNDP), Belgium (1997-1998), a M.Sc. in Electrical Engineering/Biomedical Engineering from University of Santa Catarina, Brazil (1984) and graduated in Electrical Engineering from University of Santa Catarina, Brazil (1990). Her research interests include artificial intelligence, data mining, machine learning, knowledge acquisition, knowledge-based systems, hybrid expert systems, virtual reality, intelligent tutoring systems, informatics in health and e-learning.

Julie Coultas is an evolutionary social psychologist. She obtained her first degree in applied psychology from University of Sussex and then went on to complete MSc in Knowledge Based Systems and DPhil in Cognitive Science, also at University of Sussex. She was the Eduserv research fellow (2004 – 2006) and produced a review of the effectiveness of e-learning in higher and medical education and work-based learning She is currently writing a book for Cambridge University Press entitled 'Conformity: Social Psychology and Cultural Evolution'. She has published in psychology and education journals and presented many papers on evolutionary psychology at international conferences. Her research and teaching focus on: social learning (including conformity and cooperative behaviour), social development (including play), the emotions (developmental aspects), and gender differences. She is a visiting research fellow in the Department of Psychology at the University of Sussex. She is currently collaborating on an international project on social learning and cultural evolution with Swedish researchers. Previously she has worked on Department for Education and Skills (DfES) and Department for International Development (DfID) projects. She is also a freelance consultant who works for a toy company providing research and advice on the developmental benefits of educational toys. She has provided advice for a BBC television series and consultancy for many public relations and commercial companies.

Gloria Millaray Curilem obtained her Professional Degree in Computer Engineering in the Polytechnic Superior Institute “José Antonio Echeverría” of La Havana, Cuba in 1992. She obtained the Doctor degree in the Federal University of Santa Catarina, Florianópolis, Brazil in 2002. She developed a Postdoctoral position in the Universidad de Santiago, USACH, Chile during 2007. She is presently working as an Assistant Professor of the Electrical Engineering department at Universidad de La Frontera, in Temuco, Chile. Her research areas involve the application of artificial intelligence techniques to intelligent learning environments and more recently to digital signal processing.

Tonći Dadić was born August 7th 1957 in Split, Croatia. He graduated 1981 at Faculty of Electrical Engineering, University of Split, and has got master degree 1991 at Faculty of Electrical Engineering, University of Zagreb. His master work titled “Proposal of graphical programming language for microcontrollers” dealt with an approach of visual programming. In period 1984 – 1990 he was with «KONCAR – ETAS» company, where implemented visual programming tool that significantly improved application of microcontrollers to industrial processes. From 1990 to 1998, he worked for Croatian Chamber of Economy, with duties of system and database administration. Since April 1st 1998, Tonci is employee of Faculty of Natural Science and Mathematics, University of Split, lecturing Operation Systems and Databases. Since 1998, he is a consultant of AutoScout24 Gmbh, Munich - Germany, helping set up the biggest European internet market of new and used cars. He developed Delta Replication system that collects, transforms and integrates data from heterogeneous data sources, finding minimal set of transactions in order to keep central database up-to-date. Besides his age, on February 2006, Tonci started doctorial study at Faculty of Electrical Engineering and Computer Science, University of Zagreb. Currently he designs an intelligent tutoring system for learning programming in procedural languages. The system is aimed to help students to understand the features of target programming language, as well as develop their program design, testing and general problem solving skills. Tonci is collaborative member of Project grant 177-0361994-1996 «Design and evaluation of intelligent e-learning systems», funded by the Ministry of Science and Technology of the Republic of Croatia, conducted by professor Slavomir Stankov.

Funda Dağ received the MSc degree in 2003 and the PhD degree in 2008, in the Kocaeli University. She is an Assistant Professor in Computer Education and Instructional Technology Department of Education Faculty in Kocaeli University. She is the vice director of the Distance Education Center of the Kocaeli University. She has been working in the area of adaptive e-learning systems and e-learning since 2000. Her research interests are e-learning standards, metadata, learning objects, and educational technology based on personalization. She teaches computer based education and programming languages courses.

Benedict du Boulay is Professor of Artificial Intelligence in the School of Informatics at the University of Sussex. Following a Bachelors degree in Physics at Imperial College London, he spent time both in industry and as a secondary school teacher before returning to university to complete his PhD at the University of Edinburgh in 1978 working on Logo. After a post-doc position at Edinburgh, a lectureship at the University of Aberdeen and a Sloan Fellowship at the University of California San Deigo, he joined Sussex as a lecturer in 1983. He has been at Sussex since then, taking many roles of responsibility including Dean of Cognitive and Computing Sciences (COGS) as well as more recently Dean of Science and Technology. He has two main research areas. The first is the Psychology of Programming where his main work has been in the area of novices learning programming and the development of tools to assist that process. The second is the application of Artificial Intelligence in Education. Here he is particularly interested in issues around modelling and developing students' metacognition and motivation. He is a former editor of the International Journal of Artificial Intelligence in Education, is on the Editorial Board of the International Journal of Technology, Instruction, Cognition and Learning and has edited/written 8 books and written some 150 papers in the areas indicated above.

Kadir Erkan is a professor Phd. in the Technical Education Faculty of Kocaeli University. Moreover, he is head of Distance Education Center of Kocaeli University. His main research interests are soft computing technologies and programming languages. Dr. Erkan teaches programming, problem solving and design courses.

Mingyu Feng is a Research Scientist at Center for Technology in Learning of SRI International. She holds a Ph.D. degree in Computer Science from Worcester Polytechnic Institute. She received his B.S. in Computer Science from Tianjin University in 1999, and her M.S. degree in the same field from Tianjin University in 2002. Her primary interests lie in the areas of intelligent tutoring systems, particularly, student modeling and educational data mining. Ms. Feng has also worked in the area of cognitive modeling, and psychometrics as well. Her paper summarizes part of her dissertation work on adaptive assessing in the ASSISTment project on which she has been working since 2004.

Fred Garnett is currently a Visiting Research Assistant at the London Knowledge Lab and part of the Learner-Generated Contexts Research Group. He was a Strategic Policy Advisor for Post-16 e-Learning at Becta, working on a range of issues concerning policy development, including the national e-strategy Harnessing Technology, from a social and digital inclusion perspective. He also lead on interactivity design strategies for policy consultation for the DfES and helped link the research and policy communities as a Visiting Research Fellow at Sussex University. From these activities he developed the concept of Policy 2.0. Formerly he managed the Community Programmes Team at Becta, which built government websites such as Help is at Hand for UK online centres, and advised various government departments on the £250m Community Access to Lifelong Learning initiative. For DCMS he was a Culture on-line Visioneer, advised on the future of libraries, and I helped set up the Participatory Media Literacy Working Group at OFCOM. He is also a specialist in Community Grids for Learning and Digital Inclusion. Previous work included lecturing on Political Science at the University of Colorado and Computer Science at Lewisham College. From 1984 he lectured on the social impact of IT, writing the first Internet Unit for Greenwich University in 1995 and creating e-learning resources from 1997. He worked with the London Borough of Lewisham on their Citizen Connects projects and set up the TaLENT Consortium, establishing the Lewisham Community Grid for Learning. He also worked as Accessibility and Usability consultant on their EU-IST GALA project. He helped set up the Creekside Environmental Education Centre in Deptford Creek as a Trustee with a focus on Urban Ecology. He is a Fellow of the Royal Society of Arts, and blog on music and learning as well as architectures of participation.

Jeroen Geuze was born in Zaandam in 1981. He received a Masters' degree in Artificial Intelligence (AI) in 2005 at the Vrije Universiteit in Amsterdam, specializing in Intelligent Internet Applications and Knowledge Management and Knowledge Technology. He received a second Masters' degree in Cognitive Neuroscience at the Radboud University in Nijmegen specializing in Psycholinguistics and

Brain Computer Interfaces. He will obtain a Ph.D. in 2012 on the topic of communication with Brain Computer Interfaces. His research interests are Brain Computer Interfaces, games and Artificial Intelligence, intelligent internet applications, and psycholinguistics.

Ani Grubišić was born in 1978 in Split. She graduated under supervision of prof. PhD Slavomir Stankov in 2001 on the Faculty of Science, University of Split, and gained a BS for mathematics and computer science teacher. The theme of her graduate thesis was "Model tracing – a diagnostic technique of intelligent tutoring systems". Since 2002 she has been employed as a scientific novice at the same faculty, and in the period 2002 – 2006 she has been collaborating on a scientific and research project "Computational and didactical aspects of intelligent authoring tools in education." She enrolled postgraduate study at the Faculty of Electrical Engineering and Computing, University of Zagreb, in 2002. She was collaborating on a technological project "Web-oriented intelligent authoring shell" from 2003 to 2005. Since 2007 she has been collaborating on scientific and research project "Design and evaluation of intelligent e-learning systems." She got her MS degree in 2007 on the Faculty of Electrical Engineering and Computing, University of Zagreb. The theme of her master's thesis was "Evaluating educational influence of intelligent e-learning systems," and it was done under supervision of prof. PhD Slavomir Stankov. The board of Faculty of Electrical Engineering and Computing gave her a silver plaque "Josip Lončar" for outstanding master's thesis. She enrolled postgraduate doctoral study at the Faculty of Electrical Engineering and Computing, University of Zagreb, in 2007. The editors of Marquis "Who's Who" (USA) have selected her biographical profile for inclusion in the 10th Edition of "Who's Who in Science and Engineering, 2008-2009". Ani Grubišić is oriented on evaluating educational influence of the e-learning systems. Her scientific interest includes e-learning systems effectiveness evaluation in general, and as well, calculation of the effectiveness of different categories of e-learning systems, especially intelligent tutoring systems, using meta-analysis. Recently, she has been involved in researching different approaches to intelligent courseware generation.

Andreas Harrer is associate professor for Informatics (Computer Science) at Catholic University Eichstätt-Inglostadt since winter 2007. He has received his PhD in Computer Science from the Technical University of Munich with a PhD thesis in the area of CSCL (intelligent support of collaborative learning interactions). He worked in the Collide group at University Duisburg-Essen from 2002 to 2007 with a research line of analysis and intelligent support of group learning as well as software engineering principles for educational systems. He was speaker of the special interest group "Artificial Intelligence and Education", the European Research Team "Computer-based Analysis and Visualization of Collaborative Learning Activities", and member of the steering group of the European Research Team "Computer-Supported Scripting of Interaction in Collaborative Learning Environments" in the "Kaleidoscope" Network of Excellence (FP6, ended 2007). He was technical coordinator within the FP6 STREP Argunaut and responsible for the design of the system architecture and the integration of the system components. His current research interests are in the field of learning process modeling, analysis of collaboration and social networks, and the application of software engineering methods to development of educational systems.

Neil Heffernan is Associate Professor of Computer Science at Worcester Polytechnic Institute, and creator of WPI's new Learning Sciences & Technology Ph.D. program. Dr. Neil Heffernan graduated summa cum laude from Amherst College in History and Computer Science, and completed his Ph.D. in

2001 at Carnegie Mellon University. For his dissertation, Neil built the first intelligent tutoring system that incorporated a model of tutorial dialog, as well as being one of the first intelligent tutoring systems on the web. He does multi-disciplinary research in Intelligent Tutoring Systems, Artificial Intelligence, Psychometrics, and Cognitive Science. Dr. Heffernan has over 30 peer-reviewed publications and has received over $9 million in funding on over a dozen different grants.

Daniel Huenteman obtained his Professional degree in Computer Engineering at the Universidad de la Frontera, Temuco, Chile in 2006. During his student years he served as assistant professor of the Computer Graphics Discipline at the Universidad de La Frontera. He also worked as a research assistant of the research project: "Intelligent Tutoring Systems for the non-violent conflict resolution" financed by Research Direction of the Universidad de La Frontera. Between 2007 and 2008 he started his professional activity developing several computational systems to support the management systems of many local companies. Currently he is working as Executive-Sales and Commercial Finance Manager at Topiary Ltd. Company in the city of Temuco, Chile.

Ali Keles is a lecturer at the Computer Sciences Application Unit, Ataturk University. Now, he works at Department of Computer Education and Instructional Technology, Faculty of Education. He received her MS from Istanbul University - Institute of Business Administration-Economy and MS in Computer Sciences from Ataturk University, and Ph.D. on computer sciences at Atatürk University in Turkey. His current research interests are in the fields of software, medical diagnosis with methods artificial intelligence and intelligent tutoring systems, expert system, image processing.

Ayturk Keles is a lecturer the Computer Sciences Application Unit, Ataturk University. Now, she works at Faculty of Engineering. She received her BS in Business Administration-Economy from Anadolu University, MS in Computer Science from Atatürk University and Ph.D. on intelligent tutoring systems at Atatürk University in Turkey. Her current research interests are in the fields of software, data mining, fuzzy logic, medical diagnosis with methods artificial intelligence and intelligent tutoring systems, expert system.

Kenneth Koedinger is Professor of Human–Computer Interaction and Psychology at Carnegie Mellon University. His background includes a BS in Mathematics, a MS in Computer Science, a Ph.D. in Cognitive Psychology, and experience teaching in an urban high school. His research has contributed new principles and techniques for the design of educational software and has produced basic cognitive science research results on the nature of mathematical thinking and learning. Dr. Koedinger directs the Pittsburgh Science of Learning Center and is co-founder of Carnegie Learning Inc., a company bringing learning research to schools in the form of the Cognitive Tutor technology.

Divna Krpan was born in 1977 in Imotski, Croatia. She graduated under supervision of prof. dr. Slavomir Stankov in 2004 on the Faculty of Science, University of Split, and gained a BS for mathematics and computer science teacher, where she now works as an teaching assistant. The theme of her graduate thesis was "Knowledge evaluation in e-learning systems". She teaches two courses in programming (Object Pascal and BASIC) and a course Introduction to computing. In 2007 she began her doctoral studies in Computer Science at the Faculty of Electrical Engineering and Computing, University of Zagreb. Her main research interests includes student modeling and group modeling in intelligent tutoring systems, artificial intelligence techniques for developing student and group model and Web-based intelligent e-learning systems.. Her previous work experience includes working as a elementary school mathematics and coputer science teacher from 2004 till 2006. She successfully passed all modules required for the granting of the ECDL Certificate in 2005. She speaks English language.

Haidi Kuvač is a teaching assistant at Information Technology Department of University Centre for professional studies, University of Split. She received B.Sc. degree in computer science in 2007, from the Faculty of Electrical Engineering, Mechanical Engineering, and Naval Architecture, University of Split. She is 3rd year PhD student in computer science at the Faculty of Electrical Engineering, Mechanical Engineering, and Naval Architecture. Her research interests include e-learning, student modelling, and intelligent (web) technologies.

Chee-Kit Looi is an Associate Professor and the Head of Centre of Excellence in Learning Innovation (CELLI), NIE, NTU. He has over two decades of experience with educational technology research in research institutes and universities. His research interests are Artificial Intelligence in Education, intelligent agents for learning, mobile learning, and Computer-Supported Collaborative Learning. He is an editorial member of the International Journal on Artificial Intelligence in Education and the International Journal on Computer-Supported Collaborative Learning.

Rosemary Luckin is Professor of Learner Centred Design at the London Knowledge Lab (LKL), a visiting Professor in Informatics at the University of Sussex and an EPSRC Advanced Research Fellow. She holds a first class degree in Computing and Artificial Intelligence and a DPhil in Cognitive Science from the University of Sussex. Her research explores how to most effectively scaffold learning across multiple technologies, locations, subjects and times. At the LKL she is part of a group of researchers who share an interest in applying participatory methods to the development and evaluation of technology enhanced learning experiences. This work is interdisciplinary and encompasses education, psychology, artificial intelligence and HCI. It investigates the relationship between people, the concepts they are trying to learn and teach, the contexts within which they operate and the resources at their disposal. Prof. Luckin has been a principal or co-investigator on 12 Nationally funded research grants, is a member of several journal editorial boards, has numerous peer-reviewed publications, was appointed by the Minister for Schools for England and Wales as a non-executive director of Becta (the government agency leading ICT and learning strategy) and is a member of the Advisory Board of the UK Technology Enhanced Learning Research Programme.

Alke Martens is Professor at the Department of Computer Science at the University of Rostock, Germany since winter 2007. She is leader of the research group "eLearning and Cognitive Systems". She has received her PhD in Computer Science from the University of Rostock in the research field of Artificial Intelligence in the context of Intelligent Tutoring Systems. Her current research interests are formal methods, software engineering, modeling and simulation, artificial intelligence, teaching and training systems, and a combination thereof, e.g. in game-based learning and in the development of inclusive eLearning systems. Current application domains of her research and her projects are system-biology, medicine and education of computer scientists.

Saša Mladenović is teaching assistant at Computer Science Department of Faculty of Science, University of Split. He received B.Sc. degree in electrical engineering from the Faculty of Electrical Engineering, Mechanical Engineering, and Naval Architecture, University of Split. From 1999 to 2006 he was acting as Technical manager of the Toll collection system department of Ecsat, Croatia, that is software development responsible for the Transportation department of CS group Designer, integrator and operator of mission critical systems, France. His research interests include interoperability, intelligent technologies like ontology and multi-agent systems, especially engineering applications of intelligent technologies. He is IEEE member since 1996.

Scott Overmyer started his career in the software field with TRW, Inc. as a user interface designer and requirements engineer on the Space Defense Operations Center project in Colorado's Cheyenne Mountain NORAD Complex. After completing several government projects with TRW, he was appointed manager of TRW's Research and Technology Center in Virginia. He earned a Ph.D. in Information Technology (Information and Software Systems Engineering), while appointed as Research Instructor in George Mason University's Center of Excellence in Command, Control, Communications and Intelligence. He has nearly 10 years of industrial experience, followed by over 12 years of academic experience. He has been awarded 2 summer faculty fellowships at NASA's Johnson Space Center. While an Associate Professor at Drexel University, he was also the Founding Director of the Pennsylvania Governor's School for Information Technology, a 5-week summer residential program for talented high school students. He served at Subject Coordinator for both Software Engineering and Information Systems while at Massey University in NZ. He is currently Professor and Director of the MSIS Program at Baker College. His research interests include: meta-languages for software requirements elicitation and modelling, as well as requirements management; creating virtual worlds for teaching students how to be "systems thinkers"; affective computing; and human-computer interface design.

Ana Maria Poo obtained her Professional degree in Psychology from the University of La Frontera in 1992 and her master degree in University Pedagogy in 2002 from Universidad Metropolitana de la Ciencias de La Educación. She is presently an Assistant Professor of Psychology at Universidad de La Frontera, in Temuco, Chile. She has done teaching to undergraduate as graduate students in the areas of general psychology, gender psychology and domestic violence. During the last fifteen years she has developed research on topics of sexual and reproductive health, domestic violence and child abuse. She also has developed multidisciplinary projects related to prevention of school violence through implementation of mediation programs at school.

Abdolhossein Sarrafzadeh is an Associate Professor and Head of Department of Computing at Unitec, New Zealand. He has been involved in research in intelligent and affective tutoring systems for over 15 years. He is internationally known for developing world's first affective tutoring system "Easy with Eve". He has been involved in the development of various cognitive tutors and software tools for detection and expression of affect in intelligent tutoring systems. He has published over eighty research papers in both pattern recognition and artificial intelligence in education forums. He is a member of IEEE and Artificial Intelligence in Education Society.

Jamshid Shanbehzadeh is an Associate Professor in the Department of Computer Engineering at Tarbiat Moallem University (TMU) in Iran. He has published over eighty international journal and conference papers in the areas of image processing, computer vision, emotion detection and affective tutoring systems. He is an expert in e-learning and artificial intelligence in education. He has developed several tools for improving the quality of e-learning systems. Dr. Shanbehzadeh is also an e-learning practitioner teaching at Mehralborz virtual university which is the first virtual university in Iran.

Maja Štula is a docent of computer science at Faculty of Electrical Engineering, Mechanical Engineering and Naval Architecture, University of Split. She received a BS in electrical engineering in 1996, a MSc in 2001 and a PhD in 2005, all from the Faculty of Electrical Engineering, Mechanical Engineering and Naval Architecture, University of Split. Her research interests include intelligent technologies like multi-agent systems, ontology and fuzzy cognitive maps, especially engineering applications of intelligent technologies. She is IEEE member since 2005.

Suzana Tomaš was born on 1975 in Split. She finished elementary and Gymnasium in Split and graduated on the Faculty of Natural Sciences, Mathematics and Education University of Split. She volunteered from October 1998 until October 1999, in elementary school Gripe, Split and deposited 1999th professional examination. She worked on replacing the elementary school Gripe since 2000 to 2002. Since 2003, today for an indefinite period the employment in Dance club Sedmi vjetar in Split. She was associated since 2003 till 2005, at the Technological project MZOS "Web oriented intelligent authoring shell" (TP-02/0177-01). She is involved since 2003. in the implementation of instruction in courses: Application of computers in teaching, Intelligent tutoring systems, Systems for e-learning, Man-machine interaction and Systems for teaching at a distance the teacher study the Faculty of Philosophy as a subcontractor. She got her Masters degree in 2007th Faculty of Philosophy, University of Zagreb, in the scientific field of social sciences, scientific field of Science Education, a branch of Teaching. The theme of her master's thesis was *Learning and teaching in primary education using tutoring systems*. She enrolled postgraduate doctoral study at the Faculty of Philosophy, University of Zagreb, in October 2009. From 1.studenog 2009th is a lecturer at the Faculty of Philosophy, University of Split (Department of the teachers).

Egon L. van den Broek obtained his MSc (2001) in Artificial Intelligence (AI) and PhD (2005) in Content-Based Image Retrieval and will obtain a PhD (2010) in Affective Signal Processing. Currently, he is assistant professor (University of Twente, NL), assistant professor / research coordinator (University Medical Center Nijmegen, NL), as well as consultant with Human-Centered Computing Consultancy. In the latter function, he works for various companies, among which Philips Research. Within the fields of AI and man-machine interaction, his primary research interests are cognitive computer vision and affective computing. He has published 100+ articles, guided 45+ students, holds various awards, is reviewer and program committee member of 50+ conferences and journals, and holds 3 patent applications. Additionally, he is editor-in-chief of the Pan Stanford Series in Artificial Intelligence, which will be launched in 2011/2012.

Rosa Maria Vicari received her PhD in Computer and Engineering at University of Coimbra, Portugal, and is Associate Professor of Artificial Intelligence at Institute of Informatics, at Federal University of Rio Grande do Sul (UFRGS), Brazil, with a large number of published papers in conferences and journals.

Beatriz Vizcarra obtained her Professional Degree in Psychology from the Catholic University of Chile in 1978. She was awarded the Diploma in Advanced Studies in Education by the University of Barcelona in 2003. She is presently an Associate Professor of Psychology at Universidad de La Frontera, in Temuco, Chile. She has done teaching to undergraduate as graduate students in the areas of psychological assessment, domestic violence and child abuse. During the last fifteen years she has developed research on topics of domestic violence and child abuse, at national, as well as internationally levels, through the World Safe Project, working together with researchers from India, USA, Egypt and Brazil. She has published numerous studies in the areas of interpersonal and domestic violence and child abuse.

Roko Vladušić was born 1971 in Split, Croatia. After secondary school he studied at University of Split on the Faculty of Natural sciences, mathematics and education where he graduated and became a teacher of biology and chemistry. He has worked in several primary schools teaching biology, chemistry, nature and informatics. His primary interest is teaching chemistry so he has specialized in that area through activities on his job and studying at the Split University Master's postgraduate program "Didactics of natural sciences" – chemistry area. He was the author and the leader of some educational projects, mentor of many pupils on the different levels of competitions in chemistry, leader of regional Council of chemistry teachers. He wrote some papers and educational books of chemistry. Now, he is working at the Faculty of natural sciences in Split where he teaches chemistry and methods of teaching chemistry.

Lung-Hsiang Wong is a Research Scientist in the Learning Sciences Laboratory, National Institute of Education (LSL, NIE), Nanyang Technological University (NTU), Singapore. He has 18 years of experience with educational technology research. His research interests are Artificial Intelligence in Education, intelligent agents for learning, mobile learning, technology-enhanced Chinese Language learning, and teachers' professional development. He is the Singapore representative for Technical Committee 3 (Educational Technology), International Federation for Information Processing, UNESCO.

Marija Zelić was born in 1979 in Knin, Croatia. She graduated in 2002 at the Faculty of Science, University of Split, under supervision of Ph.D. Professor Marko Rosić and Ph.D. Professor Slavomir Stankov. Since 2005 she has been working as an assistant at the Faculty. She teaches two courses in object oriented programming, namely C# and Object Pascal programming languages. In 2006 she began her doctoral studies in Computer Science at the Faculty of Electrical Engineering and Computing, University of Zagreb. Her main research interests include intelligent tutoring systems, intelligent agents and mobile learning, particularly modeling and development of agent-based m-learning systems. She has collaborated in the technological project TP-02/0177-01 "Web oriented intelligent hypermedia authoring shell" as well as the research and development project 036-0361994-1995 "Universal Middleware Platform for e-Learning Systems". She has authored or co-authored several research papers in journals and conferences. Her previous work experience includes working as a software developer from 2002 till 2005. During this period she gained a Microsoft certificate MCP in developing and implementing Web applications with Microsoft Visual C# .NET and Microsoft Visual Studio .NET. She speaks fluent English and Italian (FCE certificate, University of Cambridge, and DILI diploma, Accademia Italiana di Lingua).

Branko Žitko graduated (2001) under supervision of prof. PhD Slavomir Stankov at Faculty of Science, University of Split. Since then he was employ of the same faculty and postgraduate student of Faculty of Electrical Engineerin and Computing, where he reached his MsC (2005) also under supervision of prof. PhD Slavomir Stankov. The theme of his master's thesis was "Knowledge Evaluation Model in Intelligent e-Learning Systems". In past four years he is working on his PhD thesis named "Model of Intelligent Tutoring System based on Controlled Language over Ontology". As an employ, he was collaborating on two scientific and research projects: "Computational and didactical aspects of intelligent authoring tools in education" (2002-2006) and "Design and evaluation of intelligent e-learning systems" since 2007. He was one of developer and architect involved in technological project "Web-oriented intelligent authoring shell" (2003-2005). Branko Žitko's interests in general are intelligent tutoring systems and authoring shells for such systems. His specific interests are knowledge representation, ontologies, automated reasoning and natural language processing in intelligent tutoring systems.

Index

Symbols

A

B

C

G

H

I

J

K

L

Q

R

S

T

Breinigsville, PA USA
26 September 2010
246051BV00003B/3/P